Middle America

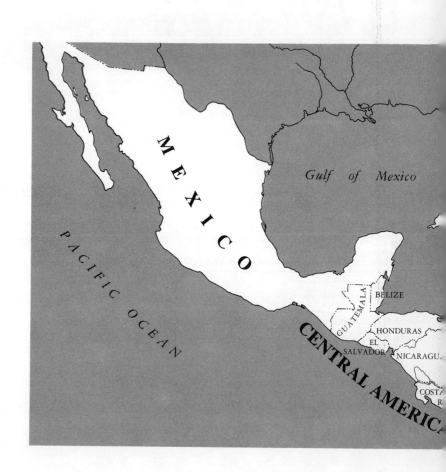

MIDDLE AMERICA

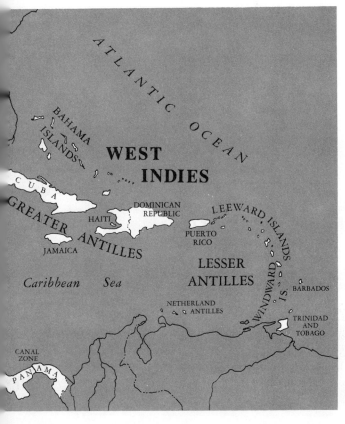

Its

Lands

and

Peoples

second edition

ROBERT C. WEST
Louisiana State University

JOHN P. AUGELLI
University of Kansas

Prentice-Hall, Inc., *Englewood Cliffs, New Jersey*

Library of Congress Cataloging in Publication Data

West, Robert Cooper (date)
  Middle America, its lands and peoples.

  Bibliography: p.
  Includes index.
  1. West Indies. 2. Mexico. 3. Central America.
I. Augelli, John P., joint author. II. Title
F2161.W42 1976   972   75-14417
ISBN 0-13-581546-0

10 9 8 7 6 5 4 3 2 1

PRINTED IN THE UNITED STATES OF AMERICA

PRENTICE-HALL INTERNATIONAL, INC., *London*
PRENTICE-HALL OF AUSTRALIA, PTY. LTD., *Sydney*
PRENTICE-HALL OF CANADA, LTD., *Toronto*
PRENTICE-HALL OF INDIA PRIVATE LIMITED, *New Delhi*
PRENTICE-HALL OF JAPAN, INC., *Tokyo*
PRENTICE-HALL OF SOUTHEAST ASIA (PTE.) LTD., *Singapore*

Contents

Illustrations

Preface

In the revised edition of this book the authors have maintained the emphasis on the cultural and historical approach to the geography of Middle America. In the chapters on the contemporary scene, however, we have tried to present the major economic, social, and political problems that are reflected in the geographic landscape of the various Middle American countries. Phenomena that have changed greatly in the past decade, such as population, urbanization, and industry, have been emphasized for the modern period. Most of the recent statistics used are based on data of the late 1960s or early 1970s.

Certain sections of the book, in particular those on the West Indies, have been completely reorganized, and the section on Central America has been considerably lengthened. To conserve space, many illustrations and tables that appeared in the first edition have been deleted, and others have been replaced by new ones. Mrs. Judy Ardoin drafted most of the new and revised maps that appear in this edition.

We are indebted to many colleagues and students who have suggested changes in the first edition and who have read portions or all of the manuscript of the second. To these individuals, too numerous to mention separately, we give our heartfelt thanks.

A NOTE ON NOMENCLATURE

There is no universally accepted or standard definition for *Middle America*. Some apply the term only to Mexico and Central America; others add the West Indies; and still others include Colombia, Venezuela, and the Guianas. Non-English equivalents of this geographic designation either do not exist or merely add to the confusion. For example, Professor Nilo Bernardes, who is the Brazilian editor of the *Revista Geografica,* unable to find a Spanish or Portuguese counterpart for the term, chose to translate it as "Mesoamerica" (Augelli 1962). The German equivalent, "Mittleamerika," appears in literature primarily with reference to the isthmian territories from Panama to Guatemala.

Inconsistency and confusion also stem from the connotations of the term "Middle America" and the names of its component territories, from the overlap of these names with the other regional nomenclature (such as "Latin America," "North America," "Caribbean America,"), and from the different contexts (geographic, historical, cultural) used to define the variety of overlapping terms. A few questions frequently posed by students may illustrate the problem. If Mexico is geographically part of North America, why do Mexicans object to being called North Americans or "norteamericanos"? Why do many Central Americans seem to exclude Panama from their definition of "Centroamerica"? Are the non-Hispanic West Indies part of Latin America?

The following definitions are intended to clarify these and other questions raised by students. Although extent and frequency of use are key criteria in defining each term, the authors cannot claim that their definitions have the sanction of universal acceptance. The sole absolute guarantee is that the definitions are applicable to this volume.

Latin America. Geographically defined, this term usually includes Mexico, Central and South America, and the West Indies and other islands adjacent to the mainland territories. As a culture-area designation, however, it excludes all territories, such as the non-Hispanic West Indies, which do not claim an Iberian heritage. Within the Iberian context, further differentiation is often made between Brazil, which has a Portuguese heritage, and the countries of Spanish heritage, which are sometimes designated as "Hispanic America."

North America. As a continent, this area includes all lands from Canada in the north to Panama in the south. Occasionally, the term is used to identify a cultural region which is synonymous with "Anglo-America" (see below), in which case North Americans, or *noteamericanos,* refers to people from the United States and possibly Canada.

Anglo-America. As a culture-area counterpart of "Latin America," this term is used with reference to continental United States and Canada but not to former British colonies in the West Indies. Presumably, French Canadian nationalists would exclude at least Quebec from the designation.

Middle America. This term is most frequently used with reference to Mexico, Central America, and the West Indies. For purposes of this book, it will also include the Bahamas, the islands adjacent to Mexico and Central America, and the Dutch islands of Aruba, Bonaire, and Curaçao off the coast of South America. (See frontispiece map.)

Caribbean America. Strictly defined, this term designates the territories with frontage on the Caribbean Sea (the West Indies; all Central America, except El Salvador, which fronts on the Pacific Ocean; Venezuela and Colombia). There are some, however, who apply the label exclusively to the West Indies, and others who exclude from it all South American countries but include Mexico.

Mesoamerica. This expression is almost invariably used to define the pre-Colombian or Indian high-culture areas, such as those associated with the Maya and the Aztecs in Mexico and Central America. It is attributed to the anthropologist Paul Kirchoff.

Central America. Geographically defined, this expression refers to isthmian territories from Guatemala in the north to Panama in the south. Unfortunately, it seems to have two Spanish equivalents—"America Central" and "Centroamerica." For those who differentiate between the two, "America Central" is considered a geographic designation which includes the same isthmian territories as "Central America." In contrast, they deem "Centroamerica" to be a historical area designation identifying the isthmian countries that, under Spanish colonial rule, formed part of the Capitanía General de Guatemala. (See Chapter 13.) Thus defined, "Centroamerica," excludes Panama and presumably British Honduras, or Belize.

West Indies, or Antilles. These terms are synonymous and identify the chain of islands extending from Cuba in the north to Trinidad and Tobago in the south. (See frontispiece map.) Less frequently, the terms also include the Bahamas and the Dutch islands off the coast of Venezuela. The West Indian archipelago is often differentiated on the basis of size into the Greater Antilles (Cuba, Hispaniola, Puerto Rico, and Jamaica), and the Lesser Antilles, which generally include all other islands in the chain. The Lesser Antilles are further subdivided into the Leeward and Windward Islands. Originally, this division was supposed to be based on the location of the islands with reference to the northeast trade winds, but such a climatological basis is not tenable. (See Chapter 7.)

Middle America

Preface to
the First Edition

Middle America: Its Lands and Peoples presents the geography of an important and diverse segment of Latin America—the West Indies, Mexico, and Central America. This is the part of Latin America that is nearest to the United States; from its strategic and commercial importance alone, this is the part of Latin America that should be best known (but unfortunately is little understood) by North Americans. We hope that this volume may aid North American readers toward a better understanding of their nearest neighbors to the south.

The approach used in this book is strongly cultural and historical. We believe that such an approach is necessary to comprehend the complex medley of peoples and cultures that characterize Middle America today. The comprehension of the contemporary cultural scene of any long-inhabited land is rooted in an understanding of its past. Consequently, chapters on the pre-European aboriginal, European colonial, and nineteenth- and twentieth-century human geography of the West Indies, Mexico, and Central America comprise much of the book.

While we share joint responsibility for the entire book, we did not feel bound to maintain complete uniformity of style or in the content emphasis of the various chapters. The division of labor was such that the sections dealing with Mexico and Central America fell to West, while the first and last chapters and those focusing on the West Indies fell to Augelli.

Several people contributed to the art work for this volume. Joseph W. Wiedel, assistant professor of geography at the University of Maryland, drafted most of the maps. Judy Josserand and Morris Morgan executed the line drawings.

We thank the Association of American Geographers for permission to include Figures 1.3, 1.4, 1.5, and 1.7, first published in the *Annals* of that organization. We are indebted to the editors of the *Geographical Review* and *Focus* for borrowing freely from their published maps in constructing Figures 6.3, 6.4, 7.44, and 7.45. We are also indebted to Otis P. Starkey, Arilin D. Fentem, and Robert C. Kingsbury for using many data from their Technical Reports (numbers 1 through 11) on the commercial geography of the eastern Caribbean, prepared under Office of Naval Research Contract 908 (13).

≡ 1 ≡

The Cultural Diversity
of Middle America

Middle America is an arbitrary geographic expression that refers to a mosaic of peoples, places, and cultures. The term provides a convenient classification for geographic analysis but does not imply a sense of social "community" or of physical and cultural uniformity in the area it defines. Mexico, Central America, and the West Indies, which constitute Middle America for purposes of this volume, share a general focus on the Gulf of Mexico and the Caribbean Sea and an intermediate location between North and South America. Each of the units formed part of the first European settlement in the New World and, in each, post-Columbian domination and exploitation by outside powers has deeply affected the patterns of land and people, the cultural institutions and values, and, perhaps above all, the economy. The three units have emerged into the twentieth century with economic structures that, for the most part, are still colonial. Each is handicapped with national markets of low purchasing power, a weak competitive position for exports in the world market, and a heavy dependence on agricultural (or mining) products for commerce. Their resources have been exploited to the point of abuse in some instances and inefficiently developed in

others, and their economies cannot provide remunerative employment for a rapidly expanding labor force.

Other problems common throughout Middle America deal with the population. In each of the component units, the population is comprised of multiple racial elements and is socially structured according to a race-class correlation that frequently places lighter-skinned groups at the top and darker ones at the bottom. Moreover, the socioeconomic stratification results in glaring gaps between the privileged few and the underprivileged many.

Still another common denominator for all Middle America is the dominant position of the United States. With few exceptions, the area's dependence on the United States for markets, loans, grants-in-aid, investment capital, and even technology is so slavish that it limits the political freedom of action of Middle American states, especially on policies opposed by Washington. True, Cuba has proven that this dependence can be broken, but only at a very high cost.

But these and other common threads that tie Middle America together are slender compared to the forces that tend to separate and differentiate its territories. Diversity rather than uniformity domi-

1

nates the geographic character of the area. Each island and each mainland nucleus of settlement is a distinctive composite of people, habitat, historical tradition, and cultural orientation. The climate ranges from the aridity of Baja California and northern Mexico to the tropical rain forest of some of the Antilles and the Caribbean lowlands of Central America. Soil, vegetation, and landforms run almost the entire gamut of possibility (see Chapter 2). Mexico and Jamaica boast useful mineral resources, but most of the territories have little exploitable mineral wealth.

Culturally, Middle America includes a variety of ethnic, social, economic, and political patterns rivaled by virtually no other area of comparable size in the world. Political processes range from the functional democracy of Costa Rica to rule by presidential whim in Haiti and the "sugar communism" of Cuba. Despite the trend to political independence among Caribbean dependencies, some territories continue to have varying degrees of political association or partnership with outside powers such as Britain, the Netherlands, France, and the United States. In addition to the Papiamento tongue of some of the Netherlands Antilles, there are at least three major linguistic communities—Spanish, English, and French—plus a proliferation of local dialects in Middle America.

Economies in the area range from purely commercial, as in Curaçao, to almost subsistence, as in some of the Indian communities of Guatemala. Poverty and limited opportunity characterize all of Middle America, but considerable distance lies between the Haitian peasant's constant flirtation with famine and the improving conditions of the Puerto Rican. The differences in living standards become glaring when we compare the conspicuous consumption of the privileged few with the lot of the masses, or each territory's cities with its rural areas.

Populations differ in number, density, and racial composition. The population of Mexico, more than 48,000,000 people in 1970, contrasts sharply with that of the West Indian island of Montserrat and the British Virgin Islands which, combined, is less than 27,000. Population density is equally varied; many of the West Indies, for example, have more than 500 people per square mile, while Central American areas such as the Petén of Guatamala and parts of Panama are almost empty. Racial and ethnic heterogeneity are apparent everywhere (Figures 1.1–1.8). The people of Costa Rica, Puerto Rico, and the Cayman Islands are largely Caucasian; those of Guatamala are predominantly Indian; the populations of Haiti and Jamaica are largely black; and many natives of Trinidad are of East Indian origin. In Mexico, marked regional differences exist in racial composition, especially between the north and south.

These are only some of the more important aspects of the diversity of Middle America, but they are sufficient to invalidate any claim that the area meets the usual criteria of homogeneity which distinguish a region. Because of the area's

Figure 1.1   East Indian Hindus, Trinidad

general focus on the Gulf and the Caribbean Sea, a weak case may be made for the existence of a nodal region, but such nodality would have to embrace the United States Gulf coast as well as the Guianas, Colombia, and Venezuela, which are not included in this particular study of Middle America.

PRINCIPAL ROOTS
OF DIVERSITY

There are many causes of cultural diversity in Middle America, but in addition to the nature and variety of the physical environment and the consequent historical adjustments to it, the most important appear to have been: (1) variety in the numbers, densities, and technological levels of the pre-Columbian Indian populations; (2) the cultural baggage, motives for conquest, and colonial methods and policies of the European groups who entered the area in the early period of settlement; (3) the origin and extent of subsequent immigration; and (4) the varying play of isolation and localism.

Pre-Columbian
Indian Populations

Middle America was an Indian world before the arrival of the Europeans and the Africans, and to a considerable extent, it still is. The degree of Amerindian influence on the racial composition and cultural patterns of any part of the area roughly correlates with the number, density, and level of civilization of the indigenous population before the Conquest. This correlation is, however, not applicable to the West Indies, where the aborigines were unable to withstand the initial cultural shock of conquest, and most were all but extinguished less than a century after the arrival of the first Europeans. A

Figure 1.2   Changing of the guard at Government House, Nassau (*Bahamas Tourist Bureau*)

further exception is found in the few areas of the mainland that have retained an Indian flavor despite low population densities and standards of culture because such areas have been remote and unattractive to the European.

We have no count of the total Indian population of Middle America on the eve of Discovery, and estimates vary enormously. A conservative approximation based on the latest studies is 30 million: more than 25 million for Mexico and Central America, and perhaps 5 million in the West Indies. This total, far larger than the combined pre-Columbian populations of all Anglo-America, probably was even greater than the Andean concentrations among the Indian populations of the New World.

The Europeans found conspicuous cultural and demographic differences among the aboriginal groups of Middle America. The high-culture areas of *Mesoamerica* (the southern Central Plateau of Mexico and Yucatan, and the highlands and the Pacific lowlands of Central America, e.g.,

Figure 1.3   Mexican boys (*Delta Airlines*)

of Guatamala, western Honduras, and western Nicaragua) were the most populous and the most advanced technologically. Here the inhabitants were densely settled, often in large communities and even cities. Their agriculture was intensive and stable enough to assure an adequate food supply; they had domesticated a large number of plants; and they often practiced terracing and irrigation. Their economy was regulated by highly sophisticated social organizations and theocratic states. In some of the West Indies, and in most of the Caribbean lowland areas on the Mainland and in arid northern Mexico, the Indian populations were smaller, primarily because of their inferior food-producing methods—slash-and-burn agriculture, gathering, hunting, and fishing. The availability of food was thus less certain; settlements were smaller and less permanent; and the entire economy was less stable. Except for the nomadic tribes of northern Mexico, which depended largely on the chase, the vast majority of the pre-Columbian people of Middle America depended on agriculture. This difference between the aboriginal population of Middle America and the smaller and culturally less advanced Indian population of what is now the United States, accounts, in part, for the superiority of the Middle American Indians, both in number and in post-Columbian influence.

The cultural shock resulting from European conquest caused vast changes among the aboriginal populations of Middle America. In the West Indies the Indians died off virtually en masse, leaving a mere handful of survivors and a few vague traces of their former occupation of the islands. Elsewhere, and particularly in the large settlements of Mesoamerica, the initial European impact resulted in a drastic reduction of population. The Indians had no immunity to imported diseases, and they were ill prepared for the brutality of the Spanish handling of labor. Perhaps more important, their food supply was sharply curtailed by the diversion of their lands to large tracts, or *latifundia,* which were conferred on the white colonists and then allowed to lie almost idle.

The small number of Spanish colonists who entered Mexico and Central America in the early colonial period used every means to pacify the Indians, including military action, economic pressure, and intermarriage. Except where the number of Spaniards was more nearly equal to the Indian population, however, pacification did not always result in assimilation to the culture of the conqueror. Today, more than 450 years after Columbus, there still exists on the mainland of Middle America an unassimilated or partially assimilated indigenous element which accounts for at least half of the population in Guatemala and one-twelfth of the population in Mexico. Both countries are keenly conscious of what they refer to as their "Indian problem."

Even where assimilation with the European pattern has gone further, however, the biological and cultural mark of the Indian past is apparent. Except in Costa Rica and British Honduras, the racial composition of the mainland of Middle America is basically Euro-Indian or mestizo.[1] Indian languages remain locally important, and the Indian motif permeates much of the artistic expression and thought of Mexico and Central America. Equally important to the student of geography are the crops, farming practices, diet, settlement patterns, house types, and other aspects of the material culture which, in varying degrees, are all part of the heritage of the Indian tradition.

The European
Cultural Intrusion

Many nations have left their cultural stamp on the people, landscapes, and institutions of Middle America. The list includes Spain, England, France, the Netherlands, Denmark, and the United States, as well as assorted African, oriental, and other elements. The role of Spain must be judged by far the most important, however, if only because the European tradition of the vast majority of the people and the territories of Middle America is Hispanic. Other ethnic groups have been significant primarily in the West Indies and in parts of the Caribbean coast of Central America, but even the West Indies—Cuba, Puerto Rico, the Dominican

Figure 1.4   Costa Rican school teachers in Guatemala

Republic, and to a much lesser degree, Trinidad and Jamaica—came under early Spanish influence. Therefore, in this section we shall deal exclusively with the role of Spain; we shall assess the influence of the other nations later in the book.

The Spaniard brought to Middle America an entirely new fabric of life which was imposed on the indigenous forms. The resulting human geography speaks loudly of the colonist's Iberian background, his motivations, and his institutions. At the time of the discovery of America, Spain was emerging from a 700-year struggle to evict the Moors, and the conquest of America was in many respects a parallel to and a prolongation of the conquest of the Moors. Many institutions and much of the national character which had developed during the fierce Moorish wars became part of the Spaniard's method and policy of colonization in the New World. Unlike England in North America, Spain never

1. *Mestizo* (feminine, *mestiza*) means a person of mixed blood, usually the offspring of a European and an Amerindian. In Middle America, the term has also acquired a cultural connotation. Mestizo culture implies assimilation with the European pattern, as distinguished from the Indian. A person whose way of life is European may be racially a pure Indian but culturally a mestizo. Similarly, a white person who lives like an Indian may be classified as an Indian, culturally. In Guatemala and other parts of Central America, the term *Ladino* is used to describe anyone whose speech and way of life are Spanish.

attempted to establish small, slow-growing colonies which could develop themselves. What Spain undertook was an imperial expansion, aimed at imposing her language, religion, and customs on millions of colonial subjects of different race and culture. The symbolism of the cross and the sword, the fanatic missionary zeal, the strongly centralized control of every phase of colonial life from town planning to trade, the tolerance of racial fusion, the fierce intolerance of contrary ideas, religious and other, the contempt of the conquering soldier for manual labor, the attitudes of the aristocratic exploiter—all these and more formed the cultural baggage which the Spaniard carried to Middle America.

Spain's approach to colonization differed radically from that of every other western European power, with the exception of Portugal, partly because many of the forces that had transformed western Europe from a feudal to a modern condition had bypassed the Iberian Peninsula. The Reformation, the Enlightenment, the industrial and mechanical revolutions, laissez-faire capitalism, and other move-ments created little impression on Spain. Thus, during much of their formative colonial period, Spanish settlements received their principal cultural nourishment from a medieval and feudalistic fountainhead which was strikingly different from the rest of western Europe.

Spain faced two major disadvantages in the conquest and colonization of the New World: a lack of surplus wealth and a small population (the population of Spain in 1492 is estimated to have been only ten million). To overcome her need for money, Spain borrowed heavily from European bankers and paid back with gold and silver from her colonies. This necessitated a strict commercial monopoly of colonial trade, so that all the profits could go back into Spain's coffers. In essence, the colonies were viewed as instruments for the benefit of the mother country. Trade was restricted, and any colonial endeavor which might compete economically with the mother country was discouraged. To overcome the disadvantage of a small Spanish population, the Spaniards incorporated Indian populations into the feudalistic structure of colonial society. The

Figure 1.5   Middle-class Central Americans and Dominicans

small group of Spanish colonists formed the aristocracy, and the indigenous people supplied the labor force.

The primary motivation of the Spanish colonists was to obtain precious metals. But when stores of precious metals were not to be had or had been depleted, emphasis was given to the creation of large landed estates owned by Spaniards and worked by Indians. Large Indian concentrations were sought out, not only to satisfy the burning missionary zeal, but also to supply cheap and abundant labor.

While the gold and missionary fevers burned, the Spaniards located their settlements very carefully. Not every piece of real estate would do—only those zones that contained large Indian populations and precious metals. This careful method of selection was the principal reason for the rapid exploration and envelopment of Middle America, which contrasts with the slow, systematic, westward movement of the Anglo-American frontier. It also partially explains the nucleated pattern of settlements separated by empty or lightly populated areas—a pattern of population distribution which has often persisted to the present.

Of the various tools used by Spain to mold the patterns of land and people in the New World—trade legislation, religion, racial fusion, and land tenure systems— the last was probably the most important. After the initial gold rush, land became the basis of most fortunes. Landed property became the chief institution of colonial production, and its ownership the hallmark of social prestige in a society that disdained trade and industrial pursuits. The large European-owned estate was firmly established at an early date in Middle America; it has remained the principal form of land tenure and one of the major obstacles to progress in most of the area.

Without a labor force, however, landed property would have been worthless, and the Spanish colonists had to be assured of an adequate supply of workers. Some black slaves were imported, particularly into the West Indies and, to some degree, into Mexico. But, on the whole, this type of labor was not an important factor in the Hispanic exploitation of the land. The African slave was too expensive for the haphazard production of the Spaniard's *hacienda;* and the *plantation,* which was geared to the intensive production of commercial crops such as sugar and so created the heaviest demand for African slave labor, was only spottily developed by the Spaniards in Middle America. More important, the large Indian populations in the principal Spanish settlements in Mexico and Central America obviated the need for black slaves.

The Spaniards used various techniques to acquire and hold Indian workers. In the early days of the Conquest, the most important method of supplying a gold mine of human labor was the *encomienda* system, perhaps the most misunderstood institution established by the Spaniards in the Americas. Its origins go back to medieval Europe, where it was the practice of peasants living in a given locality to "commend" themselves to the lord of the neighborhood manor, rendering him specified personal services in return for protection. In the Americas, the encomienda was initially instituted by the Spanish Crown to protect the Indians, establish a stable and efficient economy, and gradually incorporate the large indigenous population into Spanish colonial society. Under the terms of the encomienda, the Crown "commended" Indians to the colonists "in order that you may employ them on your lands and in your mines, and it is your duty to instruct them in the Spanish language and our Holy Catholic Faith." The grant did not *ipso facto* include ownership of land itself; it gave the colonist, as trustee, the right to collect tribute and demand certain services from his Indian wards. Since

Figure 1.6   Street in Jacmel, Haiti (*Alcoa Steamship Company*)

even the rendering of services was abolished by law in 1542, the encomienda's primary function became that of tribute payment by the Indians to the *encomenderos.* Thereafter, the labor needed for agriculture was supplied mainly through the *repartimiento,* a work-levy system which the Spanish authorities imposed on Indian villages.

As conceived in Spain, the encomienda seemed a humane method of bringing about an economic and social transition of the lands and people of the New World, and certainly it was less brutal than the slave-and-tribute systems imposed by the Aztecs on their subject tribes. In practice, however, the system resulted in abuse for at least two reasons. First, it rested on the mistaken assumption that the encomenderos were God-fearing gentlemen. The truth is that many of the early colonists represented the very dregs of Spanish society; they made magnificent explorers, soldiers, and sires of the mestizo races, but most of them proved to be miserable economists and rulers of men. The second reason was the inability of the Spanish Crown to enforce the letter of the law in the far-off colonies. The law regulated the treatment of the Indians and the amount of services and tribute that could be required from them, but it was almost impossible to enforce these regulations in the colonies. Any effort the Crown and the clergy made to improve the lot of the Indians was fiercely resisted by colonists who needed the labor.

The encomienda system never worked in the West Indies, where the natives, unaccustomed to hard labor, were rapidly decimated. In the major centers of Indian population of Mexico and Central America, however, where the natives were already organized into a well-disciplined labor force, the system largely accomplished its aims. It brought about an initial transition from pre-Columbian to Spanish colonial patterns and was an important instrument in cementing the feudal, master–serf relationship, which to this day persists in many parts of Middle America.

According to law, the encomiendas were made for two generations—for the original encomendero and for his heir—after which they theoretically reverted to the Crown. The system was gradually reduced by attrition and was abolished outright in 1720; by that date debt peonage was established well enough to assure the landholders of a continued labor supply.

The other two most important Spanish institutions that laid the groundwork for the land-and-people patterns of Hispanic Middle America were perhaps the town and the mission. Most Spanish landholders lived in the towns and went to their holdings only for tours of inspection. The estates (and the mines) were the sources of production of goods. The towns contained the consumers, and the collecting, trading, and distributing of the goods took place there.

In contrast, the religious missions were

Figure 1.7 Dutch house types, Curaçao (*Alcoa Steamship Company*)

often independent, self-contained economic units. The role of the mission in encouraging Spanish settlement, particularly in areas that lacked minerals or a large Indian population, was an important one. The Catholic mission, serving as the other arm of Spanish colonization, helped effect a less painful transition of land and people from the indigenous to the Spanish form. It placed religion above labor requirements and persuasion above force. Wherever the mission came into conflict with the encomienda, however, the encomienda won out.

Origin and Extent
of Subsequent Immigration

The diverse human geography of Middle America was molded not only by the initial wave of Hispanic settlers but by subsequent immigration as well. Following the first flush of conquest and colonization, which involved a relatively small number of settlers, the flow of Spanish colonists to Middle America dwindled to a mere trickle. This reduced flow is explicable partly by Spain's small population and her numerous interests in other parts of the world and partly by a policy of restricting the immigration of non-Cath-

olics and colonists from other nations. But perhaps its chief cause was the lack of opportunity in the Spanish colonies of Middle America. The early grants of large holdings to Crown favorites and others preempted the supply of vacant public lands that could serve as a magnet to immigrants, as it did in Anglo-America. Moreover, the restrictions imposed on commerce and manufacturing stunted the development of these activities and further limited opportunity. Thus, unless he possessed capital (and most potential immigrants did not), the new immigrant was doomed to competing with Indians and slaves in the labor market. No Spanish or other European peasant, no matter how harsh his lot at home, preferred the even harsher lot of the peon and slave of Middle America. Spanish immigration to the area did not become significant again until the nineteenth and early twentieth centuries; even then, the immigration was primarily in response to the opportunities created by the commercial development of Cuba and Puerto Rico.

The establishment of northern European colonies (by England, France, Holland, and Denmark) in the West Indies and, to a far lesser degree, along the Caribbean coast of Central America brought new European immigrants to Middle

America. But again, the number of arrivals was not large, and again, the principal restriction was lack of opportunity. The West Indian territories occupied by the northern Europeans had little arable land, and this quickly became concentrated in a few hands. True, the development of plantation agriculture in these areas created a huge demand for labor, but early experiments proved that this demand could not be met by importing European workers, even when they were brought in as indentured servants.

The development of plantations by the northern Europeans was instrumental, however, in what is perhaps the largest migration of people into Middle America —the forced slave movement from Africa. An accurate count of the number of blacks brought into Middle America during the slave period is difficult to deter-

mine, but it was sufficient to make black and part-black people the dominant population in virtually all the West Indies. On the Caribbean coast of Central America, the colonial slave population was later reinforced by the free migration of Jamaicans and other West Indian blacks who were attracted by the growth of banana plantations, work on the Panama Canal, and other employment opportunities in the nineteenth and twentieth centuries. The total of this migration has been sufficient to give this sector a strong black component.

The vast bulk of the immigrants entering Middle America arrived from the sixteenth to the first half of the nineteenth centuries. The arrivals since 1850, such as the East Indians in Trinidad, have been relatively few and are only locally significant.

Figure 1.8   Library, University of Mexico (*Eastern Airlines*)

Isolation and Localism

Isolation has been a major factor in crystalizing and perpetuating the vast diversity of human geography in Middle America. The circulation of people, goods, and ideas within the area has always been limited. This was true when much of Middle America formed part of Spain's colonial empire, and the individual colonies were forbidden to trade with one other, and it is almost equally true today. Most of the population move within an economic orbit that essentially provides only subsistence, and they have little need for commerce or contact outside their own communities. Exports, primarily plantation crops and minerals, directly involve only a small percentage of the total population, and these exports do not move within Middle America but are directed chiefly to middle latitude markets such as the United States and Europe. The nature of the economy, the nucleated pattern of settlements, the different cultural traditions, the difficulty of transportation and communication, the restriction of migration, and other isolating forces have engendered in the component units of Middle America a degree of localism that has virtually no equal in Anglo-America. This localism not only separates the territories from one another but is found even within the same political unit.

RESULTING CULTURE AREAS

Response to the varied possibilities of different locations, climate, and other conditions of the physical environment; adjustment to the diverse currents of history, economy, politics, and ethnic influences —these and other forces have given Middle America a myriad of culturally differentiated areas and landscapes. Only a vast, and perhaps impractical, number of detailed and narrowly focused studies could reveal the extent of this diversity. The culture-area classification of the following outline, which is also depicted in Figures 1.9, 1.10, and 1.11, emphasizes gross patterns rather than detailed distinctions. Consequently, it should be considered only an approximation of the truth.

Figure 1.9   The Rimland-Mainland division of Middle America

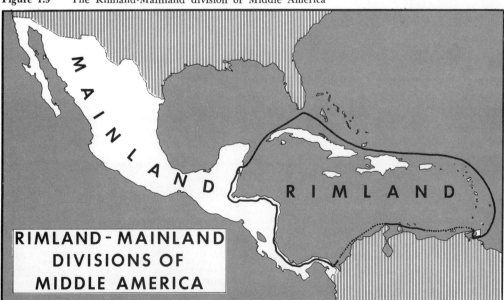

Generalized Culture Areas
of Middle America

I. The Euro-African (Caribbean) Rimland
   A. Central American sector
      1. Plantation zone
      2. Others
   B. West Indian sector
      1. Hispanic zone
         a. Dominican Republic
         b. Cuba
         c. Puerto Rico
      2. North European zone
         a. The Netherlands Antilles
         b. British West Indies
         c. French Culture Complex
            (1) Primary
               (a) Martinique and
                   Guadeloupe
            (2) Secondary
               (a) Haiti
               (b) Dominica, St. Lucia,
                   Grenada [2]

II. The Euro-Indian Mainland
   A. Mesoamerican sectors (marked Indian
      influence)
      1. Southern Plateau of Mexico and
         Yucatan
      2. Guatemala and Chiapas, western
         Honduras, and western Nicaragua
   B. Mestizo sector (moderate Indian influ-
      ence)
      1. Honduras
      2. El Salvador
      3. Nicaragua
      4. Panama
      5. Central Mexico
   C. European sectors (limited Indian influ-
      ence)
      1. Costa Rica
      2. Northern Mexico

Racial Differentiation of the Culture Areas

The primary basis for the proposed culture-area classification of Middle America

2. Dominica, St. Lucia, and Grenada, although
British territories, retain many French cultural
characteristics because of their past association
with France.

rests on a twofold division of the area between what may be termed the "Euro-
African Caribbean Rimland" (Figure 1.10)
and the "Euro-Indian Mainland" (Figure
1.11). This delineation is based in part, of
course, on the racial makeup of the population of the two segments. In general,
the dominant strain of the Rimland is
black or part-black, and even where blacks
do not form a majority (as in Cuba,
Puerto Rico, and some segments of the
Caribbean coast of Central America), they
represent a significant minority. On the
Mainland it is the Indian or, more commonly, the part-Indian (mestizo) who
forms the racial matrix of the population.
The incidence of Indian blood may vary,
but it is present to some extent everywhere, including the more European-like
areas of Costa Rica and northern Mexico.
These generalizations provide only a clue
to the complexity of Middle America's
racial patterns. One reader (Jones 1970)
has pointed out that, in addition to West
Indian and other blacks, the population
of the Central American Caribbean sector
of the Rimland includes other "cultural
groups," such as "white" Americans;
"Mediterranean" Greeks, Italians, and
Spaniards; various types of Indians; and
others. He concludes that there is no
marked homogeneity among the coastal
peoples, even though he recognizes that
these peoples share ". . . at least a common experience of separation from the
bulk of the Central American population
further inland"; and he concludes that
". . . the convenient concept of a cultural
rimland has little validity, therefore, other
than when seen from the mainland Spanish standpoint of a common non-Spanish-
ness. . . ."

Other readers have questioned the ex-
clusion from the Rimland of the Bahamas
whose population is predominantly black.
Still others have pointed to important
similarities between the Rimland and the
coastal margins of northern South America and even the United States South.

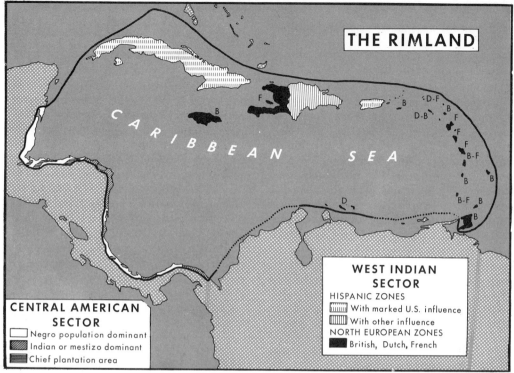

THE RIMLAND

CARIBBEAN SEA

WEST INDIAN
SECTOR
HISPANIC ZONES
⊪ With marked U.S. influence
⊪ With other influence
NORTH EUROPEAN ZONES
■ British, Dutch, French

CENTRAL AMERICAN
SECTOR
☐ Negro population dominant
▨ Indian or mestizo dominant
▤ Chief plantation area

Figure 1.10   The Euro-African Caribbean Rimland

Figure 1.11   The Euro-Indian mainland

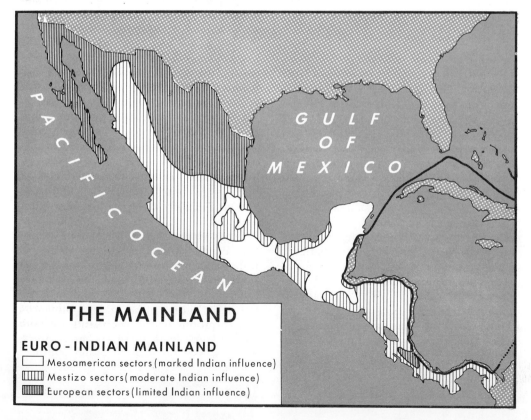

PACIFIC OCEAN

GULF
OF
MEXICO

THE MAINLAND

EURO-INDIAN MAINLAND
☐ Mesoamerican sectors (marked Indian influence)
⊪ Mestizo sectors (moderate Indian influence)
▥ European sectors (limited Indian influence)

While grateful for such reactions from readers, the authors wish to stress that: (a) they do not claim total racial-cultural homogeneity of the Rimland; (b) the Rimland-Mainland scheme is intended more as a pedagogic device than a precise instrument for measuring cultural homogeneity; and, above all, (c) race is only one of several criteria on which this scheme is based. If race were the sole criterion, for example, there would be no reason for excluding the Bahamas from the Rimland. As explained in Chapter 7, however, there is justification for excluding the Bahamas partly because their economic history was not strongly characterized by the slave plantation and partly for other reasons. The authors also acknowledge that some of the criteria used to delimit the Rimland are applicable to the coasts of northern South America and the United States South. The Rimland limits were not extended to these continental margins primarily because areas such as the Guianas, Colombia, and the United States South are not considered in this book.

Finally, the authors wish to stress that the cultural distinctiveness of the Caribbean has been recognized by others (Wolf and Mintz 1957; Segal 1968). "The common influence of a plantation society, slavery, and racial interbreeding are found not only on the islands [West Indies], but on the adjacent Caribbean coast of Central America and Panama. There is a distinct cultural belt stretching from southern Mexico across British Honduras, Central America, and Panama to the Caribbean shores of Colombia and Venezuela where songs, dances, musical forms, family structures and linguistic patterns display common traits. The Carribbean peoples of the Mainland are readily distinguishable from the white and mestizo inhabitants of the highland areas and Pacific coasts of Central America . . ." (Segal 1968:19).

Cultural Differences

The racial differentiation is only a symptom, however, of the far more important contrasts which stem from cultural orientation, human habitat, and the economic organization of land. The Mainland retains strong pre-Columbian Indian cultural remnants, and the post-Columbian culture brought to it has been almost exclusively Hispanic. The Rimland retains virtually no indigenous forms. It has some imported African traits and, in its post-Columbian history, has been exposed to a variety of European (including Anglo-American) ethnic cultures. These contrasts are responsible in part, at least, for the differences between the two areas in landscape, material culture, and other facets of man–land relations.

Viewed as a human habitat, the Rimland is essentially a tropical lowland, varying in humidity from rain forest conditions to savanna, with occasional patches of steppe. True, many of the West Indian islands are mountainous, but the vast bulk of the Rimland population lives on coastal plains and river valleys well below 1,000 feet in elevation. Because of its island and coastal character and sea location, the Rimland habitat has been more accessible to the play of outside forces than that of the Mainland. Its lowland tropical conditions are conspicuously expressed in the general landscape, the nature of the subsistence and commercial crops, the building materials, and the types of houses, as well as in other ways. The Mainland habitat is largely a tropical or subtropical highland, characterized by subhumid to arid conditions over much of its Mexican and Pacific slope components and by a wide range of humid conditions in the highlands of Central America. With the exceptions of Panama, Nicaragua, and northern Yucatan, the major population concentrations of the Mainland are both more remote from these and at considerably higher elevations than in the Rimland. The climatic variation and the location of the habitats of the Mainland population help account for their restricted contact with the outside world as well as for much of the distinctiveness of their crops, their use of the land, their diet, and other aspects of their adjustment.

The Plantation
versus the Hacienda

While it is impossible to focus on every cause and consequence of the contrasting human geography of the Mainland and the Rimland in Middle America, the story of at least one more contrast merits special attention—the difference in economic organization of the land.

The expansion of European enterprise into Middle America following the Discovery eventually gave rise to two outstanding modes of land organization: the hacienda and the plantation. The two are similar in a number of respects: (1) both are European techniques for the exploitation of land and labor; (2) both require large amounts of land and cheap labor (though labor costs have been characteristically cheaper on the hacienda); (3) both have been developed on the best land in their respective sphere, discouraging the emergence of a strong, independent class of small farmers and of a balanced economy; and (4) both have been historically characterized by agglomerated, village-type settlements of workers grouped near the big house of the landowner.

As institutions that have shaped man–land relations, however, they differ fundamentally. They mirror the differences in the surrounding environment and in the availability of indigenous labor, and perhaps above all, they reflect the gulf that separated the economic values of the Spaniard from those of the northern European. The hacienda is an almost exclusively Hispanic institution, now confined largely to Mexico and Central America. The hacienda was characteristic of Cuba, Puerto Rico, Santo Domingo, and perhaps even Trinidad during much of the colonial period, but the destruction of the indigenous population, the high cost of imported labor, and the development of the more efficient plantation largely doomed the hacienda organization in those territories.

Part of the land on the hacienda is devoted to cash crops that often supply the food for the populations of nearby towns and cities. The hacienda is fairly self-sufficient in that the workers are provided with subsistence plots and meet most of their needs from this production and from home crafts. There is far less specialization than on the plantation; capital is scarce; and family ownership of land is characteristic. Land is used extensively rather than intensively, and production is notoriously inefficient. Traditional methods of cultivation are employed; little use is made of machinery; and the movement of products to any except nearby markets is often beset with difficulties. While there has been some desire for profit, it would appear that the hacienda owner's desire to live like a proper Spanish *caballero* has been more important to him than financial gain. The acquisition of hacienda property has had more to do with the prestige of land ownership than with any desire to expand production and increase profits. Under these circumstances, much hacienda land remains unused, a testimony to the inefficient Hispanic concept of aristocratic living.

Without a large and cheap supply of indigenous labor, the hacienda might never have developed. Its inefficiency made even slave labor prohibitively expensive. In the centers of large Indian population of Mexico and Central America, however, conditions were well suited to its development. The Spaniard developed his hacienda by obtaining grants of land that once belonged to Indian nobility and of unoccupied areas abandoned by Indian villages; then he acquired a cheap labor force, first through the encomienda and repartimiento, and later by debt peonage, custom, and political legislation.

The plantation, in contrast to the hacienda, became associated largely with the Rimland and was authored primarily by Northern Europeans and later by the Anglo-Americans, who established themselves in the West Indies and the Caribbean lowlands of Central America. Hispanic groups engaged in some plantation development, particularly in Cuba and Puerto Rico during the nineteenth century, and at various times along the southern Gulf coast of Mexico. But the plantation was never a forte of Hispanic agricultural economics, and least so during the colonial period. Following the political break with Spain, the Hispanic territories of the Rimland—Cuba, Puerto Rico, and the Dominican Republic—developed important plantation economies. The so-called coffee plantation, developed chiefly by local entrepreneurs of Hispanic origin in the uplands of Central America and Mexico, is a special economic form that in many respects is more akin to the hacienda than to the typical sugar or banana plantation of the Caribbean rim.

The Rimland plantation has been more than an economic institution; with some modification, it has persisted as a way of life from the colonial period to the present. It has been an important, and often the chief determinant of racial composition, population numbers, densities and distributions, land tenure and land use, commerce, transportation, and other cultural aspects of the Caribbean.[3] Of course,

the plantation has not remained unchanged by time and space. There is considerable difference between the family-owned West Indian sugar plantation of the eighteenth century, for instance, and the corporate organization of the present. Equally significant differences exist today between a United Fruit Company banana plantation in Central America and a French sugar plantation in Martinique.

Nevertheless, certain aspects of the Middle American plantation are always the same:

1. Its location is generally on the coast, roughly the same area as the humid tropical lowlands of Middle America.

2. Production is almost exclusively for export, usually of a single crop.

3. Capital, technology, and managerial skill are often imported, giving rise to absentee ownership and the export of profits.

4. Labor is seasonal and, historically, had to be imported because the indigenous Amerindian labor force was inadequate.

5. While the utilization of land is more efficient than on the hacienda, the plantation must hold considerable idle land in reserve for expansion of production, crop rotation, grazing of work animals, and other uses.

Both the plantation and the hacienda have undergone great changes in the twentieth century. The plantation has evolved from the family-owned enterprise

---

3. Sociologists and anthropologists stress that the plantation has functioned as a political and social force as well. It represented the political organization through which the authority of the whites was imposed on colored colonial peoples; it established the framework of a system of social relationships between the European masters and black laborers, including the tradition of white paternalism and the other guiding principles of race relationships. "In short, it has fashioned the whole environment which the people. . . have inherited." (Beckford 1972:3)

The overriding impact of the plantation on land, people, and society was not restricted to the Caribbean Rimland of Middle America. It is manifest in the United States South, northeastern Brazil, and wherever else the institution became important. Gilberto Freyre's brilliant study of the Brazilian plantation as a social institution would be applicable in large measure to the West Indies and to the American South (Freyre 1956).

of the colonial period to the corporation-owned big business of the present. In Mexico, the hacienda has been dealt a heavy blow by the concept of the *ejido* and by other land legislation stemming from the Mexican Revolution. Elsewhere, social unrest and improved transportation are creating both problems and marketing opportunities which are forcing hacienda owners to produce more efficiently and for export. Despite these changes, however, the two institutions—the Rimland plantation and the Mainland hacienda—continue to differentiate the man–land relationships of the two culture areas.[4]

Secondary Division
of the Culture Areas

In most instances, the bases for subdividing the Rimland and the Mainland are self-evident. The Central American sector of the Rimland, for example, stands apart from the West Indies for several reasons: the plantation in Central America was a postcolonial development; it was developed by Anglo-Americans rather than northern Europeans; it specialized primarily in bananas rather than sugar; and, while drawing much of its labor from the black populations of Jamaica and the other West Indies, the Central American plantation also attracted some workers from the Indian and mestizo areas of the interior uplands. The distinctiveness of the Central American sector of the Rimland is further reinforced by the presence of numerous settlements of English-speaking, Protestant communities which tend to resist assimilation with the predominantly Catholic and Hispanic cultures of the adjacent Mainland.

4. Some differences also exist between the Rimland and Mainland in other forms of land organization and utilization, such as peasants' small holdings, Indian communal lands, sharecropping, and so forth, but these are less significant. They are discussed in appropriate sections of the book.

The differentiation between the Hispanic and northern European islands in the West Indies is obviously based in part on their cultural histories and in part on their history of foreign occupation, racial composition, and other factors. In the Hispanic territories the plantation did not develop significantly until the nineteenth and twentieth centuries, and it used slave labor only for a short period. As a result, blacks are less numerous in Cuba and Puerto Rico than in the northern European territories.

Differentiation within the Hispanic group itself stems in large measure from United States influence in Cuba and Puerto Rico following the Spanish American War, as opposed to Haitian influence in the Dominican Republic.

Within the northern European group of islands, the "French cultural complex" extends beyond France's current possessions, Martinique and Guadeloupe, into Haiti, Dominica, St. Lucia, and even Grenada, because of France's former occupation of and cultural influence on these territories.

On the Mainland, the Mesoamerican centers of southern Mexico and Guatemala are distinguished by a far greater influence of indigenous forms and race than is found elsewhere. Northern Mexico and Costa Rica, on the other hand, are loosely designated as "European," partly because of their racial composition and partly because of their more European-like economy, settlement patterns, and other features. The remainder of the Mainland, where Indian influence is moderate, is designated as "mestizo."

THE IMPORTANCE
OF MIDDLE AMERICA

Middle America, as we have seen, is an arbitrary geographic term for a complexity of land-and-people patterns. Although it is not a region in the sense that geographers ordinarily define one, its study as a single geographic unit is not without justification. Its very diversity provides a fertile field for the comparative study of human adjustment under different physical and historical conditions.

Moreover, Middle America is one of the two richest repositories of Amerindian cultural remnants. It was the birthplace of the post-Columbian world in the Americas; it witnessed the arrival of the first Europeans, the first Africans, the first Jews, and the first members of other religious minorities in the New Word; and it was the experimental area in which the tools, plants, animals, and political and economic institutions used for the eventual conquest and settlement of the Americas were introduced. The study of the variety of human habitats and cultural forms that have evolved in Middle America constitutes an intellectual challenge that can be found in few other areas in the world. While this challenge alone would justify our study of Middle America, the area is important, particularly to the United States, for many other reasons.

Strategic and Economic Significance

Middle America's Caribbean Sea, often called the "American Mediterranean," is one of the world's most important circulation routes. It is part of the major trade routes between the Atlantic and the Pacific which go through the Panama Canal, and, together with its mainland and insular rims, it links the Americas. For good reason, control of the Caribbean has been imperative to the defense of the United States for more than a century, perhaps as far back as the proclamation of the Monroe Doctrine. A potential enemy with bases in the area could not only disrupt the vital trade lanes that flow through the canal and those that bring strategic materials such as petroleum from South America; he could also mount an attack on the very heart of the United States. This accounts for the presence of American military establishments in Puerto Rico, the Canal Zone, and Guantánamo Bay in Cuba, and for the lend-lease bases temporarily acquired elsewhere in the West Indies during World War II. Changes in military technology and in transportation have given and may again give different expression to the strategic value of Middle America, but its location and its arrangement of sea and land are, in Sauer's words "an elemental and permanent fact" whose strategic significance does not diminish (Sauer 1954:15).

The economic importance of Middle America as a market for finished products, fuel, and food, and as a source of raw materials such as tropical products and minerals has already been implied. The annual value of goods absorbed by the area's markets jumped from about five to nine billion dollars during the 1960s, while the value of exports rose from about four to over six billion dollars per year during the same period (Figure 1.12).

The economic importance of the area also rests, however, on its capacity to absorb foreign capital investment. The pattern of foreign investment originated in the early colonial era and has continued to this day. In the past, capital came primarily from England, France, and the Netherlands, and while investments from these countries are still important, currently the vast bulk of the money comes from the United States. American capital permeates virtually every sphere of commercial activity. It is found in the plantations of Central America, the Dominican Republic, and Puerto Rico; in the oil refineries of Trinidad and the Dutch islands; in the bauxite mines of Jamaica; in the mines and ranches of Mexico; in the public utilities of Central America and elsewhere; in the industries of Puerto Rico; in the tourist hotels of the West Indies; and in countless other enterprises. Despite the unfavorable investment cli-

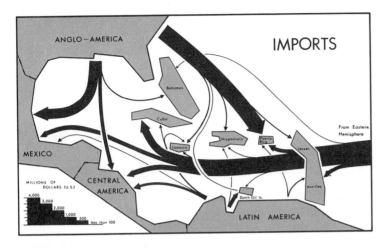

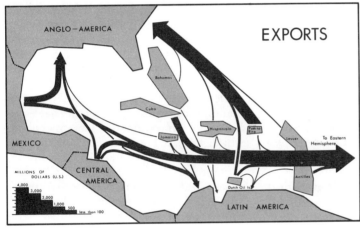

Figure 1.12   Middle America: Generalized flow maps of international commerce, imports and exports

mate created by the expropriation of American interests in the Mexican oil industry, the confiscation of United States property in Cuba, and the numerous threats that American capital has faced in Central America and elsewhere, Middle America continues to rank along with Canada and Venezuela as one of the major areas of United States investment abroad.

Partially reflecting this economic importance is the dramatic growth in air traffic to Middle America from Anglo-America (Figure 1.13). In 1973, for example, there were almost three thousand scheduled air flights per week. Of this total, over 95 percent originated in the United States.

Social and Political Challenge

The social importance of Middle America is complex, but perhaps its greatest value stems from its being a human laboratory, a potential pilot area in which to study many of the problems and issues of the "emerging" world. Such study is not only sugggested by altruistic considerations, but dictated by pragmatic reasons, for many parts of Middle America are, in Hussey's vivid summary, "boiling cauldrons of human miseries and resentment likely to blow their lids at any careless stoking of the hearth" (Hussey 1958:248). Violent upheavals of Middle American societies (such as the slave uprisings in

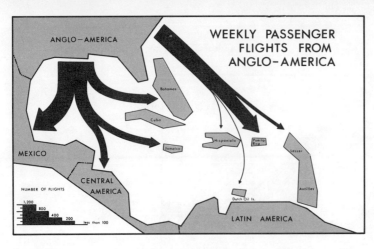

Figure 1.13 Middle America: Air traffic from the United States and Canada, 1973

Haiti during the late eighteenth century, the Mexican Revolution [1910–1917], and the more recent Communist revolt in Cuba) are well known. In the event of a generalized explosion, the West in general and the United States in particular have much to lose.

The conditions stoking the "boiling cauldrons of human miseries and resentments" are many. The human biomass of Middle America is increasing at an alarming rate and gives little evidence of slowing down. The area as a whole has an annual population growth of over 3.5 percent, as compared to a world average of 2 percent. Although less publicized than in the United States, the area's ecological problems are no less serious. Continuous use and misuse of the land, often since pre-Columbian times, has ruined more than half of Middle America's usable soil resources, and as a result, people are "fleeing from a rural environment too ecologically overtaxed to support their growing numbers" (Bennett 1971). Much of the rural environment has been ruined by profit-motivated entrepreneurs of the past who had little concern for the long-range social cost of their exploitation. Similarly, "modern entrepreneurs . . . have turned the basin of Mexico into a smog-filled tureen in which more people arrive each day . . ." (Bennett 1971).

Politically and ideologically, the countries of Middle America are struggling with the same dilemmas that wrack other emerging nations: nationalism versus internationalism, socialism versus private enterprise, protected external markets versus economic development, democracy versus dictatorship. In many Rimland areas, particularly the former British colonies, there are strong movements to seek identity with the African or Asian origins of much of the population. In these areas, nonwhites are no longer satisfied with mere political independence. Increasingly led by Black Power groups modeled after those in the United States, they are demanding control of the commercial establishments traditionally dominated by white, foreign businessmen.

Despite its proximity, its obvious importance, and the alarming challenge it poses, Middle America continues to occupy only a small portion of the international consciousness of the United States and the rest of the world. Public awareness of the area's "boiling cauldrons" appears to surface only when there is an overt threat to the established order. At other times, the American man in the street, for example, still tends to view the area as a vaguely defined backyard of banana republics, comic opera revolutions, exotic vacation spots, and attractive dance rhythms. The territories of Middle America, in the words of Sumner Welles, ". . . are among those of the American Republics with which the people of the United States are least familiar . . . [To] most of us the national problems . . . the manner of being, the culture, and the economy [of Middle America] is a closed book" (Perkins 1947:7).

It is the purpose of this text to view the

lands and peoples of Middle America against the background of their geographic, historical, and cultural settings, placing particular emphasis on the relationships between the people and the land on which they live.

SELECTED REFERENCES

ADAMS, R. N. "Cultural Components of Central America." *American Anthropologist* 58, no. 5 (1956):881–907.

AUGELLI, J. P. "The Controversial Image of Latin America: A Geographer's View." *Journal of Geography* 62, no. 3 (1963):103–12.

———. "The Rimland-Mainland Concept of Culture Areas in Middle America." *Annals of the Association of American Geographers* 52, no. 2 (1962):119–29. Translated as "O Conceito de Zonas Perifericase de Zonas Interiores nas Areas Culturais da Meso-America." *Revista Geográfica* (PAIGH) 31, no. 57 (1962):45–61.

BECKFORD, G. L. *Persistent Poverty*. New York: Oxford University Press, 1972.

BENNETT, C. F. "Development and Ecological Reality in Latin America." Paper presented at meeting of Conference of Latin Americanist Geographers. Syracuse, New York, December 2–4, 1971.

FREYRE, G. *The Masters and the Slaves: A Study in the Development of Brazilian Civilization*. 2nd ed. New York: Alfred A. Knopf, 1956.

GILLIN, J. "Mestizo America." In *Most of the World*, edited by R. Linton. New York: Columbia University Press, 1949, pp. 156–211.

HERSKOVITS, M. J. *The Myth of the Negro Past*. New York: Harper and Row, 1941.

HUSSY, R. D. "Historical Factors." In *The Caribbean: British, Dutch, French, United States*, edited by A. C. Wilgur. Gainesville: University of Florida Press, 1958, pp. 247–61.

JONES, D. R. "The Caribbean Coast of Central America: A Case of Multiple Fragmentation." *The Professional Geographer* 22, no. 5 (1970):260–66.

KLASS, M. *East Indians in Trinidad: A Study of Cultural Persistence*. New York: Columbia University Press, 1961.

McBRIDE, G. M. "Plantation." *Encyclopedia of the Social Sciences* 11 (1937):148–53.

OTS CAPDEQUI, J. M. *El Régimen de la Tierra en la América Española durante el Periodo Colonial*. Ciudad Trujillo, S.D.: Editora Montalvo, Universidad de Santo Domingo, 1946.

PERKINS, D. *The United States and the Caribbean*. Cambridge: Harvard University Press, 1947.

RUBIN, V., ed. *Caribbean Studies: A Symposium*. Kingston, Jamaica: Institute of Social and Economic Research, University College of the West Indies, 1957.

———. "Social Cultural Pluralism in the Caribbean." *Annals of the New York Academy of Sciences* 83, no. 5 (1960):796–815.

SAUER, C. O. "Economic Prospects of the Caribbean." In *The Caribbean: Its Economy*, edited by A. C. Wilgus. Gainesville: University of Florida Press, 1954, pp. 15–27.

SEGAL, A. *The Politics of Caribbean Economic Integration*. Río Piedras: University of Puerto Rico, 1968.

SIMPSON, L. B. *The Encomienda in New Spain*. Rev. ed. Berkeley: University of California Press, 1950.

WOLF, E. R. and MINTZ, S. "Haciendas and Plantations in Middle America and the Antilles." *Social and Economic Studies* 6, no. 3 (1957):380–412.

≡ **2** ≡

Physical Patterns
of Middle America

Diversity, as we have already noted, is the keynote of the physical landscape in Middle America. In few other areas of similar size are there, within short distances, such great variations of surface configuration, climate, soils, vegetation, and animal life as are found in Mexico, Central America, and the West Indies. With the exception of those features derived from continental glaciation and from frost action in high latitudes, almost the entire gamut of known landforms is represented in this area. Flattish alluvial and limestone plains are in close juxtaposition with high plateaus and rugged mountains that vary in type from fault blocks and folded ridges to volcanic cones. There is a magnificent variety of coastal forms, ranging from cliffed headlands through extensive barrier beaches and lagoons to coral reefs. This diversity of surface configuration in Middle America stems primarily from the complex geological history of the area and its position within one of the world's regions of contemporary active mountain building.

The mountainous character of Middle America is one of the important reasons for the complex pattern of climate types and associated vegetation cover. For example, on the eastern escarpment of the Mexican plateau one may, in one or two hours, drive from a hot, jungle-covered coastal plain into the cool pine and fir forests of the Sierra Madre, passing on the way through rain-drenched windward slopes and dry protected valleys. Moreover, Middle America straddles the northern limit of the tropics. Thus, climates in Mexico vary from midlatitude types to most of the subtropical and tropical ones. The diversity of plant and animal life also derives from the fact that Middle America is the meeting zone between North American (Nearctic) and tropical American (Neotropical) flora and fauna.

SURFACE CONFIGURATION
AND RELATED GEOLOGY

Because of their complexity, the landform patterns of Middle America might best be described on the basis of large physiographic regions, each of which has a general uniformity of surface characteristics. In the following section on surface configuration, Middle America is divided into 11 major physiographic provinces, beginning with those of Mexico (Figures 2.1 and 2.2).

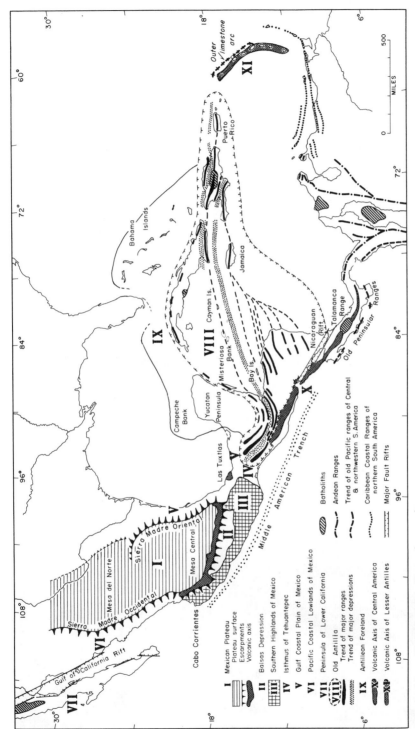

Figure 2.1 Physiographic-Tectonic provinces

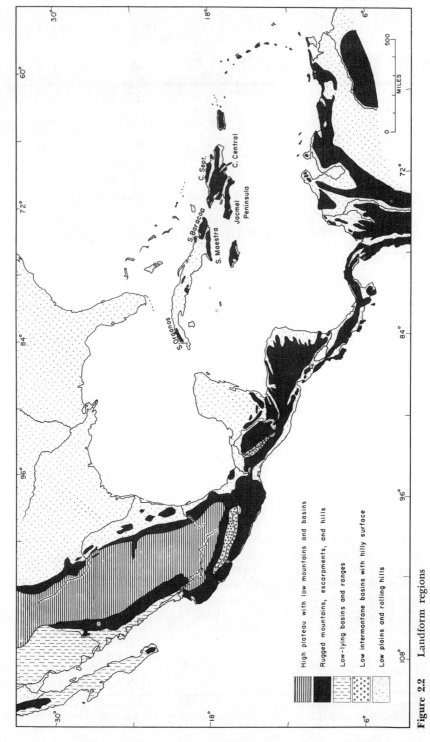

Figure 2.2 Landform regions

High plateau with low mountains and basins

Rugged mountains, escarpments, and hills

Low-lying basins and ranges

Low intermontane basins with hilly surface

Low plains and rolling hills

MILES

S. Organos

S. Baracoa

C. Sept.

S. Maestra

C. Central

Jacmel

Peninsula

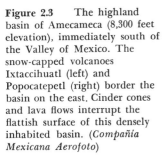

Figure 2.3 The highland basin of Amecameca (8,300 feet elevation), immediately south of the Valley of Mexico. The snow-capped volcanoes Ixtaccihuatl (left) and Popocatepetl (right) border the basin on the east. Cinder cones and lava flows interrupt the flattish surface of this densely inhabited basin. (*Compañia Mexicana Aerofoto*)

The Mexican Plateau (I) [1]

One of the largest landform units of Middle America, and one of the most significant in terms of human settlement, is the Mexican plateau. This upland is a tilted block of earth that stands a mile or more above the sea. Elevations are greatest in the southern portion, where some parts of the plateau surface rise over 8,000 feet above sea level. As one travels northward from Mexico City, near the plateau's southern edge, elevations gradually decrease to less than 4,000 feet at El Paso on the United States–Mexican frontier.

The Plateau Surface. The arid northern half of the plateau is sometimes called the *Mesa del Norte*. This part extends from the international border southward to about the latitude of San Luis Potosí (22°N.), where it blends indefinitely into the higher and more moist southern half of the plateau, often known as the *Mesa Central*. The surface of both parts of the plateau is characterized by low mountains separated by basins. Flattish basin floors occupy perhaps two-fifths of the total area. The ranges of the Mesa del Norte trend generally northwest–southeast and rise 500 to 2,500 feet above the adjacent

1. The Roman numerals in parentheses refer to areas of Figure 2.1.

basins. In the eastern section of the plateau the ranges are of limestone and shale, while on the western side volcanic materials prevail. Northern Mexico is arid, and there are few permanent streams. The desert basins (*bolsones*), flanked by sloping alluvial fans and rock pediments, form plains between the ranges. Usually lacking exterior drainage, the flat centers of these basins are often occupied by intermittent or playa lakes which contain water only after rare heavy showers.

The southern half of the plateau, or Mesa Central, is a land of geologically recent volcanic activity. A row of high, widely spaced volcanoes lines the southern rim of the plateau. This range, called the Transverse Volcanic Axis or the Neovolcanic Range of Mexico, contains the snow-capped peaks of Popocatepetl (17,900 feet), Ixtaccihuatl (17,300 feet), Toluca (15,000 feet), and, near its western end, Colima (14,200 feet). Most of these large volcanoes were formed about ten million years ago in Late Tertiary time, but some, like Colima and Popocatepetl, are still active occasionally. Mexico's newest volcano, Parícutin, which erupted in 1943, lies within the volcanic axis. Low cinder cones, crater lakes, and lava flows add to the many volcanic forms within the mountainous area (Figure 2.3).

Immediately north of the volcanic range, the surface of the Mesa Central is composed of eroded remnants of old volcanoes, between which are flat-floored basins. During moist Pleistocene times most of these basins contained lakes formed by the interruption of normal stream drainage through damming by ash fall and lava flows. Tapped by headward eroding tributaries of the main rivers and filled by sedimentation, the majority of the lakes have now disappeared, and their beds remain as the present level surfaces within the basins. Since prehistoric days, these basins have been the most culturally significant landforms of the plateau. An abundance of aquatic wildlife in and around the remaining lakes and the fertile soils on adjacent volcanic slopes and basin flats have attracted dense settlement. Today Mexico obtains much of her food supply from the crops cultivated in the originally fertile lacustrine soils. Such basins vary greatly in size, from a few square miles to extensive areas 30 by 40 miles. The largest basins include the valleys of Mexico, Huamantla, Puebla, Toluca, Morelia, Guadalajara, and a series of con-

nected basins called the Bajío of Guanajuato (Figure 2.4). Some of the basin lakes, such as Pátzcuaro, are still intact; others, such as the five original lakes of the Valley of Mexico, have been artificially drained within the last century; still others are in the process of disappearing through filling and natural dessication.

Three main river systems drain the greater part of the Mesa Central. The Santiago-Lerma system, the largest in Mexico, drains the western two-thirds of the plateau. Originating in the Basin of Toluca, the Lerma River passes through the Bajío, forms Lake Chapala within a long depression, and flows out as the Río Santiago to plunge over the western edge of the plateau in a deep canyon toward the Pacific Ocean. Much of the eastern third of the Mesa Central is drained by the Pánuco-Moctezuma river system, the tributaries of which have cut deep canyons into the edge of the plateau. Lastly, tributaries of the upper Balsas River serve as drainage for the southeastern section of the Mesa Central. Tributaries of all three drainage

Figure 2.4   Principal basins of the Mesa Central. The basins are shown with stippled pattern; the edge of the Mesa Central is indicated by the broken line.

Figure 2.5 At their northern end the folded ranges of the Sierra Madre Oriental veering westward. This sector of the Sierra is called the Arteaga Anticlinorium. The city of Monterrey (lower right) occupies a plain along the intermittent Santa Catarina River. (*Compañia Mexicana Aerofoto*)

systems, as well as those of minor rivers, are continually eroding headward, farther into the plateau surface.

The Plateau Escarpments. The most spectacular features of the Mexican plateau are the steep escarpments which flank it on the east, west, and south. Each of the escarpments is overlooked by a mountain range which forms the respective rims of the plateau. On its eastern flank the plateau is bordered by the *Sierra Madre Oriental,* a series of elongated limestone ranges. Trending generally north–south, the higher ranges of the Sierra rise from 7,000 to 8,000 feet elevation, with some peaks reaching as high as 13,000 feet. Viewed from the plateau, most of the Sierra Madre Oriental appears to be insignificant and seems to form only the eastern upturned lip of the highlands. But from the Gulf Coastal Plain, the Sierra rises in a series of parallel ridges and valleys to

create a formidable escarpment. The ridges and valleys are the result of geological folding of the bedrock and are similar to those of the Appalachians in the eastern United States. The southern portion of the eastern escarpment bordering the Mesa Central is rimmed by the eastern end of the volcanic axis mentioned above. Here towers the great snow-capped volcanic peak of Orizaba, or Citlaltepetl (18,700 feet), the highest point in Middle America. Near Monterrey, northeastern Mexico, the Sierra Madre Oriental suddenly veers westward, forming a spectacular series of folded ridges and valleys called an anticlinorium (Figure 2.5). North of Monterrey the plateau escarpment, composed of low folded ranges, gradually decreases in elevation toward the Rio Grande.

On its western rim, the Mexican plateau is flanked by the *Sierra Madre Occidental.* The elevation of this range is similar to that of the eastern sierra, but its geology and physiography are quite different. The Sierra Madre Occidental, as well as the western side of the plateau, has been built up of vast quantities of volcanic material that has issued from vents. The western side of the Sierra, which forms the plateau escarpment, has been frayed with deep canyons, or *barrancas,* by streams flowing westward from the plateau. Some of these barrancas, such as that of El Cobre, rival the Grand Canyon of the Colorado in depth and grandeur. The steepness of the escarpment and the presence of the deep barrancas make access to this section of Mexico most difficult. Not until 1945 was an auto road completed across the sierra from Durango on the plateau to Mazatlán on the Pacific coast; the first railway to cross it (from Chihuahua City to Topolobampo) was finished in 1962.

On the south the Mexican plateau is bordered by the volcanic axis, already discussed. Overlooking the deep Balsas River depression, the volcanic range forms the southern escarpment of the plateau. Low passes between the large volcanoes, as well as the presence of occasional plateau remnants and basin fills on the escarpment slope, make the southern approaches to the Mexican plateau much less difficult than those on its eastern or western sides. The valleys of Iguala and Cuernavaca, south of the Valley of Mexico, are examples of the steplike arrangement of basin fills on the escarpment that ease the climb from the Balsas depression to the central highlands.

The Balsas Depression (II)

The low, hot, and dry Balsas Depression separates the Mexican plateau from the southern highlands of Mexico. A jumble of low hills, through which the Balsas River and its tributaries twist and turn, characterizes the surface of the depression. In only a few places has the Balsas River formed sizable pockets of alluvium along

its course. Near the Pacific Ocean the river breaks through the southern highlands to the sea. Geologically, the depression continues northwestward along the foot of the Mexican plateau. In this section the lowland is occupied by the Tepalcatepec River, a tributary of the Balsas.

The Southern Highlands (III)

South of the Balsas depression lie the Southern Highlands of Mexico. The western part of this mountainous area within the state of Guerrero is often called the *Sierra Madre del Sur;* small discontinuous ranges continue northwestward along the Pacific coast as far as Cabo Corrientes. The wide eastern section of the highlands within the state of Oaxaca is known as the *Mesa del Sur.* The entire southern highlands form a mountain mass of ancient crystalline rock that represents some of the most rugged terrain in Mexico (Figure 2.6). Average elevations of mountain crests range from 7,000 to 8,000 feet above sea level, some 3,000 to 4,000 feet above adjacent stream valleys and basins. A few peaks rise to more than 10,000 feet above the sea.

Along the Pacific coast the southern highlands descend abruptly to the sea in a steep escarpment, forming in places a rugged cliffed coast. Only a few short stretches of narrow coastal plain occur from Cabo Corrientes to the Isthmus of Tehuantepec. There is little level land in this rugged mountain mass. The hundreds of small, swiftly flowing streams that drain the highlands have carved deep V-shaped valleys into the surface, creating a land of precipitous slopes and knife-edged ridges. Only scattered remnants of a former plateau area and a few basins in the Mesa del Sur have extensive flattish surfaces. The Valley of Oaxaca is the largest basin —a down-faulted trench 60 miles long and some 15 wide that lies at an elevation of 5,000 feet above the sea.

Figure 2.6 Aerial view of the Mesa del Sur east of Oaxaca City. This view shows the rugged, stream-dissected surface and the scattered subsistence maize fields of the Indian inhabitants. In the center background is Cerro Zempoaltepec (11,000 feet elevation), the highest point in the southern highlands of Mexico.

The Isthmus of Tehuantepec (IV)

The Isthmus of Tehuantepec is a lowland depression east of the Southern Highlands. It is often taken as the physical divide between North and Central America. In this section, only 125 miles of land separate the Gulf of Mexico from the Pacific Ocean. Isthmian America truly begins here. Although the maximum elevation at the drainage divide of the isthmus is only 800 feet, streams have dissected the surface into a rough hill area. Plains occur only on the Gulf and Pacific sides.

The Coastal Lowlands of Mexico (V and VI)

The *Gulf Coastal Plain* (V), which fringes the eastern side of Mexico, is one of the most extensive lowlands of Middle America. A continuation of the Gulf Coastal Plain of the United States, this lowland belt extends from the Rio Grande for a distance of 850 miles to the Yucatan Peninsula. In width, the lowland varies from a maximum of 100 miles near its northern and southern extremities to a few miles in its center, where a spur of the eastern

escarpment reaches the sea a short distance north of Veracruz. Swamps, lagoons, and barrier beaches occur along many parts of the immediate coast, such as the long stretch from the Rio Grande to below Tampico and along the shore of Tabasco. Inland from the coast are extensive plains and rolling surfaces underlain by young sediments of marl, shale, and sandstone. Toward the escarpment of the plateau, the plains grade into elongated ridges and valleys that trend north–south. Occasionally the plain surface near the coast is interrupted by isolated hills and low mountains that have resulted from past volcanic eruptions, local folding, or the uplift of young coastal sediments by large masses of granite rock that have intruded from below. The Sierra de Tamaulipas between the Rio Grande and Tampico is an example of folding and intrusion, while the Tuxtlas Mountains, which rise abruptly from the coast south of Veracruz, exemplify recent volcanic activity.

A number of rivers originating on the eastern side of the plateau cross the coastal lowlands and have built alluvial flood plains in their lower courses. With adequate water for irrigation, the flood plain of the lower Rio Grande has, in recent years, become one of Mexico's major agricultural areas. Farther south, the Río Pánuco at Tampico, the Coatzacoalcos and Papaloapan rivers in southern Veracruz, and the large Grijalva river system in Tabasco discharge a large volume of water and sediment into the Gulf, and have formed extensive deltaic plains (Figure 2.7). Such areas afford future possibilities for agricultural development.

In contrast to the Gulf area, the *Pacific Coastal Lowlands* (VI) of Mexico are much less extensive and are characterized as much by hills and low mountains as by level plains. The Pacific lowlands are widest in the north near the United States frontier, where they form the Sonoran or Altar Desert, one of the driest sections of Mexico. There low, worn-down mountains, oriented north–south with desert basins between, characterize the surface. As one goes southward into the state of Sinaloa, the lowlands form a narrow coastal strip between the western plateau escarpment and the Pacific Ocean, continuing as far as the Santiago-Lerma delta in Nayarit. Even in this narrow lowland, north–south-trending hills of granite—remnants of formerly higher ranges—dominate the landscape. Some hills abut upon the sea, forming in places natural harbors, such as that of Guaymas, Topolobampo, and Mazatlán, with small islands off coast. Some of the larger streams, such as the Fuerte and Mayo rivers, which cross the

lowlands, have formed large delta plains along the coast. These deltas afford extensive level areas of alluvium, and the rivers supply adequate water for the large-scale irrigated farming that has been developed along the northwest coast of Mexico since 1930. Numerous lagoons fronted by sand bars extend along the southern part of the coast, and swamps abound immediately back from the sea in Nayarit state.

The Peninsula of Lower California (VII)

In the extreme northwest of Mexico, the peninsula of Lower California extends southeastward from the international frontier for a distance of 800 miles. This long strip of mountainous land is separated from the Mexican mainland by the equally long Gulf of California. The latter is a rift, or down-faulted block of earth, that has been invaded by the sea; the northern part of the same rift extends into the United States in the form of the Imperial and Coachella valleys of southeastern California. Discharging its water and sediment into the northern part of the Gulf, the Colorado River has built a deltaic plain of fertile alluvium, now an area of intensive irrigated farming on both the Mexican and American sides of the frontier.

The greater part of the peninsula of

Figure 2.7 A portion of the deltaic plain of the Grijalva River in Tabasco, southeastern Mexico. In the foreground a line of settlement occupies the narrow natural levee, back of which lie marshes and lakes.

Lower California is an elongated fault-block mountain whose steep escarpment faces eastward toward the Gulf and whose backslope inclines gently toward the Pacific Ocean. Large areas of volcanic outpourings cover much of the backslope, forming rough, plateaulike features. In the north, the high, rugged granitic ranges of Juárez and San Pedro Mártir are but southern extensions of similar mountains in southern California. Another mountainous mass of granite forms the Cape area, or southernmost tip of the peninsula.

Northern Central America and the Greater Antilles (VIII): Old Antillia

The oldest and most complex physiographic and tectonic area of Middle America comprises both northern Central America (including the state of Chiapas in southeastern Mexico) and the islands of the Greater Antilles. The association of these two areas—one an isthmian portion of the continent, the other a group of large, mountainous islands, separated by the Caribbean Sea—becomes understandable in view of the similarity of present landforms, geologic structure, and tectonic history. Some investigators believe that at one time in the geologic past, probably 100 million years ago during the Cretaceous era, the two present areas formed one large land mass, to which the term "Old Antillia" is often applied.

The surface of both northern Central America and the Greater Antilles is characterized by a series of east–west-trending mountain ranges and intervening depressions. Most of these ranges are extremely rugged. Some of the mountain surfaces are composed of limestone and sandstone into which streams have carved deep canyons, exposing ancient crystalline rocks, some of which are rich in gold and other minerals. Erosion has stripped other mountain surfaces almost completely of their former limestone covering, and has exposed large masses of granite (*batholiths*) which have intruded upward from depths within the earth's crust.

Two ranges and one depression of northern Central America can be reasonably identified with those of the Antilles and can be traced across the floor of the Caribbean Sea in the form of submarine ridges and deeps. One range begins in the Mexican state of Chiapas as the plateaulike Sierra de San Cristóbal (9,000 feet elevation). Continuing into central Guatemala as the plateau of the Alto Cuchumatanes (10,000 feet elevation) and the highlands of Cobán, it joins with minor ranges in southern British Honduras to descend into the Caribbean as the Cayman Ridge. This range is expressed in the shallow Misteriosa Bank and the Cayman Islands with their adjacent shoals. Eastward it rises in southernmost Cuba as the high Sierra Maestra (5,000 to 6,500 feet elevation), continues into the island of Hispaniola where it forms the Cordillera Central, and finally ends in the central mountains of Puerto Rico (4,500 feet elevation) and the Virgin Islands. In the Dominican Republic, on the island of Hispaniola, the Cordillera Central has been intruded by a huge gold-bearing batholith, the summit of which is Mt. Duarte (Mt. Trujillo), 10,400 feet above the sea and the highest point of the Antilles. A lower mountain range, called the Cordillera Septentrional, borders the northern coast of the Dominican Republic. Between the northern and central mountain ranges lies a depression known as the Cibao, a wide alluvial-filled valley of prime agricultural importance.

A second large mountain structure of Old Antillia lies south of the one already described. It begins as the granitic Sierra de Chiapas along the Pacific coast of southernmost Mexico. Passing through Guatemala in a series of low crystalline ranges, it joins with the Sierra de Omoa in northwestern Honduras, forms the Bay Islands off Honduras and possibly Swan

Island in the mid-Caribbean, and continues toward Jamaica. Farther south, a series of east–west ranges in Honduras and northern Nicaragua dip beneath the Caribbean to form the numerous shoals and banks off the coast (the Nicaraguan Swell). Most of Jamaica is covered with limestone that has been highly eroded and dissolved to form an extremely rugged surface (a topography called "karst") averaging 2,500 feet above the sea. The island's highest elevations occur in its northeastern portion, where the Blue Mountains, a deeply dissected mass of crystalline rock, rise to 7,500 feet. The same structure continues eastward as the southern range of Haiti in the Jacmel Peninsula (elevation 8,000 to 9,000 feet).

Between the two Antillean mountain ranges described above, there occurs a depression that can be traced from the Valley of Chiapas in southern Mexico, eastward through the Motagua Valley of central Guatemala, and thence into the Caribbean as the Bartlett Deep, a submarine trench which in places attains depths of nearly 25,000 feet below sea level. An eastward

Figure 2.8   Vertically walled sink, or *cenote*, in the limestone plain of northern Yucatan, Mexico. The water level lies some 60 feet below the scrub-covered surface.

extension of this depression is seen in the lowland basins of Cul-de-Sac in Haiti and Enriquillo in southeastern Dominican Republic. The latter basin is one of the two spots of land in Middle America that are below sea level (−154 feet), the other being the southern portion of the Salton Sink which extends across the Mexican border to Mexicali in Baja California.

The Antillean Foreland (IX)

On the northern side of the extensive belt of east–west ranges and depressions that has been called "Old Antillia" lie two separate areas of similar surface configuration and tectonic history. These are the Yucatan Peninsula and the Bahama Islands. Both are low-lying, almost level plains of recently emerged limestone. Because of their peculiar tectonic nature, these two areas are often termed the *Antillean Foreland.*

Most of the Yucatan Peninsula is characterized by a karst, or limestone solution surface. In its northern half there are no surface streams, for rainwater sinks quickly through the porous rock to form underground courses. Round, steep-sided hollows, called "sink-holes" (*cenotes*), the result of the caving of surface rock above subterranean stream channels, are the most common landform and are the main sources of water supply (Figure 2.8). The red *terra rossa* soils derived from limestone are thin over most of the northern part of the peninsula. Bare, fluted limestone is exposed over large areas, and the little soil available for cultivation has accumulated through rainwash in low, scattered pockets. Farther south into the Petén of northern Guatemala, low, elongated limestone hills frequently interrupt the extensive plains. There surface streams are more common than in the drier north, and round or oval lakes of all sizes indicate shallow sinkholes and solution channels.

North and west from the peninsular

Figure 2.9   Lake Ilopango with the volcano of San Vicente, El Salvador, in the background typifies much of the volcanic landscape of Central America.

mainland lies a large submarine platform, the Campeche Banks, with depths of less than 600 feet and many shoals and reefs. The shallowness of these tropical waters has made them an ideal habitat for many kinds of fish and crustaceans, giving rise to a sizable fishing industry.

Immediately north of Cuba, the Bahama Islands—low, flat patches of porous limestone and coral—perch slightly above the sea on a vast shallow platform, or bank. Approximately 700 islands and over 2,000 reefs, cays, and rocks comprise this peculiar area. The Bahama Platform is separated from the crumpled Antillean area to the south by a submarine trench which merges eastward with the Brownson Deep (−28,000 feet) off the north coast of Puerto Rico.

The Volcanic Axes of Central America and the Lesser Antilles (X and XI)

Both the western and eastern sides of the Antillean area of Central America and the West Indies are flanked by long zones of geologically recent volcanic activity. A continuous line of young volcanoes borders the Pacific edge of Central America for 800 miles, from the present Mexico-Guatemala frontier to Costa Rica. This volcanic axis forms the longest and most spectacular mountain range of Middle America. The Caribbean counterpart of the Central American chain is the volcanic arc of the Lesser Antilles, a festoon of small islands 500 miles long, which forms the southeastern limits of Middle America.

The old Antillean east–west structure along the Pacific margin of northern Central America has been buried by recent volcanic materials. Thick deposits of older volcanic ash and lava cover much of the southern highlands of Honduras and north-central Nicaragua. The most recent volcanic activity lies near the Pacific coast, where more than 40 large volcanic peaks have ejected enormous quantities of ash, cinder, and lava. Among these volcanoes are the famous Fuego (12,600 feet) in Guatemala and Irazú (11,300 feet) in Costa Rica. Many volcanoes within the Central American axis are still active. As in the Mesa Central of Mexico, volcanic activity has formed lake-studded basins that range from 1,000 to 6,000 feet in elevation (Figure 2.9). Favored by fertile volcanic soils, these tropical highland basins and adjacent mountain slopes are the areas of densest settlement within Central America. The largest of these highland basins is the Meseta Central of Costa Rica with elevations between 3,000 and 5,000 feet. South of the Meseta Central the volcanic axis is interrupted by a huge batholith known as the Talamanca Range with elevations over 12,000 feet. In Panama, vulcanism resumes with the volcano of Chiriquí (11,410 feet) and continues in diminishing degree almost to the Canal Zone. Costa Rica and Panama have sometimes been called a volcanic bridge that connects Central and South America. Beyond the Canal Zone, the geology of Panama is closely related to a northwestern prong of the Andes, characterized by low mountain ranges along both the Caribbean and Pacific shores.

The middle of Central America is rent by a large crustal fracture, or rift, which forms the lowlands of Nicaragua. This long, narrow depression trends northwest–southeast between the Old Antillean structure and the volcanic axis of Central America. The central portion of the lowland is occupied by the largest fresh-water lakes of Middle America: lakes Managua and Nicaragua. Both drain to the Caribbean by way of the San Juan River, which flows through the southeastern part of the depression. Extending to the northwest of the lakes are plains covered with fertile soils derived from ash spewed from the volcanoes nearby. This rich lowland has been one of the most densely populated areas of Central America since pre-Conquest times. Near its northwestern end the depression helps form the Gulf of Fonseca, the largest indentation along the Pacific shore of Middle America.

The Lesser Antilles are composed of a double arc of small islands. The inner arc consists of the high volcanic islands, which are volcanic cones or groups of cones. The tops of these cones rise out of the sea to elevations of 4,000 or 5,000 feet. Most of the surface of the volcanic isles, such as those from St. Kitts to Grenada, is composed of steep slopes, with narrow coastal plains and gently sloping piedmonts of deep, rich soil which ring the mountainous centers. The outer, and smaller, arc is made up of a few low flattish islands that are covered with limestone which overlays older volcanic or crystalline materials. This section of the Lesser Antilles

includes the small isles of Barbuda, Antigua, the Grande Terre portion of Guadeloupe, and Marie Galante.

The Geological Hazards of Middle America

Situated in one of the world's most intensive zones of active mountain building, much of Middle America is subject to frequent earthquakes and volcanic eruptions. Often, in the past, these geological hazards have caused widespread damage to man and his works in Mexico, Central America, and the West Indies. In the future they will undoubtedly cause much more (Figure 2.10).

During historic times, several serious eruptions and explosions have occurred in all three of the main volcanic axes of Middle America. Probably the worst, in terms of loss of human life, was the 1902 explosion of Mt. Pelée on Martinique Island in the Lesser Antilles. A mass of fiery lava and superheated gas (*nuée ardente*) completely destroyed the town of St. Pierre and suffocated its 30,000 inhabitants within seconds. In 1835, Mt. Cosigüina, on the Gulf of Fonseca in northwestern Nicaragua, exploded. Many villages were half buried, and farmland was temporarily damaged by falling ash and dust within a radius of 100 miles. Much more serious destruction, accompanied by the loss of 6,000 lives, was wrought in 1902 by the eruption of Santa María volcano in Guatemala. Even the eruption of the relatively small Parícutin in Mexico in 1943 caused considerable damage to forests and crops over a large area through ash fall; moreover, a flow of lava completely engulfed one Tarascan Indian town. Where ash fall was light, however, soils were improved by the addition of minerals. In 1963 Costa Rica's long dormant Irazú volcano suddenly erupted, spewing vast quantities of fine, grayish ash over the Meseta Central. Coffee groves, pasture

Figure 2.10 The 1968 eruption of Cerro Negro, western Nicaragua. Lying within the volcanic axis of Central America, this small volcano has been active since 1850. The prevailing winds carry the plume of falling ash southwestward across the Pacific coastal plain, damaging large acreages of cotton around the city of León. (*Instituto Geográfico Nacional de Nicaragua*)

lands, and forests were temporarily damaged. In the long run, perhaps, the benefits of rich soils derived from the weathering of volcanic ejecta may outweigh the damage inflicted by occasional catastrophes.

As geological hazards, earthquakes have been far more destructive and widespread than volcanic eruptions in Middle America. Zones of seismic disturbance extend along most of the Pacific coast of Mexico and Central America and around much of the island rim in the Caribbean, as indicated in Figure 2.11. Severe quakes frequently occur in those coastal areas adjacent to deep submarine troughs, where slippage along faults sets up heavy shock waves within the earth's crust. Southwestern Mexico, near the Acapulco Deep off coast, and portions of the Dominican

Figure 2.11 Geological hazards

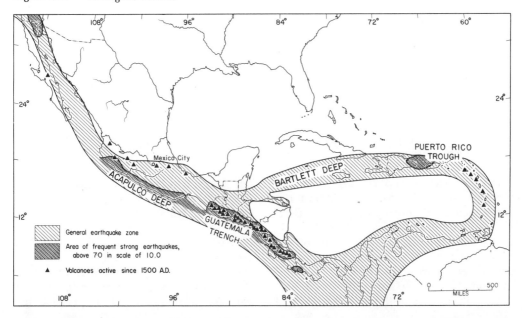

Republic and Puerto Rico, adjacent to the Puerto Rico Deep, are good examples. The Pacific coast of Central America is subject to frequent shocks that are associated with both volcanic activity and the deeply seated fault zones off coast.

The catastrophic effects of earthquakes are seen most frequently in the destruction of buildings and in the generation of landslides. A less frequent, but equally destructive, effect is the creation by submarine earthquakes of tidal waves, called "tsunamis," which may inundate extensive sections of the coast, causing great destruction of property and life. There is hardly a town or city in western and southern Mexico, the Pacific side of Central America, or the West Indies that has not experienced earthquake disasters sometime in its history. The city of San Salvador, capital of El Salvador in Central America, has been completely or partially destroyed and rebuilt nine times since its founding on the present site in 1528. The most serious earthquake disaster of Middle America in recent times was the partial destruction of Managua, the capital city of Nicaragua, in December 1972, when an estimated eight thousand people lost their lives, crushed by collapsing buildings in the city's central area.

WEATHER AND CLIMATE

The physical diversity of Middle America is expressed, again, in its weather and climate. The distribution of air temperature and precipitation, the two principal elements of weather and climate, is highly complex in Middle America. Almost the entire range of subtropical and tropical climates, as well as some midlatitude types, occur in this small segment of the earth's surface. Among the reasons for such diversity are: (1) latitudinal position; (2) complicated terrain and varied altitude; (3) influence of the adjacent seas and

oceans; and (4) the various dominant pressure areas and accompanying wind systems.

General Temperature Characteristics and Controls

Latitude. Middle America's latitudinal position near the northern margin of the New World tropics is one of the basic controls of its weather and climate. The greater part of the area is within the tropics. Approximately two-thirds of the land and most of the adjacent seas lie south of the Tropic of Cancer ($23\frac{1}{2}°$ N.). At least half of Mexico, however, lies north of the latitudinal limit of the tropics; in terms of weather and climate most of this area is subtropical or midlatitude. The effect of latitude is reflected mainly in seasonal temperatures. As Figure 2.12 indicates, within the tropics there is a relatively small difference, usually less than 15° F, between the average temperatures of the coldest and warmest months (the annual temperature range). That is, in terms of temperature, there are no distinct summer and winter periods in the tropics. The difference between day and night temperatures (the diurnal range) is usually far greater than the annual range; hence, the well-known expression, "Night is the winter of the tropics." In much of northern Mexico, which is outside the tropics, the annual temperature range increases rapidly poleward, demarcating definite summer and winter seasons similar to those in the southern United States. Killing frosts occur every winter in the Mesa de Norte, but in the Pacific and Gulf coastal lowlands of northern Mexico they are rare.

Altitude. Within the Middle American tropics, altitude strongly influences air temperature. Since the temperature of the air decreases with altitude at the normal rate of approximately 1° F per 300 feet

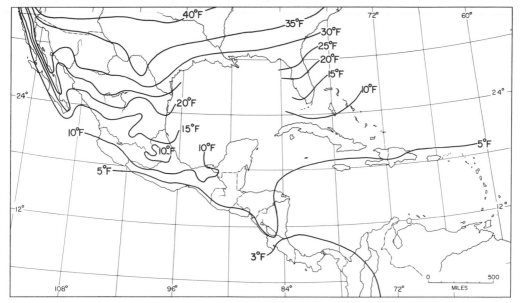

Figure 2.12   Mean annual temperature range

elevation, it follows that on high mountain slopes there occurs an altitudinal zonation of weather and climate. This fact is keenly recognized by the inhabitants of the Latin American tropics, who know the temperature belts by the terms given in Figures 2.13 and 2.14 and described below.

Within Middle America, altitudinal zonation of temperature is best seen in the escarpment areas of central and southern Mexico and in the mountainous sections of Central America. There, weather and climate, vegetation, soils, and man's use of the land vary according to altitude. In such areas, one may pass through three or four types of climate types within a horizontal distance of only 25 miles. Variation in altitude within mountainous terrain is one of the most important reasons for the great complexity of weather and climate in tropical Middle America.

Following is a brief description of the extent and general temperature characteristics of the major altitudinal zones recognized in the Middle American tropics. Varying local conditions make it difficult to indicate the precise limits of these zones but, in general, the upper altitudinal limits of each zone tend to increase equatorward, and in Central America and Mexico they tend to occupy somewhat lower elevations on the Pacific slope than on the Gulf or Caribbean slopes.

Figure 2.13   Altitudinal temperature zones

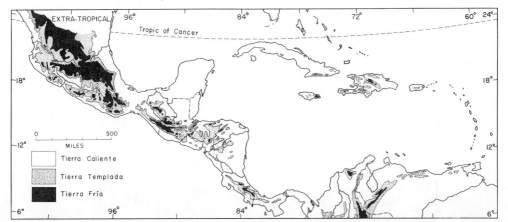

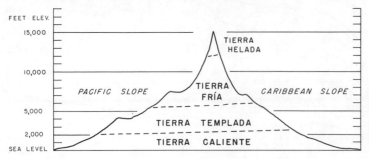

Figure 2.14   A schematic representation of the altitudinal temperature zones of Middle America, at approximately 15° N. latitude

THE TIERRA CALIENTE.   The *tierra caliente* ("hot land") of Middle America lies generally between sea level and 2,500 feet elevation. Within these limits are included all of the tropical coastal lowlands, large plains areas (e.g., Yucatan Peninsula), low interior basins (e.g., the Balsas River valley), and the foothills or low mountains of southern Mexico, Central America, and the West Indies. Thus, approximately one-half of the Middle American tropics is *tierra caliente*. In general, high but not excessive daytime temperatures (85 to 90° F) contrast with cool nighttime conditions (70 to 75° F) most of the year, with small differences between summer and winter months. Frost is unknown, and rarely do night temperatures fall as low as 50° F. The *tierra caliente,* a land of tropical agriculture, is of growing importance throughout Middle America.

THE TIERRA TEMPLADA.   The *tierra templada* ("temperate land") is roughly between 2,500 and 5,500 to 6,000 feet in tropical Middle America. This zone, together with those that lie above it, constitutes the tropical highlands. The *tierra templada* includes the intermediate mountain slopes and much of the plateau surface of Central Mexico and Central America; only the higher interior mountains of the Caribbean islands qualify as tropical highlands. Mild daytime temperatures (75 to 80° F) prevail, although hot afternoons with temperatures of 90 and 95° F sometimes occur in the warmer months of April or May, just prior to the start of the rainy season. Nights are delightfully cool (60 to 70° F). The difference between summer and winter temperatures increases poleward, so that in the Mesa Central of Mexico, on the northern margin of the tropical highlands, periods of cold and occasional night frosts are not uncommon in December and January. However, the escarpment areas of Mexico and Central America are usually frost-free. Most Latin Americans and visitors from the midlatitudes consider the *tierra templada* to have the most desirable temperatures for human comfort in Middle America. In Mexico and Central America, much of the population and the agricultural production is found in the *tierra templada*.

THE TIERRA FRIA.   The *tierra fria* ("cold land") generally lies above 5,500 to 6,000 feet elevation. Only a small part of the Middle American tropics—possibly 10 percent of the land surface—is considered to be *tierra fria*. Most of the cold land lies in the high basins and mountain slopes of the Mesa Central of Mexico and in the highlands of Chiapas and Guatemala. These are areas of warm, pleasant days (75 to 80° F) and cold nights (50 to 55° F). Frosts are common during the cooler months of December through February; even in midsummer, killing frosts have occurred in the higher basins of central Mexico, though rarely. Only hardy highland or midlatitude crops thrive at these altitudes; however, many of the cold but fertile highland basins, such as the Valley of Mexico and those of western Guatemala, are among the most densely populated spots of Middle America.

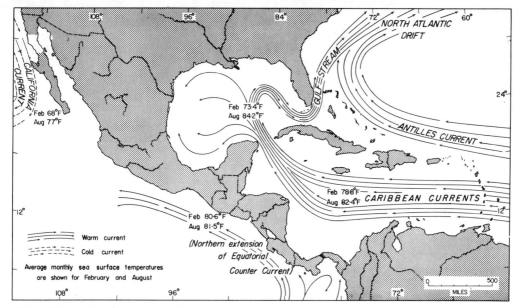

Figure 2.15 Ocean currents and sea surface temperatures

THE TIERRA HELADA. The *tierra helada* ("frozen land"), generally lying above 12,000 feet elevation, occupies only the highest mountain peaks of Mexico and Central America. Temperatures below 50° F prevail almost all year. Freezes occur nightly in the cooler months and frequently in midsummer, and permanent ice and snow occupy the upper portions of the highest peaks.

Water Masses and Ocean Currents. Although their effect on temperature is less spectacular than altitude, the influence of adjacent water bodies must be considered. Air that overlies large water areas tends to take on the same temperature as the water surface. Thus, the air temperature of the coasts and the smaller islands of Middle America is profoundly influenced by the adjacent seas and oceans. Warm water borders the shores of most of Middle America. Of prime importance to the weather and climate of adjacent land areas are the Caribbean Sea and the Gulf of Mexico, both practically inland seas fed by warm offshoots of the Atlantic North Equatorial Current (Figure 2.15). As the temperature of the surface water ranges between 73 and 84° F, these two water bodies are veritable caldrons, over which forms a tropical marine air mass. This air mass extends warm conditions somewhat northward of their normal latitudes and carries tropical air into the southeastern and central United States during the summer period.

Warm surface waters fed by the northern extension of the Pacific Equatorial Counter Current occur on the western side of Central America and southern Mexico. The Pacific maritime tropical air mass forms over these warm waters and transfers high year-round temperature and low annual range along the adjacent coasts.

In contrast, the relatively cold water of the California Current, which borders the Pacific shore of Lower California, brings cool year-round temperatures along the coast, but lowers the annual range to almost tropical proportions.

Continentality. Relatively narrow land masses, isthmuses, and islands characterize the southern two-thirds of Middle America. Thus, few points within this area are far from the influence of the sea. But toward the United States frontier, northern Mexico widens to continental proportions, introducing another temperature control, termed "continentality." Distance from

39

the ameliorating conditions of the oceans and increasing latitude combine to give north–central Mexico the cold winters and hot summers common to the interior mid-latitudes.

Rainfall and Its Controls

The rainfall map of Middle America (Figure 2.16) shows a complex areal pattern of abundance and paucity of moisture. The aridity of northern Mexico contrasts with the humidity of the southeastern part of the country. In general, the east coasts receive more rain than the west coasts, and small spots of dryness occur in the midst of areas with heavy precipitation throughout Middle America.

For the most part the rainfall is seasonal. The rainy period usually comes during the hotter months, May through October. The drier part of the year corresponds to the cooler period, December through April, and February and March are usually the months of least rain. Over most of the plateau and Pacific coast areas of Mexico and northern Central America, 75 to 80 percent of the yearly rain falls between May and October. In the tropics,

seasons are determined by rainfall distribution and not, as in the higher latitudes, by temperature.

This simplified picture of seasonal rainfall distribution, however, is complicated by several significant exceptions. In particular, the eastern sides of the Caribbean islands and Central America have short dry periods of less rain than usual, during January and February, rather than a true dry season with little or no moisture. Moreover, parts of the West Indies have double rainy and dry periods during the year, the longer dry season coming in January and February, the shorter one in June or July. Again, over most of Central America a short dry period of 10 to 15 days duration occurs in July or August, while the long dry season lasts from November through March.

Both the areal and seasonal distribution of rainfall, as of temperature, are controlled by various natural factors. In Middle America the main controls of rainfall are: (1) pressure areas and associated winds; (2) air masses; and (3) configuration of the land surface. Usually all three controls operate together to effect the lifting and cooling that is necessary to produce precipitation.

Figure 2.16   Mean annual precipitation

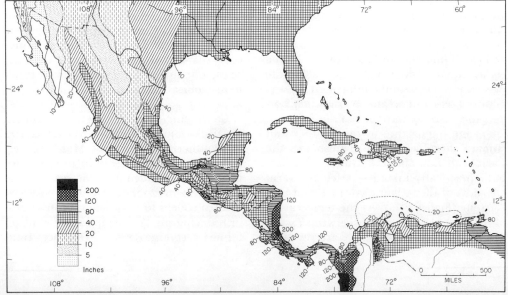

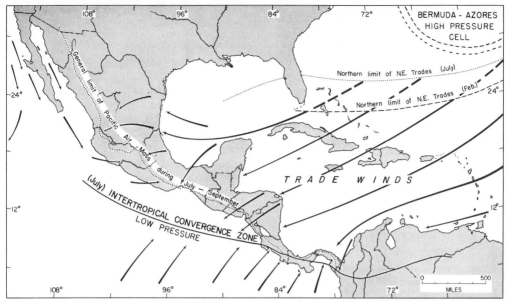

Figure 2.17   Pressure areas and prevailing winds

The northeast trade winds are the prime "weather machine" of eastern Middle America (Figure 2.17). These winds blow out of the Bermuda-Azores subtropical high-pressure cell, the center of which lies over the mid-Atlantic around 30° N. latitude. As they move toward the equatorial low pressure belt, the earth's rotation deflects the trades to the southwest. By the time they reach Middle America, they blow from the northeast and east, sweeping across the West Indian islands and the warm Caribbean Sea to Central America and southern Mexico. As the air imported by the trades sweeps over the warm waters of the South Atlantic and the Caribbean, it is heated and absorbs vast quantities of moisture, forming an unstable maritime tropical air mass. Along the windward slopes of highlands exposed to the trades, the unstable, moisture-laden air is forced to rise and cool, forming great cloud banks and precipitating abundant rain on the mountain slopes. Thus, the northeastern, or windward, sides of the West Indian islands and the eastern side of Central America and southern Mexico are the wettest areas of Middle America, with an average yearly rainfall between 80 and 120 inches. In these areas, nearly every

month is rainy, although there is a short, dry period during February and March when the tropical air mass is more stable. Interior valleys and the lee sides of mountains and mountainous islands receive comparatively little rain (20 to 40 inches), owing to the dryness of the descending air; such areas are said to be in the "rain shadow." Moreover, low-lying areas in the trade wind belt (northern Yucatan and the Bahamas for instance) receive little moisture, owing to the absence of high elevations to induce ascent and cooling of air.

During the warmer months, when the pressure areas have shifted slightly northward, the tropical air mass over the Caribbean and adjacent waters becomes quite unstable, and various kinds of tropical disturbances frequently interrupt the steady trades. Afternoon thunderstorms over both land and sea are common during this period. Also, weak tropical disturbances with ill-defined fronts, called "easterly waves," move westward and northward through the Caribbean islands and Central America, and bring prolonged rains (called *temporales* in Central America and southern Mexico) that last from three to four days. A more spectacular disturbance during the warmer period of the year is the

41

tropical hurricane, discussed below under "Weather Hazards."

Closely associated with the summer disturbances in the trade wind area is the northward movement of the equatorial low pressure belt (doldrums), or Intertropical Convergence Zone (ITC), into Central America and the Caribbean coast of South America. This zone is one of converging and rising warm, unstable air fed by the trade winds of the northern and southern hemispheres. Intense thunderstorms during the afternoon and night, and occasional weak tropical fronts, characterize the weather of this zone, which helps usher in the summer rainy season on the Pacific coast of Central America and southern Mexico. The so-called monsoonal winds that blow from the Pacific into the Central American coast during this period are probably induced by the ITC as it moves periodically into the land. Destructive hurricanes also originate over the warm Pacific waters off the southern Mexican coast, as indicated below.

Because of its aridity and its position outside the tropics, northern Mexico stands apart climatically from the rest of Middle America. Two large areas separated by the Sierra Madre Occidental comprise the arid section of the north: (1) the high, central desert of the Mesa del Norte; and (2) the low desert of Baja California and western Sonora. The low desert is the most arid section of Middle America, containing some points in Baja California which receive less than four inches of rain annually. Baja California and Sonora are often considered to be a southern extension of the Great Basin Desert of the United States, but their aridity is caused principally by the eastern end of the Pacific subtropical high-pressure cell which lies over northwestern Mexico most of the year. The dry, subsiding air of this high-pressure cell precludes much rainfall. The high, central desert of the northern Mexican plateau, on the other hand, owes its aridity mainly to its interior position, rela-

tively far from oceanic sources of moisture. Furthermore, high escarpments effectively bar the entrance of much moist air from the Pacific or the Gulf of Mexico. In summer, occasional afternoon thundershowers bring isolated rains; in winter, the southern extension of midlatitude cyclonic storms cause light rains and sometimes sleet and snow. In semiarid northeastern Mexico, tropical disturbances, including the edges of hurricanes that form in the Gulf of Mexico, occasionally bring heavy rainfall during September and October.

Weather Hazards

Middle America is plagued as much by meteorological as by geological disasters. Its position at the poleward margin of the tropics makes this area vulnerable to atmospheric disturbances that originate in both low and middle latitudes. As we just mentioned, prolonged droughts are particularly prevalent in the central Mexican plateau, at the margin which lies between humid and arid zones. Excessive, flood-producing rains occur periodically in all parts of Middle America, even in the dry northwest, though at rare intervals. The killing frosts of northern Mexico and the tropical highlands have already been mentioned; in addition, summer hailstorms sometimes destroy crops in the highlands of Mexico and Guatemala. The most spectacular and widespread of the weather hazards that affect Middle America, however, are storms of two types: (1) the tropical hurricane; and (2) midlatitude cyclonic disturbances (Figure 2.18).

Tropical Hurricanes. These destructive storms occur on both the Caribbean and Pacific sides of Middle America. Those of the Caribbean are notorious; during the normal hurricane season—July through October—from five to a dozen occur. They are usually no more than 100 miles across, but the high winds within them whirl

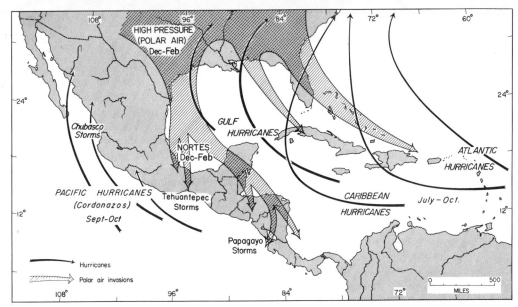

Figure 2.18   Weather hazards

about a small, abnormally low-pressure center at velocities of over 75 miles per hour. They originate within the maritime tropical air mass over the warm waters of the Atlantic, the Caribbean Sea, and the Gulf of Mexico. Once generated, the storm centers move slowly westward or northwestward and eventually recurve to the north and northeast, to be dissipated in the midlatitudes. The Atlantic hurricanes often pass through the West Indies and recurve to the northeast striking the eastern coast of the United States or dying out in midocean. The storms that originate in the Caribbean Sea affect mainly the Greater Antilles, Yucatan, Florida and, occasionally, the east cost of Central America. Those of the Gulf of Mexico often hit the east coast of Mexico and the Gulf coast of the United States. The high winds of the hurricanes cause enormous destruction of human life and property, both directly and through the creation of large tidal waves along coasts, and the torrential downpours within the hurricane structure frequently flood large sections of land. In September 1974, a hurricane devastated the heavily populated western section of the Caribbean coast of Honduras, destroying banana plantations and causing floods

and landslides that took the lives of thousands of inhabitants.

The hurricanes that originate over the warm Pacific waters off the southern Mexican coast during the months of June to October or November are little known, and are usually less dangerous than the Caribbean variety. These storms, locally called *chubascos,* frequently proceed northward from their point of origin and veer suddenly to the northeast, causing extensive damage along the west coast of Mexico as far north as Baja California and southern Sonora.

Midlatitude Storms.   The second type of destructive storm is the midlatitude cyclonic disturbance, which often invades the Middle American tropics. Winter atmospheric conditions in the United States affect the weather and climate of Middle America to a greater extent than is normally supposed. The winter cyclonic rains of northern and central Mexico have already been mentioned. From November through March, incursions of northern polar air into the Middle American tropics are frequent. Fronts (lines of contact between cool polar air and warm tropical air) often penetrate into central Mexico,

43

Yucatan, and Cuba, and sometimes extend as far as Nicaragua in Central America and Puerto Rico in the West Indies. Along these weakened polar fronts heavy rains occur, principally along the eastern escarpments of Mexico and northern Central America where uplifting takes place. On the plateaus of central and southern Mexico and of Guatemala, the arrival of the front is accompanied by extensive overcast with light rains. Such rains, as already mentioned, are highly beneficial to agriculture and grazing in the drier plateau areas. Following the passage of the weakened front, however, are stiff, cold winds which cause temperatures to drop suddenly as much as 10 or 15° F and which have caused killing frosts along the Gulf coast of Mexico as far south as northern Veracruz (as in January, 1962). These winds, which come from a northerly direction, are called *nortes* (northers) in Middle America. *Nortes* are most frequent along the Gulf coast of Mexico, where normally 15 to 20 occur each winter, prolonging the rainy season in places into December and January. Within this area and the Caribbean coast of Guatemala and Honduras, the north winds often destroy extensive sections of banana plantations and

seriously damage coastal shipping. Northers also blow through the natural corridors across Central America, causing rough seas in the Pacific south of the Isthmus of Tehuantepec, the Gulf of Fonseca, and in the Nicaraguan lowlands. The stronger *nortes* pass over the highlands of northern Central America, causing occasional freezes; they then descend to the Pacific coast as hot, dry winds, often dessicating coffee and banana plantings.

CLIMATE TYPES AND ASSOCIATED VEGETATION AND SOILS

Figure 2.19 indicates the distribution of climatic types according to the Koeppen classification. Mathematically, these types are based mainly on yearly and monthly averages of temperature and rainfall. However, vegetation is often used as a climatic indicator when temperature and rainfall data are lacking, since the area covered by each type of climate corresponds roughly to a given native type of vegetation. As we shall see, this correspondence of native vegetation and climatic type is often wanting.

Figure 2.19   Climatic areas

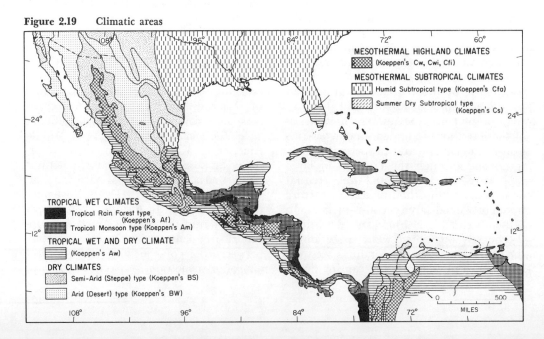

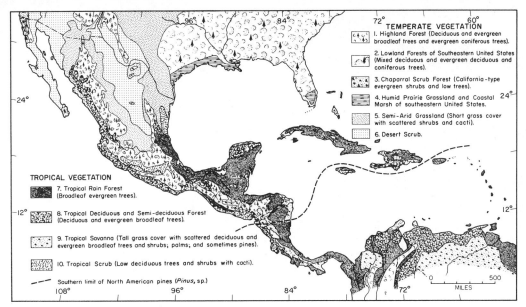

Figure 2.20   Natural vegetation

The Tropical Wet Climates: Koeppen's Af and Am

These climates have high temperatures all year, the average for each month being above 64° F. Annual rainfall is heavy, usually over 80 inches, and there is no pronounced dry season. In Middle America these climates correspond mainly to the *tierra caliente,* or hot tropical lowlands, in exposed positions within the trade wind area; that is, the northeastern sides of the Caribbean islands and the greater part of the eastern half of Central America and southern Mexico. A narrow belt of tropical wet climate extends northward along the lower eastern escarpment of the Mexican plateau where heavy orographic rains result both from the trades in summer and the occasional northern cyclonic storms in winter. On the Pacific side of Central America, two small areas of high annual rainfall come within the tropical wet climates. One includes the coast and seaward-facing slopes of southwestern Panama and southeastern Costa Rica; the other is a narrow strip along the volcanic escarpment of Guatemala at an elevation 2,000 or 3,000 feet above the adjacent coastal plain.

Most of the areas of tropical wet climate in Middle America are characterized by a short dry period during the cooler months, but sufficient rain falls during the year to support heavy rain-forest vegetation. This is Koeppen's Am type, the tropical monsoon rain-forest climate. Only a few sections of the rainiest areas, such as the windward sides of the Lesser Antilles, a few parts of the Caribbean coast of Central America, and a portion of the Tabasco lowlands in southeastern Mexico can be classed as true tropical rain-forest climate (Koeppen's Af), with no dry season.

Vegetation.   A heavy forest of tall tropical trees—properly called the "rain forest" —was probably the original vegetation that covered the greater part of the tropical, wet climate area of Middle America (Figure 2.20). Just what may have been the natural vegetation of any area, however, is often hard to determine. Man, exploiting native plants, on the one hand, and clearing by cutting and burning, on the other, has greatly modified much of the natural cover of most of the world. This human process has been going on in Middle America since the coming of the first Indians, possibly more than ten millennia

Figure 2.21   Tropical rain forest along the edge of a clearing in the Tuxtlas Mountains, southern Veracruz state, Mexico. The large trees, often buttressed and festooned with lianas and epiphytes, range from 60 to 80 feet in height. Palms and young trees form the understory vegetation.

ago, and the rate of cultural modification of the vegetation has been greatly accelerated since the beginning of European settlement in the sixteenth century. In all of Middle America, there are probably few parts of the rain forest untouched by man.

The less modified tropical rain forests in eastern Central America and the West Indies are composed of a great number of distinct species of large, broad-leaved, evergreen trees, some of which are more than 150 feet tall (Figure 2.21). Most have straight, broad trunks, and many are heavily buttressed at their bases. Pure stands of single species are rare, and in Central America they exist naturally only in swampy areas. A dense canopy of overlapping tree crowns shuts out almost all sunlight from the forest floor, making it free of dense undergrowth except for occasional clumps of shade-tolerant palms and wide-leaved aroids. A myriad of large climbing vines (lianas) and clinging epiphytes often cover the trunks and larger branches of many trees. Dense undergrowth (jungle) occurs where sunlight can penetrate, as along stream banks and in scattered tree falls (Figure 2.22).

Many valuable hardwoods, such as mahogany, tropical cedar, and guayacan, were once abundantly scattered through the rain forests of Middle America, but large specimens of these trees are now found only in isolated spots. A peculiar feature of the forest near the Caribbean coast of Honduras and on either side of the Yucatan Peninsula was the abundance of dye-yielding logwood, which was heavily exploited, particularly by English loggers, during colonial times. These stands are now badly depleted. In the dense rain forest of the Petén, or northern Guate-

Figure 2.22   Dense tropical jungle growth along a stream bank in the lowlands of northern Chiapas, Mexico

Figure 2.23   Open pine savanna, Mosquito Coast of Nicaragua, near Bluefields. This area receives an annual average rainfall of nearly 100 inches with a short dry season during March and April. (*James J. Parsons*)

mala, certain trees valuable for human food, such as the breadnut (Brosimum) and sapodilla, or chicle tree (Achras sapota), are often found in groves or solid stands, although their distribution is scattered. Such conditions seem to point to the probable influence of Indians, who planted these trees around settlements now abandoned or who protected them by cutting away competing vegetation.

Today, large areas of the once extensive rain forest of Central America and southeast Mexico have been destroyed to make way for plantations and pastures, and native farmers have reduced even greater areas to low growth by repeatedly cutting and burning in order to clear small plots for cultivation. In the West Indies, only isolated groves of rain forest remain on steep mountain slopes.

One of the most puzzling features of the natural vegetation in the tropical rainy areas of Middle America is the presence of large expanses of grassland, called "savannas," in areas that receive as much as 80 to 100 inches of rain annually, with no dry period or a quite short one. In terms of climate, such areas should be covered by a heavy rain forest. The largest of the humid savannas is found along the Caribbean margin of Nicaragua and northeastern Honduras (the Mosquito Coast). Open stands of tropical lowland pine (Pinus caribaea) add to the curious aspect of this wet area (Figure 2.23). Such vegetational anomalies may be caused by edaphic (soil) or cultural factors, and the chief reason for the Nicaraguan pine-savanna is probably the porous, gravelly soil, which will support only drought-tolerant plants. Smaller areas of humid savanna associated with open stands of pine or palms within the rain-forest zone occur in British Honduras, the Petén of northern Guatemala, the Tabasco coast of southeastern Mexico, and in Cuba. Little is known about the origin of these grassy areas; most are probably edaphic, but some may have been culturally induced through burning.

Soils. Over a long period of time, and under given climatic conditions and kinds of vegetation cover, certain types of soils tend to develop. Such soils are considered mature, or *zonal*, types. In tropical rainy climates, where high temperatures and excessive moisture permit the weathering of rocks to depths of 30 to 50 feet below the surface, a thick layer of clayey red and yellow soil, or *latosol*, tends to develop as the general zonal type. In the tropical rainy areas of Middle America, however, there appears to be a great variety of zonal soils, most of which have received little study. In the Caribbean lowlands of Central America, red and yellow latosols are often encountered in the rain forest on well-drained slopes. Latosols are usually leached of plant nutrients and, when the forest is cleared, they prove to be quite infertile for agriculture. In Cuba, on the other hand, most of the red latosols derived from the weathering of hard limestone are among the most productive of mature tropical soils.

Large sections of the Middle American rain forest contain soils that develop under special drainage conditions or are derived from a given rock that imparts peculiar soil characteristics (*intrazonal* types). For example, the tropical weathering of soft limestone and marl in the Petén of northern Guatemala has produced a leached, heavy, black clay known to scientists as *rendzina;* in spite of the leaching, this soil still contains abundant calcium and thus is more fertile than the more normal reddish latosols. It is significant that the ancient Maya Indian civilization reached its apogee in precisely this area of tropical rendzina soils. Another intrazonal soil of the rain forest is the water-logged, blue and grey, mottled clay (gley) found in the swampy Tabasco lowlands of southeastern Mexico and in other wet areas along the east side of Central America.

Probably the most fertile soils in the wet tropics of Middle America are the *azonal* types derived from the weathering of recently deposited alluvium and young volcanic ejecta. Immature, these soils have not yet been leached of valuable plant nutrients and minerals; consequently, they have been considered premium farmland since aboriginal times. Primarily because of such fertile soils, the wide alluvial flood plains along the Caribbean coast of Central America were densely occupied by Indian farmers in pre-Conquest times, and today they are the sites of large tropical plantations. Likewise, the rain-forest-covered volcanic slopes on the Pacific side of Guatemala, parts of the eastern escarpment of Mexico, and the Lesser Antillean islands contain fertile soils rich in minerals needed for the cultivation of coffee and sugar cane.

The Tropical Wet-and-Dry Climate: Koeppen's Aw

The temperature of this climate is similar to the tropical humid types, but it is distinguished by a definite dry season of four to six months during the cooler part of the year. It should be emphasized that this dry period may not be entirely without rain. However, the dryness is sufficient to induce a seasonal rhythm in vegetative growth.

In Middle America, the tropical wet-and-dry climate is characteristically developed in the lee of the trade winds, along the southern and western coasts and in interior basins of less than 3,000 feet elevation. It characterizes more than half of the *tierra caliente*. The largest continuous area of this climate is found on the Pacific side of Mexico and Central America. Smaller areas occur on the lee sides of the Caribbean islands and in extensive low plains on the east side of Mexico. The latter include the northern half of the Yucatan Peninsula and much of the central Gulf coastal plain of Mexico.

Vegetation. The long dry season has a pronounced effect on the natural vegetation. Within Middle America, most of the tropical wet-and-dry areas are covered by a low forest of mainly deciduous trees that shed their leaves during the dry period. Occasional giant trees, such as the guanacaste (Enterolobium) and the silk-cotton tree (Ceiba pentandra) rise above the general forest level; frequently, clumps of palms grow in low wet spots. In Spanish-speaking areas, this type of forest is locally called *monte alto* ("high bush"). A less luxuriant association, called *monte bajo* ("low bush"), composed of thick growths of low, thorny scrub and cacti of many forms and species, often covers hill slopes having thin, rocky soils (Figure 2.24). A similar thorny scrub is also dominant in the drier interior basins, on the leeward coastal strips of the mainland and on many of the Caribbean islands. The brilliant green foliage of both the low- and high-bush vegetation during the rainy season contrasts with the dull greys and browns of the bare trees relieved only by scattered clumps of green palms and an occasional evergreen broad-leaved tree, during the dry period.

One of the significant features of the vegetation associated with the tropical wet-and-dry climate in Middle America is the paucity of extensive areas of savanna grassland, which in South America and Africa forms the dominant plant cover in a similar climate. Only one large natural savanna, that of central Panama, occurs on the Pacific margin of Middle America. This and smaller spots of savanna elsewhere in Central America and the West Indies are more likely the result of soils and drainage conditions than of climate.

Man has altered the tropical deciduous and semideciduous forests of Middle America more than he has the rain forest. The tropical wet-and-dry lands have always been the part of the *tierra caliente* more favorable for human occupation, and they still today support a much denser

Figure 2.24   A low forest of columnar cactus and deciduous trees. The forest forms this tropical *monte bajo* vegetation characteristic of the rocky, rain-shadow mountain slopes in southern Oaxaca, Mexico.

population than the rain forest areas. Consequently, in many sections, particularly in alluvial flood plains and the more fertile hill sections, the original forest has been almost completely replaced by cultivated fields or pastures. Man-made grasslands, with scattered palms and broad-leaved trees, cover large areas of the tropical wet-and-dry climate of Middle America, giving a false impression of natural savannas. Landowners maintain such grasslands by annual burning during the dry season in order to improve forage for livestock and to destroy ticks. Once burning is stopped for a number of years, the low, woody growth begins to retake the land.

As in many other tropical areas of the world, there occurs, along the shores of quiet, muddy bays of the Middle American coasts, a special type of vegetation called a "tidal forest" or "mangrove swamp." This curious swamp vegetation may occur in all types of tropical lowland climates along muddy shores. Various spe-

Figure 2.25   Red mangrove forest along the Honduras shore of the Gulf of Fonseca, Pacific coast of Central America

cies of salt-tolerant trees compose the mangrove swamp, the most typical being the red mangrove (Rhizophora) renowned for having a mass of stilt roots which grow up from the malodorous tidal mud flats (Figure 2.25). In bays and lagoons along the Central American coasts the mangrove forest is tall, some trees reaching 100 feet or more. Northward, along the Mexican coasts and in many sections of the West Indies where the winters are cooler, the mangrove becomes a scrubby growth. The swamps, almost impenetrable except along tidal channels, form an effective barrier between the coast and the interior. Much of the taller swamp growth has been altered in the past century as red mangrove has been cut down for its tannin-rich bark, and white mangrove for wood to make charcoal.

Soils.   The soils, like those of the tropical rain-forest area, are various. Owing to the dry season, soils that develop in the tropical wet-and-dry climate are not as deeply weathered or leached as those of the rain forest.

The highly infertile red lateritic soils that cover the surface of so much of the tropical savannas of South America and Africa are found only rarely in Middle America. However, such soils, with the characteristic hard-pan layer of iron oxide nodules, may underlie the natural savannas of western Panama, the Mosquito coast of northeastern Nicaragua, and the savannas of Tabasco in southeastern Mexico, as well as parts of Cuba and Hispaniola. Young azonal soils, derived from volcanic material, are found in most of the Pacific coastal lowlands of Central America, and they may be responsible for the luxuriant, semideciduous tropical forests that once covered this area. In the wet-and-dry lowlands of Mexico there is a bewildering variety of zonal, or mature soils, which seem to defy attempts to associate them with climate. According to recent surveys, many of the soils of the Mexican Pacific lowlands and some of the Gulf coast are *chernozemic,* a general type that is usually associated with semiarid regions of the midlatitudes. Alkaline, little leached, and red-brown to black in color, such soils are quite fertile and often contain an abundance of lime. The northern half of the Yucatan Peninsula is characterized by its thin, red, limey soil (*terra rossa*), which has been cultivated for centuries by Maya Indians.

**The Mesothermal
Highland Climates:
Koeppen's Cw, Cwi, Cfi**

These climates correspond generally to the *tierra templada* and *tierra fría,* or the tropical highlands. As indicated previously, the tropical highlands of Middle America are confined almost wholly to Mexico and Central America; only scattered patches occur in the Caribbean islands. Because of their elevation, the temperatures are lower than in the tropical lowland climates, at least one month of the year averaging less than 65° F. Seasonal temperature differences are slight; the highland climate in southern Mexico and Central America is *isothermal;* that is, it has an annual temperature range of not more than 9° F. In Mexico, a wide strip of mesothermal highland climate follows the Sierra Madre Occidental northwestward almost to the United States border. The northern half of this range has cold winters, often with snow, and warm summers.

In most of the tropical highlands of Mexico and Central America, precipitation is seasonal, the rains coming as thunderstorms during the hotter months. Annual total precipitation is 30 to 80 inches (Koeppen's Cw, Cwi). Occasional light winter rains of cyclonic origin are common in the Mesa Central of Mexico. On high slopes exposed to the trade winds, particularly along the eastern escarpment of southern Mexico and the Caribbean side of Central America, heavy rains fall every month; the annual total is 80 to 120 inches (Koeppen's Cfi).

Vegetation. The mountainous relief and the consequent variety of slopes exposed to wind and sun makes for a multiplicity of types of vegetation in the highlands. The most widespread highland plant association is an oak and coniferous forest, which extends from northern Mexico southward into Central America. The coniferous trees, however, extend only as far as the highlands of northern Nicaragua, where the North American pine (Pinus) reaches its southern limit. Both evergreen and deciduous oaks continue along the volcanic axis of Central America into Costa Rica and Panama. In the West Indies highlands, oak and pine forests are found in the higher mountains of Cuba and Hispaniola. The Cordillera Central

in the Dominican Republic and the Jacmel Peninsula of Haiti form another equatorial limit of the genus Pinus.

An altitudinal sequence of plant associations usually occurs in the forested highlands of Mexico and Central America. Within the Mesa Central of Mexico, for example, grass and scattered oaks probably formed the original vegetation of the basin floors. On the slopes of adjacent volcanic mountains (e.g., Popocatepetl), this association grades into forests of evergreen and deciduous oak. At approximately 7,000 feet, pines begin to appear in these forests, and at 10,000 feet solid pine predominates. Above the pine zone, fir (Abies) is found. It appears at 11,500 feet and continues as solid stands almost to the tree line, between 12,500 and 13,000 feet. A similar vegetational sequence occurs as far south as northern Central America, where the pine zone usually begins at a lower elevation than in central Mexico. Throughout the pine-covered mountain areas of Mexico and northern Central America, the solid forest is interrupted by grassy meadows in small flat-floored basins which afford pleasant sites for settlements and pastures.

In Central America and southern Mexico, on windward slopes, a highly interesting vegetation association, called the "cloud forest," occurs above the pine zone. Beginning at elevations of 6,500 or 7,000 feet, these are almost continually enveloped in cloud even during the drier part of the year, and they drip with moisture. Giant evergreen oaks, laurels, deciduous sweet gums (Liquidambar), and thickets of tree ferns make up the greater part of this eerie forest (Figure 2.26). Owing to the abundance of moisture, the trunks and lower branches of the larger trees are covered with epiphytes such as bromelias, orchids, and mosses, which enhance the fairyland aspect of the vegetation. Somewhat similar cloud forests occur on the higher windward sides of the volcanic

Figure 2.26   A remnant of the cloud forest, much of which is now practically destroyed by man, in the Talamanca Range, Costa Rica. Giant buttressed oaks comprise the bulk of the formerly magnificent vegetation.

mountains in the Lesser Antilles and along the upper edge of the eastern escarpment of central Mexico.

Of all the vegetation types of Middle America, probably the oak-pine highland forests of central and southern Mexico have been the most seriously altered by human action. The process of destruction by man, principally by clearing for cultivation, has been in progress for at least 3,000 years. Large areas of the Mesa Central of Mexico, once oak and pine forest, now appear to be semiarid grass and bushland. Since the Mesa Central has for so long been an area of dense rural population, the amount of forest destruction is not surprising, especially when one realizes that since the Spanish occupation in the sixteenth century, cutting for lumber and fuel has increasingly diminished the extent of the pine and fir forests. Today, the only extensive reserve of pine in Mexico is in the Sierra Madre Occidental. On the other hand, in Honduras and northern Nicara-gua, man may have accidentally extended pine growth by destruction of an original tropical forest; the latter appears to have been replaced by pine on eroded mineral soils.

Soils.   The soils of the tropical highlands and the adjacent mountains of Mexico and Central America are extremely complex in type and distribution, as would be expected in an area of rugged relief and varied geology. The most important, in terms of human occupance, are the azonal soils derived from volcanic material found in the Mesa Central of Mexico and in the highlands of Central America. Two kinds of volcanic soils prevail. Those weathered from recent basic volcanic ejecta (basalt, andesite) are the most fertile and widespread. The second type, derived from older acidic material (rhyolite), as in the southern highlands of Honduras, are thin and infertile. On the Mexican plateau, many of the old volcanic basins contain mature, dark-colored chernozemlike soils derived from ancient lake-deposited alluvium. High in calcium and organic material, these soils are renowned for their fertility. Unfortunately, overcropping and overgrazing on the lower slopes of the basins have caused serious gullying and sheet erosion. The erosion so caused has often exposed an underlying hardpan of lime (caliche, or *tepetate*), rendering sizable amounts of land useless for cultivation.

The Mesothermal Subtropical Climates: Koeppen's Cfa, Cs

In Middle America, these climates occur in only two small areas of northern Mexico. The southernmost *humid subtropical climate* (Koeppen's Cfa, typical of southeastern United States) is found in the extreme northeast of Mexico on the Gulf coastal plain and adjacent hill lands. In this area, winter temperatures are lower than normal for the latitude because of the frequent incursions of cool polar air from Texas. Hot, muggy summers are induced by the presence of the tropical maritime air mass from the Gulf of Mexico. Rain, although relatively meager (20 to 40 inches), falls every month, reaching its maximum during the hot summer; frequent cyclonic storms bring most of the winter rainfall. The low annual precipitation and the porous, limestone-surface rock encourage a thorny semideciduous bush vegetation which covers most of northeastern Mexico. True forest occurs only in the higher elevations (such as the Sierra de Tamaulipas) and along streams, where cottonwoods and bald cypress are common. The soft limestone and marl of the lower coastal plain is responsible for the development of a belt of rendzina soils, a southern extension of the black soils of Texas.

The extreme northwestern part of Baja California is the southernmost limit of the summer-dry mesothermal climate (Koeppen's Cs), which characterizes the coastal valleys and ranges of upper California. Marked by severe summer drought and light winter rains (15 to 20 inches), this subtropical climate embraces the pine-covered mountains of the northern part of the peninsula and extends to the chaparral-covered plain around the city of Ensenada.

The Dry Climates: Koeppen's BS and BW

The dry climates of Middle America, including the *semiarid,* or *steppe* (Koeppen's BS), and the *desert* (Koeppen's BW) types, are confined mainly to the northern interior and the northwest of Mexico. Small areas of dry climate, principally of the semiarid type, occupy rain shadow positions in deep valleys and in the lee of high mountains in many parts of the Middle American tropics. For example, a narrow corridor of semiarid climate extends southward from the dry, northern plateau of Mexico into the central and southern parts of the country that lie directly behind the eastern sierra. The Tepalcatepec Valley south of the Mesa Central in Mexico, the middle Motagua Valley of Guatemala, and the Enriquillo depression of Hispaniola in the West Indies are rain-shadow basins. Another area of dry climate that borders Middle America includes a portion of the Venezuelan coast of South America and islands offshore.

Moisture deficiency is, of course, the outstanding characteristic of the dry climates. Generally, the semiarid type receives twice the rainfall of the desert, but this is still insufficient for the growth of forest vegetation. In north Mexico, most of the scant precipitation comes during the summer months in the form of scattered thundershowers, but occasional winter cyclonic rain and drizzles are of exceptional importance where dry farming is practiced. In the northern part of Baja California, however, winter cyclonic rains and summer drought prevail.

In terms of temperature, the Middle American dry climates are mainly subtropical (Koeppen's BSh and BWh), with hot summers and mild winters. On high mountain slopes within the northern plateau, there are probably many spots of cold steppe and desert (Koeppen's BSk and BWk) with severe winter temperatures. Owing to the unusually clear, dry atmosphere and rapid radiation, the difference between day and night temperatures is extreme. In winter, nightly freezes are not uncommon in north central Mexico, while midday temperatures may be uncomfortably hot.

The Steppe Lands.   In terms of human occupation, the semiarid steppes of Middle America are the more significant of the dry climatic areas. Generally, the steppe is a transition zone between the true desert and the more humid climates. In north central Mexico, the steppe occupies the higher plateau surface that flanks the sierras on the west and east and the Mesa Central on the south. In northwestern Mexico,

a wide belt of semiarid climate covers the ridge and basin lands between the Sierra Madre and the Altar Desert, narrowing southward along the Sinaloa coast. In northeastern Mexico, a semiarid climate extends almost to the Gulf coast south of the Rio Grande. The annual rainfall on these steppes averages between 15 and 20 inches.

The relatively small amount of rainfall in the semiarid regions is sufficient for the growth of a short grass, the most distinctive landscape feature of the steppe (Figure 2.27). Low, spiny shrubs, such as mesquite and cat's-claw, and various cacti grow in scattered fashion as associates of the low grasses. In low swales and along intermittent stream courses where the water table is high, mesquite bushes grow in dense thickets, and on the higher mountain slopes open stands of scrub oak and juniper prevail. The nutritious grasses and the protein-rich mesquite pods afford a natural basis for the development of the Mexican livestock industry.

Soils of the steppe areas of north Mexico are typical of those that develop in semiarid climates; they are principally chernozemic, with a layer of lime accumulation that lies a few inches below a humus-rich, black-to-brown, upper soil layer. Except in irrigated areas, however, the deficiency of

Figure 2.27   Steppe, or shortgrass pasture lands, in the semiarid portion of the Mexican plateau, near Durango City. Scattered huisache trees and mesquite shrubs form the sparse woody growth.

Figure 2.28 Desert shrub in Coahuila State, north central Mexico. The spiny plant at the right is ocotillo; the dark-toned ones are creosote bush. Lechuguilla forms low clumps between rocky outcrops.

moisture unfortunately precludes intensive cultivation of these rich soils.

The Deserts. The true deserts of Middle America are limited to northern Mexico. That of Baja California and Sonora in the northwest is the most arid, a large area receiving less than four inches of rain annually. Along the Pacific coast of Baja California, the cold California current reduces air temperature; warm air from the Pacific, drifting over the cold water, produces extensive fog banks. Thus, the coastal areas present the anomaly of a cool, foggy desert with atmospheric conditions similar to those of the Peruvian coastal desert in South America. The temperature range of the desert that borders on the Gulf of California, however, is quite distinct, with extremely hot summers and mild winters. Some of the highest summer temperatures in Middle America have been recorded along the arid coastal plain of Sonora and northern Sinaloa, where extremes of 115 to 120° F are not uncommon.

Less extreme temperatures and somewhat more rainfall (5 to 15 inches) prevail in the interior plateau desert of northern Mexico. Some of the higher mountain slopes may receive more than 20 inches of precipitation yearly. As in most deserts, the amount of annual rain is highly variable. Prolonged droughts of several years duration may be followed by periods of plentiful moisture and even floods.

Climatically and botanically, the deserts of northern Mexico are southward extensions of arid zones in the southwestern United States. Compared to the barren deserts of the Sahara and Arabia, the Mexican areas support a relatively lush plant cover. Plants are low xerophytes having special adaptations to long periods of drought. On the rocky hillsides and alluvial fans, the spindly ocotillo, the creosote bush, and the palm-like yucca form the dominant woody vegetation; between these plants grow succulent-leaved agaves, a bewildering variety of cacti, and a few widely spaced clumps of bunch grass (Figure 2.28). Areas completely devoid of vegetation are found in the few small shifting dune fields, such as those of Salamayuca in Chihuahua, 100 miles south of El Paso, Texas. In contrast, the mountain crests above 10,000 feet elevation often support scrub oak and occasional pine forest, forming spots of semiarid or even humid climate within the desert.

The desert vegetation of north central Mexico appears to be invading the margins of eroded or overgrazed steppe lands. That even the desert plants have not been free of destructive exploitation by man is evidenced by the depletion, in many areas, of various wild agaves and spurges collected for fiber and wax during the past few decades.

A definite zonal soil type is associated with the desert climate of Mexico in those areas where there has been sufficient accumulation of weathered material, as in basin fills and old alluvial fans. These desert soils are generally called *sierozems*. Because of the deficient rainfall and the slowness of plant decay, they are low in organic matter, high in lime and other soluble salts, and usually grey-brown in color. The soil is often so alkaline as to be useless for cultivation, but with proper treatment large sections of basin floor in the north Mexico deserts have been brought under irrigated agriculture. On the rocky hill slopes of the desert, however, little soil forms.

It should be obvious to the reader that acquaintance with the physical characteristics of any geographical area serves to aid him in understanding how people have settled the land and utilized its natural resources. The interaction of man and habitat has long been a subject of inquiry in the social sciences, and that subject is a subtheme that runs through the course of this text. In this chapter we have presented mainly the general aspects of land configuration, climate, natural vegetation, and soils of Middle America. In the chapters that follow, references will be made to these characteristics, and in some cases the physical scene will be given in more detail.

SELECTED REFERENCES

BENNETT, C. F. "A Review of Ecological Research in Middle America." *Latin American Research Review* 2, no. 3 (1967):3–27.

DENEVAN, W. M. "The Upland Pine Forests of Nicaragua: A Study in Cultural Plant Geography." *University of California Publications in Geography* 12, no. 4 (1961):251–320.

JAEGER, E. C. *The North American Deserts.* Stanford, Calif.: Stanford University Press, 1957.

JOHANNESSEN, C. L. *Savannas of Interior Honduras.* Ibero-Americana, no. 46. Berkeley: University of California Press, 1963.

LAUER, W. "Klimatische und Pflanzengeographische Grundzüge Zentralamerikas." *Erdkunde* 12, no. 4 (1959):344–54.

LEOPOLD, A. S. "Vegetation Zones of Mexico." *Ecology* 31, no. 4 (1950):507–18.

ORDÓÑEZ, E. "Principal Physiographic Provinces of Mexico." *Bulletin of the American Association of Petroleum Geologists* 20, no. 10 (1936):1277–307.

PARSONS, J. J. "The Miskito Pine Savanna of Nicaragua and Honduras." *Annals of the Association of American Geographers* 45, no. 1 (1955):36–63.

PORTIG, W. H. "Central American Rainfall." *Geographical Review* 55, no. 1 (1965):68–90.

ROSENDAL, H. E. "Mexican West Coast Tropical Cyclones, 1947–1961." *Weatherwise* 16, no. 5 (1963):226–29.

SCHUCHERT, C. *Historical Geology of the Antillean-Caribbean Region.* New York: John Wiley & Sons, 1935. Reprinted, New York: Hafner, 1968.

TAMAYO, J. L. *Geografía General de México.* 2nd ed. 4 vols. Mexico, D. F.: Instituto

Mexicano de Investigaciones Económicas, 1962.

VAN DEN BERG, C. A. "The Caribbean: Battle Field for the Weatherman." *Weather* 23, no. 11 (1968):462–68.

VIVÓ, J. A., and GÓMEZ, J. C. *Climatología de México.* No. 19, Mexico, D. F.: Instituto Panamericano de Geografía e Historia, 1946.

WALLÉN, C. C. "Some Characteristics of Precipitation in Mexico," *Geografiska Annaler* 37, nos. 1–2 (1955):51–85.

WEST, R. C., ed. *Natural Environment and Early Cultures: Handbook of Middle American Indians.* Vol. 1. Austin: University of Texas Press, 1964.

≡ 3 ≡

Geographic Parameters
in West Indian History

EARLY SETTING

It is impossible to dissociate geography and history; the landscape is made up of their synthesis. Nature gives us the frame, but men, even in their most humble manifestations, are caught up in the currents of history. Almost always the present can be explained only by the past. It is by the integration of history into geography that one attains the very soul of a country.—Jean Sermet

The important changes that have taken place in the human occupance of Middle America from pre-Columbian times to the present may be grouped historically into a series of formative periods during which major forces reshaped the area's land-and-people relations into new and distinctive forms. Since historical continuity makes overlap inevitable, it is seldom possible to cite the specific beginnings of such periods and even less possible to fix endings. At best, historical divisions are approximate and often arbitrary guides for surveying the evolution of spatial patterns and relationships.

The historical picture is further complicated in that the critical formative periods of Middle America's various segments do not coincide. On the Mainland, for example, the Amerindian past and the sixteenth-century Spanish Conquest have had far more important long-range effects on human geography than the same periods in the Caribbean Rimland. Plantation agriculture, the vital agent of post-Columbian change in the Rimland, did not reach its peak in most of the West Indies until the eighteenth century, while in Cuba, Puerto Rico, the Dominican Republic, and the Central American coast, the plantation was only of limited importance until the nineteenth and twentieth centuries. The human geography of Middle America is so deeply rooted in the past, however, that it is mandatory to assess and classify the play of time within its geographic context despite the complications.

For the West Indies, five major periods are suggested: (1) the pre-Columbian, Amerindian prologue; (2) the European Conquest and spread of settlement, which may be dated from 1492 to the latter seventeenth century; (3) the sugar revolution and the colonial plantation, encompassing roughly the 200 years from the latter seventeenth to the latter nineteenth centuries; (4) the transition from the late nineteenth century to World War II, characterized by the modern plantation; and (5) the contemporary, with its postwar sociopolitical developments and old eco-

58

nomic problems. This chapter will deal primarily with the first three of these periods.

THE PRE-COLUMBIAN
AMERINDIAN PROLOGUE

The patterns of the Amerindians in the Antilles on the eve of the Discovery defy detailed reconstruction. None of the Indian groups possessed a written language, and most of the indigenous cultures were so quickly wiped out by the shock of the European Conquest that our knowledge of them is derived primarily from the limited writings of early explorers and settlers and from later archaeological study of burial caves, middens, and village sites.

Evidence indicates that the West Indian islands were swept by at least three Amerindian cultural waves before the arrival of the Europeans. The first of these was the primitive hunting and gathering Ciboney culture, whose origin is unknown.

This was followed by the Arawak and the Carib cultures, both of which originated in South America and island-hopped their way into the Antilles. By the time of the Conquest, the Arawaks were centered on the Greater Antilles but also occupied the Bahamas and southern Trinidad. They had eliminated Ciboney holdings everywhere except for pockets on the coast of western Cuba and southwestern Haiti (Figure 3.1). The Caribs, who arrived later, had displaced the Arawaks in the Lesser Antilles and northeastern Trinidad and were raiding eastern Puerto Rico when the arrival of the Spaniards checked their expansion.

The Ciboneys subsisted primarily on fish, turtles, sea cows, and other sea animals, on iguanas, and on the wild fruits of the forest. Their villages were small, semipermanent settlements made up of rock shelters and caves. They practiced no cultivation, and aside from the crudest tools and weapons, their chief possession was the dugout canoe.

The Arawaks and, to a lesser degree, the Caribs had more advanced material

Figure 3.1   Pre-Columbian Indian cultures of the Antilles

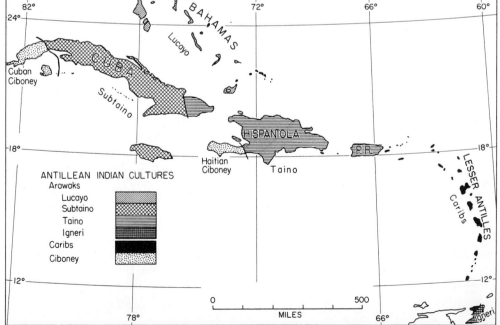

cultures than the Ciboneys. Both groups practiced agriculture, although the economy was far better developed among the Arawaks. The crop production of the Arawaks rested primarily on the *conuco,* a farming system that is widely practiced in the Hispanic West Indies to this day.

Arawak conuco farming began with the heaping of the soil into roundish mounds that were often knee-high and several feet in diameter. The basic plantings in the mounds were starchy root crops, chief of which were the bitter yuca (manioc or cassava) and the sweet potato (Ipomea batatas), followed by yautia (Xanthosoma), arrowroot (Maranta), and peanuts or maní (Aranchis). Also part of the conuco system were maize, beans, and squash, with the result that different kinds of plants—root, upright, and climbing— were placed together in the same mound and provided effective cover against erosion.

Seemingly primitive to the early European colonists, the conuco system represented a sophisticated adjustment to the ecological conditions of the Greater Antilles and the needs of the Arawaks. Heaping the earth into mounds provided a loose, well-aerated soil; clusters of mounds reduced sheet erosion, and "multistoried" plantings provided not only a ground cover against erosion, but also a variety of crops. Equally significant, this method of tillage resulted in high yields even on the mountain slopes that characterize much of the land in the larger West Indian islands. Sauer concluded that, "Conuco planting gave the highest return of food in continuous supply by simplest methods and moderate labor" (1966:69). Little wonder that the system is still in use among West Indian peasant farmers!

In addition to food crops, the Arawaks also raised tree cotton for netting, calabashes, or gourds; fruit trees such as the mamey (*Mamea americana*); and tobacco, which was used as a drug and as a means of exchange. Their diet, like that of the Caribs, was supplemented by large quantities of fish, fowl, and other food yielded by the surrounding waters and forests.

The Caribs were far fewer than the Arawaks, culturally less advanced, and much more warlike. They depended more heavily on fishing, hunting, and gathering than on agriculture. In addition, the practice of eating the flesh of their captured male enemies, whether for ritual purposes or merely for food, was sufficiently widespread so that the very name "Carib" came to mean cannibal. According to their own legends, the Caribs came into the West Indies about a century before the Discovery. They established their small villages either on the windward side of the islands or on low hills adjacent to the coast, where they were safest from surprise attacks. Their houses were either oval or rectangular structures of poles thatched with palm leaf. Outstanding among their material possessions were canoes, some of which could carry 40 or 50 Carib warriors. The canoes played an important part in the Caribs' northward push along the Lesser Antilles.

Estimates of the total Indian population of the West Indies vary enormously. Las Casas, who observed the initial European impact on the Indians, sets the figure at 6 million, at least 3 million of whom were in Hispaniola (1909). Later, the German naturalist Alexander von Humboldt (1856:232–39) reasoned that the indigenous population of Cuba must have been well below the figures suggested by the early Spanish observers. The opinions of more recent scholars are equally varied. Rosenblatt, for example, concluded that the total number of Arawaks in the Antilles when the Europeans arrived was roughly 200 thousand (1954:102–7). Carl Sauer gives no specific estimate, but on the strength of the high food-producing capacity of the conuco system and other conditions, he is inclined to a higher figure (1966:65–69). Even the lowest estimates, however, give the Greater Antilles a much higher pre-Columbian population density than Anglo-America.

It is noteworthy that none of the Antillean Indians had developed the concept of private ownership of land. Land existed only to satisfy the necessities of life; it was never bought or sold or used for commercial profit. Since Rimland cultures included no wheeled vehicles or other sophisticated tools, and no beasts of burden or sources of energy other than human muscle, this attitude toward the land made for a relatively low standard of living, but it also usually meant security. Subsistence was never a problem, and famine occurred only if war and the forces of nature destroyed the productive effort of man.

EUROPEAN CONQUEST
AND SPREAD OF SETTLEMENT

The conquest and settlement of the West Indies by the Europeans between 1492 and the latter seventeenth century may be divided into a number of phases. First came the Spaniards, who discovered the area and who immediately proclaimed an exclusivist policy of trade and colonization. For almost a century, the Spanish claims to lands discovered by Columbus went largely unchallenged, and Spain attempted to legitimize her possessions by occupance. Eventually, however, northern Europeans, lured by the possibility of trade, loot, and new lands, invaded the Spanish monopoly and ushered in a period of intense political, economic, and cultural competition. French, English, Dutch, and other north European powers not only attacked Spanish settlements and trade monopolies, they also established their own colonies, bringing into the Caribbean a multiplicity of national interests and cultures.

Less spectacular but equally important is the fact that, during this period of conquest and settlement, the Antilles served as a testing ground and dispersal base for the plants, animals, and new techniques that European man was to use in his conquest and colonization of the rest of the Americas.

Discovery
and Spanish Colonization

Spanish discovery of the Caribbean borderlands at the close of the fifteenth century was followed by rapid envelopment of those areas that were deemed economically desirable. Within 50 years of the arrival of Columbus, the conquistadors had established themselves on the larger islands of the Antilles and had pushed on to Panama, Mexico, and other segments of the Mainland. Occupation of these territories, however, was never total. The preferred settlement sites possessed such advantages as proximity to gold deposits, facility of external communications, abundant land for agriculture and grazing, and an ample Indian population to supply labor. If gold was the only consideration (and it generally was), the settlement was often either abandoned or allowed to die when the metal gave out.

The first locus of Spanish colonization was Hispaniola, in the West Indies, and the initial objective was to found a mining and farming colony that could produce its own food, send gold back to Spain, and serve as a base for further exploration. To this end, the Spaniards imported a whole society in miniature—tools, seeds, plants, livestock, and colonists who included not only priests and soldiers but also farmers, artisans, and miners. The earliest settlement was established at Isabela on the north coast of the island (Figure 3.2). Moving southward through the Paso de los Hidalgos across the Cordillera Septentrional, the Spaniards discovered the great lowland of the Cibao, which Columbus himself named the *Vega Real* ("Royal

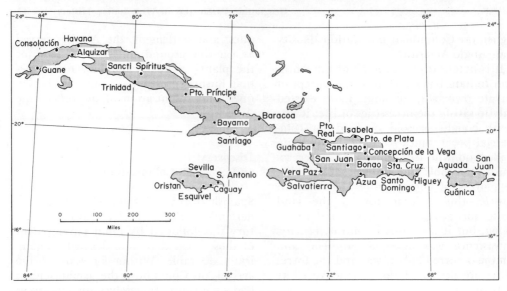

Figure 3.2   Early Spanish settlements in the West Indies

Vale"). From here, they moved rapidly through the Cordillera Central toward the south coast, founding the city of Santo Domingo in 1496.

Within a few years, the Spaniards had founded numerous small settlements on Hispaniola (Figure 3.2). These original settlements, formed by miners and *encomenderos* and by such merchants and craftsmen as served their needs, relied on gold and Indian labor, and most of them (including the original settlement of Isabela) proved to be almost as ephemeral as the gold deposits and the Indians. Only the city of Santo Domingo, which was founded near the Jaina gold mines and which had the advantage of a good harbor at the mouth of the Ozama River, achieved and retained even modest importance during the colonial period. In fact, this city was so dominant that its name was used to designate the entire island.

Hispaniola, an object of colonization in itself, also served as a base for the conquest and settlement of the adjacent Antillean islands and the continent. From Santo Domingo, Ponce de León settled Puerto Rico; del Campo and Velásquez went to explore Cuba; Esquivel colonized Jamaica; Balboa set out to discover the Pacific; Pizarro conquered Peru; Heredia founded Cartagena on the Caribbean coast of Colombia; and Díaz Solís discovered the Plata estuary on the southeast coast of South America.

The settlement of the other West Indian islands from the Hispaniola base was also determined largely by the lure of gold. The Spaniards tended to occupy permanently only those islands where this precious metal was available. Where there was no gold, as in the Lesser Antilles, Jamaica, the Bahamas, and even western Hispaniola (Haiti), Spanish settlement was either limited or nonexistent. These vacuums were later filled by north European colonists.

The West Indies remained at the center of Spanish interest for only a few decades after the Discovery. Once Mexico, Peru, and other more desirable areas of the Mainland were found, the islands quickly fell into decay. With their gold and Indian labor force largely exhausted by 1530, the insular economies were reduced to virtual subsistence. The flow of colonists from Spain ceased; even worse, most of the original settlers joined the bands bound for the continent, taking with them much of the wealth of the islands in the form of horses, arms, tools, and other supplies. *"Qué Dios me lleve al Perú"* ("May God take me to Peru") became the prayer of the colonists who remained, and total depopulation of the islands was avoided only by invoking the sternest penalties—including cutting off a leg of any settler who tried to leave the islands. Nevertheless, many escaped in small boats to join their fellows in Mexico and Peru.

Spanish Policy and the Colonial Economy of the Antilles. The guiding principle of Spanish colonial policy in the Antilles (as elsewhere) was that the colony existed for the benefit of the mother country. Spain implemented this policy by establishing a highly centralized monopolistic control under the supervision of the Council of the Indies. While the restrictions imposed by the Council varied from time to time, the general controls included:

1. Only Spaniards could trade with the colonies, all goods had to be carried in Spanish ships and, for protection, all ships had to move in convoy from designated ports at specified times.

2. Colonies were prohibited from producing any product that would compete with the merchants and manufacturers of the home country.

3. Colonies were forbidden to trade directly with each other, and for many years goods from one colony to another had to be transshipped through Spain.

4. Only proven Spanish Catholics could migrate to the colonies (though this rule was not always enforced, and the early colonists in the Spanish Antilles included small groups of Italians, Germans, Flemings, French, and Portuguese).

To make matters worse, a large number of taxes were levied on colonial goods, so that by 1600, many products cost from three to ten times as much in the colonies as they did in Spain. And the Antilles, in particular, were beset by two additional disadvantages which had negative economic ramifications: They had to bear the brunt of attacks by pirates and by Spain's north European enemies in the Caribbean; and Spain considered them of little commercial importance in comparison to other colonies.

Following the expansion of Spanish colonization to the Mainland, the Antilles ceased to be an economic end in themselves and became only a means to an end. Spain came to view them as possible supply bases and strong points guarding her imperial lines of communication with Mexico, Peru, Panama, and even the Philippines. To this end, all the major Antillean ports—Havana and Santiago in Cuba, San Juan in Puerto Rico, Santo Domingo—and others (such as St. Augustine, Florida) were heavily fortified and garrisoned. The defenses of San Juan illustrate the extent and costliness of these fortifications. The entire town was enclosed in a wall 50 feet high, into which was set the fortress of San Felipe del Morro, which rises 140 feet above the sea. The fortifications mounted 400 guns and spread over 200 acres of land, although the town itself occupied only 62 acres. Its construction continued intermittently from 1525 to 1785, and its ultimate cost was six million pesos. These colonial fortifications are still very much a part of the picturesque landscape of San Juan and other Caribbean cities.

Not all the fortified harbors, however, proved to be equally important. Ultimately, Havana rose to be the chief fortress city of the Indies, not only because of its superior harbor but also because of its prime location with respect to the Spanish fleet movements under the convoy system.

Under the convoy system, which operated from 1561 to 1748, two fleets were supposed to leave Spain every year for the

Caribbean. The ships would depart from Cadiz or Seville and proceed to the Canaries in order to enter the belt of the northeast trades for the westward journey. The first landfall in the Caribbean was usually near Dominica or on an island to the north. Here the fleet divided, one segment going to Cartagena and Puerto Bello, the other going to San Juan, Santo Domingo, and Veracruz (Figure 3.3). Then the entire fleet would reassemble in Havana for the journey back to Spain. From Havana, adjacent to the Florida Passage along the line of shortest distance between Veracruz and Spain, the ships entered the northeast-flowing Gulf Stream, which carried them into the westerlies and thence into European "waters."

It was never certain, however, that the Spanish fleet, which was the only legal link between the Antilles and the outside world, would always call. War, a shortage of ships, or other obstacles would prevent sailings, and Caribbean ports might go for two or more years without seeing a single Spanish ship. These and other conditions of the Spanish monopoly blighted com-

mercial developments on the islands, discouraged free immigration, and caused finished products to become so scarce and costly that contraband trade with the English, Dutch, and French became necessary to survival.

With the exhaustion of gold and the shift of Spanish interest to the continent, the chief obstacle to economic development in the Spanish West Indies became shortage of labor. By 1530, immigration had come to a virtual standstill, many of the colonists had moved out, and the Indian population had been all but destroyed. African slaves began to be imported early in the sixteenth century to fill the labor gap, but this proved unprofitable in the Spanish islands until the nineteenth century, when plantation agriculture took significant hold. The labor shortage, coupled with other restrictions imposed by Spanish colonial policy, left open only two avenues of production—a largely subsistence agriculture and grazing.

In addition, there was some lumbering in the Spanish Antilles during the early colonial period. Exports included logwood,

Figure 3.3   Route of the Spanish convoy system

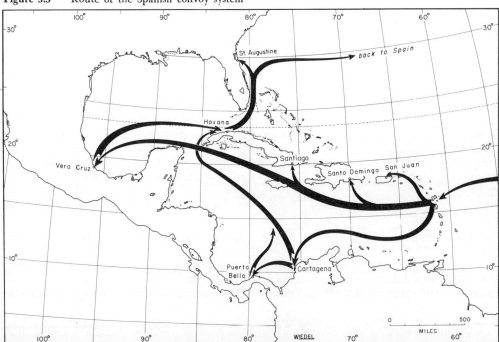

mahogany, and tropical cedar. A byproduct of lumbering was shipbuilding, particularly in Havana. Slave raiding among the Indians of the unoccupied islands (the Bahamas and the Lesser Antilles) was a noteworthy economic activity, as was the production of salt, which was used to cure hides and meat.

The North European Intrusion

In answer to Spanish claims of monopoly in the Caribbean and elsewhere in the New World, Francis I of France is reputed to have said, "The sun shines for me as for others. I should very much like to see the clause in Adam's will that excludes me from a share of the world." A comparable attitude was adopted by other ambitious maritime nations of Europe, such as England and Holland. Their challenge to Spain and to each other converted the Caribbean and its Rimland into a focus of intense international rivalry from the latter sixteenth century to the end of the eighteenth century.

The north European challenge to Spanish monopoly did not at first involve colonization. Searching for new routes to the great markets of Asia, privateering and pirating for booty, trading in contraband with Spanish colonists, cutting logwood, and making salt were the principal activities of the intruders, and these they carried on without establishing bases. Privateering expeditions were often business ventures financed by the merchants of Dieppe, London, Amsterdam, and other north European cities. In theory, privateers were supposed to operate against Spanish commerce only in wartime, but since "no peace beyond the line" (i.e., west of the longitude of the Azores and south of the Tropic of Cancer) was recognized even when there was peace in Europe, privateering continued as long as it was profitable.

As hopes for finding the straits to the Orient vanished and the profits from privateering began to decrease, however, the unemployed adventurers and their financial supporters turned their attention to the possibility of establishing colonies that might produce commodities such as tobacco and indigo, which commanded good prices in European markets. The result was a rapid colonization of the unoccupied Lesser Antilles, western Hispaniola, and other parts of the Rimland, beginning in about the first quarter of the seventeenth century.

The methods of the north European colonizers differed from those of the Spanish in almost every instance. Spain employed direct conquest, and her settlements were under the strict, centralized control of the home country. Her aim was to create a monolithic empire that would faithfully mirror the language, religion, political institutions, and other cultural facets of the Castilian fountainhead. The north European nations used the trade and plantation company as the principal instrument of colonization. These companies were generally composed of merchants who subscribed capital for settlement and trade and received profits on a share basis from the enterprise. While the relationship between the company and the national government that granted the charter was a close one, there was far less political control and far less required cultural integration with the mother country. Trade and profits were, from the very beginning, recognized as sufficient reasons for colonization.

EUROPEAN IMPACT AND EXPERIMENTAL ADAPTATIONS IN THE CARIBBEAN

The Europeans who colonized the Caribbean had to function in a milieu very different from anything they had previously encountered. The physical environment, the cultures of the indigenous people and of the later African imports, and the potentials of a new world presented the European with new situations to which he had to adjust and new problems for which he had to find solutions. In the process of adjustment and experimentation, he caused a radical alteration in the natural and cultural scheme of things that he found in the area; at the same time, his own cultural baggage was conspicuously modified. New features appeared on the land; new social and political forms evolved; and new values replaced old ones as European man adapted himself and his institutions to the new surroundings.

Impact on the Indian

Perhaps the most immediate consequence of European colonization in the Caribbean was the virtual annihilation of native peoples and cultures, especially in the West Indies. With the exceptions of some of the forest dwellers of the Central American coast, the Amerindian past in the Caribbean is now hardly a memory. In the Greater Antilles the destruction of the once numerous Arawaks at the hands of the Spaniards was so rapid and complete that, 75 years after the Discovery, there were essentially no survivors. The Caribs of the Lesser Antilles survived a little longer, but only because the Europeans came to these islands later. Within a half-century of the start of north European colonization in 1623, the Caribs had been destroyed or had been driven off all their islands except Dominica and St. Vincent. Today, the only noteworthy remnant of the Caribs is a group of approximately five hundred on a reservation in Dominica, and even most of these have a large admixture of black blood. There are also the Black Caribs, who live along the Central American coast, from Stann Creek in British Honduras to the Black River in

the Republic of Honduras. The Black Caribs are, for the most part, descendants of the Carib Indians of St. Vincent and a cargo of black slaves which was shipwrecked off the island in 1675—a mixture that proved so hostile to the Europeans that the English exiled them from St. Vincent to Central America in 1797.

Many reasons have been advanced to account for the decimation of the Antillean Indians. The most basic appears to be that their technologically weak native culture was unable to compete for survival in the face of ruthless European methods. The Indian was at a disadvantage in military organization and weapons; he had no immunity to diseases such as smallpox brought in by the Europeans; he lacked the disciplined capacity for sustained hard work; and in the Antilles, the islands were too small to afford him refuge from the European onslaught. Perhaps equally important, the Indian lost his food supply when his European competitor took the land that produced it. A few survivors fled to the forested mountain interiors of the larger islands and became known as *Cimarrones* ("dwellers of the summits"). There they retained their way of life and continued to war against the European settlements on the lowlands. Eventually they were joined by runaway slaves, and black blood became dominant. Maroon bands persisted for a considerable time in a few of the islands, and in Jamaica the Maroons are still a distinct element of the population.

Even leaving aside the exaggeration of the Black Legend,[1] the history of the An-

1. The Black Legend originated with the publication, by Bartolomé de las Casas in 1552, of the *Brevisima Relación de la Destrucción de las Indias*, in which it was charged that 15 million Indians had perished on account of the cruelty of the Spaniards. The book was eventually translated into virtually all the principal languages of Western Europe (including 18 Dutch editions, 8 German, 6 French, 4 English, 3 Italian, and 3

tillean Indian is a tragic one. The Europeans deprived him of his land, exposed him to smallpox, and permitted him to live only as a virtual slave laborer. The Indian either chose death over slavery, as did the Caribs, or he died because he lacked immunity to new diseases or was unable to adjust to the rigors of hard labor, as did the Arawaks. And about all that remains to prove his former occupancy of the Antilles is the tradition of raising tuber crops for subsistence, the *bohio* as a rural house type, the hammock, place names such as "Cuba" and "Haiti," and other Indian terms such as "hurricane."

The destruction of the Indian created both a labor and a cultural vacuum in the Caribbean, and history has filled the vacuum with a predominantly African labor force and a modified Euro-African culture.

The Plant and Animal Factors

Colonization of the Caribbean lands also had a disturbing impact on the plant and animal associations of the region, particularly in the more densely populated zones such as the Antilles. Today, all the domestic animals and many of the useful plants of the Caribbean are Old World imports. Even some of the wild plants and animals were originally introduced from without and have since displaced some of the native species.

Descriptions of early travelers indicate that the Central American coast was al-

most entirely forested. In the Antilles, also, the vegetation was dominated by trees, the more humid islands being forested right down to the water's edge. The forest of the Caribbean Rimland, however, was not everywhere the same. The Antilles, for instance, had far fewer species [2] than the Mainland coast. Moreover, it may be assumed that on the drier leeward sides and on the islands of low elevation, the true forest gave way to scrub woodland, savanna, and even steppe. Much of the area currently under grass or scrub vegetation in the Indies, however, was probably once forest that was altered by burning for agriculture, or by logging, charcoal making, and other post-Columbian disturbances. At present, small remnants of virgin forest in the Indies may be found only in remote mountain terrain such as in Dominica. In the Greater Antilles, even the mountain forests have generally had to give way to the need for farmland.

The native animal life of the insular sectors of the Rimland also consisted of a limited number of species, except in Trinidad, where proximity to South America resulted in a much richer fauna. Even these few, however, have been largely destroyed by post-Columbian man or by his animal imports, such as the mongoose and the rat. The iguana (a herbivorous lizard), the agouti, the hawksbill turtle, the green turtle, the manatee, and other animals have been nearly destroyed or sharply reduced on the islands.

In an effort to become self-sufficient in food, the Europeans, particularly the Spaniards, introduced a wide variety of domestic plants and animals to supplement the indigenous food supply. The vine and olive

Latin). The report was welcomed as an exact picture of conditions in the Spanish colonies and of the inherent qualities of the Spaniards, who were hated by the Protestant people of that day as the leading Catholic power and by other people as the strongest nation in Europe. Despite the apparent exaggerations, this propaganda piece formulated an attitude toward Spain that survives to this day.

2. Gordon Merrill (1958) indicates that three species—gumlin trees (Dacryode excelsa), mountain cabbage (Enterpa globosa), and guava sweetwood (Aniba bracteata)—make up more than three-fourths of the forest in the upper slopes of several of the Lesser Antilles. In the Greater Antilles and on all the lowlands, the flora is richer.

brought from Iberia proved unsuited to the climate, as did stoned fruits and wheat and other European cereals. Oranges, lemons, and limes throve, however, and before long had passed from cultivated groves to a wild state in the forests. Bananas and plantains imported from the Canaries were an immediate success, as were sugar, rice, and numerous vegetables—lettuce, onions, cucumbers, cabbage, and others. Indian maize was used as a substitute for European cereals. Later plant imports included coffee, breadfruit, and the ubiquitous mango.

As we have already noted, grazing soon exceeded agriculture in the Spanish Antilles. The cattle, pigs, and horses imported from Spain and (more often) from the Canaries multiplied so rapidly that, by 1503, no further imports were necessary. Livestock was released on newly discovered islands so that permanent colonists who came later would have meat, and the Spanish Crown established farms and ranches to supply colonies on the Mainland. A grant to the city of Panama (1521) from a Crown farm in Jamaica, for instance, included 500 cows, 500 yearlings, 1,000 pigs, and 200 loads of maize. In this way, the islands became suppliers to the conquerors of Mexico, Peru, and New Granada, and functioned as dispersal points from which animals, as well as plants, spread to the continent.

Because of the limited size of their territories and their greater emphasis on commercial agriculture, food was a more acute problem for the north Europeans than for the Spaniards, and initially they had to rely more heavily on indigenous food supplies. The diet of the early English and French colonist was built around sea food (turtles, sea cows, and fish) lizards, cassava, and maize. Later, the introduction of sugar and the consequent rapid increases in slave populations made land so valuable and food so scarce that large-scale importation became necessary. Sugar cane changed the drinking habits of the less well-to-do European colonists, from wine and ale to rum and *aguardiente*.

Settlements and Houses

The evolution of settlements and house types in the Caribbean was dictated in part by European tradition and in part by local exigencies. In the Hispanic territories, the town was always the anchor point of European culture. Grazing and mining were somewhat seasonal and could be left to overseers. The leading settlers preferred to live in the towns, and the corporate town, rather than the country house, became the stronghold of the ruling class. The pattern of dispersed rural settlement characterized by the *bohio*—now in evidence in Cuba, Puerto Rico, and the Dominican Republic—developed later, authored primarily by the poorer whites and by blacks.

The Spanish had a simple, standard plan of town construction. The central point was invariably a square plaza, around which were built the church, the *casa de ayuntamiento* ("town hall"), the prison, and other public buildings. If the town had a garrison, the barracks, facing a *plaza de armas* ("parade ground"), was located nearby. The streets were laid out in a chessboard pattern, intersecting at right angles where possible. The settlement tended either to be square or to develop on two sides until it acquired an oblong shape. Public buildings and the homes of the wealthier colonists were generally of stone; the others were frame, of local wood with palm thatch roofing. Except for major centers like Havana, most Spanish settlements in the Caribbean during the first three centuries of the colonial period were very small, consisting of from 10 to 30 *vecinos* ("families").

The *bohio,* which became the most widespread house type in the rural areas of the Hispanic Antilles, was a simple structure, often containing one all-purpose room, and closely resembling its Arawak namesake. It was generally rectangular, and was constructed of thin poles or boards with a thatched palm roof. In the wetter zones, the entire structure was set on four short poles above the ground, and a floor of boards was added. There were virtually no furnishings. The family slept in hammocks which were folded and put away during the day, and cooking was done in the *batey,* or yard.

The town houses of the wealthier colonists had a strong Andalusian flavor. They were built flush with the street, with walls of thick masonry to keep out the heat and to give protection against hurricanes. Enclosed patios with an outside kitchen were characteristic, and the central bedrooms were often windowless. Major churches, such as the cathedral of Santo Domingo, were often designed by Italian architects and had a markedly Romanesque style.

Dutch settlements, like the Spanish, were also urban-oriented. The emphasis on commerce made the warehouses, port facilities, and the counting house the characteristic landmarks of the Dutch pattern. The merchants often lived in the rear or in an upper story of their business establishments, much as they did in Amsterdam.

In contrast, the English and the French tended more to rural living. Even before the profitability of sugar made expensive manor houses and estates possible, these two groups preferred to reside directly on the land. As a result, while the Spanish towns developed into well-planned settlements with imposing churches and public buildings, those in the English and French colonies were often haphazard collections of buildings. By the same token, however, there was nothing in the countryside of the Hispanic territories to equal the Georgian "great houses" of Jamaica and Barbados or the lavish estate residences that once dotted French St. Domingue.

Eventually, each European group left its cultural stamp on the architecture of its colonies. The visitor to Havana, Curaçao, or once Danish St. Thomas has no difficulty in determining architectural origins. Where more than one culture has been at work (as in Trinidad), a variety of cultural forms are evident.

NATURE AND IMPACT OF THE WEST INDIAN COLONIAL PLANTATION

The present patterns of land and people in the Antilles are in a state of change, but they still mirror the effect not only of the varied tropical environment, but also of a history marked by colonialism, black slavery, mercantilism, monoculture, and absentee ownership. The origin of much of this history centers around the classical device used by Europeans for the agricultural exploitation of newly acquired tropical areas—the colonial plantation. This early form of the plantation was developed to supply European markets with cane sugar and other tropical products. It became well established during the latter seventeenth century, reached its maximum development in the eighteenth century, and declined in the nineteenth century, to be replaced by today's modern plantation.

Initially conceived as an instrument for organizing the commercial possibilities of tropical land and labor, the colonial plantation in the Antilles had wide repercussions. It served as the vehicle for importing large numbers of black slaves and became a major determinant of racial composition and population patterns; it mined the soil and created a temporary but spectacular wealth over which European nations fought numerous wars; it made impossible the development of a European population composed of independent farmers and tradesmen, and gave rise to a two-class society divided by racial and economic gulfs. Whenever it took root, ". . . the plantation has been the dominant economic, social and political institution in the past, continues to be in the present, and from all indications will continue to be in the future. . . . In short, it has fashioned the whole environment . . ." (Beckford 1972:3). No other institution is so vital to the understanding of past and present in the West Indies as the colonial plantation, for none has so deeply affected the patterns of land and people.

The colonial plantation based on sugar did not develop uniformly throughout the Rimland; in fact, it was confined almost exclusively to the West Indies. Along the Caribbean coast of Central America, sugar and the early plantation failed to take root, and when plantations began to emerge in the 1880s, they were the modern type, based on bananas and free labor rather than on sugar and slavery. But there were differences in development even within the West Indies. In the Spanish colonies (including Trinidad until 1797), the sugar plantation worked by black slaves tended to be an exceptional feature of the economy until the nineteenth century. Its late development, as well as other circumstances, suggests that the nineteenth-century Spanish plantation was a transitional type between the colonial and the modern forms.

On the basis of equipment, land tenure, labor force, time of occurrence, and other characteristics, the evolution of the colonial sugar plantation in the Caribbean may be classified into two phases and forms— the *trapiche* and the *ingenio*. The two Spanish terms described types of mills used for grinding sugar cane, but they may also be applied to the distinctive forms of the colonial plantation with which the mill types were generally associated.

The *trapiche* was a small primitive mill worked by animal power, although wind and even water were sometimes employed (Figures 3.4, 3.5). Its grinding capacity was so limited that each farm had to have one or more, depending on the amount of land under cane. The *trapiche*, family-owned land worked by black slaves, was the first plantation type everywhere. It had its beginnings in Santo Domingo, Cuba, and other Hispanic areas in the sixteenth century, but it reached its peak in the north European islands during the eighteenth century.

The *ingenio,* a larger and better-equipped mill that characterized the nineteenth-century sugar plantation in much of the Caribbean, was run by water power and later by steam. Most *ingenio* plantations were large, family-owned estates, but corporate ownership was also present, especially in Cuba during the latter nineteenth century. Depending on time and place, the labor force was either slave or free. In many respects, the *ingenio* was transitional between the earlier *trapiche* and the modern *central,* or factory in the field, which is discussed elsewhere in this text.

Regardless of specific form, the characteristic colonial plantation, with its slave labor force and its emphasis on sugar production, was primarily a phenomenon of the English and French colonies. On the eve of the American Revolution, for example, there were approximately 3,900 sugar plantations in the West Indies, of which 1,830 were English and 1,350 were French. The remainder were Spanish, Dutch, and Danish (Sheridan 1969:21–22). Thus, it is to the British and French colonies that we must turn for an analysis of the nature and impact of the colonial plantation as an institution in the Caribbean.

THE COLONIAL PLANTATION IN THE ENGLISH AND FRENCH WEST INDIES

Several conditions paved the way for the rise of sugar and the plantation that began in the English and French Antillean colonies about the middle of the seventeenth century. As already noted, tobacco production, which had initially been the commer-

Figure 3.4   Surviving example of a primitive, *trapiche*-type cattle mill common to the colonial plantation, Plaine du Nord, Haiti

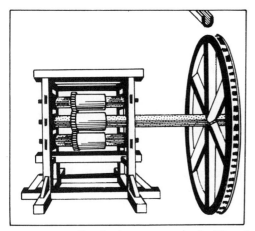

Figure 3.5   Sketch of a water-powered mill used on a West Indian sugar estate during the eighteenth century

cial mainstay of many of these territories, was being undermined by competition, in the European markets, from the higher-quality Virginia and Maryland product. Other possible cash crops, such as ginger and indigo, had only limited markets, and extensive cotton cultivation required more land than was available on the small islands. Coffee growing had modest possibilities and eventually achieved some importance, particularly in the mountain lands of St. Domingue and Jamaica. It was sugar, however, that offered the most promising alternative, not only because the

islands were climatically suitable for the crop but also because an expanding European market promised the planters rich rewards.[3]

Once established, sugar caused a virtual revolution in the land-and-people complex of the Indies. Beginning in Barbados in 1640, the revolution swept through the Leewards a generation later and reached its climax in Jamaica and St. Domingue in the eighteenth century. Land values rocketed, and the pattern of land tenure rapidly changed from small holdings to large estates. Successful sugar planters squeezed out the failing tobacco farmers, who left the islands in droves, and this, together with increased demands for labor, resulted in the importation of large numbers of black slaves. The population composition changed from dominantly European to dominantly African. The very appearance of the land was altered. As sugar planting expanded, the lowland forests were rapidly cut down and cane fields became the chief feature of the agricul-

3. The technical know-how, as well as the credit and the shipping often needed by the early English and French planters, was supplied by the Dutch, who had learned the sugar business in Brazil. Expelled by the Portuguese from Bahia in the seventeenth century, the Dutch (including many Jews) moved to the Caribbean and supplied the necessary catalyst for sugar production.

tural landscape. The big house of the planter, with its villagelike slave quarters, replaced the dispersed homestead of the small tobacco farmer. The sugar mill and its boiling house became an integral part of the West Indies scene.

AFRICAN SLAVERY AND
ITS WEST INDIAN IMPACT

The keystone of the colonial sugar economy was an abundance of cheap labor. Economically speaking, it mattered little whether this labor was African, European, Asian, or Amerindian; the emphasis was on cost. Approximately one field hand was needed for every acre of land in cane, and workers were needed for domestic service and other tasks, besides. Where was this labor to be obtained?

The dwindling Amerindian population was unused to hard labor. Records indicate that some Indians worked on plantations on a few of the islands such as Barbados, but from the beginning, the Indian was never a major source of labor. Every effort was directed to the importation of European indentured workers, and the conditions of the European peasantry in the seventeenth and eighteenth centuries were so wretched that many poor people voluntarily indentured themselves for five years in the hope of getting a fresh start in the West Indies. Their treatment at the hands of the planters was so brutal, however, that the voluntary movement ceased quickly, and other methods of recruitment had to be resorted to. Prisoners, prostitutes, religious nonconformists (including many Irish Roman Catholics), and other people were shipped to the islands. When all else failed, kidnapping, even of children, was used. "To be barbadoed" (sent to Barbados) became an infamous verb in the English language.

Ultimately, however, white labor proved too expensive as well as too difficult to obtain. If the indentured European managed to survive his term of service, he had to be given some kind of compensation in money or land. More often he succumbed to the arduous plantation labor and to malaria, yellow fever, and other tropical disease, against which the poor diet and poorer sanitation provided little protection.

There is evidence that the Spaniards experimented in importing Filipinos and Malayans, but the large pool of Asian labor was too far removed to be tapped. This left Africa as the only large, available source of labor.

Many reasons have been advanced for the heavy importation of black slaves to the West Indies. Western Africa, particularly around the Gulf of Guinea, had a large population located at a comparatively short distance across the Middle Passage from the Caribbean. The blacks were felt to be inherently strong; they possessed some agricultural know-how; and many were already accustomed to slavery in their African habitat. Remote from his own cultural hearth and thrown in with fellow slaves who did not even speak the same language, the black could be easily controlled. Finally, the Africans seemed to possess some immunity both to tropical diseases and to the European varieties which had been the scourge of the Indian populations.

Slavery's Impact
on Population

Everywhere that plantation sugar and slavery took hold in the West Indies the population changed: (1) the total population, as well as the ratio of blacks to whites, increased rapidly; (2) miscegenation gave rise to a mixed-blood group that stood apart both from their maternal black and paternal white racial heritage; (3) population became concentrated on the coastal plains and other lowlands where sugar was cultivated; and (4) settlements took the form of black slave villages grouped around the great houses.

The impact of slavery on population is perhaps best illustrated by Barbados, the first territory to experience the sugar revolution. In 1640, the island had 43,000 people, of whom 37,000 were white and 6,000 black. By 1678, the white population had dropped to 20,000 and the black had risen to 40,000. By 1809, the island had 84,685 inhabitants, and the blacks outnumbered the whites about five to one. The actual drop in the European population resulted from the departure of the small farmers, who could not compete with the large cane planters for land or with slaves in the labor market.

Elsewhere, the population trends illustrated by Barbados differed only in degree, mirroring differences in the size of the territory, the date of the sugar revolution, the history of settlement prior to sugar, and other local conditions (Table 3.1). Not unexpectedly, the largest population totals were ultimately achieved in Jamaica and St. Domingue, and the highest densities occurred in Barbados and the smaller is-

lands, particularly the Leewards. An actual decrease in the size of the European population tended to take place only in the early-settled islands, which already had a sizable number of small tobacco farmers.

The rapid importation of large numbers of black slaves gave rise to very high population densities, particularly in the smaller islands. Barbados, for example, had densities of 400 people per square mile by 1684. In the other territories densities were lower, but everywhere the pressure of people on land was vastly greater than in the British North American colonies or the adjacent Spanish areas. The high densities of population in the West Indies today owe their origin in large measure to the influx of slaves authored by the colonial sugar plantation. But, as we have observed, the mountain lands were relatively lightly occupied, a contrast that survives to this day on many of the islands.

Miscegenation occurred in all the slave-holding territories but was probably most widespread in the French. The white planter, manager, or bookkeeper often chose an overlapping succession of concubines from among the slaves, and the

Table 3.1 CONTRASTS BETWEEN SEVENTEENTH- AND EIGHTEENTH-CENTURY TOTAL POPULATION AND RACIAL COMPOSITION OF COLONIAL PLANTATION TERRITORIES

Territory	End of 17th Century			End of 18th Century		
	total	white	black	total	white	black
St. Domingue	10,000	7,091	2,909	640,000	40,000	600,000(?)
Guadeloupe	11,000	6,009	4,981	99,970	13,261	86,709
Martinique	16,500	5,000	11,500	91,815	11,619	80,196
Jamaica	48,500	8,500	40,000	280,000	30,000	250,000
Barbados	60,000	20,000	40,000	78,282	16,167	62,115
Grenada		Windwards		24,926	1,000	23,926
St. Vincent		largely		13,309	1,450	11,853
Dominica		unoccupied		16,203	1,236	14,967
Antigua	?	5,000	?	40,398	2,590	37,808
Montserrat	3,775	2,783	992	11,300	1,300	10,000
Virgin Islands	?	?	?	10,200	1,200	9,000
St. Kitts	7,381	3,521	3,860	22,335	1,900	20,435

Note: Data gathered from several sources; figures should be considered only approximate.

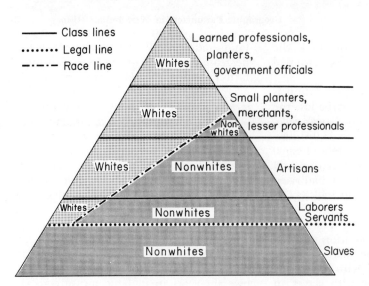

Figure 3.6 Race and class in a slave society

mixed-blood group which developed ranged from 3 to 10 percent of the total population. The importance of the mulatto group rested less in its size, however, than in the intermediate socioeconomic position it occupied. The possession of a lighter skin in a society obsessed with a black slave tradition gave the mulattoes a higher status. Even when they were not freed by their white fathers, as was customary, they were often considered too light to work in the fields and were used as domestic servants. Degrees of rank, depending on the exact admixture of race, developed, and society took careful note of the individual's composition (Figure 3.6). Light skin became the badge of the European, of racial superiority and high status, and dark skin was associated with slavery, field work, and low status. This prejudice has tainted the attitude of the West Indian toward agriculture and manual labor ever since.

**Other Consequences
of Slavery**

Contrary to much opinion, the black slave did not arrive in the Caribbean a culturally naked savage. The region of West Africa that furnished most of the slaves to the sugar plantations was an area of well-developed cultures, including those of the Fula and Mandingo empires, the Hausa Kingdom of northern Nigeria, the Fanti and Ashanti states of the Gold Coast, and the eastern kingdoms of Dahomey, the Yoruba, and the Benin. In most of these places, the people lived in villages and even cities. They subsisted by means of complex systems of agriculture and animal husbandry; they possessed sophisticated social and political organizations; and, in some instances, they had developed handicrafts such as wood carving and working with metals.

The African culture brought by the slaves was not uniform, however, and crossing the Atlantic usually meant a radical break with African cultural tradition. The slave often assimilated, in varying degree, the European culture of his master. But there was some African cultural carry-over, and it left its mark on the social forms and the man-land patterns of the West Indies.

The blacks seemed to have retained at least part of the African view of land tenure. Private ownership of usefully occupied or cultivated land was widely recognized in West Africa, but vacant land was considered the property of the tribe (or its king) and could be worked by any individual willing to invest the effort. After emancipation, the blacks stubbornly asserted that unoccupied or unused land was open to settlement. They rejected the idea that perfectly good land could be left unoccupied at the mere whim of its owner.

Other African carryovers are discernible in agricultural tools and practices. In much of West Africa, farming resembled Amerindian cassava culture, which emphasized root crops and used fire for clearing the land. The chief tool was the hoe (often short-handled). Cultivation was done in gangs, with the laborers swinging their hoes in parallel rows to the beat of a drum. Friends and neighbors often worked together in cooperative, mutual-help groups. The slaves used these familiar tools and practices in plantation work or on their provision grounds, and the West Indian peasantry continued to use them after emancipation. Cooperative work, for example, variously called "combite," "jollification," and other names, is still practiced.

With the black slaves came new food plants. Among the more important were the ackee fruit, okra, the congo bean or blackeyed pea, the yam, millet, sorghum, and the mango, an Asian fruit that had been introduced into West Africa by Arab slavers. Breadfruit was introduced from the Pacific primarily to satisfy the need for cheap slave food; but the slaves refused to eat it, and it did not become an important food crop until after emancipation. African influence has left its mark on the material culture of the West Indies in a host of other ways including the wooden mortar for grinding grains, ways of preparing certain foods and even palm wine, and materials and modes for constructing huts such as the already-mentioned wattle and daub. In addition, modified African carryovers may be discerned in the role of women in rural life, the operations of rural markets, the nature of the family, and a wide range of artistic forms from folk tales to music and the dance.

DECLINE OF
THE WEST INDIAN
COLONIAL PLANTATION

After reaching its height in the eighteenth century, the West Indian colonial plantation underwent a general decline in the nineteenth century and was ultimately replaced, in most instances, by the modern plantation. This decline and transition rocked the land-people complex of the West Indies into new forms, particularly in the English and French territories where the colonial system had been most completely established. On the Hispanic islands, where the colonial institution was not deeply rooted, the transition from the colonial to the modern plantation was smoother. In fact, the Spanish possessions experienced an upsurge in plantation production precisely while production in the English and French territories was declining. Therefore, the following analysis of the decline of the colonial plantation will focus primarily on the English and French territories.

There was no one major cause that led to the decline of the colonial plantation, nor were all causes equally important in all territories. For the Caribbean as a whole, the list includes:

1. Slave uprisings and unrest.

2. The exhaustion of the soil.

3. The abolition of the slave trade and the emancipation of slaves.

4. The growing competition from other sugar producers, especially Cuba, as well as from beet sugar, which became established in Europe after the Napoleonic period.

5. The loss of monopoly of the home-country market, especially by the English territories after 1846.

6. The independence of the American colonies which obstructed the once-free commerce and increased the cost of food and lumber for the British sugar colonies.

7. Absentee landlordism and heavy indebtedness.

8. New industrial and marketing arrangements and techniques.

9. The destruction caused by the numerous wars in the Caribbean.

The collapse of the colonial plantation caused revolutionary changes. The mainspring for most of these changes was the necessity to readjust land-people relations in the face of a sharp reduction in the production of sugar, the financial bankruptcy of the planter class, and an emancipation that freed a race but did not create a society.

Populations were profoundly affected. Their numbers, densities, distributions, movements, racial compositions, and modes of settlement were changed. Land use and land tenure were altered, and the organization of commercial production was revolutionized. In virtually all the islands, the white population decreased. Many planters were killed in slave uprisings, and many left for England, France, Louisiana, and elsewhere. The numerical loss was more than compensated for, however, by an increase in the black population. Once emancipated, the black population, which had generally been unable to reproduce itself under slave conditions, began to increase—a trend that has continued unabated to the present. In turn, the rise in black population increased population densities and pressure of people on land, and thereby set the stage for the current discrepancy between the population and the land resources of the West Indies.

"After the experience of the brutality of the plantation, the ex-slaves sought every opportunity to secure an existence for themselves as independent of the plantation as possible" (Beckford 1972:47).

Wherever possible, the newly freed blacks abandoned the coastal estates and occupied land in the hilly interior. This movement created in the larger territories a labor shortage that could be met only by the importation of cheap labor from the Orient and elsewhere; it tended, by transferring people from the crowded coastal plains to the interior, to more nearly equalize the population distribution; it emphasized the economic and social difference between the commercially utilized plains with their estates and their planter groups, and the uplands with their subsistence peasant groups; it modified the settlement patterns, which had mainly been coastal cities and the slave villages of the estates, by creating dispersed settlement and free villages.

Eventually, the subsistence plots established by the ex-slaves were able to produce marketable surpluses, thus diversifying the insular farm production and expanding the money economy. Moreover, the trend strengthened the internal marketing system; it led to the development of a network of footpaths and rudimentary roads; and it fostered the creation of linkages between the different production and service sectors of the local economy.

Ultimately, the tendency of the freed blacks to abandon the estates and establish themselves on small plots created a class of small farmers that came to be called "peasant." But the peasant class in the West Indies differed then, as it differs now, from its counterpart in Europe and Asia. There was little love for the land, little association with place, and little respect for manual toil. The association of field labor with slavery left a stigma on agricultural labor that continues to this day. And, since there was never enough land to go around, many of the blacks came to form a landless peasantry whose unemployment or underemployment add to the poverty of the present. In most of the West Indies, even those who were fortunate enough to acquire plots of land were unable to divorce themselves completely from the plantation system. Their tiny plots on marginal land simply did not produce enough to provide a livelihood, and they had to offer their services as part-time estate laborers.

Readjustment also gave rise to change in the patterns of land use and land tenure. With the drop in production and price of sugar and the bankruptcy of a large number of planters, many estates were placed in receivership. Some of the estates were divided into small plots and sold or sharecropped to the ex-slaves. This caused a sharp increase in the number of small holdings and, as in the post–Civil War American South, it created the practice of sharecropping. The general reduction in the amount of land in cane condemned marginal lands to other uses. As a result, land values tumbled. Those estates that remained sugar producers had to be made more efficient to stay solvent, and this set the stage for the modern corporate plantation.

SELECTED REFERENCES

BECKFORD, G. L. *Persistent Poverty*. New York: Oxford University Press, 1972.

BENNETT, J. H., JR. "The Problem of Slave Labor Supply at the Codrington Plantations." *Journal of Negro History* 36, no. 4 (1951):406–41; 37, no. 2 (1952):115–41.

DEBIEN, G. *Une Plantation de Saint-Domingue: La Sucrerie Galbaud du Fort: 1690–1802*. Cairo: Les Presses de l'Institut Français d'Archéologie Orientale du Caire, 1941.

DEBIEN, G., and HOUDAILLE, J. "Les Origines Africaines des Esclaves de les Antilles Françaises." *Caribbean Studies* 10, no. 2 (1970): 5–29.

DEERR, N. *The History of Sugar*. London: Chapman and Hall, 1949.

DEFFONTAINES, P. "L'introduction du Bétail en Amérique Latine." *Les Cahiers d'Outre-Mer* 10 (1957):5–22.

EDWARDS, B. *History, Civil and Commercial, of the British Colonies in the West Indies*. Dublin: Luke White, 1793.

HARLOW, V. T. *A History of Barbados: 1625–1685*. Oxford: Clarendon Press, 1926.

HUMBOLDT, A. *The Island of Cuba*. New York: Derby and Jackson, 1856.

INTERNATIONAL LABOUR ORGANISATION. *Definition of the Term "Plantation."* Geneva: International Labour Office, 1953.

LAS CASAS, B. *Apologética Historia de las Indias*. Madrid: Biblioteca de Autores Españoles, 1909.

LÓPEZ DE VELASCO, J. *Geografía y Descripción Universal de las Indias desde el Año 1571 al de 1574*. Madrid: Establ. tip. de Fortanet, 1894.

LOWENTHAL, D. "Caribbean Views of Caribbean Land." *Canadian Geographer* 5, no. 2 (1961):1–9.

MERRILL, G. C. *The Historical Geography of St. Kitts and Nevis, The West Indies*. Mexico, D.F.: Pan-American Institute of Geography and History, no. 232 (1958).

———. "The Historical Record of Man as an Ecological Dominant in the Lesser Antilles." *Canadian Geographer*, no. 11 (1958), pp. 17–22.

OVIEDO Y VALDÉS, G. F. DE. *Historia General y Natural de las Indias, Islas y Tierra-Firme del Mar Océano*. 4 vols. Madrid: Real Academia de la Historia, 1851–1855.

PAN-AMERICAN UNION. *Plantation Systems of the New World*. Social Science Monograph, no. 7. Washington, D.C.: Pan-American Union, 1959.

PARES, R. *Merchants and Planters*. London: Cambridge University Press, 1960.

PARRY, J. H., and SHERLOCK, P. M. *A Short*

History of the West Indies. London: Macmillan, 1956.

PARSONS, J. J. "San Andrés and Providencia: English-speaking Islands in the Western Caribbean." *University of California Publications in Geography* 12, no. 1 (1956):1–84.

————. *The Green Turtle and Man.* Gainesville: University of Florida Press, 1962.

PITMAN, F. W. "The Settlement and Financing of British West India Plantations in the Eighteenth Century." In *Essays in Colonial History Presented to Charles McLean Andrews by His Students.* New Haven, Conn.: Yale University Press, 1931.

REID, M. *The Maroon: Or, Planter Life in Jamaica.* New York: R. M. DeWitt, 1864.

ROBERTS, W. A. *The French in the West Indies.* Indianapolis: Bobbs-Merrill, 1942.

SAUER, C. O. *Agricultural Origins and Dispersals.* New York: American Geographical Society, 1952.

————. *The Early Spanish Main.* Berkeley: University of California Press, 1966.

SHERIDAN, R. B. "The Plantation Revolution and the Industrial Revolution, 1625–1775." *Caribbean Studies* 9, no. 3 (1969):5–25.

STEWARD, J. H., ed. "The Circum-Caribbean Tribes." *Handbook of South American Indians.* Vol. 4. Washington, D.C.: Smithsonian Institution, 1948.

WILLIAMS, E. *Capitalism and Slavery.* Chapel Hill: University of North Carolina Press, 1944.

ZELINSKY, W. "The Historical Geography of the Negro Population of Latin America." *Journal of Negro History* 34, no. 2 (1949): 153–221.

≡ 4 ≡

Economic Geography
of the Present-Day West Indies

Generalizations about the West Indies are seldom equally valid for every island or island group in the archipelago. As already suggested (Chapter 1), local differences in physical environment and resources, in historical experience and current political connections, and in an array of other influences tend to give virtually every territory a noteworthy distinctiveness. However, the impact of powerful formative forces such as colonialism, the plantation, slavery, and emancipation has been felt on virtually every island, and as a result, there is often striking similarity of economic patterns and problems, man-land relations, institutional equipment, and other aspects of material culture in the archipelago. Traditionally, the differences and the resulting distinctiveness have been emphasized. Currently, however, "The West Indies are beginning a painful process of self-discovery. Part of this discovery is a growing of awareness of related problems, mutually relevant experiences, and common interests" (Segal 1968:36). This awareness has already spurred modest regional efforts such as the Caribbean Free Trade Association (discussed at the end of this chapter), and it may eventually lead to even greater regional cooperation. Partly for these reasons, Chapters 4 and 5 will present a composite view of the West

Indies, with particular stress on the common denominators among the islands. The distinctiveness of the various territories will be assessed in Chapters 6 and 7.

SALIENT CHARACTERISTICS

Many of the earmarks of the current economic geography of the West Indies are discouragingly similar to those of the colonial plantation period (Chapter 3). In recent decades, for example, some of the territories have diversified their traditional "one-crop" economy through the development of tourism, mining, and even manufacturing, but for the region as a whole, farming is still the economic mainstay. Cash crops, such as sugar, which were introduced during the colonial era, continue to make up a large part of the region's exports. The patterns of land use have been moderately modified by the growth of peasant farming and other developments, but land tenure and tenancy are still dominated by the plantation as they were in preemancipation days. Internal markets remain small, and interregional trade is still restricted by similarity of agricultural export products. The West Indies are as heavily tributary to more developed non-Caribbean countries as ever, producing raw materials in exchange for finished products. While several of the territories are no longer political "colonies" in the eighteenth-century sense of the word, their slavish dependency on external markets makes them politically vulnerable to the countries that buy their products. Virtually everything the islands have to sell, whether it be sugar, coffee, or tourist attractions, is in greater supply than demand, and most of the region's exports, especially its high-cost farm products, cannot compete effectively in an open market and preferential treatment must be sought for them abroad. Compared to the colonial period, the region's current labor force is no longer made up of slaves, but it is still predominantly black. Widespread famine among workers is no longer common (Chapter 3), but the landless peasantry and urban proletariat of the present labor force still live in constant economic distress. In fact, partly because of the population explosion that followed emancipation (Chapter 5) and partly for other reasons, unemployment and partial employment are greater now than in colonial times.

The West Indian agricultural resource base is still handicapped by small size, mountainous terrain, fragmentation, and the danger of such natural hazards as hurricanes and droughts (Chapter 2). If this base has undergone any change in the past century, it has been for the worse. The pressure to cultivate slope land and poor management have made erosion a major problem. Where soils are not eroded, their nutrients have become so depleted by constant use and misuse, that only the barest yields are possible without heavy inputs of fertilizer. Destruction of the original vegetation cover, already serious in the lowlands prior to emancipation, engulfed the uplands and become worse as the ex-slaves sought farmland away from the estates. Currently, a patchy forest cover remains only in the steepest and most inaccessible mountain zones. On most islands a "settlement frontier" of arable, virgin land had disappeared before the end of the nineteenth century. Since then, the rapid growth of population has been constantly reducing the ratio of cultivable land to people. Also reduced are the once considerable opportunities for the emigration of surplus West Indian labor (Chapter 5). With farming still the leading occupation, with a growing population attempting to wrest a living from a depleted resource base, and with other economic options severely restricted, it is not surprising that the economic geography of the West Indies continues to be a geography of poverty and even hunger, of frustration and even desperation. Nor is it surprising that there is political restiveness and even revolution in the region.

AGRICULTURE

The economic crisis that followed emancipation and the decline of the colonial plantation gradually brought about a drastic reorganization in West Indian commercial production of export crops. The principal instrument of reorganization was the corporately owned modern plantation based on large land holdings (latifundia). The plantation emerged in the late nineteenth and early twentieth centuries, and with rare exception, it still dominates the economic life of much of the region. Although the modern plantation is associated with various cash crops. including bananas and coconuts, its primary ties by far are with sugar cane.

Paralleling the emergence of the modern plantation was peasant farming, a sharply contrasting agricultural system based on small holdings (minifundia). While the roots of peasant farming can be traced back to the colonial era to slave provision grounds and conuco plots worked by poor whites, maroons, and manumitted slaves (Chapter 3), its major growth began after emancipation as the ex-slaves sought economic freedom in the production of food crops on the unused lands away from the estates. Currently, peasant farming still places major emphasis on food crops for subsistence and for sale in the local market, but it is also becoming increasingly involved with the production of export products.

As will be demonstrated, the modern plantation and peasant farming have become symbolic of opposing economic interests and viewpoints. Translated into social and political language, the conflict between the two agricultural systems provides the economic background for much of the current turmoil in the West Indies.

The Modern Plantation

The modern sugar plantation in the Antilles resembles its colonial predecessor in a number of ways, including physical requirements, the need for an abundance of cheap labor, and heavy dependence on non-Caribbean markets with high purchasing power. Among its major physical requirements are a climate that is frost-free to assure a year-round growing season, and which, while humid, has a relatively dry period immediately before and during the cane-cutting season; a terrain that is level to rolling to obtain the best yields and to keep the costs of transporting the cane from the fields to the mills low; and proximity to cheap ocean transportation to facilitate the export of sugar. In the West Indies these requirements generally restrict the modern plantation to coastal plains and to the alluvial flats of connecting interior valleys, which also represent the most productive farmlands in the archipelago.

In contrast to the colonial plantation, the modern version requires much larger amounts of capital and land, more responsible and efficient management, and

a more sophisticated production technology. Such requirements can only be provided by a large-scale corporate or government enterprise capable of marshaling money, machinery, and skills not readily available in an underdeveloped tropical region. Thus, the modern plantation in the West Indies has become synonymous with the contemporary "big business" corporation (or "big government," as in Cuba), and the region has all the advantages and disadvantages stemming from corporate organization.

Although there is state ownership of plantations in Cuba and some local ownership in other territories, a large percentage of the sugar plantation economy of the West Indies is owned by foreign corporations whose stockholders are nationals of the countries that buy sugar. British firms, for example, account for the bulk of the sugar production and trade in the British-connected islands. United States enterprises play the same role in Puerto Rico, the Dominican Republic, and Haiti, and French corporations are dominant in the French Antilles.

In order to assure an adequate supply of cane and to provide for future expansion of production, the corporations have acquired ownership or control over vast holdings of the most productive land in the archipelago. According to Beckford (1972:253), a single American company is reputed to own or control some 400,000 acres of land in the Dominican Republic and Puerto Rico; subsidiaries of a British sugar refining firm handle virtually the entire sugar production in Jamaica and Trinidad; and two American corporations produce three-fourths of the sugar crop in the Dominican Republic. Control of sugar lands is exerted either through direct ownership of the land itself or through the ownership of milling, transportation, and other facilities for processing and marketing the crop.

Instead of the small, numerous, inefficient mills of the colonial period, the mod-

highways have been built, and trucks, trailers, and other types of rapid transport have come into use (Figure 4.2). Despite this and other efficiencies, the unit cost of processing cane is high because of the central with its expensive machinery and its highly skilled technical staff; even the transport network connecting the central to the fields can be utilized only for the few months when cane is being milled.

The modern plantation has been aptly described as a modern factory in the field, and like any other modern factory, its survival depends on a continuous supply of capital, the ability to adapt to technological change as quickly as is feasible, and a relatively stable market. Equally significant to survival in the case of the West Indies is a political climate which does not threaten the land monopoly of the plantation or arouse demands for increases in labor costs.

Regional Variations. While the modern plantation is crucial to the economy of the West Indies as a whole, there are significant variations from place to place both in its comparative importance and in some of its basic characteristics. In some territories, such as the Bahamas, the plantation never took root; in others, such as the British Virgin Islands, which were marginally suitable for the colonial plantation, the amount of arable land and

Figure 4.2 French West Indies: Transferring cane from field cart to truck for rapid transportation to a central (*French Government Tourist Office*)

ern plantation processes in a comparatively few *centrales,* or large mills, located so as to service the largest amount of sugar land at minimum transportation cost (Figure 4.1). Once the milling begins, efficiency dictates that the central have sufficient cane on hand to operate around the clock. Since the mills have to be accessible both to vast areas of cane land and to ports, narrow gauge railroads and other conditions were inadequate for the development of the modern plantation. Also among the exceptions to plantation-dominated economies are the Netherlands Antilles; the tiny territories of Barbuda, Nevis, Anguilla, and Montserrat; and the Windward Islands. The modern plantation is economically dominant in Cuba, the Dominican Republic, the French Antilles, the Leeward Islands, and Barbados (Figure 4.3). In these areas it often controls half or more of the best arable land, and its products make up half or more by value of the exports. In Jamaica, Puerto Rico, and Trinidad the export value of plantation crops is exceeded by that of other economies, but the amount of land under the control of the plantation is high. Within the Greater Antilles, the plantation is least important in Haiti.

Other salient characteristics of the modern plantation in the West Indies are the same everywhere in the archipelago except Cuba, where the plantation concept has been altered by the revolutionary government headed by Fidel Castro, who came into power in 1959. The large plantations formerly owned by foreign and local corporations have been expropriated. At first, Castro's government made an effort to maintain sugar production on the expropriated estates by means of cooperatives.

When this failed, the sugar areas were organized into state plantations. Thus, the most obvious Cuban departure from the typical West Indian plantation model is the substitution of state for private ownership. It is also claimed with some justification that public ownership of Cuban plantations has eliminated or reduced some of the traditional evils associated with the privately controlled plantation: unemployment or partial employment; the white-owner–black-worker syndrome; and disregard for the social needs of plantation workers.

But there are other traditional drawbacks of the plantation that have not been eliminated. Cuba is more dependent than ever on a one-crop economy. The sugar plantation still dominates foreign trade and exchange earnings, the use of land, and employment. Above all, Cuba's dependence on a non-Caribbean industrial country for a protected market is still crucial. The only change is that Cuba is now economically tributary (and politically vulnerable) to the Soviet Union and other Communist countries instead of to the United States.

The Balance Sheet. In retrospect, credit is due to the modern plantation for many positive achievements in the West

Figure 4.3   Barbados: The dominance of sugar cane (*W. G. Haag*)

Indies. It has placed sugar and other plantation crops on sounder economic footing; its scientific agriculture has often improved worn-out land; it has been an incentive for new transportation construction; and through increased yields and lower production costs, it has made sugar available to a much larger market. But the modern plantation is also responsible for a variety of problems in the Antilles. It is a more efficient instrument for land and labor organization than the colonial *trapiche* and *ingenio* but has done little to bring about a more equitable distribution of resources and income. The best land has continued to be concentrated in the hands of the few, and the relationship between the rural and often black proletariat that has replaced the slaves and the generally white landowners has been marred by increasing mutual resentment and conflict. With only rare exceptions, the economy of the islands is still painfully dependent on monoculture. A large share of the considerable profits go to foreign stockholders, leaving the local population with only incidental benefits. Large amounts of idle land, which might be used by the peasantry, are tied up in corporate holdings as a hedge against future needs. Work is, at best, seasonal, and the management is not obliged to give its workers year-round care, as were the colonial slave-owning planters. (As already noted, Cuba is free of some, but not all of these drawbacks.)

Such conditions, in a region of rapidly increasing population and limited resources, often result in a social environment of abject poverty and dangerous restiveness. The modern plantation in the Caribbean can be defended on many grounds, but there is little doubt that the bulk of the local people resent it as an instrument of exploitation, often a foreign-owned instrument, at that. The Cuban Revolution under Castro indicates that this resentment can sometimes become explosive.

Table 4.1   SUGAR PRODUCTION IN THE WEST INDIES,
SELECTED YEARS, 1960–1970
(in thousands of metric tons)

	1960–61	1964–65	1969–70
Antigua	21	14	15 *
Barbados	162	207	145
Cuba	6,767	6,082	5,534
Dominican Republic	873	583	886
Guadeloupe	175	194	148
Haiti	71	65	65
Jamaica	447	497	397
Martinique	94	74	26.9 *
Puerto Rico	1,001	816	438
St. Kitts-Nevis	47	39	27.16 *
Trinidad-Tobago	250	255	248

Note: Table includes only data for territories that produced 15,000 metric tons or more from 1969 to 1970.

Sources: Starred data from *West Indies and Caribbean Yearbook, 1972;* all other data from pertinent United Nations statistical yearbooks.

The Sugar Crisis

Sugar is still king of the West Indian economy, but its reign is becoming shaky (Table 4.1). Labor and other problems resulted in a sharp decrease in the 1960s, and except for Cuba, the forecast for the 1970s is even gloomier. In 1970, for example, the British-connected territories in the Caribbean had their lowest sugar production in 11 years; Barbados had such a poor harvest that it was unable to meet its limited Commonwealth Sugar Agreement Quota. Puerto Rico's 1970 production was less than half of its record-breaking 1961 harvest, and the island was able to meet slightly more than one-third of the 1,275,-000 tons assigned to it by the United States Sugar Quota. Despite all-out effort and fanfare, Cuba fell short of its ten-million-ton goal in 1970, and Cuban officials scaled down their goal for 1971 to seven million tons.

The causes of the West Indian sugar crisis are many. In addition to the vagaries of weather, rising production costs and the uncertainty of future market quotas laid the foundation for the crises. In turn, rising production costs stem in part from worn out soils which require costly inputs of fertilizers and in part from high labor costs, labor shortages, inefficiencies of scale and management, and low level of mechanization.

Labor unrest, including numerous strikes, have led to higher wages without a corresponding increase in productivity. Unlikely though it may seem in a region of high unemployment, the West Indian sugar industry is frequently plagued by scarcity of labor. Because farm work is associated with the hated heritage of slavery, many young workers regard field labor as demeaning. Given an opportunity for work in industry, mining, business, or any other "urban" employment, they quickly abandon wage work on farms. Much of the drastic drop in Puerto Rico's sugar production between 1961 and 1970, for example, was due to rising wage levels and opportunities for the younger generation to work in factories or migrate to the United States (Chapter 6). Comparable effects are apparent from the labor impact of bauxite mining in Jamaica, oil production in Trinidad, and increasing tourism in Antigua and Barbados.

Sugar producers have attempted to overcome labor shortages and rising costs partly through the importation of workers from other islands and partly through increasing mechanization and other means. Significantly, the stigma attached to field labor such as cane cutting on one's own island does not apply away from home. As Momsen has observed, Jamaicans will cut cane in United States territories but not on their own island. Overcrowded Barbados, with its high rate of unemploy-

ment, found it necessary to import workers from St. Vincent and St. Lucia to bring in the 1970 harvest; and the Dominican Republic is finding it impossible to replace migrant laborers from Haiti (1971: 338).

Efforts to counteract labor shortages and costs through increased mechanization have not always been welcome or successful. Given the high rate of unemployment on the islands, any labor-saving device is viewed with suspicion and resentment. Moreover, unlike the past, farm labor is now organized, and the labor unions have considerable political clout. In Trinidad, for example, the Industrial Court accepted that increased mechanization was the only means of raising the productivity of the Caroni Sugar Company, but it deferred decision on the company's request to expand its mechanization (Momsen 1971: 339). In Barbados an increase in harvesting machinery is being allowed, but the Sugar Producers' Association has been ordered to phase out the importation of cane cutters from elsewhere. On St. Kitts, experiments with cane-cutting machines in 1970 were deemed a failure because of the island's terrain. Labor difficulties in Cuba have spurred some mechanization, but in 1970 it was estimated that less than 5 percent of the island's cane crop was cut mechanically.

On some islands, more traditional labor-saving devices, such as cane burning, have been employed. Cane firing permits an easier and more rapid harvest, but it is not without disadvantages. Burnt cane must be processed more quickly, usually within 24 hours of being cut. Moreover, fire destroys the cane trash, which deprives the soil of mulch and results in correspondingly lower cane yields the following year.

Because the sugar industry is still the largest employer in the West Indies, the insular governments have no choice but to try to save it from collapse. Each government is seeking its own solution to the crisis, ranging from consolidation through merger of sugar companies, as in Barbados, to nationalization, as in Antigua and Trinidad. But the outlook is not encouraging. Among its many problems, the industry faces the harsh dictates of the law of supply and demand. World demand for sugar (both from cane and beets) is substantially lower than potential supply. For example, when the huge flow of Cuban sugar to the United States was abruptly cut off for political reasons, the American consumer experienced no serious shortage of the product. The United States quota for the island was simply reassigned to other producers. In contrast, loss of the American market seriously disrupted the Cuban economy, and the island was saved from economic collapse only by the financial aid and the markets made available by the Soviet Union and other socialist countries. Except for Cuba, which has by far the most favorable conditions for production, indications are that the sugar economy of the West Indies is moribund. It is being kept alive partly by the lack of other economic options but more by subsidies, guaranteed price arrangements, and an international quota system. Where other options are available, as in Puerto Rico, production is decreasing rapidly. Elsewhere, as in the British-connected islands, Britain's entry into the European Common Market and the lack of favored treatment for West Indian sugar in the British market may wipe out the industry.

Other Export Crops

In a desperate effort to adjust to the vagaries of midlatitude export markets, the West Indies have experimented with a wide range of tropical cash crops in the last three centuries (Chapter 3). Currently, only sugar cane continues to be widely cultivated. Of the remainder, some, such as indigo, Sea Island cotton, and ginger have passed into the realm of historical curiosities. Others, such as coffee, hang on only in certain favored areas.

Tobacco, one of the earliest cash crops in the archipelago, fell before the onslaught of sugar in Barbados and elsewhere in the non-Hispanic islands where it had taken root. Efforts to revive its production, including experiments with varieties for cigarettes, have seldom succeeded. The crop remains of some importance in the Greater Antilles, especially Cuba, and is used primarily for cigars. In Cuba, survival has been possible because of special soil and other physical conditions which yield a high quality leaf that has become justly famous for the island's Havana cigars (Chapter 6). Elsewhere, as in Puerto Rico and the Dominican Republic, the crop has experienced numerous ups and downs, but it survives because of special ties with the United States market.

Coffee, once an important export of all the Greater Antilles and whose production had spread as far south as Trinidad, now is important only in the commerce of Haiti and the Dominican Republic. On other islands, such as Puerto Rico, where the crop continues to be cultivated, production is not even sufficient to meet local demands. Cacao is still produced on various islands in the archipelago, but it is of noteworthy importance only in the Dominican Republic and, to a lesser extent, Trinidad.

Among the later innovations, citrus and pineapple have obtained a foothold in Jamaica, Puerto Rico, Trinidad, and Martinque, but for the region as a whole, their importance looms well below that of bananas. Introduced as an export crop in Jamaica during the late nineteenth century, bananas have proven a boon to plantation and peasant farming alike. With rapid transportation, effective corporate organization, and a ready market in the United States and Europe, banana production has become almost as widespread as sugar cane in the West Indies.

Figure 4.4   St. Lucia: Bananas replacing sugar in Dennery Valley (*W. G. Haag*)

In fact, on some islands it is replacing sugar cane (Figure 4.4). During the early 1970s, bananas loomed as the only export crop in the entire region whose future is brighter than its past.

It is significant that, with the exception of sugar cane and bananas, West Indian cash crops are seldom produced on large, corporately owned land holdings associated with the modern plantation. Most of the region's coffee, cacao, and tobacco, for example, is produced on family-owned, farms ranging in size from small to medium. Even banana production is being increasingly shifted to small holders who contract to sell the fruit to a corporate buyer.

One reason for the reluctance of the corporate plantation to get involved in the farming phase of secondary export crops is that the volume and value of production is often too limited to warrant large-scale investment. Perhaps more important, there is far greater risk of crop loss and damage from weather and other causes in the farming of coffee, bananas, cacao, and tobacco than in that of sugar cane. Because of such risk, corporations have found it more profitable to buy the harvested crop from the farmer rather than raise their own. In this way any damage and loss during the actual farming operation is absorbed by the farmer.

Peasant Farming

Characteristics and Conflict. Currently, West Indian peasant farming is often classified in two categories. The first is an extension of the plantation, and its farming operations consist of producing sugar and other export crops. Peasants in this category are completely dependent on the plantation, producing crops either on a share basis or as "associate producers" (Figure 4.5). They may use their own plots, but more frequently they rent or use estate lands. In any case, they have to depend on the plantation for milling, as

Figure 4.5 Grenada: Colono farmstead on Mt. Rich estate (*W. G. Haag*)

in the case of sugar cane, or for transportation, refrigeration, and other services for bananas; and the price they are paid is set by the sugar or banana plantation. The other category of peasant farming concentrates on the production of food crops and other products for the domestic market or for subsistence, and is less dependent on the plantation.

Regardless of category, peasant farming as an agricultural system stands in sharp contrast to the plantation. It is relegated to hilly slopes and other low-yielding marginal lands which have been deforested and scarred by erosion. Inheritance has fragmented and reduced the size of holdings so that most farms are less than five acres of noncontiguous, oddly shaped plots. On the typical plot, cultivation involves no plows and little rotation, terracing, or fertilizing; labor inputs are high, and capital investments are low; and tools are primitive, often consisting of a hoe, the ubiquitous machete, and a sharpened stick. When animals are kept for food, they are generally of the scavenger type such as chickens, goats, and swine. The peasant farm that can provide the owner and his family a complete living is exceptional; the majority of peasants must supplement their income with wage work on estates or elsewhere.

Many of these characteristics and problems of peasant farming spring from its competition and conflict with the plantation. Small-scale cultivation by freeholders or peasants has always been counterposed against the estate in the West Indies. In fact, the two systems have been so competitive in the past that the flourishing of one has often been possible only at the expense or in the absence of the other. More specifically, the amount and the quality of land available to peasant farming has varied according to the fortunes of the sugar plantation. Thus, the absence of significant plantation development in the Hispanic territories until the nineteenth century (Chapter 3) kept land values low and made possible a marked growth of peasant farming even on some of the better lands of Cuba, Puerto Rico, and Santo Domingo. Once the plantation became established, however, the peasantry was gradually pushed off the better lands into the mountains or to other zones of less productive soils. The plight of the peasant farmer in the Hispanic territories seems to have become especially difficult after the Spanish American War when the influx of American capital gave rise to the archetype of the modern plantation. In fact, the deteriorating conditions of peasant farming and farmers may have been among the causes for Castro's revolution in Cuba, for the violence which swept the Dominican Republic after the fall of Trujillo, and for the strong appeal which the reform programs of Munõz Marin have had in Puerto Rico (Chapter 6).

The competition and conflict of peasant farming with the plantation has been equally apparent in the non-Hispanic West Indies. For example, peasant farming is currently dominant in Haiti primarily because the plantation system was largely destroyed by slave revolts (Chapter 3). The early English yeoman farmers of Barbados and the other British Antilles were virtually wiped out by the advent of the colonial plantation, and there was no room for peasant farming during the sugar boom period of the eighteenth century (Chapter 3). Immediately following the downfall of the colonial plantation, however, the amount of land available for peasant use in many of the British territories was considerable. Along with the interior uplands, which had never been used for sugar production, many of the bankrupt planters sold or rented even some of the better estate lands to the peasants. As a result, peasant farming underwent rapid expansion in the latter nineteenth and early twentieth centuries. Later, with the population explosion that eventually followed emancipation, and with the recovery of the sugar economy through the efficiencies of the modern plantation, the amount of land for the peasantry was again in short supply.

In addition to its weak position in competing for land, peasant farming has been at a disadvantage to the plantation because of a variety of economic and political institutional arrangements. The infrastructures for transportation, manufacturing, and marketing, for example, are more attuned to the processing and distribution of plantation export crops than to peasant production of food crops for local consumption. Though most insular

governments have now established agencies to help in the marketing of peasant-grown food crops, such agencies are weak in comparison to corporations which handle the sale of sugar and other products for the overseas trade. Peasants have difficulty in obtaining agricultural credit from the private sector, and the public sector often lacks the resources to provide it. Government policy, whether made by outside colonial powers or by local legislators, whether ideologically capitalistic as in Jamaica or socialistic as in Cuba, has always shown greater concern for the plantation than for peasant farming. No matter how genuine the government's interest is in the well-being of the peasants, plantation products are still the lifeblood of the export economy. Without them the economic structure of the West Indies would collapse—a truism that even Castro cannot escape.

Equally disadvantageous, because of the quota systems, preferential treatment, and other arrangements, plantation crops have had an assured market abroad. Food crops from peasant farming have not only lacked such assurances, they have been forced to compete both with other local producers and with imported food products. The peasant farmer who raises large quantities of yams or plantains for the local market may face financial ruin because of oversupply and low prices. It is hardly surprising, therefore, that whenever possible, peasant farmers will choose to cultivate sugar cane or some other export crop with a guaranteed market.

Finally, while weather hazards such as droughts, hurricanes, and floods do not differentiate between peasant and plantation farming, the former is far more vulnerable. Unlike the corporate plantation, the peasant farmer cannot afford crop insurance even if it were available; he has no cash reserves to fall back on in case of emergency; and his ability to borrow is severely limited. The passage of a hurricane can leave a peasant community destitute and worse. Destructive winds with velocities of over 100 miles per hour and a heavy, damaging rainfall of an inch or more per hour trigger floods and landslides. Not only is the peasant's economy wiped out, but his house may be reduced to fragments and scattered all over the countryside. In the past, starvation and disease followed almost inevitably upon the heels of a hurricane. Today, these dreaded consequences are less likely, but looting is still common. Even more common is the temporary demoralization of the peasant community.

Variations. Like most generalizations about the West Indies, those concerning peasant agriculture are also subject to significant exceptions. Variations occur from group to group, as between the *petite culture* of the Haitian *habitant* and the East Indian rice farmer of Trinidad (Chapter 7); from territory to territory, as between densely populated but technologically more advanced Barbados and less-populated and less-developed Dominica; and even from one locale to another in the same territory, as between wet northern and drier southern Puerto Rico. The production of West Indian peasant farming ranges from the totally subsistent to the highly export-oriented. Most peasant plots depend exclusively on the family for labor, but others rely heavily on paid workers; some peasants own their own land which others must sharecrop or rent. Comparable differences are apparent in the technological inputs made, the intensity of land use, the types of crops and yields, and other characteristics of the system. A recent study by Momsen of peasant farming on Barbados, Martinique, and St. Lucia indicates, for instance, that patterns, such as land tenure, did not differ greatly in the three territories; but others, including land use and crop emphasis, varied according to physical conditions,

population pressure, and culture (1971: 78–83). [1]

Achievements. The conclusion is inescapable that the plantation legacy has imposed definite restrictions on West Indian peasant farming, and that as long as the plantation continues to dominate the re-

1. The study found that in each of the three islands, two-thirds of all farms sampled were held in freehold ownership and the remainder were sharecropped; the number of parcels making up the farm ranged between one and two; the most common occupation of the peasant farmers was plantation laborer; peasant plots were located on less fertile, shallow-soiled slope land, while the best land was held by the plantation; all farms kept some livestock; and the farm children preferred nonfarm labor upon reaching working age. Also, on each of the three islands peasant farms located near large towns fell into two groups: the first were operated on a part-time basis, raising food for home consumption by people who worked in town; the second specialized in the production of vegetables and other food products for the nearby urban market.

Among the major differences Momsen encountered are the facts that: farms were largest in St. Lucia and smallest in Barbados, "reflecting differences in population pressure and settlement history"; the cost of land was highest on heavily populated Barbados; the ratio of cash to subsistence crops ranged from 71 percent in Barbados to 24 percent in Martinique. In food crop production, St. Lucians showed a preference for tannia; Barbadians for yams, maize, and the sweet potato; and Martiniquans for dasheen. Martinique and St. Lucia used only family labor, but Barbados used hired hands for at least a few weeks out of the year. Also, the proportion of farmers with nonfarm jobs was 62 percent in Barbados, 56 percent in Martinique, and only 36 percent in St. Lucia (". . . these figures reflect the greater diversity of the economies of Barbados and Martinique, with consequent larger job opportunities . . ."). Technical inputs (transport, water supply, fertilizer) were also highest in Barbados. Momsen concluded that physical differences reinforced cultural differences between small, limestone Barbados and larger, volcanic St. Lucia and Martinique. In Barbados, the peasant farm is smaller; very little land is left uncultivated, and there is much intercropping and double cropping, "whilst in St. Lucia and Martinique . . . the acreage . . . is less intensively used."

gion, there is little likelihood for the expansion of peasant farming activities. But the impact of this legacy has had at least one positive consequence. Because the plantation has been linked with external markets, the peasantry has not been isolated from outside influences. Unlike many peasants elsewhere, the West Indian peasant is not hampered by a tradition that resists innovation. His awareness of the economic possibilities of foreign markets has made him strongly prone to experiment and change. In some respects, he has been more progressive and responsive than the plantation owner. It was the peasant and not the plantation owner, for example, who was responsible for the introduction of bananas in territories like Jamaica, for developing a local marketing system, and for supplying local markets with food crops, thereby reducing the drain of heavier food imports on the regional economy. The peasant also deserves much of the credit for developing a road network and for producing significant amounts of sugar, coffee, arrowroot, ginger, and other crops that contribute to the external trade of the Caribbean. In the process of responding to innovation, in the face of a wide range of physical and historical handicaps, West Indian peasant farming has contributed to real economic growth as much as, and perhaps more than, the plantation system.

The Food Problem. The West Indian peasant farmer is heir to a wide range of food crops. As already noted, some of these, like manioc, were inherited from the Indians (Chapter 3); others such as millet, sorghum, okra, the akee, and the mango were introduced from Africa; and still others such as the breadfruit came from the Pacific. Food crop production, already well established during the slave era, expanded rapidly in the period immediately after emancipation as the ex-slaves settled in the upland interiors and cultivated the land. Whenever possible, the peasant attempted to produce not only enough for his own needs but a small surplus to sell in the local market as well.

Despite the rich variety of food crops and the long tradition of their cultivation, the food problem is acute throughout the West Indies. At the root of the problem are the aforementioned emphasis given cash crops, the relegation of food farming to the least desirable land, and the difficulties in marketing and other areas, stemming from the competition between the plantation and the peasant food crop farmer. Nor are these the only handicaps that limit peasant crop production and give rise to shortages and high food prices throughout the archipelago. The surging migrations from rural to urban areas are reducing the production of food crops, especially the surpluses for sale in local markets. Tastes are changing, and there is a marked preference for the more expensive food imported from the United States and Europe over the native food crops. On many islands local produce is disdained, and there is a certain prestige attached to the consumption of canned or otherwise processed food from abroad. The same prestige applies to imported whiskey and beer as compared with the locally made rum. Hotels have been known to serve canned Hawaiian pineapple when the fresh, local fruit was readily available, and the visitor who requests plantains and breadfruit at a tourist hotel might raise eyebrows if not create downright consternation. Such attitudes furnish at least some of the reasons why food imports represent such a heavy drain on the economies of most islands.

Most of the conditions that inhibit food crop production are also applicable to meat and fish. Except for the period preceding the advent of large-scale sugar production and slavery (Chapter 3), the West Indies have never been able to produce enough meat and fish for their needs. During the slave period, heavy imports of salt pork and salted fish, especially cod, from North America provided the primary protein food for the large slave population. Currently, imported salted cod is still an important item in the diet of the poorer classes in the West Indies. Although there is a growing effort to increase the catch of fish and the production of cattle, the chief source of locally produced protein foods are scavenger animals such as the chicken and the pig.

The Agricultural Outlook

It is difficult to be optimistic about the future of West Indian agriculture. On most of the islands the economy is simply burdened by too many people and too many handicaps imposed by nature and history. Even without most of these handicaps, it would be difficult to provide for the archipelago's large and increasingly restive population. Some conditions affecting agriculture, such as those imposed by nature, are impossible to modify. Others, such as the inequities of land holding, the problem of food production, and vulnerability to foreign markets, are almost equally resistant to change.

Measures for improving the conditions affecting agriculture often vary from island to island, but nowhere in the archipelago is the solution easy. Revolutionary Cuba, for example, has made agrarian reform, increased food production, and diversification of its one-crop economy major planning goals at various times since 1959. But while eliminating private ownership of large land holdings, the country in the 1970s is still characterized by (state-controlled) latifundia and peasant farms; sugar is still economically dominant; and crucial dependency on foreign markets is still present. While the food problem may not be so grim as reported by anti-Castro refugees, rationing of certain foods is still necessary.

Elsewhere in the West Indies, as in Jamaica and other British-connected islands, the governments have attempted to increase food production and provide land for landless peasants through numerous settlement schemes. Jamaica's Yallahs Valley Authority, one of the older and more successful of the settlements, was established to restore eroded land, increase food production, and raise the living standards of the peasant communities relocated on it. On the whole, the Yallahs experiment has achieved most of the planned goals, but its success is more the exception than the rule among the hundreds of settlement schemes in various parts of the archipelago. Handicapped by marginal lands, inadequate financing, poor management, and inexperience on the part of the peasants, settlement schemes have done little to solve the problems that led to their establishment.

Since sugar cannot be efficiently produced by small landholders, as long as this crop remains crucial to the insular economies there is little hope for basic agrarian reform. This has been demonstrated not only in the case of Cuba, but elsewhere as well. In Puerto Rico, for example, the famous "500 Acre Law," aimed at limiting the holdings of large sugar corporations (Chapter 6), currently is not being as vigorously enforced as in the 1940s. In an effort to arrest the rapid decline of the sugar industry, the Puerto Rican government is turning a blind eye to the restoration of large-scale exploitation.

Finally, there is little indication that the current West Indian sugar crisis will disappear in the immediate future. On the contrary, new developments such as Britain's entry into the European Common Market actually threaten to intensify the crisis. Under the circumstances, the West Indies are desperately trying to diversify their economies. Unfortunately, not all the islands have the means necessary to achieve diversification.

OTHER MAJOR ECONOMIES

While no insular economy in the Antilles has become highly diversified, some, as already noted, have managed to reduce their traditionally heavy dependence on farming through the development of mining, manufacturing, tourism, and other activities. Significantly, the territories that have been most successful in developing their nonfarming sectors are those that have capitalized on a natural or other advantage. Thus, Jamaica has parlayed its rich bauxite resources into an important mining economy; Trinidad has utilized both its own limited petroleum deposits and its proximity to Venezuelan oil fields to nurture a significant refining industry; and Puerto Rico has made maximum use of the opportunities provided by its unique connection with the United States (Chapter 6) to mount a major industrial effort. Since every island possesses at least the minimum advantages of climate and sea coast to attract visitors, for the archipelago as a whole, the most widespread and fastest growing new economy is tourism.

Tourism

Many conditions have combined to trigger the recent rapid development of the Caribbean tourist trade. Nature has provided a tropical island setting which is often dramatic in its beauty; history has contributed a cultural variety which smacks of Africa, Europe, and even Asia. In a single vacation the tourist can visit French-, English-, Spanish-, and Dutch-speaking islands. Modern technology and business enterprise have added a dense network of air routes (Figure 1.13) with special air fares and package tours; a fleet of luxurious, island-hopping cruise ships; and a Madison Avenue publicity which paints a Caribbean vacation in almost irresistible exotic hues. Above all, the Caribbean has the good fortune of being located relatively near the large and generally affluent block of middle-class populations which lives in the eastern United States and Canada.

There was a significant West Indian tourist economy with heavy concentration on Cuba well before World War II, but it was in the postwar period, and particularly in the decade of the 1960s, that the economy underwent spectacular growth. For example, the number of tourists arriving at the United States Virgin Islands rose from 200,000 in 1960 to 650,000 in 1966 and had reached more than 1.25 million by 1969. During the same period the tourist flow doubled in Jamaica and quadrupled in the Bahamas. Even a small and virtually unknown island such as St. Lucia boasted an increase of 78 percent in tourism between 1967 and 1969. Counting the Bahamas and the Dutch Islands of Curaçao, Aruba, and Bonaire, the total number of visitors reported by the West Indies in 1969–1970 was almost five million (Table 4.2). This rapid increase of visitors since World War II has made the Caribbean one of the most outstanding tourist regions of the world.

Regional Patterns and Variations. There may be a sprinkling of millionaires among the tourist hordes that descend on the Caribbean every year, but the vast majority spring from the economics of American and, to a lesser extent, Canadian suburbia (Figure 4.6). The average visitor comes from east of the Mississippi equipped with middle-class tastes and pocketbook. He arrives by air, visits one or two Caribbean islands, remains less than a week, and spends under $300. A much smaller number of visitors (less than 10 percent of the total) arrive on cruise ships and "island-hop" to several territories. They may remain in the region for as long as two weeks, but while there, they do not necessarily spend more than the airborne visitors because they often

Figure 4.6   Nassau, Bahamas: American tourists (*Bahamas News Bureau*)

sleep and eat aboard their ship instead of at local hotels.

While virtually every territory in the West Indies has been affected by the increasing flow of visitors, the development of tourism is by no means uniform. There are marked differences from place to place in the number of visitors, the duration of their stay, the amount they spend, the comparative importance of tourist spending on the local economy, and other characteristics. The giants of the Caribbean tourist trade are Puerto Rico, the United States Virgin Islands, and the Bahamas, each of which received over one million visitors in 1970. These leaders are followed by Jamaica, the Netherlands Antilles, and the French West Indies. Among the least important of the West Indian tourist territories are Cuba, the Dominican Republic, and Haiti (Table 4.2). Cuba, which once had a $100 million per year tourist economy based primarily on American visitors, now receives virtually no tourists. Haiti and the Dominican Republic are somewhat better off, but still far below their potential. During the boom tourist

Table 4.2   TOURISTS AND OTHER VISITORS IN THE WEST INDIES, 1970

Territory	Number of Visitors (in thousands)
Bahamas	1300
Cuba	?
Puerto Rico and U.S. Virgin Islands	2368
Jamaica	407
Haiti	65
Dominican Republic	30
Leeward Islands	75
French West Indies	175
Windward Islands	160
Barbados	156
Trinidad-Tobago	117
Total	4853

Note: Not all these visitors were tourists. A small number were seasonal laborers moving from one island to another. Also, many tourists included in the five million figure were counted more than once because they visited more than one territory.

Source: West Indies and Caribbean Yearbook, 1972.

94

period of the late 1960s, for example, neither country received as many visitors as the tiny islands of Antigua or Grenada or St. Lucia.

Puerto Rico and Jamaica are the only West Indian territories that are sufficiently large and varied and possess the necessary accommodations to handle large numbers of tourists the year round. As a result, these islands experience less marked seasonality in the tourist trade, and visitors tend to stay longer. In most other territories, the length of stay is briefer and there is only one tourist season during the year. Seasonality and duration of stay are, of course, important determinants of tourist expenditures.

There is also regional variation in the relative importance of tourist spending within the total insular economy. In the Bahamas, it is estimated that, directly or indirectly, tourism accounts for three-fourths of the economic activity. The industry's importance is almost as high for the United States Virgin Islands. For Jamaica, it is second only to bauxite as a means of earning foreign exchange. For Puerto Rico, tourism is comparatively less important in the total economy, even though the expenditure of more than $200 million by visitors in 1970 placed the commonwealth at the very top of the region's tourist centers. In contrast, the far smaller income from tourism in places like Grenada or St. Lucia or Barbados loomed much more important in their total economic picture (Chapter 7).

Problems and Outlook. The present regional patterns and variations suggest that many factors, including the territory's "image" and political ties with the United States, influence the flow of visitors to the various Caribbean islands. The case of Cuba is self-evident. The breaking off of diplomatic relations with the United States virtually wiped out the island's substantial tourist industry. The special po-

litical and economic ties which Puerto Rico and the Virgin Islands have with the United States are an important explanation for their dominance in the Caribbean tourist trade. The Dominican Republic is still saddled with the negative image of the Trujillo dictatorship and the political instability that followed his fall. Similarly, the image of Haiti under "Papa Doc" Duvalier resulted in a sharp drop in tourism. According to the *New York Times* (May 9, 1966), only about one-third of Haiti's tourist hotel capacity was being occupied at that time. Under the younger Duvalier, tourism has begun to increase.

Other conditions that may affect the outlook of the Caribbean tourist economy include the competition both within the region and from other tourist areas such as Mexico, the rising cost of international air travel, and above all, the state of the United States economy. The Caribbean tourist trade has much to gain through regional cooperation. For example, many potential American tourists perceive of the archipelago as a "region." They think more in terms of a Caribbean vacation than one spent on Curaçao or Antigua or Grenada. As has been observed, no tourist agency can induce Americans to visit such little-known places unless they can first be located "in the Caribbean." A cooperative effort in advertising, in encouraging island-hopping, and in catering to a truly Caribbean vacation would benefit the entire region. Instead of cooperation, however, there is competition in advertising and in other aspects of the tourist economy. Insular governments use tax concessions and other inducements to compete among themselves in attracting foreign capital needed for tourist development. An almost ridiculous expression of competition for the American tourist dollar is the recent rush in some territories to modify laws for granting "quickie divorces." There is competition and conflict even at the local level because the indus-

Figure 4.7   Barbados: Stone quarry (*Barbados Tourist Board*)

try is dominated by numerous small entrepreneurs who are hostile to government regulation.

But the most important single determinant of the present and future outlook of Caribbean tourism is the health of the American economy. Compared to the booming American prosperity of the 1960s, which helped fuel the rapid expansion of Caribbean tourism, the early 1970s were economically discouraging for America, and thus for the West Indies. Not only had the West Indian tourist growth rate slowed down, but some of the large and more expensive centers, such as Jamaica, Puerto Rico, and the Bahamas, were actually experiencing a decline. Like every other aspect of the West Indian economy, tourism is saddled with a high degree of dependency.

Mining and Manufacturing

Like much of the Third World, the people of the West Indies also dream of being propelled up the steep road to economic development and modernization by the sudden discovery of rich mineral deposits and rapid industrialization. To date, however, this dream has become only a limited reality, and then only in a very few of the island territories. The contribution of mining or manufacturing to the gross national product has surpassed agriculture only in special circumstances such as those of Jamaica for mining and of Puerto Rico for industry. True, virtually every West Indian territory reports some mining and manufacturing activities, but these are often more symbolic than significant. In most territories, mining centers on the quarrying of local stone and sand for construction (Figure 4.7); and manufacturing consists of processing local farm products such as sugar cane. Even where mining and manufacturing have achieved more than symbolic importance, they are heavily dependent on capital and conditions outside the West Indies.

Viewed in the light of mineral wealth, the West Indies are characterized by sharp contrasts. Because of differences in geologic history (Chapter 2), the Greater Antilles are, on the whole, better off than the smaller islands (Figure 4.8). Among the larger territories, Jamaica is the undisputed leader. The island ranks (1970) as the world's largest exporter of bauxite and alumina,[2] deriving over one-third of its foreign exchange earnings from such exports. Cuba with its wide range of alloy minerals such as manganese, chrome, nickel, cobalt, and an estimated three billion tons of iron ore reserves also ranks

2. Bauxite, the claylike ore of aluminum, consists mainly of hydrated aluminum oxide (alumina) but includes other substances. It is found primarily in tropical areas where water has dissolved the soluble minerals from the soils, leaving a residue of insoluble aluminum oxide and iron.

high in mineral resources, although the island's foreign exchange earnings from mining are negligible compared to Jamaica's. Third in mineral importance in the Greater Antilles is Hispaniola where the Dominican Republic and Haiti exploit bauxite and other minerals. Ranking last in the Greater Antilles is Puerto Rico, whose major mineral assets are copper deposits that may eventually be exploited. Within the Lesser Antilles, the only noteworthy mineral exploitation is the petroleum of Trinidid, an island that is geologically part of the adjacent South American mainland. The territories of recent volcanic origin in the Lesser Antilles (such as the Windwards) are without petroleum or metallic minerals of any kind, and the situation in the small limestone islands is only theoretically better.

Much of the recent Antillean mineral dream has focused on petroleum and bauxite. The effort to find oil has been widespread, but except for Trinidad, success has been limited to a few wells in Cuba and the Dominican Republic. Most of the petroleum, which is the principal energy source in the archipelago, is refined locally in the Greater Antilles (Figure 4.8) and in Trinidad, Curaçao, Aruba, and Antigua, but the vast bulk of the crude oil has to be imported. The effort

to find bauxite has been more rewarding, and currently, the West Indies have achieved worldwide importance for the production of this mineral. Together with the output of nearby Surinam and Guyana, the Antilles supply over three-fourths of United States bauxite needs and virtually all those of Canada. Bauxite provides still another illustration of West Indian economic dependency because control of production, of markets, and of processing the ore into aluminum is vested in the hands of a small number of American and Canadian firms (Chapter 7).

Within the context of the archipelago as a whole, manufacturing in the West Indies permits a number of generalizations. Because workers are abundant and capital is scarce, industry is labor-intensive, using a large labor input per unit of capital investment. Even so, industry employs a much smaller labor force than agriculture. Like tourism, mining, and commercial farming, much of the capital for manufacturing is imported. The largest industrial establishments are connected with the refining of sugar cane, petroleum, and bauxite. Except for the processing of minerals and agricultural export crops, industrial production is geared to a local market with emphasis on import substitution. The average man-

Figure 4.8   Greater Antilles: Mineral exploitation, 1970

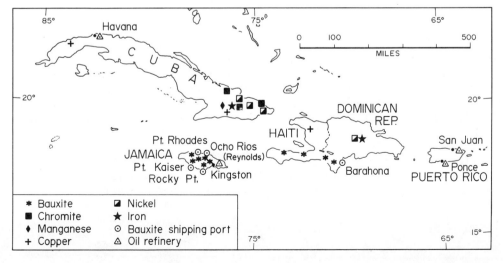

ufacturing unit tends to be a small factory, employing less than 100 workers; it uses local raw materials to produce for the local market; and its operations are often more akin to traditional handicraft than to modern industry.

But like so many generalizations about the West Indies, these (and others) concerning manufacturing say nothing about the considerable variety that exists from place to place. For purposes of identifying some of this variety in the industrial patterns of the archipelago, three representative models may be used. The first, or "Puerto Rico" model, typifies those territories where industrial production is both highly diversified and the leading contributor to the Gross National Product (GNP). The second, or "Trinidad" model, represents those islands where industry makes a major, or even the leading, contribution to the GNP but lacks diversification. The third, or "St. Lucia" model, is applicable to territories in which manufacturing lacks both diversity and importance in relation to the GNP.

The Puerto Rico model is in a class by itself. Since the 1940s the island has been involved in a major industrial revolution (Chapter 6). At present, the dollar value of its industrial production exceeds that of agriculture, tourism, and other economies; and the range of manufactured goods runs from the traditional sugar and rum to newly introduced and highly sophisticated electronics and petrochemical products. Metropolitan San Juan has emerged as the largest and most important industrial center in all Middle America outside Mexico.

The Trinidad model is also applicable to the Dutch "oil islands" of Curaçao and Aruba, Jamaica, and to a lesser extent, Cuba. In each case the value of industrial production is comparatively high but derived in large measure from the processing of a limited number of raw materials from farms and mines. The most important of

these raw materials include sugar cane and tobacco in Cuba, bauxite in Jamaica, and petroleum in Trinidad, Curaçao, and Aruba.

The characteristics of manufacturing in the majority of the West Indies generally fit the St. Lucia model. Such characteristics may be inferred from the report that, in the early 1970s, the industrial establishment of St. Lucia consisted of a traditional component represented by two rum distilleries and small factories for the production of lime, edible oil, aerated waters, soap, bricks, and furniture; and by new industries such as a fertilizer plant built by Esso Standard Oil (now Exxon Corporation) and a factory each for paper products and electrical components. The value of all the island's industrial production ranked well below that of agriculture.

Because of its striking success, the most prestigious industrial model in the West Indies is, of course, the Puerto Rican model. As a result, virtually every island except Cuba [3] is attempting to emulate the Puerto Rican experience. The effort to emulate generally begins with the passage of some kind of "industrial incentive act" by the government. In varying degree these acts feature a public industrial development corporation to provide seed capital and a planning apparatus for development; and rent-free "industrial park" sites, tax holidays, and other inducements to attract outside capital and industry. Unfortunately, there are a few crucial ingredients in the Puerto Rican success story that cannot be duplicated elsewhere. Not the least among these are the advantages stemming from Puerto Rico's special political and economic connection with the United States (Chapter 6).

3. Because of the vast changes that have taken place since 1959, many aspects of Cuba's industrial structure are more akin to those of socialist countries than to the "capitalistic" patterns of other Caribbean countries (Chapter 6).

Trade and Transportation

As noted in Chapter 1, the historical circulation of people, goods, and ideas in the West Indies has had closer linkages with non-Caribbean countries than with other Antillean territories. Whether for trade, transportation, political models, or cultural institutions and values, the islands have traditionally looked abroad rather than to each other. And despite some recent changes, the traditional patterns of circulation and marked dependence on non-Caribbean powers are still dominant. At the economic level, this is perhaps best illustrated by current trade flows and statistics (Figure 1.12, Tables 4.3, 4.4). The establishment of the Caribbean Free Trade Association in 1968 (discussed later in this chapter) and other recent developments are prompting some increase in intra-island trade, but the vast bulk of West Indian commerce continues to be with non-Caribbean states. Similarly, al-

Table 4.3   SOURCES OF IMPORTS TO THE WEST INDIES
BY PERCENTAGE VALUE (based on percentage of
total value in United States dollars, 1970)

Territory	Other West Indies and Latin America	United States and Canada	Euroasia and Others
Cuba	10	—	90
Jamaica	10	42	48
Hispaniola	7	50	43
Puerto Rico and U.S. Virgin Islands	2	78	20
Lesser Antilles	23	26	51
Dutch "Oil Islands"	79 *	11	10
Bahamas	—	81	19

* All except 2 percent represents the value of petroleum imported from Venezuela.

Table 4.4   DESTINATION OF EXPORTS FROM THE WEST INDIES
BY PERCENTAGE VALUE (based on percentage of
total value in United States dollars, 1970)

Territory	Other West Indies and Latin America	United States and Canada	Euroasia and Others
Cuba	15	—	85
Jamaica	5	40	55
Hispaniola	6	80	14
Puerto Rico and U.S. Virgin Islands	2	90	8
Lesser Antilles	6	33	61
Dutch "Oil Islands"	10	50	40
Bahamas	5	75	20

though post–World War II trends have given rise to some diversification of products, the archipelago's trade is still characterized by the export of raw materials or semi-processed agricultural and mining products, and by imports dominated by finished goods and foodstuffs. Also in keeping with the historical record of the past century, the Antilles are handicapped by a generally unfavorable balance of trade and by the weak competitive position of their exports on the world market.

Obvious conditions account for these characteristics of West Indian commerce. Despite some variety in production structure, the economies of the archipelago tend to be competitive rather than complementary. Too many of the insular economies are forced to depend on the export of tropical cash crops, or on tourism, to earn foreign exchange. Moreover, paucity of arable land, worn-out soils, limited mechanization, and other factors make for high production costs. Further weakening the competitive position of the islands, is the existence of a greater supply than demand for most West Indian products and services. These drawbacks deprive the insular economies of any bargaining power in export trade and make them vulnerable to the dictates of external markets. In fact, the vulnerability is such that the agricultural export economy of virtually every West Indian territory would face collapse without preferential treatment abroad. More than three-fourths and perhaps as much as 90 percent of West Indian farm exports depend on some form of special consideration. The role of the United States quota system in providing favored treatment for the sugar exports of Puerto Rico, the Dominican Republic, and other West Indian territories has already been cited. In 1970 virtually all of Cuba's sugar (and most of the island's other exports) was sold under preferential arrangements with the USSR and other socialist countries. Similar treatment from the European

Common Market, the United States, Canada, and Britain [4] was given to the export of West Indian bananas, citrus fruit, cacao, and tobacco. The only West Indian agricultural export that is not receiving such preference is coffee. The archipelago's mineral exports do not depend on special treatment and are less vulnerable than farm exports, but as already noted, Jamaica's bauxite, the region's leading mineral export, is controlled by United States and Canadian companies.

The West Indies are equally vulnerable in the import component of their international trade. Dependence on food imports, which began in the slave plantation period (Chapter 3), has grown with the rapid increase of population and the virtual monopoly of the best land by producers of sugar cane and other cash crops. The cost of imported foodstuffs has always been high, but it threatens to rise even higher. The decrease in the catches of New England and Canadian fishermen, for example, is already pushing up the price of salt cod, which has long been important in the West Indian diet. The cost of other foodstuffs purchased abroad may be similarly affected, especially if the shortages that threaten the USSR, Japan, China, and even the United States continue. Also expected to add to the rising bill for West Indian imports is the real or contrived world shortage of petroleum (the archipelago's chief energy fuel) and the growing inflation in the industrial countries from which the islands buy finished products.

Thus, if it is true that profitable international trade is based on the principle of "comparative advantage," which stresses the export of those products for which a country possesses a competitive edge, then the West Indies seem to be hopelessly handicapped. In the face of

4. The impact on West Indian farm exports anticipated from Britain's entry into the ECC was not clear in the early 1970s.

rapidly increasing population, limited natural resources, and a small domestic market, they have to depend heavily on international trade. Yet, their comparative advantages for such trade are so few that they are constantly caught in a classic economic "squeeze play": the price which they receive for their exports remains relatively low while the cost of their imports rises.

Like commerce, West Indian transportation and communications are also more closely linked to the outside than to other territories in the archipelago. Despite the recent rapid growth of an interisland air network, the amount of extraregional air travel by West Indians is still far greater than interisland visiting. The sea lanes over which the bulk of the goods are shipped to or from the archipelago provide even less of a regional link. Given the nature of trade described above, most sea lanes help tie the islands with Anglo-America, Europe, Asia, and other parts of the world, but not with each other (Figure 1.12). Similarly, interisland telecommunications and the flow of ideas is improving, but they are still held down by linguistic barriers, long-standing parochialism, and marked differences in educational systems.

The limited sea transportation linking the archipelago's territories to one another has been traditionally based on small steamers or boats utilizing sails or gasoline engines for power. This type of sea transport is still important, especially for the movement of low-value goods. In recent decades, however, a significant interisland air network for the movement of passengers, mail, and high-value cargo has developed. This network provides a concrete illustration of the characteristics of current interisland circulation.

In 1973, the international edition of the *Official Airline Guide* listed over 6,000 weekly interisland flights for the West Indies (Table 4.5). Most of the flights are made by small planes that carry a cor-

Table 4.5   WEEKLY INTERISLAND FLIGHTS IN THE WEST INDIES, 1973

Territory	Number of Flights (in hundreds)
Puerto Rico	15.0
U.S. Virgin Islands	14.4
Antigua (Leeward Islands)	4.3
Barbados	3.4
French West Indies	3.1
St. Martin	2.9
St. Kitts-Nevis-Anguilla (Leeward Islands)	2.9
Trinidad-Tobago	2.7
St. Lucia (Windward Islands)	2.5
Grenada (Windward Islands)	2.0
British Virgin Islands	1.7
Jamaica	1.2
St. Vincent	1.0
Bahamas	—*
Dominican Republic	—
Haiti	—
Dominica	—
Montserrat	—

Note: Flights that connect segments of the same territory, such as the various islands in the Bahamas, are not included in the data.

* Less than 100 flights.

respondingly small number of passengers and cargo loads. Except for Puerto Rico, there is little correlation between the number of flights and the territory's economic importance (or its size and population). For example, the combined total of interisland flights listed for Jamaica and Trinidad is less than the listing for Antigua. Some of the larger territories, such as the Dominican Republic and Haiti, have less than 100 such flights. Also noteworthy is that much of the interisland air movement is between territories that "fly the same flag." For example, of the roughly 1,400 flights that touch on the American Virgin Islands, almost 1,200 originate in Puerto Rico; the largest number of interisland flights received at Port of Spain, Trinidad, are from Barbados,

Antigua, St. Lucia, and Grenada respectively. Reaffirming the greater importance of extraregional connections, there are fewer than two daily flights between Jamaica, Puerto Rico, and Trinidad, compared to several dozen flights connecting these same territories with non-Caribbean centers.

ECONOMIC INTEGRATION

CARIFTA

Like Western Europe and Latin America, the Caribbean region is also responding to the potential advantages for trade and development stemming from economic integration. To date, the most concrete response to such integration has been the Caribbean Free Trade Association (CARIFTA). Implemented in May 1968, the organization counts as members Jamaica, all the territories with a British connection [5] in the Lesser Antilles except the British Virgin Islands, and Guyana. CARIFTA's general goal is to promote trade expansion and diversification and to encourage more rapid economic development of its member territories. To these ends the participating governments have agreed to eliminate tariff barriers among themselves as quickly as possible and to establish a common tariff policy for purposes of trading with nonmember countries.

The potential advantages of CARIFTA are varied. It pools a dozen small markets into a larger market of over five million people, thereby providing greater attraction for foreign investments in manufacturing and other economic activities. The

5. Other than the British Virgins, the territories with a "British connection" in the Lesser Antilles are Barbados, Trinidad-Tobago, Antigua, Dominica, Grenada, Montserrat, St.Kitts-Nevis-Anguilla, St. Lucia, and St. Vincent.

"strength in numbers" also may provide the association greater bargaining power to negotiate favorable trade agreements with nonmember countries, and to obtain developmental capital and technical help. The association gives each member relatively free access to the markets of the others even for some of the ubiquitous farm products. For example, no member may import from abroad any one of a special list of 22 agricultural items unless these items are not available from members of the association.

But such advantages are offset by disadvantages. The members of CARIFTA are widely scattered along the northern and eastern rim of the Caribbean Sea, so that Jamaica at one extreme is separated from Guyana at the other by more than 1,000 miles. The distance factor, coupled with poor communications, the small volume of goods generated by the small islands, and other conditions result in high transportation costs. At least some of the products that make up the trade among CARIFTA territories can be more cheaply obtained abroad. Moreover, the member territories can absorb only a small part of each other's total exports and can provide only a small percentage of each other's import needs. For instance, in 1967 prior to CARIFTA, the trade among members was less than 5 percent of their total commerce. This figure has been increasing since 1968, but the vast bulk of both the export and import trade continues to be directed to the outside. Significantly, the CARIFTA compact does not affect contractual agreements that members had with outside markets prior to 1968.

Another disadvantage is the considerable difference in the stage of economic development and per capita income among CARIFTA members. Trinidad's per capita income in 1970, for instance, was more than four times greater than those of smaller territories such as Montserrat or St. Kitts. Such differences often favor the larger and better developed territories over the smaller ones and thereby foster conflicting viewpoints on important questions such as the location of new industries and the treatment of farm products.

The vast bulk of the CARIFTA trade (some 70 percent of imports and 95 percent of exports in 1970) centers on Guyana, Jamaica, Trinidad, and Barbados. Guyana, with its abundance of agricultural land and surplus production of rice, led in the export of foodstuffs; Jamaica and Trinidad dominated the trade in petrochemical products and, together with Barbados, led in the commerce of manufactured products.

There are those who look upon CARIFTA as a "pooling of misery" and who predict that it will founder as did the West Indies Federation (Chapter 5). Others stress that the association has already survived its fifth anniversary (1973), and are moderately optimistic about its future. It may be too early to predict the outcome, but in July 1973, CARIFTA's four most developed members (Jamaica, Trinidad, Barbados, and Guyana) formed a new grouping called the Caribbean Economic Community. The stated purposes of CEC are to promote measures leading to cooperation in agriculture, industry, and financing, as well as trade among the CARIFTA members. The CARIFTA territories also agreed to launch the Caribbean Investment Corporation to foster investment, especially in the less-developed, smaller islands.

Caribbean Development Bank

A final example of the trend to economic integration in the West Indies is the establishment of the Caribbean Development Bank. In addition to the CARIFTA territories, which provide 60 percent of the capitalization, the bank's members also include the Bahamas, the British Virgin Islands, the Cayman, Turk, and Caicos Islands, and for certain purposes, Puerto Rico, Britain, and Canada. The bank's aims include helping members to coordinate their development programs and providing technical assistance and capital.

SELECTED REFERENCES

BARCLAYS BANK. *Barclays International Review.* London, 1970–1973.

BECKFORD, G. L. *Persistent Poverty.* New York: Oxford University Press, 1972.

DONNELLEY, R. H. *Official Airline Guide.* International Ed. 17, no. 3 (1973).

INTER-AMERICAN DEVELOPMENT BANK. *Socio-Economic Progress in Latin America.* 10th Annual Report. Washington, D.C., 1970.

LEWIS, S., and MATHEWS, T. G., eds. *Caribbean Integration.* Río Piedras: University of Puerto Rico Press, 1966.

MOMSEN, J. "Crisis in the Caribbean Sugar Industry." *Geography* 56, no. 253 (1971).

———. "Small-Scale Farming in Barbados, St. Lucia and Martinique." *Proceedings of the Fifth West Indies Economic Conference.* Trinidad, 1971.

MULCHANSINGH, V. C. CARIFTA. Occasional Publication no. 3. Kingston, Jamaica: University of the West Indies, Dept. of Geography, 1968.

ORGANIZATION OF AMERICAN STATES. *America en Cifras.* Washington, D.C., 1971.

PAXTON, J., ed. *The Statesman's Year-Book.* London: St. Martin's Press, 1970.

RUDDLE, K., and HAMOUR, M., eds. *Statistical Abstract of Latin America 1970.* Latin American Center, U.C.L.A. Los Angeles: University of California Press, 1971.

SEGAL, A. *The Politics of Caribbean Economic Integration.* Institute of Caribbean Studies.

Río Piedras: University of Puerto Rico Press, 1968.

VELIZ, C., ed. *Latin America and the Caribbean: A Handbook.* New York: Praeger, 1968.

West Indies and Caribbean Year Book, 1972. Croydon, U.K.: Chapel River Press, 1971.

Population and Political Geography
of the Present-Day West Indies

The economic problems assessed in Chapter 4 and the geopolitical problems to be discussed later in this chapter are deeply rooted in the population context and characteristics of the West Indies. Overall population densities in the archipelago are already the highest in the Americas, and yet on most islands annual birth rates continue to range between 3 and 4 percent, or roughly double those of the world's developed nations. Despite the emigration of almost two million people in recent decades, the discrepancy between economic production and spiraling population still exists, and grinding poverty is still very much the lot of the West Indian masses.

There is nothing new about the current poverty stemming from the gulf between production and population in the archipelago except a growing popular resentment over the causes of such conditions and the political expression of this resentment. Many West Indians, particularly among the black majority, justifiably blame their slave past, white political domination, and economic exploitation by outsiders for their present fate. Whenever possible they are assuming control of their insular governments and are even declaring themselves politically independent from their former rulers. Unfortunately, political change rarely erases the scars of a slave colonial past, and it does little to reduce the pressure of a growing population on a limited and generally impoverished resource base. Herein lies one of the threats to the fabric of West Indian society.

POPULATION

Because of the large labor demands of sugar cane and other tropical crops (Chapter 3), most West Indian territories were characterized by a comparatively large population even before emancipation. In the mid-nineteenth century, for example, the British-, French-, and Dutch-connected territories had a total population of over two million people and an average population density that was already above 100 persons per square mile. As long as slavery continued, there was a bar to rapid population growth. Under slave conditions, the rate of natural increase (excess of births over deaths) among blacks was actually negative in most territories. Slave mortality from disease, malnutrition, inhumane treatment, and other causes[1] has been estimated at about 20 percent per year. In fact, the excess of deaths over births among slaves was so high that an adequate labor supply could be maintained only by the constant importation of new slaves from Africa. About five million slaves were brought to the British, French, and Dutch West Indian colonies from the mid-seventeenth to the mid-nineteenth century, but on the eve of emancipation these colonies had only two million people.

In the century following emancipation, the West Indies experienced a "population explosion" despite a substantial emigration. The chief cause of this explosion was the rapid rise in the rate of natural increase. Freed from the more inhibiting psychological and other conditions of slavery, and aided by the gradual improvement of sanitation and the control of killer diseases such as yellow fever and malaria, the black population of the West Indies began to increase at a rapid rate. Also contributing to the West Indian population explosion in the century following emancipation was the heavy immigration from India, Europe, and elsewhere and the rapid growth of the poor white and mixed populations of the Hispanic territories.

Numbers, Densities, and Distribution

Although the causes and consequences of the West Indian postemancipation population boom were not the same everywhere, by 1960 the archipelago as a whole counted a total of 17 million inhabitants; and a decade later this total was in excess of 25 million. With an area of about 90 thousand square miles (including the Bahamas), the population density of the ar-

1. It has been hypothesized that many slave women resorted to birth control methods, including abortion and even infanticide, to keep from having children.

chipelago averaged over 280 persons per square mile in 1970 (Table 5.1), and there was every indication of further increase. Comparable densities per square mile for the same year were about 64 for Mexico, 27 for Peru, and 58 for the United States. In fact, no other general region in the Americas had higher average densities than the West Indies.

But high average densities account for only a general measure of the actual population pressure and resulting poverty in the West Indies. They do not reflect the irregular distribution of population or the local differences in the quality of the resource base, in the productive capacity of

Table 5.1   AVERAGE POPULATION
DENSITIES IN THE
WEST INDIES, 1970

Territory	People (per square mile)
Cuba	183
Puerto Rico	789
Jamaica	443
Dominican Republic	231
Haiti	551
Trinidad-Tobago	476
Barbados	1542
U.S. Virgin Islands	473
British Virgin Islands	178
Bahamas	38(?)
Antigua	368
Montserrat	384
St. Kitts	409
Dominica	231
Grenada	783
St. Lucia	424
St. Vincent	594
Martinique	782
Guadeloupe	586
Curaçao	830
Aruba	866
Bonaire	85
St. Martin	440
St. Eustatius	112
Saba	193
REGIONAL AVERAGE	285

specific insular economies, or in birth rates and other pertinent differences. For example, with reference to average densities (Table 5.1), Barbados at one extreme has in excess of 1,500 persons per square mile, while the Bahamas and Cuba at the other extreme have 38 and 183 respectively; Puerto Rico's average may be 789 people per square mile, but the island's north coast, where most of the population is concentrated, has much higher densities than other parts of the territory.

Of the more than 25 million inhabitants of the West Indies, 15 million, or about 60 percent, are concentrated in the Hispanic territories (Cuba, Puerto Rico, and the Dominican Republic); Haiti and the French départements of Martinique and Guadeloupe account for another 25 percent; and the remainder are represented by the islands with British and Dutch connections. Thus, despite widespread heterogeneity of cultural influences, viewed in terms of total population, the Antilles are predominantly Roman Catholic and "Latin." Cultural influences, however, seem to have little to do with the current population growth rates of the various territories. In the two decades between 1950 and 1970, the Dominican Republic

had the sharpest increase in the West Indies, while Puerto Rico had one of the lowest; almost at par with the Dominican Republic was the growth rate in the Netherlands Antilles; Trinidad, Haiti, and the French dependencies had roughly similar high rates of increase; and the rest of the archipelago ranged from moderate increases such as those in Cuba and Jamaica to actual decreases of population such as those in the Turks and Caicos Islands.

Given the widespread importance of farming in the West Indies, the ratio of people to unit of cultivated land (agricultural density) provides a more realistic indicator of population pressure than overall average densities. Assessed in terms of agricultural density, it is noteworthy that Cuba and the Netherlands Antilles have less than one person per acre of cultivated land (Figure 5.1). Most of the archipelago has a ratio of two to four people per acre, while Martinique and Barbados go even higher. Also noteworthy, agricultural density does not always correlate directly with population pressure and the level of poverty. For example, Haiti has a lower ratio of persons per cultivated acre than Barbados (Figure 5.2), but be-

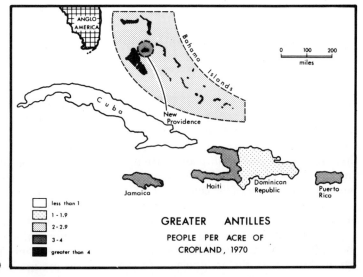

Figure 5.1   Greater Antilles: People per cultivated acre, 1970

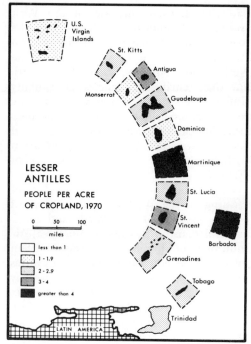

Figure 5.2   Lesser Antilles: People per cultivated acre, 1970

cause the quality of the Haitian resource base and other conditions are vastly inferior, the population pressure as reflected by per capita income and poverty level is higher in Haiti than in Barbados. Where the insular economy depends primarily on oil refining as in Curaçao or on tourism as in the Bahamas, agricultural density may have even less meaning.

Race

Racial composition in the West Indies defies detailed classification. Not only has the archipelago received people from a large number of racial and ethnic groups, but the intermarriage (or cohabitation) of these groups during almost five centuries of post-Columbian history has resulted in a wide spectrum of mixtures. Moreover, the racial meld varies considerably in different segments of the archipelago. In the

territories with a British or French connection, including Haiti, black in a variety of shades predominates, and whites generally make up less than 5 percent of the total population. In the Hispanic and Dutch islands, whites or near-whites outnumber the blacks except in the Dominican Republic where most of the population "thinks white" but is essentially mulatto. But even these generalizations have numerous exceptions. Thus, in the tiny British-connected islands of Barbuda and Carriacou, the population is almost exclusively black, but the French Les Saintes and St. Barthelemy are predominantly white. There are communities of poor but "pure" whites such as the "Redlegs" of Barbados, Grenada, and St. Kitts; the Germans of Seaford in Jamaica; the English of the Grand Caymans; the "Chachas" of St. Thomas; and similar groups in Guadeloupe. Although the population of both is black, that of Martinique is more visibly light skinned than that of Jamaica. The white majority of Cuba was slightly more than half and may have decreased because of the recent departure of primarily white middle- and upper-class groups escaping from Castro. In contrast, Puerto Ricans, who in the United States are frequently considered less white than Cubans, have a white majority of almost 80 percent. East Indians (Chapter 3) constitute small minorities on several British-, French-, and Dutch-connected islands, but in Trinidad their higher birth rate is rapidly pushing their numbers to parity with the blacks. In addition, many of the islands include small groups of Chinese, Syrians, and Lebanese in their populations.

Despite the efforts of some groups, especially the whites, to avoid miscegenation, racial purity in the West Indies is at a minimum, and the trend toward further mixing is obvious. In Trinidad, for example, the Chinese are already half mixed, and the "pure" unions among East Indians are gradually breaking down as the younger generations rebel against family-arranged marriages. In Puerto Rico, which has the largest percentage of whites in the Hispanic territories, the percentage of blacks in the total population tends to decrease with each census count. This suggests that the black minority is gradually being absorbed into the white majority. It also indicates that, unlike the United States, a small quantity of black blood does not automatically place a person in the black racial classification.[2]

To summarize the complicated character of West Indian racial composition, there are practically no American Indians left. In the territories with British and French ties, whites are in a small and diminishing minority; about one-third of the population in these islands is already a mixture of black and white, and the evolution of racial mixture is toward increasing blackness. In the Hispanic territories, roughly one of every five Puerto Ricans, one of every three Cubans, and possibly three of every four Dominicans may be classified as black, but there is a general tendency toward increasing whiteness, at least for purposes of classification. Finally, the process of racial mixing continues at a more rapid rate than in the past, and there are indications that, with few exceptions, those segments of the West Indian population that are not already mixed will become so within a few generations. Among the exceptions to this trend are the aforementioned poor whites in the non-Hispanic territories who appear determined not to mix even at the price of consanguine degeneracy exacted by inbreeding.

The trend toward increasing racial mixture does not mean, of course, that color consciousness and the scars of a slave his-

2. Census classification of race often has little meaning in the West Indies. Much depends on the bias of the individual census-taker. As a result, for example, the "coloured" percentage of the total population in Dominica was reported at 30 in 1921, 75 in 1946, and 33 in 1960.

tory have disappeared. Contrary to the belief of some tourists and other casual observers who often view the archipelago as a model area of harmony among various races, the West Indies are still a long way from achieving racial integration. While friction between the races is low-keyed in comparison to South Africa and even the United States, color differences are important—in part because they still tend to correlate with social classes, and in part because of the area's slave history and other reasons. "Racial distinctions have mattered longer in the West Indies than anywhere else in the Americas." (Lowenthal 1972:26). Nor is black always considered beautiful. Whether in Puerto Rico, Trinidad, or Haiti, whether the group is poor white or the emerging black elite, the preference among most West Indians continues to be for the lighter skin pigmentation and for other European physical characteristics. The sense of color shame stemming from the slave past still manifests itself by the desire to "put some cream in the coffee" in choosing a mate (Coombs 1970:32).

But race relations are undergoing some change. As recently as a generation ago, conspicuous racial segregation was an accepted fact of life in the West Indies. There was a relatively rigid correlation between race and class, and nonwhites were seldom able to rise to positions of power and prestige. The small (2 to 5 percent of the population) upper class was white or nearly white; the middle class, which made up from 5 to 15 percent of the total was predominantly of mixed blood ("coloured," "mulatre," "gente de color"); the lower class was predominantly black; and other ethnic groups such as the East Indians, Chinese, and Syrians lived on the fringes of the basic social structure with no clear-cut class association based on race. Also in a social limbo were the poor whites in the non-Hispanic islands who were in the anomalous position of being lower class economically but claiming upper class on grounds of race and cultural origins. Frequently looked down upon by both upper-class whites and blacks, the poor whites maintained their "racial purity" through isolation and inbreeding. Currently, with the possible exception of the French Antilles, the once-marked correlation between color and class is fading. Institutionalized racial segregation ended during World War II, and the elites in many island societies are no longer exclusively white. The middle class has been absorbing increasing numbers from the lower class; and nonwhites as a group have gained greater prominence. Political power and privilege, once exclusively in the hands of upper-class whites, is being rapidly transferred to the black masses.

Migration

Many of the present salient population characteristics of the Antilles are closely related, either as causes or consequences, to the numerous migrations experienced by the archipelago in post-Columbian times. West Indians have been migration-prone almost from the very beginning of European colonization (Chapter 3). The early Spanish colonists of Santo Domingo, Cuba, and Puerto Rico desperately sought to leave the islands for the promising rewards of Mexico and Peru on the Mainland. Later, British and French colonial planters yearned to return "home" to England and France, and so many of them left the islands that absentee ownership became characteristic of the West Indian colonial plantation. Still later, emancipated slaves readily moved from their native islands to seek a living elsewhere, and judging from the outward movement of hundreds of thousands of Puerto Ricans, Cubans, Jamaicans, and other islanders in the past few decades, the urge to migrate is very much a force in contemporary West Indian societies.

But these population movements have not been uniform. They have differed through time with reference to causes, destination, scale of flow, impact on the archipelago and other characteristics. Viewed historically, for example, the principal movements in the period from the Discovery to the postemancipation years of the late nineteenth century were in-migrations (immigrations). There were some important examples of outward movements (emigrations) during this period, but in the balance, far more people arrived in the West Indies than departed. In contrast, the major trend since 1900 has been to emigration, and despite the arrival of additional East Indians and Europeans, more population actually left than entered the archipelago.

Immigration. As partially explained in Chapter 3, the chief immigration movements to the West Indies prior to 1900 included (1) the initial settlers from Spain, Britain, France, the Netherlands, and elsewhere in Europe; (2) the small but economically significant groups of Jews who settled primarily in Curaçao and Jamaica; (3) the forced migration of millions of African slaves in connection with the development of the plantation economy; (4) the arrival of miscellaneous small groups such as French and Spanish colonists following the annexation of the Louisiana territory by the United States, unreconstructed Confederate sympathizers after the American Civil War, Corsicans following the defeat of Napoleon, and others. Significant immigration of European colonists to the British, French, and Dutch colonies came to a virtual standstill during the eighteenth century as plantation development concentrated most available land into a few hands and African slaves provided labor. European immigration to the Hispanic colonies also dwindled following initial colonization, but it resumed on a noteworthy scale in the nineteenth century as plantation development took place, especially in Cuba and Puerto Rico.

The African slave trade, legally abolished early in the nineteenth century, continued to bring contraband slaves to the Caribbean until the 1870s.

Emancipation and the refusal of many former slaves to work on the sugar estates set in motion another major immigration to the Caribbean—the entry of indentured laborers. The major sources of contracted or indentured labor were India and China, though significant numbers also came from Java, Indo-China, Africa, and Portugal. During a period of roughly 70 years beginning in the 1850s, nearly a half-million Indians (called "East Indians" to distinguish them from West Indians and American Indians) were brought to the British and French West Indies and to the Guianas; well over 100,000 Chinese were contracted for work in the British islands, Cuba, and Surinam; the French islands received small numbers of Annamese; and the Dutch islands and Surinam received more than 10,000 Javanese. In addition, the British imported a small number of Portuguese plus thousands of free Africans released from captured contraband slave ships. The latter, unable to return home, had no choice but to accept a three-year contract of indentured servitude in exchange for a grant of free land.

Other than the decreasing flow of indentured workers, the only numerically significant group of immigrants were European laborers who arrived in Cuba in connection with the rapid expansion of the island's sugar economy following the Spanish American War (Chapter 6). From 1902 to 1920, for example, more than 450,000 immigrants were attracted to Cuba from Europe. The vast majority of these (almost 95 percent) came from Spain, but small numbers came from many other European countries and even from Turkey. The movement of Spanish workers to Cuba continued until the early 1930s when the island's sugar economy almost collapsed under the stress of the Depression (Chapter 6).

Emigration. On the basis of destination, West Indian emigration flows may be grouped into three classes: those bound for areas outside the archipelago (extraregional); those from one West Indian territory to another (interregional); and those taking place from one sector to another of the same territory (internal). Prior to emancipation, extraregional emigrations were few and involved only small numbers of persons. As already noted, the most prominent movements were the migration of early Spanish *conquistadores* from the Caribbean island bases to the Mainland, the exodus of English yeoman farmers from Barbados and other plantation colonies to North America and elsewhere, and the return to Europe of many white planters both before and after the decline of the colonial plantation. In the postemancipation decades of the late nineteenth century, however, there was an extraregional exodus of black workers, especially from the heavily populated territories of Jamaica and Barbados. During the unsuccessful French attempt to build the Panama Canal (1881–1888), for example, it is estimated that Jamaica alone furnished in excess of 25,000 laborers. Most of those that were not victims of the high mortality rate in Panama returned home when the French abandoned the project, but the stage was set for renewed black emigration to Central America after 1900 (Figure 5.3). When the United States resumed work on the canal (1905–1913), some 35,000 Jamaicans plus additional thousands from Barbados and other British territories responded. The Panama Canal Zone continued to attract Jamaicans and others after the canal was opened until as recently as World War II. English-speaking Jamaicans, some still retaining British citizenship, are much in evidence in Panama to this day. Job opportunities in the banana and sugar plantations of other Central American countries (Costa Rica, Nicaragua, Honduras, Guatemala) and of South American areas such as the

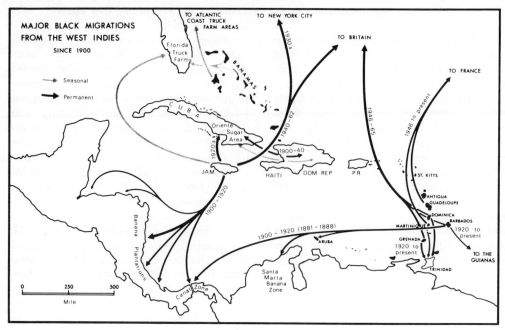

Figure 5.3   Major black migrations from the West Indies since 1900

Guianas and Colombia also drew West Indian migrants, especially Jamaicans and Barbadians.

Other extraregional emigrations of black workers from the British West Indies between 1900 and 1930 were triggered by the development of the Maracaibo oil fields in Venezuela during World War I and the subsequent establishment of oil refineries on Curaçao (1916) and Aruba (1925), and by the high wages paid even for unskilled labor in the United States and, to a lesser degree, in Canada. Between World War I and 1930, for example, more than 100,000 British West Indian workers emigrated to North American cities, particularly New York and Boston. This flow was virtually cut off by the Depression, but was renewed during World War II to relieve the acute labor shortage in the United States.

West Indian extraregional emigrations from both the British islands and elsewhere assumed mass proportions following World War II. Most of these movements were permanent, but a few were seasonal (Figure 5.3). Jamaicans, for ex-

ample, continued to emigrate and to settle permanently in the United States, often entering on unfilled United Kingdom quotas until 1952. From this date until 1965, much of the Jamaican emigration to the United States became seasonal. The permanent extraregional movements of both Jamaicans and other black West Indians focused on Europe, and by 1960 there were roughly 400,000 black West Indians in Britain, 150,000 in France and over 20,000 in the Netherlands. In Britain, a growing fear of "coloured" immigrants resulted in the Commonwealth Immigration Act (1962) which restricted the once free migration from Commonwealth countries including the West Indies. With Britain virtually closed to them, British West Indians have again turned to the United States and Canada. When the United States immigration law (1965) eased entry, resident visas for Jamaica jumped from 5,000 in 1966 to 17,000 in 1968; and Jamaican migration to Canada has been averaging over 3,000 per year.

Two other West Indian extraregional mass emigration flows in recent decades have affected primarily the Hispanic territories. These are the large movement of Puerto Ricans to United States cities, especially New York, Philadelphia, Chicago, and other large cities (Chapter 6) and the political emigré flow of Cubans to the United States after 1959. By the early 1970s there were several hundred thousand Cuban refugees in the United States with over 300,000 concentrated in Miami alone. A successful campaign has been waged to resettle Cuban refugees in other parts of the United States, but Florida (especially Miami) still remains the major focus of Cubans who have fled from Castro. Many of these retain their refugee status and mentality hoping for the day of return to their homeland. Many others, however, particularly among the younger generation and those that have left the refugee "cultural hearth" in Miami, are becoming Americans in both citizenship and outlook.

The scale and frequency of West Indian interregional emigration suggests that people have moved more readily than commerce in the Caribbean. Interregional movements, whether permanent or seasonal, have been primarily from the more heavily populated territories such as Jamaica, Barbados, Haiti, and the Windwards to less densely settled areas such as Cuba, the Dominican Republic, and Trinidad (Figure 5.3). They have involved primarily unskilled agricultural workers, and the migrants have been black for the most part. Nonblack migrations such as the recent movements of Puerto Ricans to the American Virgin Islands or of refugee Cubans to Puerto Rico have involved far fewer people.

The enormous potential for Cuban sugar in the United States market following the Spanish American War (Chapter 6) set the stage for a rapid expansion of the island's cane lands and created a large demand for labor. As already noted, part of the labor need was met by European immigration, but part had to be met by importing workers from Jamaica, Haiti, and the Lesser Antilles. Although the intent was to have the imported black workers return to their own islands, many managed to stay on in Cuba permanently. It is estimated that between 1912 and 1924 over 200,000 Jamaicans and Haitians took up residence on the island. The flow continued to be heavy until the early 1930s when, as a result of a drastic fall in sugar prices and the "50 percent law" requiring half the workers in any island enterprise to be Cuban, the Antillean emigration to Cuba was drastically reduced.

The movement of Haitians into the Dominican Republic is of long standing (Chapter 6), prompted primarily by the vast differences in population pressure between the two countries. All of the permanent Haitian movement into Dominican territory has taken place despite strictly enforced laws against it and has affected primarily the border region. Despite the periodic expulsion (and even a wholesale massacre during the 1930s) of Haitians, many have managed to stay, and with the assassination of the fanatically anti-Haitian Trujillo, the illegal movement undoubtedly continues. Even Trujillo, however, sanctioned the controlled seasonal movement of cheap Haitian labor to harvest the Dominican sugar crop. This seasonal flow is legal and continues to this day.

Other interregional emigration flows have involved primarily workers from the smaller islands. Among these are the movements to the American Virgin Islands of blacks from the British Virgins and other Lesser Antilles, of poor white fishermen from the French islands, and of Puerto Ricans (Chapter 7). Much of Trinidad's black population is made up of arrivals (or their offspring) from the smaller islands to the north, especially the Windwards, and despite strict new controls this movement continues. On a seasonal basis there is a considerable circulation of workers among such Lesser Antillean territories as Barbados, the Windwards, Guadeloupe, and others.

By far the most important type of internal emigration that has been taking place in the West Indies is the country-to-town movement. Of less importance have been movements such as those of Cuban population eastward toward the Oriente Province with the spread of sugar during this century, the often-forced migrations of Dominicans toward the Haitian frontier during the Trujillo regime, and, in Trinidad, the movements of blacks to the oil fields and East Indians to the more sparsely populated sectors of the island (Chapter 7).

General Causes and Consequences of Migration. Because of differences in time of occurrence and duration, in places of origin and destination, in the scale of movement, and in other conditions, generalizations concerning the causes and consequences of West Indian population movements are risky. What may be true of a migration originating in Cuba may be less true of one originating in Puerto Rico and may not apply at all to one involving Haitians. It is possible to say, however, that except for political refugee movements, the most widespread cause of migration has been population pressure and limited job opportunities at home compared to lower population pressure and either real or imagined employment opportunities in the destination areas of the migrants. Jobs for the unskilled have rarely been abundant or more than seasonal in the West Indies since emancipation. More important, with the constant growth in the unskilled labor force and the decreased demand for such labor in modernizing agriculture and industry, the number of jobs available is decreasing proportionately. Half a century ago, for example, the largely unmechanized West Indian sugar economy required twice as many workers to produce half of what the growingly mechanized industry pro-

duces today. Such technological improvements have not only displaced labor and created unemployment but have also increased the seasonality of employment. As a result of mechanization and of improved, faster-growing varieties of sugar cane, the number of work days needed to plant, raise, and harvest the crop is substantially less than it was at the turn of this century. The causes for the small but significant migrations of skilled and professional West Indians also stem primarily from economic considerations such as better pay away from their home islands. There is evidence, however, that many of the most talented professionals migrate to escape the boredom and lack of creature comforts which are often characteristics of small, relatively secluded places.

The most obvious generalization concerning the consequences of migrations is that population movements have a wide-ranging impact on West Indian economy, culture, insularity, and even sex habits. Many consequences of migration are negative. For example, the West Indian territories suffer a constant attrition of the younger, the more ambitious, and often the most talented and trained groups in their population. The typical migrants are young men who can find no work at home. Their departure creates a skewed sex ratio in the population which results in considerable social stress. If the migration is permanent, young females follow the men, often leaving children behind to be cared for (or not cared for) by older relatives and friends. Large-scale emigration may often undermine the insular economy by decreasing the size and increasing the cost of the labor force. In the British Virgin Islands and Montserrat, for instance, much of the arable land lies idle or is used for grazing due to labor shortages. Also negative is the hostility, frequently expressed in racial terms, that the migrants encounter abroad. The relatively affluent or intellectual West Indians such as the Jamaican student, or

Puerto Rican businessman, or Trinidadian government official may meet with some racial difficulties in the United States or Europe, but the situation seems to be improving for them. The same is not true, however, of the poor nonwhite workers who concentrate abroad. Note the reaction to poor Puerto Ricans in New York, or to Jamaicans in Britain, or to Dutch West Indians in Amsterdam.

On the positive side, migration often provides the only safety valve for the escape of surplus labor, and the money sent home by the migrants is an important source of "hidden" income for the insular economies. Thus, Puerto Rico's substantial trade deficit is offset in part by tourist spending but more by the remittances of Puerto Ricans who have migrated to the United States. Jamaicans living in Britain sent home almost £9 million in 1967, and on small islands such as Barbuda and Anguilla, emigrant remittances may represent the principal income of the resident population.

The Outlook

There are too many people for the number of available jobs in the West Indies, and even without further demographic increases, the archipelago is overpopulated. Unfortunately, all evidence points to further growth. The rate of natural increase on most territories is so high that the present population could easily double itself by the end of this century. The archipelago's resource base and even its most optimistic dreams of economic development are finite, while its potential for population growth seems infinite. Are there any solutions to this untenable dilemma? In extreme cases such as Haiti, it is difficult to see any solution except a totally Malthusian one. In others, the most obvious key is to reduce the birth rate to or even below the level of the death rate. Many West Indian governments (Puerto Rico, Jamaica, Trinidad,

Barbados, the French Antilles) have established programs for family planning and birth control, but to date, the results are generally not encouraging. Whether due to the emphasis on *machismo* in Hispanic groups, or the pride in procreation of black societies, or the advantages that many parents feel stem from large families, or plain ignorance of birth control, most West Indian birth rates remain high, and the pressure of population continues to increase.

Another possible solution is a vast increase in the current rate of emigration. Again, however, there is little room for optimism. There is every evidence of conscious efforts to restrict the flow of West Indian immigrants not only in Europe, Anglo-America, and Latin America, but within the archipelago itself. The Dominicans have long-standing fears and legal barriers with reference to Haitian immigrants; Haitian and Jamaican migrations to Cuba have been halted; the Netherlands Antilles have halted the influx of the British and French territories and have actualy carried out some repatriation; Jamaica and Barbados forbid the entry of unskilled labor; Trinidad, much of whose population initially came from the Windwards and Leewards now has legal barriers against further entry. The only West Indian immigrants who are not discouraged are the skilled and professional groups, and this kind of "brain drain" is precisely what the archipelago does not need.

Finally, it is becoming increasingly apparent that a change in political ideology and status is not per se a solution to the discrepancy between population and economic production in the West Indies (Chapter 5). The switch to socialism in Cuba, to independence in Jamaica, to a "freely associated commonwealth" in Puerto Rico and to the status of *départments* in the French Antilles is not without importance, but it is not the answer to the deep-rooted demographic and economic problems of the West Indies.

Settlement Types and Patterns

Prior to emancipation, West Indian settlement patterns were relatively uncomplicated, and the variety of settlement types was limited (Chapter 3). Most of the population was concentrated on coastal lowlands and interior valleys, and the plantation village with its great house and slave quarters was the most common settlement type, particularly in the British and French colonies. In such colonies with a highly specialized plantation economy there was only one so-called city that served as the chief seaport, commercial center, and political capital. The wealthy British and French planters tended to avoid the city except for business, preferring to live in the great houses on their estates. Other types of nucleated settlements were the exception rather than the rule in the north European territories. There were a few Maroon villages in the Jamaican highlands, and a small number of upland communities stemming from early black freedman occupation as in Martinique. Along the coast, there was an occasional fishing village of poor whites and a few small port settlements used by the more removed plantations as transportation links with the capital, in preference to the nonexistent or poorly maintained roads. In the Hispanic territories where the plantation economy was less well developed and where the number of white peasants was larger than in the north European territories, there tended to be more peasant freehold villages. Also, in the Hispanic tradition, the city was more important as a residential focus for the upper classes and as a cultural center than in the British and French territories.

Emancipation and the subsequent population explosion initiated important changes in this simple settlement structure. In the north European territories, wherever possible, the former slaves abandoned the coastal estates for the unoccupied highlands, establishing an increasing number of black peasant communities. The importation of indentured servants led to the creation of other distinctive ethnic communities such as the East Indian villages of Trinidad. Increasing population pressure forced many peasant families to forego village life and seek out the scattered pockets of cultivable land in the more remote uplands, thus creating a dispersed pattern of individual peasant farmsteads on many islands. In the Hispanic territories, where emancipation came during a period of plantation expansion (Chapter 3), settlement change was of a different order. Poor whites could not compete for land with the expanding plantation on the coast and continued to retreat to the highlands or to less desirable swampy lands. Later, settlement patterns everywhere in the archipelago were further complicated, first by the emergence of new economies such as bauxite mining in Jamaica and oil refining in Trinidad, and most recently, by a surging country-to-town movement of population.

Urbanization. The most dramatic current impact on West Indian settlement stems from the migration of the rural population to the urban centers, particularly to the chief city in each territory. Precisely when and why this movement began is still subject to controversy. There was a limited shift of rural population to the towns at various times earlier in this century, especially in Cuba, but the movement became large-scale only since World War II. The causes of this rampant urbanization in the West Indies, as in other sectors of Latin America and the underdeveloped world, are not convincingly clear. Those that are most frequently cited include:

1. The uprooting of resident workers on large estates as a result of mechanization, change in land use, or landowners' fears of future claim of squatter's rights by the workers.

2. The increasing tempo of industrialization and other urban economic activities in the cities.

3. The greater concentration of schools, hospitals, and other social service facilities in the urban centers.

4. The role of the city as a first step in overseas emigration.

5. The twin psychological force exerted by the pull of the city's bright lights and the push of poverty and boredom in the countryside, particularly on the young.

None of these and other causes that are mentioned provide a wholly rational explanation for the urbanizing phenomenon in the West Indies. For example, it is true that some industrialization is taking place, but with the possible exception of Puerto Rico, industry is not creating enough new jobs to warrant the large influx of unskilled labor from the countryside.

Regardless of cause, however, many of the consequences of West Indian urbanization are abundantly clear. Even though the criteria for the census classification of the urban-rural ratio of the population are not uniform throughout the archipelago, it is obvious that the ratio is changing rapidly in favor of the urban segment everywhere. In Puerto Rico, for example, the percentage of the population classified as urban jumped from 30 in 1940 to over 50 in 1970, and it continues to rise so rapidly that the island's 100-mile north coast may soon merge into a megalopolis. Despite efforts by Castro's regime to stem the flow to the cities, three-fifths of Cuba's population is currently considered urban. The Barbadian census still classifies the bulk of its population as rural, but this is because only the population of the city of Bridgetown *proper* is listed as urban. In fact, the urban sprawl of *metropolitan* Bridgetown continues beyond the political boundaries of the city and includes almost half of the island's population.

One spinoff of the changing urban-rural ratio in the West Indies is an actual decrease of population in some of the rural areas of numerous islands, including most of the Lesser Antilles, Puerto Rico, and Cuba. The drop in rural population often creates labor shortages in the countryside even though the cities have serious unemployment. In extreme cases, such as the British Virgin Islands and Puerto Rico, the scarcity of labor results in shifting land use from crop production to a less intensive use such as grazing.

The most obvious consequence of urbanization is, of course, the rapid growth of cities. In 1950 the archipelago counted only seven cities with a population of over 100,000, and three of these were in Cuba. By 1970, there were at least 12 such cities (Figure 5.4), and the number would be greater if centers such as Marianao in Cuba or Bayamon and Carolina in Puerto Rico were counted separately instead of being lumped together into the metropolitan areas of Havana and San Juan. But while urban growth has been relatively widespread, not every city and town in the West Indies has grown at the same rate. In certain territories such as Puerto Rico (Table 5.2), a few of the smaller cities and towns have actually experienced a net loss of population. The most dramatic growth has taken place in the primary or largest urban center of each territory. In fact, the urban explosion in the West Indies as elsewhere in Latin America, has been largely a phenomenon of the primate city.[3]

---

3. By general definition, a primate city is one whose population is at least two times greater than that of the second largest city and is frequently greater than the combined population of a country's next three largest cities. The index of primacy is a measure of the extent to which the primate city predominates over the next three largest centers. It is derived from the equation $I_p = \dfrac{P_1}{P_2 + P_3 + P_4}$ in which I_p is the index of primacy and P_1, P_2, P_3, and P_4 are the populations of the four largest cities.

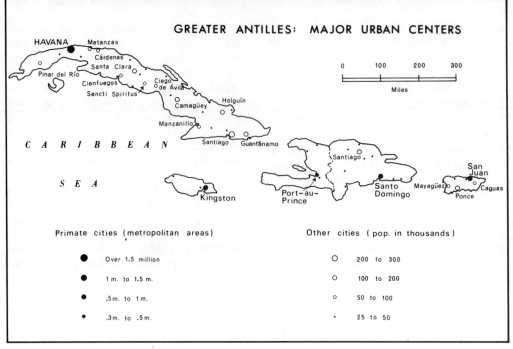

Figure 5.4   Greater Antilles: Major urban centers

Table 5.2   POPULATION CHANGES IN PUERTO RICAN CITIES, 1960–1970

	1960	1970	Percentage of Change
METROPOLITAN AREA			
San Juan (proper)	451,658	454,705	+0.7
Bayamon	72,221	154,440	+114
Carolina	40,923	107,988	+163
Trujillo Alto	18,251	30,351	+66
Guaynabo	39,718	65,557	+65
OTHER SELECTED MUNICIPALITIES			
Ponce	145,586	156,498	+7
Mayaguez	83,850	86,267	+3
Lares	26,922	24,897	−7
Ciales	18,106	15,422	−9

Source: West Indies and Caribbean Yearbook, 1973.

Primate Cities. In every West Indian territory the metropolitan area of the primary urban center has a population greater than those of the next three largest centers. This was generally true even before World War II, but in recent decades the extent or index of primacy has risen sharply, in part because the country-to-town movement has often bypassed secondary urban centers in favor of the primary one. Equally significant, the outward expansion of the primate city has frequently resulted in the absorbing of smaller nearby cities into its metropolitan area. For example, the city proper of San Juan, Puerto Rico, consists of the old nucleus on San Juan Island plus the adjacent communities of Santurce and Rio Piedras. In the process of urban growth, however, the once-rural areas that separated San Juan from surrounding municipalities such as Carolina, Bayamon, and Guaynabo have been filled in and now form the contiguous urban zone of metropolitan San Juan. As may be inferred from Table 5.2, the population flow toward Puerto Rico's primate city has been on such a vast scale that San Juan proper is no longer able to contain it. After absorbing almost 100,000 people between 1950 and 1960, the city proper became virtually saturated. In the 1960–1970 decade the flow spilled into other municipalities of the metropolitan area; the growth rate of San Juan proper was reduced to less than 1 percent, while that of nearby cities such as Bayamon and Carolina jumped more than 100 percent. Also indicative of the predominance of the San Juan metropolitan area, the growth rate of Puerto Rico's second and third largest cities, Ponce and Mayaguez, was comparatively low, and smaller urban centers such as Lares and Ciales have been losing population in recent years. The primacy index of greater San Juan as compared with the island's next three largest cities was about 1.07 in 1950, 1.86 in 1960, and 2.4 in 1970.

The post–World War II population growth of other West Indian primate cities, particularly those in the Greater Antilles was almost of the same order as San Juan's. Between the early 1940s and (ca.) 1970, the population of greater Havana increased from less than 900,000 to two

million; and the populations of greater Kingston and Santo Domingo rose by 100 percent or more. Both the index of primacy and the percentage of a territory's total population concentrated in the primate city vary (Table 5.3), but the average for both is exceptionally high throughout the archipelago. In 1970, for example, the primate city accounted for one-fourth or more of the total population of every territory in the Greater Antilles except Hispaniola. In addition to population, the West Indian primate city (like its counterpart elsewhere) tends to attract to itself a disproportionately large share of a territory's wealth, political power, professional talent, skilled labor, and health, education, and other social services. Whether it be doctors, plumbers, or politicians, the primate city often has a surplus while the rest of the territory has an inadequate supply.

Not unexpectedly, urbanization that creates this sort of imbalance also generates an array of problems. Frequently, the primate city fails to relate to the rural areas and small urban centers of the territory which it is supposed to serve; it consumes, often conspicuously, more of the country's wealth than it produces; and it charges a high price in human misery to those who are pouring in from the coun-

Table 5.3   SELECTED POPULATION CHARACTERISTICS OF
PRIMATE CITIES IN THE GREATER ANTILLES, CA. 1970

City (metropolitan area)	Population (in thousands)	Percentage of Country's Total Population	Index of Primacy
Havana, Cuba	2,335	30	3.3
San Juan, Puerto Rico	813	27	2.4
Santo Domingo, Dominican Republic	671	15	2.8
Port-au-Prince, Haiti	386	6	3.9
Kingston, Jamaica	506	27	3.9

Sources: America en Cifras, 1972, and official censuses and yearbooks.

tryside. Most of the flow from the rural areas consists of poor, unskilled worker families who cannot afford adequate housing. They are either forced to crowd together in old, dilapidated buildings with an entire family often living in a single room, or they construct makeshift housing on tidal flats or patches of steep hillside. The result is that, in varying degree, festering urban slums have become characteristic of every West Indian primate city. Such slums always generate a host of sociological problems, but in some cities (Santo Domingo, Kingston, and Port-au-Prince, for example) their deprived occupants are a potential threat to political stability. There is not much hope of rapidly eradicating slum conditions either. In Puerto Rico, which has been the most successful territory in attacking urban problems, it has been estimated that the annual decline of slum population has been averaging less than one-half of one percent, a rate which, if unchanged, guarantees the continuation of the slum for another 200 years.

Other problems triggered by the rapid growth of the West Indian primate city include inadequate supplies of water, sewage disposal facilities, and in a few cases, even environmental contamination from industrial wastes. In Puerto Rico, for example, the Condado Lagoon in San Juan is so contaminated with sewage from surrounding apartment houses and hotels that it is no longer safe either for swimming or for fishing; and near Ponce wastes from the new petrochemical industries are blighting vegetation and killing fish along the shoreline.

Many problems of West Indian primate cities are compounded by conditions inherent in their history and geographic settings. Most of the present cities began as small port towns in the sixteenth and seventeenth centuries when the primary considerations were defense and safe anchorage for sailing ships. With a few exceptions, such as Havana and San Juan,

they were established on the leeward sides of the island for protection from the trade winds. The typical site was on the shore of an embayment protected on the landward sides by commanding hills on which forts overlooking the sea approaches were built. Houses in the town, whether of stone or timber, huddled together along narrow, winding streets which could be more easily defended in case attackers breached the outer defense perimeter. Such town sites and internal structures were well suited to the sea transport needs, the small population, and the limited urban functions of the colonial period, but they are frequently inadequate in terms of current conditions and needs. The narrow streets of the old town core are ill suited to the automobile traffic of the twentieth century. Urban expansion in answer to the influx of more people or new industry is frequently limited to coastal flats which may be poorly drained, or it must make a costly upslope push into the surrounding hills (Figure 5.5). The same hills increase the cost of road construction from the city to the interior and oblige modern airports to locate at a considerable distance from the city center.

Other West Indian urban centers may face less of a challenge than the primate cities, but they are also less well equipped to meet the challenge. The disproportionate concentration of a territory's wealth, political power, and social services in the chief urban center inevitably shortchanges the smaller cities and towns. Whether it be government allocations for new schools, roads, and public housing, or the location of new industry or attracting tourists, the smaller urban communities get far less than their share. As a result, many of these communities are stagnating and even declining. Since they cannot compete with the primate city in providing new jobs, education, and other attractions, they often lose their most ambitious youths, their professionals, and other human talent to the lure of the "big town."

Figure 5.5   Guadeloupe: Pointe à Pitre, capital and chief seaport *(French Government Tourist Office)*

Figure 5.6   Haiti: Tiny peasant village in the highlands *(Delta Airlines)*

Rural Settlement. The postemancipation changes in the West Indies resulted in some modification of rural settlement patterns and types, but they did not lessen the traditional influence of commercial agriculture. On the smaller, more densely populated plantation islands such as Barbados, the emancipated blacks had no choice but to continue to live on or near the sugar estates; there was no mountainous interior with unoccupied lands to which they could move. Elsewhere, as in Jamaica, the freedmen left the estates to establish themselves in freehold communities in the highlands, but their economic dependency on the lowland estates continued.

Currently, the most widespread rural settlement types in the archipelago include:

1. The dispersed peasant farmstead, which is generally found in the uplands or in scattered areas of poorer soils in the lowlands.

2. The traditional plantation settlement always associated with the lowlands.

3. Peasant freehold villages in the mountains (Figure 5.6) or in the foothills along roads

leading to the lowland plantations, as in Jamaica.

4. Coastal fishing villages.

5. Settlements, whether dispersed or nucleated, associated with large highland coffee or tobacco farms and consisting of landless sharecroppers, as in Puerto Rico.

Whether a territory's settlement is widely dispersed or heavily concentrated depends on a variety of conditions including land tenure systems, population pressure, transportation networks, and other considerations. Unless the landless peasant is able to squat on public land, his only option is to live in worker villages on the sugar plantations or in sharecropper villages on the coffee estates. Even the land-owning peasant who can live on his own plot or in freehold villages is affected by the need for part-time work on the plantation or elsewhere. As already noted (Chapter 4), West Indian peasant plots are so small and of such poor quality that they rarely provide an independent livelihood for their owners. At best, the small peasant freeholder is a part-time farmer on his own land. He has to spend the remainder of his time working on the lowland plantation or on government road projects or in some other capacity to supplement the puny income from his plot. For this reason much of the peasant settlement in the archipelago forms linear patterns along the roads leading to the plantations or to other supplementary sources of work. Many coastal fishing villages are also "plantation oriented." Like the peasant in the hills, the coastal fisherman cannot make an independent living and must seek additional work elsewhere, and the nearby plantation is often the sole source of such work.

GEOPOLITICAL
PATTERNS AND PROBLEMS

The West Indies have been a colonial area *par excellence.* Few areas in the world have been more selfishly exploited for the benefit of outsiders; fewer still have as long a record of political vassalage; and no region of comparable size has been disputed by such an array of foreign powers or has had a more peculiarly international history. With the exception of Portugal, every European country that competed for colonies in the New World flew its flag in the West Indies. Some of these foreign flags, including that of the United States, are still in evidence, like symbolic reminders of past and present colonialism.

From the Discovery to the end of the nineteenth century, most of the important political decisions bearing on the West Indies were made in western European capitals such as those of Spain, England, France, and Holland. During this period, the islands were variously perceived by European statesmen as a new frontier for settlement and imperial expansion, as a network of bases for guarding the lifelines of empire, and as a trading area to be exploited for the benefit of the "mother" country. Later, much of the initiative for decision-making in the Caribbean shifted to Washington, D.C., where it still remains. Americans have also had various perceptions of the West Indies and the Caribbean in general. Chief among these are views of the region as:

1. A natural "Mediterranean," a "soft underside" vulnerable to foreign attack, whose control is vital to the defense of the United States.

2. A logical area for trade and investment, and a source of tropical products.

3. An area of political instability which has to be carefully patrolled lest it flare up in revolutions inimical to United States interests.

In retrospect, regardless of historical period or of the external locus of political control, colonialism in the West Indies seems to correlate most closely and persistently with two conditions. The first is the region's economic geography whose foundation, as already implied, rests largely on climate and soils suitable for the production of tropical crops, on a location that makes the area easily accessible to ocean transportation, and on a combination of climate and location suitable for attracting tourists and for easy access to the rich markets of the United States. The second condition that correlates with colonialism is the region's strategic geography, discussed below. It should be stressed, however, that West Indian colonialism has been determined not so much by nature and geography as by history and culture. "It is nurture, not nature, which has produced . . . the Balkanization of regional government . . ." (Lewis 1968:18) and the political oppression of the West Indies.

Strategic Geography

The strategic importance of the Caribbean stems from its geographic proximity to the United States and from its function as a funnel for trade and communications flows between the Atlantic and Pacific oceans, North and South America, and the east and west coasts of Anglo-America, especially the United States. The eastern rim of the Caribbean Sea is formed by the curve of the Antillean archipelago, which, for strategic purposes, may be likened to a fence separating the Gulf-Caribbean area from the Atlantic (Figures 5.7 and 5.8). This fence has gateways of varying size through which sea lanes pass. The most important of these gateways are, from north to south, the Straits of Florida, the Yucatan Channel between Cuba and Mexico's Yucatan Peninsula, the Windward Passage between Cuba and Haiti, the Mona Passage between the Dominican Republic and Puerto Rico, the Virgin Passage lying between the tiny island of Culebra (Puerto Rico) and the American Virgin Islands, and the Anegada Passage between the islands of Anegada and Sombrero. Several smaller and less important channels, including the Serpent's Mouth between Trinidad and Venezuela, occur further south in the Lesser

Figure 5.7   Greater Antilles: Sea gates and United States installations

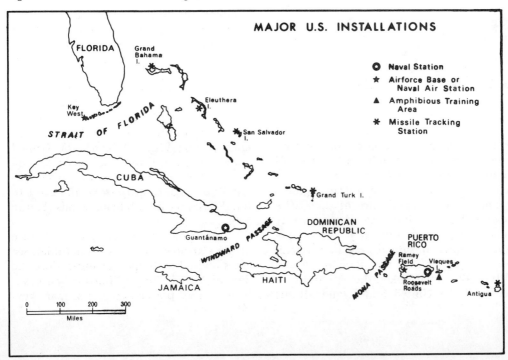

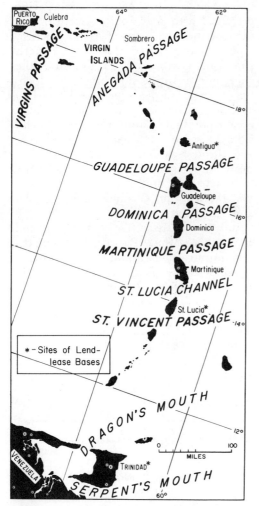

Figure 5.8　　Lesser Antilles: Sea gates and World War II lend-lease bases

Antilles (Figure 5.8). Control of these sea gates, of course, is tantamount to control of the sea-borne movements between the Atlantic and the Gulf-Caribbean region.

The strategic significance of the Caribbean and the Antillean sea gates, already at a high point in the early colonial period (Chapter 3), surged even higher with the completion of the Panama Canal (1914). The canal linked the east and west coasts of the United States (and all the Americas) with cheap ocean transportation; it shortened the distances to the Orient and Europe from the American east and west coasts respectively; and it vastly increased the sea trade from other parts of the world through the Caribbean "funnel." While virtually the entire world benefited from the seaway, it was ultimately the United States that derived the greatest advantages from it. The Panama Canal was not only a boon to American transportation and trade, it also increased the mobility of all but the largest warships of the United States fleet and reduced the need for a two-ocean navy.

Safeguarding the Panama Canal became of such paramount importance to the United States that steps for its defense were taken even before its completion in 1914. Since the defense of the eastern approaches to this vital waterway rested in large measure on the control of the Antillean sea gates, the United States made every effort to assure their control by a network of bases. The Straits of Florida could be guarded by bases on the American mainland. Following the Spanish American War, bases were established in Guantanamo, Cuba, and in Puerto Rico to assure the control of the Windward and the Mona Passages respectively. Control of the Virgin and Anegada Passages was assured a few years after the completion of the canal by the purchase of the (American) Virgin Islands from Denmark in 1917. Significantly, when German submarine warfare threatened the Caribbean sea lanes during World War II, the United States moved to shut even the smaller sea gates in the Lesser Antilles by giving Britain 50 overage destroyers for the right to build bases on British-held islands (Figure 5.8).

Some aspects of the strategic significance of the Caribbean and its West Indian sea gates undoubtedly have changed since the days of Alfred Thayer Mahan when naval bases and sea power were the primary keys to the defense of the Caribbean.[4] Since then, the strategic equation has been modified by the advent of air power, intercontinental ballistic missiles, and other new weapons and concepts of warfare. Yet, the geographic factors underlying the Caribbean's strategic significance have not changed. If anything, air power and missiles increase the region's geographic proximity to the United States and, by inference, increase its strategic significance. (President Kennedy risked all-out war to eliminate the threat of Soviet missile bases in Cuba.) The amount of sea trade moving through the Panama Canal and the Antillean sea gates is greater than ever. In fact, partly because the present canal is too small to handle large tankers and other craft and partly because of increasing traffic and security considerations, explorations preliminary to the possible construction of an additional canal are well under way.

Safeguarding the Panama Canal and controlling the Antillean sea gates do not,

of course, encompass the total strategic importance of the Caribbean to United States security interests. American policy has given almost equal priority to warding off the real or imagined threat of a great power or combination of powers becoming established in the region and to maintaining "safe" political regimes in the area. Two of the more recent expressions of this policy are the firm measures taken by President Kennedy to eliminate Soviet missile bases in Cuba and President Johnson's decision to land troops in the Dominican Republic to forestall a possible take-over by leftist groups. Significantly, the Monroe Doctrine, which has been used to justify United States intervention in all of Latin America, has been primarily applied to those countries that border on the Gulf-Caribbean region.

But whether strategically or economically motivated, colonialism is still rampant in the West Indies. Even those territories that fly their own flag and are supposedly independent live with the ever-present threat of intervention by a non-Caribbean power. More important, the entire region is economically so vulnerable to external markets that its political freedom of action is in danger of being compromised.

4. Alfred Thayer Mahan (1840–1914) was perhaps the most articulate and influential spokesman for American strategic interests in the Caribbean in the decades preceding the completion of the Panama Canal. His writings provide the springboard for many of the policies which precipitated the Spanish American War and resulted in the acquisition of American bases in the Antilles, the United States construction of the Panama Canal, and the record of American intervention in the region. In an article entitled "The United States Looking Outward," Mahan argued that the completion of the Panama Canal would represent "nothing but a disaster to the United States, in the present state of her military and naval preparation." In a second article, "The Strategic Features of the Gulf of Mexico and the Caribbean Sea," he assessed the importance of the West Indies and their sea gates, and developed his version of the analogy between the Mediterranean and Caribbean Seas. Although he did not coin the phrase "American Mediterranean," he gave it the geopolitical significance which, for many, it continues to have to this day. (Mahan 1898:1–27; 269–314).

Transition to
Current Political Status

The nineteenth-century collapse of the colonial plantation and the abolition of slavery had widespread economic and social ramifications in the West Indies, but they had little effect on the region's political status quo. Only Haiti, the Dominican Republic, and later, Cuba, had achieved a nominal independence. In the rest of the archipelago, political control continued to rest in the hands of non-Caribbean powers. The vast majority of the West Indians, whether black former slaves as in Jamaica or poor Spanish whites as in Cuba and Puerto Rico, had little voice and less vote in the political process. To the extent that local political power existed anywhere in the archipelago, it was held by a tiny, local elite which, even in Haiti, boasted of a lighter skin than the masses.

Among West Indians, particularly those of the poorer classes which include a high percentage of blacks, there developed a tendency to blame the largely white upper classes, the foreign corporations, and the non-Caribbean powers for the plight of their communities. This feeling gradually intensified class and racial frictions, and gave rise to a growing demand for greater political autonomy and a stronger voice for the masses. Popular unrest in search of such goals was generally frustrated until the post–World War II period. Since then, universal suffrage has been accepted, at least in theory, everywhere; government, which used to be the privilege of the lighter-skinned upper classes, has fallen increasingly under popular control; and former colonies have reached a variety of accommodations with the metropolitan powers that ruled them.

As a result of these changes and accommodations, the current variety of West Indian political forms and processes verges on the bewildering (Table 5.4). Seven of the territories are independent. Of these, four (Jamaica, Barbados, Trinidad, and the Bahamas) are members of the British Commonwealth; one (Cuba) belongs to the Communist block; and all are members of the Organization of American States except Cuba and the Bahamas. Although each of the seven independent countries claims to be a democracy based on universal suffrage, the elective process prompts skepticism in the Dominican Republic and is meaningless in Haiti and Cuba, which are essentially dictatorships.

Table 5.4   POLITICAL STATUS OF THE WEST INDIES, 1970

I. British-connected units
  A. Independent members of British commonwealth
    1. Jamaica
    2. Trinidad-Tobago
    3. Barbados
    4. Bahamas
  B. West Indies Associated States *
    1. Antigua
    2. Dominica
    3. St. Lucia
    4. St. Vincent
    5. St. Kitts
    6. Grenada
  C. Colonies (varied local autonomy)
    1. British Virgin Islands
    2. Montserrat
    3. Turks and Caicos Islands
    4. Cayman Islands

II. United States–connected units
  A. Associated commonwealth
    1. Puerto Rico
  B. Unincorporated territory
    1. U.S. Virgin Islands

III. French–connected units
  A. Overseas Départments of France
    1. Martinique
    2. Guadeloupe

IV. Dutch–connected units
  A. Member of Tri-partite Kingdom of the Netherlands
    1. Netherlands Antilles
      (a) Aruba
      (b) Bonaire
      (c) Curaçao
      (d) St. Martin
      (e) St. Eustatius
      (f) Saba
  V. Other (independent)
    A. Cuba
    B. Haiti
    C. Dominican Republic

* Although each of the territories is officially designated as "The Associated State of _____," the association is not a federated unit. Each state is separately associated with Britain.

The will of the total electorate is adequately expressed only in the four British Commonwealth countries.

It is the political status of the non-independent territories which really taxes the vocabulary. The Netherlands Antilles are incorporated (with Surinam) in the tri-partite Kingdom of the Netherlands; French Martinique and Guadeloupe (and their respective smaller island dependencies) constitute two overseas departments of metropolitan France. The *Estado Libre Asociado de Puerto Rico,* designated in English as a commonwealth "freely associated" with the United States, has local autonomy. Most of the Leeward and Windward Islands are similarly autonomous in association with the United Kingdom. The remaining British-connected units, such as the Cayman Islands, are colonies whose rule rests largely in the hands of the British Colonial Office.

The causal factors for this political variety defy analysis in detail, but a few generalizations are possible. Former colonies whose size, resources, economy, and total population could meet even the barest viability requirements for separate existence have become politically independent. The major exception to this trend is Puerto Rico, which has a comparatively large population and a well-developed economy. In recent decades, the people of Puerto Rico have achieved a wide measure of local autonomy but, to date, have chosen to avoid the potential economic hardship of independence and the cultural pitfalls of requesting statehood from the United States Congress (Chapter 6). The territories that cannot meet the minimum requirements to be viable as independent countries have made other adjustments. The French and Dutch units made the choice to become politically integrated with their respective metropolitan powers, while the British-connected smaller islands are struggling to find a suitable solution

by working for increased local autonomy without abandoning the protection and aid afforded by Britain.

The Outlook for Stability and Cooperation

The process of political adjustment in the West Indies is not over. Unrest and uncertainty are actually increasing in much of the region. For example, few consider the present commonwealth form of government in Puerto Rico to be the final solution to the question of political status. Most observers agree that sooner or later Puerto Ricans must decide either for independence or for statehood. In the meantime, political status continues to be the most controversial issue in every insular election, and political violence among students and other dissident groups is on the increase.

Virtually everywhere in the region, politics are becoming increasingly viewed in light of race and class conflict. In some of the British-connected territories militant Black Power groups are not only demanding a stronger voice in the government but are also pushing for local control of commercial enterprises traditionally owned by foreign interests. Racial militancy against foreign economic enterprises and the traditional "establishment" surfaced in Trinidad in early 1970, and several months of disorder followed. When the government declared a state of emergency, junior officers in the Trinidad Regiment mutinied. The mutiny was quelled, but the incident undoubtedly struck a sympathetic note among black and other militants in the Caribbean.

In varying degree, heightened race and class consciousness also affect the electoral process, especially in the non-Hispanic territories. A candidate's political party or the ideology he professes are often less important in capturing votes than the color of his skin or his social class association. Regardless of party sponsorship, a black running against an East Indian in a dominantly East Indian ward of Trinidad has little chance of success. There is no law barring a white upper-class Jamaican from running for political office, but the obstacles he faces are virtually insurmountable.

"West Indianization," often defined in racial terms, seems to be a policy and a goal everywhere except on the French islands. In the territories where the population is predominantly black, no head of government dares to make many white appointments for fear of antagonizing his constituents. Elsewhere, as in Puerto Rico, posts in the University and other public institutions once occupied by Americans are being filled by Puerto Ricans.

But neither race consciousness nor West Indianization policies nor a history of colonial rule by the same metropolitan power has created a widespread sense of common identity among the various insular communities of the West Indies. The past is strewn with the failures of schemes devised by the ruling metropolitan powers aimed at achieving some measure of regional cooperation and unity. For instance, the efforts of Britain's Colonial Office to unite all British colonies in the region into an independent West Indies Federation were frustrated in the 1950s by the economic self-interests of Jamaica and Trinidad. Another failure was the Caribbean Commission (later called the Caribbean Organization) whose creation was due primarily to the initiative of Britain, France, the Netherlands, and the United States. Those who are optimistic about the future of West Indian cooperation point to the establishment of CARIFTA (Chapter 4) and to increasing evidence of a Pan-Caribbean movement. West Indian writers, for example, have begun a marked pursuit of West Indian themes, and several professional groups are organizing themselves into loose associations that cut across territorial boundaries. It remains, however, that to date the notion of Pan-Caribbeanism is restricted primarily to a small minority of intellectuals and professional persons. Among the masses and even among the new breed of black leaders there is still no strong sense of a West Indian identity shared in common with all the peoples of the archipelago.

There may be obvious advantages to West Indian regional cooperation and unity, but there are also formidable barriers: (1) the islands are spread over a distance of more than 2,000 miles; (2) communications, although improving, are still poor; (3) the people are of differing religion, language, and outlook as a result of their different histories; (4) the rate of economic progress achieved varies from one territory to another; (5) some of the islands are densely populated and poverty stricken, and the less crowded and more economically developed islands fear that they would be swamped by migrants from the former; (6) the insular economies tend to be competitive rather than complementary; and (7) the archipelago is characterized by important differences in political forms, processes, and ideologies. Under the circumstances, it is difficult to foresee the development of a strong sense of community and an urge to unity in the immediate future.

SELECTED REFERENCES

COOMBS, O. "West Indians in New York." *New York Magazine* (July 13, 1970), pp. 28–32.

DE BRUIJNE, G. A. "Surinam and the Netherlands Antilles: Their Place in the World." *Geografisch Tijdschrift* 5, no. 4 (1971).

FRANCO, J. L. *Presence Africaine au Nouveau Monde*. Dakar, Senegal: University de Dakar, 1967.

LEWIS, G. K. *The Growth of the Modern West Indies*. New York: Monthly Review Press, 1968.

LEWIS, L. A. "Spatial Properties of Population Mobility within Puerto Rico." *Journal of Tropical Geography* 29 (1969).

LEWIS, S., and MATHEWS, T. G., eds. *Caribbean Integration*. Río Piedras: University of Puerto Rico, 1967.

LOWENTHAL, D. "Race and Color in the West Indies," *Daedalus* 96, no. 2 (1967).

———. *West Indian Societies*. New York: Oxford University Press, 1972.

MAHAN, A. T. *The Interest of America in Sea Power, Present and Future*. Boston: Little, Brown, 1898.

MITCHELL, H. *Contemporary Politics and Economics in the Caribbean*. Athens: Ohio University Press, 1968.

PEACH, C. *West Indian Migration to Britain: A Social Geography*. London: Oxford University Press, 1968.

PEREZ DE LA RIVA, J. "La Population de Cuba et Ses Problemes." *Population* 22 (1967).

PERON, Y. "La Population des Départments Francais d'Outre-Mer." *Population* 21, no. 1 (1966).

TAMBS, L. A. "Latin American Geopolitics: A Basic Bibliography." *Revista Geografica*, December 1970.

THOMAS, R. N., ed. *Population Dynamics of Latin America: A Review and Bibliography*. East Lansing, Mich.: CLAG Publications, no. 2, 1973.

WELCH, B. "Population Density and Emigration in Dominica." *Geographical Journal* 134, Part 2 (1968).

≡ 6 ≡

The West Indies:
The Hispanic Territories and Haiti

Despite current differences in political ideologies, stage of economic development, and other conditions that affect their national life styles, the Hispanic territories of the West Indies continue to share much in common. The cultural landscapes of Cuba, Puerto Rico, and the Dominican Republic still carry the unmistakable imprint of their Spanish origins. It is reflected by place names, the architecture of public buildings, the plaza patterns of the towns, the patio-focus and grilled iron work of many residences, and countless other details. Although the population of these Hispanic territories includes a significant number of blacks, especially in the Dominican Republic, the racial root stock, like the language, is of Spanish origin. To the extent that a religious ethic and a "national character" are present in the three societies, they have a traditional Roman Catholic Spanish flavor, even among those Puerto Ricans who have become Protestants or among Cuban Communists who may view religion as the opiate of the people.

In contrast, the people, landscape, and culture of contemporary Haiti carry only vague reminders of the country's original European colonists. Much of the French influence was consciously obliterated by the slave uprisings of the late eighteenth century when the blacks sought to destroy every vestige of the hated *blancs* (Chapter 3). Thus, bracketing Haiti with the Hispanic territories in this chapter can be justified primarily in terms of convenience. The only other justification is that many of Haiti's fortunes (and misfortunes) in the last four centuries have been closely linked with those of its neighbor, the Dominican Republic.

Cuba and Puerto Rico have run surprisingly parallel courses through much of their post-Columbian history, even though the role of the larger island (Cuba) has been more important. Both were among the first colonies established by Spain in the Caribbean. Through the early colonial history both served as springboards for the exploration of the Mainland and as island fortresses guarding the sea lanes between the mother country and the richer settlements on the Mainland. Except for these functions, however, neither island was given much importance by Spain following the conquest of Mexico and Peru; and the growth of population and economy was consequently retarded in the two colonies.

While sugar and slaves were introduced in Cuba and Puerto Rico in the sixteenth century, neither island experienced an early plantation development comparable to the English and French West Indies colonies. Until the nineteenth century, the limited economy of both islands remained essentially subsistent. Grazing, food crops, and small quantities of tobacco, sugar, and other cash crops were the mainstays of the largely white population.

In the first quarter of the nineteenth century, when Spain's Mainland colonies achieved independence, Cuba and Puerto Rico were left behind. Agitation for freedom swept both colonies, but their small size and insularity enabled Spain to retain control until the Spanish-American War (1898). Nevertheless, the long-delayed economic and population growth finally overtook the two colonies during the 1800s. The plantation became firmly established, and blacks came in large numbers, first as slaves and then as free workers. The economy became increasingly commercial— sugar and tobacco in Cuba; coffee, sugar, and tobacco in Puerto Rico.

Both islands became pawns in the Spanish-American War. Following the war, Cuba was granted a questionable independence, and Puerto Rico became a territory of the United States. This difference not withstanding, however, the economic and political destinies of both islands became intimately enmeshed with those of the United States.

On paper at least, the commercial economies of the two islands forged strongly ahead during the first part of the twentieth century. With preferential treatment in the rich United States market, the production of sugar, tobacco, and other cash crops expanded at a prodigious rate. This spelled wealth for a number of Cubans, Puerto Ricans, and foreign investors, but it left the growing masses of people on both islands far from satisfied with their lot.

Following World War II, the restive populations called for change. Both islands achieved change of a sort: Puerto Rico chose the road of political and economic evolution to improve the lot of its

people; Cuba followed the path of revolution. The destinies of the two islands seemed to have parted company.

CUBA

In the mid-1960s, it could be said that Cuba had become "an enigma with a beard." Fidel Castro's revolution and the swing to Communism had effectively closed the island to most foreign observers. Whatever information was available on insular developments tended to be skimpy, second-hand, and unreliable. Geographers and others familiar with pre-Castro conditions could do little more than speculate about changes that were being wrought by the revolution.

Recently, Cuba seems less enigmatic. A growing number of outside observers are gaining entry into the island, and there is an encouraging increase in published analyses and data based on actual field studies. Unfortunately, the foreign observers that have had access to the island have included only a small number of Americans, and the authors of this book have not been among them. As a result, the following summary lacks the authority of direct field observation. It relies exclusively on published data in its outline of current changes, and it measures such changes primarily with the yardstick of pre-Castro conditions in Cuba.

Physical Setting

With an area of 44,218 square miles, Cuba is easily the largest of the Antilles. The long, narrow island stretches southeastward for almost 800 miles, from Cape San Antonio on the Yucatan Channel to Punta Maisí on the Windward Passage, and its width ranges between 25 and 120 miles. Cuba is the least mountainous of the Greater Antilles, and its soils are well

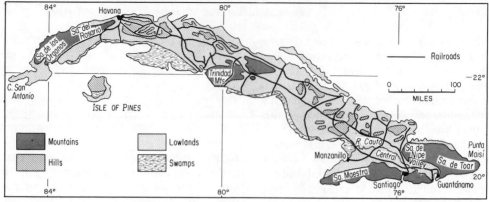

Figure 6.1   Cuba: Surface configuration and railroads

adapted to large-scale, machine agriculture. Most of the terrain consists of gentle slopes and lowlands which form the Peneplain of Cuba. This "almost plain" runs the length of the island and represents the final states of great erosional cycles that have reduced large limestone accumulations to gentle relief. There are three distinct mountain systems (Figure 6.1), all roughly oriented east–west and generally known in Cuba as the *oriental,* the *central,* and the *occidental.* In extent, altitude, mass, and complexity, the eastern system is the most striking.

The interaction of this generally moderate relief and the trades results in less contrast in precipitation than is found between the windward and leeward sides of the more mountainous Antilles. Rainfall ranges from over 65 inches annually in the Sierra de los Órganos and the Trinidad Mountains, to less than 40 around Guantánamo, in the rain shadow of the Sierra Maestra (Figure 6.2). No part of Cuba is truly deficient in moisture.

The historical and strategic values of Cuba's location have already been cited. The island sits astride three important narrows: the Straits of Florida, the Windward Passage, and the Yucatan Channel (see Figures 3.3 and 5.7). For much of the colonial period, Spain looked on Cuba (and especially Havana) as the "bulwark of the Indies" and "the key to the New World." The acquisition of Guantánamo Bay by the United States following the Spanish-American War was further recognition of the island's strategic position at the principal gates to the Gulf of Mexico and the Caribbean Sea.

Figure 6.2   Cuba: Soil groups and rainfall

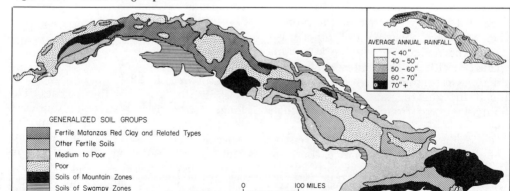

Cuba's location has also paid rich economic dividends. Within a radius of 1,500 miles from Havana lies the vast market of east-central United States, much of it accessible by cheap water transportation. Before Castro, this market absorbed virtually all of Cuba's tropical products and minerals. Proximity to a large group of well-heeled Americans also meant a tourist income of almost $100 million a year.

The island's ocean-borne commerce is aided by a highly articulated coastline. Because of its narrow width, no part of the island is far from one of the 200 harbors that dot the coast. Except for Matanzas and Cárdenas, all the principal harbors are pouch-shaped, and as a result, Cuba has an extraordinarily large number of well-protected anchorages.

Land and the Cuban Economy

Land Use. There are a few economic facts of life that even a profound socialist revolution have not changed in Cuba. Agriculture is still the heart of the insular economy, and sugar is still its commercial life blood. An abundance of land continues to be Cuba's outstanding natural resource, and the utilization of this resource is still governed by the interplay of physical conditions, market possibilities, and land tenure systems. The changes authored by Castro's revolutionary government since 1959 have had to adjust to these constants.

A favorable combination of climate, relief, and soils gives Cuba one of the highest ratios of cultivated to cultivable land in Middle America. Of the 28 million acres which constitute the island's total land area, approximately 5 million are under crop, 10 million are in meadow and pasture, and 3.2 million are under forest cover. If permissive physical conditions were the sole criterion, almost two-thirds of the island's land surface could be classified as arable.

In 1973 sugar cane occupied more land than it did in 1953, accounting for well over one-half of all the cultivated land in Cuba. No other single crop takes up as much as 10 percent, although food crops, including corn, yucca, plantains, beans, rice, yams, and others, account for about one-third of the land in crops. No significant percentage of the land is planted either in tobacco or in coffee. The amount of land in pasture indicates the importance of livestock, the practice of rotating pasture and cropland, and the conditions that have kept land use extensive rather than intensive.

Land Tenure

PRE-CASTRO TIMES. While the switch to socialism did not seriously affect the use of land, it radically altered its ownership. Cuba's land tenure patterns (and other economic earmarks) when Castro came to power smacked strongly of the heyday of American capitalism on the island (1900–1959). As the nearest and most accessible of the low-latitude lands to the United States, Cuba had become a convenient source of tropical farm products and other raw materials for the American market and a reciprocal buyer of American finished goods. On the eve of the revolution, the United States supplied an average of three-fourths of the island's imports and absorbed almost four-fifths of its exports. This relation gave the island favorable access to the world's richest marketplace and to a large supply of development capital, but it also entailed some serious disadvantages. Cuba's dependence on its northern neighbor verged on being slavish. Everything from food, machinery, and lipstick to airplanes and roller skates came neatly wrapped from the United States and was expensive. The exploitation of Cuba's land resources, which was determined by the needs of the American market, became grossly uneven, and the unbalanced economic posture that resulted was a classic illustration of monoculture. Heavy emphasis on the production of a few profitable commercial crops, such as sugar, retarded agricultural diversification; the pressure to buy American finished goods tended to discourage industrialization; and above all, ties with the United States helped intensify the spread of the plantation and the *latifundium,* with all their inherent drawbacks.

Although neither the *latifundium* nor the plantation was a twentieth-century innovation introduced by American investors in Cuba, both institutions were strengthened by such investment. Before 1900, the island still had a large number of small independent farms and family-size *ingenio* plantations. Land values, while higher than they had been before the increase in sugar production during the nineteenth century (Chapter 3), were moderate, particularly in the thinly settled eastern provinces. Squatting was widespread, and squatters were seldom evicted from private property. Landless peasants did not have a significant cash income, but under the easygoing paternalistic system of the times, money was not essential to survival.

Then came the Americans with their profitable market potential, their genius for corporate enterprise, and more than a billion dollars to invest in Cuba's sugar industry. The effects of this invasion on the island's land tenure structure and economy were revolutionary. Land values shot upward; the small owner was squeezed out; and the corporation, whether foreign or national, became the chief instrument of agricultural organization and land ownership. Many of the small farmers who lost or sold their holdings became *agregados* (hired hands). With the emergence of a highly specialized sugar plantation agriculture based on *latifundium* and efficient corporate management, Cuba was transformed into an industrial wage economy. This helped destroy the traditional paternalistic relation between landowner and worker; it made squatting more difficult

for the increasing number of landless peasants; and it pegged the well-being of the *guajiros* (peasants) to a money-wage. REVOLUTION AND REFORM. Castro's initial Agrarian Reform Law (May 17, 1959) was an emotional testament against foreign ownership, monopoly, and the *latifundium.* It provided that only Cubans could buy or inherit land, and it barred sugar manufacturers from operating their own plantations. The law also abolished sharecropping and prohibited private ownership of land of more than 400 hectares (988 acres). Privately owned land in excess of this limit as well as public property could be distributed in one of two ways: in the form of individual small holdings of no less than 67 acres, the "vital minimum" for a family of five persons; or through assignment to agricultural cooperatives whose establishment was to be strongly encouraged. The instrument for implementing these measures was the INRA (*Instituto Nacional de Reforma Agraria*). Later legislation, such as the second Agrarian Reform Law of 1963, reduced even further the legal size of private holdings and made state-owned and cooperative farms the principal form of land tenure on the island.

At present (early 1970s) less than one-third of Cuba's arable land is still privately owned and indications are that even this proportion will decrease in the future. The private farming sector consists of approximately 150,000 peasant holdings, most of which are 67 acres or less in size. Many of the peasant holders are former sharecroppers who qualify for a "vital minimum" grant of land under the 1959 Agrarian Reform Law. They continue to receive some help from the government, but are expected to sell part of their production to the government at less than market prices. Privately owned farms tend to emphasize the production of food crops, coffee, and tobacco.

The government sector of the Cuban agricultural economy encompasses roughly

70 percent of the land in farms and is represented by two principal types of holdings, *granjas*, or "people's estates," and sugar plantations. Both types consist for the most part of land expropriated from the large holdings of foreign corporations and Cuban landlords, and both are organized along the lines of the state and collective farm models of the Soviet Union. *Granjas* vary in size, but many encompass more than 50,000 acres. They produce small amounts of sugar cane, but the bulk of their production is diversified, including food, fodder, and industrial crops as well as meat. Although called people's estates, *granjas* are essentially state-owned farms whose profits go directly to the government. The permanent laborers are paid a fixed salary and may receive some supplies from the *granja's* production, but they may not cultivate garden plots or keep livestock. Like their Russian counterparts, *granjas* are provided with some machinery but must rent the rest from state rental agencies. They are managed by INRA-appointed administrators who must comply with production plans laid down by the government.

More important to Cuba's export economy is the sugar plantation type of holding. According to one Soviet observer (Semevsky 1967:12–25), these are organized on the basis of cooperatives and are highly specialized, with as much as 80 percent of their land in sugar cane. In most other respects, including management and planning goals, the sugar plantation is similar to the *granja*.

A less important type of land holding in the government sector is the *finca*, which Semevsky (1967) calls a "state farm." This type consists of relatively small farms abandoned by refugees from the Castro regime. Many such farms have already merged with *granjas*, suggesting that this type of holding may be a transitional one. Apparently, the future trend in Cuban land tenure under Castro will be toward the strengthening of government control, in-

cluding the remaining segment of land that is still in private hands.

Thus, the revolution has eliminated the foreign ownership of land and drastically reduced both the size of holdings and the total amounts of privately owned land. But to date, the revolution has not abolished either the *latifundium* or monopoly. It has merely transferred them from the private to the government sector.

Sugar

Environment and Diffusion. Sugar cane has been called "the grass of Cuba," and for good reason. The island possesses an almost ideal environment for growing the crop. It has large areas of level-to-gently-rolling land which facilitate harvesting and the rapid transportation of the cane; its tropical climate generally provides sufficient rainfall and the necessary dry season for the *zafra* (harvest); and the sugar lands are within easy distance of the coast with its numerous pouch-shaped harbors.

Despite these natural advantages, a combination of inadequate land transport, political instability, and other obstacles restricted sugar to a few select zones until 1900. The bulk of production was concentrated in the western part of the island, particularly in the provinces of Habana, Matanzas, and Las Villas. The larger, eastern end of the island was devoid of sugar, except for spotty development such as that along the coast southwest of Manzanillo and the Central Valley–Guantánamo Basin area of Oriente.

With the influx of American capital after 1900, Cuba's sugar frontier started to move out in all directions. Ultimately, however, its major direction became eastward, toward the unoccupied or thinly settled lands of Camagüey and Oriente provinces. There was some penetration into Pinar del Río, but there the Sierra de los Órganos, poor soils, and a high population density of small tobacco farmers

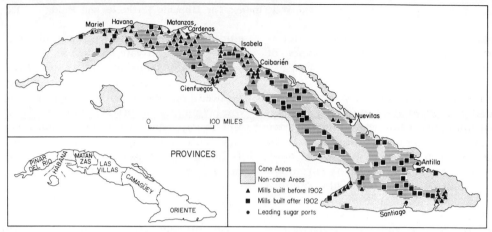

Figure 6.3   Cuba: Sugar lands and *centrales*

posed obstacles. Cane also was blocked from most of Cuba's south coast by widespread swamps or by the rugged relief of the Trinidad and Sierra Maestra ranges (Figure 6.1).

Sugar's initial thrust outward from its western center after 1900 generally followed the line of the productive Matanzas red clay soils to eastern Camagüey. These soils are deep (in places exceeding 25 feet), and are composed of residues from dissolved limestone. They are so fine-grained and permeable that, despite a clay content of 75 to 90 percent, they may be cultivated even after heavy rains. The Matanzas soils, which extend from Artemisa in Pinar del Río to Ciego de Ávila in Camagüey (Figure 6.2) provided the first avenue for cane's expansion and still account for fully one-third of Cuba's sugar production.

Relief and precipitation also played a significant part in the spread of sugar production across Cuba. As already indicated, cane was ruled out of mountain zones. Practically no cane took hold on elevations higher than 1,000 feet above sea level. Currently, over three-fourths of production is concentrated in areas below 300 feet, and gentle slopes, which assure good drainage without serious erosion, are preferred. As to rainfall, most cane areas on the island receive between 50 and 60 inches per year. When other conditions

are positive, cane may be grown where totals drop to as low as 40 inches.

Transportation Impact. The eastward push of the sugar frontier in Cuba not only authored the occupation of new lands and the intensification of the *latifundium* and plantation, it also carried with it waves of population and brought about the development of modern transportation facilities, mills, and other major features of the landscape. Of these, perhaps the most obvious were transportation and the *centrales* (Figures 6.1 and 6.3).

Under Spanish rule, Cuba's land transport system had grown little, and most of this growth coincided with the zones of denser settlement in the western provinces focusing on Havana. The spread of cane, which must be moved rapidly from field to mill, gave rise to a widespread rail network after 1900. At present, roughly two-thirds of Cuba's more than 9,000 miles of railroads consist of narrow-gauge tracks built directly by sugar corporations. The remainder were constructed by English and American capital attracted by the sugar boom. The much-maligned sugar interests gave Cuba the densest rail network in Latin America. Over 90 percent of the island's population are within hearing distance of a train whistle (Figure 6.1). If fewer highways than railways were built, one important explanation is that the sugar industry took less interest in automotive transport.

Centrales and Regions. The large sugar mills (*centrales*) are more than factories for grinding the crop. Before Castro, they functioned as mechanisms for owning land and controlling the *colonos,* as reference points for the transportation network, and as nerve centers for administering the total operations of the large sugar plantations. The amount of sugar land needed to feed the *centrales* varied, but the average mill owned (or controlled through *colonos*) about 40,000 acres, and the largest serviced 165,000 acres.

The *centrales* came into their own in Cuba after 1900. Prior to that, the island's cane was milled for the most part in moderate-sized, closely spaced *ingenios.* In 1860, for example, Cuba had about 2,000 such mills, but by 1900, the destruction ensuing from the Wars of Independence had reduced their number to 207. Only about 100 of the larger *ingenios* were subsequently retained, and most of these were in the old sugar areas of the western provinces (Figure 6.3).

The need for larger modern mills to facilitate the development of sugar production resulted in the construction of over 60 *centrales* between 1902 and 1927. Most were constructed by American companies on their newly acquired cane lands in Camagüey and Oriente in eastern Cuba. In contrast to the older, smaller, and largely Cuban-owned mills, which controlled relatively small plantations, the modern *centrales* built by foreign capital eventually controlled huge blocks of land.

During the 1950s, Cuba's sugar areas could be grouped into three major regions: (1) the eastern, consisting primarily of Camagüey and Oriente provinces; (2) the central, which focused on Las Villas; and (3) the western, which included the provinces of Matanzas, Habana, and Pinar del Río. These regions were serviced by more than 160 mills of varying size and age, and the bulk of their production was exported through 11 ports, the most important of which were Nuevitas in Camagüey and Santiago in Oriente. The eastern region, which was the most recently developed of the three, included most of the largest, foreign-owned *centrales.* In the central region, the mills were smaller, more numerous, and were owned primarily by Cubans. The western region included both small, Cuban-owned mills and large *centrales* constructed by outside companies.

Since 1959 the socialization of Cuba's sugar industry, its market reorientation from the United States to the USSR, eastern Europe, and Red China, and other developments have resulted in significant adjustments in the patterns of the island's sugar mills, ports and, to a lesser extent, its sugar regions. Numerous mills have been dismantled for spare parts. Most of the dismantled mills (such as Escambray in Las Villas province and La Francia in Pinar del Río) were in the central and western regions. Also noteworthy, virtually all the remaining mills have been renamed in keeping with new revolutionary values. Thus, *Amistad* became *Amistad de los Pueblos* ("Friendship of the People"); *Manatí* was renamed *Argelia Libre* ("Free Algeria"); and *Patria* became *Patria o Muerte* ("Fatherland or Death"—the battle cry of the revolution). Reflecting the antichurch bias of the revolution, all of the 27 mills that formerly carried the names of Catholic saints were "rebaptized." Most of the new names are in honor of Cuban revolutionary heroes, selected foreign liberators, and Latin American countries.[1]

1. Typical of the name changes are Trinidad (Trinity) to Federación Nacional de Obreros Azucareros; Conchita to Puerto Rico Libre; San Cristóbal to Jose Martí; Fajardo to Comandante Manuel Fajardo; Andorra to Abraham Lincoln. Also prominent among the new names are important dates commemorating the revolution (1 de Mayo, 10 de Octubre, and so on).

The most significant change in the sugar ports since the revolution is the emergence of the newly developed facilities at Guayabal on the coast of Camagüey province (Figure 6.4). The sugar hinterland of Guayabal stretches from northern Oriente to Jatibonico on the Las Villas–Camagüey border. Guayabal draws on the output of more than 20 mills and ranks as Cuba's leading sugar port. Second in importance is Matanzas, whose volume of sugar exports has vastly increased since 1959 primarily at the expense of Havana and Cárdenas. The increasing importance of both Guayabal and Matanzas is due in large measure to the installation of bulk-loading equipment. Nuevitas, once the leading sugar port of the island, now ranks third. Much of its former trade, like that of Manzanilla and Antilla, has been "captured" by Guayabal.

Changes in the pattern of mills and ports also coincide with some changes in the regional structure of Cuban sugar. Both the western and the central regions have experienced a relative decline in the production and export of raw sugar since 1959. The eastern region (Camagüey and Oriente provinces) has had a relative increase in importance for sugar since the revolution despite the closing of two small mills, one of which was near Guantánamo.

Problems and Production. Cuba's sugar economy was beset with a multiplicity of problems well before the change ushered by the socialist revolution added to its woes. It had been technologically stagnant ever since the middle of the 1920s. No new *central* had been constructed in Cuba after 1927, and, while existing mills were kept in repair before Castro, the equipment and techniques for grinding cane were not efficiently up-to-date. Also, before Castro the sugar industry had been plagued by a market fluctuation that had affected both production and national income. Sugar output rose rapidly during the first decades of this century, increasing from less than one-half million tons in 1900 to four million in 1919; it continued to be high until market saturation and the effects of the Great Depression caused a drop (from five million tons in 1930 to two million in 1933); and thereafter, output rose irregularly to an all-time high in 1952, only to tumble later.

Not unexpectedly, the revolution caused an almost fatal dislocation of Cuba's sugar economy. Rupture of trade and diplomatic

Figure 6.4   Cuba: Sugar lands and *centrales* served by ports of Guayabal, Matanzas, and Nuevitas

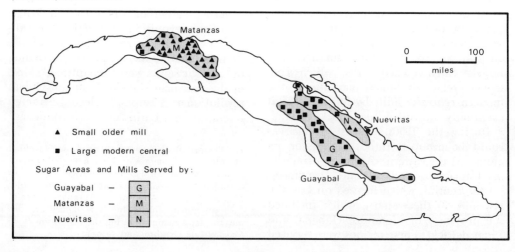

relations with the United States deprived the industry of its principal market and its chief source of capital, transportation equipment, spare parts for mill machinery, and the entire array of other equipment needed to produce and process the crop. In addition, the exit of American and Cuban technicians stripped the industry of most of its managerial and technical know-how. Only the prompt intervention of the Soviet Union and other Communist countries saved the sugar industry (and the entire Cuban economy) from total collapse.[2] New markets for the island's sugar (and other exports) were opened behind the "Iron Curtain"; Russian technicians and machinery were sent; and large subsidies and loans to bolster the Cuban economy were provided by the Soviet government.

But while Soviet help prevented collapse, it did not stabilize Cuba's sugar industry. Nor did it prevent serious planning errors by the politically motivated but economically inexperienced revolutionary regime. Production rose to slightly under 7 million tons in 1961 and then plummeted to less than 4 million in 1963. The drop was due to a variety of causes, including the reallocation of funds to other sectors of the economy in an effort to diversify and lessen the island's dependence on sugar. After this, the plans for economic diversification were modified, and emphasis was placed on dramatic increases in sugar production. For 1970, the unheard-of target of 10 million tons was announced, and Castro pledged the "honor of the revolution" to achieve it. Other sectors of the insular economy were temporarily neglected as every available Cuban (and even sympathetic American students of the *Venceremos* brigade) took to the fields during the 1970 *zafra*. One result was a record-breaking 8.5 million

ton harvest. Perhaps a more important result was Castro's realization that such high goals were unrealistic and could be achieved only at the cost of dislocating other sectors of the economy.

Other Cash Crops and Grazing

There are many crops other than sugar in Cuba, but they are of limited importance. Cane has so completely dominated land use during this century that other products, even when commercial in nature, have been relegated to lands considered unsuited for sugar plantation requirements. Since "big money" was interested solely in sugar before the revolution, production of other cash crops was left largely to the small landholders and the sharecroppers. Land use for subsistence food crops was at an even greater competitive disadvantage; the amount of land devoted to subsistence was large, but of poor quality. With some exceptions, grazing also was associated with the small holder and poor land.

The revolution wrought only minor changes in this pattern of land use and crop structure. True, sharecropping was abolished, and many once landless peasant families received "vital minimum" plots for the production of food crops. But total agricultural self-sufficiency is not a national goal. In fact, the amount of land in sugar cane has been increased at the expense of other crops. Castro's planners seem to have concluded that it is more advantageous for Cuba to import corn, rice, wheat, potatoes, and vegetable oils and to increase the export of those farm products most desired by the island's new trading partners. In addition to sugar these products include tobacco and animal products.

Tobacco. Despite its worldwide fame and ready markets, tobacco occupies less than 3 percent of the land under cultiva-

2. It became apparent that American officials counted on the collapse of the sugar industry as a major weapon to oust Castro.

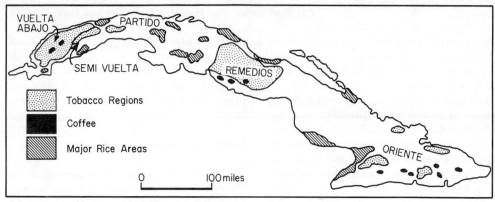

Figure 6.5   Cuba: Tobacco, coffee, and rice

tion and provides less than 5 percent of the exports by value. Cultivation of the crop began in the seventeenth century, and during most of the colonial period it ranked as Cuba's leading export. Unlike sugar growing, however, tobacco production received little impetus from the establishment of the United States connection in 1900. Neither American nor Cuban investors showed interest in producing the crop. Tobacco farming was too risky, required far too much care and labor and, compared with sugar, promised too few profits to attract the investment dollar. As a result, Cuba's tobacco production experienced only a modest increase between 1900 and 1960, and the export of quality cigars actually decreased. On the eve of Castro's revolution, there was little *latifundium* associated with tobacco, although sharecropping was widespread. In Pinar del Río, for example, the average *vega* measured less than two *caballerías* (66 acres). Even such small plantings required 20 to 30 hired hands or sharecroppers. Except for eliminating sharecropping, the revolution did not change the association of tobacco with small holdings. Much of the crop continues to be produced on small, privately owned peasant farms.

While tobacco is grown practically everywhere on the island, Cubans traditionally have recognized five major regions (Figure 6.5). The most important of these is the famous Vuelta Abajo, which is concentrated for the most part along the low-

lands and foothills south of the Sierra de los Órganos in Pinar del Río. There, a combination of undulating terrain with excellent drainage, red to gray-brown soils with a high sand content, and tobacco farming know-how that goes back more than two centuries produces the island's finest crop. This leaf is bright brown, aromatic, and mild, and is used for better-grade cigars. The region consists of several districts (Llano, Lomas, Remates, Guane, Costa Norte, and Costa Sur), and the tobacco of each district is recognizably different, the very finest wrapper leaf being grown under cheesecloth in the Llano. A smaller region, called the Semi-Vuelta, adjoins the Vuelta Abajo to the southeast. In the Semi-Vuelta, the leaf has a heavier body and a stronger aroma, and is blended with other tobaccos as cigar filler. The soils of the tobacco lands in Pinar del Río are too poor for sugar, and there has been little competition for their use.

In contrast, the rich red soils of the Partido region to the southeast of Havana have been increasingly taken over by winter vegetables and sugar. Production has dropped from over 7 million pounds of tobacco before World War I, to less than 1.5 million pounds at present. Much of the Partido tobacco is grown under shade to produce a large, light-colored leaf of fine texture that is used as wrapper on clear Havana cigars manufactured for the English export market.

Another area of production is the Remedios (also called Vuelta Arriba), most of which is in Las Villas province. A combination of swampy coasts and generally mountainous terrain in this province has functioned to keep much of the area the domain of the small farmer. The tobacco leaf grown on the slope land of the Remedios is of poorer quality and is characterized by a heavy, gummy texture. However, it blends well with lighter leaf for cigar fillers, and before Castro, it was largely exported to the United States for use in machine-made cigars. The tobacco grown in the four widely separated districts of the Oriente region is of even lower quality. Most of the production is too poor for export and is sold in the Cuban market.

Coffee and Rice. Both coffee and rice are cash crops primarily sold in the Cuban market, and the production of both has suffered since the revolution because of the heavy emphasis on sugar. Introduced into Oriente province by French refugees from St. Domingue in the late 1700s, coffee flourished during much of the Spanish colonial period. At mid-nineteenth century, for instance, Cuba counted over 2,000 coffee *fincas,* producing over 50 million pounds per year. This was sufficient not only for the island's needs, but for considerable export as well. With the advent of sugar, coffee was neglected, particularly at the turn of the century. Later attempts by the Cuban government to aid the industry resulted in an occasional export surplus prior to 1959. The Castro regime has made self-sufficiency in coffee production a goal and has created a new government agency, Cuba-Café, which has charge of all phases of the crop's production from planting to harvesting.

As in Puerto Rico, coffee grows in the highlands. The chief producing region continues to be in the mountains of southern and eastern Oriente province, where the French introduced it. A second region is in the mountains between Cienfuegos and Trinidad in southern Las Villas province, and the third is in the uplands of Pinar del Río (Figure 6.5). Most of the crop is grown under shade trees on small farms.

Rice with beans makes up a substantial part of the Cuban's food intake. Prior to World War II Cuba imported over 90 percent of its rice, mostly from the Orient. The small amount of rice produced locally was of the dry or upland type, because Cubans feared the mosquito and malaria-breeding potentialities of wet rice fields. When the war cut off imports from the Orient and forced the importation of much more expensive rice from the United States, wet rice production in Cuba became potentially profitable as long as the needs of the wet rice industry for level land did not displace any sugar. Most production was clustered on poorer soils around Manzanillo in Oriente, La Florida in Camagüey, Consolación de Sur in Pinar del Río, and elsewhere (Figure 6.5).

In 1958, Cuba produced 280,000 tons of rice, which represented three-fifths of its national needs. By the late 1960s, production had dropped to less than 100,000 tons, and rice became one of the more stringently rationed food items on the island.

Grazing. Grazing was Cuba's first industry (see Chapter 3), and together with tobacco, it remained in the lead until surpassed by sugar in the late 1700s. It was unable to compete with plantation agriculture and was pushed off the best lands during the nineteenth century. Grazing was dealt a further blow during the Wars of Independence, when more than three-fourths of the island's cattle were wiped out. After 1900, the herds were slowly built up again, aided by imports from Venezuela and the introduction of special breeding stock from the United States and India.

Currently, the Cuban government is placing special emphasis on increasing animal products for both local consumption and export. A program to expand and improve both the beef and dairy herds has been established. Prize bulls have been imported from Britain and Canada; enough artificial insemination centers have been created to serve more than half the island's cattle; and pastures are being improved by planting pangola grass.

Cuba's potential for grazing is considerable. The climate permits almost year-round feeding. More than one-third of the island's total area is classified as natural pasture, and there is a tradition for stock raising throughout rural Cuba. The major concentration of beef cattle is still in the poorer lands in the east-central region (Camagüey-Oriente) where, before Castro, there were large ranches.

Trade Indicators

Partially because of economic interests but more for political reasons, more than three-fourths of Cuba's foreign trade in the early 1970s was with the USSR and other socialist countries. Political considerations were also paramount in the annual subsidies and loans (estimated at $500 million) that Castro was receiving from the Soviet camp. These facts suggest that Cuba is as economically dependent on (and potentially vulnerable to) the USSR today as it was to the United States in 1953.

Cuba's economic isolation from the United States remains total, but Castro's efforts to improve trade relations with other non-Communist countries is increasingly successful. By 1970 trade with Japan and Western countries such as Canada, Britain, Italy, and France accounted for more than 20 percent of Cuba's total, and all indications pointed to further increase in the future. The United States policy of discouraging economic ties between Cuba and the West was becoming obsolete.

Except for market reorientation, there were few important differences in Cuba's foreign trade between the decade preceding the revolution and that which followed it. The island's imports in both periods consisted primarily of finished products, machinery, oil, and food; and its exports were made up primarily of sugar. In 1970, for example, the breakdown of Cuba's exports was 85 percent for sugar, 10 percent for nickel and 5 percent for tobacco, beef, shrimp, and lobster. It is noteworthy that one of the more successful undertakings since the revolution has been the development of a fishing industry. Aided by an expanded program of marine research and by the importation of boats, machinery, and know-how from Japan and the Soviet Union, Cuba's fish catch has grown large enough to satisfy local needs and provide a surplus for export. Fish is one of the few foods items that is not rationed on the island.

Population

Historical Growth. The growth and the composition of Cuba's population may be closely correlated with the island's commercial economy, especially plantation agriculture based on sugar (Figure 6.6). Other important influences include the impact of political disturbances and the elimination of tropical diseases such as malaria and yellow fever.

The history of Cuban population growth lends itself to a fourfold division: (1) the preplantation period, from the early sixteenth century to the British capture of Havana in 1762; (2) the *ingenio* plantation period, from 1762 to the outbreak of the wars of independence in 1868; (3) the war period, from 1868 to 1900; and (4) the *central,* or modern plantation period, from 1900 to Castro's revolution.

The growth of Cuba's population in the preplantation years (1512–1762) was slow and erratic. Such colonists as arrived during the first decade or two of colonization were largely siphoned off by Cortes'

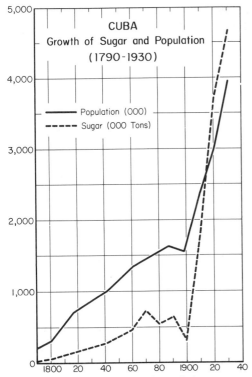

Figure 6.6   Cuba: Sugar and population

The brief English occupation of Cuba (1762–1763) set the stage for the expansion of sugar production based on the plantation and slavery. The first census, in 1774, counted a total population of 171,620, composed 56 percent of whites and 44 percent of blacks. Despite some political unrest before 1868, population expanded rapidly, along with sugar production (Figure 6.6). A small part of this was due to natural increase, but most of it was due to new arrivals, including French refugees from the slave uprising in Haiti, a steady flow of Spanish immigrants, the arrival of Chinese indentured servants and, above all, the importation of roughly one million black slaves.

During the period of instability resulting from the Wars of Independence, 1868–1899, the population of Cuba tended to decrease. The insular economy was badly disrupted; immigration was drastically reduced; slavery was abolished (1886–1887); and large numbers of people died. In an effort to deprive Cuban rebels of popular support, the Spaniards herded much of the rural population into concentration camps. There are no precise figures as to the number of people who died from famine and disease in these camps, but estimates place the number of dead at almost 200,000 under the regime of the infamous Valeriano Weyler alone.

With the coming of independence, integration with the huge United States economy, and an unprecedented expansion of sugar and other industries, Cuba's population again rose dramatically, increasing more than fourfold between 1899 and 1959. Large-scale immigration again played an important role, although natural increase, prompted by general political stability and the elimination of dreaded diseases such as malaria and yellow fever, was also responsible. The major growth (ranging from 3.1 to 3.4 percent annually) occurred from 1899 to the eve of the Depression of the early 1930s. Thereafter,

venture to Mexico and other expeditions. In 1537, the estimated population of the island was 5,800, of which 300 were Spaniards, 500 were black slaves, and 5,000 were Indians. Thereafter, the Indians were largely wiped out, and European immigration dwindled to a trickle except for a block of 8,000 Spaniards that arrived from Jamaica following the English capture of the island in 1665. The total number of African slaves imported during the preplantation period is estimated at 60,000. A few of these were employed in the tiny *trapiche*-type sugar industry, but most of them were absorbed by the more important occupations of grazing and tobacco-food crop agriculture. Except in and around Havana, Cuba remained thinly occupied through most of this period. In 1762, the population was probably less than 150,000.

the rate of increase dropped as immigration was substantially reduced.

The correlation between population growth and sugar production has been all but absolute in the history of Cuba. Not only has the total number of inhabitants risen in almost direct proportion to sugar output, but the greatest population increases have taken place precisely in the provinces of rising cane production. For example, in 1911, the eastern provinces of Oriente, Camagüey, and Las Villas contained 52 percent of the total population and accounted for 60 percent of the island's sugar output; in recent years the percentage of population and sugar production in these same provinces has risen to roughly 60 and 75 percent, respectively. The correlation is even more striking when one considers the fact that the three western provinces (Pinar del Río, La Habana, and Matanzas) include the huge urban concentration of metropolitan Havana.

Migration and Racial Composition. Migrations in Cuba have been the chief determinants not only of population growth but also of racial composition. With the destruction of the Indians, the leading elements in the racial matrix became Spaniards, blacks, and a wide range of mixtures between the two. As noted above, Spanish immigration to the island was limited during the first two and one-half centuries of colonization. The first major wave of Spaniards was attracted to Cuba by the growth of sugar plantations between the latter eighteenth and the end of the nineteenth centuries. This influx was small, however, compared to the Spanish migration in the first half of the twentieth century. In the three decades from 1903 to 1933, 723,381 Spaniards entered Cuba, and, while the number of later entrants was much smaller, Cuba remained a favorite of Spanish immigrants until the revolution. Spaniards on the island tend to be identified with the regions of Spain from which they came

(chiefly Galicia, Asturias, and Santander). Before Castro, numerous regional clubs called *Centros Asturianos, Gallegos,* and so forth, were foci of cultural and social activity.

Immigration of other European groups to Cuba has been far less than the Spanish and has varied according to economic and political conditions. The arrival of 30,000 French refugees from Haiti at the end of the eighteenth century has already been mentioned. At various times before 1900, Cuba also received small groups of Italians, Germans, and other Europeans, but the major influx of non-Spanish whites occurred after 1900. Among the more than one and one-quarter million of immigrants between 1900 and 1950, there were more than 25,000 Americans and, after 1919, considerable numbers of European Jews.

The blacks, who constitute the other important racial ingredient in Cuba's population, fall into two groups. The first, and by far the most numerous, arrived as slaves between the 1520s and the abolition of slavery in 1887. The bulk of the slaves were brought in after 1790, and the influx was so great that, by 1817, the colored population outnumbered the white. The colored continued to form the majority until past the middle of the nineteenth century. Then their number decreased partly because of the heavy toll taken by the Wars of Independence. Blacks made up a large percentage of the rebel armies, and lived in the rural areas most devastated by the wars. Also, because they lived more poorly than the whites, they were felled in larger numbers by the epidemics of cholera, yellow fever, and other diseases. After independence, the percentage of blacks decreased, in part because of the heavy Spanish immigration and in part because of widespread miscegenation.

The second black group arrived in Cuba as free laborers, primarily from Haiti and Jamaica after 1900. In the 30-year period from 1902 to 1932, approximately 190,000 Haitians and 121,000 Jamaicans entered the island, the peak years of this immigration coinciding with the sugar boom of World War I and its aftermath. The collapse of the sugar market in 1921–1922, coupled with the growing desire to "keep Cuba white," sharply reduced the importation of West Indian blacks.

Other nonwhites brought to Cuba include Chinese and small numbers of Yucatan Indians. Labor shortages during the nineteenth century resulted in contracts for 132,435 Chinese indentured laborers (13 percent of whom died in passage) between 1853 and 1873. Small numbers of Chinese came in later as free migrants, but the total of pure Chinese in Cuba now is less than 20,000, and the shortage of women is causing the gradual extinction of this Oriental group. The number of Yucatan Indians brought in probably did not exceed a few thousand, and no trace of these is left.

It is significant that from its very beginnings the Castro regime has strived to overcome racial prejudice (and traditional male chauvinism) in Cuba. As a result, the social progress of blacks and women on the island has been outstanding. According to all reports, institutionalized racial discrimination has disappeared on the island, although personal prejudice among some whites may still be present. This fact helps explain why blacks, including some in the United States, have been among the more enthusiastic supporters of Castro and the revolution.

Emigration has been of minor importance in Cuba except in times of political stress. The largest single block of emigrants (over 600,000) has been composed of refugees from Castro's regime. Most went to the United States, but also to other Caribbean areas, such as Puerto Rico, Costa Rica, and Venezuela.

Density and Distribution. With a present population of eight million, the ratio of people to arable land in Cuba is the lowest in the West Indies. Despite the rapid population increase following independence, the island has not experienced land hunger except when it has been man-made. If arable land were the sole criterion, it would take almost 150 million people to saturate Cuba to the present densities of Puerto Rico.

The spread of settlement in response to economic growth since the colonial period has periodically altered the relative distribution of population on the island. Until the end of the eighteenth century, Havana and its immediate hinterland contained the only significant population nucleus in Cuba. With the beginnings of large-scale sugar production, population movement tended to be to the western lands lying closest to the capital city and chief port. By the middle of the nineteenth century, the western provinces of Pinar del Río, La Habana, and Matanzas —only one-fourth of the island's area—had almost two-thirds of the total population. Transportation to the rich lands of the eastern interior remained so poor during the Wars of Independence that Cuba's population center remained well to the west until the twentieth century. After 1900, the growing pressure for new sugar lands and the construction of railways and roads pushed settlement eastward. By 1943, the center of population coincided with the east–west geographic center of the island, and the shift to the east continues slowly, counterbalanced by the rapid growth of Havana.

The spread of settlement was by no means uniform, however. It varied according to soil fertility, accessibility, transportation, and the growth of industry. As a result, the density and distribution of population is still quite irregular. The lowest densities occur on the poor and often swampy soils of the Isle of Pines and on the peninsulas of Guanacabibes in Pinar del Río and Zapata in Las Villas. Poor soils or poor drainage are also responsible for the scarce population of the coastal regions of Camagüey and the north coast of Las Villas. Other areas of low densities are the result of low precipitation, as exemplified by Oriente's leeward coastal strip from Guantánamo to Cape Maisí or are associated with the more rugged mountain zones, such as parts of the Sierras Maestra and de los Órganos. It is significant, however, that despite the abundance of land, many of the mountain areas in Cuba have considerable populations. Small farmers, squeezed off the more desirable lowlands by the plantation, have found refuge in the highlands, as they have elsewhere in the West Indies.

At the opposite end of the density scale are the immediate vicinities of the larger cities such as Metropolitan Havana, and the *municipios* of Santiago, Camagüey, and Holguín. These, of course, include many of the major commercial, industrial, and political centers. Following these urban zones are the Vuelta Abajo tobacco region of Pinar del Río and the sugar lands of northwestern Matanzas, central Las Villas, western La Habana, and the Central Valley focusing on Holguín. The high density pattern of the Vuelta Abajo stems from the large numbers of small tobacco farmers. The densities of the sugar lands reflect chiefly soils of high fertility, such as the famous red clay Matanzas varieties and the alluvial deposits of the Central Valley.

Settlement

In the decades preceding the revolution, urbanization in Cuba proceeded with exceptional rapidity, and the gulf of difference in living conditions that separated the city from the countryside was exceptionally wide. Although relatively well paid during the *zafra* (cane harvesting period), the rural worker earned little during the rest of the year. Such partial employment and other handicaps (Chapter 4) gave the rural workers a low annual income both in absolute terms and in comparison to the income of workers in the cities.

More recently, both the rate of city growth and the urban-rural gulf have been lessened by policies of the revolutionary government. The differences in living standards between town and country have been reduced by measures such as giving rural districts a large share of new housing and roads; establishing state-owned *tiendas del pueblo* (people's stores) which sell at comparatively low prices; and rapidly electrifying rural areas and increasing health and medical services. In addition, the establishment of minimum wages and year-round employment on *granjas* (people's estates) also has aided in improving living standards in the countryside.

The rise in rural living standards was in itself a major factor in reducing the flow to the cities. In addition, however, government propaganda gives greater prestige value to work and workers in the countryside than in the city. Many urban dwellers, especially bureaucrats and students, are expected to spend weekends and vacation periods in the country performing "voluntary work." Life in the cities, especially Havana, has lost many of its prerevolutionary attractions. Strict puritanism seems to have replaced the "swinging" night life, the gambling, and the easy virtues which were the earmarks of Havana before Castro.

The Balance Sheet and the Future

Agriculture is the heart of the Cuban economy, and sugar is its commercial life blood. This was true in the heyday of American capitalism prior to 1959, and it is equally true under Castro socialism today. Nor has the switch from capitalism to socialism changed other important characteristics and problems of the insular economy. A disturbing continuity of inadequate institutional equipment and external forces have plagued resource utilization in Cuba from the colonial period to the present. The *latifundium* of Spanish grants and the monopoly of colonial trade created the beginnings of a landless peasantry and limited the utilization of land to a few products. The connection with the United States after independence intensified both the *latifundium* and monoculture and added the burden of large foreign ownership of land and resources. Castro's brand of Communism eliminated foreign ownership, but actually intensified the *latifundium*. The fact that the *latifundium* is now based on state rather than private ownership has not altered its negative effect on the *guajiro* (peasant). He may be better off under socialism than he was under capitalism, but he has yet to benefit fully from the advantages of his country's favorable location, well-articulated coastline, good climate and topography, and plentitude of arable land and other resources.

A major cause of this unfortunate discrepancy has been international interference, attracted by Cuba's favorable location and economic potential. From its earliest post-Columbian history, the island has been buffeted by international stress which placed the strategic, political, and economic interests of outsiders above the welfare of the Cubans. Under Spain, the island had neither economic nor political independence. Cuba rid itself of Spanish colonialism only to fall victim to the economic colonialism imposed by sugar and the American market; and now its break with the United States has plunged it into an even more brutal colonialism as a satellite of the USSR.

But while Cuba's future, like its past, will depend only in part on the efforts of the Cubans themselves, prospects appeared less bleak in 1973 than in 1963. Somehow Cuba has managed to survive the traumas of social disruption that made refugees of a large segment of the island's technicians and professionals; of a United States "blockade" that has isolated Cubans from trading with much of the non-Communist world and blocked the replacement of American-made equipment as it broke down or became obsolete; and of serious economic planning errors made by the Castro regime and its Soviet advisors. Despite the absence of luxury goods and the rationing of food and clothing, there is evidence that many (perhaps most) Cubans are enjoying a higher standard of living now than before 1959. Housing is better and rents are cheaper than before. ". . . I didn't see any Cubans who looked underfed, and the ones I heard complaining about the rations invariably were hostile to everything else about the revolution." (Nicholson 1973: 56) Certainly no one suggests that Castro will soon be overthrown, and the once-serious threat of direct intervention by the United States has abated. In fact, there are even a few who dare hope that United States–Cuban relations may be "normalized" in the foreseeable future.

PUERTO RICO

There may be another territory on earth whose transformation in the last three decades equals that of Puerto Rico, but there is none which surpasses it. In the early 1940s, the island was still burdened with the handicaps of colonial rule—first under Spain and later under the United States. The annual per capita income was less than $125. Agriculture, the chief economy, rested primarily on high-cost sugar production. The best land was owned by American corporations and a small number of wealthy Puerto Ricans. The vast majority of the island's *campesinos* (peasants) were either sharecroppers or owned plots too small and infertile to provide a living. To make matters worse, a high birth rate was widening the gulf between a large population and a small resource base; unemployment and underemployment affected almost three-fourths of Puerto Rican families; and the resulting poverty, malnutrition, and disease killed the average Puerto Rican before he reached his fiftieth birthday.

By 1973, Puerto Rico's per capita income compared favorably with many European countries and even some regions in the United States. An effective agrarian reform program had sharply limited *latifundium*. Dependence on the virtual monoculture of sugar cane had been reduced by economic diversification, with emphasis on manufacturing and tourism. The parallel political and social progress was reflected by a large measure of local autonomy in government, and by a relative drop in the birth rate and a dramatic rise in life expectancy (70-plus years). Such progress has not been achieved without cost, but given the choice, even the most frustrated Puerto Rican would give preference to the conditions of 1973 over those of 1943.

The Puerto Rican Economy

Resource Base. In contrast to Cuba, Puerto Rico is a mere 3,500 square miles of eroded mountain land and tired alluvial soils. The island is slightly over 100 miles long, with an average north–south width of 35 miles. More than three-fourths of its surface consists of mountains and hills. The main mountain chain, called the Cordillera Central in the west and the Sierra de Cayey in the east, forms the island's backbone. Its average elevations are roughly 3,000 feet, and it reaches a maximum of 4,388 feet at Cerro de Punta south of the town of Jayuya. Other mountain masses are those of Luquillo in the northeast and the Atalaya range in the

northwest. The remainder of the island consists of interior valleys, such as the Caguas lowland and a narrow ribbon of coastal plain that reaches a maximum width of 13 miles on the north side of the island.

Puerto Rico's mountainous terrain gives rise to sharp windward-leeward contrasts. Precipitation varies dramatically from over 200 inches in the northeast-facing mountains to less than 30 inches at Cabo Rojo in the southwest corner of the island. Most of the land to the south or leeward side of the central mountains is too dry to be cultivated without irrigation.

Compared to Cuba, Puerto Rico is more removed from the rich American market and her coastline is less well articulated. San Juan, the capital, is 1,600 miles from New York and 1,700 miles from New Orleans. The island has several harbors, such as San Juan, Mayagüez, and Playa de Ponce, but the number of anchorages with sufficient depth and protection are few, and they are often located on the less-developed south coast.

Natural resources other than soil and water are conspicuous by their absence in Puerto Rico. Virtually all the forests that once covered much of the island have been cut to provide crop land and pasture for a growing population. The most important mineral wealth is represented by an abundance of clay, sand, limestone, and gravel, which is used for building materials and for producing cement, ceramics, and glass. Thus, Puerto Rico's impressive economic progress has been achieved not because of rich natural resources but despite the lack of them.

Agriculture. Once the backbone of the Puerto Rican economy, agriculture has been declining rapidly in importance. It now ranks second to manufacturing both in the number of people it employs and in its contribution to the gross national product. The decline in agriculture might have been even more rapid without the basic overhauling of traditional farming that has been taking place since the latter 1940s. Among the major changes are agrarian reform, significant mechanization and modernization, and the retirement to other uses of marginal farm land.

LAND TENURE AND LAND REFORM. Viewed historically, large-scale sugar monoculture, with its typical patterns of large plantations, developed only to a modest extent in Puerto Rico during the last century of the Spanish regime. Before the United States occupation, about three-fourths of the cultivated land on the island was in small holdings averaging about 12 acres. The United States military reported in its census of 1899 that "this general ownership of farms has unquestionably had a great influence in producing the contented conditions of the people on this island, as contrasted to the restlessness of Cuba, where a large proportion of the cultivated area is in the hands of comparatively few landlords."

Between the time of United States occupation and World War II, however, profound changes occurred in the island's pattern of land tenure. Small growers were swallowed up by great plantations, which were owned by a handful of wealthy local families and absentee Americans. Sugar farming spread to areas previously used for food production, and the cost of living behind the protection of United States tariff walls proved very expensive. The patrimony of the small farmers was bought by the sugar companies, and people often found themselves working as *agregados* (hired hands) on land that their fathers had owned for centuries. By 1940, only 16 percent of the cultivated land was in small farms of less than 20 acres. Most of these were in the mountains or on marginal lands unsuitable for sugar, and few were sufficiently productive to provide a living for their owners. More important, the bulk of Puerto Rico's farm workers had no land at all. The plight of Puerto Rico's landless population grew steadily worse, especially during the Great Depression (1929–1940).

In an effort to avoid land monopoly by large corporations, the United States Congress had added the Five-Hundred-Acre Law as part of the original Organic Act for the newly acquired territory. This law was conveniently disregarded and, 40 years after its passage, 51 corporations controlled 249,000 acres of Puerto Rico's best land. One of these actually had over 50,000 acres. This was the situation and the problem on the eve of Puerto Rico's famous *jalda arriba,* the "uphill push" under Governor Luis Muñoz which began transforming Puerto Rico into a showcase for progress.

In brief, the Muñoz reform program began with the enforcement of the Five-Hundred-Acre Law. About half the land illegally held by the corporations was purchased by the government for various uses. Some of it is incorporated into proportional profit farms owned by the government, with profit-sharing by workers, and some has been sold to small farmers in plots not exceeding 25 acres; other land, while owned by the government, was given in usufruct to communities of landless farm workers. Land that was not suitable for farming was turned over to the forestry service. In addition, the Insular Land Authority was empowered to acquire barren and swampy lands for purposes of reclamation.

Not all the corporate land in excess of 500 acres was forced into sale, but enough was acquired to drastically weaken the stranglehold of large landowners on the farming economy. Today, the sugar corporations of Puerto Rico are primarily industrial enterprises that run the *centrales.* Government farms and *colonos* supply most of the cane.

LAND USE AND PRODUCTION STRUCTURE. The diversity of terrain, climate, and soils permits a wide range of agricultural activity in Puerto Rico. Until the 1960s such physical diversity, coupled with a high density of rural population, had resulted in the utilization of even the marginal lands of steep mountain slopes; so almost four-fifths of the total area was under crops and pasture. The infertile mountain lands were generally cultivated by the poorer, backward, small farmers. The more productive coastal plains and valley bottoms had been absorbed by the plantations and large landowners.

In recent years, however, an increasing amount of marginal land and even some of the more fertile land has been taken out of agriculture. Employment alternatives, higher wages, and other conditions created by the development of the non-agricultural sectors of the Puerto Rican economy made it unprofitable to farm marginal land. A rising demand for land for residential, industrial, and other urban uses is removing from farming substantial amounts of the more productive land of the coastal areas and valleys.

To remain competitive in the face of increasing labor costs, Puerto Rican agriculture is also rapidly mechanizing and diversifying crop production. The use of machinery, chemical weed killers, and other labor-saving devices, once opposed by rural workers who feared loss of jobs, is now being implemented without opposition. Increasing urbanization and a rising standard of living are making it more profitable to abandon traditional crops such as sugar and to use the land for dairying, truck gardening, and recreation.

But sugar still reigns supreme in the farming domain of Puerto Rico, and as long as the island remains within the United States quota system, there is little likelihood of its dethronement. The crop occupies almost half (the better half) of all the cultivated land; all other agricultural exports are relatively insignificant. Cane has traditionally dominated land use on the coastal plains and in the interior valleys, such as the Caguas lowland.

Tobacco, used largely as cigar filler in the United States, is an extremely poor second to sugar as an export product, and it occupies less land than other major crops, such as coffee, bananas, corn, and starchy vegetables. Production is confined primarily to the humid eastern half of the Central Cordillera, where it generally provides the cash income of small farms of less than 20 acres. Approximately one-fourth of each farm is planted in tobacco, the remaining land being devoted to food crops and pasture.

Coffee occupies an amount of land second only to sugar, but it is no longer an important export. It is raised by small farmers in the western highlands, along with other tree crops such as oranges and avocados. In the last days of the Spanish regime, coffee was Puerto Rico's chief export, but current production is so limited that often it is insufficient to meet local needs. Unlike sugar, the robust Puerto Rican coffee found little favor in the United States.

Manufacturing. Industrialization is at once the leading cause and the principal result of Puerto Rico's economic transformation. As recently as 1948, the island had no modern industry other than the processing of sugar cane. Since then the growth of manufacturing has been so rapid that Puerto Rico is now more completely industrialized than most European countries. How did an overcrowded, tiny piece of tropical real estate lacking in minerals, energy fuels, capital, and technical skills achieve such industrialization? FACTORS IN INDUSTRIAL GROWTH. There is no single answer to this question. Industrialization was made part of an overall developmental program that was started in 1941, initially aided by money coming into the island during World War II. The program fostered improvement in health, education, and housing to raise living standards and increase labor productivity.

It built modern roads, airports, fast communication, and supplied abundant electrical power to facilitate manufacturing and commerce. Government agencies were created to aid the development of private enterprise and, when necessary, to invest directly in industrial and agricultural ventures.

The government's role in aiding new industry has numerous facets—direct and indirect subsidies, free plant sites and factory buildings, training of workers and supervisors, and an endless number of services ranging from the entertaining of potential investors to conducting advertising campaigns in the United States. Under Puerto Rico's Industrial Incentives Act, new manufacturers are exempt from corporate taxes, personal income taxes, and property taxes for periods of from five to ten years. An additional incentive was provided by the establishment of a Foreign Trade Zone, an enclosed area near the western city of Mayagüez where foreign and domestic merchandise may be entered without being subject to customs law.

Finally, there are the all-important advantages stemming from the connection with the United States. Puerto Rico is characterized by political stability and the democratic process in government. It offers the American investor cheap labor and other incentives, without the dangers common to investments outside the United States. There are no tariff walls separating the island from the continental market, and there is complete freedom of movement for both goods and people. American rule has helped develop a well-trained officialdom and an efficient civil service system.

NATURE AND DISTRIBUTION OF MANUFAC-TURING. Through the mid-1960s, the new industries established in Puerto Rico were characterized by a large number of small factories employing an average of 70 workers each. They were often branch plants of American corporations that relied on the United States to provide the bulk of the raw materials and the markets for the finished products. Manufacturers covered a wide range of goods, from handkerchiefs to electronic equipment, and most industries could be classified as light, labor-oriented enterprises.

Most of these characteristics are still applicable, but in recent years the trend has been toward greater scale and complexity. There is a marked increase in manufacturing establishments that require more capital investment per worker and more skills. Especially noteworthy among the new industries are chemicals and petrochemicals.

Industrial establishments in Puerto Rico are generally located in large urban centers that have port facilities and other services. The San Juan metropolitan area, which contains about a third of the island's population, has received almost half the new jobs created by incoming industries. Next in line of preference are the port cities of Mayagüez, on the west coast, and Ponce, on the south coast—two cities that follow San Juan in total population. Large port cities are preferred because they afford cheap external transportation for both the raw materials and the finished products that move by sea between Puerto Rico and the United States. In addition, the major cities have larger labor pools and the necessary legal, banking, and recreational facilities.

The smaller interior towns, especially those in the highlands, have received only a small share of the new industry. Most of these interior centers have adequate electric power and are easily accessible by all-weather roads, but the added cost of transportation and the paucity of essential services have worked against them. In an effort to foster location of industry in towns outside the major urban clusters, the government offers special incentives. The island has been divided into incentive zones, and subsidies are paid in indirect proportion to the desirability of the location.

Tourism. Because of its climate and natural beauty, Puerto Ricans call their island *La Isla del Encanto* (The Isle of Enchantment). But this beauty yielded only poetry and songs until the Puerto Rican government and a series of gratuitous circumstances conspired to attract the Yankee dollar. As late as 1948, one could count the number of good hotels in San Juan on the fingers of one hand, and even these hotels tended to cater more to Puerto Ricans and visiting businessmen than to tourists. In an effort to stimulate tourism as part of the economic development plan, the government built the now-famous Caribe-Hilton hotel in 1948 and leased it to the Hilton chain, a venture so successful that the government recouped its investment and is now netting a profit of over one million dollars a year from it. The success of this and other hotels (such as La Concha) built at public expense stimulated private investment, and numerous hotels, including Laurence Rockefeller's sumptuous nine-million-dollar Dorado Beach, have been built. Other factors that have stimulated the Puerto Rican tourist trade include the high level of prosperity in the United States through the 1960s, the capture of much of Cuba's tourist business following Castro's revolution, and comparatively cheap air fare between the island and major United States cities.

By 1970, Puerto Rico boasted almost 10,000 hotel and other guest rooms, and received about one million visitors who spent an average of $200 each. The island's peak tourist season is late fall and winter, but with reduced room rates, "package" tours and other inducements, tourism has become a year-round source of income.

But the once-optimistic estimate of 1.5 million tourists for 1975 no longer seems realistic for a variety of reasons. The cost of a Puerto Rican vacation has risen more steeply than one in competing areas such as Mexico. Equally important is rising inflation and the increasing cost of living, including air travel in the United States. The vast bulk of the tourists who visit Puerto Rico are from middle-income groups of eastern urban centers such as New York, whose income was being seriously affected by a drop in real income (as of 1973–1974).

The American Connection

As already implied, Puerto Rico's leap forward to development and modernization has been fueled at least in part by the advantages stemming from its economic and political ties with the United States. The island looks to the United States as its principal market, its chief source of imported products and investment capital, and the major outlet for its surplus labor. Whether in the form of tourist spending, federal aid, the payrolls of American firms on the island, or the money remitted by Puerto Ricans living in the United States, the insular economy depends heavily on American dollars. Moreover, federal funds pay for the island's postal system, defense, weather bureau, and diplomatic representation abroad. Federal expenditure in Puerto Rico in 1970, for example, was estimated at over $260 million. Added to this, the island pays no federal income tax, and all custom duties, excise, and other taxes collected on Puerto Rican goods by the federal government are returned to the insular government.

But these and other advantages stemming from Puerto Rico's ties with the United States are offset, at least in part, by disadvantages. The same tariff regulations that give the island's products free entry into the large and rich American market also oblige Puerto Ricans to buy high-cost American goods and services. Trade between the island and mainland ports must be carried in American ships, which charge the highest rates in the world. Imported food and other products that are costly to begin with, become even costlier with the addition of the high shipping bill. As a result, Puerto Rican workers whose wages are well below United States averages often pay more for food and other basic necessities than American workers.

Potentially, however, the most serious disadvantages stem from the fact that the island has no vote in the United States Congress. A change in federal legislation could seriously cripple the insular economy. For example, if Congress were to pass a law forbidding federal aid to Puerto Rico unless it paid federal taxes, the results could be disastrous. And there is no constitutional provision that bars Congress from passing such a law.

Population

Growth and Racial Composition. For almost three centuries following its initial colonization in 1508, Puerto Rico's population grew very slowly and remained essentially European. The first official census (1765) counted fewer than 45,000 inhabitants, of whom about 5,000 were black slaves. Most of this population was thinly distributed along the humid north coastal plain, the island's interior being largely unsettled. The dominantly subsistent economy and the small importance which Spain attached to the island effectively controlled population growth.

Beginning in the latter eighteenth century, the tempo of population growth began to increase, and the frontier was rapidly pushed to the mountainous interior. During the nineteenth century, 35 new towns were founded, mostly in the highlands—almost the number of settlements that had been established in the previous three centuries. By 1830, the island had 315,000 inhabitants, and by 1899, the population had almost trebled to 953,000.

The growth in population was stimulated largely by the expansion of the island's commercial economy, coupled with some immigration. Land under cultivation increased from 117,000 acres, in 1830, to 183,000 acres, in 1862, and reached a total of 274,000 acres by the end of the century.

This increase in land under cultivation was prompted primarily by the expansion of commercial crops such as sugar and coffee. With the Schedule of Grace in 1815, Spain opened the island to world commerce. Significant plantation development occurred, aided by the immigration of French and Spanish planters from Louisiana, by royalist refugees from the revolutions in Venezuela and Colombia, and by immigrants from France and Corsica after the fall of Napoleon. These newcomers bought Crown lands on liberal terms and engaged in the production of commercial crops.

The growth of plantations created the usual shortage of labor. Large numbers of black slaves were imported, and the plantation altered the racial composition in Puerto Rico as it had done elsewhere in the Antilles. In 1845, the island had over 50,000 slaves and about 175,000 free blacks; by 1898, there were 570,187 whites, 239,808 people of mixed blood, and 75,824 blacks. The plantations and their black laborers were concentrated on the coastal plains, the highland interior remaining the domain of a large number of small white farmers who raised coffee and food crops.

Following the American occupation, there was a gradual decline in the death rate, which, coupled with further expansion of commercial agriculture, kept the rate of growth of Puerto Rico's population high (Figure 6.7). By 1940, the total had reached 2 million, and a decade later

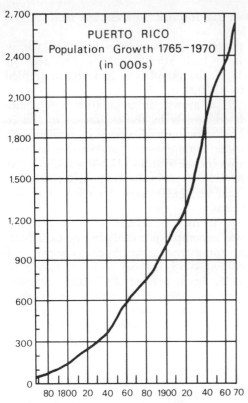

PUERTO RICO
Population Growth 1765-1970
(in 000s)

Figure 6.7   Puerto Rico: Population growth

it had surged above 2.2 million despite considerable postwar emigration. Gradually, birth control, a rising standard of living and emigration have begun to take effect. The birth rate has begun to drop, and future population increases are expected to be more modest.

The current population of Puerto Rico represents a blend of several racial and ethnic groups. Spanish Caucasian is by far the largest ingredient in the mixture,[3]

3. Puerto Rico's population includes the smallest number of nonwhites in the West Indies, including Cuba. It is ironic, therefore, that for many people in the United States, "Puerto Rican" means nonwhite while "Cuban" stands for predominantly white. This may be due in part to the fact that most recent Cuban immigrants to the United States have been from the middle and upper classes, while Puerto Rican immigrants are generally from the poorer classes. In the Caribbean, as in most of Latin America, the upper classes include fewer nonwhites than the lower.

but the island's population has absorbed various other people since the sixteenth century. In addition to the small number of native Indians who survived the shock of conquest and the larger number of blacks brought in as slaves, these include a few representatives of more than a dozen ethnic stocks. Puerto Rico's telephone directory includes such non-Spanish names as Mullenhoff (German), O'Neill (Irish), Azize (Lebanese), Bird (English), Pellegrino (Italian or Corsican), Bouret (French), and Pereira (Portuguese). Names alone provide no clue to the origin of people of African origin on the island. Their ancestors were forced into the practice common to all slave areas in the Americas; they had to adopt the family names and much of the culture of their white masters. As a result, today's black Puerto Ricans are, for the most part, as Hispanic in culture as whites on the island.

Currently, about 20 percent of Puerto Rico's population is classified as black. It is significant, however, that the percentage of blacks in the population tends to decrease with each census count. This suggests first, that the black minority is being gradually absorbed into the white majority of the population; and second, that unlike the United States, a small quantity of black blood does not automatically place an individual in the black racial classification.

Density and Distribution. Population densities in Puerto Rico are close to the highest in the world. The simple ratio of people to land is almost 800 per square mile, but the number of persons per square mile of arable land is about 2,900, and many rural areas of the islands have densities as high as comfortably spaced American suburbs.

Not unexpectedly, the zone of highest population density is the humid north coastal plain, which runs from Luquillo in the east to Aguadilla in the west. Sugar, pineapples, dairying, and other farm enterprises make this the richest agricultural area on the island. Its cities are also the leading industrial and commercial centers. The major regional focus is the San Juan metropolitan area, with a population of over 500,000. There are other cities, however, with the result that the northern plain has the largest number of urban dwellers in Puerto Rico.

The eastern interior valleys and highlands focusing on the city of Caguas are the second most densely settled areas. Here agriculture is the dominant economy—sugar cane in the valleys, and tobacco and food crops in the mountains. During the recent industrial surge, some small factories have been established in the towns of this region.

Other zones of high density are the east coast, with its sugar and pasture lands; the western mountains, with its coffee; and the irrigated sugar lands of the south coastal plain. In fact, there are only a very few areas of low density. Chief among these are the Sierra de Luquillo in the northeast and the dry leeward margins of the southern uplands and unirrigated plain.

With well over 50 percent of its 2.6 million people living in towns and cities, Puerto Rico ranks as one of the most urbanized islands in the West Indies. The movement from country to town has been especially strong since World War II. The flow, especially to greater San Juan, including the cities of Santurce and Río Piedras (but also to other urban centers, which have been growing rapidly), has been prompted by various forces, including industrialization and expanding education. For many people, the move to the city is the first leg of their emigration to the United States.

Cultural Characteristics of the People. Puerto Rico remains a Caribbean island of Hispanic culture. More than 60 years of involvement with the United States have failed to alter the basically Spanish cultural values of the people; in fact, it has often strengthened them. While English is widely taught, only about one-fourth of the people are truly bilingual, and most of these are urban middle- and upper-class people. The once-obligatory teaching of American history evoked little enthusiasm. The Anglo-Saxon, Protestant virtues illustrated by the tale of George Washington and the cherry tree were out of place in a tropical Catholic land without cherry trees. Despite the widespread efforts of American Protestant missionaries, the vast majority of the population remains Catholic.

There has been some selective borrowing from Americans. The democratic process in government is more firmly established in Puerto Rico than anywhere else in Latin America. Puerto Ricans have recognized the advantages of American managerial skills, planning, and technical know-how and are applying them with some modifications to their own environment, and they measure economic progress by United States rather than Caribbean standards. In most other respects, however, Puerto Rico is determined to retain its Spanish cultural heritage. Were it not for the economic advantages accruing from its relations with the United States, the island might well ask for total independence.

¿ A Dónde Vas, Puerto Rico ?

Puerto Rico, once the "poorhouse of the Caribbean," is now glowingly referred to as the "Laboratory for Democracy" and the "most rapidly developing territory in the Western Hemisphere." By Latin American standards the island is well ahead of the pack, but by United States standards the island's progress is less impressive. For example, it has not provided a long-range solution to either the economic problem or the ever-present question of political status. Economically, there is still a dangerous discrepancy between population and production. Despite emigration and a sharp rise in the number of jobs, the island's unemployment rate continues to be more than four times higher than that of the United States. Even more dangerous, the insular economy is highly vulnerable to conditions over which Puerto Ricans have little control. For example, the devaluation of the dollar and inflation in the United States has already hurt tourism. Expiration of tax-free privileges and rising labor costs could increase the movement of small, labor-oriented industries from Puerto Rico to areas of lower labor costs such as Jamaica.

Nor has recent progress provided a solution to the question of Puerto Rico's political status, which has been the most burning issue in virtually every insular election since the American occupation. The present, ill-defined "commonwealth" status which gives the island a wide measure of local political autonomy is, at best, a transitional political arrangement with the United States. The vast majority of Puerto Ricans realize that, sooner or later, the island must opt either for statehood or for independence. The problem is that the Puerto Ricans themselves cannot agree on which of these "final" political solutions to choose.

HISPANIOLA

The boundary line separating Haiti and the Dominican Republic on the island of Hispaniola is one of the sharpest cultural divides in the Americas. To the west of the line, the Haitian landscape is characterized by a predominantly rural occupance strongly reminiscent of West Africa. Irregularly oriented thatched houses are dispersed through the countryside or come together haphazardly to form tiny agricultural villages. Surrounding the rural settlements are patchy networks of fields owned largely by the peasantry and devoted primarily to subsistence crops. The hoe and machete are the chief farm tools, and in line with African custom, farm surpluses are sold by women who carry the products to periodic markets in the towns. There is little on the Haitian landscape which suggests either the twentieth century or a European colonial origin. Transportation is largely accomplished by human porters and overloaded donkeys who walk along narrow trails; industry is all but absent; facilities for social services are rare; and enterprise is on the penny-ante scale. Racially, the descendant of the prosperous eighteenth-century French colony of St. Domingue is essentially black and culturally more African than European. Only the ruins of European estate houses, sugar mills, and irrigation canals which dot the Haitian countryside speak of the prosperous past.

To the east of the international boundary on Hispaniola is the Dominican landscape, also dominantly rural, but with differences. Large estates, worked by landless tenants and devoted to commercial crops and cattle grazing, are more conspicuous than small peasant holdings. The plow, and even an occasional tractor, may be found side-by-side with the machete on the large farms. A sizable network of roads connects the major settlements and facilitates circulation; Dominican products move to market largely by trucks and rail. Industry is less conspicuously absent than in Haiti, and buildings, housing, hospitals, schools, and other services are not so rare as to evoke surprise from the passing observer. The Dominicans are primarily mulatto, but a history of bitter opposition to black Haiti makes them fiercely Hispanic and European in their cultural attachment and orientation. It has been said that "the Dominican thinks white," regardless of his color.

The contrasts are due, in some measure, to differences in man-land ratios and relations. Haiti has few empty areas. Although its population is concentrated on the heavily mountainous western third of the island, it has well over five million people, and overall densities exceed 500 persons per square mile. There is virtually no exploitable land (even in marginally productive soil zones) that is unused, and crop land is rarely available at any price. The intense search for land and living has often driven the Haitian *paysan* to the Dominican frontier, Cuba, and elsewhere. In the Dominican Republic, on the other hand, land hunger, and hunger in general, is far less acute than in Haiti. With a population only three-fourths as large as Haiti's, the Dominicans occupy a territory almost twice as large. There are still many thinly settled areas suitable for colonization, particularly in the border provinces facing Haiti. In fact, one of the oldest themes in Dominican history has been the search for a means of safeguarding their borderlands against the burgeoning population pushing eastward from Haiti.

This theme, and its inherent danger, is still very much present.

Physical Setting

"Beyond the mountains are more mountains," runs an old Haitian saying, and it is an apt description of Hispaniola's rugged and complex terrain. Steep-sided highlands dominate the physical landscape virtually everywhere on the island. While the four major mountain systems and the parallel ribbons of lowlands that separate them are oriented roughly east–west, individual ranges and valleys within the system strike out in a variety of directions. The relief patterns of Hispaniola are the most complex in the West Indies, and generalization with reference to landforms is possible only at the sacrifice of important detail.

A simplified landform classification of the island points up several major regions (Figure 6.8). Beginning in the north, the first of these is the Cordillera Septentrional or Sierra de Montecristi, which lies

Figure 6.8   Hispaniola: Generalized surface configuration

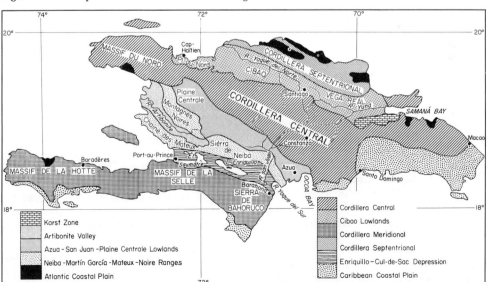

wholly within the Dominican Republic. This region consists of several parallel ranges and isolated mountain blocks separated by intermontane valleys and patches of coastal plain. Elevations in the northern highlands seldom exceed 2,500 feet, but the steep, narrow-crested ranges form a distinctive landscape feature running southeast from near the Haitian border toward the Peninsula of Samaná.

To the south of these mountains are the extensive Cibao lowlands, which continue westward into Haiti under the name of the Plaine du Nord. The Cibao varies in width from about 10 to 35 miles, and it includes within its limits a variety of drainage, relief, soil, and climatic patterns. Near the city of Santiago, the Cibao is divided into two parts by a low, hilly watershed. To the east of the divide, drainage follows the Yuna River to Samaná Bay, passing through one of the most impressive fertile districts in the world. This eastern portion of the Cibao, called the Vega Real, is easily the richest agricultural area of Hispaniola and contains one of the island's large population clusters. West of the watershed, near Santiago, the Cibao region is less well favored. In the valley of the Río Yaque del Norte, increasing aridity and less fertile soils limit both agricultural production and population concentrations.

Paralleling the southern edge of the Cibao is the Cordillera Central (called the Massif du Nord in Haiti), the main mountain backbone of Hispaniola. Formed from a checkered array of volcanic, metamorphic, and sedimentary rocks, the central mountains present a tangled maze of peaks and ridges with, here and there, a flat-bottomed intermontane valley. The system reaches both its maximum width (about 80 miles) and its highest elevations (over 10,000 feet) in the east central part of the island. Together with the geologically related highlands of the Samaná Peninsula, the Cordillera Central makes up more than one-third of Hispaniola.

It is a significant divide between the northern population nuclei, such as those of the Cibao and Cap-Haïtien, and those to the south focusing on Santo Domingo and Port-au-Prince.

On the southwest flank of the Cordillera Central is a complex of alternating lowlands and ranges. Included in this complex are:

1. The Azua–San Juan Valley–Plaine Centrale lowlands.
2. The Sierra de Neiba range, which continues into Haiti as the Chaîne de Mateux and Montagnes Noires.
3. Haiti's Artibonite Valley.
4. The Enriquillo–Cul-de-Sac Depression.

The sierras are for the most part rugged limestone mountains trending WNW–ESE. The adjacent lowland troughs are dry because of the rain shadow cast by the mountains. Geologically, the most arresting of the lowlands is the Enriquillo–Cul-de-Sac Depression. It resembles a rift valley which was once a marine strait. The depression was uplifted in such recent geologic times that it still remains largely unchanged by erosion. Parts of its dry surface are below sea level and are covered by large salt lakes such as those of Enriquillo and the Étang Saumâtre.

The only significant stretch of coastal plain in Hispaniola is on the Caribbean side of the island, between Ocoa Bay and Macao. In the Dominican Republic this coastal lowland is second only to the Vega Real in agricultural production and population concentration. It is the principal sugar plantation zone and forms the rich hinterland of Santo Domingo, the country's chief port and capital city. Smaller areas of coastal plains are also found on the peninsulas of Bahoruco and southeast Haiti, but inadequate rainfall limits the value of these lowlands.

The last of Hispaniola's major landform regions is sometimes called the Cordillera Meridional. It consists of the Serra de Bahoruco in the Dominican Republic and the Massifs de là Selle and de la Hotte in Haiti. This region includes several small interior lowlands, of which the most important is the Asile Valley south of Baradères in Haiti.

The complexity of terrain in Hispaniola is matched by a comparable complexity of climate and other physical elements Tropical conditions stemming from the island's low-latitude location are modified by insularity, altitude, and the trade winds. Mean annual temperatures in the lowlands are about 78°F, except in a few walled-in spots such as Gonaïves, Port-au-Prince, and the Enriquillo Depression, where averages go above 80°F. In contrast, winter temperatures in the higher mountains, such as at Constanza, frequently drop below freezing. Thus, temperature conditions on Hispaniola vary with altitude, from those of the *tierra caliente* to those of the *tierra fría* (see Chapter 2). Temperatures also tend to increase from north to south and from windward to leeward as the trades sweep across the complex terrain.

Precipitation totals and distribution are equally varied, and humidity patterns on the island run the gamut from tropical rain forest to virtual deserts. As a general rule, rainfall decreases from northeast to southwest, from highlands to lowlands, and from windward to leeward exposures. For example, at Samaná, where the northeast trades sweep in off the ocean, precipitation is over 100 inches per year; at Barahona, in the southwest, totals drop to 25 inches; and in the San Juan Valley, which lies in the rain shadow of the central mountains, the total is 20 inches or less. This makes irrigation necessary or desirable for farming in much of western and southern Hispaniola, including the Artibonite Valley, the Plaine du Nord and the Western Cibao, the Cul-de-Sac, and other lowlands.

The patterns of vegetation of Hispaniola are as kaleidoscopic as the climate and terrain. There is considerable overlap, but differences in elevation, rainfall, and other factors create plant associations ranging from the xerophytic groupings of the desert to the lush growth of the tropical rain forest.

THE DOMINICAN REPUBLIC

A bountiful nature and an unstable history seem to have been at loggerheads with each other in the Dominican Republic. Where nature might have encouraged development, political instability has impeded it. Dominicians have seldom enjoyed the political equilibrium necessary to realize the potential of their environment and, today, after more than four and a half centuries of post-Conquest occupance, their land and resources are rarely well used.

The legacy of history was a bitter one almost from the start. Spain lost interest in her Santo Domingo colony soon after the discovery of Mexico (see Chapter 3). During the seventeenth and eighteenth centuries, while the French settlers in western Hispaniola imported large numbers of African slaves and developed the richest plantation economy in the Caribbean, Spanish Santo Domingo in the eastern part of the island remained small, economically stagnant, and largely white in racial makeup. Three hundred years of Spanish colonization had made only a dent on the landscape. By the end of the eighteenth century, Santo Domingo, with twice the territory of the neighboring French colony, had barely half the population. Its mountains and western border zones were uninhabited; its fertile savannas were divided into great haciendas, haphazardly used for cattle grazing and subsistence crops; and its Creole population, with a small number of slaves, led a slow-paced, isolated, and self-sufficient existence. This was the state of things in

1795, when Spain ceded all of Hispaniola to France and exposed Santo Domingo to the turmoil of slave uprisings that began against the French planters in the west (see Chapter 3).

From this period on, the Dominican's history has been scarred with savage bloodletting engendered by the racial and cultural hatreds of the Haitians and with alternating periods of foreign domination and domestic dictatorships. To the Dominicans, the dark age of this history was the Haitian occupation (1822–1844), during which trade came to a virtual standstill; most of the white families of wealth left the country; and a planned policy of Haitianization bore heavily on the Hispanic culture of the remaining population.

Independence, achieved with the expulsion of the Haitians, did little to bring peace and economic growth. Between 1844 and the United States occupation (1916–1924), the Dominican Republic was wracked by scores of revolutions, further armed invasions from Haiti, another period of Spanish domination (1861–1865), and a war to expel Spain. Fear of Haiti remained constant even after armed attacks ceased, kept alive by the peaceful penetration which occurred as the pressure of population mounted in Haiti, and its peasantry began to spill over the thinly settled Dominican border provinces.

Despite this instability, some progress was achieved in the late nineteenth century. A group of unreconstructed United States southerners arrived in 1865, established a colony on Samaná Peninsula, and began to raise cacao. From there, cacao spread westward into the rich lands of the Vega Real, where it ultimately became a major cash crop of the rural population. Refugees from the Cuban wars of independence came during the decade 1868–1878 and created the impetus for sugar production. Later, American capital helped make sugar plantations an important feature of the landscape, especially on the southern coastal plain.

Along with this limited economic development the population began to increase, but, except for the Vega Real and the southern plains, much of the country's territory was still sparsely occupied at the end of the nineteenth century. The mountains were uninhabited, and the western borderlands contained almost as many Haitians as Dominicans. Equally important, the chief population clusters of the Cibao and the south remained sharply separated by inadequate transportation and the barrier of the Cordillera Central.

The economic development of the Dominican Republic in the twentieth century was achieved largely during two periods of political stability. The first of these was the United States occupation (1916–1924), during which there were considerable advances in transportation. The second period of stability came with Trujillo's absolute dictatorship from 1930 to 1961.

At the cost of all personal freedom, the era of Trujillo fomented vast changes on the landscape and in the general structure of the Dominican Republic. Population increased rapidly; new areas of settlement were opened up; and planned colonization bolstered the settlement of the borderlands on the frontier facing Haiti. Agriculture was strengthened by irrigation and the introduction of new crops. An impressive network of roads, linking all the major centers of population, was constructed. In addition, the foreign debt was paid off; new industries were created; and foreign investment capital received an encouraging welcome. Unfortunately, only a small measure of this progress filtered down to the bulk of the people, and the present patterns and problems of population, land, and resource use indicate that a continuing struggle for adjustment lies ahead.

Economic Patterns

Land is the fountainhead of the Dominican economy, but the economic structure erected on the land is far less sophisticated than that of Cuba or Puerto Rico. Most Dominican peasants are self-sufficient to the extent that often their only cash needs are for *sal y candela* ("salt and candles"). Even the commercial phase of the national economy is distinctive in the Caribbean. The Dominican plantation is of very recent vintage. It has not achieved the intensity of production, the monopoly of land, nor the marked dependence on foreign markets that plantations have in most of the other Antilles. Under Trujillo, the Dominican economy resembled a feudal, patriarchal state of the past. The serflike peasants worked for and owed allegiance to the landowners, particularly to *El Benefactor,* the biggest landholder of them all. In turn, the lords of the land were supposed to take care of their peasants' minimum needs. With Trujillo's assassination in 1961, this antiquated socioeconomic structure began to change.

Agriculture

LAND TENURE. One of the critical problems facing the Dominican Republic in the post-Trujillo period is the impossible legal tangle of land titles. Nowhere else in the Caribbean is the pattern of land ownership so thoroughly confused.

Originally, most land titles were derived from grants made by the Spanish Crown or by the government of the republic after independence. Many of the records of these titles are nonexistent, having been destroyed or lost during the turbulent period of Haitian occupation or in subsequent wars and revolutions. Much of the land now held was acquired through adverse possession, that is, through unchallenged claim or squatting over a period of years. Acquisition through adverse possession is seldom supported by clear-cut legal title.

The land tenure problem has been further complicated by the expulsion of the Trujillo clan. Trujillo and his numerous relatives and favorites acquired vast holdings between 1930 and 1961. These acquisitions, including the finest sugar and grazing areas in the country, came in part from the public domain or from newly irrigated areas, but in most instances they were bought at arbitrary prices or confiscated from enemies of the state. The new government has consequently fallen heir to a large number of well-developed properties, but it has also inherited a myriad of unsatisfied claims against these holdings and must work out a rational plan for their redistribution.

While there are some exceptions, Dominican land tenure continues to be dominated by the extremes of large land holdings and a landless peasantry. The most important exception is in Vega Real, where there is a long-standing tradition among the farmers never to sell their fertile land. As a result, inheritance has fragmented holdings until they are little more than garden plots of a few tareas (1 tarea = 628.8 square meters). Elsewhere the grip of the *latifundium* remains strong, largely untouched by the changes that have taken place since the Agrarian Reform Law of 1962. The dozens of settlement projects launched by the *Instituto Agrario Dominicano* under this law have involved primarily public lands and have benefited only a small percentage of the country's landless farm families. Thus, despite a comparatively low overall ratio of people to land, the tenure system is subjecting the expanding rural population of the Dominican Republic to severe land scarcity. The largest public areas available for settlement by small holders are in the arid western valleys, but these cannot be effectively occupied before the construction of additional expensive irrigation projects. In the meantime, the landless peasantry that cannot find work on the large estates is pushing upward into the wooded zones of steep mountain slopes, triggering deforestation and erosion.

CROP STRUCTURE. The commercial phase of Dominican agriculture rests on the trinity of sugar, cacao, and coffee, reinforced by rice, tobacco, and bananas.

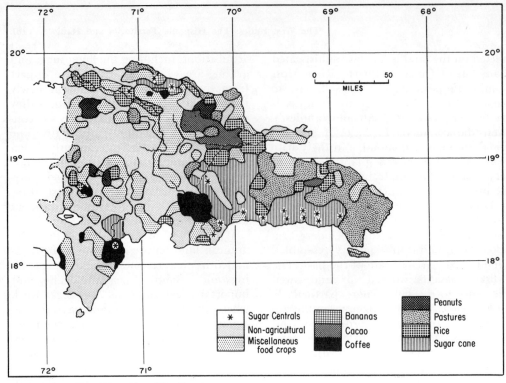

Figure 6.9 Dominican Republic: Land use

Crops for local consumption include peanuts, which supply the national needs for vegetable oil, corn, beans, peas, and the usual wide range of tropical vegetables and fruits. Stock raising is sufficient to supply both local demands and to make this one of the very few countries in the West Indies that has an exportable meat surplus. Food has been relatively cheap, and the peasants, who continue to be largely self-sufficient, are among the best fed in the Caribbean.

The cornerstone of cash farming is sugar, which normally makes up more than half the country's exports. Small quantities of sugar are raised in many places, but the major production comes from the southeast coastal plain and adjacent interior lowlands (Figure 6.9). Secondary sugar regions are found in the Cibao, on the north coast near Santiago and Puerto Plata, and in the lower valley of the Río Yaque del Sur. As we noted earlier, cane was brought to Santo Do-

mingo in the sixteenth century, and small quantities of sugar were produced throughout the colonial period. Significant production based on the modern plantation, however, did not begin until the arrival of Cuban refugees in the latter nineteenth century. Since then, production has increased steadily, rising from less than 5,000 tons in 1870, to over 1 million tons in 1970. Most of the Dominican sugar was exported to the United Kingdom and other European countries, but with the abolishment of the Cuban quota, an increasing amount is being sold to the United States. Trujillo, who owned much of the country's sugar industry, introduced the most modern machinery for both farming and processing, and approved the importation of cheap, seasonal labor from Haiti to keep wage costs low.

In contrast to cane, cacao and coffee are raised by small farmers using primitive tools and simple agricultural techniques. The machete, the hoe, and, where terrain permits, the ox-drawn plow are the chief instruments of cultivation. Cacao is largely grown on the rich soils of the Cibao between Moca and San Francisco de Macorís. In this region, the typical cacao farm consists of a small property set off by a live fence of a spiney plant called the *malla*. The cacao trees are generally invisible because they are shaded by amapola trees whose falling flowers and leaves help conserve the humidity around the sensitive cacao roots. The soil on these small farms is coal-black and produces a variety of food crops. A characteristic feature of the landscape is the small drying platform for cacao beans.

Coffee and rice growing are less localized than cacao farming (Figure 6.9). Coffee is raised on the lower slopes of many mountain areas, including the Cordillera Central. Upland or dry rice is also widely scattered, but paddy rice is produced primarily in the irrigated districts of the western Cibao and the reclaimed marshlands near the mouth of the Yuna River in Samaná. With the expansion of irrigation since 1930, the production of paddy rice has increased sufficiently to change the Dominican Republic from a large-scale importer to a modest exporter of the crop. Bananas are widely raised for local use, but those for export are concentrated in the irrigated lands of the western Cibao. A substantial part of the country's banana trade is in the hands of the American-owned Grenada Company, which raises the crop on its own plantations and also buys from small farmers.

Population and Settlement

If Dominican statistics are trustworthy, the population of the country increased from roughly 1 million in 1930 to over 4.3 million in 1970. This exceptionally rapid rate of growth, even for Latin America, took place during the only significant period of stability that Dominicans have enjoyed since the end of the eighteenth century. Except for the clandestine infiltration of Haitian settlers and workers, immigration has played only a slight role in the rise. Most of the population growth has been due to higher rates of natural increase.

Sharp increases in population are exceptional in Dominican history. Santo Domingo was the first European colony in the New World, but its post-Columbian population growth was probably the lowest in Middle America before 1930. The total destruction of the colony's Amerindian groups, its lack of attraction for Spanish and other European immigrants, the absence of the plantations and their need for slaves, political instability, and economic stagnation—all these served as barriers to population growth until recent times.

There are no accurate data, and only a few estimates, about Dominican population trends before this century. The early sixteenth-century concentration in Santo Domingo was rapidly decreased as adventurers left to conquer the other Antilles and the Mainland (see Chapter 3). Thereafter, virtually abandoned by Spain, the population of the colony increased at a snail's pace. By the latter eighteenth century, it is estimated, the total number of inhabitants in the territory came to about 150,000, of whom 20 percent were black slaves. The Haitian invasions reduced this figure by almost two-thirds, partly through slaughter and starvation and partly by prompting the wholesale emigration of the better-to-do white families. Estimates of population at the beginnings of independence in 1844 vary from 80,000 to 125,000. There were modest increases during the rest of the nineteenth century, but as we have noted, the total did not reach one million until 1930.

With a current population in excess of four million and a national territory of 18,817 square miles, overall densities in the Dominican Republic approximate 230 people per square mile. This ratio is low compared to other West Indian islands, but high in comparison to most Latin American countries. The distribution of people on the land is very irregular, however, and mathematical densities are only a crude index of actual densities.

The country's major population clusters continue to coincide with the historical nuclei of the Cibao and the southern coastal plains. The Cibao, together with adjoining parts of the north coast such as Puerto Plata and Montecristi, contain over half the Dominican population. Densities are especially high (over 600 people per square mile) in the black-soil belt of the Vega Real between Santiago and San Francisco de Macorís. Concentrations in the semiarid Cibao lowlands west of Santiago are small, except in the irrigated zones; and east of San Francisco de Macorís to Samaná Bay, densities are lower than in the heart of the Vega Real because of less favorable soils and poorer drainage. The metropolitan zone of Santo Domingo and the sugar lands of the Caribbean coastal plain between San Cristóbal and La Romana account for roughly one-third more of the population. The remainder is distributed along the approaches to the Haitian frontier, on the grazing lands of El Seibo, and in the various mountain regions.

Among these nuclei, the largest proportional increase in recent decades has taken place on the southeast Caribbean coastal plain. This has been caused by the rapid growth of the capital city of Santo Domingo and its environs and by the increasing importance of sugar cane, which is the agricultural mainstay of the area. Proportional increases have also been high along the frontier and its lowland approaches, such as the Enriquillo Depression, the San Juan Valley, and the westernmost Cibao. Population growth in the traditionally empty borderlands was due primarily to a policy of planned colonization under Trujillo. Since much of the

frontier is subhumid, the expansion of irrigation played a leading role in this colonization. Finally, it is noteworthy that the rapid overall increase in population, the expansion of plantation agriculture through large landholdings, and the tendency to import cheaper Haitian labor for seasonal work on the estates is forcing population into the higher mountain zones, including the Cordillera Central. Unlike Puerto Rico and Cuba, the Dominican peasant did not have to occupy mountain areas in the past, because limited plantation development on the lowlands left ample room for settlement. Currently, however, there is a marked push into the mountains, and many of the forested mountain zones, even in the *tierra fría,* are being cleared for occupation.

Population movements such as those to the mountains, the frontier, and the city are all of comparatively recent origin. Historically, Dominicans have exhibited a strong tendency to stay put. Unlike the Haitians, Puerto Ricans, and other West Indians, the Dominican peasantry has never been forced to migrate because of land hunger at home. On the contrary, the Dominican Republic has experienced immigration rather than emigration in this century.

In addition to comparative lack of mobility, the Dominican population is also distinctive in the Caribbean in terms of racial composition. Cuba and Puerto Rico, the other Hispanic islands of the region, are primarily white. The territories of north European colonial association are largely black. Only in the Dominican Republic is the bulk of the population mulatto. As we noted earlier, Spanish Santo Domingo continued to be primarily white during the colonial period. A small number of slaves were imported, but the low profits from cattle grazing did not warrant the importation of any large number of slaves. As usual, some miscegenation took place between white masters and slave women, but, still, at the end of the eighteenth century, the population of Santo Domingo was basically European. The change to mulatto composition must be largely attributed to the Haitian invasions and occupation. Many white families fled, as we have said, and the death rate among the remaining white Dominican males rose sharply. It was not uncommon for invading Haitian troops to slaughter the men and boys in a captured town and mate with the women. The Hispanic family names have been retained, but much of the mulatto population of the Dominican Republic issues from nineteenth century Haitian soldiery and captured white women.

In round numbers, the racial distribution is as follows: about 25 percent are more or less white, 12 per cent are black, and the remainder of the population falls into a wide range of mixture between the two. In addition, there are a few thousand Chinese, concentrated in the cities where they all but monopolize the restaurant trade. Blacks are heavily concentrated along the Haitian border, particularly in the Montecristi area, and above-average concentrations of blacks are also characteristic of the sugar lands of the southeast.

Types and patterns of settlement in the Dominican Republic attest to the importance of farming and to the rural orientation of most of the people. The percentage of the population classified as urban rose from 16.6 percent in 1920, to 30 percent in 1970, and the trend to urbanization continues; but most Dominicans are attached to the land and dwell in agricultural settlements, both dispersed and nucleated.

The average Dominican peasant lives in a *bohio* constructed of split royal palm siding and thatched with palm leaves. The unit usually consists of two rooms with a dirt floor, plus an occasional secondary shelter that serves as a kitchen or a storage shed. *Bohios* are often built by a *junta* of neighbors, in a cooperative effort which resembles the old house-raising bees in the

United States. Furnishings are few—a table, a few chairs, a bed for the parents, and hammocks for the children.

Traditionally, the *bohios* were dispersed through the countryside, and some dispersed settlement is still apparent, particularly in the Cibao and in the mountain areas of *conuco* or slash-burn agriculture. More recently, however, the general trend has been to village groupings that often develop stringlike along the roads. This trend has been encouraged by the growth of a highway network in the last 30 years and also by the government, which has found it easier to provide social services for village nuclei than for scattered homesteads.

Under Trujillo, the government-sponsored agricultural colony emerged as a distinctive rural settlement on the Dominican landscape. There are now dozens of such colonies scattered over the country, particularly along the Haitian borders (Figure 6.10). Their functions include bolstering the frontier against the growing pressure of Haitian population, developing previously unexploited areas, resettling surplus population from both urban slums and overcrowded farm zones, and attracting foreign immigrants.

Most of the larger towns and cities are in the Cibao or along the southern coastal plain. The road running eastward through the Vega Real from Santiago passes in

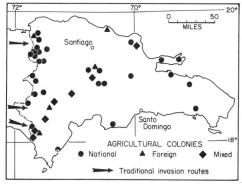

Figure 6.10   Dominican Republic: Agricultural colonies, 1960

rapid succession through important centers such as Moca, Salcedo, San Francisco
de Macorís, and Sanchez. Similarly, on the
south coast, La Romana, San Pedro
de Macorís, Santo Domingo, San Cristóbal, and Baní follow each other in close
order. Outside the two major population
regions, towns such as San Juan, Barahona, and Azua are more widely spaced,
reflecting lower economic production and
smaller population concentrations.

All the country's urban centers have
been experiencing rapid growth, but none
comparable to that of Santo Domingo
(formerly Ciudad Trujillo). The population of the capital increased more than
twentyfold in recent decades, jumping
from about 30,000, in 1920, to over 600,-
000, in 1970. Santo Domingo was largely
destroyed by a hurricane in 1930, and its
subsequent growth mirrors a rapid expansion of its government and port functions,
as well as of its role as the country's chief
center of industry, transportation, and
banking. Trujillo lavished huge sums of
money on this city, which bore his name
until 1961. At its center, Santo Domingo
is one of the cleanest and most attractive
cities in Middle America, but even Trujillo was unable to wipe out the odoriferous slum fringes that characterize Caribbean urban centers.

The Outlook

At an incredible cost in terms of liberty
and other human values, Trujillo brought
about major economic improvements that
left an impressive mark on the Dominican
landscape. The task of maintaining and
improving on the material achievements
of Trujillo has not been easy. The rapid
and continuing growth of Dominican population is wiping out the traditionally
favorable land-people ratio; the problems
of land titles and redistribution are more
complex and acute than ever; and political instability is again rampant. Above

all, there is the great difficulty of changing
the relation of a quasi-feudal society to the
land, so that the peasant will give up the
security and shackles to which Trujillo
accustomed him and match his new freedom with economic initiative and political responsibility. The beginning of the
revolution following Trujillo's death was
easy; it is the unfinished business of the
revolution that is hard.

HAITI

There is no more arresting theme on the
Haitian landscape than the hopeless dis-
equilibrium of its people, land, and resources, and the grinding human poverty
which ensues from this. All of Haiti's potentials appear submarginal, save the
child-bearing capacity of its women. The
mountain lands that make up almost 80
percent of the national territory's 10,240
square miles are eroded; the lowlands often suffer from inadequate rainfall; minerals are virtually nonexistent; the forests
have largely been cut down; and fishing
makes only a puny contribution to the
food supply of the nation.

On this weak resource base live over
five million people; some accounts place
the figure at over six million. No truly
accurate count has ever been made. Population densities are high almost everywhere, for people have had to spread over
mountains and plains, wet areas and dry
ones, regardless of conditions. And still
the population increases.

Under these conditions, poverty is
etched on the landscape in bold relief.
In Port-au-Prince it can be seen in the
distended bellies of children begging for
tourist nickels, in the eyes of the men and
women scavenging alongside the pigs in
the city dump, and in the swampy slums
of La Salene. The countryside is equally
bad (Figure 6.11). People "forage on the
hillsides like nature's lesser creatures. As

Figure 6.11   Haitian fisherman from Gonaïves. Note the ravages of disease and malnutrition.

soon as something green grows . . . they chop it down, to eat or burn as fuel" (Wolfe 1960:1).

Haiti's change, in less than two centuries, from the richest plantation colony in the Caribbean to the poorest independent nation in the Americas is due to a multiplicity of causes. First of all, much of the equipment and organization for production developed by the French went up in the flames of slave revolts (see Chapter 3). Estate houses and sugar mills were symbols of slavery and of the hated *blancs,* and they were destroyed outright; other features, such as roads, aqueducts, irrigation works, and coffee groves, were not maintained and often reverted to nature. The turmoil and instability that began with the slave uprisings at the end of the

eighteenth century did not end with independence. They have continued in varying degree of intensity to this day. When the Haitians stopped fighting Europeans, they fought the Dominicans, and they fought each other—north against south, republic versus kingdom, mulatto against black. Added to this instability were the burdens of inexperience, lack of know-how, political corruption, and perpetual distrust of the white world.

Through this turbulent history the pressure of people on the poverty-stricken land has gradually increased to saturation and beyond. As in other slave societies, freedom from bondage was often interpreted as freedom from work—at least freedom from supervised work (see Chapter 3). The blacks took to the hills to scratch out a bare but independent living, and the peasant plot replaced the large plantation. In this way the national economy became dominantly subsistent; estate agriculture became an anomaly; erosion of mountain lands became rampant; and poverty became the way of life for the constantly increasing population. While many Haitians deny it, the most constructive period in recent times seems to have been the United States occupation (1915–1934). As in the Dominican Republic, the Americans were not popular, but they built roads, improved sanitation, stabilized the budget, and left the national treasury with a surplus. The surplus had disappeared by 1937, and it now requires a strong back and a sturdy jeep to traverse some of the roads built by the Americans.

Agricultural Patterns

The mark of economic activities other than agriculture is barely legible on the Haitian landscape. Mining, forestry, grazing, and transportation are of minor consequence; tourism is of modest significance, and only in a few centers such as Port-au-Prince and Cap-Haïtien; and manufacturing installations are few in number and largely associated with the processing of farm products.

The chief molder of the landscape and the backbone of Haiti's economy is the *petite culture* of peasant farmers. Plantation agriculture *(grande culture),* so important in most West Indian territories, is insignificant except for a few minor cash crops such as sisal. The dominance of peasant farming throughout the production structure is reflected in land ownership and use, local marketing and foreign trade, agricultural practices and tools, and a variety of other characteristics.

Land Tenure. The current patterns of land ownership in Haiti may be grouped into three major categories: (1) peasant plots, (2) bourgeois holdings, and (3) the public domain. Of these, peasant ownership is the most important, both in terms of cultivated acreage and overall crop production. Peasant plots vary from a fraction of an acre to upwards of 100 acres. Estimates are that average holdings are less than 1.5 *carreaus* or 5 acres (1 *carreau* = 3.33 acres or 1.2 hectares). Peasant properties of over 10 *carreaus* are exceptional, and their owners form a rural middle class called *gros habitants.*

Bourgeois holdings include both the estates of Haitian nationals and the lands owned by foreign corporations and individuals. There are probably about 1,000 estates (of 300 acres or more) owned by the local town-dwelling elite. Only a few of these holdings are intensively cultivated under the direct supervision of owners. Most are haphazardly exploited through rental and sharecropping under a peasant *gérant* ("manager"). The owners who prefer to live in town are interested only in the income from their land. They seldom visit the properties, and as a result, the estates are undercultivated and mismanaged. Prior to the United States occupation (1915–1934) there were considerably more of such holdings. The elimination of many

town jobs by the efficiency-minded military government forced many of the unemployed elite to sell their lands in order to live.

The United States occupation also resulted in the repeal of laws against foreign ownership of land in Haiti. Presently, there are several large holdings that are owned and operated in typical plantation fashion, using agricultural wage labor for the production of crops (see Chapter 4).

The extent of Haiti's public domain has never been accurately established, but most of it consists of marginal lands in the mountains and in arid areas. In order to produce revenue and relieve the pressure on private lands, the government rents parts of the public domain for annual fees. The rental theoretically varies according to environment and productivity, being highest in well-watered mountains and favored locales. In practice, however, local politics are more important than environmental considerations in determining rent.

Renting land from the government and estate owners goes hand-in-hand with widespread sharecropping, or *métayage,* in Haiti. Both practices reflect the growing pressure of population on the limited supply of land. Fragmentation of small holdings through inheritance has forced many families to sharecrop additional land to eke out a living. Even when a peasant's total inheritance is large enough, it is often scattered in patches over a wide area, and, unable to farm the scattered properties, the small owner is forced to relinquish some of the land to *métayage.* References to the preponderance of small properties in Haiti tend to obscure the fact that many of these holdings no longer provide an independent living to the peasant owners. Moreover, the small holders are constantly haunted by insecurity of tenure. With no adequate cadastral survey, a long tradition of squatting, widespread illiteracy, and increasing land hunger, many property titles are subject to legal challenge.

Coffee and Other Export Crops. Haitian exports are almost exclusively agricultural. In recent years, coffee has accounted for almost three-fourths of the total trade, and sisal and sugar together make up 15 percent more. Other noteworthy commercial products are essential oils, cacao, cotton, and bananas.

The position of Haitian coffee (see Chapter 4) has undergone a number of modifications since the end of the eighteenth century: it has surpassed sugar as the leading export; it has changed from a plantation product to a peasant cash crop; and its chief center of production has shifted from the hinterland of Cap-Haïtien to the southern massifs. Coffee production was able to survive the destruction of the colonial plantation. Its exportation surpassed that of sugar, and it became the leading cash crop of the peasants—largely because the plantings were self-perpetuating. In the chaos that followed the ousting of the French, little care was given to the coffee estates. The crop would have died out, except that berries which fell to the ground were decorticated by rats, and thus provided seed for the new trees which began to grow wild on the mountain sides. The postrevolutionary population that occupied the former estates seldom attempted to restore the groves, and coffee came to be gathered as a wild fruit from the forest. Even today, there is little actual cultivation of the crop. Most thickets from which the peasantry gathers berries are natural growth, *café rat,* derived from the French colonial plantations.

The southward shift of major coffee production from its old eighteenth century locus around Cap-Haïtien is due in part to the nineteenth-century struggles that separated the Haitian north from the south, making the Artibonite a no-man's land. The north, under radical black militarists such as Christophe, experienced greater destruction and instability than the south, which was ruled by moderate mulattos such as Pétion and Boyer. The

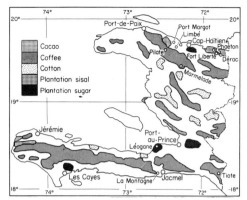

Figure 6.12   Haiti: Commercial crops

shift of the coffee-growing areas may also be explained in terms of land distribution policies, climate, and other factors.

Currently, Haiti's chief coffee area is the mountainous Southwest Peninsula between Tiote and Jérémie (Figure 6.12). Production in the Massifs de la Hotte and de la Selle amounts to over three-fifths of the national total, making the south's production well above that of the north and the Artibonite. Since the south experienced less destruction from slave revolts and has had greater stability in the postindependence period, the investment of the region's highlands by peasant farmers was more orderly. Under the enlightened land distribution policies of Pétion and Boyer, the property rights of small holders were more firmly established and respected, and as a result, the peasantry seems to have taken better care of the land. Deforestation and erosion, which are major threats to the coffee economy in mountain zones, have occurred less in the southern massifs than elsewhere. Equally important, the rainfall of the windward slopes of the southern highlands is almost ideal for coffee, especially the dry fall period when the crop is reaching maturity. These favorable historical and climatic conditions for the crop were also reinforced by the region's proximity to Port-au-Prince, Haiti's chief port and coffee mart.

The coffee areas of the north and the Artibonite rank a poor second and third, respectively, to those of the south. The heart of the coffee country in the Massif du Nord is on the windward slopes, extending from the vicinity of Port Margot eastward through Limbé, Marmelade, and Pilate. The crop is also found on the lowlands, such as those near Port-de-Paix, Milot, and Cap-Haïtien, where it is often raised in association with cacao and bananas. Production in the Artibonite centers on a number of upland fringes, including the Chaîne de Matheux and the Montagnes Noires.

Despite the vital importance of coffee as Haiti's chief cash crop, production is beset by numerous difficulties. The peasant farmers who produce the bulk of the crop seldom prune or top the trees, with the result that plantings have become dense thickets of stems and leaves that yield only about 100 pounds of berries per acre. There are very few large plantations, and most peasants own only a few hundred trees. Equipment for processing the crop is very primitive; the berries are dried in the sun and then pounded in mortars to remove the dry pulp. Pounding breaks many of the beans and improperly cleans others, and the overall quality of the product is greatly reduced.

Sugar and sisal, the other two significant exports, are primarily associated with the *grande culture* of the plantations. Both crops are of comparatively recent commercial development, and both are largely tied to United States corporate ownership. While some sugar continued to be produced in Haiti after the downfall of the colonial estates, the modern sugar plantation of the *central* type had to await the United States occupation (1915–1934). The Americans not only abolished the laws against ownership of land by foreigners, but they also improved the transportation and provided the capital necessary to stimulate plantation development. The chief regions of commercial sugar produc-

tion are the irrigated lowlands of the Cul-de-Sac, the plain of Léogane near Port-au-Prince, the Plaine du Nord south of Cap-Haïtien, and the coastal zone of Les Cayes (Figure 6.12). An unknown quantity of cane is also raised on peasant plots for local use. This goes into making *rapadou* (a solid sweetner) and *tafia* and *clairin,* the favorite alcoholic beverages of Haiti.

Sisal production received a major boost during World War II. Currently, a few large plantations, located mainly on the north coast between Cap-Haïtien and Fort Liberté (Figure 6.12), raise the crop. Mills for processing sisal in this area have been built at Phaéton and Dérac. Chief among the plantations is the American-owned Daphne holding of over 10,000 acres, in northeast Haiti.

Peasant Farming. As already implied, the *petite culture* of Haitian peasant farming rests upon the intensive cultivation of small plots. Labor input is large; capital investment is limited and is largely restricted to the ownership of the land itself; tools are few and simple; the use of animal power is restricted primarily to marketing; and farming practices are primitive. While generally described as subsistent, *petite culture* shows considerable market orientation at the local level.

Peasant production emphasizes numerous food crops, of which the more important are cassava (*manioc*), yams (*igname*), sweet potatoes (*patate*), and other root varieties. In the drier areas the African grains, sorghum and millet (*petit mil*), are widely cultivated. Other food crops brought from Africa and grown by the Haitian peasant include the vegetables, okra (*gombo*), and pigeon bean (*pois congo*); the cooking banana, or plantain (*banane*); and the all-important yam. Virtually all the fruit, vegetables, and grains (especially maize) of Middle America's *tierra caliente* and *templada* zones are raised, and in addition there are some cooler latitude plants (such as peaches, strawberries, and figs) that are grown at higher elevations. Fibers such as cotton, native sisal, and others (used in making rope, cloth, and so forth) are second to food crops in importance.

Peasant farming practices and tools may appear primitive to outsiders, but they are often convenient adaptations to local physical and economic conditions. The principal tools include the hoe, the machete, the billhook (*digo*), an iron bar or dibble (*louchette*), and various types of knives, such as curved *serpette* and the *collins*. The machete is used for clearing, and the hoe, billhook, and dibble are variously used for cultivation, depending on slope and type of crop. In some especially steep mountain lands where the peasant can only work with a rope to hold him up, even the hoe is ruled out. No use is made of the wheel; crops are carried by man or animals in baskets; and the mortar serves as decorticator. The plow has never won acceptance, in part because of the small size of holdings and in part because of the broken surface of the ground. Actually, plows and other less primitive tools would have loosened the mountain soils more deeply and thus increased erosion.

Farming practices are roughly comparable to those of *conuco* agriculture elsewhere in the West Indies, but with some suggestion of African influence. In planting, for example, the peasant drops seeds from a calabash and covers them with his feet, as is done in parts of West Africa. Plural-storeyed, mixed planting is common, with maize and beans above and root crops below. In the absence of fertilizers, crop rotation and fallowing are necessary for even the barest yields, but they are not always practiced. Burning weeds and brush before cultivation is common, even though forbidden by law. Burning impoverishes the soil by consuming some of the humus content, but it does add some needed potassium to the land.

The heavy work of clearing and hoeing is done by the men who often invite their neighbors to form a working *combite*. Although comparable in spirit to the American husking bee, the *combite* is supposed to be a West African carryover. The workers line up and hoe in unison to the beat of a drum or the cadence of a chant. Payment by the farmer to the members of the *combite* may be made in a variety of ways, including return services, cash, or a large meal and a measure of white rum (*tafia*). Once the heavy work has been accomplished, women and children take over the weeding and other light tasks.

Women play a vital role in Haitian peasant agriculture, not only in light farm work but in management and marketing as well. As we have already noted, peasant holdings are often fragmented and scattered, making it impossible for the farmer to work all his plots. Under the circumstances, he may either give part of his land to others for sharecropping or he may take a second wife (*placé*) and put her in charge of his plot. Thus, if a peasant increases his holdings or inherits a second plot on the other side of the mountain, it is only common sense for him to take a second woman, raise a family by her, and assure himself of an overseer, a labor supply, and a marketing agent on each of his properties. Practical needs determine the number of women to each man.

Marketing in Haiti, except wholesale and export, is also largely in the hands of women. The surplus of peasant farming is walked to market in loads of anywhere from 20 to 50 pounds on the heads of women or on donkeys (Figure 6.13). Every town and hamlet has a market, and there are others in the countryside, at crossroads or other convenient locations. Groups of walking women may spend half the week on the road and in the marketplace. They sleep wherever nightfall catches them, and many walk as much as 30 miles to a more distant market to get a slightly better price. If all the produce carried by the woman or burro is sold at a fair price, she may return home richer by a few *gourdes*

Figure 6.13   Haitian peasant women walking to market

(20 or 30 cents). If, as often happens, the market is glutted, she has to sell for less or carry the stuff back home. Markets serve a social as well as economic function. The market women are the rural gossip columns of Haiti, and often they will not sell until they have had a chance to socialize and gather news.

Marketing by women began in revolutionary times with the breakdown of the French communication system. During the troubled periods, men had to hide to escape death or the army, and women had to take over the disposal of farm surplus. Once established, marketing by walking women was reinforced by custom and economic conditions. Inadequate transportation and lack of refrigeration and other facilities make any other form of collecting and marketing too difficult and costly.

While most of the production of Haitian peasant agriculture is for subsistence, the widespread local marketing suggests a significant commercial emphasis. The peasant depends not only on the disposal of such obviously cash crops as coffee, but also on the small surpluses of virtually everything his plot produces. Part of the peasant surplus goes to feed the country's urban population and to supply export, but much of it is sold within the rural peasant population itself. The walking women often buy from each other the different produce grown under different climatic conditions only a short distance away. There is an obvious exchange between lowlands and highlands, between the *tierra caliente* (*té cho*) farmers and those of the *tierra templada* and *fría* (*té fret*) zones, and between the coast and the interior.

Population

Densities and Movements.   The growth of Haiti's population was comparatively slow until this century. The territory contained over 500,000 people, the largest block in the West Indies, in the eighteenth century, but the subsequent proportional increases have been well below those of Puerto Rico, Cuba, and even the Dominican Republic. Historical turmoil served as a Malthusian barrier to rapid population growth, but this is of little comfort in the light of current population pressures and patterns.

Estimates in 1970 indicated an overall density of roughly 500 persons per square mile, but the figure is over 1,000 per square mile when population is related to arable land. The rural population concentration tends to be high over much of the country, but densities vary considerably with climate, terrain, soil productivity, and other factors. The heaviest concentrations are generally on well-watered or irrigated lowlands, and on the lower and middle slopes of windward-facing uplands; the lowest densities are associated with dry, leeward areas on the upper slopes of the high mountains.

Composition, Caste, and Culture.   With the exception of a tiny colony of white business families in Port-au-Prince, Haiti's population is about 95 percent black (*brun*) and 5 percent mulatto (*jaune*), the latter descendants of eighteenth-century French fathers and African mothers.

The slight difference in eighteenth-century ancestry has burgeoned into a wide gulf between the minority of *jaunes* and the masses of *bruns*. There are few Caribbean areas where color and classes are so closely related as in Haiti. The mulattoes constitute the elite and are separated from the black majority by class barriers which have the rigidity of caste. The elite do not work with their hands; they live in the urban centers and are engaged primarily in business, the professions, industry, and government. In contrast, the black majority constitutes a rural peasantry whose life is bound to the cultivation of the land. The two groups are also sharply differentiated by language, religion, dress, education, cultural orientation, and other ways of life.

Haiti is actually a bilingual country. French, the official language, is spoken only by the elite. The peasantry speaks a Creole patois that is a mixture of French, Spanish, and English, with some African and Indian vocables. The two groups can communicate only because the elite learn the Creole dialect, as children, from the servants. The masses dress in cotton and go barefoot, but the mulatto aristocracy copies the latest European fashions. The elite adhere to Catholicism as a badge of their part-European ancestry and wholly European cultural values and orientation; the blacks may be nominally Catholic, but they also practice *voudon* ("voodoo"), an African carryover. In short, while the *jaunes* represent the veneer of sophisticated twentieth-century French culture in Haiti, the *bruns* symbolize the more primitive African cultural forms stemming from the colonial slave period. Money breaches the barriers however: "a poor *jaune* is a *brun,* and a rich *brun* is a *jaune.*"

Settlement

Rural Patterns.   Nine out of ten Haitians live in a rural setting, either in dispersed homesteads or in tiny villages consisting of from four to ten dwellings. In general, the peasant hut (*caille-paille*) is a one- or two-room thatched cottage whose walls are loosely made of twilled bamboo or other flexible creepers and coated with mud and lime (Figure 6.14). The shelter tends to be small, averaging 10 by 12 feet; it has a beaten-earth floor but no ceiling; and its roof thatching is of straw, palm leaves, or similar materials. Cooking is done outside or over a charcoal fire in a metal brazier. Furnishings are few. Perhaps one *caille-paille* in four contains a bed. The others have hammocks or straw mats for sleeping. A few crude chairs, occasionally a table, cooking utensils, and the family chest complete the list of household goods. The more fortunate village groupings may have a community privy nearby. In the colder mountain zones, families shiver around small braziers, or simply shiver. About three-fourths of Haiti's rural housing consists of vermin-infested hovels that are wet during the rainy season and suffocating at night when the doors and windows are shut tightly against ghosts and the night air.

Figure 6.14   Haitian peasant's *caille-paille* on the Plaine du Nord

The presence of rural dwellings on the Haitian landscape is generally denoted by clumps of fruit trees. These trees are most commonly banana, plantain, breadfruit, avocado, and mango, but there is some variation with climate and region. At higher elevations, such as in the mountains around Kenscoff, there are peach and other middle-latitude trees. Beyond the fruit groves that screen the houses are cultivated patches of field crops and occasional thickets of coffee trees. Not infrequently, the family tomb, built of masonry and much sturdier than the cailles, is also hidden by foliage.

Dispersed rural settlement is much more frequent in Haiti than elsewhere in the Antilles. In part this is due to the necessity to seek out the small patches of cultivable land, but in part it stems from historical insecurity. In the turbulent past, agglomerated settlements were frequently pillaged by roving bands of marauders and soldiery. The peasant learned that there was less danger in dispersed settlements hidden by a screen of thick foliage. Even today, the unwary observer may walk for miles through densely settled rural zones without seeing a *caille*.

The village grouping of four to ten houses, less common than the dispersed homestead, seems to be disappearing altogether in some parts of the country. Neither highways nor social services are sufficiently developed to play any important role in stimulating the growth of agglomerated rural settlements in Haiti, as they have in the Dominican Republic. Most of the tiny villages of Haiti are inheritance groupings that develop on family lands, and the *habitants* are usually blood kin, with common parents or grandparents.

Urban Patterns. Despite the practice of census officials of designating even hamlets of a few hundred inhabitants as *villes*, cities and urban settlements in general have made only a slight dent on the Hai-

tian landscape. This is due in part to the limited importance of commerce, industry, and other city-building activities. Perhaps equally important, however, is the strong psychological attachment of the Haitian *habitant* to the land. From the time that the emancipated slaves escaped from the French plantation villages and the colonial towns, the Haitian masses have avoided the urban centers except for marketing. Currently, Haiti is one of the few countries in Latin America without a burgeoning (and often artificial) country-to-town movement.

The Haitian town (*bourg* or *bouc*) is smaller than the city and located inland, and its major function is to serve as a marketplace for Haiti's "walking women." The size of the *bourg* appears to be proportional to its market. In turn, the size of the market depends on the population density and the productivity of the immediate hinterland, plus the nature of the terrain over which the peasant woman must walk. The internal structure of the average town includes a *place* ("square") around which are grouped the church and public buildings. The houses of the better-to-do residents are on the principal streets leading to the *place*. These residences are small, rectangular constructions that are built of wood plastered over with clay, painted in bright colors, and roofed with sheet iron. Most houses near the center of the town have a veranda and an interior courtyard that has a cookhouse and a storage shed. The huts of the poorer elements on the edge of town are no different than the *caille-paille* of the rural *habitant*.

The Balance Sheet

Probably nowhere else in Middle America is man so closely tied to nature as he is in Haiti, but it would be difficult to find another place where man's struggle to wrest a living from the land is so bitterly unrewarding. History and environment seem to have conspired to foster hopelessness in Haiti.

Economically, the country appears to be worse off today than under French rule. In 1789, fewer than 10,000 French planters, aided by about a half million slaves, cultivated almost as much land as do over 3 million Haitian peasants today; and the value of the plantation exports in 1789 was over $75 million, roughly double the amount of Haiti's current annual exports. The contrasts are almost equally sharp in terms of transportation, irrigation, the processing of plants for crops, and other features of the economic landscape. After more than a century and a half of independence, Haiti has not only failed to recover from the destruction of the French colonial plantation, but has actually retrogressed.

This retrogression may be attributed in part to the lack of order in man's relation to land. A growing pressure of population on a limited resource base has been compounded by deforestation and erosion, by fragmentation of holdings to a point where they are no longer viable, and by disregard of the most elementary rules of conservation. But Haiti's current plight can also be attributed to lack of order in man's relation to man. Until recently, a Western world, obsessed with the notion of European racial and cultural superiority, looked upon the black republic as a hopeless throwback to Africa and made no effort to lend a hand. The negative attitude of the outside world has been more than matched by that of the Haitian elite itself. In a society almost wholly dependent on agriculture, the governing aristocracy has shunned the countryside for the towns and poured its talents into professions largely unrelated to farming. Legislation that might have aided the peasant in making better use of the land has been inept because the legislators themselves have known little about the problems. Burdened with this legacy of disorder, the Haitian peasantry has had to forego progress in an elemental struggle simply to survive.

SELECTED REFERENCES

AUGELLI, J. P. "Agricultural Colonization in the Dominican Republic." *Economic Geography* 38, no. (1962):15–27.

———. *Puerto Rico.* Boston: Ginn, 1973.

DE YOUNG, M. *Man and Land in the Haitian Economy.* Latin American Monographs, no. 3. Gainesville: University of Florida Press, 1958.

DYER, D. R. "Cuban Sugar Regions." *Revista Geografica* 67, no. 2 (1967):21–30.

———. "Distribution of Population on Hispaniola." *Economic Geography* 30, no. 4 (1954):337–46.

———. "Sugar Regions of Cuba." *Economic Geography* 32, no. 2 (1956):177–84.

GUERRA Y SÁNCHEZ, R. *Sugar and Society in the Caribbean: An Economic History of Cuban Agriculture.* New Haven, Conn.: Yale University Press, 1964.

HANSON, E. P. *Transformation: The Story of Modern Puerto Rico.* New York: Simon and Schuster, 1955.

HOLLY, M. A. *Agriculture in Haiti.* New York: Vantage Press, 1955.

JONES, C., and PICÓ, R. *Symposium on the Geography of Puerto Rico.* Río Piedras: University of Puerto Rico Press, 1955.

"La Historia Azucarera y su Evolución en la República Dominicana," *Revista Secretaria Estado Industria Comercio Banca* 42 (1955): 59–86.

LOGAN, R. W. *Haiti and the Dominican Republic*. London: Royal Institute of International Affairs, 1963.

MARRERO, L. *Geografía de Cuba*. Havana: Editorial Minerva, 1950.

MATTHEWS, H. L. *Cuba*. New York: Macmillan, 1964.

MINTZ, S. W. "The Culture History of a Puerto Rican Sugar Plantation, 1876–1949," *The Hispanic American Historical Review* 33, no. 2 (1953):224–51.

MORAL, P. "La Culture de Café en Haïti." *Les Cahiers d'Outre-Mer* 8 (1955):233–56.

———. "La Maison Rurale en Haïti." *Les Cahiers d'Outre-Mer* 10 (1957):117–30.

———. *L'Économie Haïtienne*. Port-au-Prince: Imprimerie de l'État, 1959.

———. *Le Paysan Haïtien: Étude sur la Vie Rurale en Haiti*. Paris: G. P. Maisonnueve et Larose, 1961.

NICHOLSON, J. "Inside Cuba." *Harper's* 246, no. 1475 (1973):54–69.

ORGANIZATION OF AMERICAN STATES. *Haiti, Mission D'Assistance Technique Integrée*. Washington, D.C.: General Secretariat of the OAS, 1972.

———, Natural Resources Unit, *Survey of the Natural Resources of the Dominican Republic*. Washington, D.C.: General Secretariat of the OAS, 1969.

ORTIZ FERNANDEZ, F. *Cuban Counterpoint: Tobacco and Sugar*. New York: Alfred A. Knopf, 1947.

PICÓ, R. *The Geographic Regions of Puerto Rico*. Río Piedras: University of Puerto Rico Press, 1950.

SCHAEDEL, R. D., ed. *Research and Resources of Haiti*. New York: Research Institute for the Study of Man, Columbia University, 1969.

SEERS, D., ed. *Cuba, the Economic and Social Revolution*. Chapel Hill: University of North Carolina Press, 1964.

SEMEVSKY, B. N. "Social and Natural Conditions of Cuban Agriculture." *Soviet Geography: Review and Translation* 8, no. 1 (1967).

STEWARD, J. H., et al. *The People of Puerto Rico: A Study in Social Anthropology*. Urbana: University of Illinois Press, 1956.

WOOD, H. A. *Northern Haiti: Land, Land Use and Settlement*. Toronto, Canada: University of Toronto Press, 1963.

≡ 7 ≡

The West Indies: Jamaica, the Lesser Antilles, and the Bahamas

The geographic variety that characterizes the Hispanic territories and Haiti is no less pronounced in the rest of the eastern or insular rim of the Caribbean. Behind the seemingly uniform facade of tropical insularity and the predominantly black population of Jamaica, the Lesser Antilles, and the Bahamas, are significant economic and cultural differences. Some of these differences stem from a varied historical experience (see Chapter 3); others seem to correlate with current adjustments to differences in location, size, resources, and political options.

Agriculture is the economic cornerstone of Jamaica and most of the Lesser Antilles, but land use, crop structures, and other particulars of farming are far from uniform. Tourism ranges in importance from providing the life blood of the Bahamian economy to being virtually negligible in some of the Lesser Antilles. The relative importance of mining and manufacturing from territory to territory is even more varied.

Patterns of population, language, religion, and political orientation are also diverse. Many of the islets and reefs are too small or inhospitable for human occupance; others, such as Barbados, are among the world's most densely populated territories. The official languages are Eng-

lish, French, and Dutch, depending on current political connections (see Chapter 5), but the language of the people may have older origins. Thus, a French patois is spoken in British-connected Dominica and St. Lucia; Hindi is heard in the East Indian villages of Trinidad; and the Barbadian peasant's English is unique. As for religion, Trinidad alone probably has as great a variety as most of mainland America.

JAMAICA

It is not surprising that Jamaica was the first to withdraw from the West Indies Federation (see Chapter 5). With almost 1.9 million inhabitants and a territory of 4,411 square miles, the island had more than half the land area and population of the tentative union. Many Jamaicans reasoned that they had problems enough of their own and that separate independence was preferable to political association with the other small, widely scattered, and poorly endowed British colonies. But, as in other newly emerging Third World nations, political independence has not solved Jamaica's formidable physical and social problems.

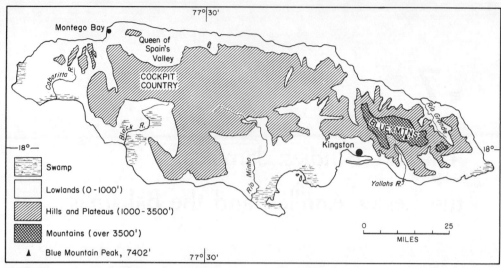

Figure 7.1   Jamaica: Gross surface features

Physical Setting. Jamaica's resource base is handicapped by numerous disadvantages—some natural, and others resulting from man's misuse of the land. Level areas suitable for farming are scarce. Well over half the island's surface consists of rugged slopeland lying 1,000 feet or more above sea level (Figure 7.1). In the east, an uplifted core of igneous and metamorphic rocks has been heavily dissected by rivers into a topography of twisting valleys and sharp crested ridges dominated by the Blue Mountains. Elevations in this sector average well above 3,000 feet and reach a maximum of 7,402 feet at Blue Mountain Peak. Except for a fringe of coastal plain, the rest of the island consists of a limestone plateau that has been considerably broken up by faulting, and on which the erosive action of water has etched a typically karst landscape.

The widespread karst terrain is both an asset and a liability. In some areas, such as the Cockpit Country (Figure 7.1), the honeycombed limestone, with its network of collapsed caverns and sinkholes, diverts drainage underground and causes inadequate surface water supply despite heavy rainfall. Here farming is difficult and population is sparse. Elsewhere, erosion of the limestone has produced a rolling upland of rounded hills that provides a living for a larger number of people. The heaviest rural settlement in the limestone areas, however, is to be found in the great solution basins with their deposits of rich, red soils. The largest and most productive of these are: St. Thomas in the Vale; the valleys of the Black, Minho, and Cabaritta rivers; and the Queen of Spain Valley near Montego Bay. A number of solution hollows also contain a byproduct of limestone weathering that is rich in alumina. This is bauxite ore, now Jamaica's leading mineral export.

As a mountainous trade wind island, Jamaica receives its heaviest precipitation in its northeast highlands. The higher slopes of the Blue Mountains, for example, are drenched by 200 or more inches of rain per year. In contrast, the southern lowlands (such as those west of Kingston), which lie in the rain shadow of the mountains, are often too dry for agriculture without irrigation. The island's humid zones once had a dense forest cover, but most of this has been cut down, and many of the woodland areas shown in Figure 7.2 represent secondary growth of limited value for lumbering.

Deforestation has deprived Jamaica of useful timber resources and has also intensified soil erosion and leaching. Without a protective cover, a combination of

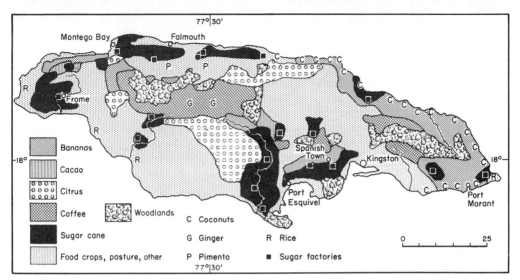

Figure 7.2   Jamaica: Land use

steep slopes, high temperatures, and (in humid areas) torrential rains has washed away much of the topsoil. Often the entire upper horizon has been removed; where it still remains, the rate at which nutrients have been leached from the soil has increased.

Natural disasters have added to the problem. Crustal instability periodically gives rise to severe earthquakes, such as the tremor that largely destroyed Kingston in 1907. Hurricanes are even more of a problem. At least once in every decade of this century, the island has suffered from varying degrees of destruction from the "dread wind of the Caribees." Loss from these storms was particularly heavy in the 1940s.

Economic Patterns.   The meagerness of Jamaica's resource base is strikingly revealed by land use. Despite the vital importance of agriculture, only about 15 percent of the island's area is considered cultivable, and much of this is marginal land or land devoted to tree crops. Unbridled exploitation of the lowlands by the plantations and of the uplands by the peasantry has ruined much of Jamaica's soil resource. Perhaps as much as three-fourths of the area now classified as unused and unproductive can be restored to

productivity for farming and forestry. Officially, agriculture contributes slightly more than one-tenth of Jamaica's Domestic Product, and employs about one-third of the labor force. Unofficial estimates, however, indicate that roughly 60 percent of the island's total population "are dependent largely upon the soil for their livelihood" (Floyd 1968:9).

The usual West Indian contrast, between the plantations (called "estates" in the British-connected territories) in the lowlands and small peasant plots in the uplands, characterizes land holdings in Jamaica. At one extreme well over one-half of the agricultural land is held by less than 1 percent of the population in the form of large, well-organized estates. Many of these larger holdings encompass several thousand acres and are foreign-owned. At the other extreme, the peasant group, which constitutes some three-fourths of the farming population, controls about 12 percent of the land. The average peasant plot measures about 1.8 acres of mountain slope in the interior, with some spillover into the least productive lowland zones.

Also in keeping with West Indian patterns, the contrast between peasant farming and estate agriculture in Jamaica goes far beyond the differences in size, location,

179

and fertility of holdings. Except for a limited number of large holdings in drier areas that emphasize cattle production for local consumption, most Jamaican estates have the typical organization and production structure of the modern plantation (see Chapters 1 and 4). They emphasize the production of a few crops for export, using machinery and hired labor under an efficient corporate management. In contrast, the peasant farmer uses hand tools and family labor to raise a large number of crops. A small part of his production may be for export, but the vast bulk is for subsistence, or for sale (by his "higgler" spouse) in local markets. His holding, reduced in size and fragmented into small, scattered plots by successive inheritance, seldom provides an independent living; he must either sharecrop additional land or seek wage labor on the estates and elsewhere. Without reserve capital, the peasant can be devastated by drought, hurricanes, cold spells, and by his neighbors' bad habit of stealing crops.

The land use patterns shown in Figure 7.2 are, at best, a highly generalized version of reality. With only 15 percent of the island under cultivation or in orchards, much of the area shown in crops includes considerable acreage that is not farmed at all or is used only for grazing. This is particularly true in the eroded uplands and on the drier leeward coast.

Sugar and bananas, the leading export crops, can be traced across Jamaica's agricultural landscape from Frome in the west to the vicinity of Port Morant in the east (Figure 7.2). In addition, the island produces a variety of secondary agricultural exports. The most important of these used to be coffee, including the world-famous Blue Mountain variety. In recent years, however, citrus fruit, pimento (allspice), and even cacao have commanded a higher value in the overseas trade. Most of the secondary exports are raised on small upland farms, and their chief importance is that they provide a cash income for the peasantry. But the most valuable products of Jamaican farming are food crops that are grown by the small farmers for both subsistence and local sale. The cultivation of such crops is so widespread that items such as corn and yams often make up the bulk of the farmed land even in the zones shown to be under bananas, coffee, and other largely commercial products (Figure 7.2).

MINING.   Thanks to the recent growth of the bauxite industry, minerals now surpass agricultural products in Jamaica's foreign trade. Bauxite was discovered in the course of wartime explorations in 1942, but the first shipment was not made until 1952. Since then, however, the island has become the world's leading exporter of the ore.

A number of factors have favored the rapid rise of Jamaican bauxite production. Chief among these are the huge ore reserves (500 to 600 million tons) which the island possesses, and the ease and low cost of mining operations, including the shipment of the ore to market. Most of the bauxite is found in limestone solution hollows averaging 20 to 30 feet deep, with only a thin overburden of soil covering the ore. This makes it possible to carry on inexpensive open-pit mining with power shovels and scrapers (Figure 7.3). And the mines are located a short distance inland, on the north and south flanks of the limestone plateau, so that the bauxite can be hauled cheaply to port or to local processing plants by truck, rail, and even aerial tramway for eventual shipment to overseas markets (Figure 7.4).

In 1971, Jamaica's annual bauxite production had risen to more than 12 million tons, and further expansion was anticipated. Most of the ore still undergoes little more than kiln-drying before being shipped overseas, but an increasing amount (about one-third in 1970) is being processed into alumina in local plants. One such plant, completed in 1969 at Nain in St. Elizabeth Parish (Figure 7.4), is the largest of its kind in the world, outside of the United States. Two other plants are located at Ewarton and Kirkville, and a fourth one will soon begin operating in the Parish of Clarendon.

Capital and know-how for the development of bauxite, Jamaica's "red gold," has come primarily from the United States and Canada. Of the five aluminum corporations operating on the island in 1970, four were American and one was Canadian. Other American companies are expected to begin mining in the future.

Many Jamaicans deplore this wholesale foreign ownership of bauxite resources, but few can deny the benefits it has brought to the island. The export of bauxite and alumina accounts for most of Jamaica's foreign exchange earnings. American and Canadian mining interests also pay a large share of the island's taxes; they employ thousands of workers; and they have either improved existing transportation and shipping facilities or, as in the case of Port Kaiser, have actually built new ones.

Equally significant are the consequences of the laws that oblige bauxite companies to restore mined lands to at least previous fertility and to maintain agricultural production on land being held in reserve for future mining. Before bauxite can be dug in a given area, six or more inches of topsoil must be stripped and stockpiled for restoration to the same location later. In

Figure 7.3   Jamaica: Open pit mining of bauxite (*G. Murison*)

most cases, the companies fertilize the restored soil. In addition, the bauxite firms have undertaken reforestation, planted food crops, improved water supplies and pastures, and developed considerable herds of beef and dairy cattle on their properties. Of the 80,000 acres owned by Reynolds, for example, 60,000 are under some form of cultivation, including a large area

Figure 7.4   Jamaica: Mining

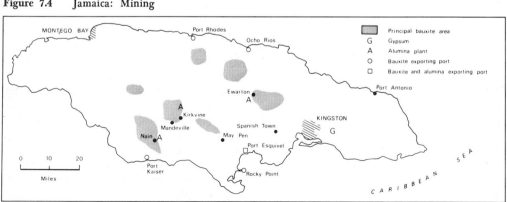

planted to pangola and Guinea grasses. The companies have also imported Santa Gertrudis, Charolais, and Brahman stock to improve the island's cattle strains.

In addition to bauxite, Jamaica also mines gypsum, a nonmetallic mineral widely used in cement, plaster of Paris, and other building materials. Rich, 85 percent pure, massive deposits of gypsum are located near Bull Bay about ten miles east of Kingston. Most of the production is sent to New Orleans and Jacksonville, but some is retained for use in local cement and plasterboard factories.

INDUSTRY, TOURISM, AND TRADE. Like Puerto Rico, Jamaica is making a strong bid to encourage the establishment of new manufacturing industries on the island. Since achieving independence, the government has passed legislation such as the Laws for Industrial Incentives, Export Industries, and Pioneer Industries, and has created the Jamaica Industrial Development Corporation. As a result, the island's manufactures have grown both in number and diversity. Virtually all the new establishments can be classed as labor-oriented light industries, and their products range from textiles to frozen foods and electronics. Also as in Puerto Rico, most industries tend to concentrate in the chief urban center (Kingston), but the government is using special incentives to induce location in smaller towns.

The importance of tourism to the Jamaican economy has been already noted (Chapter 4). Except in the World War II years, tourism has grown constantly ever since the flow of visitors first assumed significant proportions in the mid-1920s. Prior to the war, most tourists came by sea, on cruise ships and even banana boats. Port Antonio, for example, once ranked along with Montego Bay and Kingston as a tourist center, largely because it served as a port of call for vessels in the banana trade. Since the war, the rapidly increasing movement of vacationers to the island has been largely by air.

Like Puerto Rico, Jamaica's tourism depends on the prosperity of the United States and Canada, which supply most of the visitors. The less-than-prosperous conditions of the American economy in the early 1970s was reducing both the number of tourists and the amount of money they spent in Jamaica. Still, tourism ranks second only to bauxite as a dollar earner.

In addition to the expansion of facilities in the old tourist centers of Montego Bay and Kingston, the large influx has given rise to new developments on the north coast beach zones between Falmouth and Port Maria, and more recently, in the Negril district at the western end of the island. Interestingly, some of the old manor houses of the colonial plantation period are serving the tourist trade, in addition to the new hotels and guest houses.

The pattern of foreign trade has also been undergoing growth and change. In 1950, for example, sugar and bananas accounted for 65 percent of the exports, and the bulk of the trade was with Britain and the sterling block. By 1970, bauxite and alumina had replaced sugar and bananas as the chief exports; and the primary export markets had shifted to the United States and Canada. Britain continues to take most of the island's farm products.

Population and Settlement.   As already suggested in previous chapters, the historical occupance of Jamaica may be broadly divided into two stages: (1) the colonial plantation-slave period, during which there was settlement of lowland areas suited for sugar production; and (2) postemancipation, roughly to 1910, during which a population of peasant farmers invested the unoccupied limestone uplands to the limits of cultivation. With the disappearance of the settlement frontier in 1910, the gross patterns of population distribution were complete. Thereafter, there was no significant extension of the settled area; instead, land use became more intense; densities continued to rise; and, above all, there began a marked trend to urbanization that has continued at an ever-accelerating tempo.

The current distribution of population tends to be correlated closely with terrain, the history of settlement and urbanization, and the productive capacity of agricultural land. The heaviest concentration is the urban sprawl of Kingston–St. Andrew which continues westward along the irrigated southern lowlands, through Spanish Town, to Port Esquivel. Densities are also high in St. Thomas in the Vale and other well-watered solution valleys, such as those of the Black and Minho rivers; in the Montego Bay area and south through the lowlands of the Great River; and along the humid north and east coasts from Falmouth to around Morant Bay. Elsewhere, population densities are less, and ratios are especially low along the driest sectors of the southwest coast, the Cockpit Country, and in the highest mountain zones of the central and eastern parts of the island.

With an annual rate of natural increase of almost 30 per thousand, Jamaicans rank among the most prolific people in the West Indies. The island's total population zoomed from less than a half million in the mid-nineteenth century to almost 2 million at present (1973). Similarly, overall population densities (86 per square mile in 1844) had jumped to 365 by 1960 and 443 in 1970. Such densities would be even higher had it not been for more than a century of emigration during which Jamaicans moved to Central and South America, other West Indian islands, Anglo-America, and Britain.

Most of the current population increases are taking place in the island's predominantly rural parishes. There has been hope that increasing urbanization would help reduce the high birth rate, but to date these hopes have not been realized. Almost one-half of Jamaica's population is under 16 years of age, suggesting that future rates of demographic growth may be even higher than at present. And herein lies the major cause of the island's socioeconomic problems.

The bulk of Jamaica's population lives in dispersed homesteads or in small clusters which, depending on size and function, may be classified as neighborhoods or villages (Figure 7.5). In most parishes,

Figure 7.5   Jamaica: Settlement types and patterns

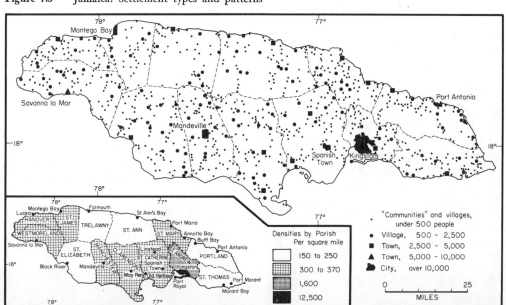

the chief town is on the sea coast and serves as a port. Except for Kingston, Montego Bay, and Spanish Town, the term "city" is difficult to apply to the urban centers.

Some differences exist, however, between the interior uplands, with their large number of small holders and subsistence agriculture, and the lowlands, with their estates, commercial farming, ports, and fishing villages. In the hilly interior, dispersed settlement is the rule, although discontinuous ribbon clusters of households often form neighborhoods along the motor roads. At more important road junctions, the clusters of buildings are more closely spaced and form the typical village. In addition to residences, the village also includes shops, a primary school, a post office, and facilities for a weekly market. While the lowlands also have some dispersed settlement, one sees more village clusters here than in the uplands. This is especially true of the sugar estates and the fishing settlements. Often the estate villages consist of barracks and other housing built by the landowners for the workers. The lowland village tends to be more nucleated and less ribbonlike than its upland counterpart.

Kingston, which, together with its suburbs, had a population of over 500,000 in 1970, is by far Jamaica's chief city. Founded in 1693 after the destruction of Port Royal, the city has been aided by a sheltered and once easily defended harbor and a rich agricultural hinterland. Kingston suffered heavy damage by earthquakes in 1907, but was rebuilt and now functions as the island's chief port, as well as its major administrative, financial, and transportation center. In recent decades, its suburbs have spread rapidly into the parish of St. Andrew across the Liguanea Plain and up into the encircling foothills. Kingston has been, by far, the leading terminus of Jamaica's country-to-town movement since 1911.

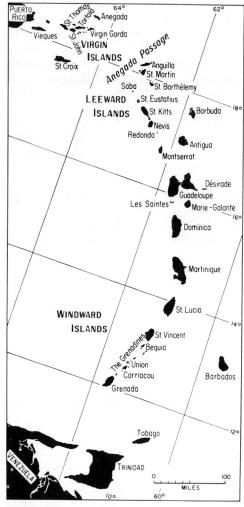

Figure 7.6   The Lesser Antilles

THE LESSER ANTILLES

The Lesser Antillean chain, which traces an arc between Puerto Rico and the Venezuelan coast (Figure 7.6), is a bewildering array of islands, islets, and reefs.[1] As al-

1. We include among the Lesser Antilles, Trinidad, Barbados, all the territories from the Virgin Islands in the north to Grenada in the south, and Aruba, Bonaire, and Curaçao, which lie well to

ready noted, no segment of comparable size in Middle America has been so completely fragmented and diversified by nature and history. The following summaries can provide only a hint of the striking physical and cultural variety in this insular mosaic.

Trinidad

Although each of the Lesser Antilles has its own geographic flavor, none approaches the distinctiveness of Trinidad. The island is the largest and most populous in the archipelago, the richest in natural resources, and the most heterogeneous in ethnic composition. It is also one of the two Lesser Antillean territories with sufficient economic viability to be politically independent.[2] These advantages stem partly from its physical geography and partly from its unique history of settlement and exploitation.

Physical and Historical Setting. A detached fragment of South America, Trinidad shows the imprint of close connection with the continent in both its physical and historical geography. The island's geology, including the oil-bearing tertiary formations, its surface configuration, and its plant and animal life, is more akin to the adjacent Orinoco region of Venezuela than to the more distant volcanic and limestone arcs of the Lesser Antilles.

In contrast to the rugged Windwards,

for example, Trinidad's relief is generally subdued. The major exception is the Northern Range, a line of steep-sided mountains that rises abruptly from the sea to elevations of 3,000 feet. Even this range is punctuated on its southern flank by several large, pouch-shaped valleys. The only other uplands are two low, narrow ridges of hills, within elevations of 1,000 feet or less, that extend across the center and south of Trinidad. The rest of the island is lowland, whose chief handicap is poor drainage. Because of its comparatively large size (1,864 square miles) and its gentle relief, the island has more level, cultivable lowland than any of the other Lesser Antilles.

Trinidad also possesses a major climatic advantage. It lies south of the main path of hurricanes and seldom experiences them. Because of its lower latitude and other influences, the climate is distinctly hot for the West Indies. The high temperatures and generally high precipitation often create hot-house weather, uncomfortable for people but ideal for tropical crops such as cacao. Soils vary widely, but on the whole, the most fertile are along the west coast and in the southern valleys and foothills of the Northern Range.

Trinidad's unarticulated coastline, however, is a drawback. A combination of steep barrier mountains in the north, widespread coastal swamps, and winds and currents make sea communications difficult, except in a few spots along the western margins of the island.

Its soil, its adequate rainfall, its year-round growing season, and its relative protection from hurricanes provide Trinidad with an agricultural potential far exceeding that of the other Lesser Antilles. Yet, Spain, which controlled the island from its discovery until the British annexation, in 1797, sent only a few colonists, and these developed little agriculture. There was little cultivation, particularly of cacao, during the seventeenth and

the west of the Antillean chain. There is no absolute agreement about the inclusiveness of the designation. For many students, especially geologists, the Lesser Antilles begin with the islands east of the Anegada Passage, such as Sombrero and Anguilla, and end with Grenada or Tobago in the south (Figure 7.6).

2. Trinidad followed Jamaica's example both in withdrawing from the West Indies Federation and in electing for independence within the British Commonwealth.

eighteenth centuries, but by 1783 the total population of Trinidad was only 2,763.

In that same year, Spain liberalized its colonization policies, permitting all Roman Catholics to enter, remitting taxes, and conceding land to new settlers. As a result, the island began to receive a moderate flow of immigrants, largely planters from revolt-torn St. Domingue and other French West Indian colonies. On the eve of the British occupation, there was some production of sugar; the population had risen to about 20,000; and settlement had expanded from a tiny nucleus around Port of Spain to adjacent areas on the Caroni Plain and in the valleys of the Northern Range.

The tempo of economic development and the spread of settlement picked up dramatically after 1797. The plantation-minded British settlers expanded commercial agriculture, and cash crops such as sugar and cacao provided a firm economic foundation throughout the nineteenth century. The economy was further strengthened by petroleum after 1910 and, more recently, by manufacturing, tourism, and other sources of income.

The steady demand for workers attracted immigrants not only from nearby islands but also from India, China, and other distant places (Chapter 5). As the population increased, the frontier was gradually thrust southward from Port of Spain. By the 1870s, much of the western part of the island had been occupied. The settlement of lands in the east came later, with the development of cacao plantations.

Economic Patterns. In most respects, Trinidad's economy is typically West Indian. Agriculture employs most of the people; export crops occupy so much of the best land that much food must be imported. For its food, as well as for a wide range of other imports, including most finished goods, the island is slavishly dependent on the export value of a limited number of products. Unlike most of the other Antilles, however, Trinidad exports more petroleum and related products than agricultural commodities.

PETROLEUM AND ASPHALT. Leases for oil exploration have been granted for more than 90 percent of Trinidad's surface, including its offshore areas. Currently, explorations are being conducted in a 3,000-square-mile offshore zone lying between northern Trinidad and southeastern Tobago. Most of the island's oil however, comes from a small area adjacent to the Pitch Lake (Figure 7.7) and from the offshore Soldado and North Marine fields in the Gulf of Paria. Proven deposits are associated primarily with the tertiary formations located in the southern part of the island, opposite the delta of the Orinoco, and may be considered a geological extension of Venezuela's Orinoco oil province.

Trinidad's oil industry was developed after 1910, primarily by British capital. In 1956, however, Texaco, an American firm, bought the English-owned Trinidad Oil Company and became the largest owner. Texaco together with British Petroleum and Shell now account for most of the production; the remainder is pumped by more than a half-dozen small companies.

Trinidad refines far more oil than it pumps. Two major refineries are in operation, one at Point Fortin and the other at Point-à-Pierre. The latter, owned by Texaco, is reputed to be the largest in the British Commonwealth and one of the largest in the world. Crude oil is imported chiefly from nearby Venezuela and Colombia, but smaller quantities may come from as far away as Saudi Arabia and Libya.

Geologically associated with oil are considerable reserves of natural gas and asphalt. Although most of the asphalt is a by-product of oil refining, the island is famous for the natural deposits at Pitch Lake, near La Brea (Figure 7.7.). The lake's natural asphalt is a semisolid bituminous material that results from the mixing of gas and oil with clay. In a few spots

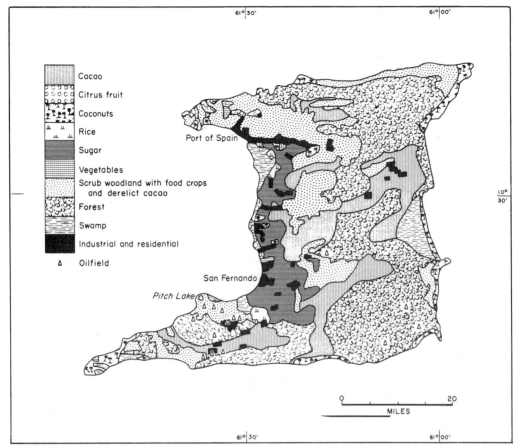

Figure 7.7   Trinidad: Land use

the material is soft and sticky, but over most of the surface, it is hard enough to cut into blocks. The asphalt is then loaded on light railway cars and carried up the steep lip of the lake to a factory where asphalt cement and other by-products are made, and the finished product is hauled by overhead cable to a nearby pier.

Pitch Lake is the world's chief deposit of natural asphalt. Annual output is over 150,000 tons; cumulative production since mining began in 1867 is about ten million tons; and reserves are estimated at several million tons. Removal of the asphalt causes the lake to drop a few inches every year, and the surface is now over 30 feet below the rim.

AGRICULTURE. Nearly half of Trinidad's total area is in forest, but the woodland cover appears even more extensive because tree crops occupy more than half the cultivated land. The remaining farmland is mostly in sugar cane and food crops (Figure 7.7).

The land is held both in estates and in small peasant plots. The estates, which comprise less than 1 percent of the farms but control over 40 percent of the farm land, dominate sugar and coconut production; the smaller holdings produce all the food and half the cacao and coffee. The peasant plots are of more commercial importance in Trinidad than in most of the other Antilles.

For several decades following the British occupation, Trinidad's sugar production was based on a modification of the colonial plantation (Chapter 3). Estates were generally family-size farms, widely dispersed in the valleys of the Northern Range and along the west coast; virtually every estate was equipped with a *trapiche;* and transportation and milling costs were high.

Despite these inefficiencies and the "labour problem," an abundance of virgin land enabled Trinidad to weather the postemancipation sugar crisis of the West Indies until the 1870s. By that time, however, the island's competitive position in the world sugar market had become weak, and there ensued a rapid changeover to the modern plantation. The family estates gave way to corporate ownership and the *central.* The more remote cane lands were planted in cacao and other crops, and sugar production was increasingly concentrated in a belt running south of Port of Spain to the Oropuche Lagoon. Here were the best conditions—level terrain, better soils, a more favorable climate, and easy access to ports. Little cane is now grown elsewhere on the island.

Currently, cane occupies about a quarter of the cropland, the ownership being about equally divided between the estates and some 11,000 small holders. The capital resources, mechanization, and efficiency of the estates, however, enable them to produce twice as much sugar as the small holdings and to process the entire crop. Many of the small sugar farms are owned by East Indians who also work as wage laborers on the estates. Great Britain is the chief buyer, and Canada and the United States also purchase significant amounts.

As we noted earlier, cacao was grown very early in the colonial period, but it became a significant crop only in the late nineteenth century. When sugar declined, the cultivation of cacao increased rapidly, and by 1900, it had become the island's leading export. Eventually, cacao occupied much of the former cane land in the west and spread over the unsettled virgin lands in the eastern part of the island.

Cacao prospered until the 1930s. Then, the witch's broom disease, combined with competition from the African Gold Coast and the Great Depression, brought about a decline. Many cacao farms were abandoned; others became coffee or citrus groves; and still others became cane fields or were put to other use. In the valleys of the Northern Range, for example, the cacao lands closest to Port of Spain became urban areas; those more removed from the capital became citrus groves.

At present, more of Trinidad's land is classed as "cacao" than "sugar" (Figure 7.7), but this is misleading because many of the cacao plantings are derelict. Moreover, cacao is generally intercropped with other plants and seldom occupies more than half the land. Currently, cacao production centers in the Central Range, northeast of San Fernando. The crop is produced both on estates and on small holdings, but the estates use superior methods so that, even with substantially less acreage, they produce more.

Other Trinidad export crops of some importance include citrus fruit and coconuts. Citrus fruit has replaced cacao, especially in the valleys of the Northern Range. Coconuts grow on the sandy soils of virtually all the island's coasts (Figure 7.7), and almost three-fourths of the output comes from large estates. The bulk of the harvest is dried to make copra for the manufacture of edible oils, soap, and cosmetics. Most of these products are consumed locally, but some are exported to other West Indian territories.

Food crops are grown largely in an area of small holdings that skirts the sugar belt and runs to the south of San Fernando. Rice, the most distinctive food crop, is raised mainly in the low, wet areas of the Caroni Swamp. It is grown during the wet season between June and December; the rest of the year the fields are often planted in vegetables. Rice is produced almost entirely by East Indians who plow the land with the water buffalo and use other

Asiatic techniques. Most of the harvest is consumed by its growers, and a large part of the island's rice, as well as other food, has to be imported.

Population. As noted elsewhere, the economic development of Trinidad following the British occupation was accompanied by the rapid growth and ethnic diversification of the population. From a mere 20,000 in 1797, the population climbed to 75,000 by 1851, to 300,000 by 1911, and reached over 800,000 in the early 1960s. Besides the East Indians who came between 1845 and 1917 (see Chapter 4), there arrived, at various periods, smaller numbers of Chinese, Madeiran peasants, Syrians, European Jews, Venezuelans, and others. The largest group came, after emancipation, from overcrowded territories elsewhere in the British Caribbean, especially from Barbados and the Windward Islands. Even today, about one Trinidadian in ten was born in one of the other British territories in the Lesser Antilles.

DISTRIBUTION. The current distribution of the population reflects Trinidad's settlement history, terrain, land use, and a variety of other conditions. The lowest population densities coincide with the rugged terrain of the Northern Range and the zones of poorer soils, inadequate drainage, and inarticulate coastlines in the east and south. The heaviest concentrations are in the west, which was settled earlier and has a more articulate coastline, and whose fertile soil is more intensively and commercially cultivated. The western counties also include most of the oil fields and refineries, the Pitch Lake, and the urban complexes of Port of Spain and San Fernando (Figure 7.7).

Trinidad's people have been moving to the towns, particularly since 1940, and it is now one of the most urbanized territories in the West Indies. By the 1970s, the population of metropolitan Port of Spain was well over 300,000, and the en-tire area between the capital and Tuna Puna, 10 miles east, was gradually fusing into one urban sprawl. The urban thrust of the metropolitan zone was being felt even in the island's third largest city, Arima, 24 miles to the east. San Fernando, the second largest city, has also grown vigorously.

In the rural areas, population densities tend to vary with the labor requirements of the dominant crop. Thus, sugar cane, which requires a large labor force, is associated with high concentrations, and many parts of the sugar belt, which extends south of Port of Spain, contain over 200 persons per square mile. Rice and vegetable gardening are associated with comparable, and even higher, densities. Cacao, which requires about one-half the labor force needed for sugar cane, is associated with less dense populations. Coconuts, the chief cash crop along much of the southern and eastern coastal margin, require a small labor force and hence are associated with low population densities.

RACIAL AND CULTURAL DIVERSITY. While there has been some mixing among Trinidad's diverse racial and ethnic groups, the island has not been a melting pot. The various segments have retained their distinctiveness and, as a result, Trinidad's landscape is marked by a variety of cultural features and flavors. The diversity of the population is expressed in distribution, as well as its settlement, its land use, its agricultural systems, its place names, and in other areal phenomena; it is also mirrored in differences in religion, architecture, language, diet, class association, dress, and even politics. There is virtually no aspect of the island's culture that does not somehow express the diversity of its people.

Distributional contrasts between the blacks and East Indians are especially sharp. The blacks (or Creoles) markedly prefer the urban areas. They comprise about 57 percent of the total population, but account for a far greater percentage of

Figure 7.8   Hindu temple, Port of Spain, Trinidad

people in the cities and towns, in the oil fields, and in the Pitch Lake district; they comprise much less than 57 percent of the population in the intensively cultivated countryside. The distribution of the East Indians is almost the reverse. They make up about 40 percent of the population, but contribute far less than this ratio to the urban areas and the oil fields; they form a much higher percentage of the population in the more intensively cultivated areas, especially the sugar belt.

Place names are truly diverse. Town names are French (Blanchisseuse), Span-ish (Sangre Grande), Indian (Fyzabad), English (St. Mary's), as well as Irish and Scotch (Flanagin Town and McBean). In Port of Spain, O'Connor, De Vertueil, and Petra are adjacent streets, and Fraser and Carlton run alongside others named Madras, Calcutta, and Bengal.

Religious architecture is equally heterogeneous (Figures 7.8 and 7.9). There are stately English Gothic churches, Moslem mosques, and Hindu temples. There are many sects, but the major religious division is between the Christian population, which includes practically all the Euro-

Figure 7.9   Episcopalian church, Trinidad

pean and black groups, and the non-Christians, which include the East Indian Hindus and Moslems, the Jews, and others.

The Christians are mostly Roman Catholics, but Presbyterians, Methodists, and Baptists are well represented. About 70 percent of the East Indians are classified as Hindus, and the remainder are, in almost equal numbers, Moslems and Christians. In addition to the established religions, there are sects with a strong African flavor, such as the Shango, the Rada, and the Shouters.

Language is less varied. English is the official tongue and Creole English the ordinary language, but remnants of Spanish, French patois, and Urdu and Hindi survive.

Tobago

Tobago, which has an area of 116 square miles, is politically bracketed with Trinidad, but its history, economy, and landscape are noticeably different.

In size and general character, Tobago bears a closer resemblance to the Windward Islands than to Trinidad, which is only 20 miles away. The uplands of the Main Ridge, which dominates the northeast, consist of igneous materials; the lower, southwest portion of the island is made up largely of coral terraces. Tobago was settled early, unlike Trinidad, and during the seventeenth and eighteenth centuries, its sugar, cotton, and indigo made it a bone of contention among France, England, and Holland. Before British rule was established in 1814, the island had changed hands more often than any other West Indian territory.

At that time, Tobago was an intensively cultivated plantation island with a prosperous, slave-supported sugar economy. The economy began to collapse, however, after 1838, when over 10,000 slaves were emancipated, and by 1886, exports had

fallen 90 percent. Economic distress forced Tobago to unite with its more prosperous neighbor, Trinidad, in 1888.

Tobago has since experimented with several other cash crops, of which the most important are now cacao, which is raised on the humid windward side, and coconuts, which are more characteristic of the leeward side. About 40 percent of the total area is under cultivation (Figure 7.10), but the economy is weak. A long history of exploitation has depleted the soil, and yields are low. Erosion is a major problem on the interior slopeland, where most of the peasant plots are located, and even the coastal estates have suffered.

Tobago's dominantly black population has a high birth rate, but large-scale emigration to Trinidad has kept the net population increase relatively low in recent years.

Barbados

Barbados has been appropriately described as "a city with sugar cane growing in the suburbs." Over 250,000 persons are crowded into an area of 166.3 square

Figure 7.10   Tobago: Land use

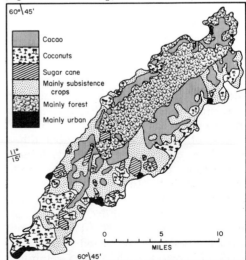

miles, producing urbanlike population concentrations; yet, the island depends primarily on farming, and on one crop at that. For the past three centuries, almost all the cultivated land has been in sugar.

Barbados was the first of the West Indies to experience the sugar revolution in the seventeenth century, and the first to experiment successfully with the slave plantation (see Chapter 3). But emancipation caused relatively little disruption in Barbados. So many slaves had been imported that population densities had reached 700 people per square mile by 1834–1838, the period of emancipation. And, since nearly all the land was in the hands of the planters, the freed blacks were unable to obtain holdings of their own and either had to continue to work for their former masters or migrate. The abundant supply of cheap labor enabled the economy to survive the sugar crisis of the nineteenth century. Barbadian planters were under less pressure to incorporate or to invest in new machinery and mills than were planters in Jamaica and Trinidad. Nor did they have to diversify; Barbados' land and labor force could still produce sugar more profitably than any other crop.

The Land. Barbados is the most easterly of the West Indies, located at least 100 miles further out in the Atlantic than its nearest neighbor, St. Vincent. From the west, the island looks flat and uniform. Closer observation, however, reveals considerable variation in relief. Rainfall, soils, and other physical characteristics are also varied.

Most of the island consists of a limestone layer over a core of strongly folded sedimentary rocks such as clays, sandstones, and shales. In the northeastern, or Scotland, district, the limestone cap has been eroded, and the underlying rock has been weathered into rugged ridges and ravines. Elsewhere, the island is mostly a series of terraces, each with a retaining

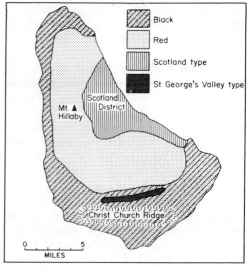

Figure 7.11   Barbados: Major soil types

wall of coral rock, which ascend from west to east and culminate in Mt. Hillaby (1,115 feet) in the central uplands (Figure 7.11). East of the upland mass, the land often drops abruptly, forming cliffs that plunge hundreds of feet to the windward coast. South of the uplands, the land descends to St. George's Valley and rises again to about 400 feet at the Christ Church ridge.

Soils in the limestone areas, while shallow, are very fertile. In zones of higher elevation and rainfall, they are red or brown and, like the Matanzas clays of Cuba, especially suited for cane. On the less wet limestone lowlands, the soil is black and less fertile. In the Scotland district, the soils vary in fertility, but are often so eroded as to be untillable. The black soils of St. George's Valley are highly productive when properly plowed and drained. All the soil is admixed with volcanic materials, which presumably were carried to the island from the Windwards, especially from Mt. Soufrière on St. Vincent.

The productive capacity of the land also depends on the water supply and drainage. Rainfall is irregular, both from year to year and from place to place. The annual average rainfall is about 63 inches, most of which falls during the rainy season (June to November), but it may be less than 40 inches or soar to almost 90. And 25-inch differences between the wettest zones in the Central Uplands and the driest zones on the leeward coast are common (Figure 7.12).

Economic Patterns. Except for a very modest tourist industry, a scattering of manufacturing enterprises, and some entrepôt trade, the Barbadian economy rests almost exclusively on farming. The enormous pressure of population has resulted in much more intensive farming here than elsewhere in the Caribbean. Every bit of productive land is used. The forests and thickets that once covered the island have vanished; over 55 percent of the total area is tilled; and what land cannot be worked is put to other uses. On the steep flanks of the terraces grass for fodder and for cane mulch is grown, while "rab" land, unfit even for pasture, is being planted with hardy trees or supports peasant dwellings. Farming practices are similarly intensive.

Figure 7.12   Barbados: Mean annual rainfall

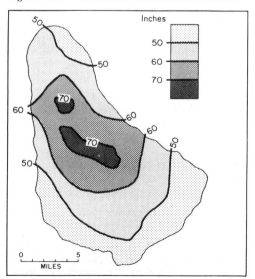

Agriculture and cane cultivation have been virtually synonymous on Barbados for three centuries. The crop occupies almost 90 percent of the cultivable land; sugar and its by-products, rum and molasses, constitute up to 95 percent of the exports. The well-being of every person, be he merchant, peasant, or politician, is tied to cane. Nowhere else in the Caribbean has sugar reigned so long and so absolutely, and nowhere else is its reign more secure.

The sugar plantation or estate is the dominant holding. Four-fifths of all the land is held in about 240 estates, which range from 10 to 1,000 acres and average between 150 and 200 acres. The remainder of the land is held in small peasant plots, but the estates with more and better land and more efficient management produce almost six times as much sugar as the small holders.

Farming practices, as well as yields, reflect the pressure of population. Labor-saving machinery is not extensively used. Holes for planting, for example, are still dug by hand. Production has been increased largely through the use of fertilizer and better plant varieties and by the elimination of pests and plant diseases. Efforts have also been made to cut production costs by reducing the large number of antiquated mills or factories, especially those that were powered by wind.

While cane is grown throughout the island, the center of production is in the parishes of the central uplands. The heavier and more reliable rainfall, together with the fertile red and black soils, result in the best yields (Figures 7.11 and 7.12). In this area, cane occupies virtually all the cultivated land, and the large landholders control over 90 percent of the acreage.

The sugar industry of Barbados has little prospect of further growth. There is no unused land; the unreliable rainfall is a major problem; irrigation is costly and subsurface water supplies are limited; yields are already almost maximum; mechanization is of dubious advantage when labor is overabundant. Moreover, the sugar market is glutted; prices are low, and could the island produce more, there would be few buyers. The continuing growth of the island's population in the face of its limited economic future is Barbados' greatest problem.

Population and Settlement. Barbados is extremely populous. By 1970, there were over 1,500 persons per square mile, and despite emigration and one of the lowest birth rates in the West Indies, the ratio continues to climb. It was estimated (Lowenthal 1957:445–501) that the island's densities are equal to those of suburban London and exceed those of suburban Philadelphia and most United States cities. Along with a few spots in the Nile Valley and the Orient, Barbados heads the world list of densely occupied agricultural areas. The island now has over four persons per cultivated acre. As we noted earlier, Barbados was densely populated before emancipation. Periodic waves of emigration to Trinidad, the Guianas, Central America, the United States, and the United Kingdom, have served only to slow the rate of growth. Current emigration is a mere trickle, primarily to the United Kingdom.

The distribution of population on Barbados is somewhat irregular. Over one-third of the people are in metropolitan Bridgetown, which extends well beyond the municipal limits of the city proper. Here, densities range from ten to twenty thousand per square mile. The least crowded areas, the rugged and eroded Scotland district and the semiarid southeast coast, have densities of about one person per acre.

Compared to Trinidad, and even to Jamaica, the population is relatively homogeneous. About four-fifths are descendants of African slaves; slightly over 5 percent are whites; and the remainder are Euro-African mixbloods, locally called "coloured." Since the island had a surplus

of labor after emancipation, there was no need for immigrants from India, China, or elsewhere.

The correlation between race and class is more obvious on Barbados than in the other West Indies. In general, the whites occupy the top of the social hierarchy, and the mixbloods and blacks rank below them, but there is considerable stratification within each group. The poorest whites, the Red Legs, have a standard of living lower than that of most blacks, and are looked down on by everyone. But the island's "colour bar" excludes even the highest officials of black blood from membership in elite white social clubs. Despite such distinctions, however, racial relations have been comparatively peaceful. The average Barbadian has an English respect for tradition and the law, born of over three centuries of uninterrupted British rule. This helps explain why the island is sometimes described as "a little bit of England, and Victorian England, at that."

Clustering is the predominant settlement pattern. Outside of the urban nuclei such as Bridgetown and Speightstown, most Barbadians live in village clusters located on estates or on "rab" land along highways or at crossroads. On the estates, the workers' villages stand apart from the factories and the residences of the managers and owners, as they did in the slave era. The other villages are extremely compact and generally have a few shops, a church, and a school. Only in the less fertile and less populous eastern areas, where peasant plots are common, does one find dispersed houses.

The Leeward Islands

The Leewards and Windwards [3] (discussed below) underwent the full, stormy

3. There is no rational basis for the trade wind nomenclature applied to these islands. The Leewards are not to the west, or leeward, of the Windwards, but to the north. To complicate matters, Saba and other Netherlands territories, which lie

Table 7.1 AREA AND POPULATION IN THE LEEWARDS AND WINDWARDS

Territory	Area (in square miles)	Population 1960	Population 1970	Density (people per square mile)
LEEWARDS				
Antigua and Barbuda	170.5	54,000	63,000 (1969)	368
St. Kitts, Nevis, and Anguilla	152.0	56,600	56,118 (1968)	409
Montserrat	32.5	12,000	12,300	384
WINDWARDS				
Dominica	305	60,000	70,302	231
St. Lucia	233	86,000	101,064	424
St. Vincent	150	80,000	89,129	594
Grenada	133	89,000	104,188 (1968)	783

history of conquest and counterconquest by France and England before finally becoming British (Chapter 3). Both groups experienced the growth of the colonial sugar plantation in the eighteenth and early nineteenth centuries, and both felt the impact of its downfall.

Most of the islands have suffered almost continuous economic depression since emancipation, and their prospects seem as bleak as their past. Small, limited in resources, and with expanding populations (Table 7.1), they cannot maintain themselves without outside help.

Antigua

LAND AND ECONOMY. Although classified as a low-lying, semiarid, limestone island, Antigua's geology, relief, and rainfall are sufficiently varied to permit a threefold regional division. The southwest consists of eroded volcanic remnants, where steep-sided hills rise to an average of 1,000 feet. Paralleling these volcanic uplands is the central plain, a lowland some ten miles long and three miles wide, consisting of lagoon-deposited clays with elevations that seldom rise above 50 feet. The third region is a belt of low limestone hills that

---

in the midst of the British Leewards, are called *Bovenwindse* ("windwards") by the Dutch. The nomenclature is used here only as a device for distinguishing two British administrative units.

extends from the northeast to the southwest coasts. The average rainfall varies from less than 40 inches over much of the coastal lowland to slightly over 50 inches in the volcanic uplands but may fluctuate sharply from year to year. Drainage is a problem; it is poor in the clay soils of the central plain and is too rapid through the porous limestone areas. Surface streams are rare, yet floods are not unknown, especially after the heavy downpours associated with hurricanes. Water is in such critical supply that much of the farm work on the island consists of repairing catchments, making ponds, and drilling wells.

The scarcity of water, as well as other physical limitations, is sharply mirrored in Antigua's agriculture. The uncultivated areas are generally those with less than 40 inches of rain on the steep, eroded slopes of the volcanic uplands; pastures are located primarily in the most poorly drained sections of the central plain; and subsistence farming is practiced only where commercial crops are ruled out (Figure 7.13). Sugar cane, the leading cash product, occupies the best lands in the central plains and valley bottoms, and cotton, which is second in commercial importance, dominates the limestone hills. Yields are comparatively low and drop dangerously in the dry years.

Sugar, which comprises about four-fifths of Antigua's exports, is raised both on

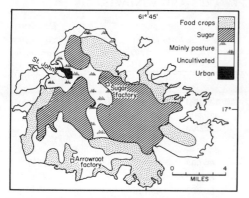

Figure 7.13   Antigua: Land use

estates and on peasant plots. As elsewhere, the estates own the best lands, use more scientific methods, and obtain the higher yields. The estates control the single sugar factory, which mills all the island's cane.

Cotton is also raised on both large and small holdings, but the greater part of the cotton crop is produced by peasants. Antigua now has the largest cotton acreage in the Antilles; unfortunately, this is no panacea. Production fluctuates with rainfall and price, both of which are highly unreliable, and the crop is often ravaged by insects.

The rest of Antigua's farm production consists largely of food raised on peasant plots, mostly roots, such as yams and sweet potatoes; tree crops, such as bananas; and pigeon peas. The government is encouraging the production of arrowroot as a peasant cash crop and has established a factory for processing it.

POPULATION AND SETTLEMENT. Antigua's population fell from over 40,000, in the heyday of the eighteenth-century sugar boom, to less than 30,000 in 1921. This decline was largely the result of emigration (to Cuba, Panama, Central America, and the United States), which reached its peak in the early twentieth century. Emigration was largely cut off after 1921, and the population increased to over 60,000 by 1970. The average density of population per square mile is about 400, but

there are 2,000 people per square mile of cultivated land. Almost three-fourths of the population is concentrated in the more productive northeast half of this island.

Except for the capital, St. John's, settlement is rural and typified by clusters of tiny wooden houses. Most of the more than 60 rural settlements that now dot the island began as plantation villages.

Barbuda. The wealthy Codrington family, which owned Barbuda from 1691 to the latter nineteenth century, used it as a hunting preserve and as a stud farm to provide livestock and slaves for their sugar plantations on other islands. Today, making a living on this administrative outlier of Antigua poses a challenge.

Barbuda's 62 square miles form a flat, low-lying plain that rises to a height of 200 feet at its eastern edge, in a series of steepsided limestone terraces. An alternation of droughts and occasional torrential rains discourages all but hardy bushes and grass. The population of about 1,200 maintains itself by fishing, keeping cattle, making charcoal, and catering to a few tourists. Such farming as exists is of food crops and cotton.

St. Kitts. St. Kitts, the largest territory in this administrative unit, is a sugar plantation island par excellence. It rivals Barbados as a striking example of a one-crop economy and a landholding system dominated by estates. Equally striking, it has maintained cane production for almost three centuries without serious deterioration of its soil. The island is the most agriculturally efficient and prosperous of the Leewards and Windwards.

LAND AND ECONOMY. Except for the tail-like southern peninsula, most of St. Kitts has a backbone of rugged volcanic mountains that rise steeply to average elevations of almost 3,000 feet and reach a maximum of 4,314 feet at Mt. Misery, in the northwest. Surrounding the base of this highland core is a gently sloping apron of volcanic ash cut by deep ravines known as "gats" or "guts." The southern peninsula consists of a cluster of volcanic hills and the large Salt Pond.

Precipitation, more than 90 inches in the mountain zones at about 1,200 feet, decreases downslope to as little as 50 inches in parts of the ash apron and even less in the southern peninsula. Virtually all the troughlike "guts" are dry, but heavy rains often result in disastrous floods. The island is also subject to hurricanes.

These physical conditions impose definite limitations on land use. The semiarid southern peninsula, with its scrub trees, low bushes, and cacti, is used primarily for grazing. The wet upper slopes of the highland core above 1,000 feet remain under a dense cover of rain forest and palm brakes, except for scattered patches of peasant cultivation. Only the ash apron and lower mountain slopes lend themselves to intensive agricultural use (Figure 7.14).

Of the 16,000 acres currently under cane in St. Kitts, all but a few hundred are estate-owned. And, since the estates often extend from the sea to the mountain crests, they control much of the other land as well. The marginal slopeland at the edge of the forests is usually rented to peasants.

All other economic activity is slight compared with sugar production. Sea island cotton, which occupied over 4,000 acres in the early 1900s, now occupies less than 200, and experiments with other cash crops, such as citrus fruit and tobacco, have failed. Food crops, grown on peasant plots and in rotation with cane on estate lands, are insufficient for local needs.

POPULATION AND SETTLEMENT. Population densities on St. Kitts are the highest in the Leewards, despite considerable emigration of black workers to Trinidad, the Dutch oil islands, Britain, and the Dominican Republic. The outflow of younger men in search of employment is so great that there is a large surplus of women.

Much of the population is concentrated along the lower courses of the "guts." The estate mansions are of stone; the houses in the peasant villages are built of imported lumber or, more recently, of cement blocks. The only town of any size is Basseterre, the capital. It is the chief port, though its harbor is little more than a sheltered roadstead.

Nevis. Like St. Kitts, Nevis is a relatively humid, high-lying volcanic island. At its center is the steeply rising cone of Nevis Peak (3,232 feet), whose base is surrounded by a volcanic ash apron. Like its larger neighbor, Nevis experienced a sugar boom in the eighteenth century, but only the ruins of estate houses and sugar works

Figure 7.14   St. Kitts–Nevis: Land use

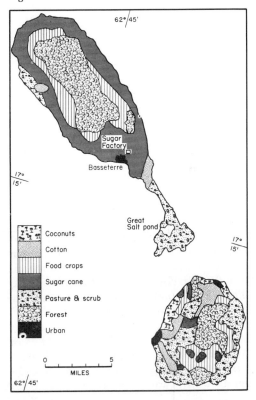

are left. The soils on Nevis are stonier and less fertile than those on St. Kitts, and most of the sugar estates were unable to weather the crisis in the nineteenth century.

Land use and tenure has changed greatly since the eighteenth century. Much of the cane land has reverted to scrub, and the approximately 7,000 acres still under crop are largely in cotton, coconuts, and provisions (Figure 7.14). Coconuts are estate-grown; the rest are produced by peasants who cultivate their own plots or sharecrop estate land. The coconuts are raised primarily along the north and west coasts, and provide the copra for the margarine produced in a small local plant.

The peasants grow enough food for the island and some, especially fresh fruits and vegetables, for export to St. Kitts. They also raise small quantities of sugar cane which is sent by lighter to St. Kitts for milling.

Anguilla. In contrast to volcanic St. Kitts and Nevis, Anguilla, which lies 60 miles north, is a dry, low-lying limestone island. With a maximum elevation of about 200 feet and an annual precipitation of 40 inches, most of the island is too dry or has soil too thin to support agriculture. Except for a few of the more favored spots, where peasants cultivate cotton and food, the land is used only for grazing or is not used at all.

Anguilla's second most important export is salt, which is produced by evaporating sea water. Her most important export is her young men, many of whom become sailors or migrate to the Dutch oil islands and elsewhere in search of work. The island's population in the 1960s numbered approximately 5,000.

Montserrat. The "little world" of Montserrat is a troubled one. Only 32.5 square miles large, its only resource is its land, which was depleted by the early

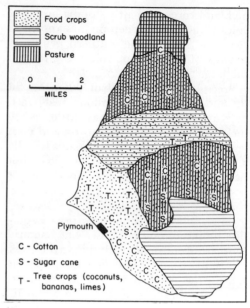

Figure 7.15   Montserrat: Land use

sugar plantations and which has been heavily eroded by poor farming practices. It is burdened by a slavish dependence on cotton, the most unstable of West Indian cash crops. Yet the territory has a population density of almost 400 people per square mile.

Montserrat is a rugged, high-lying core of volcanic hills surrounded by a narrow ribbon of coastal plain. Annual precipitation averages over 70 inches on the wet, cool uplands and well below 50 on most of the coast. Heavy rains ravage the soil on the deforested slopes and create destructive floods.

About one-third of Montserrat is cultivated (Figure 7.15). Sea island cotton, the chief cash crop, is grown on the ash aprons and up to about 500 feet on the slopes. Most of the cotton is raised on peasant-owned plots, although there is still some sharecropping on the larger landholdings. The value of the fruit and vegetables produced probably matches that of cotton, but they are used locally, and only about one-tenth of the harvest is exported. Tomatoes, onions, and carrots are the most

important food exports. Most of the vegetables are sent to nearby islands, such as
St. Kitts and the British Virgins, but they
have also been shipped to Bermuda and
even Canada.

The scrub and grass support several
thousand head of cattle, enough for the
island's meat and milk and an occasional
exportable surplus. Montserrat's economy
is rounded out by income from minor occupations such as charcoal burning and
boat building and, more important, by
remittances from islanders who have migrated. The gap between exports and imports is so wide that, without these remittances and British Colonial Development
and Welfare funds, the island would face
disaster.

Emigration has become a way of life for
the men of Montserrat. The island has
the dubious distinction of being the only
one of the Antilles whose population has
seriously declined in the last century.
Originally settled by Irish Roman Catholics from St. Kitts, Montserrat lost all
but a handful of its white planter families
after emancipation. These remnants, plus
a few Syrian merchants, are now the only
nonblack elements on the "Emerald Isle
of the Caribbean."

The Windward Islands

All the larger islands in the Windwards
fall into the humid, high-lying volcanic
arc of the Antilles. The Windwards were
settled later than the Leewards (see Chapter 3), but experienced an even more frequent alternation of French and English
ownership than their northern neighbors.
Their French heritage is still apparent in
the language and customs of most of the
islands. All the territories, except Dominica, experienced the rise and fall of the
colonial sugar plantation. Bananas are
now the chief cash crop of the group as a
whole, but each territory also has at least
one other important agricultural specialty.

Dominica

LAND AND ECONOMY. A mountainous terrain, easily the most rugged in the Lesser
Antilles, dominates Dominica's landscape.
Patches of isolated alluvial flats, which
comprise less than 3 percent of the total
area, are the only level land. The remainder is a tangled backbone of steep,
volcanic ranges with peaks, such as Morne
Diablotins and Morne Trois Pitons, which
rise to almost 5,000 feet. Geologically, the
island is completely volcanic, and the presence of fumaroles and hot springs attests
to continuing, albeit subdued, vulcanism.
Rainfall and vegetation vary with elevation and exposure to the trades, but both
are heavy.

This forbidding environment has
stamped every important phase and facet
of post-Columbian occupance in Dominica. The fierce Caribs, fighting from the
forested mountain fastness, delayed European conquest until well into the eighteenth century (Chapter 3). After the conquest, the scarcity of level land and other
impediments limited the growth of the
sugar plantations. Except for a few decades
after the 1830s, when an effort was made
to develop cane, the island's chief exports
have been coffee, limes, cacao, vanilla, and
bananas—all tree crops vulnerable to hurricanes. The environment has intensified
the island's isolation, and the difficulty of
the terrain still discourages effective settlement of the interior.

Probably less than 15 percent of Dominica's total area is under crop, and most
of that area is a narrow coastal strip
within 2,000 yards of the sea. Even this
strip includes sea cliffs and other impediments, and is not uniformly developed.
Only the vicinity of Roseau and sections
of the windward coast in the northeast and
southeast are intensively farmed. Most of
the interior is either not used or is haphazardly exploited by shifting cultivators
(Figure 7.16). Shifting cultivation is more
widespread on this island than anywhere
else in the Antilles.

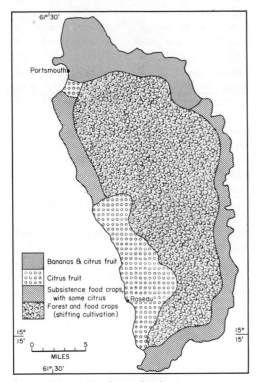

Figure 7.16   Dominica: Land use

The most productive coastal land is owned by approximately 85 estates. Compared to St. Kitts, Barbados, and other sugar islands, however, the estate system is but weakly entrenched on Dominica. Only a few of the tree crops that have been the mainstay of the island's exports lend themselves to large-scale production. As a result, much of the land now cultivated is peasant-owned or unalienated public land which the peasantry feels free to use.

Bananas, which became the chief cash crop after World War II, occupy more than a fifth of the cultivated acreage and are raised wherever transportation permits. About a fourth of the crop is produced on the estates, the largest of which are on the humid northeast coast. Citrus fruits, which are second only to bananas in commercial importance, are largely grown on estates on the southwest coast

near Roseau. Grapefruit and oranges are shipped fresh to Britain, and most of the limes are first processed into preserves, juice, and oil. Other tree crops, such as cacao and vanilla, are raised mostly by the peasantry.

Dominica has the most extensive forest resources in the Lesser Antilles, but lack of transportation has so far prevented their exploitation.

POPULATION AND SETTLEMENT.   Because it was colonized late and the growing of sugar was limited, Dominica had a comparatively small slave population at the time of emancipation (1834–1838). The island's population is still less than that of the other Windwards, and its population density is far below the average. In Dominica, however, average densities are meaningless, because about 90 percent of its people are concentrated in the narrow coastal band of cultivated land within a mile from the sea. Here, the pressure of population and the lack of economic opportunity are such that permanent emigration to the United Kingdom and seasonal migrations of farm workers to nearby Guadeloupe are common.

The paradox of emigration and overconcentration on the coast while the interior remains uninhabited stems in no small measure from the inadequacy of transportation. The steep terrain and the heavy rains, which cause landslides, make roads prohibitively costly. Even the seacoast is, in places, so rugged that no continuous coastal highway has been built.

St. Lucia. Like Dominica, St. Lucia is a high-lying, humid, volcanic territory, but without the high relief and great rainfall of its neighbor. The island's major surface divisions include a heavily eroded northern upland with an average elevation of about 1,000 feet, central *pitons* with a maximum height of more than 3,000 feet, and a southern zone of worn-down volcanic cones covered with thick deposits of ash and rocks. Level land is scarce and scattered, consisting mostly of alluvial bottoms in the lower courses of the valleys.

As in Dominica, the Caribs stemmed colonization of St. Lucia until almost mid-eighteenth century. The French effected the first permanent settlement in 1744, and between that time and the establishment of a permanent British connection in 1803, the island changed hands 14 times. The influence of the French, reinforced by proximity to Martinique immediately to the north, is still evident in place and family names, the French patois and Roman Catholicism of much of the population, and in many customs, including the law governing property.

The economic history of St. Lucia has been almost as unstable as its political history. The earliest economy, based on cotton and tobacco, gave way to cane. Emancipation created the same problems it created elsewhere, and, despite the importation of East Indians and the construction of modern mills, the sugar industry never fully recovered. With the decline of cane, St. Lucia's economy ran a checkered course. The planters experimented with other cash crops, such as limes, with varied success, but the labor shortages resulting from emigration and nonfarm employment forced many large holders to subdivide their estates.

For almost a half-century beginning in the 1880s, Castries, which has an excellent harbor, was a major coaling station in the West Indies and provided a livelihood for hundreds of workers. When oil replaced coal as ship fuel in the 1930s, however, the island experienced a severe economic depression, and many of the laborers returned to the land. Then came the unprecedented prosperity of World War II, when the United States used St. Lucia as a lend-lease base. Agricultural workers left the farms in droves to work for the free-spending Americans. But the closing of United States installations after the war created new economic distress, compounded by the reluctance of many of the workers to return to farming, the only economy of any importance on the island.

At best, less than one-third of St. Lucia's total area is devoted to agriculture. Bananas, sugar, coconuts, and cacao are grown for export, and the usual variety of vegetables and fruit is grown for local consumption.

There are roughly 70 estates and more than 10,000 smaller holdings. The lack of clear titles, often stemming from the old French practice of vesting ownership in the family rather than in the individual, complicates the problem of land tenure, especially among the peasantry. Much of the land is worked by squatters who have no legal title.

Over 40 percent of St. Lucia's population lives in towns, such as Castries, the capital, Soufrière, and Vieux Fort. Castries, which is built on a small alluvial flat, was largely destroyed by fire in 1948 and had to be rebuilt. Rural settlement tends to be dispersed; isolated huts are scattered along, or adjacent to, the roads. There are also clusterings around estate houses and hamletlike groups of huts at the intersections of paths or tracks.

Population distribution is uneven. Almost four-fifths of the people live in two nuclei: the alluvial valleys and hills in the north, which include Castries; and the southern hills and lower mountain slopes. The remainder are scattered over the drier zones of the extreme north and south. The rugged mountain country in the center of the island is the most thinly populated.

St. Vincent. St. Vincent's natural landscape bears the deep brand of vulcanism. The island is composed almost entirely of ash and other porous volcanic materials, and of lava flows. In the north, Soufrière, one of the two most active volcanoes in the Antilles, rises abruptly from the coast to a height of over 4,000 feet. Its eruptions are sporadic, but violent; in 1902 they killed more than 2,000 people, devastated the entire northern part of the island, and choked the valleys with heavy deposits of ash. Arable land is limited not only by the rugged terrain but also by rainfall and drainage. No part of the island receives less than 60 inches of precipitation, but seepage through the porous volcanic soils is so rapid that drought sometimes occurs on the leeward coast.

European settlement came late to St. Vincent, as to the other Windwards. The island was the chief stronghold of the Caribs, and resistance to white encroachment was especially strong. The French, who began to establish cotton plantations on the west coast in 1719, made little progress, but after the British seized the territory in 1763, large numbers of slaves were imported for the sugar plantations, and settlement was greatly expanded.

Plantation cane dominated St. Vincent until the latter nineteenth century. Then, a labor shortage and changing market conditions brought about a shift to arrowroot, and peasant-owned plots increased at the expense of the estates.

ECONOMY. St. Vincent's economy differs from that of most of the Lesser Antilles in at least one important respect. There is a healthy balance between large plantations and commercial crops, on the one hand, and peasant food farming, on the other.

The relative importance of the small holder in the economy gives rise to better farming practices, such as mixed cropping, intensive cultivation, and careful attention to conservation. The volcanic soils of St. Vincent are very fertile, but their steep slopes expose them to erosion. To prevent rapid runoff, the farmers resort to extensive terracing, strip cropping, grass barriers, and other conservation techniques. Such farming is unusual in the haphazard West Indies.

St. Vincent's commercial crops are diversified. In addition to bananas, which rose to first place in the 1950s, the island exports arrowroot, sugar, cotton, coconuts, and even sweet potatoes. Bananas have

proven so profitable a crop in the postwar years that their cultivation has become widespread. They are grown on the estates, and virtually every peasant raises at least a few stems, even if he has to plant them at his doorstep. Since fruit is typically interplanted, its expanding production has not encroached seriously on the established crops.

St. Vincent's most distinctive crop is arrowroot. The island produces 98 percent of world consumption of the starch derived from the roots of the plant. Arrowroot is raised on slopeland and grows to a height of about five feet. The harvested roots are trucked to one of approximately 20 estate factories or to a large government-owned plant at Belle Vue where they are processed for starch.

The major share of the export products are raised in the coastal margins and up to 1,000 feet on the mountain slopes on the windward side of the island (Figure 7.17). Food crops are grown chiefly on the leeward coast, though provisions are also raised in a zone of shifting cultivation between the forest and the permanently cultivated fields everywhere on the island. Food production is sufficient for most of the local demand, and there is significant exporting of sweet potatoes and other vegetables to nearby islands, especially to Trinidad.

POPULATION. Despite some recent emigration to Trinidad and elsewhere, St. Vincent's population rose to almost 90,000 in 1970. The average population density is about 600 per square mile, and the ratio of people to cropland is almost 1,500 per square mile. In the British Leewards and Windwards, only Grenada has a higher pressure of people on its land.

The racial composition of the population almost rivals Trinidad in diversity. While the vast majority are black or "coloured," there are also British whites, Portuguese, and East Indians who descend from laborers imported after emancipation, and a tiny remnant of Caribs. The

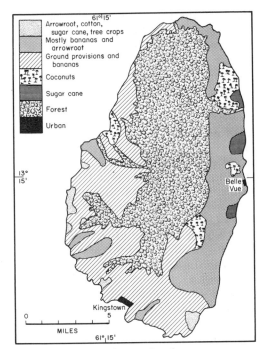

Figure 7.17   St. Vincent: Land use

whites include a small group of "Red Legs," who live in the hills overlooking Kingstown and trace their ancestry to Irish slaves originally sent to Barbados following Cromwell's conquest of Ireland. The total number of people classified as Caribs comes to slightly more than 1,000, but so many of the purebloods were wiped out in the Soufrière eruptions of 1812 and 1902 that only 200 remain. The others are Black Caribs, descendants of a black-Indian mixture that resisted the Europeans so fiercely that most of them were deported to Central America at the end of the eighteenth century. The bulk of St. Vincent's population hugs the coastal periphery of the island, especially the southwest coast near Kingstown, the capital and chief port.

Grenada

PHYSICAL AND HISTORICAL SETTING. Agriculturally, Grenada's terrain leaves much to be desired, but its soil and climate could be worse. The island is a high-lying volcanic mass consisting almost wholly of mountain slopes and ridges. The level land consists of scattered patches of alluvial flats in the small valleys and narrow ribbons of coastal plain compressed between the uplands and the sea. Grenada shows little evidence of recent vulcanism. Except for a few crater lakes, such as Grand Etang, its surface has been shaped primarily by the erosion of older volcanic deposits.

The island's best soils are associated with the alluvial flats. The next best are the red and red-brown types in the less humid lowlands. But even the poorest of the gray or yellow-brown soils of the wet uplands is arable.

The climate is generally adequate, except in the hurricane seasons, and other conditions are also generally favorable for farming. Temperatures are high enough to permit a year-round growing season even on high mountain slopes. Precipitation, though marked by the usual extreme differences between windward and leeward exposures is sufficient everywhere but in the driest segments of the southwest coast.

Post-Columbian exploitation of Grenada began early. Carib resistance was weak, and the French were able to establish the first agricultural colony by 1650. Initially, tobacco and indigo were stressed, but by the mid-eighteenth century the chief cash crops were cotton, coffee, and sugar. The French, who held the island until its capture by the British in 1762, left a heritage still found in the language, religion, and place names.

As on St. Vincent, the arrival of the British resulted in a swift increase in the slave population, an expansion of cane, and the entrenchment of the plantation system. Also as on St. Vincent, Grenada's rapid development continued up to the mid-1800s, only to be followed by an equally rapid decline.

The postemancipation labor shortage was especially acute because more favorable working conditions in nearby Trinidad attracted many of the freed blacks. Those who remained left the estates to occupy mountain lands in the interior, just as did their counterparts on other West Indian islands (Chapter 3). Efforts to attract indentured workers from India, the Madeiras, and elsewhere were largely unsuccessful.

Eventually, the labor shortage and other unfavorable circumstances brought about major changes on the land. Cane production dropped 75 percent between 1840 and 1880; cacao replaced sugar as the chief export; and the hard-pressed planters sold small plots to the peasantry. The plantation did not disappear, but its grip was weakened.

ECONOMY.   Agriculture is Grenada's leading economic activity, but the growing pressure of population is a serious problem.

Cultivation has been pushed over two-thirds of the island's total area. Even the poorest slopes are now under crop, and there is no room for further expansion. Only the highest and most inaccessible mountain peaks have been left in forest. The patches of thorny scrub in the dry southwest are given over to grazing. Elsewhere, even the steepest slopes immediately below the forest hold nutmeg trees. Cacao follows nutmeg downslope and merges with bananas in the humid valleys. Food crops and sugar are raised in small quantities on the leeward coast, and coconuts occupy the sandy beaches of the sea margins.

The pattern of land tenure on Grenada has changed little in the twentieth century. About half the land is held in estates of 100 or more acres, and the remainder is in peasant plots of 5 acres or less. The smaller properties are owner-operated, but many of the estates are run by managers for absentee owners. The arrangement is unusual in that a large number of the peasant plots are at lower elevations along the coast, while the estates are frequently located in the interior hills. This pattern is probably due to the fact that the slopeland is used for the commercially important tree crops.

The most distinctive tree crops are nutmeg and mace. Small quantities are raised in other West Indian territories and in Indonesia, but Grenada is the chief source of these spices. The nutmeg tree is raised on the higher mountain slopes, where temperatures range from 70 to 75° F and precipitation exceeds 80 inches. The center of the fruit is a dark brown nut, covered with a fine web of mace, which splits when ripe. Most of the mace is sent to Britain, where it is used for baking and in the manufacture of cosmetics; the bulk of the nutmeg is sold to the United States.

Nutmeg production illustrates some of the peculiar problems of Grenada's agriculture. The slow-growing trees require 20 years to reach peak production, but they can be quickly destroyed by heavy winds. In 1955, for example, a hurricane reduced the crop over 90 percent. The same storm also caused huge damage to cacao, bananas, and coconuts. Only ground provisions, such as yams, escaped injury, and this was scant consolation since the island depends on its cash products to finance the purchase of its food. Tree crops, especially bananas and cacao, are also more susceptible to disease than field crops. But with a dense population and a land that consists almost entirely of mountain slopes, what choice is there?

POPULATION AND SETTLEMENT.   With 783 inhabitants per square mile in 1970, Grenada is the most densely populated island in both the Leewards and the Windwards. The increase in population was relatively moderate between the two world wars. Since 1946, however, a drop in emigration and in the death rate, coupled with a rise in the present birth rate, has resulted in a huge net increase.

Except for a small number of whites and an East Indian minority of about 5 percent, the population is black or "coloured." English, well-laced with French and even African phrases, is the chief language, but a dominantly French patois continues to be spoken in many communities.

Settlement is largely rural. Farmsteads are scattered through the hills or strung out on roads leading to the coast, and hamlets consist of a dozen or so houses. These tiny villages often mark the site of former slave quarters on plantations. The only town of any size is St. George's, the capital, chief port, and major commercial and administrative center.

The French West Indies

Martinique and Guadeloupe, together with the latter's dependencies, are all that remain of the once-considerable French holdings in the Caribbean. Even these remnants probably adhere to France as much from economic necessity as from sentiment. Small in size (1,112 square miles) and heavily populated, the islands suffer from many disadvantages. Arable land is their only significant resource, but the terrain is rugged and there is less than an acre per person. There are periodic hurricanes and very destructive volcanic eruptions and earthquakes, especially on Martinique. The agrarian economy is beset by monoculture, latifundia, and other liabilities characteristic of West Indian tropical plantation agriculture.

Thus handicapped, Martinique and Guadeloupe desperately need the protected market for exports, the government subsidies, and the outlet for surplus population which the French connection provides. This need was strongly manifested in 1946, when the islands overwhelmingly elected to end more than three centuries of political dependency and become overseas *départments* of metropolitan France. Their new status provides both territories with direct representation in the French parliament and gives them all the advantages and disadvantages of being integral parts of France.

Economy. Emancipation in 1848 and the subsequent downfall of the colonial plantation created the problems with which the reader is by now familiar. A labor shortage developed as the freed blacks abandoned the estates; much of the white planter class was bankrupt and returned to France; the amount of land under cultivation dropped, and so did the harvest; and the population increased.

In the readjustments, a class of small peasant holders emerged; sharecropping was introduced; and the sugar plantations were consolidated. The black peasantry acquired small plots either by squatting on unused land in the mountains or by buying it from hard-pressed estate owners, but their plots were not large enough to provide them with a living. Sharecropping was an attempt to meet the postemancipation labor shortage; once established, however, it remained, especially on the less desirable estate lands. The consolidation of family-size estates presaged the rise of the modern plantation (see Chapter 4). Corporate ownership, financed by French capital, became established in both territories, especially on Guadeloupe. With the emergence of the small peasant holders, however, agriculture became more diversified. The peasants grew food, and, whenever possible, small quantities of coffee and cacao for sale.

Cane occupied the best land even at the height of the nineteenth-century sugar crisis. Sugar production was bolstered by an expanding demand for rum in Europe, and many planters, especially in the more isolated areas, began to convert their cane into alcohol. Later, the sugar economy received additional help through the establishment of a quota system which guaranteed the Antillean territories a share of the protected French market. French tariff protection, coupled with widespread hurricane damage of coffee and cacao crops in the 1920s, was also instrumental in effecting the last important change in land use. A 1928 law that gave preferential treatment to bananas from French possessions resulted in a gradual elimination of coffee, cacao, and even cane, in favor of commercial banana production in zones suitable for the fruit on both Martinique and Guadeloupe. At present, hardly enough coffee and cacao is produced for local needs, and the value of the banana exports surpasses that of sugar.

Despite these changes, the economy of the French Antilles differs only in degree from that of a century ago. It is still dominated by plantations controlled by local planters and absentee stockholders; its exports are few, with bananas, sugar, rum, and molasses accounting for over 90 percent of the total; and its dependence upon the French market is almost absolute. While the plantations have undergone some modernization, they continue to use hand labor, animal power, and simple tools. The planters have felt little need to increase efficiency until recently, because French tariffs have shielded them from competition. Mechanization has recently been increasing, however, because of the French minimum wage law which became applicable on the islands after they became *départements* in 1946.

Subsistence farming is a very poor second in the agricultural structure. Export crops monopolize the best areas, and the consequent necessity of importing food from France is the principal drain on the insular economy. But virtually all the arable acreage is already under crop, and expansion of subsistence farming is a dubious solution.

Industry is restricted to the processing of cane, the production of rum, and the manufacture of a few simple products such as textiles. Some fishing is carried on, but not enough to supply local demand. Tourists are attracted by the inexpensive French wines and perfumes, but hotel accommodations are sparse and poor. In a

way, perhaps the second most important economy on the islands is the French government. Both *départements* receive much more from Paris, in the form of subsidies and public aid, than they pay in taxes.

Population. Except for the decade from 1895 to 1905, when the loss of life from the Mont Pelée disaster caused a slight drop (discussed later), the population of the French West Indies has grown steadily since 1635. Prior to 1848, the gain was due to immigration but, after 1848, the non-European population increased rapidly. More than 78,000 Orientals and 16,000 Africans were imported between 1852 and 1887, and the birth rate of the freed blacks rose sharply. On the other hand, the white population decreased. Many emigrated, and those remaining suffered a disproportionately heavy loss of life in the destruction of St. Pierre. In addition, their birth rate was low, compared to that of the nonwhite groups.

The overall growth of population has increased the pressure on the land. By the early 1970s, population totals were approaching 650,000, and average densities were over 580 persons per square mile. A mounting tide of migration to France, especially by the younger element, has been the only safety valve.

Except for the whites (who number less than 10,000) and the descendants of the imported Orientals, the racial composition of the French islands is black. Traditionally, the whites have possessed a disproportionate amount of economic and political power, but in recent decades, and especially on Martinique, they have been ousted from political power, and their economic position is being weakened by the rise of an aggressive colored middle class.

The gross characteristics described above stem primarily from broad influences such as French colonial policy, the impact of the plantation, and the tropical environment—influences shared by all the

French Antilles. The details of land-people patterns, however, tend to vary in accordance to the play of local factors.

The Netherlands Antilles

The Netherlands Antilles consist of two groups of widely separated islands. One, which the Dutch call the *Bovenwindse* ("windward") islands, is located almost at the head of the Lesser Antillean chain, and includes St. Eustatius, Saba, and the southern part of St. Martin; the other, named the *Benedenwindse* ("leeward") islands is in the southernmost Caribbean adjacent to Venezuela, and consists of Aruba, Bonaire, and Curaçao—the ABC islands. The islands differ in their landscape, history, economy, demography, and in other ways. In fact, the six territories are so different that they seem to be held together by little more than the mechanics of Dutch administration.

Physical Landscape and Historical Setting. Of the three northern islands, St. Eustatius (sometimes referred to as Statia) and Saba belong geologically to the inner, or volcanic, arc of the Lesser Antilles, and St. Martin falls in the outer, or limestone, arc (Chapter 2). St. Eustatius is dominated by two high-lying extinct volcanic peaks; Saba consists of a single cone which rises to 2,887 feet (Figure 7.18). Lower-lying St. Martin has a core of older igneous rocks beneath its calcareous cap, but is devoid of recent volcanic forms. In contrast, the southern, or ABC, islands are worn-down remnants of crystalline rocks from which most of an overlying limestone layer has been removed. Their terrain is thus less striking, except for the distinctive, fan-shaped, bottle-necked embayments that were formed when a rise in sea level after the last ice age flooded the coastal valleys. The prime example of these is the Schottegat, St. Anna Bay, which forms the magnif-

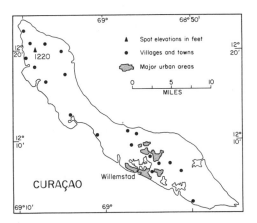

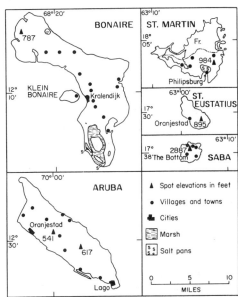

Figure 7.18   The Netherlands Antilles

icent harbor of Willemstad on Curaçao (Figures 7.19 and 7.20).

The Netherland Antilles receive scanty rainfall, but the northern trio, which has a higher elevation and is closer to the hurricane paths, receives roughly twice as much as the southern. On Curaçao, for example, the annual total of 22 inches is so low in comparison with the mean annual temperature, 81° F, that the island's sparse vegetation is primarily xerophytic, or drought-resistant. Water for domestic

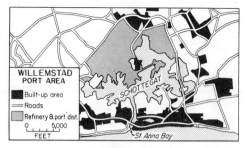

Figure 7.19   Curaçao: St. Anna Bay and the Schottegat

use is obtained by catching rain in cisterns or is pumped from wells, often powered by windmills. On Curaçao and Aruba, the large population and the heavy demands of the oil refineries have made necessary the distillation of sea water. Equally discouraging, everywhere in the Dutch West Indies, is the scarcity of level land, the poorness of the soils and, except for small deposits of phosphate at Sta. Barbara on Curaçao, the absence of valuable minerals.

Obviously, it was not resources that first attracted the Dutch to their Antillean holdings. The southern islands, and especially Curaçao, with its excellent and easily defended harbor, were occupied in the seventeenth century primarily as bases for preying on Spanish commerce. When

privateering became less profitable, Curaçao was converted into an important slave-trade center. St. Martin, with its salt-rich lagoon, provided salt for Holland's herring industry. The Dutch made some effort to raise sugar and other cash crops, but the chief function of the Antillean islands during the seventeenth and eighteenth centuries was to serve as entrepôts and trading centers (Chapter 3). Compared to the rich profits made from the trading marts at "Statia" and Curaçao, the return from farming was slight. With the destruction of "Statia" by Rodney, the English admiral, in the late eighteenth century and the subsequent abolition of the slave trade and collapse of the West Indian colonial plantation system (Chapter 3), all the Netherlands Antilles entered a decline from which most have never recovered.

Economic Patterns

OIL REFINING.   In August 1918, a tugboat called "Don Alberto" with the lighter "Willstad" in tow, sailed from Lake Maracaibo with the first shipment of oil for the newly built Curaçao refinery. For Curaçao, and later for Aruba, this was a revolutionary event. Immigrants began to pour in;

Figure 7.20   Harbor entrance at Willemstad (*Foto Fischer*)

banking and business assumed proportions unheard of in the Caribbean; and, almost overnight, the two islands were transformed from sleepy, subsistence areas to places of world-wide commercial importance. This revolutionary change started with the construction of large refineries by subsidiaries of Royal Dutch Shell on Curaçao, in 1916, and was given a tremendous boost when Standard Oil of New Jersey built its refineries on Aruba in 1929.

Curaçao and Aruba were selected as sites for the refineries for political and geographic reasons. Dutch oil interests were among the first to negotiate with Venezuela for the development of the Maracaibo fields. These interests wanted their refineries located on the Dutch islands because of Venezuela's political instability and because she lacked adequate ports near her oil fields. Curaçao, only 216 miles away and possessing the excellent natural harbor of Willemstad, was the logical location. Similar reasons probably prompted Standard Oil to choose Aruba for their refineries.

Currently, oil dominates the economy of the Dutch Antilles. It comprises over 85 percent of the imports and 98 percent of the exports; it enables Curaçao and Aruba to support a large population at one of the highest standards of living in the Caribbean; and it indirectly provides income and social services for the four agricultural islands in the federation.

Despite the prosperity of the last few decades, however, many a sober Dutchman views the economic future of the oil islands with apprehension. What would happen if the oil ran out or if it were refined elsewhere? Farming cannot be expected to support the large population now making its living from oil. Minor occupations—fishing, phosphate mining, the manufacture of Panama hats—are not the answer, and mass emigration, particularly of the black peasantry, seems out of the question.

OTHER ECONOMIES.   Farming in the Netherlands Antilles has always been precarious. The southern islands have a rocky surface and a paucity of water; the northern islands have a rugged terrain and a paucity of arable land. Small qauntities of cotton are grown on St. Martin and Statia, and aloes are grown on Aruba and Bonaire; elsewhere, agriculture is generally confined to small-scale food growing on peasant plots. Local food supplies, including livestock and fish, are so inadequate that virtually all the food, especially on Curaçao and Aruba, must be imported.

Since the islands' agricultural potential is so limited, the Dutch have pinned their major hopes for an economic future on tourism and manufacturing. Luxurious new hotels have been built; duty-free zones have been established on Curaçao and Aruba; and widespread advertising has been undertaken.

Population and Settlement. The demography of the Netherlands Antilles is so closely linked with their economies that the contrast between the oil-refining islands and the others is enormous (Table 7.2). Between them, Curaçao and Aruba now account for 80 percent of the total population and have densities of 830 and 866 persons per square mile, respectively; but the other four islands have had a quite different recent history. The outflow of persons, especially men, from the agricultural islands to Curaçao and Aruba has been so marked that on Bonaire, for example, the females outnumber the males more than three to one. The northern islands, also, are now populated by females and by males who are too old or too young to seek work elsewhere.

The people of the Netherlands Antilles are predominantly African, but there are some Europeans. The history of settlement and recent migrations, however, has given rise to somewhat different racial balances on each of the territories. On Saba, for example, Europeans have traditionally

Table 7.2 AREA, POPULATION, AND DENSITY IN
THE NETHERLANDS ANTILLES, 1970

Territory	Area (in square miles)	Population	Density (people per square mile)
Curaçao	170	143,778	830
Aruba	70	60,733	866
Bonaire	108	8,099	85
St. Martin (Dutch section)	13	7,475	440
St. Eustatius	12	1,341	112
Saba	5	965	193

outnumbered blacks, but the recent emigration of whites to the oil islands and elsewhere, coupled with the higher birth rate of the blacks, is reversing the ratio. The same trend is apparent on St. Martin, whose population also included a high percentage of whites.

On Curaçao, the pre-oil population included descendants of black slaves, of seventeenth-century Jewish settlers from Brazil and Holland, and of Dutch, German, Danish, and Swiss colonists. On Aruba, the old peasant stock is of Amerindian ancestry. Oil has brought a variety of new groups to both islands, chiefly blacks from the other West Indian islands and from Surinam. But there has also been significant immigration from the Netherlands and the Madeiras, and by smaller groups of Chinese, Syrians, and East Indians.

The islands' racial and ethnic pluralism is matched by their cultural pluralism. While the Dutch language has official recognition and is spoken by an increasing number of people, the most common tongue in the ABC group is *Papiamento,* a remarkable mixture based mostly on Iberian linguistic forms. *Papiamento* reflects the close contact with the Hispanic peoples of nearby Venezuela and the probable influence of Portuguese-speaking Jews. In addition, many of the immigrant minorities continue to use their own languages. The colored peasantry of the northern islands, for example, speak an English dialect.

Similarly, the vast majority, especially in the southern islands, are Roman Catholic, reflecting both Hispanic contact and the strong missionary effort of Dutch Roman Catholic priests. Various Protestant denominations, Jews, and others are also represented, however.

Settlement in the Netherlands Antilles tends to be agglomerated rather than dispersed, with villages predominating. The chief urban center is Willemstad. With its distinctive harbor and drawbridges, the Amsterdam-like flavor of its architecture, and its cosmopolitan population, Willemstad is rated by many as the most colorful city in the Caribbean.

The Virgin Islands

Between the Anegada Passage in the east and Puerto Rico in the west are several dozen small islands and numerous reefs which, collectively, are called the Virgin Islands (see Figure 7.6).[4] Politically, the archipelago is unequally divided; two-thirds of its 200 square miles is governed by the United States, and the remainder is British.[5] The bulk of the population and economic activity in the American islands is centered on St. Thomas, St.

4. Geologically, the Puerto Rican islands of Vieques and Culebra, sometimes called the "Spanish Virgins," are also part of the archipelago.
5. The British Virgin Islands have often been administered as part of the Leewards. They are treated separately here, partly for convenience and partly because of their close ties with the American Virgin Islands.

Croix, and St. John; the most important of the British holdings are Tortola, Virgin Gorda, Jost Van Dyke, and Anegada (Figures 7.21 and 7.22).

Physical and Historical Setting. Most of the Virgins are of volcanic origin and are characterized by rugged slopes that rise abruptly from the sea to elevations of 1,000 to 1,700 feet. The remainder are low-lying limestone islets, such as Anegada, whose average height is barely 30 feet.

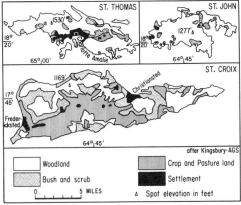

Figure 7.21   The American Virgin Islands

Except on St. Croix, level farmland is restricted to a few dry stream bottoms or "guts." The soil is not rich. On the limestone islands, it is either nonexistent or consists of small pockets of an early substance composed of coral sands and humus. Elsewhere, the soil is a brown loam derived from volcanic material. Serious erosion, the result of deforestation, overgrazing, and the cultivation of slopeland, is widespread. Even the best soils tend to be shallow and are exhausted from long use.

However, the Virgins' greatest physical drawback is the scarcity of water. The average annual precipitation in the archipelago is about 50 inches, but with year-round temperatures of 65 to 90°F, the rate of evaporation is high. Moreover, the seasonal distribution is highly variable; most of the rain falls in short, heavy showers during summer and fall. The runoff on the steep slopes is so rapid that the moisture is sufficient only for xerophytic vegetation.

"Water is our most precious resource, please conserve it," reads a sign found in many Virgin Island hotels. There are no rivers or lakes on the islands, and only a few perennial streams. Water comes from

Figure 7.22   The British Virgin Islands

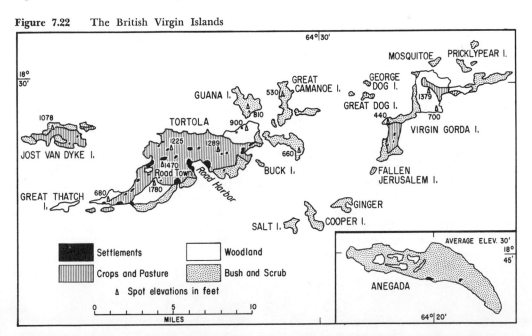

wells, a few springs, home cisterns, and, especially on St. Thomas, from stone or cement catchment basins built on the hillsides. It is imported in ever-greater quantities from Puerto Rico.

In the seventeenth and eighteenth centuries, this poor environment was contested far more than its economic potential warranted. The various islands have flown the flags of Holland, France, England, Spain, Denmark, the Knights of Malta and, intermittently, even the Jolly Roger of the buccaneers. Eventually, the Danes gained firm control of the western islands and the English of the eastern. The last political change occurred in 1917, when the United States purchased the Danish territories for $25 million.

The archipelago's economic history has been almost as chequered as its political history. Following early experiments with indigo and tobacco, the island's economy was a slave-based estate sugar and cotton agriculture. While market and labor conditions remained favorable, the plantations enjoyed a small measure of prosperity. In 1787, for example, the sugar exports of Tortolan estates came to £164,000.

Handicapped by a mountainous terrain, poor soils, and a limited water supply, however, the marginal plantation agriculture of the Virgins was ill equipped to withstand the problems created by emancipation and the drop in sugar prices during the nineteenth century. Its collapse on Tortola and other British islands was so complete that, by 1860, virtually all the white planter families had migrated, leaving the land to black subsistence farmers. The Danish islands were also severely affected. Only St. Croix, which is less mountainous, managed to retain a meager sugar economy. St. John was taken over by the black peasantry, and its mansions became relics. St. Thomas suffered not only from the downfall of sugar but also from a major reduction in shipping and warehouse revenues. In the days of slow-moving sailing ships, the island's excellent harbor at Charlotte Amalie (Figure 7.21) was an important transhipping and supply base. Its relative proximity to Africa and Europe made it the first port of call for vessels in need of stores. With the advent of the faster, wider-ranging steamship, Charlotte Amalie became an important coaling station, but it lost much of its former income.

Economy

THE AMERICAN TERRITORIES. Like Puerto Rico, the United States Virgin Islands have been reaping major economic benefits from being American-owned, especially since World War II. Federal subsidies and aid, the influx of tourists and small industries from the continent, an outlet for surplus labor—these and other advantages of the American connection are transforming the islands that Herbert Hoover once called a "poor-house." There has been marked improvement in social services, including the establishment of the College of the Virgin Islands in 1963. Per capita income, which was $412 in 1950, has risen so dramatically that the American Virgin Islands now rank with Puerto Rico as among the most prosperous territories in Middle America. In addition, the insular government, which was once virtually controlled by the United States Navy, has been given back to the Virgin Islanders together with a large measure of local autonomy.

This progress has been achieved despite an absence of natural resources and the stagnation of the traditional economies— agriculture and fishing. On St. Thomas, farming has disappeared except in a small northern area where fruit and vegetables are planted on terraced plots. The peasant farming on St. John is largely subsistent, but production is sufficient to allow some exporting to the growing urban market of Charlotte Amalie. St. Croix continues to have a plantation economy based on sugar, but only by the grace of federal quotas and supports. Efforts are being made to induce a switchover to provision farming on St. Croix, and for good reason. Food, like water, is scarce, especially on St. Thomas. The cost of food imports is rising steeply, causing a substantial drain on the insular economy.

While the new industries attracted to the islands have made some contribution, the major economic gains in the Virgins have resulted from tourism (Chapter 4). Tourist expenditures, less than $5 million in 1952, were over $35 million in 1962, and by 1972 had become the cornerstone of the insular economy.

St. Thomas is less than 20 minutes by air from San Juan, and much of the heavy traffic bound for Puerto Rico spills over into the Virgin Islands. A major attraction is the free-port status of the islands, which enables the visitor to purchase luxury goods for 20 to 50 percent less than he would have to pay in New York.

THE BRITISH TERRITORIES. The British Virgin Islands have changed only slightly in the last century. Tourists are beginning to discover them, but a semisubsistent peasant farming is still their characteristic economy. If the people of these islands were permitted to do so, they would probably emigrate en masse to the American territories.

With crop cultivation largely ruled out by steep slopes, small rainfall, and poor soils, land in the British Virgins is mostly given over to scrub growth or pasture (Figure 7.22). Probably not more than one-tenth of the land is under crops, and the amount is constantly decreasing. Most of the cropland is in the bottoms and on the more fertile slopes; even so, the soil is so marginal that a modified shifting cultivation has to be practiced. Food crops are generally followed by pasture, croton thicket, and secondary woodland. Stock raising, particularly of cattle, is the principal farming activity.

Many of the islanders engage in secondary occupations such as fishing and boat building. Fish is the second most important export, cattle being the first, and is also an important part of the local diet. On islands such as Anegada, Salt, Peter, and Jost Van Dyke, where farming is even more difficult than on the main island of Tortola, fishing is often the principal economic enterprise.

Despite the poverty of their economy, the islands have a higher standard of living than the people in most of the other British Lesser Antilles. The key to this paradox is hidden income, especially that derived from temporary employment of the British Virgin Islanders in St. Thomas and St. Croix. Such employment in the more prosperous American territories is a long-established practice, and it has reached major proportions since the recent boom in tourism. It is estimated that, at any given date, as much as one-fourth of the labor force of the British islands is temporarily residing and working in the American Virgins. This, as well as other interaction between the two politically separated groups of islands, has led to a surprising degree of social and economic integration.

Population. In 1970, the total population of the entire Virgins archipelago was about 70,000. Most of the inhabitants were concentrated on the American islands of St. Thomas and St. Croix; Tortola accounted for more than 85 percent of the 10,500 people living in the British islands.

The vast majority of the islanders are black. There are not 50 whites in the British islands. The Caucasian population of the American Virgins, especially of St. Thomas, has increased with tourism, but blacks still constitute more than three-fourths of the total.

Two minorities in the American islands are the Puerto Ricans of St. Croix, who are recent arrivals, and the French of St. Thomas, who came from St. Barthélemy in the eighteenth century. These French are one of the most interesting cultural groups in the Caribbean. They have retained their language, customs, and racial homogeneity despite two centuries of exposure to other cultures and races. They are concentrated in Charlotte Amalie, where the colors and the neatness of their tiny houses catch the eye. Even the straw hats worn by *Chachas,* as the French are called, are distinctive. Most of the group fish or make handicrafts; the rest are farmers who work the terraced plots on the north side of the island.

The Danes who once ruled the American Virgins have also left their mark, especially on the architecture of the older buildings and in place names. The Danish language, never widely used, is no longer heard at all.

THE BAHAMAS

The people of the Bahamas have some justification for rejecting identity with the West Indies. In the last two centuries, their destinies have been more closely linked with continental United States than with the island world of the Antilles. Moreover, their way of life has never been typically West Indian. Plantation agriculture was an ephemeral development, and even today farming is of little importance. The Bahamians are a race of seamen, and it is the sea that provides the key to understanding their island habitat. In the words of one Bahamian, "We rely upon the sea for everything . . . through the centuries it has given us our food and our wealth . . . our products and our people move by boat."

Setting. The Bahamas are a sprawling archipelago of some 700 islands and more than 2,000 reefs and rocks which rise above shallow submarine banks to form the eastern rim of the Florida Passage (Figure 7.23). None of the islands rises as high as 400 feet above sea level, and on most of them, the highest point is well below 200 feet.

The archipelago is composed largely of calcareous materials derived from sea shells. At higher elevations on some of the islands, these materials were consolidated into rocks and have subsequently been weathered into a typical karst landscape of caves and other features; elsewhere, the calcareous sand has been piled into low ridges by the action of wind and water. Brackish water swamps cover large insular areas.

The soils of the Bahamas are therefore poorly developed and of low fertility. They have little depth or humus content; they retain little water; and, once disturbed by cultivation, they are prone to erosion and depletion. Moreover, the islands are subject to hurricanes. Annual precipitation varies between 40 and 60 inches, and most of it falls in heavy showers between May and October and soaks quickly through the thin, sandy mantle, reducing its usefulness to the farmer. As on Barbados, well water is drawn for domestic use from subsurface reservoirs, but there is little for irrigation.

The land is not otherwise rich. A few of the islands have exploitable forests, but the vegetation elsewhere tends to be sparse. Except for bat phosphate found in the caves and used for fertilizer, mineral wealth is insignificant. Resources are so limited that only about 22 of the several hundred islands have permanent populations.

Such prosperity as the Bahamas have experienced has stemmed largely from the advantages of their sea environment and their strategic location vis-à-vis the United States. These advantages have frequently made illegal activities profitable. During the seventeenth and eighteenth centuries, for example, the archipelago provided an ideal base from which pirates could prey on shipping sailing through the Florida Straits. The "wreckers," who lured un-

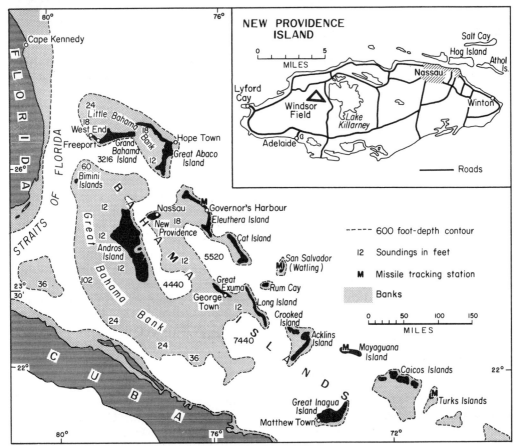

Figure 7.23   The Bahamas

suspecting ships to their destruction among the uncharted reefs, also prospered from stripping and selling the cargoes. The Bahamas experienced another brief prosperity during the American Civil War, when Confederate blockade runners came to the islands to exchange cotton for English munitions, medicines, and machinery. And the Bahamians also profited from the smuggling of liquor into the United States during Prohibition.

It was the location of the Bahamas and the difficulties of navigating among them which made possible these dubious but profitable activities. Channels deep enough for large ships are few, and they are difficult to follow in the shallow waters surrounding the maze of islands and reefs (Figure 7.23), so that people familiar with them could easily elude pursuit. The pres-

ent economic upsurge in the archipelago, while less spectacular and more legal, also stems in part from the advantages of location and a unique sea environment.

Economic Patterns

AGRICULTURE.   In addition to the drawbacks we have already enumerated, there is little arable land in the Bahamas. Moreover, transportation is poor and agricultural practices are primitive.

Less than 2 percent of the archipelago's total area of roughly 4,000 square miles is considered suitable for crops. The arable pockets, widely scattered, are often so remote from Nassau, the chief market, that it takes a week for sailboats to transport produce and livestock. The peasantry clears the land by slashing and burning, a practice that destroys the humus, dries the soil, and subjects it to erosion. In general, yields are low and profits discouraging.

Nevertheless, the peasants produce enough fruit and vegetables for themselves and for the Nassau hotels. In addition, small quantities of tomatoes, onions, okra, and pineapples are exported to the United States and Canada. Livestock production has been associated with this haphazard peasant farming, especially on Exuma and Long Island, but there are now some large and modern livestock farms, such as that established by a former president of the Chicago Stockyards on Eleuthera Island.

FISHING AND FORESTRY.   Fish is the major staple of the Bahamian diet, partly because farming is so difficult and partly because the shallow waters of the archipelago provide rich catches. Fishing, from small boats and with primitive equipment, is practiced throughout the archipelago, but it is especially important on Grand Bahama, Abaco, and Harbour Island. Most of the catch is consumed locally, but there is some export, especially of crayfish, to the United States.

Forest products, especially pulpwood, account for over a third of the value of the exports. Most of these come from the extensive pine stands of Grand Bahama, Abaco, and Andros. In addition, there are mahogany and other hardwoods for constructing small boats, an industry of vital importance.

TOURISM AND TAX REFUGE.   The current economic boom in the Bahamas results largely from tourism and tax dodging. The islands are near the populous east coast of the United States, and they offer a subtropical climate without extremes of temperature, excellent fishing and bathing, and spectacular marine scenery. These natural advantages, combined with the United States ban on travel to Cuba and an effective advertising campaign, have resulted in a year-round tourist industry.

The center of tourism, and of everything else in the archipelago, is Nassau on New Providence, but as transportation improves, an increasing number of visitors are discovering the charms of the other islands.

The Bahamas have also acquired some well-heeled permanent guests from the United States and elsewhere. Some who came to the islands to retire have contributed know-how and capital for economic development. For example, the Ericksons, a Boston family who came to Great Inagua Island in 1934, found evidence of a once-important salt industry based on the solar evaporation of sea water, revived the industry, and now produce hundreds of thousands of tons of salt for annual export.

But the major attraction for most of the new settlers is an extremely liberal tax law. Except for import duties, there are virtually no taxes. As a result, the Bahamas have become the legal residence of numerous American, Canadian, British, and other foreign firms, as well as of many wealthy individuals.

Population and Settlement.   After the destruction of the Indians by Spanish slave raiders in the early sixteenth century, the Bahamas remained virtually unsettled, except for pirates, until the "Eleutherian Adventurers" arrived in 1647. But these settlers and those who followed, including Palatinate Germans in 1721, were so few that by 1731 the archipelago had only 1,378 inhabitants. The major influx of settlers took place at the close of the American Revolution, when loyalists from the Carolinas arrived with their slaves to settle on Abaco and several other islands, at the time to raise sea island cotton. They prospered for the few decades during which the virgin soil lasted and slavery was permitted. But their plantations were wiped out in 1834, when slavery was ended, and many moved to Nassau or left the archipelago altogether.

The present population of the Bahamas is less than 175,000, but aided by the steady influx of new settlers, it is increasing rapidly. Totals increased by 54 percent between the 1953 and 1963 censuses, and climbed an additional 30 percent between 1963 and 1970.

Among the 22 inhabited islands, there are enormous differences in the distribution and density of population. New Providence, with an area of 60 square miles, accounts for more than half the total and has a population density of more than 700 per square mile. The Bahamians apply the term "out islands" to all the Bahamas except New Providence, the site of Nassau "and therefore the capital of the world." Of the 21 inhabited "out islands," Andros, Grand Bahama, Abaco, and Eleuthera have a few thousand inhabitants each; the others have from less than a dozen to several hundred inhabitants.

SELECTED REFERENCES

AUGELLI, J. P., and TAYLOR, H. W. "Race and Population Patterns in Trinidad." *Annals of the Association of American Geographers* 50, no. 2 (1960):123–38.

DE BRUIJNE, G. A. "Surinam and the Netherlands Antilles." *Geografisch Tijdschrift* 5, no. 4 (1971).

EYRE, L. A. *Geographic Aspects of Population Dynamics in Jamaica*. Boca Raton, Florida: Atlantic University Press, 1972.

FENTEM, A. D. *Commercial Geography of Antigua*. Office of Naval Research Technical Report no. 11. Bloomington: Indiana University, Department of Geography, 1961.

———. *Commercial Geography of Dominica*. Office of Naval Research Technical Report no. 5. Bloomington: Indiana University, Department of Geography, 1960.

FINKEL, H. J. "Patterns of Land Tenure in the Leeward and Windward Islands and Their Relevance to Problems of Agricultural Development in the West Indies." *Economic Geography* 40, no. 2 (1964):163–72.

FLOYD, B. "Jamaica." *Focus* 19, no. 2 (1968).

HAREWOOD, J. "Population Growth in Trinidad and Tobago in the Twentieth Century." *Social and Economic Studies* 12, no. 1 (1963): 1–26.

HOY, D. R. *Agricultural Land Use of Guadeloupe*. National Research Council Publication no. 884. Washington, D.C.: National Academy of Sciences, 1961.

KINGSBURY, R. C. *Commercial Geography of Trinidad and Tobago*. Office of Naval Research Technical Report no. 4. Bloomington: Indiana University, Department of Geography.

LASSERRE, G. *La Guadeloupe: Étude Géographique*. Bordeaux: Union Francaise d'Impression, 1961.

LEWIS, G. K. "An Introductory Note to the Study of the Virgin Islands." *Caribbean Studies* 8, no. 2 (1968).

———. *The Growth of the Modern West Indies*. New York: Monthly Review Press, 1968.

LOWENTHAL, D. "The Population of Barbados." *Social and Economic Studies* 6, no. 4 (1957):445–501.

———. "The Range and Variation of Caribbean Societies." *Annals of the New York Academy of Sciences* 83, no. 5 (1960):786–95.

———. *West Indian Societies*. New York: Oxford University Press, 1972.

MACPHERSON, J. *Caribbean Lands: A Geography of the West Indies*. London: Longmans, Green, 1963.

MULCHANSINGH, V. C. "The Oil Industry in the Economy of Trinidad." *Caribbean Studies* 11, no. 1 (1971).

NIDDRIE, D. L. *Land Use and Population in Tobago.* The World Land Use Survey, Regional Monograph no. 3. Bude, Cornwall, England: Geographical Publications, 1961.

O'LOUGHLIN, C. "Economic Problems of the Smaller West Indies Islands." *Social and Economic Studies* 11, no. 1 (1962):44–56.

PAGET, E. "Value, Valuation, and Use of Land in the West Indies." *Geographical Journal* 127, no. 4 (1961):493–98.

PERON, Y. "La Population des Départments Francaise d'Outre-Mer." *Population* 21 (1966).

STARKEY, O. P. *Commercial Geography of Montserrat.* Office of Naval Research Technical Report no. 6. Bloomington: Indiana University, Department of Geography, 1960.

THOMAS, C. Y. "Coffee Production in Jamaica." *Social and Economic Studies* 13, no. 1 (1964):188–217.

WELCH, B. "Population Density and Emigration in Dominica." *Geographical Journal* 134 (1968).

West Indies and Caribbean Year Book, 1973. Croyden, U.K.: Chapel River Press, 1972.

YOUNG, B. S. "Jamaica's Bauxite and Alumina Industries." *Annals of the AAG* 55, no. 3 (1968):449–64.

≡ **8** ≡

Pre-Conquest Mexico and Central America

To understand adequately the human geography of present-day Mexico and Central America, one must consider the aboriginal background as it existed in these areas before the European invasion in the early sixteenth century. Much of Mexico and parts of Central America are still considered to be largely Indian in character, although they have been variously modified by European culture. Probably one-third of Mexico's total population, and more than half of Guatemala's, is of pure Indian blood. In Mexico, some 3.2 million people (6.5 percent of the population) still speak Indian languages; in Guatemala, more than 2 million (40 percent) speak native tongues. But more significant than race and language are the great number of Indian customs that are retained in the cultural heritage of Mexico and Central America. Among these are food crops and food habits, farming practices, and rural dwelling types, all of which give an aboriginal cast to the landscape of many areas. To be sure, most of the present dominantly Indian sections are found in isolated areas. On the other hand, many Indian customs, mainly food crops and diet, have become an integral part of rural life throughout much of Mexico and Central America. Moreover, certain aspects of ancient Indian systems of land tenure have been retained in many areas, and in Mexico the aboriginal custom of communal land use has been incorporated into the current agrarian program.

ABORIGINAL ECONOMIES IN ABOUT 1500 A.D.

Immediately prior to the Spanish invasion, two fundamentally different types of aboriginal economies were present in the Mexico–Central American area: (1) A *primitive hunting, gathering, and fishing economy,* which was practiced by the scant population that inhabited the steppes and deserts of northern Mexico; and (2) an *agricultural economy,* which prevailed over the rest of Mexico and Central America (Figure 8.1). The bulk of the Indians were farmers living in villages or in scattered dwellings and practicing a rudimentary slash-burn cultivation, although in various sections advanced farming techniques such as irrigation and terracing were utilized. The advanced methods were particularly important in parts of central and southern Mexico and of northern Central America. This was the area of highly developed aboriginal culture that

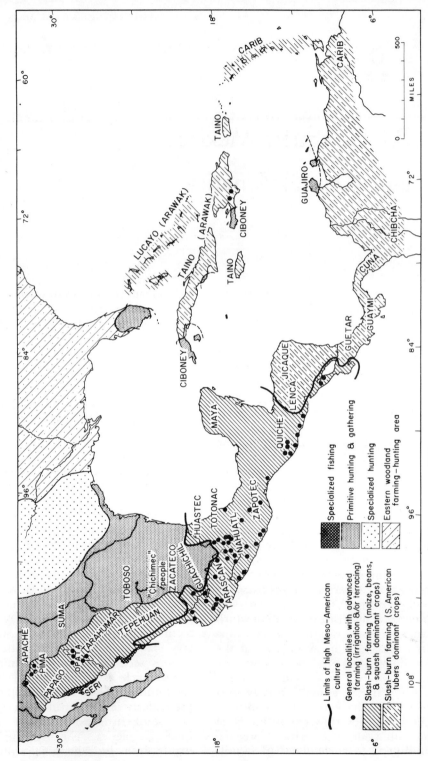

Figure 8.1 Pre-Conquest economy and culture areas, 1500 A.D.

the anthropologists call "Mesoamerica," the locale of the renowned Aztec, Maya, and other Indian civilizations.

The farming population of Mexico and Central America may be further classified into two groups on the basis of crop types. In the southeastern part of Central America, Indians of relatively low cultural status cultivated mainly tubers of South American origin, such as manioc and sweet potato. In contrast, within northern Central America and Mexico, the Indian farmers relied principally on three seed plants of local origin: maize, beans, and squash. These three plants still comprise the major crop complex in the same area. The maize-beans-squash region may, in turn, be divided into two areas: (1) Mesoamerica, distinguished by its high native cultures, advanced farming techniques, and a great variety of domesticated plants; and (2) northwestern Mexico, characterized mainly by people of relatively low culture, but related culturally to both the Mesoamericans to the south and the well-developed farming cultures of southwestern United States.

Summary of Aboriginal Economies in Mexico and Central America

I. Primitive hunting, gathering, and fishing economy: desert nomads of northern Mexico
II. Agricultural economies
   A. Maize, beans, and squash farmers of Mexico and northern Central America
      1. Primitive and advanced farmers of Mesoamerica
      2. Primitive farmers of northwestern Mexico
   B. Primitive tuber farmers of southeastern Central America

PRIMITIVE HUNTING, GATHERING, AND FISHING

The desert nomads of northern Mexico held the lowest cultural status of any Indian group on the mainland of Middle America. They wandered in small bands from place to place, gathering seeds, roots, and fruits of desert plants; hunting with traps and bow and arrow for rodents, reptiles, and sometimes deer, and often fishing with nets in the streams and more permanent desert lakes. Along the eastern coast of the Gulf of California, some nomads, such as the Seri and Guasave, became specialized fishermen.

The rudimentary shelters of these people were crudely built lean-tos and domed huts of desert plant materials. Such dwellings could be quickly constructed where fruit and game were abundant and abandoned when the surrounding resources were depleted. Owing to the scantiness of the desert resources for people of such low culture, the number of the nomads was never large.

The Indians of Baja California, one of the least desirable areas of Middle America, were the least numerous and culturally lowest of the desert nomads. The Pericú in the southern Cape area, the Cochimí in the central Vizcaino Desert, and the Kiliwa in the north were some of the important language groups of the arid peninsula. Missionized by Spanish priests in the seventeenth century, these Indians were practically wiped out by diseases brought over from Europe, and today only a handful remain scattered in isolated areas.

The nomads of the north-central Mexican desert and steppes were more numerous and more culturally advanced than the lowly Baja Californians, particularly in social organization. Warlike and mobile, they were the scourge of the northern Aztec frontier, having more than once raided the settled farming areas near the Valley of Mexico. Quite likely, these people were the source of the periodic invasions that often overthrew the high cultures of central Mexico, with the intruders finally being assimilated into the culture, much as the Mongol invaders were absorbed into the central Chinese civilizations. The Aztecs themselves were probably descendants of desert nomads from the north.

Collectively, the northern hunters and gatherers were known as "Chichimecs," an Aztec term of derision. Linguistically, they comprised many groups, such as the Pame, Guachichil, and Zacateco in the south and the Toboso, Suma, and Coahuilteca in the north. Women gathered desert products and men hunted deer and smaller animals with their strong bows. One of the favorite foods of many bands was the pod of the mesquite bush. Stripped of their indigestible seeds, the pods, rich in protein and sugar, were pounded into a meal and eaten as a gruel mixed with water. This is still a famine food for many people in isolated villages in northern Mexico.

We shall see later how the Chichimecs became a cultural barrier to northward expansion of Spanish settlement during the colonial period. Never numerous, these aborigines gradually died away or mixed with Spaniards or with settled Indians from central Mexico, so that today probably no Chichimecs are left. Quite in contrast to the civilized farmers of Mesoamerica, the desert nomads left no cultural heritage in northern Mexico. Today northern Mexico is largely non-Indian, providing a contrast to the central and southern parts of the country, which have a strongly aboriginal character.

THE MESOAMERICAN CIVILIZATIONS

Mesoamerica was the cultural hearth of ancient Mexico and much of Central America. It was one of the two areas of the Americas in which both high Indian civilizations and a major center of plant domestication developed, the other being the central Andes of South America. Thus, we are dealing now with the most significant aboriginal area of Middle America. It is precisely within the bounds of ancient Mesoamerica that we find today the bulk

of Indian population, the greatest number of spoken aboriginal languages, and most of the Indian ways of life that are retained in the culture of Mexico and Central America.

Significantly, the civilizations of Mesoamerica developed within the tropics of Mexico and Guatemala, in the high- and lowlands. On the northern periphery of aboriginal American civilization, the Mesa Central of Mexico, the home of the Aztecs and their predecessors, was the largest and probably the richest of the tropical highlands (Chapter 2). The rugged uplands of Oaxaca and the volcanic highlands of Guatemala were secondary foci of cultural development. In the tropical lowlands, the hot, damp Petén of northern Guatemala and the Yucatan Peninsula fostered the magnificent Maya civilization; almost equally advanced cultures, such as the Totonac, evolved on the Gulf coastal plain of Veracruz.

About 1500 A.D., on the eve of the Spanish invasion, the northern limit of Mesoamerican high cultures began on the Gulf of Mexico, at the latitude of present Tampico, and followed the Pánuco and Moctezuma rivers southwestward to the Río Lerma on the Mesa Central. Thence it extended northwestward, forming a narrow prong of high culture along the Pacific coast to the present town of Culiacán in central Sinaloa. This northern limit between high and low aboriginal cultures represents one of the most significant cultural boundaries in Middle America. It persisted through colonial times, and though now blurred, it is still expressed as a transition zone between northern Mexico's predominately European-mestizo way of life and southern Mexico's prevailingly Indian and mestizo cultures.

Prior to 1500 A.D., this cultural line had not been a stable one. On their arrival in Mexico, the Spaniards found the Chichimecs pressing southward into the area of high culture. Moreover, archeological evidence reveals that, probably during the ninth century A.D., Mesoamerican civiliza-

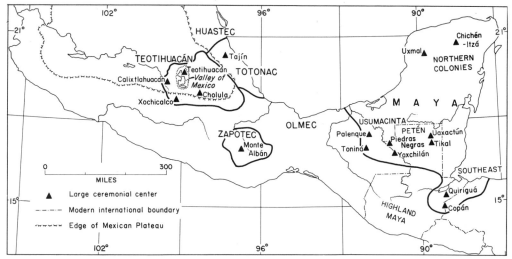

Figure 8.2   Mesoamerican classical cultures, 200 B.C. to 900 A.D.

tion extended northward into the steppe lands of Zacatecas and Durango along the eastern foothills of the Sierra Madre Occidental. By 1500 A.D., the Mesoamericans had abandoned their ceremonial sites and cultivated fields within this area, which was subsequently occupied by desert nomads and simple farmers.

The southern limit of Mesoamerica bordered on the simple farming culture of Central America. The boundary passed through western Honduras and thence southeastward, to include the Pacific coastal areas as far south as the Nicoya Peninsula of Costa Rica. This southern extension of high culture resulted from early (perhaps ninth century A.D.) migrations of Central Mexicans into the coastal lowlands of El Salvador (Pipil culture) and the lake shores in the Nicaraguan Depression (Nicarao and Mangue cultures).

Anthropologists have defined Mesoamerican culture on the basis of various attributes indicative of a civilization. Among these are advanced architectural knowledge, illustrated by the construction of large ceremonial centers with stonefaced or plastered, truncated, pyramidal temple bases; ball courts; and palaces. The ruins of these sites form part of the present cultural landscape throughout central and southern Mexico and northern Central America. Such centers imply the existence

of a highly organized religion with an elaborate priesthood and ritual. A well-developed agriculture based on maize, beans, squash, and other plants; organized trade and markets; and knowledge of metallurgy are other significant characteristics of this culture level.

History of Mesoamerican Cultures

The Aztec, and other Indian civilizations that the Spaniards found in the Mesoamerican area, had been preceded by many highly evolved cultures entailing centuries of human development. Since remote times, man has favored the tropical highlands and lowlands of Mexico and northern Central America. One of the oldest human skeletal remains in the Americas, dated at approximately 7000 B.C., was found in the Valley of Mexico near the village of Tepexpan. Following a long period of slow cultural development, the immense ceremonial centers of Teotihuacán, Cholula, Xochicalco, and Monte Albán represented the culmination of native American art, architecture, and religion in the brilliant classical civilizations that developed between 200 B.C. and 900 A.D. in central Mexico (Figure 8.2). These cultures were followed by the Toltec period

223

(900–1170 A.D.), when the great site of Tula was constructed north of the Valley of Mexico.

From approximately 300 to 900 A.D., the renowned classical Mayan civilization flourished, paradoxically, in the tropical rain forests of northern Guatemala, Tabasco, and British Honduras. The ruins of hundreds of large Mayan ceremonial centers today lie hidden by dense forest within this region. After the sudden and, as yet, unexplained abandonment of these centers in the last years of the ninth century, the Mayas continued their culture in the drier northern half of the Yucatan Peninsula. There the famous ceremonial centers and cities of Chichén-Itzá, Uxmal, Mayapán, and scores of others were occupied from around 850 to 1300 A.D. (Figure 8.3). Many of these sites had already been established during the classical period. In the north, practically every ceremonial center was located near a *cenote,* or sinkhole, which in many parts of the dry limestone peninsula is the sole water supply. When the Spaniards first penetrated Yucatan in the 1520s, the Mayan civilization, through a series of civil wars, had disintegrated into a group of 18 native states. Although most of the large ceremonial centers lay in ruins, an estimated population of 500,000 Mayans at that time were carrying on a thriving agriculture and trading extensively with their Mexican and Central American neighbors. Today, approximately 300,000 Maya-speaking Indians inhabit the northern part of the peninsula.

To the south of Yucatan, in the highlands of Guatemala and Chiapas, lived close relatives of the Mayas. Although they lacked the pretentious ceremonial centers characteristic of the lowlands, they practiced advanced agriculture and were probably far more numerous than their lowland counterparts. Among the many linguistic groups related to Mayan speech were the Quiché and Mam of the volcanic highlands of Guatemala; the Kekchi or Pocomam of the limestone plateaus in the Alta Verapaz; and the Tzeltal and Tzotzil of the Chiapas highlands. The descendants of these groups who still speak the Indian languages number over two million.

By 1500 A.D., two powerful military states had evolved in the highlands of central Mexico. These were the Aztec domain in the east and the Tarascan state in the west (Figure 8.4). The Aztecs, who spoke Nahuatl, or Mexicano, had established the larger and more populous of the two states. According to legend, these people were migrants from the north who established themselves in the Valley of Mexico

Figure 8.3   A portion of the Maya ceremonial center of Chichén-Itzá in northern Yucatan. In the foreground are two stone-faced, truncated pyramids topped by temples. The Temple of the Warriors (*lower center*) and the Castillo were rebuilt under Toltec influence after 950 A.D. In the background are older Maya buildings of the eighth and ninth centuries A.D. (*Compañia Mexicana Aerofoto*)

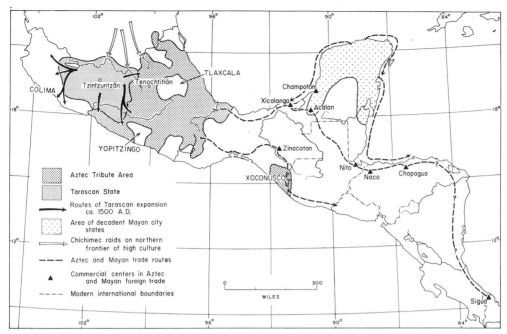

Figure 8.4 Ancient political states, 1500 A.D.

during the fourteenth century A.D. As all of the available land around the basin lakes was already occupied by sedentary farmers, the Aztecs were forced to settle on a small island near the western shore of Lake Texcoco. There, in 1325, they established a village and ceremonial center called Tenochtitlán, which later became a magnificent city and capital of the Aztec realm. The old central square (the Zócalo) and adjacent parts of the present metropolis of Mexico City lie over the ruins of Tenochtitlán, destroyed in 1521 by the Spanish conquerors. Through an alliance with the neighboring states of Texcoco and Tlacopán (Tacuba), the Aztecs gained political and military control over the Valley of Mexico. In 1429, the rulers of the alliance began the spread of empire with well-disciplined armies. Within 75 years, the Aztecs had extended their political hegemony from the Pánuco River in the northeast to the modern frontier of Guatemala in the south. The Totonac and Huastec Indians of the eastern escarpment and Gulf coastal plain, the Otomí on the northern Chichimec frontier, the Mixtec and Zapotec of the southern highlands of Oaxaca—all became vassals of the Aztec.

Only the Tlaxcalans east of the Valley of Mexico, the Tarascans to the west, and minor chiefdoms in the south were able to resist Aztec domination. When Cortes arrived on the Gulf coast of Mexico in 1519, the Aztecs were slowly pushing their realm southward into Central America.

The Aztec domain was not an empire in the modern sense. Rather, it was a tribute state. All conquered towns were subject to the payment of an annual or semiannual tribute in the form of grain, gold, textiles, cacao, or other economic products of the land. These were carried to the capital, Tenochtitlán, and there placed in the storehouses of the ruler or apportioned among the nobility. Although the Aztecs established military garrisons at strategic points within their realm to encourage the payment of tribute or to protect trade routes, they made no attempt to impose their language (Nahuatl), government, or religion on the conquered.

Aztec conquests were motivated principally by the desire for economic gain through tributes. The hot lower escarpments bordering the plateau, the Balsas Basin, and the Pacific and Gulf coastal lowlands were particularly prized. These areas were the main sources of cotton and cotton cloth; of cacao, the beans of which were employed both as a beverage for the nobility and as currency; and brilliant plumes of tropical birds and jaguar skins used in priestly and military garb. One of the last territories conquered before the landing of the Europeans was that of Soconusco (Xoconusco), along the Pacific coasts of Chiapas and Guatemala, famed for its extensive groves of cacao. For gold for ceremonial ornaments, the Aztecs depended mainly on the stream placers of the upper Balsas Basin; however, professional merchants undertook long trading expeditions as far as the Caribbean coast of Honduras and Panama to obtain the precious metal, as well as other products. The Aztec state thus spread southward and eastward into the rich tropical lowlands; the dry northern plateau, inhabited by marauding nomads, was unattractive.

On the western part of the Mesa Central, the Tarascan Indians also established a native state, which, although not comparable in size and wealth to that of the Aztecs, was a cohesive political unit. Pre-Conquest Tarascan territory corresponded roughly to the present Mexican state of Michoacán. The principal ceremonial center, Tzintzuntzan, like the Aztec capital, occupied a lake site—the eastern shore of beautiful Lake Pátzcuaro. Today the small remnant of Tarascan-speaking Indians lives around the lake and in the adjacent pine-covered volcanic highlands (*La Sierra*) in central Michoacán.

Like the Aztecs, the Tarascans expanded their frontiers outward from their highland core during the 75-year period preceding the Spanish conquest. To the east, approximately along the present Mexico-Michoacán state boundary, a stable military frontier, lined with forts of log and stone, was set up against the Aztecs. Tarascans made their military advances mainly to the south and west of the highland core. Southward they took over the hot, lower Balsas and Tepalcatepec basins, the sources not only of tropical products, but also of copper. Westward they conquered the highland areas occupied by culturally advanced Indians south of Lake Chapala and penetrated into the rich lowlands of southeastern Colima near the Pacific shore. Another likely incentive for westward Tarascan expansion was the silver ore within the present state of Jalisco, south and west of Lake Chapala. The Tarascans and their subject peoples were the foremost metallurgists of Middle America; they were good goldsmiths and knew the art of refining silver and copper. Early Spanish assay records from Mexico are replete with references to plates and ingots of silver taken as booty from various Tarascan towns, and there have been many archeological finds of ceremonial copper axheads, bells or rattles, and other copper objects in Tarascan or pre-Tarascan graves.

The Tarascan state was probably more of a political empire than that of the Aztec. The Tarascans not only exacted tribute from conquered populations, but also colonized their own people in frontier towns and, by this means, spread their language and culture by methods not used by the Aztecs.

Population and Settlement in Mesoamerica

During pre-Conquest times, the southern half of Mexico and northern Central America formed one of the most densely occupied areas of the New World. The actual numbers of people can never be known, but historians and anthropologists have made serious though highly discrepant estimates of the population of this area. Estimates for Mexico vary from 3 to 25 million persons, but the latter figure may be nearest the truth.[1] The in-

1. In recent studies on Indian population in Mexico, Woodrow Borah and S. F. Cook of the University of California, present convincing evidence that central and southern Mexico, alone,

Figure 8.5 Dispersed *ranchería* type settlement and small fields of Otomí Indians on the western slope of the Sierra de las Cruces, overlooking the basin of Toluca, central Mexico

habitants of the highlands of Chiapas and Guatemala may well have numbered over one million; of the Yucatan Peninsula, one-half million; and of southernmost Mesoamerica (El Salvador and western Nicaragua) perhaps another quarter million or more.

At the time of the Spanish Conquest, over 80 different languages belonging to more than 15 language families were spoken within Mesoamerica. The multiplicity of tongues and the fragmented areal distribution of many of the languages within this small, densely settled area indicate that a great number of immigrations had occurred over a long period of time.

The dense aboriginal population was by no means evenly distributed. Undoubtedly, the highland basins of Central Mexico and Guatemala were the most favored spots for settlement, just as they are today. Nevertheless, the accounts of sixteenth-century Spanish chroniclers and the evidence of modern archeological surveys indicate that the tropical lowlands of Mesoamerica were far more densely occupied in the pre-Conquest period than at any time since.

The Valley of Mexico, 30 by 40 miles in size and the center of the Aztec realm, was the most densely inhabited spot of all Middle America. Recent studies indicate that between one and two million people probably lived in this basin during the early years of the sixteenth century. Since most of the basin floor was covered by five large lakes, settlement was heavily concentrated around the narrow lake plain and the adjacent slopes of the surrounding mountains. The most striking settlement feature of the Valley of Mexico was the large cities, almost unique in the aboriginal civilizations of the Americas. Estimates of the population of Tenochtitlán vary from 50,000 to 250,000. The cities of Texcoco and Chalco, on the eastern side of the basin, were less populous. Smaller compact towns and villages dotted the basin's periphery, probably much as they do today.

The most common type of aboriginal settlement throughout most of Mesoamerica and adjacent regions, however, was the small, semidispersed, rural village (*ranchería* or *caserío*), whose individual dwellings were scattered haphazardly over a large area and connected by footpaths (Figure 8.5). Such settlements are now typical of those in isolated mountain areas and are not uncommon in more accessible valleys and foothills. As we shall see (Chapter 9),

---

may have supported as many as 25 million people on the eve of the Spanish Conquest. See bibliography for references.

the Spaniards eventually forced most of the Indians to live in the compact European-type rural village that is so common in Latin America today.

One of the most conspicuous features of human settlement of any area is the individual dwelling, the style of which may vary from place to place with the available construction materials and the cultural heritage of the inhabitants. In aboriginal Mesoamerica, there were a confusingly large number of house types, each characteristic of a given area. In many parts of rural Mexico and Central America, aboriginal types of house construction, little modified from those of pre-Conquest times, still prevail. Such houses are usually single-family units with but one room and a dirt floor—*chozas,* or huts.

In the highlands, houses were characteristically square or rectangular, and had walls of stone, adobe (sun-dried brick), or wattle and daub (mud-covered lattice of saplings) and roofs that were steep, highly pitched, and thatched with dried grass. In certain sections, however, such as the Valley of Mexico and adjacent areas, flat-roofed adobe houses, similar to those of the Pueblo Indians of the American Southwest, were common. In the tropical lowlands, there was a much greater variety of types. Floor plans were square, oval (apsidal), or round; walls were of loose wattle, sometimes covered with mud but more frequently left unplastered to permit the free entrance of air; roofs were of palm or grass thatch. The roofs of round houses were conical; the roofs of square or rectangular houses were either steep-hipped and four-sided or gabled and two-sided. Windows and chimneys were unknown (Figure 8.6).

Associated with the main dwelling were various outbuildings. These included the kitchen, a separate structure usually built in the rear of the main house. This was the place of the women, who prepared food and cooked over the hearth—three stones arranged in a triangle for placing

Figure 8.6   Two examples of aboriginal house types in Mexico. The round structure above is a Huastec house, northern Veracruz. Below, a Tzotzil house in Chiapas, southern Mexico.

clay pots over the fire (Figure 8.7). The granary, which had many forms, and often a semisubterranean structure known as the *temazcal,* or sweatbath, completed the house assemblage (Figure 8.8).

Figure 8.7   A typical hearth in an Indian kitchen, Valley of Mexico

Figure 8.8 Aboriginal granary types of central and southern Mexico. All three types shown here are used for storing shelled maize. On the left is the *cuezcomatl,* a vasiform granary of clay and thatch.

Food and Agriculture

The dense pre-Spanish population of many parts of Mesoamerica was supported by a well-developed agriculture. A large number of domesticated plants were cultivated by farming techniques sufficiently advanced to produce a food surplus. In Mexico and northern Central America, Indians cultivated nearly 90 different species of plants. Seventy of these were native to the area; the remainder, imports from South America (Table 8.1). We have already noted that the most important food crops of Mesoamerica were maize, beans, and squash, still the basis of life for millions of Mexicans and Central Americans. This plant triad affords a fairly well-balanced diet. Maize furnishes the starch or carbohydrate element and is also rich in oil and protein; beans provide the protein component, largely taking the place of meat; and squash offers a variety of essential vitamins in its oil-rich seeds, which are roasted, and in its flowers and flesh, cooked as vegetables. Indians cultivated all three crops together in the same plot, as they do today. Through centuries of cultivation, something of a symbiotic relationship has developed among these three plants: the tall maize stalks serve as supports for the climbing bean vines, which in turn enrich the soil with nitrogen; and the squash, being a creeper, covers the ground beneath the maize and beans with its wide leaves, protecting the loose soil from undue erosion by the heavy afternoon downpours characteristic of the summer rainy season.

The Indian farmers of Mexico and northern Central America made five important starch foods from maize, just as their pure- and mixed-blood descendants do today.

1. The *tortilla,* a thin, round pancake of maize dough baked on a large clay plate (*comal*), was the most common food.

2. *Tamales* were made by filling maize dough with meat, beans, or chile peppers, wrapping in corn husks, and boiling.

3. *Pozole* was a thick soup of hominy (whole, cooked kernels of corn) with other vegetables, highly seasoned with chile pepper. In southern Mexico, *pozol* (spelled without an *e*) was a watery gruel of corn meal flavored with chocolate.

4. *Atole,* perhaps the most ancient of the maize foods, was a thick, starchy gruel of boiled maize dough, flavored with chile pepper, and drunk from a clay bowl.

5. *Pinole,* made by grinding toasted maize kernels to a coarse flour and often flavored with honey, could be carried on long trips without spoiling, and a gruel could easily be prepared from it. Pinole was the road provision for travelers, merchants, and soldiers.

Tortillas, tamales, and atole were prepared from a heavy dough (*masa,* or *nixtamal*) made by grinding boiled maize

**Table 8.1   MAJOR DOMESTICATED PLANTS CULTIVATED
IN MESOAMERICA, 1500 A.D.**

Plant	Scientific Name	Place of Origin
SEED PLANTS		
Maize	Zea mays	S. Mexico; Guatemala (possibly)
Beans	Phaseolus (4 species)	S. Mexico; Guatemala
Amaranth	Amaranthus cruentus	S. Mexico; Guatemala
Sunflower	Helianthus annuus	S.W. United States or western Mexico
Chía	Salvia hispanica	Mexico
	Chenopodium nuttalliae	
TUBER PLANTS		
Sweet potato	Ipomoea batatas	South America
Sweet manioc	Manihot esculenta	South America
Jícama	Pachyrrhizus erosus	Mexico
VEGETABLES		
Tomato	Lycopersicon esculetum	S. Mexico; Guatemala
Husk tomato	Physalis ixocarpa	S. Mexico; Guatemala
Chayote	Sechium edule	S. Mexico; Guatemala
Squash	Cucurbita (4 species)	S. Mexico; Guatemala
FRUITS		
Cacao	Theobroma cacao	S. Mexico; Guatemala
Avocado	Persia americana	S. Mexico; Guatemala
Pineapple	Ananas comosus	South America
Papaya	Carica papaya	S. Mexico; Guatemala
Tuna cactus	Opuntia	Mexico
Chirimoya	Annona cherimolia	South America
Mamey	Calocarpum mammosum	S. Mexico; Guatemala
Chicosapote	Achras sapote	S. Mexico; Guatemala
Mexican cherry (*capulín*)	Prunus capuli	Mexico
Hog plum (*jocote*)	Spondias mombin	S. Mexico; Guatemala
Guava	Psidium guajava	S. Mexico; Guatemala
Vanilla	Vanilla planifolia	S. Mexico; Guatemala
FIBER PLANTS		
Agaves	Agave (5 species)	Mexico
Cotton	Gossypium hirsutum	S. Mexico; Guatemala
CONDIMENTS		
Chile pepper	Capsicum (various species)	S. Mexico; Guatemala
DYE PLANTS		
Achiote	Bixa orellana	South America
Indigo	Indigofera suffruticosa	Central America
CEREMONIAL PLANTS		
Tobacco	Nicotiana (2 species)	South America
Copal	Protium copal	S. Mexico; Guatemala
ORNAMENTALS		
Dahlia	Dahlia (4 species)	S. Mexico; Guatemala
Marigold	Tagetes (2 species)	Mexico
Tigerflower	Tigridia pavonia	S. Mexico; Guatemala

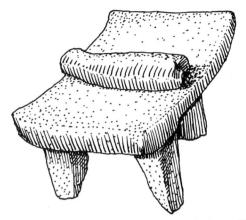

Figure 8.9 An Indian metate, or grinding mill, still used in most parts of Mexico and northern Central America

kernels on the metate, or stone quern (Figure 8.9).

In addition, fresh green corn was parched as roasting ears, and dried kernels of specific varieties were either parched or popped on the *comal*.

Besides maize, the Indians of southern Mexico domesticated another grain, amaranth, a weedlike plant that yields a colorful spike of tiny seeds rich in starch and oil. In pre-Conquest times in the Mesa Central of Mexico, this grain was almost as important a food as maize. Its significance as a ritual food presented to native gods in Aztec temples attests to its antiquity. Today only small plots of amaranth are cultivated in isolated localities in Mexico and Guatemala. Curiously, the small village of Tulyehualco, a few miles south of Mexico City, specializes in the cultivation of this tiny seed for making small cakes that are eaten only during Holy Week and Christmas.

Other food plants cultivated aboriginally included at least two starchy tubers—the sweet potato and the sweet variety of manioc (yuca), both of South American origin. Among the vegetables, besides several kinds of squash, were the tomato and the piquant condiment, chile pepper. High in vitamin C and an active stimulant of the salivary glands, chile en-

livens the bland maize foods and adds to the human dietary requirements. Over 30 different species of fruits, most of them tropical plants of Mexican or Central American origin, were cultivated in Mesoamerica. Among the most important were pineapple; cacao, or the chocolate bean tree; avocado, or alligator pear; papaya, or melon tree; many kinds of soursops, such as the chirimoya; at least five species of sapotes; the hog plum; and many others.

Most of the American food plants that we have mentioned have now spread to many parts of the world, particularly to the tropics and subtropics of Africa and Asia, where they have revolutionized native food habits and have increased the efficiency of human diet severalfold. Undoubtedly, their domesticated plants were the American Indians' greatest gift to the world.

The Mesoamerican Indians cultivated many plants for purposes other than food. Cotton and agave (the century plant) furnished fiber for weaving cloth. Several species of agave, called "maguey" in Mexico and Central America, were put to many uses. Not only do these plants produce a stout fiber in their large, fleshy leaves, but they also yield a sweet sap, which, when fermented, becomes the famous pulque of central Mexico. Since this mild intoxicant contains ascorbic acid and many kinds of vitamins, it was, and still is, an essential part of the diet of the maize-beans-squash eaters in many parts of the highlands of Central Mexico. Tobacco for smoking and copal for incense were cultivated mainly for ceremonial use, while *achiote* was raised for its red dye, which was used to color food and to paint the body. Several flowers, such as marigold and dahlia, were domesticated in central Mexico and used for decorating temples and graves.

In contrast to their wealth of agricultural plants, the Indians of Mexico and northern Central America had only three truly domesticated animals. These were the dog, one variety of which was the short-legged, hairless, edible type; the turkey, domesticated probably in southern Mexico; and the small stingless bee, kept for its honey and wax. Two small scale insects were semidomesticated. One was the cochineal bug, which feeds on the nopal, or prickly-pear cactus, and was reared for a scarlet dye. Another scale bug, called *aje* or *ajin,* was raised on certain trees for its wax, which was used as a base for paint, lacquer, and for burnishing pottery.

The Mesoamerican Indian supplemented his predominantly vegetable diet by fishing, hunting, and gathering wild animal life within his environs. It was particularly around the environment of highland lakes within the volcanic areas of central Mexico and Central America that these activities became well developed among the farming population. Lakes usually afford a great variety of food for man, the edible animal life ranging from fish and aquatic birds to insects, including their eggs and larvae. At the time of the Spanish Conquest, the highland Indians of Mexico and Guatemala appear to have hunted little large game, which may have been a reflection of the depletion of wild life after centuries of human occupation. For these people, the lake fauna had become the main source of animal food.

Fishing was an important occupation around the lakes of the Mesa Central, especially in the Valley of Mexico and the lake-studded Tarascan country. Most of the lacustrine fish resource was composed of small, sardinelike varieties, formerly caught by the thousands in nets and dried for later consumption. So important was lake fishing among the Tarascans that the Aztecs called their neighbors' area Michhuacan ("place of the fishers"), the origin of the present state name, Michoacán.

The hunting of aquatic fowl was probably as significant as lake fishing. Every year, myriads of migratory waterfowl (mainly ducks and coots) from North America nested in the reed-clogged lake shores in central Mexico. For fowling, the Indians employed long nets and forked spears thrown with the spear thrower, or the atlatl, one of man's most ancient weapons, still used today by a few Tarascans on Lake Pátzcuaro.

Probably the various insects, crustaceans, reptiles, and rodents hunted and gathered within the shallow, marshy sections of the lakes were equally as important as food. Frogs, tadpoles, turtles, crayfish, and a larval salamander which the Aztecs called *axoxotl,* were netted and gigged in large numbers. Of especial esteem in the Valley of Mexico were the eggs of various waterbugs that the Indians gathered from reeds growing along the lake shores. These eggs formed the famous ahuauhtle ("Aztec caviar"). Until a few years ago, villagers in the southern part of the valley gathered and ate ahuauhtle. Moreover, the larvae of the salt fly as well as green algae were skimmed from the lake surface for food. Away from the lakes, Indians habitually gathered and ate as delicacies toasted grasshoppers, various ants and their larvae; the maguey grub, which feeds on the agave plant; and other insects. Although such animals are not considered proper food in Western society, they are rich in protein, niacin, riboflavin, and several minerals essential to the human diet. These seemingly weird foods helped to supply dietary deficiencies that might have occurred among a population dependent mainly on maize, beans, and squash, and, in times of drought (not infrequent on the central plateau), the lake resources served as famine food. During the past 200 years, the various activities that once centered around the lakes in central Mexico have greatly declined, owing to natural desiccation and artificial draining of the water bodies.

Systems of Tillage

To cultivate their many domesticated plants, the Indians of Mesoamerica developed various methods of farming consonant with natural conditions and their technical knowledge. At least two general systems of tillage prevailed in Mexico and Central America before the arrival of Europeans: (1) migratory slash-burn cultivation; and (2) advanced farming, which involved (a) systematic fallowing of permanent fields and, occasionally, (b) terracing and/or irrigation. Despite the availability of numerous European agricultural practices and tools during the past 450 years, Indian farming techniques persist in various parts of Mexico and Central America.

Several features were common to the two systems of cultivation. For instance, since farming was mainly for subsistence, fields were small, probably no larger than one-half to three acres in size. Moreover, the Indian farmer practiced horticulture, rather than the single-crop field agriculture characteristic of Western culture and now common in most of Latin America. The Indian gave special care to individual plants, cultivating a great variety within his small plot. Not only were maize, beans, and squash raised together; but a few tomato, chile, or amaranth plants, and perhaps one or two fruit trees were also scattered about, until his holding took on an unordered, unkempt appearance. These practices are retained today in subsistence agriculture in many parts of Mexico and Central America, particularly on hillside plots, in kitchen gardens around the house, and even in permanent, plowed fields. Again, the same farming implements were employed in the two systems of cultivation. These were: (1) the simple planting stick, or dibble, with a sharpened, fire-hardened point; and (2) in some sections of central Mexico, the *coa,* a kind of spade with a triangular-shaped blade parallel with the handle (Figure 8.10). In the Tarascan area, *coas* with copper blades were used, but elsewhere they probably were wooden. Although today these aboriginal tools have been largely displaced by the European hoe and plow, they are still employed in some areas of Mexico. For instance, Indian

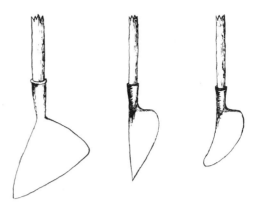

Figure 8.10   Types of metal *coa* blades used in central Mexico

farmers living in the Xochimilco area, only 20 miles from the center of Mexico City, still use the triangular-bladed *coa* to cultivate flowers and vegetables.

Migratory Slash-Burn Cultivation. Probably man's most ancient tillage system, this was the simplest and most widespread type of farming in all the Americas. Fundamentally, it is a woodland type of agriculture. It was practiced on steep, wooded slopes in the highlands, and on both slopes and level land within the lowland tropical forests. Today this relatively primitive method of cultivation still prevails in subsistence farming throughout the tropical lowlands of Mexico and Central America; and its persistence in the West Indies has been mentioned frequently in previous chapters of this book. In the highlands, however, it is now practiced only on the higher or more isolated mountain slopes where forest remains.

The system involves the clearing of small plots within the forest during the dry season and the burning of the dried branches and logs. The wood ash, rich in various minerals such as potassium and phosphorous, serves as a good fertilizer for crops. At the start of the rains, seeds and tubers are planted in holes punched into the ash-covered soil with the dibble. Yields are good the first year, but after two or three years of cultivation the soil is usually ex-

Figure 8.11   A slash-burn plot in the coastal lowlands of Veracruz State, Mexico, showing charred logs and patches of ash after burning. Maize and bean seeds will be dibbled into the ash and thin soil after the first rains.

hausted and weeds become such a problem that the plot is abandoned for perhaps 8 to 20 years, to permit the rejuvenation of the soil and the reestablishment of second-growth forest. After that time, when the decaying leaves and roots of the forest plants and microorganisms have renewed soil fertility, the same plot may be recleared and the cycle repeated. Meanwhile, in the surrounding forest, the farmer has cleared new plots which go through the same cycle of cropping and abandonment. Thus, the farmer is continually shifting his small cultivated fields. In central Mexico today, subsistence farmers call such slash-burn plots by the Nahuatl terms *tlacolol* or *coamil;* the Spanish terms *roza* and *desmonte* are sometimes used [2] (Figure 8.11).

It is readily apparent that, owing to the frequent shifting of cultivated plots, a large forested area is needed for the continued operation of the slash-burn system.

2. Slash-burn cultivation is often mistermed "milpa" agriculture. In Mexico and Central America, the word "milpa" is applied to any cultivated field (but principally one in which maize is grown), regardless of the system of agriculture used.

Being an extensive type of cultivation, therefore, it can normally support only a low density of population. Yet with only this simple farming technique at their disposal, the lowland Mayas were able to produce sufficient food to support a highly advanced culture.

Another attribute of present-day slash-burn cultivation in Middle America is an associated settlement pattern of either small hamlets (*rancherías*) or completely dispersed dwellings scattered on the forested mountain slopes. Archeological findings and early Spanish accounts indicate that a similar settlement pattern existed in pre-Conquest times, in the Mayan area of Yucatan and in the Totonac and Huastec regions along the Gulf coastal plain and adjacent eastern escarpment of Mexico. Then, however, settlements were usually scattered around the vicinity of ceremonial centers.

One of the most serious effects of long, continued use of the slash-burn system in a given area has been the alteration and, often, the eventual destruction of the forest cover. This has been especially true when the need for food causes the period of abandonment of the plots to be unduly shortened, preventing the complete restoration of the forest and with it, the renewal of soil productivity. One of the hypotheses presented to explain the collapse of the classical Mayan culture in southern Yucatan and northern Guatemala involves possible overcropping by the slash-burn system, which led to forest destruction, soil exhaustion, and even erosion and encroachment of a heavy grass cover. Probably the destruction of much of the oak and pine forest that once covered portions of the Mexican Mesa Central has been partly due to the overuse of slash-burn cultivation in pre-Conquest and colonial times.

Advanced Farming: Fallow Land.   Although somewhat akin to slash-burn cultivation, the fallowing of permanent fields in Mesoamerica was a more advanced agricultural technique and was more productive of foodstuffs. This method involved the initial clearing and burning of the vegetarian cover, but two or three years of successive cropping was followed by an equal period of letting the land lie fallow. The farmer thus confined his attention to a few more or less permanent fields within a small radius, a system conducive to permanent village settlement and fairly dense population. Indians fallowed land generally in the cool highlands, particularly around the fertile volcanic basins on the Mesa Central of Mexico and in southwestern Guatemala and Chiapas, where the population was extremely dense. They kept mainly to the lower, gentle slopes surrounding the basins; it is doubtful that they would have been able to till the flattish basin floors, characterized by heavy soils and thick grass cover, with only the dibble and *coa*. The fertile lacustrine soils of most of the highland basins, now so important in the economy of Mexico and Guatamala, were probably seldom farmed until the Spaniards introduced the plow in the sixteenth century. Today the ancient fallow system is occasionally seen on slopes in the eastern part of the Mesa Central and in Oaxaca, Chiapas, and Guatamala.

Advanced Farming: Irrigation, Terracing, and Land Reclamation. A more advanced and productive system of cultivation practiced in pre-Conquest Mesoamerica involved irrigation, sometimes accompanied by terracing on hill slopes. As far as we know, Mesoamerican irrigation was extremely spotty, but the technique was, of course, utilized in areas subject to a long dry season or to frequent drought. Archeological evidence indicates that Indian farmers used canal irrigation as early as 300 B.C. in the Tehuacan Valley, in the southeastern part of the Mesa Central. Early sixteenth-century Spaniards reported the use of irrigation at various points along the southern escarpment of the Mesa Central and the upper Balsas Basin. Moreover, most of the native cacao groves along the Pacific slope from Colima in Mexico to Nicaragua were cultivated by canal irrigation. But the Valley of Mexico and its environs was the most significant center of irrigation and hydraulic engineering in Mesoamerica. The Aztecs and their neighbors commonly employed canal irrigation on the eastern side of the Valley of Mexico, as well as in the basin of Puebla to the east. Aqueducts were also constructed to bring potable water from the springs of Chapultepec on the western side of the Valley of Mexico to the center of Tenochtitlán.

Still another advanced agricultural technique occasionally practiced by the Mesoamerican farmers was directed toward soil conservation on permanently cultivated slopes. Stone retention walls, forming crude terraces (most of which are now abandoned), are found from central Mexico southward to British Honduras. A more common soil-retention device was to plant hedges of agave along the contour to hold the soil and reduce the gradient of the slope. This technique, called *bancal* or *metepantli*, is still widely practiced in east-central Mexico (Figure 8.12).

The most fascinating advanced farming technique that the Indians developed in central Mexico was the *chinampa* (sometimes called "floating gardens"), a system of land reclamation in shallow lakes and marshy areas. This ingenious system was one of the most sophisticated and productive kinds of farming practiced by the American Indian. Chinampas were artificial plots, in some cases made of long strips of aquatic vegetation cut from thick masses of flotant that had accumulated on the lake surface. These strips, sinking at first to the shallow lake bottom, were placed one above the other until the top one barely extended above the water. Then layers of rich mud scooped from the lake bottom were spread over the chi-

Figure 8.12   The *bancal*, or *metepantli,* a semiterrace technique used today on slopes near Apam, central Mexico. Rows of maguey (agave) serve as low retention walls to prevent excessive erosion. (*Compañía Mexicana Aerofoto*)

nampa to form a planting surface. In other cases, chinampas were formed by digging drainage ditches in marshy areas and spreading the soil between the ditches to raise the ground above the water level. In either case, long artificial fields, 8 to 12 feet wide, more than 100 feet long, and separated one from another by narrow canals, resulted in the chinampa field pattern familiar today to most tourists who visit Xochimilco, south of Mexico City. To anchor the plots securely, native willows were planted along the edges. Such trees give the present chinampa areas their pleasant sylvan appearance (Figure 8.13).

From two to three harvests of maize, beans, chile, flowers, and other plants could be taken annually from one plot, for the crops were started in seed beds and transplanted to the chinampa surface. Continuous natural irrigation was effected by seepage from the canals through porous chinampa material, or water could be scooped from the canals to irrigate crops. Young plants were protected from winter frosts with mats of grass. Fertilizer in the form of lake mud, rotted vegetable matter, and probably even human excrement was applied before each planting.

There is little doubt that the dense rural population and the large cities in the

Figure 8.13   A chinampa plot bordered by willows and canals near Xochimilco, Valley of Mexico. The chinampa surface has been recently planted.

Valley of Mexico in pre-Conquest times were based mainly on the tremendous amount of food produced on these intensively cultivated plots. Recent studies within the valley show that in late Aztec times the chinampa area covered much of the beds of fresh-water lakes Chalco and Xochimilco and extended northward along the western edge of Lake Texcoco beyond Tenochtitlán (Figure 8.14). To prevent periodic incursion of the saline water of Lake Texcoco into the chinampa area and to regulate the lake levels, an elaborate system of dikes was constructed. Each of the causeways that connected the Aztec capital with the Mainland served both as a road and as a dike.

Chinampa agriculture continues to be practiced in the Valley of Mexico, and vestiges of the system can still be seen in low wet spots in the Basin of Puebla. But since the final desiccation of the lakes in 1900, the chinampa area in the Valley of Mexico has dwindled to a narrow strip along the south shore of former lakes Xochimilco and Chalco. Water for the canals is obtained from springs, and vegetables and flowers are still grown in the traditional manner for the Mexico City market.

Land Systems

Among most of the high cultures of Mesoamerica, agriculture was of such fundamental importance that rules of land tenure were carefully formulated. Especially in Mexico, some of these ancient Indian rules have persisted or have been reestablished despite 450 years of Spanish domination. Throughout most of Mesoamerica, the landholding village was at once the basic unit of settlement and the principal form of land tenure. Surrounding arable and wooded land belonged to the village. The village council assigned tillable land to each native family, and the family members held it as long as the land was farmed.

Thus, individuals held only use rights to the land; private individual ownership of land did not exist. This tradition of village land is retained in practically all Indian areas of Mexico and Guatemala today, and Mexico's recent agrarian program has incorporated many elements of the ancient landholding village into its program for redistributing the property of former large estates to the landless peasants.

The concept of the landholding village was best formulated in the Aztec area of the Mesa Central of Mexico, where much of the cultivated land was in permanent fields. There each village was organized into wards called *calpullis*. Each *calpulli* was given a tract of land in which tillable plots were assigned to each family of the ward.

By the time of the Spanish Conquest, a second type of land tenure, somewhat like the European feudal estate, had been established among the Aztecs. Through various means, Aztèc nobles had been able to acquire large tracts of land from village holdings, and these private estates were worked by serfs who were attached to the land. After the Conquest, these estates formed the first Spanish haciendas, the system of land holding that remained typical of Mexico's land tenure until the Agrarian Revolution of the present century.

Crafts, Trade, and Transport

Though the Mesoamericans were basically farmers, their society was sufficiently advanced to have developed some degree of craft specialization and an organized system of trade and transport. The ordinary farmers, like most pretechnical rural folk, were also craftsmen who fashioned household utensils during their spare time. But in the large urban centers, there were guilds of craft specialists—stonecutters, featherworkers, and goldsmiths—who made

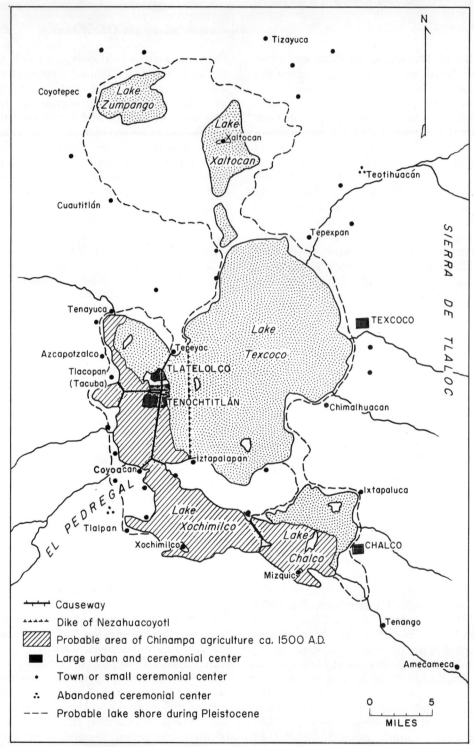

Figure 8.14 Central portion of the Valley of Mexico at the time of the Spanish Conquest

Figure 8.15 Native market scene, village square of Santiago Atitlán, Guatemalan highlands. Women, wearing the village costume, squat before their wares as did their ancestors in pre-Conquest times.

products for the nobility and the priesthood and sold their surplus wares in markets. Moreover, certain villages, favored by nearby supplies of raw materials, specialized in pottery, basketry, or weaving, much as many rural towns do today in Mexico and Central America. Thus, in certain strategically located villages, the periodic market (*tianguis*) where handicrafts and surplus agricultural products could be exchanged, became an integral part of Mesoamerican economic life. The largest markets were often held in or near large ceremonial centers. Within the Aztec realm, the great market of Tlatelolco, adjacent to Tenochtitlán, was one of the big centers of Mesoamerican commerce. In many respects, the present picturesque Indian village markets of Mexico and Guatemala are probably quite similar to those of pre-Hispanic times (Figure 8.15).

Both the Aztecs and the Mayas were great traders, engaging actively in foreign commerce. On their arrival in Yucatan, the Spaniards found the Mayas exporting large quantities of salt (from coastal lagoons), as well as cotton cloth, in large seagoing canoes to the Gulf Coast of Mexico and the Caribbean shore of Honduras.

In those areas, the Mayas traded their products for cacao, which was cultivated in abundance in the alluvial river valleys and piedmont slopes of Tabasco and Honduras.

Among the Aztecs, foreign commerce was in the hands of a group of traveling merchants, called the *Pochteca,* an official trading guild with special social status. With long trains of human carriers and protected from attack by armed guards, the *Pochteca* traveled southward to Tehuantepec, and into Central America as far as Nicaragua and Costa Rica, where they traded fine Mexican cloth, obsidian, and slaves for gold dust, jade, cacao, feathers, and jaguar skins. These merchants also served as spies in hostile territory, gaining information for Aztec rulers on rich areas ripe for conquest. Both their extensive trading activity and their tribute system helped spread the Aztecs' Nahuatl speech. Nahuatl became the *lingua franca* of much of Mesoamerica, and it remained a trade language long after the Spanish Conquest.

Lacking large domesticated animals and utilitarian knowledge of the wheel, the Indian himself served as beast of burden on land. Professional carriers (*tamemes*), both freedmen and slaves, hauled on their backs loads weighing up to 200 pounds and supported with the tump line, or forehead strap. In isolated sections of Mexico and Central America today, it is not uncommon to see both Indians and mestizos using this ancient means of transport (Figure 8.16). For water transport, the Indians used dugout canoes of various designs, and at the time of the Spanish Conquest, thousands of canoes plied the lakes of the Valley of Mexico. Canoes remained the principal means of transport for the peasant farmers of the valley until the lakes were finally drained at the beginning of this century.

Since land travel was exclusively by foot, only paths served as roads. With the exception of the causeways of the Aztec capital, all well-made ancient roads that have been discovered archeologically in Mesoamerica were for ceremonial purposes. The Aztecs and their predecessors established several main pathways leading from the Valley of Mexico into the tropical lowlands. Some colonial and modern roads followed these same paths. But as Indians on foot usually employed the most direct routes, their trails were often too steep and arduous for the wheeled traffic later introduced by Europeans.

Eastward from the Valley of Mexico, the trail to the Totonac country in the coastal lowlands of Veracruz passed between the volcanoes of Ixtaccihuatl and Popocatepetl to Cholula; thence it continued through the basins of Puebla and Huamantla and, through a series of easy steplike valleys, descended the eastern escarpment probably near the present Mexico City–Veracruz highway via Jalapa. Another trail went northeastward into the Huasteca of northern Veracruz, following approximately the route of the present highway by way of Jacala and Tamazunchale. The most important trails, however, led southeastward to the Maya country and into Central America, which, by the beginning of the sixteenth century, had become the Aztec's biggest market and source of imports. One of the southern roads passed through the Mixtec and Zap-

Figure 8.16   Indians in Guatemala hauling pottery attached to a boxlike carrying frame called the *huacal,* or *cacaxtli.* The load is steadied on the back by means of the tump line placed over the forehead. (*Delta Air Lines*)

otec areas of Oaxaca, approximating the present Pan-American Highway; from Oaxaca the trail proceeded southeastward to Tehuantepec, the Soconusco cacao area, and Guatemala. An even more ancient and significant footpath ran south and east, along the coastal lowlands of Veracruz and Tabasco to the great Aztec-Mayan trading center of Xicalango on the Laguna de Términos; thence it followed rivers and paths through the rain forest of northern Guatemala to the Mayan trading posts of Nito and Naco near the Caribbean coast of Guatemala and Honduras. Probably this same trail continued along the Caribbean coast as far as the present Costa Rica–Panama frontier (Figure 8.4). Soon after the Spanish Conquest, trade areas and modes of transport changed, and this famous road was forgotten.

On the western side of the Mesa Central of Mexico, a trail that has been used possibly for thousands of years descended the escarpment following a series of step-basins via present Tepic, approximating the modern railroad and highway from Guadalajara to the coast. The northwestern extension of high Mesoamerican culture into the Pacific coastal plain probably followed this route.

PRIMITIVE FARMERS OF NORTHWESTERN MEXICO

On the northwestern periphery of Mesoamerica lived the primitive farmers of the Sierra Madre Occidental and the coastal plain of northwest Mexico. Since their farming was based on the maize-beans-squash complex, this area might be considered as a northern extension of simple agriculture from the cultural core, Mesoamerica. Within the northwestern area, however, there were small islands of advanced farming, such as the irrigated terraces of the Ópata in mountainous eastern Sonora and the irrigated fields of the Pima in southern Arizona and the Sonoran lowlands. Both Ópata and Pima may have derived their advanced farming knowledge from the Indian cultures of southwestern United States, particularly from the ancient Hohokam culture of southern Arizona. Most of northwestern Mexico, however, was inhabited by simple farmers practicing migratory slash-burn cultivation on hill slopes and along stream bottoms. Within the Sierra Madre Occidental, the Tarahumar and the Tepehuán were the largest groups of simple farmers, while on the coast, various tribes, such as the Cahita and Yaqui, planted along the river flood plains, utilizing the moist alluvial soils when the annual floods receded. Farther north, in the desert of western Sonora, the Pápago Indians were known as cultivators of the drought-resistant tepary bean (still the commonest bean in the more Indian parts of Sonora), which they cultivated with maize and squash along intermittent water courses by flood irrigation. Most of the coastal farmers lived in small, permanent villages and supplemented their agricultural diet with seafood. The mountain people were more nomadic, living in scattered seasonal dwellings and relying on hunting and fishing for sustenance as much as on farming. Although greatly reduced in numbers, some Indian groups persist in the Mexican northwest. The Tarahumar, isolated in the rugged Sierra Madre in southwestern Chihuahua, are the most numerous; a few coastal people, mainly the Cahita, still cultivate their lands along the rivers as did their forefathers.

PRIMITIVE FARMERS OF SOUTHERN CENTRAL AMERICA

The Central American Indians who lived south and east of Mesoamerica had a much lower culture status than the Mayas or

Aztecs and their neighbors. Most of them were primitive forest farmers of South American origin, speaking languages related to Chibchan speech of Colombia. People speaking Cuna and Guaymí inhabited Panama. A large number of Chibchan languages were spoken in Costa Rica, but the Huetar of the central volcanic highlands were probably the most numerous group. In eastern Nicaragua, the Miskito and the Sumu lived on the coastal savannas and in the interior rain forest. Non-Chibchan groups, such as the Lenca, Jicaque, and Paya, occupied the rugged forested highlands of central Honduras along the contact zone with high Mesoamerican culture.

Like some of their more highly cultured neighbors to the north, the Central American Indians practiced only simple slash-burn farming. Hunting and fishing, however, was as important to their economy as agriculture. Moreover, the food crops of the Central Americans were much different from those of the Mesoamericans. Various tuber plants, all of South American origin, were raised from cuttings or part of the root, rather than from seeds. The tubers included sweet manioc, arrowroot, sweet potato, and the American yam. Another significant food was the boiled and roasted fruit from the cultivated peach palm, called *pejibaye,* also a native of South America. Maize, beans, and squash, except in a few areas, were secondary as food crops. Maize was grown principally for preparing *chicha,* a South American beer made by fermenting grains of corn. The tortilla was unknown. After the Spanish Conquest, maize became a more important food crop in southern Central America, but still today, in most rural sections of eastern Nicaragua, Costa Rica, and Panama, the tubers predominate in the ordinary dishes. In addition to their food crops, the Central Americans, like the Mesoamericans, raised cotton (but not agave) for fiber, tobacco for ceremonials, and various dye plants. Their only animal

domesticates were the dog, the stingless bee, and the small waxproducing scale insect.

Besides crops and food habits, other South American culture elements prevailed among the Indians of southern Central America. Among these were large, round communal houses of wattle and thatch, in which several families lived; the hammock for resting and sleeping; the blowgun as well as the bow and arrow for hunting and fishing; and weaving techniques similar to those used in the central Andes.

Although most of southern Central America was inhabited by forest farmers of low culture, there were at least two densely settled areas in which there existed a more advanced way of life. These were (1) the area of Coclé culture and Cuna speech in south central Panama, including the Azuero Peninsula and the savanna lands along the Pacific coast eastward to the present Canal Zone; and (2) the area of Huetar culture, which centered on the volcanic highlands of Costa Rica and extended southward along the flanks of the Talamanca Range. Both areas contained various chiefdoms organized into social classes of nobles, commoners, and slaves who lived in large villages around small religious centers. One of the most outstanding cultural achievements in both areas was skilled metallurgy in gold, a skill derived from northwestern South America, where the Quimbaya Indians of Colombia produced some of the best gold work known in indigenous America. Huetar and Coclé goldsmiths fashioned ear and nose pendents, breastplates, pins, figurines, bracelets, necklaces, and even fishhooks by casting, hammering, and soldering nearly pure gold but more often a gold-copper alloy (*guanín* or *tumbaga*). Since practically all the golden objects were ceremonial, they were usually placed in graves of chiefs and others of high social rank. Thus, after the Conquest, grave robbing became one of the main activities of the

Spaniards, particularly in Panama and Costa Rica, as well as in Colombia. Other advanced skills of the Coclé and Huetar people included the manufacture of finely decorated polychrome pottery, well-woven cloth and, among the Huetar, elaborate ceremonial stonework. Moreover, the Coclé people developed a fairly extensive trade, involving the export of salt, hammocks and other cotton goods, gold dust and gold objects, and slaves in large sail-rigged canoes to various points along the Pacific coast of Central America and possibly even to Mexico.

Today nothing is left of these cultures. The Huetar are completely gone, and only a handful of Indian descendants of various Talamanca groups now live in isolated sections of the Costa Rican highlands. The present Indians of Cuna speech who now inhabit the San Blas coast of northeastern Panama are far removed in space and culture from their ancestors.

SELECTED REFERENCES

ARMILLAS, P. "Land Use in Pre-Columbian America." UNESCO *Arid Zone Research*, no. 17 (1961):255–76.

———. "Gardens on Swamps." *Science* 174 (1971):653–61.

BARLOW, R. H. *The Extent of the Empire of the Culhua Mexica*. Ibero-Americana, no. 28. Berkeley: University of California Press, 1949.

BERGMANN, J. F. "The Distribution of Cacao Cultivation in Pre-Columbian America." *Annals of the Association of American Geographers* 59, no. 1 (1969):85–96.

BORAH, W., and COOK, S. F. *The Aboriginal Population of Central Mexico on the Eve of the Spanish Conquest*. Ibero-Americana, no. 45. Berkeley: University of California Press, 1963.

CHAPMAN, A. "Port of Trade Enclaves in Aztec and Maya Civilization." In K. Polany, *et al.*, eds. *Trade and Market in the Early Empires*. New York: Free Press, 1957, pp. 114–53.

DRESSLER, R. L. "The Pre-Columbian Cultivated Plants of Mexico." Harvard University Botanical Museum Leaflets 16, no. 6 (1953):115–72.

HEISER, C. B., JR. "Cultivated Plants and Cultural Diffusion in Nuclear America." *American Anthropologist* 67, no. 4 (1965):930–49.

MACNEISH, R. S. "The Origins of New World Civilization." *Scientific American* 211, no. 5 (1964):29–37.

MORLEY, S. G., and BRAINERD, G. W. *The Ancient Maya*. 3rd ed. Stanford, Calif.: Stanford University Press, 1956.

SAUER, C. O. *Agricultural Origins and Dispersals: The Domestication of Animals and Foodstuffs*. 2nd ed. Cambridge, Mass.: M.I.T. Press, 1969.

———. "The Personality of Mexico." *Geographical Review* 31, no. 3 (1941):353–64.

STANISLAWSKI, D. "Tarascan Political Geography." *American Anthropologist* 49, no. 1 (1947):46–55.

VAILLANT, G. C. *Aztecs of Mexico*. Rev. ed. New York: Doubleday, 1962.

WEST, R. C. "Population Densities and Agricultural Practices in Pre-Columbian Mexico, with Emphasis on Semi-terracing." *Verhandlungen des 38. Internationalen Amerikanistenkongresses*, 2 (1970):361–69.

WILKEN, G. C. "Drained-Field Agriculture: An Intensive Farming System in Tlaxcala, Mexico." *Geographical Review* 59, no. 2 (1969): 215–41.

———. "Food-Producing Systems Available to the Ancient Maya." *American Antiquity* 36, no. 4 (1971):432–48.

WOLF, E. R. *Sons of the Shaking Earth*. Chicago: University of Chicago Press, 1959.

≡ 9 ≡

Conquest and Settlement
of Mexico and Central America

In many respects, the sixteenth century is the most significant period in the development of the cultural landscape in Mexico and Central America. Through their conquest and occupation of the land during that century, the Spaniards established a cultural pattern that prevailed during most of the colonial period. This pattern, which still exists in modified form over much of the area, stamped its impress on the land and in many places altered the relationships of the native inhabitants to their environment.

Fundamentally, the colonial cultural pattern and its manifestations in the landscape evolved from a fusion of native Indian and medieval Iberian peoples and customs. The degree of cultural and racial mixing, however, varied from place to place. In remote sections and in areas where the aborigines were especially resistant to change, as in the southwestern highlands of Guatemala, the Indian way of life prevailed and is even now little modified by Spanish culture. Where the Indians were of low cultural status and few in numbers, as in northern Mexico, or where they were quickly destroyed, as in Costa Rica, Hispanic culture took over almost wholly. The most complete mixing of old and New World cultures seems to have occurred in central Mexico, particularly in the Mesa Central. In this tropical highland, the Spaniards found choice lands favorable for European settlement, but since the area was already occupied by a large Indian population with a civilization based on a well-developed agricultural economy, the Spaniards were forced to incorporate the Indian and his culture into colonial society. Thus, in central Mexico, as well as in other areas of Mesoamerica, there resulted a partial fusion of the two races and of the two sets of cultural patterns. The present kaleidoscopic cultural landscape of Mexico and Central America derives in large part from the uneven distribution of the Hispano-Indian cultural amalgam that developed in the sixteenth century.

In this and the next chapter, we shall trace the development of the cultural landscape in Mexico and Central America during colonial times—a period of some 300 years (1519–1821). Of prime significance in this development are: (1) the spread of Spanish conquest and occupation, (2) the impact of conquest on the physical aspects of the aboriginal population, and (3) the processes by which Spanish culture combined with the Indian to mold the landscape to its colonial form.

SPANISH CONQUEST
AND SPREAD
OF SETTLEMENT

As elsewhere within the Iberic sphere of the New World, the Spaniards' original motive for the discovery and settlement of Mexico and Central America was economic. Foremost in the minds of those who made up the conquering expeditions was the acquisition of quick wealth by exploiting the human and natural resources of the land. To the Spaniard, gold and silver, the standards of exchange in mercantilist Europe of the sixteenth century, were most desirable, but any other exploitable resources were acceptable, provided they could be sold for a huge profit. Thus, the Spaniards were first attracted to areas rich in mineral wealth and also to those with a dense native population that could supply large forces of labor and quantities of tribute. It was usually after the initial conquests had been effected that a more humanitarian motive of Span-

ish colonization—the spread of the Christian faith—came into play.

After the tragic decimation of the native population in the Greater Antilles and the consequent decline of gold production in Hispaniola, the Spaniards looked toward the Middle and South American mainlands to recoup their fortunes. By the second decade of the sixteenth century, various exploratory expeditions from the Antilles had touched many points along the eastern shores of Mexico and Central America. From these reconnaissance voyages, the Spaniards obtained sufficient information to realize that the Mainland probably contained great wealth.

The first successful points of Spanish conquest and occupation on the Mainland occurred in two widely separated areas: (1) the isthmus of Panama, and (2) the highlands of central Mexico (Figure 9.1). Once these two areas were firmly occupied, they became dispersal centers for the conquest and settlement of the remainder of

Figure 9.1   Spanish Conquest and settlement of Mexico and Central America, early sixteenth century

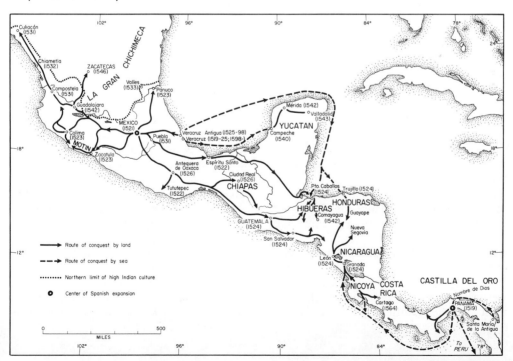

the Middle American mainland. The Spaniards were not slow to realize that both Panama and central Mexico were strategic spots. Panama, because of its isthmian character, was to serve as the transit zone between the Atlantic and Pacific oceans, a function it has performed ever since. Central Mexico, on the other hand, was the cultural focus of high Mesoamerican Indian civilizations, the center of the Aztec and Tarascan tribute states— a land of dense population with a productive agriculture and great mineral wealth.

Conquest of Panama

Panama was the first of the two dispersal centers to be occupied. Drawn by Balboa's discovery of the Pacific Ocean in 1513 and by the gold-rich Coclé Indian cultures within the southern coastal plain of the isthmus, Spanish officials established the town of Panama as the capital of Castilla del Oro (the isthmus area) in 1519. The Coclé area of south central Panama was quickly overrun; the golden artifacts looted from houses and graves were melted down into ingots; and the Indian population was either enslaved or dispersed into the surrounding hills. During the first half of the sixteenth century, a few small Spanish towns, such as Natá, were founded in the Coclé savannas. Small-scale stock raising was introduced, and various attempts were made to exploit the gold placers of Veraguas on the heavily forested Caribbean slopes of western Panama. But throughout the colonial period, the main function of the isthmian area remained that of a transit zone between the two oceans. Between Nombre de Dios and Puerto Bello, the Caribbean termini, and Panama City, on the Pacific side, mule trains and fleets of canoes hauled merchandise that came from Peru and Spain.

By 1524, expeditions exploring northwestward from the isthmus had brought most of the southern part of Central America into the jurisdiction of Panama. The most important *entrada* was that of Hernández de Córdoba, who conquered the culturally advanced Chorotega and Nicarao peoples of the densely settled Pacific lowlands of Nicaragua. In 1524, he founded the town of Granada on the northwestern shore of Lake Nicaragua and that of León on the northern edge of Lake Managua.

Within the densely settled Nicaraguan Pacific lowlands, the Spaniards engaged chiefly in taking Indian slaves during the first years of occupation. Before Indian slavery was abolished in 1542, thousands of these docile Nicaraguans were branded and taken in chains to Panama and later to Peru. Others, granted in encomiendas to various Spaniards, were forced to wash gold in the Nicaraguan highlands (Nueva Segovia) 100 miles east of the lakes. From 1527 to 1540, these gold fields became one of the main areas of Spanish activity in Nicaragua.

Later in the sixteenth century, following depletion of the gold placers and a drastic decrease in native population, the Spaniards turned to stock raising in the savannas around the lakes. Minor colonial activities, all based on Indian labor, included cultivation of cacao and indigo in the fertile isthmus of Rivas which separates Lake Nicaragua from the sea, the gathering of naval stores in the interior pine forests, and the cutting of tropical timbers for ship construction along the Pacific coast. This pattern of resource and land use persisted in the Nicaraguan lowlands well into the nineteenth century. Still today, most of Nicaragua's population and economic activity centers within the lake lowlands and in the adjacent volcanic hills along the Pacific.

A southern appendage of the colonial province of Nicaragua included the Nicoya Peninsula and adjacent Guanacaste lowlands (today the northwestern extremity of Costa Rica). The conquerors of Nicaragua quickly occupied the Guanacaste plains, for they were densely settled by Indians of Chorotegan culture, similar to that of the lake area. Throughout the colonial period, Guanacaste was a part of Nicaragua province and became a land of cattle ranches and mixed Indian-Spanish blood, as it is today.

During the early period of northward expansion from Panama, the Spaniards bypassed the high mountainous area called Costa Rica. It was not until the 1560s that settlers from Nicaragua, drawn by rumors of rich gold deposits, finally penetrated the cool volcanic basins of the Meseta Central. In 1562, disappointed by the lack of abundant gold placers in this area of young volcanic rock, the settlers founded the town of Cartago in the damp eastern basin of the Meseta Central. By that time, disease had already decimated the warlike Huetar Indians of the highlands, and the low-cultured forest tribes of the Talamanca range to the south were few in number and little inclined to work for Spanish masters. Thus, the small group of white settlers in the Cartago area remained free of Indian blood, a contrast to the mixed racial pattern in most of the Spanish provinces of Central America. They became small subsistence farmers who tilled the land themselves, without the aid of Indian laborers. These settlers formed the nucleus from which developed the present white highland-farming population of Costa Rica.

For almost a century, less than 100 Spanish peasant families living in the Cartago Basin comprised the only permanent European settlement in Costa Rica. Late in the sixteenth century, the Cartago farmers began to raise substantial amounts of wheat that were transported into the cacao-producing area of the Matina valley on the Caribbean lowlands of Costa Rica, into the Pacific lowlands of Nicaragua, and even to Panama and Cartagena by ship. Later, tobacco became an important crop exported from the highlands. By the end of the seventeenth century, the Cartago

basin was so crowded that farmers began to move to other parts of the Meseta Central. In 1706, the town of Alajuela was founded in the western part of the plateau and, by 1736, San José, the modern capital of Costa Rica, was laid out on its present site. At the end of the colonial period, the density of population in the Meseta Central exceeded 100 persons per square mile, and the expansion of white settlement into other parts of the forest-covered highlands and adjacent escarpments, which is still going on in Costa Rica, began.

Conquest from Central Mexico

The central highland of Mexico was by far the most significant area from which Spanish conquest and settlement spread over most of the Middle American mainland during the early sixteenth century. The true center of dispersal was the Valley of Mexico, the heart of the Aztec realm. In 1519, Cortes and his band entered the city of Tenochtitlán, after their initial journey up the eastern escarpment from Veracruz, and finally conquered and sacked it in 1521. Upon the ruins of the Aztec capital, the Spaniards slowly built the city of Mexico, which became the administrative center of New Spain, the name given to much of the conquered territory of Mexico and Central America.

Spanish conquest and colonization outward from central Mexico occurred in two phases, each encompassing a definite geographical area. The first phase was characterized by a relatively easy and rapid overrunning of the areas of high Indian culture, or Mesoamerica, including central and southern Mexico and the northern third of Central America. The second and later phase dealt chiefly with the relatively slow conquest and settlement of northern Mexico, the arid lands of low Indian cultures described in the preceding chapter. It is significant that the two phases of Spanish conquest in Mexico, distinguished in time, area, and process, are also distinguishable on the basis of the differing Indian cultures they supplanted.

Conquest of Mesoamerica. Within 12 years after their landing at Veracruz, Cortes's men had taken over most of the area of high Mesoamerican culture, from Culiacán and Tampico in the north to Honduras in the south. Various factors contributed to the rapidity and ease of Spanish conquest. The docile nature of the Indian peasant farmers, accustomed to outside rule, may have played a part, but more important was the fact that the Spaniards who took the place of the defeated native overlords retained the Indian institutions that corresponded with those of feudal Europe, such as the tribute system and slavery. Other factors include the weakening of the native will to resist conquest through the accidental introduction of European diseases and the Spaniards' superior military tactics and weapons, including firearms, the awesome horse, and the large, fierce, hunting dog.

Two factors were especially significant in directing the course of the early conquests from Central Mexico. One was the location of areas of dense Indian population, the source of tributes and labor under the encomienda system. Immediately after their submission to Spanish authority, Indian villages were granted as encomiendas to members of the conquering force. Thus, the densely populated basins of the Mesa Central and the adjacent escarpments, as well as the Valley of Oaxaca in the southern plateau, were areas highly prized by the Spanish encomenderos. During the early colonial period, the main income from the encomiendas was tribute in the form of gold, cacao, cotton cloth, and other products of the land that could be sold for profit. Until the mid-sixteenth century, the encomendero also forced his Indians to commute tribute to personal

services, which could include labor of almost any sort. Thereafter, the use of encomienda Indians for personal services was prohibited by law, and the Spanish Crown began to regulate Indian labor under a system called the *repartimiento,* a rationing of Indians to Spanish applicants of certain kinds of workers. The tribute system, however, continued for much of the colonial period.

The second factor that influenced the direction of conquest was the location of the major sources of Aztec and Tarascan gold. These were the placer deposits of stream beds that drain the areas of old crystalline rock in the highlands of southern Mexico and the rugged Caribbean slope of northern Central America. The major gold belt extended westward from the Isthmus of Tehuantepec, through Oaxaca and the Balsas depression to Colima. The Spaniards' early routes of conquest thus led southward from the Mesa Central into the hot lowlands and the gold country, following the earlier pattern of Aztec and Tarascan expansion.

Even before the fall of the Aztec capital, the Spaniards, working out from the friendly independent chiefdom of Tlaxcala, had secured most of the densely settled highland basins and and the adjacent escarpments east and south of the Valley of Mexico. Cortes had sent out small parties to reconnoiter the main sources of Aztec gold in the Balsas Basin as far as the Pacific and in the upper Papaloapan River basin, to the southeast. A few months after the final conquest of the Valley of Mexico in 1521, most of the former Aztec state was securely in Spanish hands. Cortes acquired for himself many of the best areas of central and southern Mexico. One of these was the rich valley of Oaxaca, where, in 1526 the town of Antequera (now Oaxaca City) was founded in the center of the Zapotec Indian country (Figure 9.2).

In 1522, other expeditions overran the Tarascan state in the western part of

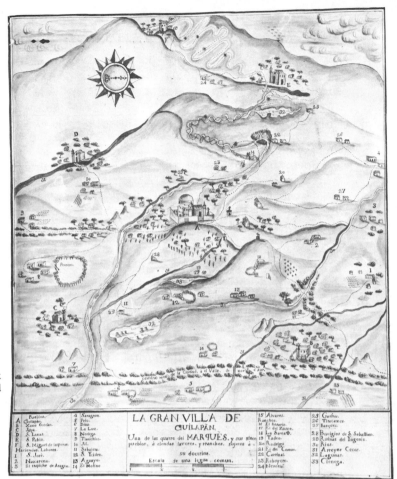

Figure 9.2 An eighteenth-century map of settlement within the jurisdiction of Cuilapan, near Oaxaca City. Around 1775, Cuilapan was one of the four villas of the once vast holdings of Cortes that remained in the hands of his descendants. Besides the villa of Cuilapan (*center, marked A*), the map shows five Indian pueblos and various haciendas, ranchos, and smaller holdings. (*Biblioteca Nacional, Madrid*)

the Mesa Central and continued down the southern escarpment of the plateau to the lower Balsas Basin and the mountainous Pacific coast. There the Spaniards found gold in abundance, especially in the isolated Motines area northwest of the Balsas River mouth. Still another expedition, in search of the source of Tarascan silver and copper, descended the western escarpment to establish the town of Colima within an area of dense Indian population, gold placers, and cacao orchards. About the same time, punitive forays from the Valley of Mexico pushed southeastward into the cacao-rich chiefdom of Coatzacoalcos in the Isthmus of Tehuantepec and northeastward into the Huastec country as far as present Tampico, to quell rebelling Indians. Far from the cen-

tral authority of Mexico City and lacking gold, the dense population of the Huastec area was ruthlessly exploited, and thousands of Indians were shipped as slaves to the island of Hispaniola in the Caribbean.

Until the 1540s, gold placering and collection of tributes from their encomiendas formed the main economic interests of the Spaniards in central and southern Mexico. By midcentury, new activities and associated settlements had been introduced. One was the mining of silver ore from small deposits found on the southern and western escarpments of the Mesa Central. Other activities included the farming of newly introduced Old World crops, such as wheat in the highland basins and sugar cane in the warmer escarpment valleys and, even more important, establishment

249

of a livestock industry based on the herding of Old World animals on the highland pastures and the tropical lowland savannas.

Both the religious orders and lay Spaniards engaged in most of these new occupations. To administer their various activities and control the Indians, the Spaniards founded towns, or *villas*, at strategic points. By 1531, some 15 towns, including Veracruz, Mexico City, and Puebla, had been established within the former Aztec area. To control their economic interests and spread the Faith, the religious orders founded convents and churches in Spanish towns and Indian settlements throughout the area.

Subsequent conquests from the Valley of Mexico were directed southeastward beyond the Isthmus of Tehuantepec, into Chiapas, Guatemala, and other parts of northern Central America. As was indicated in Chapter 8, most of this territory was occupied by advanced Indian cultures of Mayan affinity, such as the Quiché and Cakchiquel. In 1524, accompanied by thousands of Aztec and Tlaxcalan warriors, the Pedro de Alvarado expedition penetrated the Guatemalan highlands and the hot Pacific coastal areas into what is now El Salvador. In contrast to the easy penetration of central and southern Mexico, the conquests of Guatemala and Chiapas were bloody affairs, owing to the stiff resistance of the natives, and Indian uprisings in those areas persisted into the mid-sixteenth century. Moreover, the Spaniards found little gold in the young volcanic materials and the limestone of the Guatemalan-Chiapas highlands.

Although the two important Spanish towns of Santiago de Guatemala and Ciudad Real de Chiapas (now San Cristóbal de las Casas) were founded by 1526, most of the highlands were not tightly controlled, and the native cultures were little disturbed for much of the colonial period. In these same areas today, Indian blood and culture predominate. In northern Central America, the Spaniards exploited chiefly the Pacific coastal areas and the low volcanic lands of El Salvador, where the cultivation of tropical products such as cacao, sugar cane, and indigo with Indian and black labor became the main colonial activities.

North of the Guatemalan and Chiapas highlands, the Mayan Indians of the Yucatan Peninsula offered even greater resistance to Spanish conquest. Not until the 1540s, when the towns of Mérida and Valladolid were founded, were the Yucatecan Mayas subdued and Spanish authority established. Again, the low, infertile limestone plain of Yucatan contained no precious metals and offered little promise to Spaniards bent on the acquisition of quick wealth. Like the Guatemalan-Chiapas highlands, Yucatan retains a predominantly Indian culture.

The farthest southeastward thrust of Spanish conquest from Mexico was directed toward Honduras, a mountainous land of old, highly mineralized rocks that comprise the western side of Old Antillia. There the Spaniards found another center of gold production in the placer deposits of streams draining into the Caribbean. Spanish forces from Mexico, dispatched via sea by Cortes in 1524, took over points along the Caribbean shores of Honduras near fertile, densely populated alluvial valleys, such as the Aguán and Ulúa. By 1540, the Spaniards had partially subdued the recalcitrant Lenca and Jicaque Indians of the rugged interior, and had founded the towns of Gracias a Dios and Comayagua near gold and silver deposits. It was not until the 1570s, however, that the Spaniards discovered and developed the large silver mines of Tegucigalpa, which were to give the province of Honduras its colonial fame. Together with stock raising, mining continued to be the chief occupation of Honduras until the end of the nineteenth century. Owing chiefly to the early collapse of the native Indian population and the disinterest of the colonial government, the province of Honduras was never to approach the importance of Mexico as a producer of wealth for Spain.

Although nominally under the jurisdiction of the viceroyalty of New Spain, Central America was so distant from Mexico City that, in 1543, the Spanish Crown established the captaincy-general of Guatemala to administer the southern area. The captaincy comprised the Central American provinces from the Isthmus of Tehuantepec to Panama, including the present Mexican state of Chiapas. Colonial Panama, however, became part of New Granada (Colombia) and thus fell into the jurisdiction of the Viceroyalty of Peru. In 1548 Santiago de Guatemala (Antigua) was chosen the capital city of the captaincy-general and the seat of the *audiencia,* or circuit court, of Guatemala. It is significant that, with the exception of Chiapas, the major provinces of the captaincy later became the present nations of Central America.

The last important line of conquest within Mesoamerica was directed northward along the Pacific coastal lowlands of Mexico, following the northwestern extension of high Indian culture. This conquest was carried out in 1531 and 1532 under the leadership of the infamous Nuño de Guzmán who was in quest of gold and the fabled land of the Amazons. After desolating the northern part of the Tarascan area, Guzmán founded the towns of Guadalajara and Compostela on the western side of the plateau. Following a well-worn Indian trail down the western escarpment, the expedition continued into the hot, wet lowlands of Nayarit. Although some gold and silver deposits were uncovered within the western foothills of the Sierra Madre Occidental, the Guzmán party turned to slave raiding, ravaging the densely populated lowlands of Nayarit and Sinaloa. Near the limit of high aboriginal culture in northern Sinaloa, the Spaniards founded the town of Culiacán, which was to serve as a frontier base for slaving and subsequent expansion northward.

Conquest of Northern Mexico. The second phase of Spanish conquest and settlement from central Mexico was concerned entirely with the occupation of the land north of the area of high Indian culture. The presence of the warlike Chichimec nomads who occupied most of the deserts and steppes in the north, as well as the apparent poverty of the land, at first dampened Spanish ardor for further conquest beyond the Indian agricultural frontier. The north looked so formidable to the Spaniards that they gave the regional terms *la Gran Chichimeca* and *Tierra de Guerra* ("Land of War") to the dry interior that stretched for nearly 800 miles from near the Lerma River in central Mexico to beyond the Rio Grande into Texas. Thus, during the 1530s, northward expansion halted momentarily at the zone of contact between the high Indian cultures of the south and those of low culture to the north.

Two events during the next decade finally breached this cultural barrier and permitted the start of Spanish conquest northward. One was the Mixton War (1541), in which the Spaniards defeated a large Indian force of allied Cazcán farmers and Guachichil nomads on the Chichimec frontier north of Guadalajara. The subsequent retreat of the Guachichil to the east opened an approach northward from Guadalajara into the grasslands of Zacatecas. The opening of this route led, in turn, to the chance discovery, in 1546, of the vast silver deposit of Zacatecas, which set off a veritable rush of Spaniards into the new area. The exploitation of silver deposits thus became the prime motive for further expansion into the Chichimec country and eventually made New Spain the most lucrative of the Spanish colonies.

In contrast to the rapid overrunning of

the areas of high culture to the south, effective occupation of northern Mexico took nearly 200 years. Although the chief silver-producing areas were rapidly blocked out, other sections, such as northeastern Mexico, portions of the central desert, and Baja California, were not settled until the mid-eighteenth century. Moreover, the Spaniards had to employ different methods of conquest and settlement than those used in the south. Among the intractible nomadic Chichimecs the encomienda system was impossible, and the few primitive farmers of the Sierra Madre Occidental who were subjected could offer little in way of tribute. For labor, the Spaniards were forced to rely on free Aztec, Tarascan, and Otomí Indians from the south, and on sporadic importation of black slaves. Furthermore, the mining camps, rather than the villas, or the town corporations that operated so well in the south, became the chief centers of permanent Spanish settlement. Often, the richer mining camps (reales de minas) grew into large and opulent cities such as Zacatecas, Guanajuato, and Parral.

Because of repeated depredations made by the desert nomads, the Spanish administration in the north was chiefly military; the presidios, or forts, along the main trails became a common type of settlement and the origin of many present towns in the north. In addition, missionary endeavors were far greater among the lowly northern Indians than among the more cultured peoples in the south. Especially in those northern areas lacking in mineral wealth, the Church orders were often more important than the civil administration in advancing the frontier of settlement. Many present-day agricultural towns of northern Mexico and the southwestern United States can trace their origin to the colonial missions.

The discovery of the Zacatecas mines led to the settlement of the northern part of the Mesa Central, occupied since pre-Conquest times by the hostile Chichimecs.

This area included the fertile Bajío, immediately north of the Lerma River, and the extensive grass-covered plains around Querétaro. Since the direct route of communication between Zacatecas and Mexico City traversed this territory, its occupation was imperative. By 1555, Spanish military forces had established fortified towns along the cart road over which silver bullion from Zacatecas was hauled to the capital. Gradually, Otomí and Tarascan Indian farmers from the south, followed by Spanish missionaries and ranchers, took over the Bajío and the Aguascalientes Valley, both of which soon became thriving livestock and agricultural centers, supplying grain and animal products for Zacatecas. Most of the large towns, such as Celaya and León, that today serve as market centers in the Bajío, grew out of villages and ranch centers established in the mid-sixteenth century. In 1563, when the large Guanajuato silver mines were opened, the Bajío gained additional importance.

The importance of the Zacatecas mines also led to the establishment in 1548 of a new political province, called the "Kingdom of New Galicia." Initially, this province encompassed the entire northwestern part of New Spain, but it was later confined to an area that approximates the present states of Jalisco, Nayarit, and Zacatecas (Figure 9.3). Guadalajara was chosen as the administrative and religious center of New Galicia.

After the Zacatecas strike of 1546, the main line of Spanish advance northward followed a series of silver-bearing ores that outcrop along the eastern foothills of the Sierra Madre Occidental (Figure 9.4). Within 20 years, Spanish miners had opened many rich deposits, such as those in Fresnillo, Sombrerete, and around Durango, and had reached as far as the Santa Bárbara mines in southern Chihuahua. From this frontier outpost, the famous Oñate expedition departed in 1599 to settle the upper Rio Grande Valley of

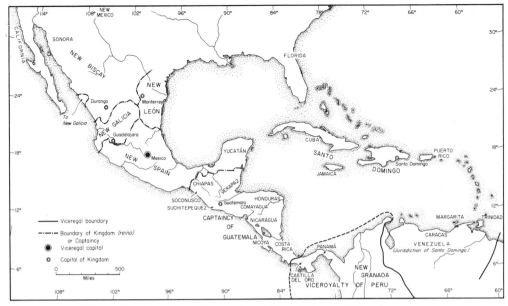

Figure 9.3   Major political divisions: Viceroyalty of New Spain, ca. 1625

New Mexico, 600 miles to the north within present United States territory. Later silver discoveries along the route of northward expansion included the famous Parral mines (1631) and those of Santa Eulalia (1703), the northernmost of the large silver lodes, near which Chihuahua City was founded.

This great Silver Belt of northern Mexico lay within a zone of semiarid grassland, or steppe, bordered on the west by the pine and oak-covered Sierra Madre and on the east by the lower central desert. This grassland served as the natural basis for the growth of a livestock industry that furnished the adjacent mines with

Figure 9.4   Spanish settlement of northern New Spain

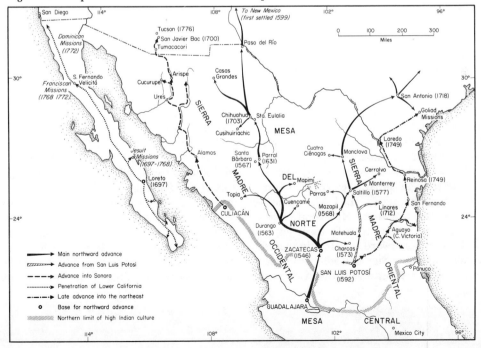

meat, hides, and tallow. Moreover, streams flowing eastward from the Sierra afforded water for irrigating narrow stretches of fertile valley land to help supply wheat, maize, and other foodstuffs to the mining centers. Thus, along the main line of northward advance there evolved a mine, stockranch, and grain farm settlement complex that was to characterize much of the Spanish occupation of northern Mexico. So significant was the northern silver area to the Spanish government that the northwestern quarter of colonial Mexico was made a separate province, Nueva Vizcaya ("New Biscay"), with Durango as its political and religious capital.

The spread of Spanish settlement outward from the Silver Belt of northern Mexico was slow, sporadic, and often accidental. The Sierra Madre Occidental discouraged settlement to the west. Gold and silver lodes within the sierra, covered by recent volcanic rock, were exposed only in the deep, almost inaccessible barrancas on the western slopes. Throughout the colonial period only one trail, via the mines of Topia, led across the sierra to the Pacific coast. To the east of the Silver Belt, aridity and the Chichimec menace combined to discourage effective settlement. Nevertheless, during punitive forays into the desert to destroy or enslave marauding bands of Chichimecs, Spaniards accidentally discovered mines such as Charcas and Mazapil. They also found the grasslands on the eastern side of the plateau along the foothills of the Sierra Madre Oriental.

The final defeat of the combined Zacateco-Guachichil nomads in 1562 cleared the way for settlement across the desert to the eastern edge of the plateau, where Saltillo was founded in 1577. Shortly thereafter, the discovery of several small silver and lead mines drew Spanish settlement farther northward to Monclova and eastward across the Sierra Madre Oriental, to the sites of Monterrey and Cerralvo

overlooking the Gulf coastal lowlands. Attracted by the grass-covered plateau basins along the western side of the sierra, stockmen from Zacatecas soon entered the Saltillo-Monclova area to establish large cattle ranches. By the beginning of the eighteenth century, ranchers and missionaries, pressing northward from Monclova, had crossed the Rio Grande into the grassy inner coastal plain of Texas, where San Antonio was established in 1718. This northward line of settlement from Saltillo and Monclova was eventually to reach the Sabine River bordering on French Louisiana.

Eastward from the Sierra Madre Oriental, the lowland basins and coastal plain of northeastern Mexico were, as early as 1579, formed into the province of New León, with the small village of Monterrey as the political capital. Sparsely settled and economically poor, with stock raising as the main activity, this isolated province remained a weakly held frontier area for most of the colonial period. Not until the mid-eighteenth century was the coastal area of northeastern Mexico finally settled under government supervision. A new province, New Santander (now the state of Tamaulipas and southernmost Texas), was formed to administer this forced colonization, which was carried out to subdue troublesome nomadic Indians and to discourage French designs for westward expansion from Louisiana.

Colonization directly northward from the Bajío of Guanajuato was blocked for a half century by the Chichimecs, especially by remnants of the Guachichil people who had taken refuge in the desert east of Zacatecas. With the final subjugation of these nomads in 1592, the town of San Luis Potosí was founded near a group of rich silver deposits. Spanish settlers soon entered to open mines on the mountain slopes and to establish cattle ranches in the surrounding grassy plains. Settlement northward, along a narrow belt of semiarid grassland, brought the Spaniards to the important silver deposits of Matehuala. Communications were established with Saltillo and Monterrey, forming an eastern trail continuous from Mexico City to New León. By the end of the sixteenth century, the settlers had overcome the Chichimecs in the southern part of the central desert. However, the Sumo, Apache, and Toboso bands in the far north continued to plague ranches and mining settlements until well into the nineteenth century.

A third significant line of northward expansion proceeded up the western side of Mexico from the frontier base of Culiacán in Sinaloa. In the early 1530s, slaving parties under Nuño de Guzmán had reached the Fuerte River in northern Sinaloa, but no permanent settlements had been established above Culiacán. In 1540, enthused by Cabeza de Vaca's reports of large towns far to the north, Francisco de Coronado departed from Culiacán on his famed expedition in search of the legendary Seven Cities of Cíbola. Coronado followed an ancient Indian trail north through the Ópata Indian country in central Sonora to the Zuñi Pueblos on the Colorado Plateau. Throughout the colonial period and into the nineteenth century, this road was an important artery for trade and settlement. It connected Sonora and southern Arizona with Guadalajara and Mexico City on the central plateau.

Jesuit missionaries were the first to make permanent European settlements north of Culiacán, but not until the end of the sixteenth century. A few small missions were established along the main rivers in northern Sinaloa and southern Sonora among the Cahita and Yaqui tribes. However, the chief area of Jesuit mission settlement centered in northern Sonora among the Ópata, who practiced irrigation farming along the rivers within the low north–south trending basins west of the Sierra Madre Occidental. The principal mission towns of Ures, Arispe, and Cucurpe, founded in the mid-seventeenth century, occupied sites within the upper Sonora and the San Miguel river valleys, the most densely occupied areas of the Ópata and the heart of colonial Sonora. Within the fertile, grassy basins the Jesuits established large herds of cattle, using Indian neophytes as stock hands. Spanish stockmen and miners followed the missionaries, forming settlements and opening small gold and silver mines in the parallel ranges overlooking the valleys. During the eighteenth century, the mining town of Álamos in southern Sonora grew into one of the largest silver producers of New Spain and became the center of white settlement in the northwest.

At the end of the seventeenth century, the Jesuits extended their missions into the Pima country of southeastern Arizona. There they founded the missions of Tumacacori (1687), north of present Nogales and San Javier Bac (1700), near the site of Tucson. Again, Spanish stockmen followed, attracted by the lush pastures on the open oak- and grass-covered hills. Southeastern Arizona represents another northern terminus of a line of Spanish settlement into what is now United States territory.

The initial settlement of the arid peninsula of Baja California, like that of Sonora, was left to the Church. The Jesuits were the first to enter, founding Loreto mission on the barren gulf coast in 1697. Other missions, spreading north and south from the mother settlement, were established in the interior oases, where the Jesuits congregated the few nomadic Indians into agricultural villages. After the expulsion of the Jesuit order in 1767, the Franciscans and Dominicans completed the missionizing of the peninsula northward, as far as the present United States–Mexico border. But although colonists had followed the missionaries into Sonora, few followed them into the desolate peninsula. After the decimation of the Indian population by disease, the mission settlements declined, and only a few interior oases and one or two villages in the more humid Cape region at the southern tip of the peninsula survived into the post-colonial period.

A final northward thrust of Spanish settlement in North America took place during the last half of the eighteenth century, along the coast of Upper California. Alarmed by the gradual encroachment of Russian trading settlements from Alaska down the coast of northern California, the Spanish government in 1769 established San Diego, the first of the garrison-mission towns of the new province. Other garrison settlements, such as Los Angeles and Monterey, the capital, were founded soon after. By the close of the century, a line of 21 Franciscan missions extended from San Diego to Sonoma, north of San Francisco Bay. Moreover, Spanish stockmen established large ranches in the pleasant oak- and grass-covered coastal valleys and were soon profitably engaged in exporting hides and tallow. Upper California was the largest area that the Spaniards occupied within present United States territory. It also was the northward limit of Spanish colonial culture in the Americas.

North Americans often forget that the southern half of the present United States west of the Rocky Mountains was once part of New Spain and later of Mexico. But since this vast territory was ineffectively held and was settled by the Spaniards or Mexicans in only a few spots, it was easily acquired by the United States government as the aftermath of the war with Mexico in 1848. Nevertheless, Spanish cultural heritage is still strong in New Mexico and southern Arizona, and it is still cherished in California, if only in legend, mission remnants, and place names.

EVOLUTION OF THE COLONIAL LANDSCAPE

The Spanish Conquest and occupation of Mexico and Central America during the sixteenth century brought many changes in the cultural and physical landscapes, and many of these modifications have persisted into modern times. One set of changes resulted from the impact of the Conquest on the physical characteristics of the Indian populations. Another kind of change came from the introduction of various aspects of Iberic culture, such as the Spanish language, Mediterranean settlement and architectural types, Old World plants and animals, Spanish agricultural methods, stock raising, and other economic enterprises. These innovations, often blended with the existing Indian culture, have given the greater part of the Middle American mainland its present geographical personality.

Conquest and the Indian Population

The impact of conquest on the physical aspects of aboriginal population resulted in an early and drastic decrease in the number of Indians and racial intermixtures. The latter process was to result in the mestizo racial element now so predominant in the area between the Rio Grande and the Panama Canal.

Decrease of the Indian Population. On the mainland of Middle America the decline of native population was less severe than in the Greater Antilles, where the Indians were virtually exterminated. Nevertheless, it is estimated that the approximate pre-Conquest population of 25 million in Mexico was reduced to about 1.2 million after the first century of Spanish occupation. Even by 1550, one of the most frequent complaints of the encomenderos of New Spain was the great decrease in tribute due to deaths among their Indians. The population of most highland villages had been more than halved, and many lowland settlements had disappeared completely.

Various factors attributed to this appalling mortality. Warfare took a large toll of Indians in Mesoamerica during the first years of the Conquest. Enslavement of many Indians during the first half of the sixteenth century also contributed to death and dislocation of population. Since the Spaniards followed the medieval custom of legally enslaving rebellious subjects, traffic in Indians early became a lucrative business, and remained so until it was outlawed in 1542. As we have already indicated, Spanish slaving parties based in Panama were particularly active in southern Central America, where they desolated the Nicaraguan lowlands and the Pacific side of Costa Rica. In Mexico, the Huasteca of the Gulf Coast and the Indians of the Pacific lowlands of Nayarit and Sinaloa supplied large numbers of slaves to the mines and plantations of Central Mexico and in the Caribbean Islands. Harsh treatment, disruption of normal food production, and psychological despair may also have contributed to the death rates. The latter phenomenon is attested to by numerous contemporary reports of systematic abortion and infanticide, as well as mass suicide, among the Indians of Central America during the early sixteenth century.

The most important cause of Indian mortality, however, was Old World disease. As in the Caribbean islands, the most virulent killers were smallpox, measles, and typhus, against which the natives had no immunity. The first smallpox epidemic swept central Mexico in 1520, even before the fall of the Valley of Mexico. The ability of the Aztecs and the Tarascans to resist the Spanish invaders was probably greatly weakened by this and subsequent epidemics of smallpox, measles, and other diseases which occurred throughout Mesoamerica at 10- to 15-year intervals for the rest of the sixteenth century. The worst were the measles epidemic of 1545 to 1548 and a scourge of typhus from 1576 to 1581. In the seventeenth century, the drastic decline of the Indian population of Mexico and Central America was to have significant economic and social repercussions.

Little is known of other Old World diseases that the Spaniards or their African slaves carried to the Middle American mainland. Quite probably, influenza, mumps, typhoid, and malaria took their toll. Still less is known about the diseases of the native Indians, who seem to have previously been surprisingly free from contagious ailments. Only syphilis has been definitely classified as an American disease, but various intestinal ailments were probably also endemic and may have become epidemic during periods of famine.

The Indian population in Mexico and Guatemala continued to decline until the seventeenth century. Thereafter, a gradual increase in numbers followed (Figure 9.5). The Indians slowly developed partial immunity to smallpox and measles, possibly through natural selection and the increasing miscegenation of white, Indian, and black.

The decrease of population brought about changes in the location of Indians in Mexico and Central America during the early colonial period. Many of the heavily settled lowland areas were almost depopulated within a century after the Conquest. With the exception of those living in the well-drained Yucatan Peninsula and the Nicaraguan depression, the lowland Indians seems to have suffered a far greater mortality from disease than did the people of the cooler highlands. The hot, damp, insect-infested coasts of the Gulf and Caribbean were particularly good breeding areas for the introduced diseases, especially for malaria, which was acquired and carried by the native anopheline mosquitoes.

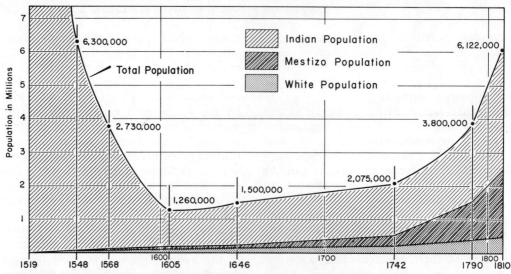

Figure 9.5 Estimated population trends (by number and racial composition) of central and southern Mexico during the colonial period (after Borah and Cook 1963)

Later in the seventeenth century, yellow fever from Africa, and its transmitter, the Aëdes mosquito, appeared on the east coast of Mexico and Central America.

As the lowlands were depopulated by disease and slave raids, the highlands acquired a relatively greater significance as the areas in which lived the remnant Indian populations. Throughout the colonial period and even into the present century, the fertile, nearly empty coastal lowlands of southern Mexico were feared by highlanders as places of sickness and hunger. Only in the last few decades has the reconquest of the lowlands, through health controls, gained real ground.

Racial Mixing. Probably the most lasting physical effect of the Spanish Conquest on much of the native population of Mexico and Central America has been the gradual dilution of Indian blood with that of the European Caucasian and the African black. The interbreeding of these three races has produced the present mestizo element which now predominates in all Middle American mainland countries except Guatemala (predominately Indian) and Costa Rica (predominately white).

The mixing of Spanish and Indian blood began slowly. By 1570 there were perhaps 50,000 Spaniards in Mexico and far fewer in Central America, compared with an aboriginal population of possibly four million. As Figure 9.5 indicates, a sizable mestizo element was not created in Mexico until the mid-eighteenth century. Thereafter, the number of people of mixed blood increased rapidly, accounting at the close of the colonial period for about 30 percent of the total population. In Mexico, interbreeding of whites and Indians occurred mainly in the Spanish towns in the central part of the country, where groups of native servants and laborers lived close at hand in the native quarter (*barrio*). Secondary centers of racial mixing were the mining camps, especially those in the north. Since Spaniards were legally forbidden to live in Indian villages, racial purity was maintained until rather late in most of the densely settled rural areas of central and southern Mexico and of Guatemala. In these areas, today, are most of the pure Indians remaining in Middle America.

Black slaves were imported into colonial Mexico and Central America in sizable numbers. It is estimated that nearly 250,-000 blacks were taken into Mexico, and an unknown but smaller number into Central America, during the colonial period. In any given year, however, the number of blacks in New Spain was small, rarely exceeding 35,000. The Spaniards used their black slaves as personal servants, as laborers in the mines and in sugar and indigo processing, and as cowhands on stock ranches. Thus, blacks were spread throughout most of the area of Spanish occupation, a few being employed even in the northernmost mines of Mexico. Most blacks, however, were concentrated along the hot coastal areas and in the port towns where the Indian population had been greatly reduced by disease. Blacks were particularly numerous in Panama, where they served as muleteers, canoemen, and carriers in transisthmian transport.

During the early colonial period, the Indians interbred with blacks probably as much as with whites, and whites with blacks, in spite of regulations to the contrary. Nearly 50 different racial castes were recognized in Mexico and Guatemala by the end of the eighteenth century.

Today, black blood in Mexico has been almost completely absorbed into the mestizo element. Occasionally one sees predominant black physical characteristics such as short, kinky hair and broad, flat noses in some sections of the Veracruz coast. A single definitely black group, stemming from colonial times, lives along the Costa Chica, eastward from Acapulco in Guerrero state. In Panama, the black element is quite evident in the mixbloods living in the savanna areas west of the Canal Zone. The predominance of blacks along the Caribbean coast of Central America, however, is a comparatively recent development, only 60 to 100 years old.

In 1810, despite racial mixing, probably more than half the total population of Mexico and Central America was still of pure Indian blood. The mestizos appear to have become predominant within the last

century. After independence, the fine distinctions in racial types, according to skin color and facial features, tended to disappear, and the term "mestizo" now has a socioeconomic rather than a racial meaning.

Introduction of Iberic Culture

The cultural changes that the Spaniards effected in Mexico and Central America during the colonial period were many and complex. Some Iberic importations, such as various domesticated plants and animals, were quickly adopted by the Indians; others, such as settlement forms and various economic enterprises were either forced upon the Indians or had little effect on their own way of life; still others, such as the Spanish language, filtered slowly into the Indian way of life.

Language Changes. Like the development of a racially mixed population, the supplanting of Indian speech by Spanish in Mexico and Central America appears to have been extremely gradual. Obviously, Spanish replaced the native tongues most rapidly in the lowland tropics, where the Indian populations were most reduced, and in northern Mexico, where the aboriginal population was quite sparse. In the densely peopled highlands and on the Yucatan Peninsula, however, native speech did not begin to give way to Spanish until the end of the colonial period. This persistence of native language was in part due to the Church, which usually taught the Faith in the local Indian tongue. Moreover, Nahuatl remained the language of trade in much of Mexico and Central America as late as the nineteenth century. Spanish tended to replace the Indian languages where European economic activity was greater and racial mixing more common, as around the Spanish towns, mining centers, stock ranches, and processing mills. Where European activity was weak or nonexistent, particularly in isolated areas, the Indian languages are still spoken. In scattered areas over east-central Mexico, nearly one-half million Indians and mestizos still speak Nahuatl, despite almost 450 years of contact with Hispanic culture. Still more striking is the persistence of the Maya-Quiché languages in the relatively isolated highlands of Guatemala, where two million speak them, and in the Yucatan Peninsula, where more than a quarter million speak Maya.

Changes in Settlement Forms. One of the Spanish activities that profoundly altered the Indian cultural landscape during colonial days was the establishment of the compact European-type town and its associated architecture. The Spaniard was traditionally a town dweller, and it was only logical that he establish this type of settlement in Hispanic America. Today most people of Mexico and Central America, including many in the rural sections, live in compact towns or villages patterned after the sixteenth-century colonial settlements.

The first and one of the most important types of Spanish settlement was the Spanish town, or *villa,* to which we have already referred. An ancient Iberian institution, the villa was a municipal corporation, made up of a group of citizens (*vecinos*), governed by the town council (*cabildo*), and headed by an alcalde, or mayor. By custom, the town was given certain privileges enjoyed by its namesake in Spain and also a rank, according to its size or prestige. The more highly ranked towns carried the title of *ciudad* ("city"); the more lowly ranked ones were simply "villas." After a ceremony of formal establishment, streets were laid out, house lots and tracts of surrounding farmland were assigned to the citizens, and the town common (*ejido*) was delimited for pasturing animals near the exit of the settlement. By 1575, the Spaniards had founded nearly 35 towns in Mexico and more than 20 in Central America.

Since the prime function of the towns was administrative, their sites were selected with reference to trade routes or control of tributes and native labor. Hence, during the early years of occupation as many towns were established in the hot lowlands as in the cooler highlands. Following the decline of Indian population within the coastal areas, however, many of the lowland towns were abandoned or became insignificant, whereas in the highlands, where population declined less, most of the old Spanish towns grew to be large settlements, from which have developed many present-day cities, including national and provincial capitals.

Although the medieval towns of their homeland had no regular pattern, the villas that the Spaniards established in the American colonies were carefully laid out with a regular grid street pattern. A public square, or plaza, occupied the center of the town (Figure 9.6). Facing the square were the public buildings, often the church, the main business houses, and usually the dwellings of the richer and more socially prominent citizens. Commonly, the weekly or daily market was held in the square. Consequently, the central plaza became the economic and social center of the town. As is well known to every tourist who has traveled in Spanish America, most of the towns and cities have retained the grid street pattern and the central plaza (Figure 9.7).

Other types of Spanish agglomerated settlements established during the colonial period included the mining towns and the habitation centers associated with various economic enterprises, such as the large estates, or haciendas, and the sugar processing plants. These settlement forms are discussed in relation to their respective economic activities (Chapter 10).

Indian Congregations. The most numerous new settlements were the Indian villages established in Mexico and Guatemala during the colonial period by both

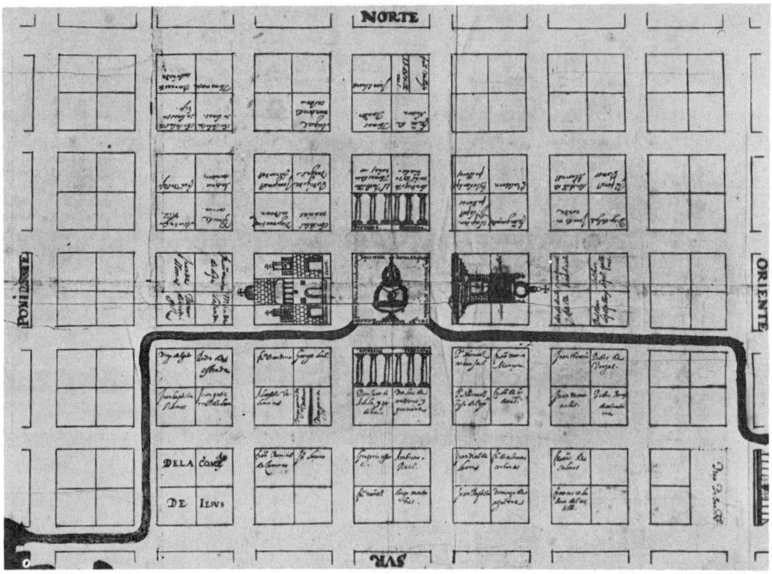

Figure 9.6 Original town plan of Nuestra Señora de la Concepción, a villa founded in 1603 near the mines of Sierra de Pinos, northwest of San Luis Potosí. The plaza forms the center block of the grid plan and is surrounded by the church, the official buildings, and portalled residences. Each block is divided into four lots, which were granted to the *vecinos*, or corporate members, of the town. (*Archivo General de Indias, Sevilla, Planos, Mexico*)

Figure 9.7 The city of Tepic in western Mexico, laid out on a grid plan in the sixteenth century. The main plaza lies near the center of the city. (*Compañía Mexicana Aerofoto*)

the Church and the civil government. The main objective of resettlement was to congregate into compact, Spanish-type towns the Indians living in dispersed hillside hamlets, in order to better foster the Christian faith, collect tribute, and recruit labor gangs. The Indian congregation of the sixteenth century was the prototype of the present-day agricultural village, now the prevailing rural settlement in Mexico and Guatemala.

The forced resettlement of much of the aboriginal population of central and southern Mexico sometimes had dire consequences. The environs were often unsuitable for Indian agriculture, with the result that food production decreased and famine ensued. Moreover, the compactness of the villages may well have encouraged the spread of contagious disease. Nevertheless, by the middle of the seventeenth century the compact agricultural village had become an essential part of the Mexican cultural landscape. Only in isolated Indian areas has the semidispersed hamlet, or *ranchería,* survived.

During the latter half of the sixteenth century another type of Indian congregation was begun in northern Mexico. Hoping to attract the desert nomads to sedentary life, the Spanish government established a number of colonies of Mexican (Nahuatl), Tarascan, and Tlaxcalan farmers from central Mexico at various points in the north. The first successful colony was Nombre de Dios, near Durango, founded in 1563 with Mexican and Tarascan Indians. In the 1590s, a large number of Tlaxcalans were induced to settle near Saltillo, San Luis Potosí, and other spots in the Chichimec country. From these centers the Tlaxcalans later established small agricultural villages in various parts of the desert, and many Chichimecs were induced to live with them. Indian blood is still much in evidence in the towns, such as Nombre de Dios, that have grown from these old colonies.

Figure 9.8   House type of southern Spanish origin introduced into Mexico and Central America. The roof of hollow red tile and ornately carved beams are characteristic.

Architectural Introductions. Probably one of the most attractive aspects of the cultural scenery of Mexico and Central America is the Spanish colonial architecture—the old dwellings, public buildings, and religious structures that remain in the countryside and towns. These architectural forms are perhaps the most impressive reminder of the area's Spanish heritage.

Of all the types of buildings that the Spaniards introduced into America during the colonial period, the rural dwellings have been the least studied. Among the great variety of rural houses found in Mexico and Central America today, it is often difficult to determine which may be purely aboriginal and which are European; many are conglomerates of Indian and Spanish architecture.

It appears, however, that during the sixteenth century Spaniards introduced two main types of rural houses, both from southern Spain. One was the one-story, rectangular dwelling of whitewashed stone or adobe walls, with a gabled roof of hollow tile or straw thatch (Figure 9.8). This house is in widespread use in central and southern Mexico and in most parts of Central America, particularly in mestizo areas. It has also been adopted by many Indian groups, such as those of the Guatemalan highlands. The other general type, probably of Berber origin, was the squat, flat-roofed adobe house, often windowless, but frequently having a built-in hearth with a chimney (Figure 9.9). The adobe, somewhat similar in form to the flat-roofed Aztec dwelling, was spread along with

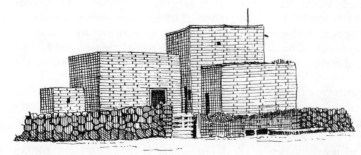

Figure 9.9   Flat-roofed adobe house, common in northern, and parts of central Mexico

Figure 9.10 The Tarascan plank house, Michoacán, Mexico. The shake roof, wide eaves, and carved doors are typical of this distinctive dwelling.

Figure 9.11 Granary of notched-log walls and thatched roof, commonly used by Indians in southern Mexico. The technique of corner notching is probably of European origin.

Spanish settlement into the dry mining areas of north-central Mexico, where it was adapted to the arid and semiarid climate.

The simpler Spanish dwellings were one- or two-room affairs; the larger and more pretentious ones, found mainly in the towns, were often of two stories and were constructed around a courtyard, or patio, a feature of Moorish and Roman antecedents. Invariably, the town houses abutted directly on the street, just as they do today in most Latin American towns.

Other types of rural and town houses introduced during the colonial period in-

cluded the charming one- or two-story Asturian dwelling (of northern Spain), now found chiefly in the state of Michoacán, Mexico. Its gently pitched, gabled, or hipped, tiled roof, its wide, projecting eaves, its carved rafters, and its wooden balconies distinguish this house from all others in Mexico. Another very interesting house, probably European and possibly introduced in the eighteenth century, is the notched-log or plank dwelling (Figure 9.10), found today in many spots in Mexico. It has been adopted by the Tarascan Indians in Michoacán and by the Mije in Oaxaca, and it also is found along the upper eastern escarpment in Puebla, Hidalgo, and Veracruz states. The notched-log house, which is used in Scandinavia, in mountainous areas of central and eastern Europe, and in the Russian plains, may have been introduced into Mexico by German miners.

Some European architectural elements have found their way into Indian architecture. The log or plank house of the Tarascans and Mije and the Andalusian gabled house of the Quiché of Guatemala have been mentioned. In central and southern Mexico there is widespread use of notched-log construction for outbuildings such as granaries and animal pens (Figure 9.11). Moreover, many highland Indian groups have been gradually replacing the native palm and grass thatch roofs with the Spanish, hollow red tile, which has considerable prestige value. We do not know how early the Indians began to adopt these new building techniques, but the Tarascans were constructing notched-log houses by the end of the eighteenth century. The adoption of other features of Spanish architecture may not have occurred until after the colonial period, for the process is still going forward.

Most of the public buildings and many of the private houses of the rich were more pretentious and durable than the small rural and town dwellings. The architecture of such structures followed Roman antecedents long established in southern Spain. Usually of stone and mortar, each building was normally constructed around a courtyard or patio, with colonnaded porticoes or arcades facing outward on the plaza. Arcaded buildings of colonial style still grace the plazas of many old Mexican towns, such as Oaxaca, Morelia, and Puebla. Other public structures of colonial

Figure 9.12   The cathedral at Campeche City, completed near the end of the seventeenth century. This cathdral is typical of the colonial religious structures of Middle America.

days included long, arched Roman aqueducts for bringing water into the towns. Although most of the colonial aqueducts are in ruins, some, such as those of Querétaro and Morelia in central Mexico, are still intact.

The various religious structures that were constructed in practically all types of settlements in Mexico and Central America during the colonial period were far more numerous than the civil buildings (Figure 9.12). The visitor to even the smaller villages of central Mexico is immediately attracted by the beautiful tiled domes and ornate belfry spires of the stone chapels and churches that tower high above the squat, whitewashed adobe houses. Most of the churches were constructed by Indians under the direction of missionary orders during the first great period of church building in Mexico and Guatemala—1530 to 1575. The disastrous typhus epidemic of the late 1570s so depleted the Indian labor force that religious construction was not resumed until well into the seventeenth century. Some pilgrimage towns, such as Cholula in Mexico and Chiquimula in Guatemala, became noted for the great number of their religious structures. In the larger colonial towns that were chosen as diocesan centers, the sumptuous bishop's palace, as well as convents and monasteries, added to the wealth of religious buildings.

Although probably as many colonial churches were constructed in Central America as in Mexico, few have survived the frequent earthquakes within the volcanic axis along the Pacific. Even major cathedrals in the towns of El Salvador, Nicaragua, and Costa Rica are recent wooden frame buildings covered with decorated tin sheeting.

Colonial Urbanization and Vegetation. The large amounts of timber used in the Spanish villas and for the churches seriously depleted the oak, pine, and fir forests that had covered the mountain slopes and high basins of central Mexico and Guatemala. The beautiful forests around the Valley of Mexico were rapidly destroyed as the Spaniards rebuilt Mexico City on the ruins of Tenochtitlán. The abundance of pine and fir throughout the Mesa Central of Mexico actually encouraged waste of the tall trees that furnished the long beams for construction. Moreover, the customary heating and cooking fuel of the Spaniards was charcoal made from oak and pine wood, and the Indians quickly adopted this practice. Many became professional *carboneros,* or charcoal burners, who supplied the towns with fuel. Consequently, around Indian villages and Spanish towns alike, the forest began to disappear through overcutting. By the end of the sixteenth century, deforestation of the mountain slopes near the heavily populated areas of central Mexico had become so serious that erosion and lake filling had begun. Charcoal is still the main household fuel of Mexico and Central America, and the remaining stands of highland forest are in the process of disappearing.

SELECTED REFERENCES

AGUIRRE BELTRÁN, G. *La Población Negra de México, 1519–1810.* Mexico, D.F.: Ediciones Fuente Cultural, 1946.

ASCHMANN, H. *The Central Desert of Baja California: Demography and Ecology.* Ibero-Americana, no. 42. Berkeley: University of California Press, 1959.

COOK, S. F., and BORAH, W. *The Indian Population of Central Mexico, 1531–1610.* Ibero-Americana, no. 44. Berkeley: University of California Press, 1960.

———. *The Aboriginal Population of Central Mexico on the Eve of the Spanish Conquest.* Ibero-Americana, no. 45. Berkeley: University of California Press, 1963.

COOK, S. F., and SIMPSON, L. B. *The Population of Central Mexico in the Sixteenth Century.* Ibero-Americana, no. 31. Berkeley: University of California Press, 1948.

CROSBY, A. W. "Conquistador y Pestilencia: The First New World Pandemic and the Fall of the Great Indian Empires." *Hispanic American Historical Review* 4, no. 2 (1967): 321–37.

JIMÉNEZ MORENO, W. *Estudios de Historia Colonial.* Mexico, D.F.: Instituto Nacional de Antropología e Historia, 1958.

KUBLER, G. *Mexican Architecture of the Sixteenth Century.* New Haven, Conn.: Yale University Press, 1948.

LÓPEZ DE VELASCO, J. *Geografía y Descripción Universal de las Indias desde el Año 1571 al de 1574.* Madrid: Fortanet, 1894.

MARSHALL, C. E. "The Birth of the Mestizo in New Spain." *Hispanic American Historical Review* 19, no. 2 (1939):161–84.

MORRISEY, R. J. "The Northward Expansion of Cattle Ranching in New Spain, 1550–1600." *Agricultural History* 25, no. 3 (1951): 115–21.

POWELL, P. W. *Soldiers, Indians and Silver: The Northward Advance of New Spain, 1550–1600.* Berkeley: University of California Press, 1952.

SAUER, C. O. *The Road to Cíbola.* Ibero-Americana, no. 3. Berkeley: University of California Press, 1932.

———. *Colima of New Spain in the Sixteenth Century.* Ibero-Americana, no. 29. Berkeley: University of California Press, 1948.

SIMPSON, L. B. *Studies in the Administration of the Indians in New Spain: The Civil Congregation.* Ibero-Americana, no. 7.

Berkeley: University of California Press, 1934.

STANISLAWSKI, D. "Early Spanish Town Planning in the New World." *Geographical Review* 37, no. 1 (1947):94–105.

VÁSQUEZ DE ESPINOSA, A. *Compendium and Description of the West Indies.* Miscellaneous Collections, no. 102. Washington, D.C.: Smithsonian Institution, 1942.

WEST, R. C. "The Flat-Roofed Folk Dwelling in Rural Mexico." *Geoscience and Man,* 5 (1974):111–32.

WINBERRY, J. J. "The Log House in Mexico." *Annals of the Association of American Geographers* 64, no. 1 (1974):54–69.

≡ 10 ≡

The Colonial Economy
in Mexico and Central America

A study of the major colonial economic institutions of Mexico and Central America reveals processes by which a Spanish-Indian cultural landscape developed. Spanish settlement and economic activity in the New World, as we have seen, initially centered around precious metals and native populations that would pay tribute. Yet, though the bulk of the wealth came from the mines, the cultural complex of the area was even more affected by the cultivation of the land and the breeding of animals. Agriculture and stock raising, especially, functioned to produce a fusion of Indian and Iberic culture which formed a rural way of life that still prevails in most parts of the area.

The plow and the ranch entailed extensive use of the land. To be sure, the Spaniards opened up new areas previously unused by Indian farmers; but they also engulfed cropland which, under intensive tilling of the aborigines, had been producing far more food than it would henceforth. The introduction of European ways of using the land altered the relationship between man and nature in Middle America.

AGRICULTURE

Farming in colonial Mexico and Central America was based on a sometimes uneasy combination of native Indian and European crops, techniques, and systems of land tenure. The Spaniards brought with them most of their basic food plants, particularly the small grains, including wheat and barley. Wheat bread was the Spaniard's principal starch food, his staff of life, but the Indians had maize. His legumes—the horsebean, chickpea, and lentil—were introduced, but they never successfully competed with the Mexican and Central American Indian beans as protein food. Other Old World food plants included various vegetables: onions and garlic for flavoring; potherbs such as cabbage and collards; and a few roots, like the carrot, radish, and turnip. More significant were the tropical plants of Asiatic origin: sugar cane, banana, plantain, citrus fruits, and the mango, which spread throughout the *tierra caliente* and much of the *tierra templada* of Mexico and Central America. Mediterranean fruits such as the grapevine, fig, and pomegranate, as well as the more hardy apple, peach, and quince, were introduced early into the cool tropical highlands.

Spanish Farming and the Indians

The Indian farmers of the Middle American mainland, having already had a well-developed agriculture with an adequate plant and food complex, were slow to adopt most of these Old World plants. Some of the tropical plant introductions, however, such as the plantain (for starch) and sugar cane (for sweetening), spread rapidly among the lowland people of Mexico and Central America. Curiously, onions, garlic, and collards also soon became important adjunct foods among the highland Indians. On the other hand, wheat was rejected. Maize was an established staple, and the cultivation of wheat was limited to the highlands and entailed the use of an entirely new agricultural technique—the Old World plow pulled by a team of oxen. In many instances, the Indians learned to use the plow only when they were forced to work on Spanish farms or to give tribute in wheat to their encomenderos. To this day, wheat is a minor crop among most of the highland Indians of southern Mexico and Guatemala and is grown not for food, but as a cash crop.

The Church was probably the most important disseminator of Old World crops and agricultural techniques. Around every religious establishment in Mexico and Central America, the Spanish priests planted fruit and vegetable gardens, a tradition of western European Catholic clergy. Their gardens served as colonial experiment stations and from them the priests spread European horticulture, especially among the highland Indian farmers. The cultivation of fruit trees, such as peach and apple, was admirably suited to the Indian way of farming. By the same process, Old World irrigation techniques and some agricultural instruments such as the hoe, spade, ax, and possibly the plow were introduced into Indian culture.

For most of the colonial period, subsistence agriculture in Mexico and Central America remained largely in the hands of Indians and mixbloods. In the Mesoamerican area, the native maize, beans, and squash, plus a few Old World plants, were farmed by the ancient slash-burn system of tillage on hillsides, although some use was made of the plow on valley floors and gentle slopes. The small surplus that was raised either entered the local native markets, as of old, or was given in tribute to Spanish encomenderos. Commercial farming of both native and imported crops, on the other hand, was directed by Spaniards using Old World techniques. With some change in crops and techniques, this division between subsistence and commercial agriculture has persisted in Mexico and Central America to the present.

The Highland Crops

Wheat. Wheat was the chief commercial food crop in the Spanish colonies. In Middle America, it was cultivated chiefly in the highland basins of Mexico and Central America. Spaniards preferred their traditional wheat bread to the Indian maize foods, which they felt were detrimental to the health of Europeans.

However, there were difficulties in the way of large-scale production of wheat. The grain would mature well only in the cool highlands. Moreover, fungus diseases reduced yields when the grain was planted during the warm rainy season. Consequently, most Spanish farmers in the tropical highlands of New Spain and Guatemala cultivated wheat by irrigation during the cooler dry season. However, the better farming areas were often already

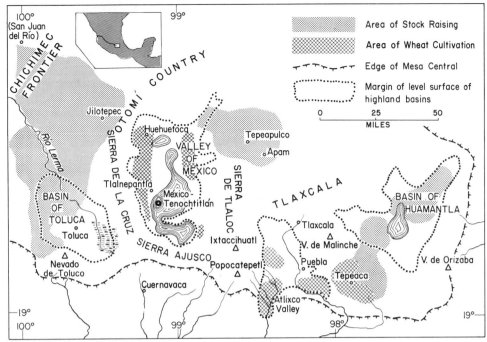

Figure 10.1 Spanish land use in the eastern portion of the Mesa Central, sixteenth century

occupied by Indians, and Spanish colonial law prohibited Europeans from usurping areas under native cultivation. The wheat farmers often acquired land titles by obtaining Crown grants of portions of former Aztec estates or of lands declared unoccupied (*baldíos*). Others, as *vecinos*, or members of a Spanish town, obtained rightful possession of agricultural plots surrounding the villa. Still others were able to amass large holdings by purchasing land from Indians or from other Spaniards.

The first large wheat-growing district in central Mexico was the Valley of Atlixco in the southwestern part of the Puebla basin (Figure 10.1). Favored by a flattish surface, light volcanic soil suitable for plowland, and plentiful water from streams fed by the melting snows from the adjacent slopes of Mt. Popocatepetl, the Atlixco Valley was by 1550 the foremost wheat-producing area of New Spain. There, and in other areas within the basin of Puebla, the Spaniards established the first commercial European-type farming

in the New World (1532). Individual holdings averaged about 640 acres. Using Indian labor from neighboring villages in encomienda, their owners often produced two crops of wheat yearly. Not only was this fertile area the breadbasket for Mexico City and Puebla; it also early became a center of European fruit production, especially of pomegranates, citrus fruits, grapes, and figs. The Atlixco Valley and its northward continuation around Cholula and Texmelucan is still noted for its irrigated farming and supplies Puebla with wheat, fruits, and vegetables.

Other wheat-growing areas were developed around Spanish villas founded in the western part of the Mexican Mesa Central, particularly near Valladolid (modern Morelia) and within the volcanic basins around Guadalajara. After the opening of the northern mining districts in the last half of the sixteenth century, Spanish farmers and Franciscan missionaries established wheat farms in the Bajío and in the Valley of Aguascalientes, both on the northern edge of the Mesa Central. By the

mid-seventeenth century the Bajío had surpassed Atlixco as the largest wheat-producing area of New Spain, and it is still considered to be a granary for Mexico. Farther
north, Spanish wheat and maize farms
were established near every large mining
center. The Jesuit and Franciscan orders
also cultivated wheat around the northern
missions. In the northern mining and
missionary frontier settlements, wheat became a more important food staple than
maize in mestizo communities.

In colonial Central America, wheat cultivation was much less widespread than in
Mexico. This might be explained by the
relatively small Spanish population, the
general poverty of the area, and the lack
of extensive upland areas. The Cartago
Basin of highland Costa Rica, with its
purely Spanish population, was the most
productive wheat area of the Central
American provinces. Elsewhere, a few
farms for the cultivation of small grains
were established around most of the Spanish highland towns, and a fair amount of
wheat was cultivated within the highland
basins of Honduras for the mines nearby.

Various agricultural tools and processes
were associated with wheat tillage and the
use of many of these was extended to the
cultivation of other crops, both Indian
and European. The most important, of
course, was the plow. In sixteenth-century
Spain, the chief farming implement was
the ancient wooden ard, or Egyptian plow,
of Neolithic origin. This instrument,
drawn by a yoked team of oxen, merely
scratches the soil; it does not turn it, as

does our modern steel moldboard plow.
The ard that the Spaniards brought to
Middle America came from the provinces
of Andalusia and Extremadura in southern
Spain; essentially the same tool is used
today in many rural areas of southern
Mexico and Central America (Figure 10.2).
With this simple instrument, the Spaniards were able to extend wheat and maize
cultivation into the extensive grass-covered
basin floors, which had been rarely cultivated by Indians, who had only dibbles
and *coas*. The Spaniards also introduced
rectangular field patterns—squares and
strips, both of which are associated with
plow cultivation. Such fields gave the rural
landscape within the highland basins a
European cast that contrasts with the irregular hillside fields of the Indians.

The plow, of course, could not be used
on steep slopes, where native slash-burn
cultivation persists to this day in Mexico
and Central America. Nor could it be employed to advantage in flat areas with shallow, rocky soil, as in the Yucatan Peninsula, where still the Maya Indians till
chiefly with the dibble. Even in areas suitable for the plow, as the coastal plains of
the lowland Totonac Indians in Veracruz,
strong native resistance to change has pre-
cluded its general use up to the present
time.

The use of the plow greatly extended
cultivation, but it resulted in the ruin
and abandonment of much land in the
most densely settled sections of the tropical highlands. In the late colonial period,
when Indians and mestizos began to em-

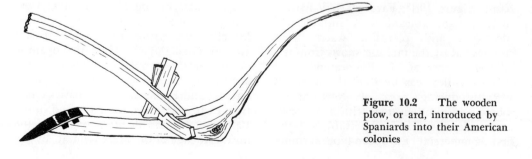

Figure 10.2   The wooden
plow, or ard, introduced by
Spaniards into their American
colonies

Figure 10.3   A noria, or wooden waterlift, operated by a donkey hitched to the long sweep. Few of these colonial-type wells remain in Mexico.

ploy the plow on low slopes, sheet erosion and, finally, serious gullying of the soil ensued. The consequence is that extensive highland areas, from central Mexico into Central America, have been lost to agriculture.

Arabic irrigation techniques were also introduced, principally with wheat cultivation. These techniques consisted of the diversion of stream water through canals (*acequias*); the construction of dams across small, intermittent streams to form reservoirs (*jagüeyes* or *presas*); and the digging of wells and the use of water lifts, such as the noria. Spanish canal irrigation was similar to, but much more highly developed than, the ancient Indian methods. Reservoir irrigation became widely employed for both wheat and maize cultivation in the northern basins of the Mesa Central, where today the *presas* form a conspicuous part of the landscape. But the noria, so common in Spain and North Africa, apparently was seldom used in colonial Middle America. Today this an-

cient waterlift (Figure 10.3) is seen only in a few farming areas in the northern Mexican states of Aguascalientes, Zacatecas, and San Luis Potosí. It also survives in the Yucatan Peninsula, where it was introduced by Spanish priests and cattlemen.

The ancient threshing floor, the grist mill, and the bakeoven are three other imports that accompanied colonial wheat culture in the Middle American highlands. A round platform of tamped earth—the communal *era,* or threshing floor—was often located on the outskirts of the Spanish towns, while private ones became a feature of every wheat farm. In many rural villages of central Mexico, wheat is still threshed by driving horses or mules over the sheaves placed on the *era* floor. Most of the flour mills were water-powered and were therefore located along streams on the farms or within the Spanish towns. Today, only the ruins of such edifices in the highlands of Mexico and Central America testify to their importance in colonial times. On the other hand, the European outside oven for baking wheat bread spread far outside the area of wheat cultivation, and is in widespread use in highland villages and isolated farm houses throughout Mexico and Central America.

Vineyards and Wine Making. Of the three plants of fundamental importance in the Mediterranean which were brought to Middle America—the small grains, the grapevine, and the olive tree—only the grains became firmly established. Climate and soils were favorable for the vine and the olive in most parts of the tropical highlands of America, but the Spanish government forbade their cultivation on a large scale except in the viceroyalty of Peru. This was done, apparently, to protect the colonial market for the wine and oil merchants in Spain. Nevertheless, in isolated spots of northern Mexico, far from central authority, both the missionaries and lay settlers succeeded in establishing small wine-producing areas. The largest vineyard district was Parras, a spring-fed oasis in the desert west of Saltillo, and during the latter half of the colonial period, the famous Parras wines and brandies were shipped to the northern mining centers. To this day, the wineries of Parras have retained their fame in Mexico. Smaller colonial vineyards were established in other northern localities, such as Aguascalientes, Saltillo, and along the Rio Grande downstream from El Paso del Río (modern Ciudad Juárez).

Commercial Farming in the Tropical Lowlands

Whereas commercial agriculture in the tropical highlands and the arid north of Middle America revolved chiefly around extensive cultivation of wheat, maize, and hardy European fruits, Spanish farming in the warm lowlands was based largely on tropical plants from both the Old and New World. Among these, the most significant were sugar cane, cacao, and the dyestuff, indigo. The commercial development of these three crops was particularly important to the colonial economy of Central America, which lacked Mexico's great mineral wealth.

Sugar Cane. Soon after their initial settlement in the 1520s the Spaniards brought sugar cane to Mexico and Central America from the island of Hispaniola, the distributing center for most of the tropical plants introduced from the Old World. In Mexico, the colonial cultivation of cane and the processing of sugar was limited to the southeastern and southern escarpments of the Mesa Central; in Central America, the crop was concentrated in the Pacific piedmont along the base of the volcanic axis. Frostless, moist, and possessing the definite dry season necessary for the proper concentration of sugar in the plant, these areas were well suited for the cultivation of cane. The rich volcanic soils supported years of continuous cropping, and the swift streams flowing down the adjacent escarpments afforded water power for turning the wheels of the grinding mills.

In Mexico, during the 1530s, the earliest sugar estates and mills were founded around Cuernavaca in the *tierra templada* south of the Valley of Mexico and at the western base of the Los Tuxtlas volcanic mountains (southeast of Veracruz). By 1550, New Spain was the foremost sugar producer of the Spanish colonies, surpassing Hispaniola, in the Caribbean, in output. In Central America, the principal sugar areas lay along the Pacific piedmont of Guatemala, while less important districts developed in the coastal provinces of San Salvador and San Miguel (modern El Salvador) and in the lake lowlands of Nicaragua. Cane has been harvested from these areas for the last 400 years, and they are still among the important sugar zones of the Middle American mainland.

Sugar cane cultivation also spread rapidly among the lowland Indian, who cultivated small plots for cane juice. The stalks of mature cane were cut into small lengths and chewed like a confection. In the markets of most Mexican and Central American villages, one sees neat piles of cut cane for sale and, in the streets, the ubiquitous litter of chewed cuds that have been spat out by children and oldsters alike. Cane juice and panela cakes of brown sugar supplemented the native honey, which had been almost the Indians' sole sweetening.

Cacao. As indicated in Chapter 8, cacao was one of the chief commercial products of tropical Mexico and Central America in pre-Conquest times. Soon after the Conquest, the Spaniards took over one of the most important of the native cacao areas—that of Soconusco along the Pacific piedmont of Chiapas and western Guatemala—and subsequently they extended cacao cultivation southwestward along the upper coastal plain of eastern Guatemala (Suchitepequez) into the Izalco area of western Salvador. The inner Pacific coastal region from the Isthmus of Tehuantepec to the Gulf of Fonseca thus became the cacao coast of colonial New Spain (Figure 10.4). The great pre-Conquest cacao area of the Tabasco lowlands in southeastern Mexico became a minor producing area during colonial times, as did other native districts such as Colima of western Mexico, the Sula valley of northern Honduras, the Rivas Isthmus of Nicaragua, and the Matina valley on the Caribbean coast of Costa Rica. In the Soconusco area, cacao production was left in the hands of the Indians, who paid most of the annual harvest as tribute to Spanish encomenderos. The new cacao areas of Suchitepequez and Izalco, however, were Spanish-owned plantations operated by skilled Indian laborers who were familiar with the starting of cacao seedlings in hot beds, with the irrigation

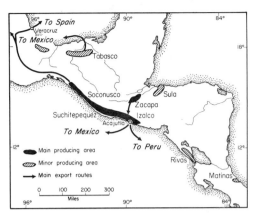

Figure 10.4   Cacao in Mexico and Central America, sixteenth and seventeenth centuries

needed during the long dry season, and with the planting of leguminous trees to shade the cacao plants.

For the first half of the colonial period, the chief market for cacao was the central highlands of Mexico, just as it had been in pre-Conquest times. In most of New Spain, cacao beans were made into a chocolate beverage drunk by Indians and Spaniards alike. They were also used as currency to pay Indian labor in many parts of the highlands.[1] Not until the mid-seventeenth century did Spain and other European countries become important markets for New World cacao. By that time, most of the groves of the Soconusco coast had declined and many had been abandoned as disease struck down their Indian cultivators. When cacao production shifted to Venezuela, beginning in the 1630s, the cacao industry in Guatemala and Salvador declined rapidly. Today only scattered groves along the Pacific coastal plain serve as a reminder of the former greatness of the cacao coast of Central America.

1. During the sixteenth century in Mexico and Guatemala, 140 cacao beans were the equivalent of one Spanish real; 1,120 beans, the equivalent of one silver peso. During most of the colonial period, however, the purchasing power of the beans fluctuated widely.

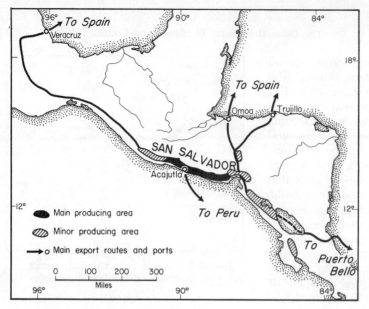

Figure 10.5 Indigo in Central America, eighteenth century

Indigo. The cultivation and exploitation of dyestuffs formed an important part of the colonial economy in Middle America. For nearly three centuries (1550–1850), American vegetable and animal dyes, including indigo, cochineal, and various dyewoods, were in great demand in the cloth manufacturing centers of northwestern Europe.

Of these dyestuffs, indigo was the most important and widely grown in the Middle American tropics. The leaves of this low, weedy plant (Indigofera suffruticosa) yield a very fast dye of deep blue. About 1570, Spanish encomenderos along the Pacific lowlands of Guatemala and Honduras began to exploit the wild indigo, called *xiquilite,* and later they formed large plantations of the cultivated plant. By the middle of the seventeenth century, the chief indigo plantations of the Middle American mainland extended along the Pacific coastal plain from northwestern Guatemala to the shores of Lake Nicaragua. In effect, indigo replaced the failing cacao industry of Central America for the remainder of the colonial period. A second important indigo center was the low Yucatan Peninsula where, by 1600, more than 50 large processing plants were in operation.

The processing of indigo involved a large investment of capital in the construction of dye factories (*obrajes de añil*) along streams or irrigation canals. Since the Spanish Crown forbade the employment of Indians in the indigo industry (it was thought to be an unhealthful occupation), black slaves were imported for labor. The black slave population was largest in the province of San Salvador, the center of indigo processing in Central America during the seventeenth and eighteenth centuries. By 1750, many tropical areas were competing with Central America for the indigo market, but the industry remained important in Guatemala and El Salvador until the introduction of analine dyes in the mid-nineteenth century (Figure 10.5).

Cochineal. Cochineal, another notable native American dyestuff, also acquired special significance in the colonial economy of Mexico and Central America. As mentioned earlier, the Aztecs used this scarlet dye, which was extracted from tiny scale insects raised on leaves of the nopal or prickly-pear cactus. Unlike indigo, cochineal was a product of the cool tropical highlands, and in pre-Conquest times it was secured as tribute, chiefly from the Mixteca of northern Oaxaca. After the

Conquest, the Spaniards also obtained the dye as tribute and forced the extension of its cultivation into the eastern part of the Mesa Central (Tlaxcala and the basin of Puebla). In Spain and northwestern Europe, this new dye commanded fabulous prices, and cochineal gained an important place in the economy of New Spain. By 1600, it ranked in value next to precious metals among Mexico's exports.

During the entire colonial period, the cultivation of cochineal remained in the hands of the Indians, who planted nopal cactus in small household plots and carefully tended the valuable insects. The red dye was extracted from the dried insects by boiling them in water (Figure 10.6).

Toward the end of the seventeenth century, Spanish officials began to encourage the spread of cochineal culture into the Central American highlands as far as Nicaragua. In the 1770s, it was taken to the Canary Islands and eventually spread to other parts of the world. The production of cochineal remained important in Mexico until 1870, when the cheaper synthetic dyes destroyed the ancient industry.

Other Plant Resources

Dyewoods. Dyewoods were scarcely exploited by Spaniards along the tropical Caribbean coasts of Central America and Yucatan. This activity was left to the English, whose settlement and exploitation of the east coasts of Central America are discussed later.

Tobacco. Tobacco, native to Indian America, was a minor agricultural product grown commercially in various localities in Mexico and Central America during the late colonial period. Although production was hardly comparable to that of the famous colonial tobacco areas of Cuba and Venezuela, sizable crops were produced for local consumption and for export in the Costa Rican highlands, San Salvador,

Figure 10.6 Early eighteenth-century drawing of cochineal harvest in Oaxaca (*Archivo General de Indias, Sevilla*)

Chiapas, and especially the Copán area of western Honduras. In the Copán area's peculiar volcanic soils was grown high-quality tobacco, which the area is still famous for. In colonial Mexico, the largest tobacco-growing area was around Córdoba and Orizaba on the humid eastern escarpment above Veracruz.

STOCK RAISING

The introduction of Old World animals and of stock raising probably did as much as any other factor to change the cultural

275

and physical landscape of Middle America during colonial times. The Indian, who lacked animal domesticates of his own in any number, was particularly affected by the incursion of this new economy. The peculiar vegetational and climatic factors of Mexico and Central America greatly favored the rapid reproduction of the new animals, and large areas of Mexico and Central America still attest to the occupance of the Spanish stockman and his herds.

In the sixteenth century, the Spanish stockman distinguished two general classes of Old World animals, all of which he introduced into the American colonies. One class he called *ganado mayor*. These were the larger domesticates, including range cattle, oxen, horses, mules, and donkeys. The other class—sheep, goats, and hogs— he termed *ganado menor* ("smaller animals"). To these we should add the barnyard fowls, particularly the chicken, the breeding of which spread rapidly among the American Indians.

The first animals the Spaniards brought to Mexico and Central America were the horse and the hog. The horse, a symbol of rank and authority, was a most effective military weapon; later, the horse helped herd other animals. Also accompanying every land expedition were droves of hogs, lean razorbacks. Easily driven and self-fed by scavenging, the hog formed a ready supply of pork and lard. Cattle, both the dun-colored, heavy-horned variety of western Europe and the black Iberian stock, were imported later, primarily for their hides and tallow, secondarily for meat; mules and donkeys were raised for transport; and sheep and goats for their wool, meat, and milk.

The Indian farmers of Mexico and Central America were quick to acquire the smaller and more tractable of the Old World animals. In almost every Indian community, the hog and chicken became household animals, supplementing the native turkey and dog. Today the hog and

chicken, both good scavengers (street cleaners, as it were), wander at will through village lanes and into doorways; they are rarely kept in pens except at night. Chicken eggs and, unfortunately, hog lard as well as the Spanish habit of frying foods, have been added to Indian cookery.

The small sheep (*rasa* variety), docile and easily handled, was readily adopted by the highland Indian farmers of Mexico and Guatemala, and wool soon replaced cotton as the chief cloth fiber in the highlands. The Indians also learned to breed sheep for certain natural colors of wool. Brown and black were the favorite hues for blankets and clothing, and the small flocks still tended by Indian children in the Middle American highlands include as many black and brown sheep as white ones. The Indians also adopted the Spaniards' hand-and-foot loom, reserving it for the weaving of woolens by men, while the women continued to weave cotton cloth on the native belt loom.

The Indians also accepted the slow, docile ox and the small donkey, or burro, which was used for transport, but feared and until late rejected the larger animals, such as the half-wild range cattle and the difficult mule. Only native nobles were permitted by the Spanish to keep or ride the horse.

Commercial stock raising remained in the hands of the Spaniards and mestizos during the colonial period. Cattle and, to a lesser degree, mules and horses were the principal range animals throughout Mexico and Central America. Raising of the merino sheep, introduced in the 1540s, was important chiefly in the cool, dry highlands and in northern Mexico.

On the Middle American mainland the Spaniards established the livestock industry in three types of natural situations:

1. The highland basins of Mesoamerica, already densely occupied by Indian farmers.

2. The tropical lowland savannas of the

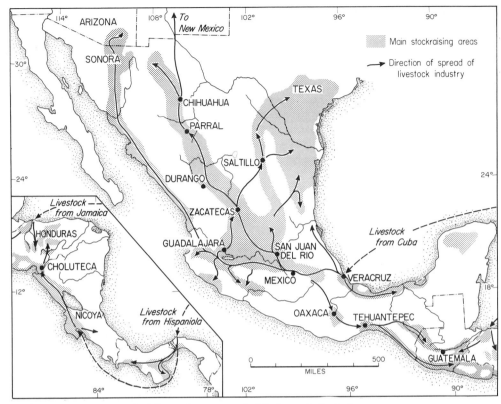

Figure 10.7 The spread of livestock economy in Mexico and Central America during the colonial era

coastal plains and the interior valleys of Mexico and Central America.

3. The steppe lands of northern Mexico.

Each of these areas presented particular problems for animal husbandry, and in each there evolved a particular pattern of stock raising with particular consequences to the face of the land (Figure 10.7).

**Stock Raising
in the Highland Basins**

In Mexico, stock raising developed first in the highland basins adjacent to the capital. By 1535, sizable herds of cattle were roaming the grassy surface of Toluca and Puebla basins and the northern, drier part of the Valley of Mexico. In all three locali-

ties, despite regulations to the contrary, the Spaniards' herds overran the unfenced milpas of the Indians, causing the natives to abandon much of their farmland and flee to the surrounding mountains; other farmland was abandoned as the Indians died off. The Spaniards quickly took over this land for pasture, for the succulent pigweeds (amaranths and chenopods) that invaded the abandoned Indian milpas afforded even better pasture than the native grasses. Moreover, the paucity of serious predators, disease, and competing wild animals favored a rapid growth of herds in the central Mexican highlands. By 1550, there were an estimated 150,000 cattle and horses in the northern part of Toluca Basin, where the abandoned Otomí town of Jilotepec had become one of the early centers of the Mexican livestock industry.

Checked by the Chichimec frontier from

277

expansion into the semiarid grasslands farther north, the Spanish stockmen drove their herds westward into Michoacán and Jalisco in the 1540s, disrupting Indian agriculture as they advanced. The same phenomenon occurred farther south, in the Valley of Oaxaca, on the highlands of Chiapas and Guatemala and, to a lesser degree, in the basins of central Honduras. In all these areas, Indian farmers were continually plagued by encroaching herds of cattle, horses, and mules. Cultivated land was abandoned, populations dislocated, and native food supplies depleted. Not until the mid-sixteenth century, when protective legislation was enforced and plow agriculture spread into the highland basins, were the herds controlled.

Within the cool highlands, commercial sheep raising became as important as cattle raising. Sheep were closely associated with agricultural areas, for they could be easily controlled by Indian shepherds and could feed on the wheat and maize stubble in harvested fields during part of the dry season. As in Spain, fields were unfenced, and harvested areas were considered common pasture for livestock. Thus, the basins of Puebla, Tlaxcala, Toluca, and of northern Michoacán in central Mexico, the Valley of Oaxaca, and the highlands of Chiapas and Guatemala all became the early sheep-raising sections of Middle America.

A colonial textile industry developed side-by-side with sheep raising. By the end of the sixteenth century, Spaniards had established small woolen mills (obrajes) in towns within the main sheep-raising areas: Puebla, Tlaxcala, Querétaro, Texcoco, Mexico City, and even Saltillo in the far north. Such mills housed scores of small European hand-and-foot looms operated by cheap Indian labor and sometimes by black slaves. The colonial woolen mills were the first Mexican factories, and Puebla and Mexico City are still textile manufacturing centers.

Stock Raising in the Tropical Lowlands

In spite of high temperatures and an abundance of parasites, the tropical lowlands of Mexico and Central America early became important stock-raising areas. Cattle, horses, and mules were the main range animals; sheep and goats did poorly in the hot and humid lowlands, and the hogs that were introduced usually went wild, feeding on roots and fallen fruits and palm nuts in the forest.

The central savanna of Panama was the first lowland area of the Mainland to be stocked with cattle and mules imported from the Caribbean islands. From Panama, Spaniards introduced livestock into the Nicaraguan lake lowlands, the Guanacaste plain of Costa Rica, and the Choluteca Valley of southeastern Honduras. By the seventeenth century, Choluteca was famous for its mules, thousands of which were annually driven to Panama for use in the transisthmian traffic. In Honduras, the savanna areas on the Caribbean coast were populated with livestock brought in from Jamaica soon after the founding of Trujillo in 1524. By the middle of the sixteenth century, stockmen in Mexico began to take cattle from the highlands into the coastal lowlands in great numbers. The Gulf coastal plain, from Tampico south to Nautla and from Veracruz into Tabasco, as well as the Pacific coast, from the Isthmus of Tehuantepec into Guatemala, swarmed with cattle.

One of the chief reasons for the rapid growth of the cattle herds in the coastal lowlands was the availability of unoccupied land—farmland abandoned as smallpox and typhus decimated the Indians. Moreover, the fresh-water marshes near the coasts, especially those of Tabasco and Guatemala, afforded year-round pasture. Inland from the marshes, however, the natural grasses of the American tropics are poor in protein, and make poor feed. The succulent weeds of recently abandoned farmlands were far more nutritious. A variety of low leguminous trees and shrubs, whose young terminal buds and bean pods are rich in proteins, also afforded excellent forage for cattle. The young shoots of coarse tropical grasses are also fairly nutritious, and the Spanish stockmen annually burned the lowland pastures to clear away the dry stalks, thereby extending the grassy areas at the expense of the tropical woodland. The present extensive coastal grasslands of Veracruz, Tabasco, and Tehuantepec are probably a product of such burning.

The underfed and ill-tended livestock in the lowland pastures were scrawny, half-wild beasts. The cattle were bred chiefly for tallow and for their hides, which were often riddled with holes by the larvae of parasitic ticks. Today, fires are set in the savannas as much to kill ticks as to clear the dry coarse grass for new growth.

Stock Raising
in Northern Mexico

Stock raising in Middle America was most highly developed in the semiarid grasslands of the north Mexican plateau. These grasslands, stretching on either side of the central desert from the Bajío of Guanajuato northward to beyond the Rio Grande, afforded an extensive open range somewhat similar to the Great Plains of the United States.

Certain physical characteristics of this great range favored the growth of the Spanish herds. The original grass cover was black grama, a highly nutritious bunch grass that afforded year-round pasture. This valuable grass, green and tender during the summer rainy season, cures to a palatable natural hay in the dry winter period. Associated with it were other less palatable grasses—bluestem, tobosa, needle-

grass, and many others. The shrubs that make up an important part of the semiarid vegetation in northern Mexico were as important as the grasses. The bean pods and young shoots of the thorny leguminous shrubs and low trees, such as mesquite and various acacias (huisache, screw bean), afforded excellent browse for cattle, sheep, and goats. Over most of the grassland area, an abundance of springs furnished water for livestock throughout the year, and these were supplemented by both intermittent and permanent streams flowing from the adjacent sierras.

Such conditions prevailed chiefly on the northern periphery of the Mesa Central and within the wide belt of semiarid grassland that lies between the Sierra Madre Occidental and the central desert. Within the latter area were the renowned pastures of western Zacatecas, central Durango, and Chihuahua, still the foremost stock-raising section of Mexico. As pointed out earlier, the zone corresponded to the great Silver Belt and the main axis of Spanish northward advance in New Spain. On the eastern side of the plateau, the main grazing areas were around San Luis Potosí and from Saltillo northward into Texas.

Spanish stockmen first penetrated the semiarid grasslands along the northern margin of the Mesa Central. This was the Chichimec frontier, which checked Spanish movement northward until the mid-sixteenth century. But by the 1550s, cattlemen had moved many of their herds into the grasslands of San Juan del Río and Querétaro, east of the Bajío of Guanajuato. Those areas, together with the previously occupied pastures to the south around Jilotepec, were the cradle of northern colonial stock raising (Figure 10.1). There Spanish herding techniques were adapted to the northern frontier; there the *vaquero* ("north Mexican cowboy") developed; and there some of the first big stock ranches, or *haciendas*, were established. From this center, the livestock industry and the mines spread northward as the Chichimecs slowly gave way. Beyond the mining districts, the Spanish stockmen and their herds joined with the Catholic missionaries to form the cutting edge of the frontier of settlement as it pressed northward into what is now United States territory. Although continually harassed by the Chichimecs, the northern cattlemen had advanced beyond the confining farmlands of the sedentary Indians to the south, and they were able to use Iberic herding techniques.

Stock-Raising Techniques

During the sixteenth century, the Spaniard introduced directly from his homeland most of the practices involved in colonial stock raising in Middle America. The rodeo, the annual or semiannual roundup to brand calves and to select stock for market; the use of the *desgarretadero,* a half-moon blade set on a long pole for hocking cattle, as well as the leather *lazo* for roping and the *garrocha,* or long lance, for controlling the herds; the emphasis on raising cattle for hides and tallow—all these practices appear to have come from southern Spain. The herder's use of leather clothing (jacket, chaps, headgear) for protection from thorny shrubs may have been a New World development. In most parts of colonial Middle America, the earliest *vaqueros* were poor whites and blacks, slaves or freedmen, for Indians proved to be poor herders of the half-wild cattle. In Mexico, the interbreeding of black and Spanish cowboys with Indian women on the frontier produced the mestizo *vaquero,* who moved north with the cattle.

Stock Raising and Land Tenure

It was from the industry of stock raising as much as from commercial farming that the vast landed estates of Mexico and Cen-

tral America evolved during the colonial period. Just as in the Greater Antilles, the Spanish stockmen of the Middle American mainland first obtained municipal or royal grants of certain pasture lands (*estancias, sitios,* or, as in Panama, *hatos*) for grazing. The size of the grants varied according to the type of animal herded. Thus, the *estancia de ganado mayor,* a ranch for cattle, horses, or mules, usually measured around 4,000 acres; the *estancia de ganado menor,* for sheep and goats, about 2,000 acres. Through the accumulation of several contiguous grants through outright royal grant, by purchase, or otherwise, rich and noble Spaniards came into possession of immense estates, particularly in arid north Mexico. For example, the estate of the Marquis of Aguayo, comprised half the present state of Coahuila. Such properties based on stock raising, together with the agricultural holdings discussed above, developed into the large haciendas that still characterize the land tenure and dominate the economy of much of Central America and, until recently, of Mexico.

Most of the livestock haciendas of Middle America consisted not only of pasture, but also of small tracts of arable land, usually along stream bottoms or alluvial terraces. Included on almost every grant of pastureland was at least one *caballería* (about 100 acres) of plowland. The wheat or maize harvested on this land was used mainly for feeding the hacienda workers and overseers. On some *estancias* in central and northern Mexico, agricultural production became even more important than livestock.

The focal point of the hacienda was a compact cluster of buildings, sometimes called the *casco* (Figure 10.8). This included the often palatial house of the owner or overseer, the huts of the workers, the corrals, granaries, and usually an elaborate chapel tended by the hacienda priest. Invariably, the structures were of stone or adobe and arranged around a central courtyard. The hacienda center was usu-

Figure 10.8   The *casco,* or habitation center, of Chimalpa hacienda, southern
Hidalgo state, Mesa Central. Now an ejido center, this large *casco* was
completely walled. Atop the wall are parapets and turrets formerly used for
defense against bandits. The hacienda church towers above all other structures.

ally walled or strongly fortified against
bandit attacks or, as in northern Mexico,
against nomadic Indians. The New World
hacienda center is highly reminiscent of
the Andalusian *cortijo* of southern Spain,
from which the architectural plan was
probably taken. These hacienda centers,
often abandoned and in ruins, dot the
landscape of Mexico and parts of Central
America.

LAND TENURE AND
THE LABOR SYSTEMS

The owners of the large colonial haciendas
developed a labor system that pervaded
New Spain. In the early colonial period,
some haciendas, situated within the area
of Mesoamerica inhabited by sedentary Indians, were able to produce sufficient labor
through the government-regulated *repartimiento* system, whereby a weekly levy of
workers was made on nearby Indian villages.

Beginning in the seventeenth century,
however, after the disastrous epidemics
had reduced Indian population, most *hacendados* were forced to resort to extralegal
means to get sufficient workers. Indians
were induced to leave their old villages to

settle on or near the estates by offers of
relatively high wages paid in kind—such
workers were called *gañanes or peones*—
and the owner or overseer advanced them
goods on credit from the hacienda store
(*tienda de raya*). In this way the workers
fell into perpetual debt to be paid in labor.
This was the origin of the pernicious system called "debt peonage," which bound
the rural peasant to the landed estates. On
the other hand, by freeing the Indian from
the conservative customs of his native village and permitting him to satisfy his
needs by exchanging his labor for food
and clothing, the hacienda system became
a powerful force for cultural change. On
the haciendas, Indian workers became mestizo in culture, if not in blood. Debt peonage continued on the large haciendas of
Mexico until the Agrarian Revolution of
1910.

A different labor system was practiced
on the ranchos, or small holdings, which
developed principally on the western and
northern fringes of the Mesa Central of
Mexico (in Jalisco and Guanajuato) and
in the highland basins of eastern Guatemala and central Honduras. The ranchos
required few workers. Occasionally the
proprietor and his family composed the
labor force; sometimes Indian workers
were obtained through the *repartimiento*

system; but, more commonly, natives and mixbloods were hired as free laborers to help cultivate crops and tend livestock. The modern, vigorous rancheros, freeholders in the Los Altos district in northern Jalisco and in the *valles* of central Honduras, are descendants of these colonial middle-class farmers who formed an anomaly within the general pattern of *latifundia* ("large estates") in Mexico and Central America. Somewhat similar in size, land system, and labor force were the properties attached to the Spanish towns. The present system of *minifundia* ("small properties") of the Costa Rican highlands evolved from colonial town holdings.

In striking contrast to all this, the Indian village lands of southern Mexico and Guatemala were set apart and, during most of the colonial period, were legally protected from encroachment by land-hungry Spaniards. In the Indian communities, the system of use rights and communal holdings of pre-Conquest days were retained, and they are practiced to this day in isolated areas. During the last years of the colonial period, and especially in the nineteenth century, the hacienda owners were permitted to acquire many of the Indian lands through illegal means, and the *latifundia* system was expanded at the expense of the Indian way of life. Such conditions were basic causes of Mexico's twentieth-century social revolution and land reforms.

COLONIAL MINING

We have observed that the acquisition of precious metals was the outstanding motive for initial Spanish settlement in Middle America, that the extraction of gold and silver became the leading business of New Spain, and that from these metals the mother country derived the greatest wealth from the Middle American colonies. On the other hand, mining engaged a rela-

tively minor part of the population; most of the people, by far, lived by subsistence and commercial agriculture. Moreover, in only one part of Middle America—northern Mexico—did mining and its adjunct activities dominate the economic scene and leave a lasting impress upon the landscape. In the southern areas, heavily populated by sedentary Indians, agriculture was economically dominant and, along with stock raising, the chief molder of the cultural scene.

Gold Placering

Gold placering was the earliest Spanish mining activity in Middle America. That carried on in the Caribbean islands has been discussed (Chapter 3). On the Middle American mainland, the Spaniards engaged in washing gold from the streams that drained the old, highly mineralized rocks of southern Mexico and from the rivers on the Caribbean versant of Central America from Honduras into Panama. These early activities did little to change the aboriginal landscape. Indians who had worked the same streams before the Conquest served as miners for the Spaniards. With the exception of a few iron tools, such as crowbars, picks, and hoes, the Indian laborers used their own placering methods, including the batea, a round, shallow, wooden bowl for panning gold dust and nuggets. Moreover, the ephemeral nature of alluvial gold deposits resulted in continuous shifting of mining camps (called "ranchos") from one stream to the next, and few permanent colonial settlements resulted from gold placering in Mexico and Central America.

Although the period of active placer mining in these areas was short-lived (1525–1560), small family-sized operations continued, for most of the colonial period, in the tributaries of the Balsas River in Mexico and along several streams in Central America, particularly the Guayape

River of northeastern Honduras. Such activity can still be seen in southern Mexico and Honduras, where a kind of folk mining with the ancient Indian placering techniques has persisted.

Vein Mining

With the abolition of cheap Indian slave labor and the depletion of the gold placers in the mid-sixteenth century, the Spaniards in Mexico and Honduras turned to the more difficult extraction of silver ores from vein deposits. This entailed permanent settlements. The exploitation of ore in veins required a large number of workers who lived in one place for long periods and a large capital investment for the sinking of shafts and the construction of mills and refining plants. Most of the silver-mining centers of Middle America became sizable towns, and some grew to be large, opulent cities.

The first silver mines exploited by Europeans were relatively small deposits found within the area of high Indian culture. A major silver-mining operation occurred

in the 1530s at Taxco, on the southern escarpment of the Mesa Central, southwest of Mexico City. Soon a series of silver deposits were discovered to the northwest of Taxco, including those of Zacualpan, Sultepec, and Temascaltepec, and these were exploited. During the same period, the mines of Zumpango were opened farther south, in the Sierra Madre del Sur. In the early 1540s, a large number of small mines were exploited in the western escarpment of the Mesa Central in the vicinity of Guadalajara (Figure 10.9). The rich mines of Pachuca, discovered in 1556 just beyond the northern limit of the Valley of Mexico, and the lead-silver workings of Ixmiquilpan and Zimapán, in Otomí country to the north, were other deposits exploited within the area of high Indian culture of Mexico.

The largest and most productive colonial mining area of New Spain was northern Mexico, the locale of the great Silver Belt in the land of the Chichimecs. The opening of this area to Spanish settlement has been described (Chapter 9). Spain derived most of its colonial wealth from the mines within the Silver Belt, from Zaca-

Figure 10.9   Spanish mining activities in New Spain, 1519–1545

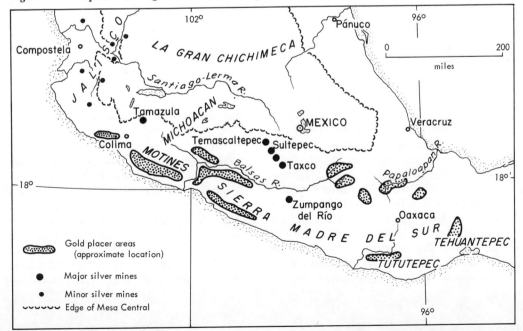

tecas and Guanajuato northward along the eastern foothills of the Sierra Madre Occidental to the mines of Santa Eulalia in Chihuahua. Outside of the main Silver Belt, other mines were opened in various sections of northern Mexico. An eastern line of deposits extended from San Luis Potosí to beyond Saltillo. In the far northwest, the mines of Sinaloa and Sonora formed a third area of silver production in northern colonial Mexico.

On the southern edge of the area of high Mesoamerican culture, within the highly mineralized highlands of central Honduras, the Spaniards developed another silver-mining area. A cluster of five mining settlements, centered around Tegucigalpa, was established soon after the initial discovery in 1569. But they were few in number, isolated from the main stream of colonial development, and neglected by the Spanish government, so the mines of Honduras, though rich in high-grade ores, could hardly compare with the opulent mining districts of northern New Spain.

The mining settlements of Mexico and Central America were physically not unlike modern ones, for both are closely associated with the peculiar nature of vein outcrops. Owing to various geological processes, mineralization of veins in underlying rock tends to occur in clusters. These individual clusters, where mineralized veins outcrop, may cover many square miles. In colonial times, as today, such clusters usually make up a mining district in which the active mines might be scattered over a large area, each corresponding to the exploitation of one or several outcropping veins. In each colonial mining district, one large town was usually established as the administrative and refining center for the surrounding mines. Such a settlement was called a *real de minas* in northern New Spain and often termed *asiento de minas* in the central and southern parts of the viceroyalty. For example, the *real de minas* of Zacatecas was the administrative and refining center for the

large number of mines within its district. Normally, the mining town was located along a stream where water was available for power and as an essential ingredient in the refining processes. Since most mineralized areas were mountainous, such streams flowed through deep, narrow valleys that afforded little level ground for buildings. Consequently, most mining towns developed an elongated shape and an irregular street plan, in contrast to the regular grid pattern of the Spanish villas. The elaborate churches and other colonial structures; the steep, winding cobbled lanes; and the picturesque plazas tucked between intersecting streets—all give the old mining towns of Mexico a charming quality rarely found elsewhere in Spanish America (Figure 10.10). Another feature of most mining centers was the *barrio,* the residential quarter for Indian and black laborers, usually perched high on the valley sides above the main part of town. These sections are now the slum districts, still serving their old function as the living quarters for poorly paid laborers.

The extraction of silver from its ore in the colonial mining centers necessitated a large array of buildings, large numbers of workers, and the development of many subsidiary activities to furnish food, reagents, and fuel. Probably no other economy in colonial Middle America developed such an elaborate and interrelated system of activities as did the mining industry.

Few of the mining and refining techniques that the Spaniards used in their New World mines were brought from Spain. If the Spaniards knew little about gold placering, they knew even less about the refining of silver ores. During the formative years of silver mining in Mexico, the Spaniards relied on Indian (mainly Tarascan) and German knowledge of vein mining and ore reduction. Many German miners were brought to New Spain from the Erzgebirge of Saxony, the chief mining area of fifteenth- and sixteenth-century

Figure 10.10 The mining city of Guanajuato, founded in 1554, crowded within a narrow mountain valley. Its winding, picturesque streets and alleys present an Old World, medieval atmosphere. Abandoned shafts of worked-out silver mines pock the surrounding hills. (*Compañia Mexicana Aerofoto*)

Europe, to impart their knowledge of metals to the Spaniards. The stamp mill, powered either by animals or water wheels and employed throughout the colonial period for crushing ores, was introduced by the Germans in the early sixteenth century. Of a similar origin were improved smelting techniques and, quite probably, the famous amalgamation process for reduction of silver ores.

Until the mid-sixteenth century, smelting was the only known method of reducing silver ores. Large numbers of small rectangular furnaces of stone or adobe, operated with water-powered or hand-driven goatskin bellows, were constructed in every large mining center. In the smelting process, large amounts of lead and litharge were used as reagents; where there was no local supply, these materials had to be imported. The only fuel used in smelting was charcoal, made from the local wood supply, and around every mining center the woody vegetation was thus almost completely destroyed. The open stands of acacia and oak that once covered the hills around Zacatecas had completely disappeared by the end of the sixteenth century, giving rise to the present barren, wind-swept landscape around this once-prosperous *real*.

Around 1556, the amalgamation process of reducing silver ores was introduced into New Spain. This process involved the mixing of mercury with finely ground silver ores puddled in water to make a sludge. Salt and chalcopyrite were other ingredients mixed with the ore mud to aid chemical reaction. Mixing was accomplished by driving mules, and sometimes human workers, through the sludge. After a long period of curing, the sludge was washed, leaving behind an amalgam of mercury and silver. The mercury was volatilized by heating the amalgam in a retort, and the remaining metallic silver was then cast into bars.

With the amalgamation process, low-grade ores free of lead compounds could be cheaply refined. This process was employed in Mexico until the latter part of the nineteenth century, when the better, modern techniques of flotation and cyanidization were perfected. Extremely rich ores and those of high lead content continued to be reduced by smelting. Smelting and amalgamation were often carried on in the same mining center.

For these operations, the colonial miners constructed large plants of stone and adobe. Stamp mills, smelters, and amalgamation plants composed the *hacienda de beneficio,* several of which were located within a given mining town. The amalga-

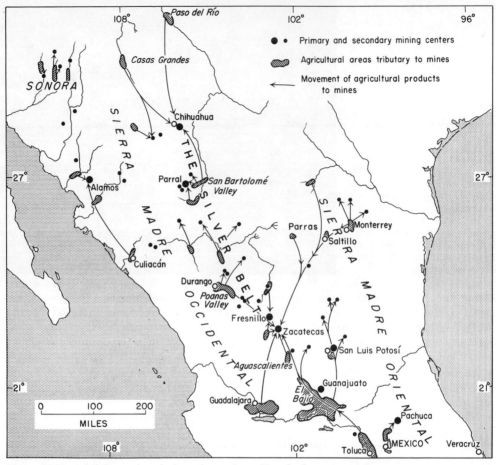

Figure 10.11 Mining and agriculture in northern New Spain, seventeenth and eighteenth centuries

mation plant consisted chiefly of large open courtyards, or patios, where the ore sludge was mixed with mercury and other ingredients for curing. Ruins of these buildings today abound in every colonial mining center of Mexico and Honduras.

The demand for reagents used in the refining processes, for animals used in mixing and hauling ore, and for food to feed the mine workers created a lively trade and the development of subsidiary activities within the mining zones. Lacking local deposits, the colonial miners imported mercury from Spain and Peru through a government monopoly. Lead and litharge were often brought in from afar. After the

introduction of amalgamation, the salt industry in New Spain and Honduras became an adjunct of the colonial economy. The close interrelationship of the mines and surrounding farms and stock ranches has already been mentioned; the ranches furnished tallow for the candles that illuminated the mine shafts, hides for ore sacks and ropes, mules and horses for mine work, and beef and mutton for food. The great demand for wheat and maize resulted in the development of small irrigated farms around the northern mines and in the expansion of commercial agriculture in the Mesa Central (Figure 10.11). Indeed, the economic survival of New

Spain during most of the colonial period was based chiefly on the mining industry and the economic institutions related to it.

TRANSPORT AND TRADE

The European modes of transport that Spaniards introduced into America during the early sixteenth century were as instrumental as the Old World types of settlement and economic enterprises in molding the landscape to its colonial form. Two new factors revolutionized land transport in the New World: the pack animal and the wheel. Pack trains of mules and donkeys and the Mediterranean two-wheeled cart gradually replaced or supplemented the native Indian carrier.

Although the colonial trails and roads in the main followed those already used by the Indian, the Spaniards opened many new routes to exploit the wealth of the land. Sea transport necessitated the establishment of new ports on both shores of Mexico and Central America and also encouraged the growth of a rudimentary shipbuilding industry as well as the exploitation of naval stores, especially in Central America.

The Indians of Mexico and Central America were slow to use the new transportation. For most of the colonial period, they continued to transport goods on their own backs with the aid of the tump line and the *cacaxtli* ("carrying frame"). Until the beginning of the seventeenth century and despite laws to the contrary, Spanish merchants and encomenderos retained the pre-Conquest system of professional Indian carriers (*tamemes*), although in reduced form. Moreover, the Spaniards first used black and mulatto slaves, rather than Indians, to drive mule trains. And, as indicated before, excepting the native nobility, Indians were forbidden to ride horses and mules.

The lowly, stubborn donkey, or burro, used as a pack animal, was probably the first European mode of transport that the Indian adopted. The two-wheeled cart, usually pulled by a team of oxen, was an expensive piece of equipment, and useful only in relatively level areas. Therefore, although they proved to be excellent cart makers, most Indians within the areas of high culture did not adopt wheeled vehicles for their own use until late in the colonial period. Today, the burro is a symbol of transport among the poorer rural Indians and mestizos of Middle America, and the ox-drawn cart is still employed in out-of-the-way places in Mexico and in many parts of Central America. Even so, in some aboriginal areas, particularly the Guatemalan highlands, the human still carries the burdens of the poorer families that cannot afford a burro or to pay freight charges on trucks and buses.

The Colonial Road Pattern

The rugged terrain of the Middle American mainland did not lend itself to a widespread system of easily traveled land routes. Fortunately for the Spaniards, however, the lines of least resistance within the areas of high aboriginal culture had been established for centuries by Indian traders and warriors. Spanish exploration, exploitation, settlement, and transport followed most of the aboriginal routes of communication. In a similar manner, many of the auto roads and some of the railway lines of modern Mexico and Central America parallel old colonial thoroughfares.

In Mexico, the general pattern of the colonial road system was relatively simple. Most of the trails extended outward from the Valley of Mexico or other parts of the Mesa Central (Figure 10.12). One set of roads led northward into the mining

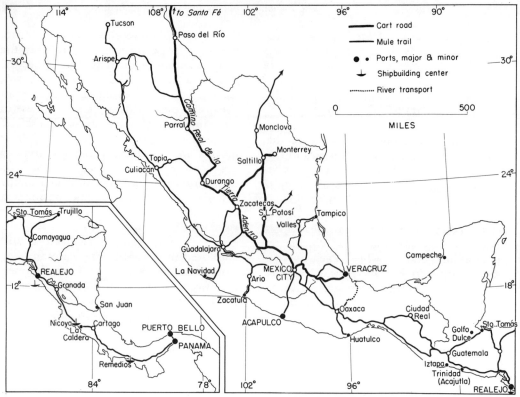

Figure 10.12   Colonial transportation in Mexico and Central America

country over the easy gradients of the plateau. Another set consisted of the more difficult trails that passed from the Mesa Central, down the steep escarpments, and into the adjacent tropical lowlands and the southern highlands beyond; these roads followed Indian routes. One led northeastward into the Huasteca and Tampico. In the eighteenth century it was extended northward, along the inner lowlands basins, to Monterrey and Laredo. Eastward from the Valley of Mexico ran one of the most vital and heavily trafficked arteries of Mexico's colonial road system —the connecting link between Mexico City and the port of Veracruz. All of New Spain's legal trade with the mother country passed over this road.

Another significant road led southward from the Valley of Mexico into the upper Balsas Basin and continued to Oaxaca in the Mesa del Sur and thence to Chiapas

and Guatemala. This was the main line of southward expansion of Aztec trade and conquest. It was the main route of trade and political contact between Mexico City, Oaxaca, and Guatemala during colonial days. And today it is the route of the Inter-American Highway.

Still another trail passed southward from the Mesa Central into the Balsas depression and thence to the Pacific coast, joining Mexico City with the colonial port of Acapulco. In the latter part of the sixteenth century this road became the famous *El Camino Real,* along which oriental trade goods imported by the annual Manila galleon were packed into Mexico City and Veracruz for transshipment to Spain. The present Acapulco highway follows the same route. In addition, an important road descended the western escarpment of the plateau from Guadalajara to the coastal lowlands, continuing northward to Sonora. All of these escarpment trails were steep and rough. With the exception of the Mexico City–Veracruz road via Córdoba, they could be traveled only by mule train or human carrier.

In contrast to the large number of escarpment trails, only two significant roads followed the easy gradients of the plateau surface from the Mesa Central into northern Mexico. One continued along the western edge of the plateau, through the great Silver Belt, from the Bajío of Guanajuato northward into Chihuahua and thence to the upper Rio Grande settlements in New Mexico. Over 1,500 miles long and heavily traveled, this road was one of the most significant of all Middle America. It was called the *Camino Real de la Tierra Adentro* ("the main road into the interior country") and, owing to its easy gradients, was the principal highway for cart traffic in New Spain. The other road into the north led through the dry basin and range country, along the western foothills of the Sierra Madre Oriental via San Luis Potosí, Saltillo, and Monclova, and into Texas as far as San Antonio. Again, modern railroads and paved highways pass near these old routes.

In colonial Central America, a little-used mule trail joined the provinces of the Captaincy of Guatemala. This road, and its many alternates, led along the volcanic axis on the Pacific side of Central America, connecting the main towns and rural population centers from Chiapas in southern Mexico southeastward into Panama. Based on old Indian trade routes, this colonial road approximated the present Inter-American Highway.

A second set of trails in Central America formed the transisthmian routes connecting the Pacific and Caribbean shores. These also served as the main outlet for local products exported to Spain from the Caribbean ports. One led from Guatemala City, down the Motagua River depression, to the port of Santo Tomás, near present Puerto Barrios. Another crossed Honduras via the Comayagua Basin, from the Gulf of Fonseca on the Pacific side to the lower Ulúa River valley on the Caribbean. A third trail crossed through the Nicaragua lake depression and the San Juan River. The most important transisthmian highway was that between Panama City and Puerto Bello, near the site of the present canal, over which the products from Peru were packed by mule trains from the Pacific to the Atlantic side.

Transport Systems

With the rise of commercial agriculture and mining, freighting by pack train and carts became an important enterprise in colonial Mexico and Central America. The mule and donkey trains, called *recuas,* formed the most common type of commercial transport over the mountainous trails. Blacks and mixbloods were the original Middle American muleteers (*arrieros*), who packed the animals and drove them on their long and arduous journeys from production center to market or port.

The demand for animals for the transport business gave rise to the development of many mule-raising areas in various parts of Middle America. The pastures of Saltillo in northeastern Mexico supplied many of the northern freighters with mules; the highlands of Chiapas, especially the Comitán area, furnished animals for the pack trains operating in southern Mexico and Guatemala; mention has already been made of the renowned savannas of Choluteca in southeastern Honduras, which supplied mules for the transisthmian transport of Panama. Today the pack train and the ancient institution of the muleteer persists in the back country of Mexico and Central America where

Figure 10.13 A mule train entering the old mining town of Sultepec, on the southern escarpment of the Mesa Central. In most parts of Mexico today *recuas* and *arrieros* such as these have been almost wholly supplanted by motor transport.

modern auto roads and railways have not yet penetrated (Figure 10.13).

Until the middle of the sixteenth century, small two-wheeled carts (*carretas*, Figure 10.14) were the wheeled transportation in Middle America. These served for short local hauls in the basins of the Mesa Central. With the opening of the northern mining districts of Mexico after 1550, the big two-wheeled cart (*carro*) was introduced. Pulled by 8 to 12 mules and equipped with iron-rimmed wooden wheels 5 to 6 feet in diameter, the *carro* hauled tons of heavy bulky merchandise over the level surface of the northern plateau to and from the mines. Today the *carro* has disappeared completely, and

the small ox-drawn *carreta* is used only for short hauls and on isolated farms.

Sea Transport and Trade

On the Middle American mainland, colonial sea transport and trade consisted of local coastwise traffic and overseas commerce with Spain, the viceroyalty of Peru, and the Philippines. Spain prohibited her colonies from trading with foreign powers, but this law was often circumvented by smugglers.

Trade with Spain and the Philippines. The most extensive ocean transport and

Figure 10.14 The *carreta*, or two-wheeled Spanish cart

290

trade was, of course, with the mother country. French, English, and Dutch pirates operated in Atlantic and Caribbean waters, so that Spanish merchant vessels plying between Seville and the Middle American ports were required to sail in convoy escorted by men-of-war (see Chapter 3).

The greater part of the fleet for New Spain put in at Veracruz. Veracruz, protected by a group of coral and sandy reefs off her coast, was one of the largest and most strongly fortified ports of Spain's American colonies, and the official gateway into New Spain. The arrival of the annual fleet was the occasion for the big fair at Jalapa, on the cool eastern escarpment above the heat and filth of Veracruz.

Vessels occasionally broke from the convoy to call at the smaller Caribbean ports of Central America, such as Trujillo and Puerto Caballos in Honduras and Santo Tomás in Guatemala. Although insignificant in size and often occupied only when the ships arrived, these ports on the hot, sparsely inhabited Caribbean coast handled a large part of the trade of the Captaincy of Guatemala with Spain. The Central American sea transport has the same pattern today, since the large markets for its products lie on the Gulf of Mexico, the eastern seaboard of the United States, and in Europe.

The fleet destined for Panama was engaged chiefly in the Peruvian trade. Until the latter part of the sixteenth century, Nombre de Dios was the Caribbean port of the transisthmian route; thereafter, the terminus was transferred a few miles westward, to deeper water at Puerto Bello. Panama City, the Pacific terminus, was changed to its present location after English pirates had destroyed the old town in 1671. On the annual arrival of the fleet from Spain, a large fair took place at Puerto Bello, and Peruvian merchants, who had come up with the Pacific fleet from Lima, purchased European goods.

There, also, the silver bullion from the Peruvian mines, packed across the isthmus on mule train, was readied for transshipment to Spain.

The rise of the Philippine trade from Manila, during the final years of the sixteenth century, resulted in the development of the port of Acapulco on the southern coast of Mexico and in a flood of oriental goods into New Spain. The well-protected bay of Acapulco is the best natural harbor on the Pacific coast of Mexico. It is also the closest point on the Pacific coast to Mexico City. In colonial times, the chief disadvantage of the port was the extremely rugged terrain that separated it from the capital.

On the annual arrival of the galleons from Manila, a great fair was held in Acapulco, and merchants from all New Spain gathered to bargain for the rich oriental silks and brocades, jewelry, woodwork, and other luxuries from the Philippines and China.

With the decline of Philippine commerce at the close of the colonial period, Acapulco degenerated into an isolated fishing village. It has never regained its former significance as a port, but has become one of the world's leading resorts.

Most of the colonial ports of Middle America had large fortifications, constructed to resist the pirate raids that were common on both coasts for nearly 200 years. The famous fortress of San Juan de Ulúa, constructed on one of the reefs off Veracruz, is typical of the military aspect of the colonial ports. Today, such structures are poignant reminders of a turbulent past, adding to the colonial flavor of the old port towns.

Shipbuilding. Shipbuilding developed on the Middle American mainland as an industry subsidiary to sea transport. Most of the vessels used on the Atlantic voyages were made in northern Spain, but those that sailed on the Pacific side of Middle America were constructed locally. The principal shipyards were located on the Pacific coast of Central America, where tropical semideciduous forests supplied abundant timbers for construction. The fine-grained guayacan (Tabebuia) was the best of the tropical woods for ship construction. Durable, yet easily sawed and hewn, it was also resistant to the borings of the shipworm (Teredo), which infested the warm waters of the Caribbean and Pacific shores of Middle America and often raised havoc with wooden ships.

The main shipyards were at Realejo, in Nicaragua, and Remedios, in the Veraguas area of southwestern Panama (Figure 10.12). From these two yards came most of the ships used in the Peruvian fleets and in local coastwise trade. Hundreds of black and mulatto sawyers were imported to cut timber in the Veraguas area. The strong black element in the present-day mixbloods of western interior Panama may well stem from the African sawyers of colonial days.

Closely associated with shipbuilding in Central America was the gathering of naval stores in the highland pine forests of Honduras and Nicaragua. Pine pitch was needed in great quantities to caulk newly constructed ships and to repair old ones. Tons of pitch were shipped to Peru, not only for ship stores, but also for coating wine jugs to prevent leakage. Other ship stores supplied by Indians of Nicaragua and San Salvador included cordage of agave fiber for ropes and coarse cottons for sailcloth. In time, much of the colonial economic activity of the Central American Pacific coast centered around sea transport.

COLONIAL LANDSCAPE:
THE CARIBBEAN COAST
OF CENTRAL AMERICA

The hot, rainy Caribbean shore between northern Yucatan and eastern Panama held few attractions for Spanish settlers during the colonial period. As we have seen, in Central America the Spaniards kept to the highlands and the Pacific coast. On the Caribbean side, the rocky northern shore of Honduras, adjacent to the mineral-rich interior; the small cacao-growing area of Matina in Costa Rica; and the Atlantic terminus of the Panamanian isthmus route at Puerto Bello were the only sections that the Spaniards more or less permanently occupied. The rest of the coast, low-lying and reef-strewn, was left to native forest Indians or to foreign interlopers such as the English pirates, smugglers, and woodcutters.

During the mid-seventeenth century, the English obtained a substantial footing in at least three sections of the Central American mainland and off-shore islands. One section included the various islands off the coast, such as San Andrés, Providencia, the Bay Islands, Corn Islands, and others, which served initially as bases for pirates and smugglers operating in the western Caribbean. These islands also functioned as springboards for the English occupation of two coastal areas: (1) the portion of the east coast of the Yucatan Peninsula that lies within the Bay of Honduras, and (2) the Miskito (Mosquito) Shore of Nicaragua and Honduras, from the San Juan River to near Trujillo (Figure 10.15). The offshore waters of each of these coastal areas are shoal and strewn with coral reefs and cays. Moreover, the coastline is frayed with hundreds of small mangrove-bordered tidal inlets. Such conditions made for difficult navigation but afforded ideal hideouts for pirates and smugglers. To this day, the influence of British occupation is seen within each of these areas—in the prevalence of English speech, in English place names, in the Anglican church, and in other Anglo-Saxon cultural carryovers. The present colony of Belize (British Honduras) traces its origin to seventeenth- and eighteenth-century English settlement along its coast. Such activity might be considered a western extension of England's political

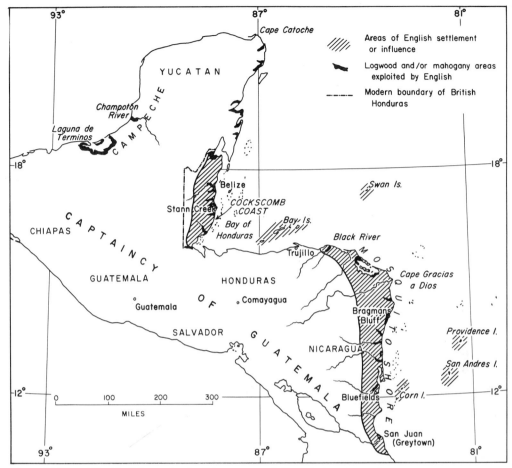

Figure 10.15 The English on the Caribbean coast of Central America and Mexico, seventeenth and eighteenth centuries

and economic interests from its holdings in the eastern Caribbean.

As early as the 1630s, English smugglers from Providence Island had established trade relations with the Miskito Indians and the sambos, or mixed Negro-Indians, on the Caribbean coast of Nicaragua. The sambos served as intermediaries in the profitable smuggling operations between the English and Spanish colonials, who were avid for cheap North European goods. About the same time, smuggling stations, called "stanns," were established along the western shore of the Bay of Honduras in an area called the "Cockscomb Coast," later to become British Honduras, or Belize. The sites of the modern towns of Belize City and Stann Creek were once occupied by such stations.

With the decline of piracy in the late seventeenth century, many of the English privateers and traders turned to the exploitation of logwood and mahogany, which abounded near the coast and inland along the river courses of the Miskito and Cockscomb shores. The heartwood of the logwood tree was a source of fast red and brown dyes and the most valuable product of the English-held coast of Central America. The main stands of logwood occurred along the shores of eastern Yucatan, exploited as far north as Cape Catoche, the northeastern extremity of the peninsula. The English log cutters and smugglers of this area soon came to be known as the "Baymen."

Although periodically harassed by small Spanish forces bent on ousting the British from the Gulf of Honduras, the Baymen of Belize, aided by their black slaves and Miskito Indian friends from Nicaragua, were able to establish a permanent hold along the Cockscomb Coast. When the supply of logwood was depleted, mahogany, which was fashionable in eighteenth-century Europe, became the main export from the Belize area. Finally, in 1862, the settlements of British Honduras were officially made a colony of the Empire.

Along the Miskito Shore during the late seventeenth and early eighteenth centuries, English trading "stanns" had been made at Bluefields, Cape Gracias a Dios, Bragman's Bluff (modern Puerto Cabezas), and along the Black River (Río Negro) in present Honduran territory. There was little logwood along this coast but, within the river forests that penetrate the interior savannas, mahogany was cut and sarsaparilla root gathered to be shipped to England. By mid-eighteenth century, a small agricultural colony had been started along Black River where, in 1761, nearly 200 Englishmen and 700 black slaves were cultivating sugar cane and tobacco. By

treaty with Spain, the British government withdrew the white settlers from the Miskito Shore in 1778. But later the area was organized as the native Kingdom of Mosquitía, with its traditional capital at San Juan del Norte (Greytown). This kingdom was a virtual British protectorate until 1856 and was not abolished until 1894, when it finally came under Nicaraguan authority. The long and cordial contact with Englishmen is still evident among the remaining Miskito Indians and the sambos, most of whom speak pidgin English and have a high regard for anyone of Anglo-Saxon descent.

The close of the eighteenth century saw another foreign cultural invasion on the Caribbean coast of Central America. In 1797, the British transferred some 5,000 troublesome Black Caribs (mixed black and Carib Indian) from the Lesser Antilles to the Bay Islands off Honduras. From there, these Carib-speaking mixbloods spread along the Honduran and Belizean coasts from Trujillo to Stann Creek, where today their descendants live as subsistence farmers and fishers.

SELECTED REFERENCES

BARRETT, W. J. *The Sugar Hacienda of the Marqueses del Valle.* Minneapolis: University of Minnesota Press, 1970.

BRADING, D. A., and CROSS, H. E. "Colonial Silver Mining: Mexico and Peru." *Hispanic American Historical Review* 52, no. 3 (1972): 545–79.

BRAND, D. D. "The Early History of the Range Cattle Industry in Northern Mexico." *Agricultural History* 35, no. 3 (1961):132–39.

CHEVALIER, F. *Land and Society in Colonial Mexico: The Great Hacienda.* Berkeley: University of California Press, 1963.

GIBSON, C. *The Aztecs under Spanish Rule.* Stanford, Calif.: Stanford University Press, 1964.

HUMBOLDT, A. DE. *Political Essay on the Kingdom of New Spain,* trans. John Black. London: Longman, Hurst, Rees, Orme, and Brown, 1811–1822.

KEITH, R. D. "Encomienda, Hacienda, and Corregimiento in Spanish America: A Structural Analysis." *Hispanic American Historical Review* 51, no. 3 (1971):431–46.

LEE, R. "Cochineal Production and Trade in New Spain to 1600." *The Americas* 4, no. 4 (1947–1948):449–73.

MACLEOD, M. J. *Spanish Central America: A Socioeconomic History, 1520–1720.* Berkeley: University of California Press, 1973.

PARSONS, J. J. "San Andres and Providencia: English-Speaking Islands in the Western

Caribbean." *University of California Publications in Geography* 12, no. 1 (1956):1–84.

RADELL, D. R., and PARSONS, J. J. "Realejo, a Forgotten Colonial Port and Ship-building Center in Nicaragua." *Hispanic American Historical Review* 51 no. 2 (1971):295–312.

SANDOVAL, F. B. *La Industria del Azúcar en Nueva España*. Mexico, D.F.: Instituto de la Historia, 1951.

SIMPSON, L. B. *The Encomienda in New Spain: The Beginning of Spanish Mexico*. 3rd ed. Berkeley: University of California Press, 1966.

———. *Exploitation of Land in Central Mexico in the Sixteenth Century*. Ibero-Americana, no. 36. Berkeley: University of California Press, 1952.

SMITH, R. S. "Indigo Production and Trade in Colonial Guatemala." *Hispanic American Historical Review* 39, no. 2 (1959):181–211.

WEST, R. C. *The Mining Community in Northern New Spain: The Parral Mining District*. Ibero-Americana, no. 30. Berkeley: University of California Press, 1949.

≡ 11 ≡

The People and Economy
of Modern Mexico

The foundations of Mexico's present geographical personality lie deep in its Indian and colonial past. True, the last 100 years, and especially the last 40, have brought great changes. Paved highways, diesel-powered trains, mechanized farms, modern cities, industrial suburbs, and rich oil fields impress the traveler. But never far away from such patches of modern Western life are the fields and villages that evoke the colonial period of which they are still a part. The varied cultural landscape of present-day Mexico is an Indian and colonial Spanish one on which an uneven veneer of modern European and North American materialism has been superimposed. Mexico, like so many other developing countries, is in a state of cultural transition that is reflected in the geographical scene.

Our purpose in this chapter is to describe and explain the more significant changes that have occurred in the Mexican landscape during the last 100 years. Many factors underlie these changes, but these are the outstanding ones: (1) the Mexican Revolution of 1910 and the breakup of the large landed estates; (2) the postrevolutionary explosive increase in population which, in a country with a paucity of arable land, has resulted in large rural-to-urban migrations that have intensified the growth of cities; (3) the geographical proximity of the United States and the concomitant ease of cultural borrowing and availability of technical knowledge and financial aid; and (4) the governmental policy to modernize the country's economy, especially agriculture, industry, and transportation and to upgrade the living standard of the Mexican people. As a force of change the latter factor may be the most significant. Mexico's centralized, oligarchical, and essentially one-party form of government maintains powerful control over the formulation and implementation of the nation's economic and social goals. As in most countries with a centralized political system, in Mexico, government action is an increasingly important factor in the changes that occur in the cultural landscape.

HISTORICAL SUMMARY
OF THE POST-INDEPENDENCE
PERIOD

Mexico's history since the close of the colonial era has been characterized by two periods of political turmoil, each followed by a phase of relative quiescence. In periods of political upheaval, the economy stagnated. With stability, it expanded; economic and social changes were effected; and the geographical landscape was transformed.

Beginning with the Wars of Independence (1810–1821), Mexico suffered nearly 70 years of intermittent political and military strife. Periodic civil wars, the Texan War (1836), war with the United States (1845–1847), and the French Intervention (1862–1867) made a shambles of economic and social progress. Although a scheme of land reform was devised by the patriot Benito Juárez in 1857, it could not be effected, and little change occurred in the colonial pattern that still dominated the economy and the landscape.

The dictatorship of Porfirio Díaz (1877–1910) gave Mexico a semblance of stability for the first time since the days of the Spanish viceroys. These 34 years of peace, often called the *Pax Porfiriana,* saw the beginning of the North American and European technological importations that have so greatly influenced present-day Mexico. The Díaz regime welcomed foreign investment and technology to build the country's railroad network, revive the declining mines with modern techniques and management, exploit the large petroleum reserves, and begin modern manufacturing. At this time, Mexico established close commercial ties with the United States, with which it still maintains the bulk of its foreign trade. In addition, the government encouraged the cultivation of new commercial crops, such as coffee in Veracruz and Chiapas, and henequen in Yucatan. In other respects, the colonial economic and social patterns of Mexico continued, and even expanded, during the *Pax Porfiriana.* The large estates become larger, although the influence of the Church declined. Most of the remaining Indian communal lands were usurped by the rich *hacendados;* Díaz gave away to foreigners and personal friends much of the public domain; and the poverty-ridden rural class became even more deeply enmeshed in the debt peonage system of colonial times.

The despotism of the Díaz regime and the problem of land distribution underlay the Revolution, which erupted toward the close of 1910. Until the late 1920s rival armies and bandit groups, led by political aspirants from the Hispanic north and by rebelling native caciques in the Indian south, periodically ravaged the country. Mexican economy slowed to a halt, and the population was reduced by warfare, starvation, and emigration. But out of this chaos came a social and economic revolution that is still in progress. The most fundamental change was the beginning of land reform—dissolution of the large estates and the reapportionment of the land into collectivized units or small parcels distributed among the poor rural population. The revolutionary government also recognized the labor unions, which were trying to better the wages, working conditions, and social security of the urban proletariat. A framework of public education was established, and the concept of gradual nationalization of the country's basic industries became a political tenet. The semisocialistic state that is present-day Mexico grew out of the Revolution of 1910.

From 1930 to the present, Mexico has enjoyed an unprecedented period of peace and stable national development, a period of rapid economic and social change as well as of fantastic population growth. The tempo of land reform, urbanization, industrialization, highway development, and colonization of new lands has steadily increased.

All these factors have helped change the face of many parts of the country. Perhaps the greatest change of landscape has taken place (1) in the arid north, where agricultural production has been greatly expanded through large-scale government-constructed irrigation projects and through mechanization; (2) in various parts of the tropical lowlands, where the government has recently opened large areas to colonization through drainage, irrigation, and road-construction projects; and (3) in various urban centers throughout the country, where large industrial suburbs have mushroomed. Poverty is still the country's most pressing problem, however, especially in the heavily populated heartland of Mexico—the Mesa Central and the southern highlands. One-third of Mexico's 50 million people live on a bare subsistence level, ill fed, ill housed, and ill clothed, and 25 percent of the population above the age of ten is still illiterate, despite a vigorous educational program of many years standing.

THE MEXICAN PEOPLE

Since the close of the colonial period, changes of varying degree have occurred in the number, distribution, movements, and ethnic composition of the Mexican people. The population patterns of the eighteenth century continued without any appreciable change for almost 100 years after Independence while Mexico awaited the twentieth century.

Numbers and Density

One of the important developments in modern Mexico is the recent growth of population. Figure 11.1 shows that at the time of Independence (1821), Mexico's population was only 6.5 million, much less than before the Conquest. When the Rev-

olution of 1910 began, the population had increased to 15 million. Today, the number has more than tripled, to 48.4 million (1970 census). Like other countries of Middle America, Mexico's population is growing about 3.4 percent annually. This is one of the fastest rates of human growth of any area on earth. It means an increase in the Mexican population of about two million people in every year of the decade 1970–1980. At the present rate of increase, Mexico will have more than 70 million inhabitants by 1980 and over 135 million by the year 2000. Future increase may be even greater than estimated, for half the country's people are under 20 years of age, with a large potential for population growth.

This great increase began in the 1930s and reached its present rate just after World War II. This is the period during which the populations of practically all developing countries "exploded" to the point of serious shortages of food supply and living space. The reason for the rapid growth in Mexico has not been increased fertility, for the Mexican birth rate has always been high, but rather a drastic decrease in the death rate, especially of infants, through the introduction of preventive medicine and increased sanitation measures. Moreover, the former killers in the tropics, yellow fever and malaria, can now be controlled with DDT sprays. The improved health of the Mexican people and the resulting population increase can

Figure 11.1   Population growth in Mexico, 1790–1970

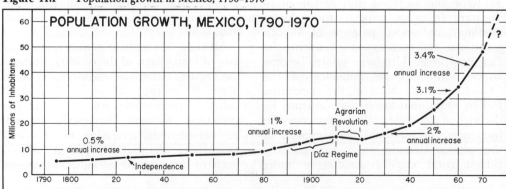

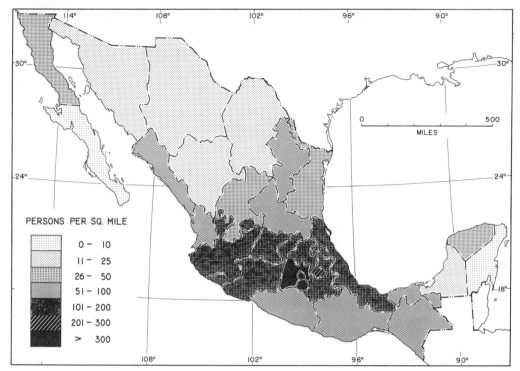

Figure 11.2   Population density of Mexico, 1970

be attributed in large part to the federal government's program of socialized medicine, begun in the 1930s.

The population boom of the last four decades has increased Mexico's overall density from 22 persons per square mile in 1930 to 65 in 1970 (the population density of coterminous United States is 68). Overall density figures, however, are misleading. The ratio of people to arable land yields a more realistic picture of potential food production per capita. Mexico has a density of about 520 persons per square mile of arable land; the United States, 290. Figure 11.2 indicates that most of the Mexican people are concentrated in the central part of the country, as they were during the colonial period.

In the Mesa Central and adjacent escarpments, densities of rural population by states range from 100 to well over 300 persons per square mile. In some sections of the plateau surface once favored by exceptionally fertile soils and plentiful water for irrigation, rural population densities exceed 500 and even 1,000 persons

per square mile, equaling some of the maximum farming area densities in Southeast Asia. Such is the area in Tlaxcala state, around the northwestern base of Malinche Volcano and extending into the Cholula-Huejotzingo plain on the western edge of Puebla Basin. Similar densities occur in the southern part of the Valley of Mexico, within the ancient chinampa farming area around Xochimilco and in Toluca Basin near the headwaters of the Lerma River (Figure 11.3). The concentration of people around the basin rims within the Mesa Central expresses an old population pattern that goes back to colonial and even pre-Conquest times. Today, overpopulation and rural poverty in the Mesa Central, the traditional core of the country, are the roots of Mexico's greatest social and economic problems.

In contrast to the densely occupied Mesa Central, the rugged southern part of the country (states of Guerrero, Oaxaca, and Chiapas) have only moderate overall population densities (about 55 persons per square mile). Within the mountainous ter-

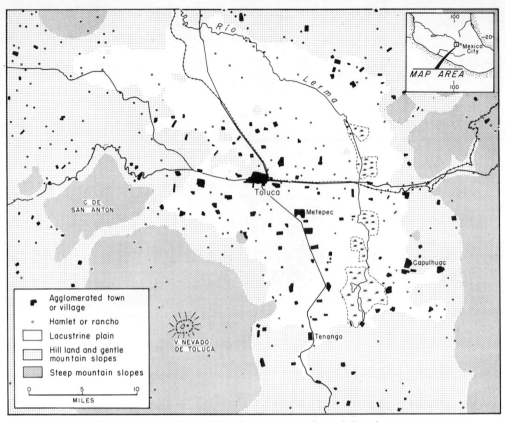

Figure 11.3 Settlement pattern of the Valley of Toluca, Mesa Central. Rural population densities between Toluca City and Tenango range from 500 to more than 1,000 people per square mile.

rain, people are unevenly distributed, many large areas being almost uninhabited, while in the highland valleys, such as that of Oaxaca, densities may be over 100 persons per square mile. Except for its well-settled northern part, the forest-covered Yucatan Peninsula and the adjacent Petén of northern Guatemala form one of the empty areas (*despoblados*) of Middle America that have densities ranging from less than 3 to only 11 persons per square mile.

As in colonial and pre-Conquest times, dry northern Mexico is distinguished from the rest of the country by its sparse population. Average densities of less than 20 persons per square mile characterize most of the dry northwest, and there are only 4 persons per square mile in the arid territory of Baja California. Since the 1930s, however, the opening of irrigation districts

and increasing industrialization have drawn many people from the Mesa Central into the north. Overall population densities of over 40 persons per square mile now occur in the northeastern states of Nuevo León and Tamaulipas; densities as high as 100 are not uncommon in the oases, such as the Laguna District in southwestern Coahuila and the irrigated river deltas of the Sonora and Sinaloa coastal lowlands. Even the state of Baja California (northern half of the peninsula) now has a density of nearly 32 persons per square mile.

Population Movements

Since the Revolution of 1910, there has been a great increase in the mobility of the Mexican people. The breakup of the hacienda system, which bound a large part of the rural population to the estate as indentured laborers, enabled people to move about more freely. Growing industrialization and improved transport have also increased the mobility of the population. But more important, the great population pressure that has developed in the Mesa Central since the 1920s has induced movements of rural folk to (1) the less densely settled farming areas and petroleum fields within the country; (2) the cities, especially the capital; and (3) the United States, as either seasonal or permanent immigrants.

Although significant numbers of poor farmers from the Mesa Central have migrated to the northern irrigated districts and the tropical coastal areas, these movements have not appreciably decreased the population pressure within the core areas. Even many of the northern oases are now overpopulated, and new irrigation districts are not being opened rapidly enough to absorb the growing local population. In the northeast, the opening of oil and gas fields in Tamaulipas, the exploitation of coal deposits in the Sabinas Basin (Coahuila), and the increasing industrialization of Nuevo León and Coahuila have attracted many migrants from central Mexico. Moreover, since the 1950s, government-sponsored colonization of the tropical lowlands has drawn some highlanders to the Tepalcatepec Basin in southern Michoacán, the lowlands of Nayarit and Colima, and the Papaloapan Valley in southern Veracruz. Even in the Tabasco lowland, once a sparsely occupied, disease-ridden land, growing petroleum production and agricultural developments are now attracting population.

The most significant movement of Mexican population in recent years has been from the rural areas to the cities. Most of these migrants have poured directly from the countryside into Mexico City and its extended metropolitan area. Others have gone to the larger state capitals, especially to those with industry, such as Guadala-

jara, Puebla, and Monterrey. Still others are attracted to the rapidly growing cities along the Mexican–United States border, where there may be local jobs and, they hope, a chance to enter the United States for temporary employment. These rural migrants are mainly young people, discouraged by the lack of opportunity and poor living conditions in the countryside. They flock into the cities in such numbers that they have created serious housing and sanitation problems, as well as unemployment. The ramshackle slums around the edges of Mexico City and other large centers are adequate testimony of this growing urban problem that stems from the pressure of a rural population chiefly within the central part of the country. Such problems, as well as the Mexican city in general, are treated more fully further on in this chapter in the section on urbanization and urban growth.

The pressure of population in central Mexico has not only set up currents of migration within the country, but also has induced emigration to the United States. At present, nearly one million Mexican citizens reside across the border, and each year 250,000 more apply for resident visas, only a fraction of which are granted. The disturbed political conditions during the revolutionary period and the present economic depression in many rural areas have been the main reasons for the outward flow of Mexicans. The permanent Mexican migrants to the United States have gone to the cities (especially to Los Angeles, where more than a half-million now live) and to many rural areas of the Southwest. Mexican nationals and United States citizens of Mexican descent now comprise the bulk of the permanent farming population of extreme southern Texas, between the international border and San Antonio.

Until recently another type of Mexican migrant to the United States was the seasonal farmhand, or bracero, who was legally contracted as a worker on United States farms and plantations during the harvest period. Seasonal labor migrations from Mexico to the United States started on an unofficial basis after 1910, but this was followed by the controlled, contract labor, based on international agreement, which began on a large scale during World War II when the United States was short of farm workers. During the period 1951–1960, each spring between 200,000 and 450,000 braceros were legally contracted to work on the irrigated truck farms and orchards of the Southwest and the Pacific coast, in the beet fields of Colorado and Michigan, in the cotton farms of Texas, and in other agricultural areas. Many thousands of Mexicans (called wetbacks) also crossed the border illegally to find seasonal work. Most of the braceros and wetbacks came from the overpopulated Mesa Central, especially from the states of Michoacán, Jalisco, and Guanajuato, but many also came from the northern states of Chihuahua and Durango, the irrigated sections of which are now overpopulated. In many remote rural sections of central Mexico, there is hardly a village where one cannot find one or two men who have worked in the United States. In 1964, the international agreement to continue the labor contracts was terminated.

The dollars that the braceros sent home to their families were an important source of income and foreign exchange for Mexico. Equally significant was the knowledge of North American agricultural techniques and of modern Western ways that the Mexican worker took back to his country. The acculturating influence of the bracero is difficult to measure, but it has undoubtedly aided bits of North American culture to penetrate even the remotest villages of central Mexico.

Despite the demise of the bracero program, many Mexican workers continue to enter the United States. In 1969, for example, 116,000 came as nonmigrants with temporary status, most of whom were employed illegally on farms, in service establishments, and in industry, chiefly within the American Southwest. An increasingly larger number (350,000 in 1971) cross the border illegally each year. Most of these are quickly apprehended and returned to Mexico.

Race and Language

Since the close of the colonial period, the mixbloods, or mestizos, have gradually become the dominant racial element in Mexico. At present the population is estimated to be about 60 percent mestizo, 30 percent Indian, and 10 percent white. More than half the Mexicans were pure-blooded Indians in 1810, but the gradual breakdown of the aboriginal community by improved communication and interracial marriage, has been accelerating their decrease. By the end of this century the proportion may be greatly reduced from its present 30 percent. For more than a century, the white element of Mexico has remained a nearly constant 10 percent of the total population, while the black blood has been almost wholly absorbed into the mestizo majority.

Mexico's Indians. In Mexico, as in most parts of Latin America where advanced aboriginal culture prevailed before the Conquest, the remnant Indian population presents a serious social and economic problem. Owing chiefly to the social stigma that the Spaniards and their descendants have attached to Indian life, the Mexican Indians are usually at the bottom of the economic scale and have the lowest living standards in the country. Since the Revolution of 1910, however, the Mexican government has attempted to improve the lot of the Indian through land reform, special educational programs, and health measures.

It should be emphasized that, in most parts of Latin America, an Indian is defined much more in cultural terms than in racial terms. In Mexico, a person is considered to be Indian if he speaks an aboriginal language (though he may also speak Spanish), if he practices more aboriginal than European customs and uses more Indian than European tools, and if he thinks of himself as an Indian living within a recognized aboriginal community apart from his mestizo or white neighbors. Thus, a mixblood who conforms to these norms is considered an Indian, while pure-blood aboriginals who no longer speak their language and have adopted predominately European ways are considered to be mestizos. Since many of the culture traits are hard to measure, government officials have usually taken language as the main criterion for determining the Indian population of Mexico.

In Mexico today, about 40 different native languages are spoken by nearly 3.2 million people (only 6.6 percent of the entire population), and two-thirds of these also speak Spanish. From 1900 to 1940, Indian-language speakers comprised about 15 percent of the population, but in the years following, this proportion decreased drastically, mainly because the non-Indians are increasing at a far greater rate than the aboriginals. Moreover, as the Indians

come into closer contact with modern Mexican culture, they are slowly discarding their native tongues. The decrease in the number of monolinguals (Indians who speak no Spanish), from 1.2 million, in 1930, to about 0.8 million, in 1970, has prompted some students of Mexican population to predict that the monolingual Indian will have disappeared by the year 2000.

Of the large number of aboriginal tongues still spoken in Mexico, only ten are used by groups of more than 50,000. Nahuatl, or Mexicano, the language of the Aztecs, is spoken by about 600,000 people scattered in fragmented groups in the east-central part of the country. Maya is spoken by 300,000 people in Yucatan. Zapotec (200,000) and Mixtec (185,000) are the main languages of the Indians of Oaxaca state. Otomí (185,000) is heard in the eastern section of the Mesa Central, north and northwest of Mexico City and Totonac (100,000) in northern Veracruz and Puebla states.

Figure 11.4, which shows areas of high concentration of aboriginal speech, also indicates the predominately Indian areas of Mexico and Central America. Almost

Figure 11.4   Areas of Indian speech concentration in Mexico and northern Central America

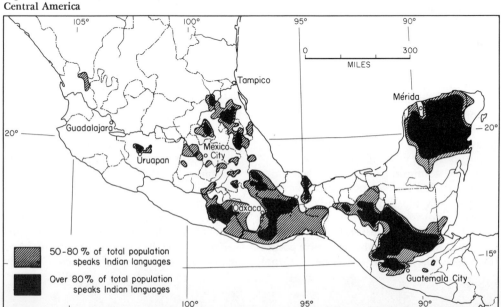

the entire present Indian population is concentrated within the bounds of ancient Mesoamerica, the most populous part of Middle America before the Conquest. In Mexico and Guatemala, the present distribution of predominately Indian speech corresponds with the ancient Aztec and Mayan areas.

Today there are four outstanding Indian areas in Mexico: (1) the eastern Mesa Central and adjacent escarpments in which reside the fragmented aboriginal groups; (2) the rugged Sierra Madre and Mesa del Sur of Oaxaca and eastern Guerrero; (3) the Chiapas highlands of southeastern Mexico, which can be considered a western appendage of the Guatemalan highland Indian area; and (4) the northern Yucatan Peninsula, where Maya speech is concentrated. Within these areas live over 95 percent of Mexico's Indians. The only significant groups outside these areas are the Tarascans of Michoacán, the small Cora and Huichol groups of Nayarit, and the Tarahumar Indians in the Sierra Madre Occidental of Chihuahua.

Except for the Maya of Yucatan, most of the Mexican Indians occupy isolated mountainous areas where modern transport is poorly developed or nonexistent and where there is extremely limited agricultural potential. The Yucatan Peninsula, though a plains area, is covered by poor, thin soils, and until quite recently was an isolated cultural island only loosely attached politically to Mexican territory. In the more accessible and fertile areas of Mexico, the Spaniards and mestizos pushed out or assimilated the Indians. Thus, most of Mexico's aborigines now occupy refuge areas that are usually characterized by isolation, poverty, and high death rates. Difficulty of communication encourages the retention of old ways and discourages the entry of new ideas from outside.

The recent aim of the Mexican government has been to acculturate the remaining Indians sufficiently to incorporate them into the national life. The National Indian Institute (*Instituto Nacional Indigenista*), created in 1948, has established various educational centers in key Indian areas. Schools, roads, hospitals, and economic aid will in time destroy the remaining vestiges of ancient life. But, until that is accomplished, the Indian areas, with their steep hillside fields, their scattered *rancheria* settlements, and their picturesque markets and wares, will remain an integral part of the Mexican landscape.

Mexico's White Population. The comparatively small white group, less than 10 percent of the population, descends from Spanish colonial families and from European or North American immigrants who entered the country within the last century. As in colonial times, most of the whites live in the cities, forming the core of the remaining aristocracy and of the urban professional groups.

Mexico has received few white immigrants since the close of the colonial period, for political, economic, and social conditions within the country have not been favorable. During the nineteenth century, a few Europeans and North Americans came to central Mexico to form agricultural colonies, but most of these were unsuccessful. More successful were various religious groups, such as the Mennonites, who formed farming colonies in sparsely settled areas of the north (see Chapter 12).

Besides these few agricultural colonists, there have been some individual Europeans, especially Germans and Spaniards, who have entered Mexican city life as merchants, professionals, and intellectuals, contributing a cultural influence out of proportion to their small numbers. Particularly significant to modern Mexican arts and letters was the influx of refugees from the Spanish Civil War (1936–1938), among whom were outstanding Castilian and Catalonian professors, artists, and writers. Most individual European immigrants have settled in Mexico City, but

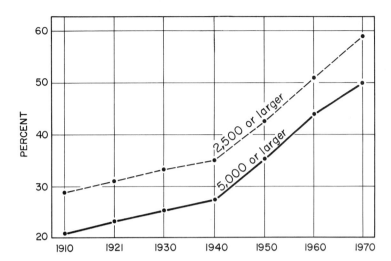

Figure 11.5 Degree of urbanization in Mexico, 1910–1970

URBANIZATION AND URBAN GROWTH

Like the inhabitants of many developing countries, today Mexicans are rapidly changing from a dominantly rural society to an urban one. About half of Mexico's people now live in towns and cities of over 5,000 population. This is approximately the urban population, for in Mexico most localities of less than 5,000 people are agricultural villages with few commercial or other urban functions.[1] In 1970, about 37 percent of the country's inhabitants lived in large cities of more than 50,000 population. (In the United States,

1. The Mexican Census Bureau (*Dirección General de Estadística*), like that of the United States, considers places of over 2,500 people as urban. According to this definition, 58.5 percent of the Mexican population was urban in 1970, versus 73.5 percent for the United States. In Mexico, however, this is an unrealistic definition, because so many of the farming villages are large. Most students of Mexican demography use 5,000, 10,000, or even 15,000 as the population that distinguishes urban from rural settlements. The United Nations has defined an urban place as one that has 20,000 or more people.

58 percent of the people live in cities of similar size.) Mexico's degree of urbanization (the percentage of urban to total population) is now approaching that of developed countries.

The city has been an integral part of Mexican life since pre-Conquest times, but until recently a relatively small part of the population was urban. As late as 1930, only 25 percent of the people could be so classified according to the definition given above. Figure 11.5 shows that the degree of urbanization began to increase rapidly after 1940, and this was due mainly to the large-scale exodus from the countryside. Mexico's present growth rate of urban population (6.3 percent annually) is among the highest in the world. It is maintained as much through natural increase of city folk as by influx of rural migrants, which has actually diminished since 1960. The high birth rates characteristic of rural people are maintained in Mexican cities, especially among the first and second generation migrants. Moreover, infant mortality is less in the cities than in rural areas, owing to the more numerous free maternity clinics and greater availability of other kinds of socialized medicine in urban centers.

The most spectacular urban growth in the country has been that of Mexico City and its metropolitan area. In 1900, the federal capital, having a population of

Table 11.1 GROWTH OF THE NUMBER OF LARGE CITIES IN MEXICO, 1900–1970

Year	50,000–99,999 population	100,000–499,999 population	500,000–999,999 population	1,000,000 and over population	Total	Percentage of Total Population
	Number of Large Cities					
1900	4	2	0	0	6	5.3
1910	5	2	0	0	7	6.2
1921	7	1	1	0	9	8.6
1930	7	3	0	1	10	11.2
1940	9	5	0	1	15	13.9
1950	14	9	0	1	24	21.7
1960	23	14	2	1	40	29.7
1970 (estimated)	31	25 *	1 *	3	60	37.8

* The separate urban municipalities of Netzahualcoyotl (570,000 population), Tlalnepantla (350,000), Naucalpan (350,000), and Ecatepec (110,000), located on the periphery of the federal district, are included within the population for the Mexico City metropolitan area.

345,000, contained but 2.5 percent of the Mexican people; in 1970, with 8.3 million inhabitants in its metropolitan area, it had nearly 17 percent. The next largest cities (Guadalajara, 1.5 million; Monterrey, 1.2 million; and Puebla, 500,000) fall much below the Mexico City metropolis. This type of disproportionately large city, which is the political, economic, and social center of the country, is one of the most characteristic features of Latin American urbanization. Such an urban structure is called *primate*. The primacy of Mexico City, however, goes back to the centralized government of colonial times and to the social prestige of its capital seat, but during this century its position has been strengthened by industrialization and the influx of people from rural areas. With the recent rise of other cities in the country having a population of one million or more, the primacy of Mexico City is now diminishing; for that reason, according to some, the country's urban structure may be said to be approaching an "intermediate" type.[2]

2. For 1970, Guatemala City's index of primacy (see Chapter 5, *n.* 3) was 7.1; Mexico City's, 2.6; and New York City's, 0.7. In 1900, Mexico City's index of primacy was 1.5; by 1950 it had risen to a maximum of 2.9.

Table 11.1 indicates another index of urbanization in Mexico—the increase in the number of large cities, especially since 1950. Growth has been striking in the number of urban centers in the 100,000–499,999 rank. Since 1940, they have quintupled in number, and since 1960 they have doubled. From 1940 to 1970 the number of all cities over 50,000 quadrupled.

Mexico now has 60 cities of over 50,000 people and 29 with over 100,000. A third of these (22), which include many of the nation's largest urban centers, are clustered in the Mesa Central and adjacent escarpments (Figure 11.6); together they contain one-fourth of Mexico's total population. Many were founded in colonial times as Spanish *villas,* and since then they have served as regional administrative and market centers. The population of the Mesa Central, however, is still mainly rural, despite the presence of many cities (Figures 11.7 and 11.8). Well-urbanized areas are scattered and include the Valley of Mexico, the western section of Puebla Basin, portions of Jalisco state, and much of the Bajío of Guanajuato. Some demographers have predicted that, if urban growth in the Mesa Central continues at its present rate, by the year 2000

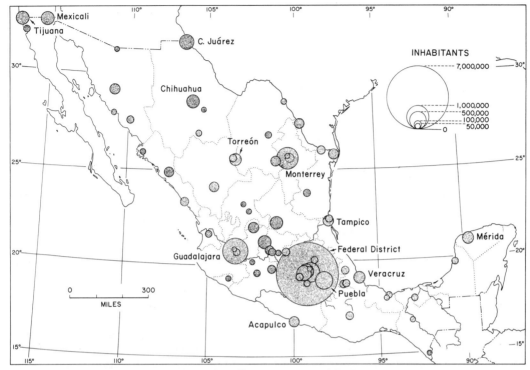

Figure 11.6   Large urban centers in Mexico, 1970. Only centers of 50,000 people and over are shown.

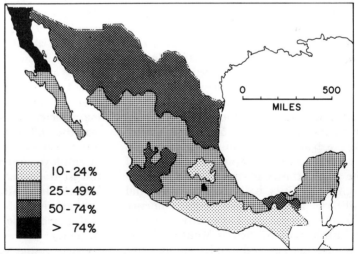

Figure 11.7   Percentage of total population living in cities of 5,000 people or more, 1960

10 - 24%
25 - 49%
50 - 74%
> 74%

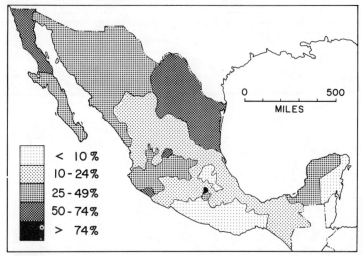

< 10 %
10 - 24 %
25 - 49 %
50 - 74 %
> 74 %

Figure 11.8   Percentage of total population living in cities of 15,000 people or more, 1960

a large megalopolis, or nearly continuous urbanized zone, will have formed between Puebla and Guadalajara. Even today there are indications of this development along the main east–west transportation axis between these two cities, with Mexico City as the central core. Along this east–west axis of highways and railroads, industrial and residential suburbs are spreading outward from the main urban centers, engulfing smaller towns in their wake.

Even more of the large cities (26), many of which have grown from small towns during the last three decades, are found dispersed throughout northern Mexico. Indeed, except for the Valley of Mexico, the arid northern border states today form Mexico's most urbanized region, where more than half the population lives in places of more than 5,000 inhabitants. The urban tradition of the north stems from the colonial period, when most of the population was concentrated in mining communities, oasis market towns, and military administrative establishments. Today, some of the larger cities include industrial centers, such as Monterrey, and regional market and service points, like Torreón (230,000 inhabitants) and Chihuahua City (290,000).

The most phenomenal urban growth in northern Mexico has occurred at the major crossing points along the United States–Mexico border. At these strategic places urban centers have developed on each side of the international boundary, forming twin cities. In all cases but one (Tijuana–San Diego metropolitan area), the Mexican twin is larger than its United States counterpart (Figure 11.9). The combined area of the two often forms an impressive urban sprawl. For example, the El Paso, Texas–Ciudad Juárez twins comprise a population of over 750,000, covering about 55 square miles of urbanized area. Almost all the Mexican border points grew from small towns of less than 20,000 people to large cities of over 100,000 between 1940 and 1970. The main factor behind this rapid expansion was the influx of migrants from the interior seeking work in the United States or employment based on the international tourist trade that boomed in all Mexican border cities after World War II. The combination of large, expanding cities and active trade at the eight major ports of entry has made the United States–Mexico border one of the most dynamic international frontiers in the world today.

The least urbanized part of Mexico is

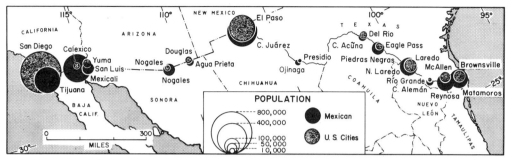

Figure 11.9   Twin cities along the United States–Mexican border, 1970

the Indian south, where to date there has been limited economic development. Although Figures 11.7 and 11.8 show much of the Yucatan Peninsula as having a fair degree of urbanization, most of the Mayan towns between 5,000 and 15,000 inhabitants function chiefly as large farming villages. Mérida (230,000) is the only large city of the region. Less then 10 percent of the population in the southern highlands of Oaxaca and Guerrero states live in cities of more than 15,000 inhabitants. The largest city of that area is Acapulco (175,000), an international resort, which does not function as a regional urban center.

Because they have grown so rapidly, Mexican cities have their full share of urban problems. Overcrowding among low-income groups; traffic congestion in narrow streets; frequent inadequacy of urban services, such as water supply and sewage disposal; and ground and air pollution are some of the ills suffered in varying degrees by most of the larger urban centers.

The influx of migrants has often resulted in the formation of squatter settlements on the urban fringe. Such shanty towns, composed of ill-constructed one-room dwellings, and lacking sanitation facilities, are common around most large cities in developing countries the world over. The vast slums on the eastern periphery of Mexico City that occupy the dry bed of Lake Texcoco are said to harbor over a million people. Similar conditions on a smaller scale are found in most of the northern border cities, but are less common in some of the older interior centers where in-migration has not been so great. Slum conditions are also developing in old central cores of some cities where commercial activity has moved outward along main traffic arteries in a pattern similar to that of North American cities. Despite the appalling living conditions in the slums, the Mexican city dweller seems to tolerate them without undue social unrest or despair. Perhaps because of their greater "proximity tolerance," Mexicans and others of Latin or aboriginal descent appear to accept overcrowding better than do North Americans. Oscar Lewis, in his book *The Children of Sánchez* (1961) described graphically the social effects of such conditions on a Mexican migrant family in Mexico City.

Increased numbers of motor vehicles, especially the diesel-burning trucks and public buses, have been the curse of Mexican cities, with their narrow, easily congested streets. One who has visited Mexico does not easily forget the impossible traffic jams and the murky air heavily polluted with exhaust fumes that develop in the larger cities. The air of Mexico City, for example, has the highest carbon monoxide level of any metropolis in the world. In most Mexican cities plagued by air pollution, exhaust emissions from motor vehicles contribute well over half the contaminants.

Because of the various problems that have arisen from the extraordinary growth of the larger Mexican cities, the federal government is now taking an active role in urban planning. In part to direct population away from the metropolitan areas, the government has planned the creation of new cities in different parts of the country, but especially in the Mesa Central. Such urban planning must necessarily be closely correlated with related economic (mainly industrial) development through government control.

MEXICO'S ECONOMY IN THE NINETEENTH AND TWENTIETH CENTURIES

Despite the recent surge of industrialization and urbanization, Mexico is still an agrarian country. Today half of the economically active people are engaged in farming. About half of these farmers eke out a bare subsistence by growing maize and beans on worn-out soils with tools not much improved over those of the eighteenth century.

Since the Díaz regime, commercial agriculture has developed at an increasing tempo. Irrigated cotton and tropical crops such as coffee and sugar are grown on some of the best lands. Stock raising is carried on in much the same way and in the same areas as in colonial times, but the livestock market has shifted from the mining centers to the United States. Mining, so important during the colonial period, has declined. Mexico is no longer the world's leading producer of silver, and the old mines are now yielding more lead and zinc than precious metals. Moreover, interest in mineral exploitation has shifted to the petroleum, natural gas, and sulphur reserves of the Gulf coast lowlands.

Some of the greatest changes in Mexico's economy have come within the last 30 years, with the rise of large-scale indus-try and tourism. In the future, increasing industrialization may reorient the entire economic structure of the country. The tourist trade, Mexico's newest addition to its economy, has been partly responsible for various landscape changes, including a large network of paved highways and resort centers.

The Agricultural Economy

Although farming is its basic economic activity, Mexico is poorly endowed with arable land. Two-thirds of the country is mountainous, and one-half is too arid to produce crops without irrigation. Today a meager 12 percent of Mexican territory is cropland. In any given year between 5 and 7 percent of the total land surface is harvested, depending on weather conditions. Government officials believe that, by expanding irrigated areas in the north and developing the tropical lowlands, between 15 and 20 percent of the total land surface can be made arable. Mexico is rapidly reaching the limit of its area suitable for cultivation.

More than three-fourths of the land now cultivated is dependent on seasonal rains; one-twentieth is considered to be sufficiently moist to produce crops even in the dry season; and less than one-fifth is irrigated.

As indicated in Figure 11.10, the larger part of the cultivated land is concentrated in the country's heartland, or the Mesa Central, where the fertile soils of the volcanic basins and the usually sufficient summer rains afford an adequate physical basis for growing the traditional Mexican food crops. As one might expect, Figure 11.10 almost duplicates the patterns on the map of population densities (Figure 11.2). Within the states that comprise the Mesa Central, an average of 10 to 25 percent of the total land surface is cultivated; in the small state of Tlaxcala, more than 40 percent of the surface is tilled. In most

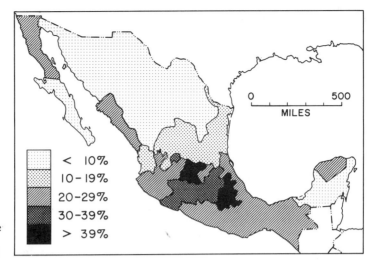

Figure 11.10 Percentage of total area planted, cultivated, and fallow, 1960

< 10%
10 - 19%
20 - 29%
30 - 39%
> 39%

parts of the densely peopled heartland, almost all the arable land has been farmed for hundreds of years. However, since the colonial period, overcropping and the unwise use of the plow have caused depletion and erosion of the soil. Over wide areas of once fertile soils derived from the weathering of volcanic ash, sheet erosion has exposed underlying layers of limey hardpan, called *tepetate,* which renders the land useless for cultivation. The gutted lands of overpopulated Tlaxcala are probably the worst examples of this process. In other sections of the plateau and adjacent escarpments, as well as in many valleys of the Oaxaca highlands, disastrous gullying has transformed former corn fields and pastures into useless badlands (Figure 11.11).

The areas of Mexico having the least arable and cultivated land are the arid north and the forested, tropical lowlands of the southeast. In the plains of northern Yucatan and the mountainous southern highlands (Oaxaca, Guerrero, and Chiapas), percentages of farmed land are much lower than in the Mesa Central. This is because of the broken terrain, the poor soils, and the predominance of slash-burn techniques, which utilize a relatively small amount of arable land in a given year.

Two fundamental changes in Mexican

Figure 11.11 Serious gulley erosion near Nochixtlán, Oaxaca highlands. Plow cultivation on slopes has induced the destruction of most of the tillable surface shown in this scene. Only small patches suitable for growing maize remain.

agriculture have been initiated during recent decades. One has been social and political in nature, involving changes in land tenure—the fall of the hacienda system and the redistribution of land to peasant farmers. The other is a technical change that began about 1930, involving the introduction of modern European and North American farming techniques, such as large-scale irrigation, mechanization, the use of commercial fertilizers, and the planting of improved crop strains. While changes in land tenure permeate all of Mexico, the technological changes have so far occurred only in a few places, chiefly in the north.

Mexican Land Systems. The colonial hacienda reached its greatest development in Mexico during the last quarter of the nineteenth century. By 1910, 8,245 haciendas covered 40 percent of the country's area. Ninety-six percent of the rural families owned no land, and the majority of the landless worked as virtual serfs (*peones de campo*) on the big estates. As in colonial times, the haciendas were seldom smaller than 2,500 acres, and most were self-sufficient. Much arable land was left uncultivated because the hacienda system was based as much on social prestige as on economic production. Through means both legal and illegal, the hacienda owners acquired the former church lands and usurped most of the Indian village properties that remained in the central part of the country. Many foreign individuals and land companies acquired vast tracts of territory, especially in the north. On the eve of the revolution, the hacienda had become the most conspicuous feature of the rural scene in Mexico.

Other Mexican land systems of the nineteenth century included (1) the rancho, or small private property of colonial origin; and (2) the few remaining Indian lands. The ranchos, 50 to 500 acres in size and operated by single mestizo or white families for subsistence, were scattered throughout the non-Indian areas of Mex-

ico. These small holdings normally occupied the less productive hill lands bordering the large haciendas, which controlled the best farming areas. Though they held a relatively small part of the land, the nineteenth century *rancheros* formed, as they do today, the nucleus of a Mexican middle-class rural society.

The unalienated communal Indian holdings, before the revolution, were chiefly in the isolated mountains of southern Mexico. Owing to misapplication of mid-nineteenth century land reforms, which sought to transfer communal property to private ownership, most of the more accessible Indian villages lost their lands to speculators and neighboring haciendas. Today the communal lands comprise only a small part of the country's total farm area. Nonetheless, the old Indian communal land organization served as a model for the present ejido land tenure system of Mexico.

Although the causes of the Revolution of 1910 are many and complex, the landless peasant's cry for land, liberty, and food was fundamental. Thus, one of the principal aims of the revolution was the expropriation of the large estates and the redistribution of the land among the rural proletariat. The redistribution program was promulgated by law in 1917, begun in 1922, and is still in progress. Under this program expropriated land may be given to agrarian communities having at least 20 eligible heads of families, usually the workers on the former hacienda or those who live in old or newly formed villages nearby. The government also apportions national lands in the same fashion. In either case, the holdings newly acquired by the community fall within the ejido type of land tenure.[3] In early years, an arable parcel, or plot, of 10 acres (4 hectares) of

3. By far most of the land reapportioned under the Mexican agrarian reform is done by this process, called "dotation." Other processes of redistribution include "restitution," by which village lands that the *hacendados* had taken illegally are restored to the rightful community; and "am-

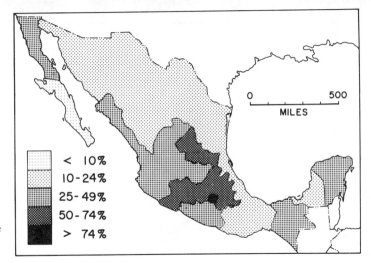

Figure 11.12 Percentage of total farm land in ejido holdings, 1960

< 10%
10-24%
25-49%
50-74%
> 74%

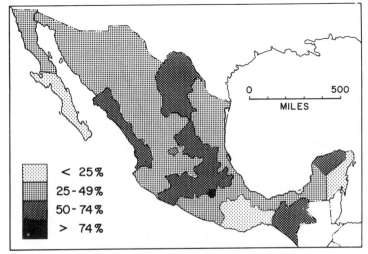

< 25%
25-49%
50-74%
> 74%

Figure 11.13 Percentage of total cropland in ejido holdings, 1960. The northern state of Coahuila ranks high mainly because of the extensive collective ejido lands in the Laguna area.

irrigated land or 20 acres (8 hectares) of seasonal land was to be provided for each of the community members (*ejidatarios*). Presently, the legal size of such parcels has been increased to 25 and 50 acres, respectively. in practice, however, hundreds of thousands of ejido families have plots of less than 10 acres, owing to insufficient land. In 1960, the average size of ejido cropland, per family head, was 17 acres.

There are two types of ejido land systems. One is the *individual* system, whereby a small unit of cropland (*parcela*) is tilled by an individual family. The ejidatario has only use rights to his parcel,

which is inheritable; but he cannot sell, lease, or mortgage it, and if he does not till it for two consecutive years, the plot may revert to the community and be reassigned. Pasture and woodland belonging to the community are used in common. These conditions are similar to those imposed under the ancient Aztec land system (*calpulalli*) and to the customs still observed in the Indian villages. The individual ejido system has been established throughout the country, but it is most common in central and southern Mexico, where it is best understood by the peasantry of Indian and mestizo descent and where subsistence farming predominates (Figures 11.12 and 11.13).

plification," by which village holdings are enlarged in cases where the original lands are insufficient for the needs of the community.

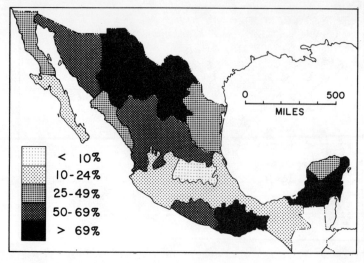

Figure 11.14   Percentage of total farm land in single holdings of 12,500 acres and over, 1960

< 10%
10 - 24%
25 - 49%
50 - 69%
> 69%

The second type of ejido system is called the *collective*. The community members do not till individual plots for family use, but work the land collectively. Theoretically, the proceeds of the harvests are apportioned among the ejidatarios, and those employed as farmhands are paid according to the type and amount of labor performed. The collective is well adapted to modern commercial agriculture, for mechanized cultivation of the large tracts, unencumbered by property lines, is possible. Only 3 percent of the ejido croplands, however, are of the collective type. The more successful ones are in the northern oases, such as the Laguna area of southwestern Coahuila and the Yaqui Valley of Sonora (where cotton and wheat are raised commercially), and in the sugar-producing districts of Los Mochis (Sinaloa) and El Mante (Tamaulipas). Other collectives include the henequen-producing area of northern Yucatan (formerly in large plantations) and the coffee area of Soconusco in southwestern Chiapas. Recently, collective ejidos based on stock raising, forestry, fishing, and tourism have been formed.

Nearly half of the cultivated land of Mexico has now been redistributed in ejidos. Most of the large haciendas have disappeared. However, relatively large holdings still prevail in the stock-raising area of the north, for grazing in desert scrub and semiarid grasslands necessitates extensive tracts (Figure 11.14). When a hacienda is expropriated, the government permits the owner to retain as private property a portion of his land, the maximum size depending on the use to which it is put.[4] Such land forms the residual estate, which is often called an ex-hacienda, or rancho.

The breakup of the large estates did not significantly change the agglomerated rural settlement pattern that typifies most of Mexico. When not retained by the owner, the hacienda headquarters (*casco*) sometimes became an ejido village inhabited by the former hacienda workers. Ejidatarios also have established many new agricultural villages on expropriated land. And, to many existing villages, the government has returned the lands that the *hacendados* usurped during the last century.

The reapportionment of land through the ejido system probably has not resulted in increased food production. The ejidatarios who have increased per-acre production of food crops are mainly those with irrigated land, as in the collectives in the northern oases and the individual

4. For example, a maximum of 250 acres of irrigated cropland may be retained or held privately; 500 acres of seasonal cropland; 375 acres for cotton; 750 acres for bananas, cacao, coffee, sugar cane, fruit trees, henequen, and so forth.

ejido parcels of the Bajío of Guanajuato. In 1960, only about one-third of the total value of farm products in Mexico came from ejido lands, in part because many individual ejidatarios, lacking the capital and technical knowledge needed to increase yields, produced just enough food to feed their families, as did their ancestors in ancient times. Moreover, the individual parcels are usually too small to raise surplus crops and are ill suited to mechanized cultivation. After expropriation of the estates was well under way in the 1930s, food production in Mexico fell, and only recently has the country been able to feed itself.

The agrarian reform, of course, has not been able to provide land to all rural families or to hold them on the land. Owing to decreased yields on overcropped soils and the inability to obtain credit to buy fertilizer and farm equipment, some farmers have abandoned their ejido plots. Furthermore, the grown children of the ejidatarios are often unable to obtain plots because there is no more land to distribute in their vicinity. Finally, for various reasons, many families have been ineligible to receive parcels. All such people make up much of the recent influx of the rural element to the cities and to the United States. It is estimated that today between 4 and 5 million Mexican peasants are still landless and eke out a precarious living as farmhands on private holdings.

The agrarian reform, however, has lessened the evils of the stagnant economy inherent in the semifeudal hacienda system by creating the ejido tenure system and the small private holdings. More important, by abolishing debt peonage, the reform has improved social conditions among the rural peasantry and has contributed to the political stability that Mexico has enjoyed since the 1930s.

Besides the ejido lands, communal properties, and the remaining haciendas, various types of private holdings have acquired increasing importance in Mexico within the last few decades. Such holdings are composed mainly of (1) old rancho properties of colonial origin; (2) the residual estates; (3) tracts that individuals may purchase and hold in fee simple; and (4) properties developed in government-sponsored colonies. These medium-sized private holdings may prove to be the solution to Mexico's land and food dilemma. Although most are small (less than 25 acres), those that range from 50 to over 500 acres are large enough to utilize modern agricultural techniques in order to increase yields and provide surplus food for Mexico's growing cities.

The larger private holdings predominate in many of the irrigated districts of the north and in the agricultural colonies opened on national lands in the Gulf lowlands of Veracruz state. Currently, however, all government-sponsored colonization projects are carried out under the ejido system and no longer grant full ownership rights to colonists. These projects strive toward the resettling of landless farmers from the overpopulated central highlands to the sparsely settled portions of the tropical lowlands.

The agrarian reform, in part, has created two contrasting facets of agriculture within the country, based on size of holding: (1) the very small holdings (minifundia), usually less than 10 acres, which occur in both the ejido and private-property sectors and are characterized by subsistence farming and rural poverty; and (2) the medium-sized holdings, usually larger than 10 acres, which are composed chiefly of private properties but also include the larger ejido parcels and are characterized by commercial farming and a fair degree of rural prosperity. On the one hand, with medium-sized holdings Mexico has greatly expanded farm production to the extent that the nation is now self-sufficient in food and agricultural products account for nearly half the country's exports. On the other hand, the reality of minifundia plagues Mexico as one of its most serious economic and social problems. Most of the *minifundistas* and landless farmers (estimated at 12 million people, or half the total rural population) live at a bare subsistence level with living standards hardly better than those that prevailed in the 1930s. One of Mexico's current political and social goals is to somehow improve the lot of these marginal farmers and to bring them into the stream of national progress. The federal government is striving to improve agricultural productivity within the ejido sector by such programs as small irrigation projects; the construction of public granaries in ejido settlements where crops can be held for sale at favorable prices; the relaxing of credit for large-risk, small-scale farming operations; and the encouragement of the development of farm cooperatives. The basic problems inherent in the ejido system, such as the existence of minifundia and the rigidity of the agrarian laws, are still to be solved.

Subsistence Farming.   Present-day farming in Mexico is characterized by great diversity in land tenure, cultivation methods, and crops. Patterns range from pre-Conquest Indian, through colonial, to modern forms. Subsistence tillage still occupies the bulk of the farming population, concentrated in the central and southern parts of the country, or within the bounds of ancient Mesoamerica.

The aboriginal crop triad of maize, beans, and squash, together with chile, is still the predominant subsistence food of most Mexicans. Maize is by far the most important single crop. In 1930, nearly three-fourths of the cultivated land of the country was planted in maize; today this proportion has dropped to about one-half, indicating a trend toward crop diversification. Although the bulk of the crop comes from the small subsistence farms of the Mesa Central and the southern highlands, where yields average less than ten bushels per acre, maize production has doubled in

the past 30 years—an increase due mainly to commercial, mechanized cultivation of high-yielding hybrid corn, which was recently introduced from the United States. The hybrid corn was developed as stock feed rather than human food, however, and most Mexicans despise its taste and cling to the low-yielding native maize.

Throughout the steep escarpment areas bordering the Mesa Central, in the mountainous southern highlands, and in the forested tropical lowlands of the southeast, the ancient system of slash-burn cultivation is still a common technique of subsistence farmers. One of the most characteristic scenes on the steep slopes of the mountainous areas is the crazy-quilt pattern of small plots, some in crops, others temporarily abandoned to forest scrub (Figure 11.15). At the height of the dry season, in March and April, the atmosphere is filled with the blue smoke from

Figure 11.15   Slash-burn milpas (*tlacololes*), or maize fields, on steep slopes, southern escarpment of the Mesa Central, Michoacán state. Old fields (*acahuales*), in various stages of secondary forest regrowth, and cultivated plots form irregular patches on the hillside.

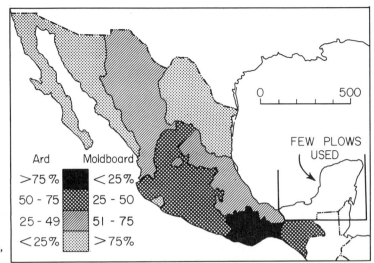

Figure 11.16 Ratio of wooden ard plows to steel moldboard plows in Mexico, 1950

Ard | Moldboard

>75% | <25%
50 - 75 | 25 - 50
25 - 49 | 51 - 75
<25% | >75%

FEW PLOWS USED

0   500

burning plots being prepared for planting after the first rains of May or June. In these areas, slash-burn farming has changed little since pre-Conquest days. And, although the steel machete and iron hoe are now the main tools, many Indian farmers still use the wooden dibble and coa. Because of the pressure of population, the plots are now abandoned for only 3 to 4 years instead of from 10 to 15, with the result that yields are declining and the soil is becoming seriously eroded. The areas devoted to slash-burn cultivation are usually Indian village lands, though some are in ejido plots, and others are national lands occupied by squatters. About 20 percent of Mexico's cultivated land is still worked by the primitive slash-burn technique.

Within the more level areas of Mexico (Yucatan and Tabasco excepted), most subsistence farms are tilled with the ancient ard or wooden plow drawn by a yoke of oxen, much as in colonial times (Figure 11.16). Although many subsistence farmers of the Mesa Central and the north have adopted, via the United States, the more effective steel moldboard plow of north European origin, some, however, are either too conservative to use it or cannot afford it.

The few tractors and modern agricultural implements now used in subsistence farming are found largely in fertile irrigated basin flats, such as the Bajío of Guanajuato and sections of northern Michoacán and Jalisco in the western part of the Mesa Central. Little slash-burn cultivation is practiced today on the steep mountain slopes of the Mesa Central. However, on the slopes surrounding the Valley of Mexico and the basins of Toluca and Puebla, one still sees in use the aboriginal semiterrace (*bancal* or *metepantli*) technique for permanent fields (see Chapter 8).

Commercial Agriculture. Commercial agriculture, begun on a modest scale in colonial times, has greatly expanded during the nineteenth and twentieth centuries, so that today a crop such as cotton, cultivated by modern mechanized techniques, has become one of Mexico's leading exports. Although some is scattered throughout the central highlands, most of today's commercial agriculture is in the irrigated oases of the arid north and in subtropical and tropical sections of the escarpments and coastal lowlands.

Mexico's commercial agriculture, unlike that of most Latin American countries, is well diversified, and many crops are cultivated for both home consumption and export. In terms of acreage, maize, beans, cotton, and wheat are the leading crops, followed by coffee, sugar cane, and oil-seeds. Although the cultivation of some crops, for example, cotton and most wheat, is highly mechanized, others, such as maguey and sugar cane, are produced by techniques that have changed little since colonial times. Commercial production is carried on under practically all systems of land tenure present today in Mexico. Small amounts of wheat and sesame are grown for sale on Indian communal lands and individual ejido parcels; irrigated cotton, wheat, truck crops, and sugar cane are cultivated on collective ejidos and private holdings. Three large areas in Mexico produce important commercial crops: the

Mesa Central, the northern oases, and the subtropical and tropical areas in the southern part of the country.

THE MESA CENTRAL.   Albeit most of the arable land of the Mesa Central is devoted to subsistence agriculture, some of the more fertile basins are noted for commercial cultivation. One of these is the Bajío of Guanajuato and northern Michoacán, since colonial times considered the bread-basket of Mexico (Figure 11.17). Maize and beans are cultivated during the summer rainy season; in winter, wheat, truck crops, and alfalfa are grown by irrigation on the small private holdings and the ejido plots. Farmers obtain water from both the large

Figure 11.17   The Bajío of Guanajuato, Meso Central. A series of coalesced volcanic basins, this fertile zone forms one of the major agricultural areas of Mexico.

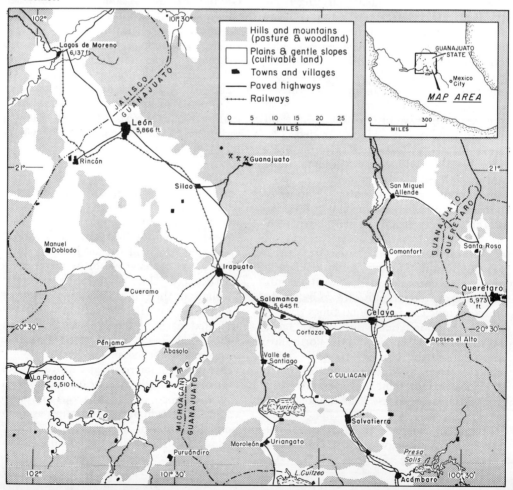

government reservoirs, such as those on the Lerma River, and the small private ones that dot the basin surface, or pump it from deep wells with the diesel-powered engines that have replaced the colonial norias. A substantial part of Mexico's commercial maize and bean crop comes from the Bajío as well as from the seasonal lands in the high basins of Zacatecas and Durango.

From colonial times until the 1940s, the Bajío produced the greater part of the country's wheat. Today, however, large-scale wheat production has shifted to the northern oases, where more than 70 percent is now cultivated by irrigation on highly mechanized ejido lands and private holdings. As in most Latin American countries, the consumption of wheat bread in Mexico is a status symbol. Bread was the food of the Spaniards, of their white descendants, and of other Europeans. Today, most of the urban population in central and southern Mexico feel that wheat foods are prestige foods, and all eat them who can afford to do so. In the north, wheat bread, and even tortillas made from wheat flour, have been staple foods since colonial times. So important is the demand for white bread in urban areas and in the north that, in past years, the Mexican government was forced to import large quantities of grain and flour from the United States, expending valuable foreign exchange. With the shift of wheat production to the northern oases, Mexico now has grain even for export in good years.

A more extensive type of commercial agriculture practiced in the Mesa Central is the large-scale cultivation of the agave plant, maguey, for the production of pulque, the ancient Indian intoxicant. Since the Revolution of 1910, the maguey-pulque producing area has shrunk to its present location in the dry, rocky lands immediately northeast of the Valley of Mexico. Today, however, the less nutritious European-type beer, introduced into Mexico in the 1880s, has largely replaced pulque as a poor man's drink in both rural and urban areas.

Closely related to maguey-pulque agriculture is the cultivation of other types of agave plants for the production of the distilled brandies called mescal and tequila. Small private holdings in Jalisco state, on the western side of the Mesa Central, produce most of this product, the center being the vicinity of Tequila, northwest of Guadalajara.

THE NORTHERN OASES. Commercial farming in Mexico is best developed in the arid north, where, in the last 50 years, the government built dams and reservoirs on streams, thus creating large irrigated oases. Nearly 20 percent of Mexico's cropland is now artificially watered, making it one of the world's leading countries in development of irrigation potential. The recent increase in food production and in the export of cotton has been due chiefly to the large-scale irrigation projects in the north.

Northern Mexico is not particularly well endowed for irrigated farming. Water is limited. Only two large rivers, the Colorado and the Rio Grande, affect north Mexican territory, and Mexico must share the water of both with the United States, which utilizes most of it. The greater portion of water for irrigation in the north derives from the modest rainfall and the melting snow of the Sierra Madre Occidental. The short streams that flow westward down the escarpment to the narrow Pacific lowland and those that run eastward into the Rio Grande or into areas of interior drainage carry most of the water used in cultivating the fertile alluvial soils of desert basins and delta plains. Moreover, the same streams maintain the ground water that is pumped from deep wells in the irrigated areas.

As we have already observed (Chapter 10), Spanish farmers maintained small patches of irrigated cropland in favored localities of northern Mexico throughout the colonial period. Much later, in the late

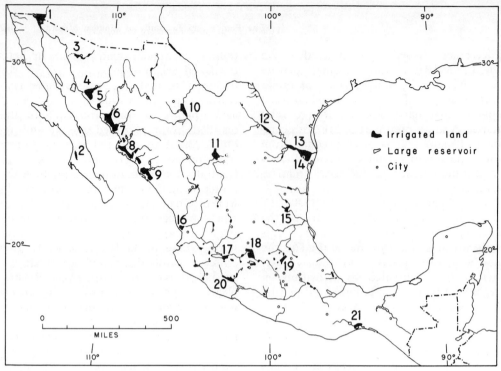

Figure 11.18 Major irrigation districts in Mexico. Numbers refer to the following districts: (1) Río Colorado (Mexicali–San Luis); (2) Santo Domingo; (3) Caborca; (4) Costa de Hermosillo; (5) Valle de Guaymas; (6) Río Yaqui; (7) Río Mayo; (8) Río Fuerte–Guasave; (9) Río Culiacán–San Lorenzo; (10) Delicias; (11) La Laguna; (12) Don Martín (Río Salado); (13) Bajo Río San Juan; (14) Bajo Río Bravo (Matamoros); (15) El Mante; (16) Bajo Río Santiago; (17) Bajo Río Lerma and (18) Alto Río Lerma (El Bajío); (19) Río Tula; (20) Río Tepalcatepec; and (21) Tehuantepec.

nineteenth and early twentieth centuries, Mexican *hacendados* and North American land speculators developed sizable private irrigation projects, especially in the Laguna area of Coahuila and the Yaqui River delta in Sonora. It was not until the late 1920s, however, that the Mexican government began construction of large dams and reservoirs to develop the present irrigation systems, which have revolutionized agriculture in the north (Figure 11.18).

The first irrigation district to be fully developed was the Laguna area of southern Coahuila, an immense desert basin once occupied by the now desiccated lakes of Mayran and Viesca and fed by the Nazas and Aguanaval rivers. The western part of the basin was converted into a large, mechanized, irrigated farming area (400,000 acres), specializing in cotton,

wheat, and alfalfa under the collective ejido system of land tenure. Deep wells that tap the once-abundant ground-water supply of the basin furnish half the irrigation water, but excessive pumping has in recent years dangerously lowered the water table. During the 1930s, the Laguna area became Mexico's foremost cotton-producing region; the cities of Torreón, Gómez Palacio, and Lerdo, which cluster around the mouth of the Nazas River, grew into the large urban complex that today serves as an administrative, market, and supply center for the district.

Northwest of the Laguna area, in the state of Chihuahua, is the Delicias irrigation district on the Conchos River, the largest tributary of the Rio Grande in Mexican territory. Most of the surface water used for irrigation is supplied by the

Boquilla Reservoir (Lago Toronto), constructed on the middle Conchos in 1916 for hydroelectric power. Other reservoirs built on the tributaries San Pedro and Florido, along with deep wells, now supplement the Conchos water supply and help irrigate 125,000 acres of fertile desert alluvium along the rivers. Wheat, maize, and cotton, grown by mechanized methods mainly on small private holdings, are the main crops of the area.

A third large region of recently developed irrigated farming lies within the lower Rio Grande drainage of northeastern Mexico. Within this area, nearly 700,-000 acres of land are now cultivated with irrigation. Most of the farmland is within the Rio Grande delta, in the vicinity of Matamoros, across the river from Brownsville; smaller irrigated areas occur along the Salado and San Juan rivers, tributaries of the Rio Grande. Developed mainly since World War II, the Matamoros area, once important for cotton, now specializes in the cultivation of sorghum, used for feeding livestock. The large international Falcon reservoir on the Rio Grande (completed in 1957) furnishes most of the water for the Matamoros area, while the Don Martín reservoir supplies the Salado section. As the lower Rio Grande carries little flow originating in the upper and middle courses of the river, the water for the reservoirs comes chiefly from erratic local rainfall, increased by the occasional passage of easterly waves and hurricanes. Slightly less than half of the Matamoros area is in ejido land, the rest being private holdings, many of whose owners have managed to circumvent the land laws and consolidate their lands into virtual haciendas.

Within the past 30 years, arid northwestern Mexico has become the agricultural hot spot of the country and one of the most rapidly developing farming areas in the world. With the recent completion of a large network of canals, water from the lower Colorado River has been diverted onto the deltaic alluvium south of Mexicali in Baja California, to irrigate a half-million acres of cotton, wheat, and alfalfa land. However, the Mexicali district receives only 10 percent of the Colorado River water for irrigation, the rest being used by the United States. Unfortunately, much of the water utilized on the Mexican side is return flow that has already been applied on American fields and is thus often heavily impregnated with salts harmful to crops. The international dispute that has arisen over this question of water rights threatens to damage Mexican–United States relations.

The most spectacular development of irrigation in arid northwestern Mexico, however, has occurred within the lower courses and deltas of the streams that cross the dry coastal plain of Sonora and Sinaloa. More than two million acres are now under irrigation along the coast, from the small Caborca district on the Magdalena and Concepción rivers in northern Sonora to the Río San Lorenzo in central Sinaloa. Beginning with the Angostura Dam on the Yaqui River (finished in 1937), the Mexican government has since completed reservoirs on most of the larger streams of the northwest, and more are under construction or planned. The largest irrigated areas comprise the flood plains and deltas of the Yaqui (550,000 acres) and Fuerte (600,000 acres) rivers (Figure 11.19). In some parts of the coastal plain, long canals bring water to the interfluve areas, so that often there are continuous stretches of cultivation from one river valley to the next.

Wheat, cotton, oilseeds (safflower and sesame), and winter vegetables (principally tomatoes) are the four main crops. Rice, sugar cane, and sorghum are also important. Most of the acreage devoted to these crops is cultivated with modern machinery on both private holdings and ejido land. Wheat production has increased so much in the recent past that the river oases of Sonora and Sinaloa have replaced the Bajío of Guanajuato as the granary of Mexico. A large part of the winter tomato

Figure 11.19 The Alvaro Obregón Dam on the Yaqui River, southern Sonora state. This dam impounds one of Mexico's largest reservoirs in the dry northwest. Water from this reservoir is used to irrigate the extensive cotton, wheat, and winter vegetable farms in the vicinity of Ciudad Obregón. (*Compañia Mexicana Aerofoto*)

crop produced in the Fuerte and Culiacán areas has long been exported to the United States. The northwestern river oases, including the Mexicali–San Luis district, now produce over half of Mexico's cotton. Although its production decreased by one-third between 1965 and 1971, Mexico is still the second leading cotton-producing country of Latin America, exceeded only by Brazil. Associated with the cotton crop are the gins and the cottonseed-oil processing plants; associated with the winter vegetable crop are the packing sheds and loading stations. All these form part of the modern landscape of the northern oases. Supply and market centers like Ciudad Obregón and Navajoa in the Yaqui and Mayo districts of southern Sonora as well as Los Mochis and Culiacán in Sinaloa, are boom towns that exemplify the rapid urban growth that is accompanying the phenomenal farming development in the northwest.

The agricultural boom that is taking place in the irrigated lands of northern Mexico is closely related to the introduction of modern technology from the United States. Such technology includes the engineering involved in reservoir and canal construction, as well as the know-how required for the use of tractors, mechanical harvesters, and other modern agricultural machines (Figure 11.20). Other new techniques include the use of

commercial fertilizers, insecticides, and improved plant strains. More fundamentally, the agricultural boom of the north is associated with Mexico's population and food problem and with direct government action in the development of water resources to increase food production. Free of the Indian conservatism and dense population that permeate central and southern Mexico, the newly developed farming districts of the north have witnessed the most spectacular and rapid changes in landscape in the country.

In 1967, the federal government began a program of constructing small irrigation projects in many parts of the country, but especially in the north and in the Mesa Central, the locale of much of Mexico's rural poverty. By damming small rivers to form reservoirs, drilling deep wells, and utilizing natural springs, the program aims at providing irrigation water for increasing commercial agricultural production on both ejido lands and small private farms. By 1971, over 300,000 acres of newly irrigated land had been brought into production under this plan.

THE TROPICAL LOWLANDS. Tropical commercial agriculture is still generally located in the areas developed by the Spaniards in the colonial period. The moist, nearly frost-free coastal lowlands and the adjacent eastern escarpment that border the Gulf are Mexico's outstanding regions

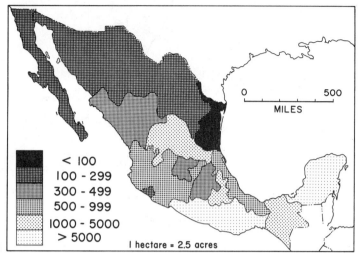

Figure 11.20   Hectares of
cropland per farm tractor, 1960

< 100
100 - 299
300 - 499
500 - 999
1000 - 5000
> 5000

0   500
MILES

I hectare = 2.5 acres

of tropical farming. This area includes southeastern Tamaulipas, easternmost San Luis Potosí, practically all of Veracruz (Mexico's richest agricultural state), Tabasco, and parts of northeastern Oaxaca and northern Chiapas. It produces most of Mexico's coffee, sugar cane, bananas, copra, cacao, and pineapple, much of the citrus and minor tropical fruits, and quantities of maize, beans, and rice. Less significant areas of production of tropical crops are the valleys and slopes on the southern and southwestern escarpment of the Mesa Central, the semiarid lowlands of the Tepalcatepec Basin in Michoacán, and the narrow Pacific lowlands and escarpments from Nayarit to Chiapas. The century-old henequen plantation area in the northern part of the Yucatan peninsula is a special development in tropical agriculture in Middle America.

Diversity of commercial crops, rather than the monoculture found in other Middle American countries, characterizes tropical farming in Mexico. Of the dozen or more significant crops, however, coffee and sugar cane predominate in terms of acreage, production, and value. Mexico has been a self-sufficient grower of sugar since colonial times, and today competes with neighboring countries as an exporter;

and, since 1950, Mexico has been the third largest coffee producer in Latin America.

The sugar-cane areas of Mexico have approximately the same distribution as in colonial days, with more than a third of today's production concentrated in the coastal lowlands and lower escarpment slopes of central Veracruz (Figure 11.21). At the close of the nineteenth century, some 30 large plantations and steam-operated processing plants (*ingenios*), plus hundreds of small animal-driven mills (*trapiches*), extended from the Nautla River to the Papaloapan lowlands. Today, the Veracruz sugar area has expanded southward, around the base of the Tuxtla volcanic mass, to the vicinity of Acayucan in the northern part of the Isthmus of Tehuantepec. The core of the sugar zone, however, still extends, as it did in the eighteenth century, southeastward from the Córdoba-Orizaba area, along the lower flanks of the eastern escarpment to the Papaloapan River basin. Within the humid Gulf region, the northernmost sugar area centers around the partly irrigated El Mante district in southernmost Tamaulipas, which was developed as a plantation just before the Revolution of 1910 and later made into large collective ejido plots.

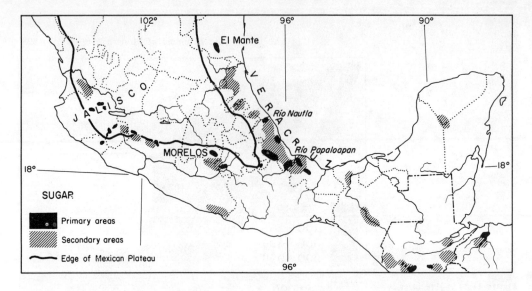

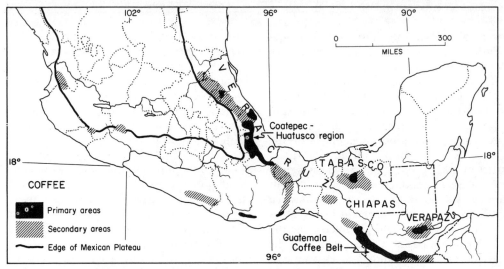

Figure 11.21   Sugar and coffee areas of Mexico

Although they were significant in colonial and prerevolutionary times, the
sugar areas along the southern escarpment
of the Mesa Central are now of relatively
minor importance. Those of Morelos state
(around Cuernavaca, Yautepec, and Cu-
autla), of southeastern Puebla (Chiautla),
and of the hot, narrow canyons and basins
of southern Jalisco (such as Tamazula
and Zapotiltic) were partially ruined during the revolution, but have since been
revived (Figure 11.22). The highly productive irrigated sugar area of Los Mochis in

northern Sinaloa is the only one in Mexico
that falls outside the humid tropical zone.

The prerevolutionary sugar haciendas
were among the few large-scale Mexican
agricultural enterprises that approximated
the tropical plantation. Few, however, acquired the size and importance of the
West Indian operations, and after the expropriation of the large estates, most of
the sugar haciendas were converted into
collective ejidos or broken down into
smaller private holdings. In most of the
sugar areas, cultivation has changed little

Figure 11.22   The sugar hacienda "Villahermosa," in Morelos state. In the foreground the *casco* is composed of the "big house" of the former owner, the sugar mill, and remnants of abandoned warehouses. In the background are extensive sugar fields. Most of the land that formerly belonged to this hacienda is now operated as a collective ejido. (*Compañia Mexicana Aerofoto*)

since colonial times. The machete is still the main harvesting instrument since the rank, irregular growth of the tropical cane hardly permits the use of the harvester. Tractor-pulled cane racks are seen in the newer, more progressive holdings, but ox-carts still haul the cane to the mills in some areas. Large, mechanized processing mills and refineries, however, have replaced the old *ingenios,* though the mule or oxen-powered *trapiches* prevail throughout the sugar zone of Mexico for making the cheap cakes of raw sugar (*panela* or *piloncillo*), consumed in large quantities by the poorer classes. An important adjunct of sugar processing, begun in colonial times, is the manufacture of the rum and cane brandies for which Mexico is famous.

Since the Communist take-over of Cuba in 1959, Mexico's sugar cane acreage has more than doubled, and production of raw sugar has nearly tripled, due mainly to increased export quotas to the United States. Sugar now vies with cotton as Mexico's leading export.

Although the coffee plant was first brought to Mexico in the late eighteenth century, commercial production did not begin until about 1860. Until recently it was a rather minor crop in Mexico, most of the harvest being consumed locally, but, between 1950 and 1960, coffee acreage doubled. The crop is now Mexico's third most valuable export and only recently was surpassed by sugar cane in acreage.

The first Mexican coffee-growing area to be developed in the nineteenth century was the humid eastern escarpment of Veracruz state, in the vicinity of Córdoba and Orizaba. From this center, coffee culture spread northward, beyond Jalapa, and southward, to the Papaloapan Basin, along an altitudinal belt of between 3,000 and 6,000 feet elevation, which corresponds to the upper part of the *tierra templada.* This belt is still Mexico's leading coffee area, particularly that section of rich volcanic soils that lies between Jalapa and Orizaba. This area, known as the Coatepec-Huatusco region, is one of Mexico's lushest horticultural areas, where citrus orchards, banana plants, coffee groves, and scattered orchid-draped mango and avocado trees blend into an almost continuous tropical garden.

Beginning in the 1880s, German planters from Guatemala extended coffee cultivation into the Pacific slope of the Sierra Madre de Chiapas (the Soconusco), creating Mexico's second coffee-producing area. Mexican colonists have recently formed a third important coffee district on the rain-drenched escarpment of northern Chiapas, overlooking the Gulf lowlands of Tabasco. There are other coffee zones along the eastern escarpment of Veracruz as far as the San Luis Potosí border in the Huastec Indian country, on the Pacific slope of Oaxaca and Guerrero, and in small patches along the southern and western escarpments of the Mesa Central (Figure 11.21).

Before the revolution, the Mexican coffee farms (*fincas*) varied in size from 50 to 5,000 acres and were chiefly owned by rich Mexicans or foreigners. Many of the large *fincas,* especially those in Chiapas, have been converted into collective ejidos; in Veracruz, many were apportioned in small individual ejido parcels. Each former *finca* owner was permitted to retain a maximum of 750 acres in coffee plantings, but many of these holdings have been enlarged by combining contiguous lands owned by relatives. As in most tropical areas of America other than Brazil, coffee is grown under shade trees, supposedly to improve the quality of the beans. Since the preparation of the beans for market involves an elaborate process of depulping, curing, and drying, many smaller growers have established cooperative processing plants; others sell their crop directly to plant owners.

Rice, although hardly comparable to sugar cane and coffee in acreage or value, is becoming an increasingly significant staple food in the tropical lowlands of Mexico, as it is elsewhere in the Latin American tropics. As mentioned in Chapter 10, the Spaniards introduced rice into Mexico early in the colonial period, but

only in the past 50 years has it become an important commercial crop. In the lowland tropics, rice is a prestige food, as wheat is in the highlands.

Traditionally, Mexico's main rice-producing area has been the irrigated valleys and basins along the southern escarpment of the Mesa Central, especially those of Morelos, Michoacán, and northern Guerrero. In those areas today, farmers grow 30 percent of Mexico's rice crop in small holdings cultivated by techniques reminiscent of those employed in the Orient. Since the 1930s, much of the Mexican rice growing has shifted to the coastal oases of the northwest and the tropical lowlands of Veracruz state; each of these areas now produces about 25 percent of the country's crop by mechanized farming.

The extent and location of many of the lesser tropical crops grown commercially in Mexico have undergone substantial changes within the past half-century. The traditional Mexican citrus district, for example, lies on the eastern escarpment between Córdoba and Jalapa, where oranges have been raised for the Mexico City market since colonial times. By 1950, the center of citrus production had shifted to Nuevo León in the northeastern part of the country, where the Montemorelos district southeast of Monterrey produced more than half of the Mexican orange crop on small private holdings. By 1970, private landowners had developed other significant orange-growing areas in the Gulf lowlands of northern Veracruz and in the tropical hill country of eastern San Luis Potosí state. About half of the Mexican orange crop is exported as fresh fruit and frozen juice concentrate to the United States, Canada, and Europe.

The banana industry has changed even more spectacularly. At the beginning of this century, local landowners established Mexico's first large banana plantations on the fertile river flood plains of the Tabasco lowlands. This development was part of the great banana boom that was taking place at the same time on the Caribbean coast of Central America. The Tabascan plantations reached peak harvests in 1936, when they produced half of the 14.5 million banana stems exported from Mexico that year. Thereafter, the expropriation of the large estates and the incursion of banana diseases caused a decline in production in the Tabasco area. In the 1960s banana production shifted to the Pacific coast, especially to the lowlands of Nayarit and Colima states, where more than half the commercial crop is now grown on small to moderate holdings (a maximum of 725 acres, by law).

Several native tropical plants, cultivated in pre-Conquest times, are now important commercial crops. Among these are tobacco, first cultivated commercially in colonial days in Veracruz but now dominant on ejido lands in the lowlands of Nayarit; pineapple, first cultivated on a large scale in 1906 around the area of Loma Bonita in southern Veracruz, which is still the foremost pineapple-producing area in Mexico; cacao, the production of which has shifted from the Soconusco on the Pacific coast to the wet foothills of northern Chiapas and the river flood plains of Tabasco; and vanilla, of which Mexico still grows half the world's production by ancient native methods in the Totonac Indian area of central Veracruz. The coconut has become an important strand crop in this century, and is grown along both the Pacific and Gulf coasts of Mexico.

An agave, or century plant called "henequen," is another commercially grown native tropical plant. The cultivation of this plant on a large scale in northern Yucatan during the nineteenth century gave rise to perhaps the best example of the tropical plantation in Mexico. Like its close relative, maguey, henequen thrives in thin, limey soil and in a hot, semiarid climate. Its thick, fleshy leaves yield a stout fiber long used by the Indians for cordage and hammocks.

During the last century, the owners of cattle haciendas in northern Yucatan began to plant henequen to obtain fiber for manufacturing ship cables and other kinds of rope. The invention of the McCormick wheat binder in 1873, and the subsequent development of wheat lands in the central United States, created a large demand for binder twine. By the turn of the century, the flat, stony plains around Mérida in northwestern Yucatan had become a zone of large henequen plantations which employed cheap Maya Indian labor to cultivate and process the fiber exported to the United States for the wheat harvest. After the revolution, several factors combined to effect a sharp reduction in Mexican henequen production. Land tenure systems changed; demand for binder twine decreased with the invention of the wheat combine; and new sisal and henequen cultivators in other parts of the world began to offer strong competition. Today, the privately held Yucatan plantations are greatly reduced in size (maximum of 750 acres), and most of the henequen comes from collectively operated ejidos established on the former haciendas. Since the 1950s, small but rapidly growing areas of henequen production have been established in northeastern Mexico, especially around Ciudad Victoria in central Tamaulipas (Figure 11.23).

Figure 11.23   Henequen near Ciudad Victoria, Tamaulipas state, northeastern Mexico. About 10 percent of the henequen grown in Mexico comes from this general area. The remainder is produced in Yucatan.

Tropical agriculture has been greatly advanced by the government's recent program for developing sparsely occupied lowland areas of the country in order to resettle landless farmers and to increase food production. In 1938, the government undertook the development of the semiarid Tepalcatepec Basin of southern Michoacán. The existing irrigation systems were enlarged; new ones were established; and large areas within the plains of Apatzingán and Bellavista were opened for the cultivation of rice, maize, cotton, and tropical fruit.

A second scheme, far larger in scope, is the Papaloapan Project, ambitiously called "Mexico's T.V.A." This involves the agricultural and industrial development of the Papaloapan River Basin in southern Veracruz. The large Alemán Dam and reservoir on the Tonto River, a tributary of the Papaloapan, now controls floods, affords irrigation water in time of need, and generates electricity. In the lower part of the basin the government has constructed roads, straightened the sinuous river channel, instituted sanitary measures, and established several agricultural colonies in which small private holdings, rather than ejido parcels, are the rule. The best lands of the lower Papaloapan, however, are the fertile natural levees along the river. These are excluded to new colonization, for they are held by residual estates and ejidos and have long been planted in sugar cane.

A third endeavor, the Grijalva Project, involves development of the Tabasco lowland, a tropical area of heavy rainfall, disastrous floods, and extensive swamps; most of the good farmland lies along the natural levees that border the active and abandoned river channels. The project involves flood control and sanitation in the lower part of the Grijalva and Usumacinta river basins, to pave the way for large-scale colonization. In 1966, work was completed on the large dam and reservoir of Netzahualcoyotl at Malpaso on the Grijalva River in northwestern Chiapas,

which now controls the flood waters of that river as it debouches from the mountains onto the coastal plain. Under a subsidiary project, the Chontalpa Plan, the government aims to drain and clear nearly a million acres in western Tabasco to resettle large numbers of landless farmers. In 1970, this project was well under way.

A fourth major government project for the development of the tropical lowlands involves the Balsas River delta in Guerrero state. More than a million acres of rich alluvial soil are to be irrigated with water from the recently completed La Villita reservoir, located immediately below the large Infiernillo hydroelectric complex. With the completion of the irrigation canal system, thousands of impoverished subsistence farmers from the Balsas Valley and the Guerrero highlands will be resettled in these fertile lands.

The Livestock Economy

Stock raising, in contrast to agriculture, has retained much of its colonial pattern. Neither the pasture areas nor the breeds of animals have changed appreciably since the eighteenth century.

Yet stock raising is still one of Mexico's most important economies. A third of the national territory is classified as pastureland; its landscape is characterized by widely spaced ranch centers, vast expanses of grassy or scrub-covered plains and hills, and scattered, ill-tended herds. According to the 1960 census, the monetary value of Mexican livestock nearly equals that of cultivated crops. However, the value of animal products sold is only half that of crops.

As in colonial times, the Mexican livestock industry is divided into (1) small-scale stock raising, including household animals associated with subsistence agriculture, which is found chiefly in the central and southern highlands; and (2) large-scale commercial ranching, which is found in some parts of the central highlands, in

the arid north, and in the coastal lowlands. Other enterprises involving animals
—dairying and poultry raising—have
evolved only recently around the larger
cities to supply produce to a growing
urban market.

Small-Scale Stock Raising.   More than
one-third of the country's livestock is kept
by the subsistence farmers of the Mesa
Central and the southern highlands. In
addition to the work animals (oxen, mules,
and burros) that he employs in cultivation
and transport, many a farmer owns a few
cattle, sheep, and goats which graze in the
common pastures and woodland or on the
stubble of cropped fields around his village. He also may have a hog or two which,
like the oxen and burros, are kept near
the house and are almost considered part
of the family. Chickens and turkeys also
comprise an important part of the household animals.

The occasional sale of a cow or hog,
and the annual wool clip (one-half of the
national production), bring the subsistence
farmers some income. The little milk obtained from cows and goats is fed chiefly
to the children or is processed into a soft,
salty cheese, common throughout the country. As in colonial times, nearly half of
Mexico's five million sheep are concentrated in the eastern part of the Mesa Central, where Indian and mestizo villagers
raise small herds.

Large-Scale Ranching.   The north, with
60 percent of the nation's natural pasture,
continues to be Mexico's outstanding commercial stock-raising area. During the Díaz
regime, North American land companies
acquired large blocks of Mexican pasture
near the international border, the Hearst
estate alone comprising two million acres
in western Chihuahua. United States
ranchers introduced improved breeds of
beef cattle, such as the Shorthorn, Hereford, and Aberdeen Angus, but most Mexican stockmen were content with the rangy
criollo descendant of sixteenth-century

Spanish stock. By the end of the nineteenth century, the market for Mexican
cattle and mules had shifted from the
local mining areas to the United States,
and thousands of head were annually
driven northward across the border.

The northern herds were devastated by
guerrilla operations during the revolution,
but have again increased to about five
million head, or one-third of the nation's
cattle. The black grama pastures of the
high plains and mountain meadows in
northwestern Chihuahua, from Chihuahua
City to the Casas Grandes area, form the
present center of the range cattle industry in Mexico. More than a million head
now graze in this area. Other large northern cattle ranges are in the steppes of
northwestern Zacatecas and central Durango and in the lowland pastures in
Sonora and northern Sinaloa. All of these
were pasturelands in colonial times. Although 85 percent of all Mexican range
cattle are still *criollos*, the Hereford is
slowly becoming the standard breed in
northwestern Chihuahua, northern Sonora, and Coahuila.

The land reforms following the Revolution of 1910 scarcely affected the size of
the large cattle estates in northern Mexico. The carrying capacity of those pastures
is so low (15 to 250 acres of land per animal) that a large holding is needed to
graze a herd of profitable size. Foreign
holdings near the United States border
have been expropriated, however, and the
land has been parceled out to ejidos for
both farming and stock raising.

The northern pastures have been overgrazed, particularly in this century. As a
consequence, the vegetation has been modified and the carrying capacity of the
pasturelands greatly reduced. The once extensive areas of nutritious black grama
grasslands in the high basins of western
Zacatecas, Durango, and Chihuahua are
now severely depleted and have been invaded by noxious weeds, some of which
are poisonous and annually cause the
death of hundreds of animals. Other in-

vaders include prickly-pear and cholla cacti, as well as mesquite and thorny acacia scrub. The invasion of desert scrub into the drier margins of the grasslands is especially noticeable in northeastern Mexico, where goats and sheep have drastically overgrazed and overbrowsed in formerly productive pastures.

Although stock raising in the tropical lowland savannas of Mexico dates from the colonial period, it is within the past 50 years that the industry has become especially significant in the Gulf coast area known as the Huasteca in southern Tamaulipas, in northern Veracruz, and in eastern San Luis Potosí. There, abundant rainfall affords year-round pasture. Most important, recent planting of nutritious African grasses, such as Guinea grass and Pará grass, has so increased the carrying capacity of the Huasteca pastures that they have become the foremost beef-fattening area of the country. Cattle from the steppes of Coahuila and Nuevo León, fattened in the lush lowlands, are shipped to Mexico City for slaughter. Like many stock-raising areas of the tropics, the pasturage in the savannas and marshes of southern Veracruz and Tabasco have been improved by the planting of African grasses. The permanent *criollo* herds in the Gulf lowlands have also been improved by crossing with Brahma stock from India and Brown Swiss from Europe. Today Veracruz is Mexico's leading cattle state.

The Dairy and Poultry Industries. The newest development in Mexican stock raising is the dairy farm, scores of which have sprung up around the major urban centers within the past 50 years. Until recently the consumption of fresh milk was not significant in Mexico; it rarely has been in areas of Spanish culture. Its consumption, of course, was unknown to pre-Conquest Indians, and still today there are large numbers of people in Mexico who have never tasted milk. With the rise of urbanism and the influence of recent govern-

ment propaganda, however, the use of milk and other dairy products has increased in Mexico.

The greatest concentration of dairy farms is near Mexico City, whose milkshed includes much of the northern and eastern portions of the Valley of Mexico, where land reclaimed by lake drainage has been planted to alfalfa. In addition, alfalfa hay and other cattle feed are shipped in quantity from the Bajío of Guanajuato for the dairy herds, composed mainly of purebred Holsteins. Although most of the city's milk supply comes from United States–style dairies within the Valley, at least one-third is furnished by small, unsanitary establishments as far away as Querétaro, Puebla, and Tlaxcala. Guadalajara's daily milk supply is shipped in from small dairies scattered over a large part of central and eastern Jalisco, while Monterrey is supplied by farms close by. Modern pasteurizing plants and plants for processing condensed and powdered milk have been built as dairying has grown.

A still more recent innovation in animal husbandry in Mexico is the spectacular development of large-scale poultry raising around the large urban centers since World War II. Financed mainly by local capital, the large chicken farms on the outskirts of Mexico City, Guadalajara, and Monterrey are equipped with modern poultry-raising techniques and purebred stock imported from the United States. Such establishments have largely replaced the small peasant farmer as supplier of fowl and eggs for the growing urban population. Overproduction now threatens the viability of this new industry.

Nonagricultural Resource Exploitation

Apart from farming and stock raising, there are other activities based on the exploitation of the country's natural resources. These include lumbering, sea fisheries, and the extraction of mineral wealth. Mining, of course, has been of true economic and historic significance in Mexico; but all three together have never attained the fundamental position that agriculture holds in the Mexican economy.

Forest Exploitation. Man's use of the forest cover in Mexico has been highly destructive, as it has been in many parts of Latin America. At the beginning of the colonial period, possibly 60 percent of Mexico was covered by tall forest; today, after nearly 450 years of indiscriminate cutting and burning, the forested area has decreased to less than 20 percent of the country's surface.

The period of greatest forest exploitation began in the late nineteenth century with the coming of the railroads and the rise of the urban population. As already noted (Chapter 9), one of the chief reasons for the overcutting has been the demand for charcoal. Moreover, the gradual spread of slash-burn farming in both the mountainous highlands and the tropical lowlands has reduced many forest stands to scrub growth. The construction of the Mexican railroads at the close of the last century, which required millions of wooden ties, added to the problem. In the past 30 years, the phenomenal growth of the larger cities has required huge quantities of lumber; and recently, the synthetic fiber plants, which use paper pulp and cellulose, have caused further inroads into the remaining forests. The recent large-scale exploitation of the Mexican forests was made possible by the introduction, from the United States, of steam- and diesel-powered sawmills, equipped with large rotary and band saws. Unfortunately, federal conservation measures have proved difficult to enforce after centuries of uncontrolled exploitation.

Today, Mexico's remaining forest reserves consist of (1) the highland coniferous forests in the northern and central parts of the country; and (2) remnants of tropical rain forest in the southeastern lowlands. The Sierra Madre Occidental contains the largest stands of unexploited pine, the main source of construction lumber. Nearly half of Mexico's annual timber harvest is cut in western Chihuahua and Durango. Smaller remnants of coniferous forests occur in the Sierra Madre Oriental, within the volcanic axis along the southern edge of the Mesa Central (where the overcut pine forests now produce chiefly turpentine), and in scattered areas of the southern highlands of Oaxaca, Guerrero, and Michoacán.

For more than 200 years, native and foreign loggers and collectors of vegetable products have exploited the tropical rain forest of the humid Gulf lowlands in southern Veracruz, Tabasco, and the Yucatan Peninsula. After the decline of the colonial dyewood industry along the coast in the mid-nineteenth century (Chapter 10), foreign interests started large-scale cutting of the mahogany and tropical cedar trees scattered throughout the Isthmus of Tehuantepec. Until the turn of the century, quantities of logs and beams were shipped to the United States and Europe through the small lumber port of Minatitlán on the Coatzacoalcos River and, by unsystematic and destructive cutting, the Tehuantepec and Tabasco forests were depleted of their valuable cabinet woods. Today, the exploitation of tropical woods has shifted to the rain forest of Campeche and Quintana Roo, in the Yucatan Peninsula. The sawmills and plywood factories of the towns of Campeche and Chetumal are busy processing mahogany and tropical cedar logs that are hauled in from the interior forests.

Sea Fisheries. Despite a long, 5,470-mile coastline and rich offshore fauna, Mexico's fisheries, like those of many Latin American countries, are underdeveloped. Throughout the colonial period and well into the nineteenth century, only a few subsistence fisherfolk lived along the coasts; commercial fishing was practically

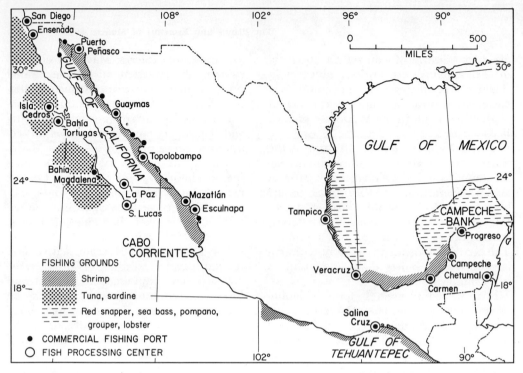

Figure 11.24 Mexican fisheries

nonexistent. Mexicans have begun to develop their fishing resources only since the 1940s, after adopting modern North American-type fishing gear, freezing plants, and canning factories. Even so, less than one-third of the fish caught in Mexican waters is consumed within the country; the rest of the catch is exported, chiefly to the United States.

Although the reasons for the poor development of Mexico's fisheries may be partly cultural, natural conditions have also been responsible. Except on the Pacific shores of Baja California, the warm seas off the Mexican coasts contain a large fish population of many species, rather than the enormous schools of a single species of finfish as are found in cooler, midlatitude waters. The difficulty and expense of catching a single marketable species of fish in warm tropical waters are somewhat analogous to those involved in lumbering a single species of tree scattered within the tropical rain forest.

The major commercial fishing grounds of Mexico lie off the Pacific coast of Baja

California; within the long, narrow Gulf of California; and along the coasts of Sinaloa and Nayarit, to Cabo Corrientes (Figure 11.24). From these areas come 65 percent of Mexico's annual catch. The nutrient-rich water of the cold California current, along the Pacific side of Baja California, teems with large schools of sardines, anchovies, and tuna. Tuna is taken mainly by United States boats operating out of San Diego and San Pedro, California, with the Mexican government collecting a tax on the catch.

Extensive shrimp beds are found in the warm waters of the Gulf of California, particularly along the shallow, muddy shores of Sonora and Sinaloa, and, since World War II, shrimping has been the mainstay of Mexican commercial fishing along the west coast. Most of the annual take is processed in freezing plants in Guaymas and Mazatlán and shipped to the United States. In recent years over-exploitation of shrimp off Sonora and Sinaloa has drastically lowered production and has prompted many trawlers to migrate southward to beds within the Gulf of Tehuantepec. At present about two-thirds of the total Mexican shrimp catch comes from beds along the Pacific coast.

Mexico's second important fishing area lies within the tropical waters of the Gulf of Mexico. From the Rio Grande southward to Veracruz, the coastal waters afford an abundance of red snapper, sea bass, and pampano. The shallow, coral-strewn bottom of the Campeche bank, off Yucatan, is even more productive of these species, which are taken by boats from Tampico and Veracruz, where the catch is processed for national consumption.

A significant fishing development of Mexico in recent years has been the rise of shrimping in the southern Gulf area. The main shrimp beds are off Tabasco and southern Campeche, where large rivers have deposited enormous quantities of silt and sand, which make an ideal habitat for these crustaceans. The Gulf shrimping fleet, consisting of over 300 modern trawlers, is based mainly at Ciudad del Carmen, in southern Campeche. There, several freezing plants process the catch for export to the United States. Shrimp exports now constitute one of Mexico's most lucrative sources of foreign exchange.

In 1969, the Mexican government began a program to encourage the growth of its fishing industry. Efforts to stem the decline of the Pacific shrimp catch involve the protection of the numerous coastal lagoons that function as nursery areas for the juvenile stage of most commercial shrimp species. Moreover, the modernization of the fishing fleet, as well as the improvement of the main fishing ports and creation of new ones, is now under way. This phase of the program aims to both increase and diversify the annual catch and thereby to decrease the reliance on shrimping as the mainstay of the industry. Another goal is to increase the national output of industrial fish products, such as fish meal, so that the country will no longer have to import them. Equally important, the gov-ernment hopes to encourage the national consumption of fish to improve the diet of low-income groups. It is estimated that less than one-fifth of the Mexican people eat seafood regularly, and that even a smaller proportion of the coastal inhabitants do so.

Mineral Exploitation. As in colonial times, the exploitation and processing of mineral resources continues to be a significant part of the Mexican economy. The bulk of the metals extracted still comes from the old mining centers within the colonial Silver Belt (Chapter 10). Since 1968, Mexico has lost to Canada and Peru its long-standing position as the world's leading producer of silver. The value of industrial metals, however, such as lead, zinc, copper, and iron, has risen to nearly 80 percent of the country's metallic mineral production. In recent years, however, petroleum, sulphur, and fluorite have exceeded the metals in value and importance.

METALS. After the Wars of Independence (1810–1821), most of the old silver mines of northern and central Mexico lay in ruins. By the mid-nineteenth century, with with the introduction of British mining techniques and capital, silver production had gradually improved. Then, during the *Pax Porfiriana* (1877–1910), the output was greatly increased by the introduction of new ore-milling and refining processes, plus capital and management, from the United States. In 1880, gold and silver accounted for 90 percent of the value of Mexico's mineral exports; at the turn of the century, lead, zinc, and copper production had surpassed that of the precious metals; and, on the eve of the revolution (1910), large North American corporations held more than three-quarters of the producing mines and smelters.

Though many new mines were opened throughout highland Mexico, the greater part of the ores came from the old mining centers of colonial fame—Pachuca, Guanajuato, Zacatecas, Parral, and others. Below the worked-out silver veins of these mines are ores abundant in zinc, lead, and sometimes copper. In the 1880s, an American company developed the rich copper deposits of Cananea in northern Sonora, and French interests opened the Boleo copper mines at Santa Rosalía in Baja California. The year 1903 saw the opening of the large Cerro de Mercado, near Durango City, one of the chief sources of iron ore for Mexico's growing iron and steel industry.

Although the mining industry faltered during the period of revolutionary turmoil, the production of silver and copper reached its peak in the late 1920s; that of lead and zinc, in the decades following. Since World War II, however, the extraction of these metals has declined, for the workable ores in the old mines are rapidly being depleted and foreign competition has depressed prices. Thus, many of the old mining centers of northern and central Mexico, such as Fresnillo, Pachuca, and several smaller towns, have become economic and social problem spots within the expanding economy of Mexico.

FUELS. A profound change in Mexican mineral production occurred at the beginning of this century with the exploitation of the hydrocarbon fuel resources—coal, petroleum, and natural gas. In the 1880s, deposits of bituminous coal yielding an excellent grade of coke were discovered in the Sabinas Basin, northern Coahuila. By 1900, Sabinas coal had become an important fuel for railroad locomotives in Mexico, and later it fueled the iron and steel industry of Monterrey.

The exploitation of the large petroleum and natural gas deposits along the Gulf coast began at the turn of the century. These fuel resources have been basic to Mexico's industrial growth for the past 30 years. Gas and oil now furnish 80 percent of the power used by Mexican industry and transport. First developed by North American and British corporations, the petroleum industry was nationalized in 1938; since that time the government agency PEMEX (*Petróleos Mexicanos*) has helped the industry to become the second largest Latin American oil producer.

In general, the petroleum zones of eastern Mexico are a southern extension of the Gulf coast fields in the United States. Similar oil-bearing structures, including ancient coral reefs, anticlinal folds, and salt domes, occur in both areas. By 1950, seven oil and gas provinces had been developed within the Mexican Gulf lowlands, extending from the Rio Grande to the Yucatan Peninsula (Figure 11.25). The most productive provinces lie in (1) northern Veracruz and southern Tamaulipas, Tampico being the main refining center and oil port; and (2) Tabasco and southern Veracruz, where Minatitlán and Coatzacoalcos serve as refining and shipping points. In 1901, a North American company brought in the first well near Tampico. Later the famous Golden Lane (*Faja de Oro*) field, which once produced 400,000 barrels daily, was developed south of Tampico. Today 40 percent of Mexico's oil comes from the Poza Rica province in northern Veracruz. Production there was increased recently by the exploitation of a rich offshore deposit, called the Marine Golden Lane. Since the 1950s, PEMEX has upped production in southern Veracruz and Tabasco. This tropical lowland now yields more crude oil than the Poza Rica province and is also Mexico's main source of natural gas. Recently, an enormous oil reserve was discovered in Tabasco and the neighboring lowlands of northern Chiapas. Future production from this zone may double Mexico's petroleum output, bringing the country into the ranks of the world's leading oil exporting nations. Although PEMEX has constructed several refineries in the Gulf area, much of the crude oil is transported to the Mesa Central, through pipelines, for refining in the Valley of Mexico (at Azcapotzalco) and the Bajío (at Salamanca). Natural gas is piped from eastern Tabasco to Mexico

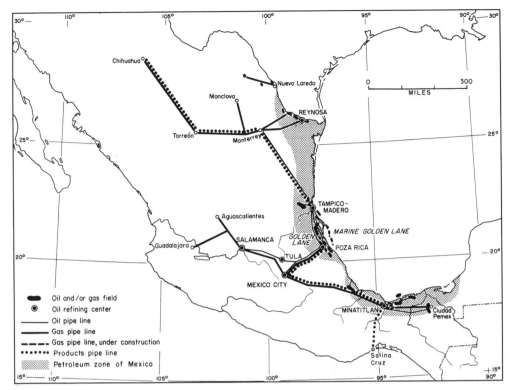

Figure 11.25 Petroleum industry of Mexico

City, and from the Reynosa fields in northeastern Mexico to the industrial centers of Monterrey, Monclova and Torreón.

The exploitation of oil and gas has changed the landscape of the Gulf lowlands. Construction and operation of drilling rigs, storage tanks, depressurizing stations, pipelines, roads, and airstrips have transformed once-isolated subsistence farming areas into semiindustrial regions. New settlements have been formed within the oil fields. Some are permanent, well-planned modern towns, such as the administrative and refining center of Poza Rica in Veracruz. Others are temporary camps for oil field workers and their families—agglomerations of wooden shacks that usually disappear with the completion of drilling operations. The network of all-weather roads within the petroleum provinces has given native farmers access to outside markets; and as laborers in the oil fields, many local inhabitants find a

new source of income and are introduced to a new way of life. This acculturating influence of the petroleum industry is clearest among the lowland Totonac and Huastec Indians of northern Veracruz. The industry has also attracted from other parts of Mexico many workers and merchants who often remain in the lowlands as permanent settlers.

The exploitation of sulphur, which is associated with the petroleum deposits of southern Veracruz and Tabasco, has been the most recent development in the Mexican mineral industry. Large sulphur deposits occur near the top of salt domes that penetrate the coastal plain. First worked in 1956 by North American concerns, the deposits in the vicinity of Jaltipan, southern Veracruz, now produce 20 percent of the Free World's native sulphur (by the Frasch process), most of which is exported to the United States and Brazil via the nearby river port of Coatzacoalcos.

With the basic ingredients of oil, sulphur, and salt close at hand, a sizeable petrochemical industry is now building up near the town of Minatitlán on the Coatzacoalcos River. Modern plants for the manufacture of commercial fertilizer, aromatics, synthetic rubber, plastics, and other products are in operation or are planned. Petrochemical plants have also been established in various industrial centers in the eastern lowlands and on the Mesa Central, all of which are dependent on the petroleum of the Gulf coast.

Manufacturing Industries

Manufacturing, partly as associated with the extractive industries discussed above, has become a significant factor in Mexico's economy and has created many changes in the landscape, particularly around urban centers. Industrialization began during the *Pax Porfiriana* of the late nineteenth century with the availability of foreign capital, the construction of railways, and the initial exploitation of energy resources (petroleum, coal, and electrical power).

Since 1940, manufacturing, like other elements of the economy, has undergone such phenomenal growth that Mexico is now one of the most industrialized countries of Latin America. The value of Mexican industrial production tripled from $6.4 billion in 1960 to $19.3 billion in 1970. Today, nearly 23 percent of the Mexican labor force is engaged in industry (versus 26 percent for the United States). It must be emphasized, however, that half of the Mexican workers are still farmers (less than 5 percent of United States workers are farmers). Moreover, in 1970, industry accounted for 34 percent of Mexico's gross national product, while agriculture's share was only 11 percent. And since 1971, the value of manufactures has exceeded that of agricultural products in Mexico's exports.

Light industries, such as textiles, food processing, paper and wood products, and the like, predominate in Mexico's manufactures; heavy industries, including iron and steel, petrochemicals, and automobile parts, are secondary but are growing rapidly. Modern industry is restricted chiefly to the large cities, primarily within the densely peopled Mesa Central and, to a lesser extent, in those of the north and of the Gulf coast lowlands.

Mexico has advantages over most Latin American countries—availability of raw materials, an adequate energy base, and an abundant pool of cheap labor. On the other hand, the low purchasing power of the predominantly rural population, the inefficiency of production, the deficiency of local capital, and the lack of outside markets have tended to hinder an industrial growth comparable to that of West European nations.

Energy for Industry. One of the most significant factors in the recent surge of Mexico's manufacturing industry is the availability of an adequate energy resource. The hydrocarbon fuels (coal, petroleum, and natural gas) discussed in the last section are, of course, fundamental. These are used directly as industrial fuels or are converted into thermoelectrical power to operate machinery. Equally important is the development of hydroelectric power.

Figure 11.26 shows that many hydroelectric plants are located on the eastern and southern escarpments of the Mesa Central, where steep gradients and adequate streams afford the natural conditions necessary for the generation of power. Most of these stations were completed between 1940 and 1960. Mexico's largest and newest hydroelectric systems, however, have been constructed on large rivers in the south. Completed in 1969, the Malpaso plant on the middle Grijalva River serves the industries of Minatitlán,

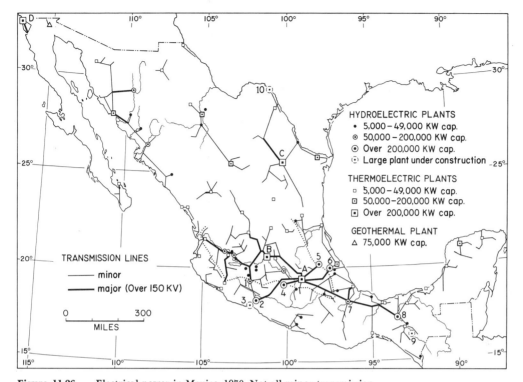

Figure 11.26 Electrical power in Mexico, 1970. Not all minor transmission lines are shown. Numbers and letters on map refer to the following: (1) Cupatizio; (2) Infiernillo; (3) La Villita; (4) Miguel Alemán complex; (5) Necaxa; (6) Mazatepec; (7) Papaloapan system; (8) Malpaso; (9) La Angostura; (10) La Amistad; (A) Mexico City (three large stations); (B) Salamanca (one large station); (C) Monterrey (two large stations); and (D) Tijuana (one large station).

Veracruz, Puebla, and the Valley of Mexico. The new Infiernillo–La Villita complex on the lower Balsas River, together with the older escarpment stations of the Miguel Alemán system, Mazatepec, and Necaxa, now furnish nearly half of the electrical energy used in the Valley of Mexico. Another large hydroelectric complex is La Angostura, recently completed on the upper Grijalva River in Chiapas.

The Mexican government considers electric power so important that the industry is almost totally nationalized and is administered by the Federal Commission of Electricity. Rural electrification is one of Mexico's major social and economic goals. In 1970, all towns and cities over 5,000 population had electricity, and the power network had been extended to cover about half of the national territory.

Even so, 40 percent of Mexico's people still live without electricity.

The Textile Industry. Two of Mexico's outstanding industries—textiles and steel—are examples of light and heavy manufacturing, respectively. Textile production is the country's oldest manufacturing industry. The colonial, hand-operated woolen mills (*obrajes*) established in the Mesa Central towns were discussed in Chapter 10. By the mid-nineteenth century, European immigrants had built water-powered woolen and cotton mills on the eastern escarpment above Orizaba in Veracruz state. With the development of hydroelectric power in the 1890s, the textile industry was greatly expanded, especially in the escarpment towns of Jalapa and Orizaba and in the

337

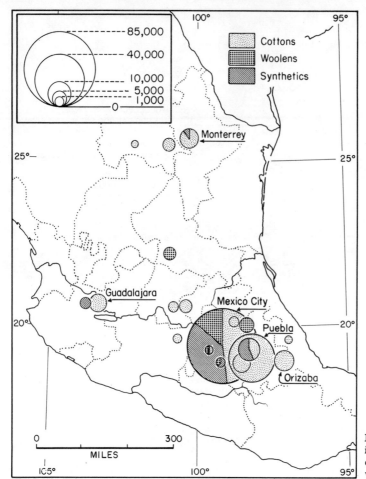

Figure 11.27 Textile industry of Mexico. Graduated circles refer to number of workers.

traditional cloth-making centers of Puebla and Mexico City. At the same time, the beginning of large-scale cotton growing in the irrigated districts of the north, plus the completion of trunk railways connecting northern and central Mexico, resulted in the rise of cotton cloth manufacturing as the chief branch of the Mexican textile industry.

Manta, heavy, coarse cloth used for clothing by low-income groups, is the main cotton textile. Finer Mexican cottons found a ready market in the United States and Latin America during World War II, but today little is exported.

The output of woolens has also declined. Synthetic fibers, chiefly rayon and nylon, are now made in Mexico. Today one-third of Mexico's manufacturing labor force works in textiles. As can be seen from Figure 11.27, the main cloth centers are Puebla and Mexico City, where over 35 percent of the textile workers are concentrated.

The Steel Industry. Most underdeveloped countries, particularly those of Latin America, which have for so long been dependent on the United States and northwestern Europe for industrial goods, consider iron and steel manufacturing the basis of industrial growth. These countries often try to force the development of this heavy industry even if they lack the balance of natural resources required for economic production. Mexico, perhaps better endowed with available raw materials for heavy industry than most Latin American countries, was the first Latin American nation to install a modern, integrated iron and steel industry. This was begun in 1903 at Monterrey, in the northeastern part of the country.

Three essential raw materials are found in the north. There is high-grade iron ore at Cerro de Mercado near Durango City, at La Perla in eastern Chihuahua, and at Hércules in western Coahuila; coking coal, in the Sabinas Basin of northern Coahuila; and limestone for flux, in the folded ranges of the Sierra Madre Oriental. But abundant water, needed in large quantities for making iron and steel, is lacking in the arid north. Monterrey, approximately halfway between the Durango iron

ore deposits and the Sabinas coal field by rail, remains an important center of the industry. In 1944, the Mexican government established a new steel mill at Monclova, near the Sabinas coal basin northwest of Monterrey. Monclova is now Mexico's leading steel-producing center. The mills of both cities produce more than half of the country's crude steel, the rest being manufactured in the Valley of Mexico, Puebla, Veracruz, Guadalajara, and in small mills in other industrial centers (Figure 11.28).

A new geographical pattern of Mexico's iron and steel industry is now emerging.

Figure 11.28   Steel industry of Mexico

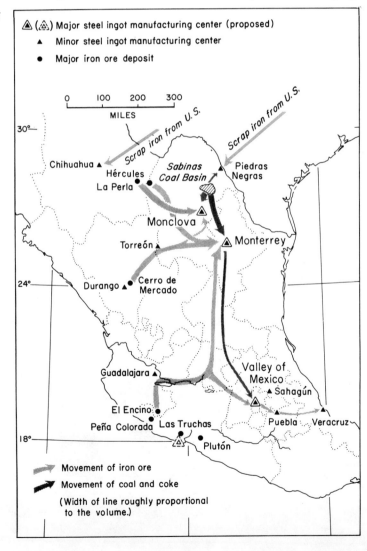

Since 1961, the government and private concerns have been mining deposits of high-grade iron ore in the Sierra Madre del Sur in the southwestern part of the country, an area that contains Mexico's largest reserves of iron ore. Presently almost one-fourth of the ore used in the mills of Monterrey, and nearly all that is employed in the new steel plants of Puebla and Veracruz, is shipped by rail for a distance of some 500 to 700 miles from the mines in southern Jalisco and Colima. More significant, in 1971, the government began construction of a new integrated steel manufacturing complex, called Lázaro Cárdenas–Las Truchas, near the mouth of the Balsas River. Planned as one of the largest steel plants in Mexico, this complex will utilize ore from a large deposit nearby, coking coal from abroad (probably Colombia), and hydroelectric power from the recently completed Infiernillo and La Villita stations.

Mexico, whose iron and steel produc-tion has increased tenfold since World War II, is now nearly self-sufficient and is even exporting some steel products. Nevertheless, to exist, the industry must be protected by high tariffs; imported United States and European crude steel is still cheaper than the local product. Although Mexicans point with justifiable pride to the rapid growth of iron and steel production in their country, in 1965 the industry employed less than 3 percent of the industrial labor force and produced only 7.5 percent of the value of total manufactures. Government plans, however, call for the doubling of Mexico's annual steel production from about 4 million tons in 1970 to 8 million tons by 1980.

Distribution of Manufacturing. In Mexico, manufacturing is localized in a few industrial centers. Figure 11.29 shows that most of the centers are within the Mesa Central and that the Valley of Mexico, including Mexico City and its en-

Figure 11.29   Relative importance of manufacturing centers in Mexico, based on number of workers, 1965

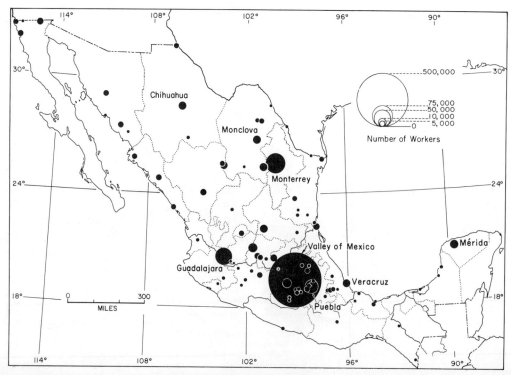

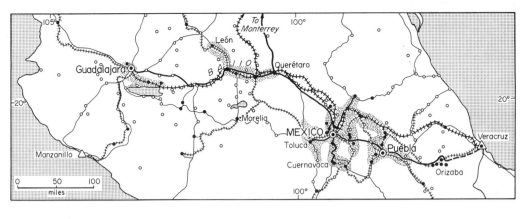

Figure 11.30   The urban-industrial corridor of Mexico

virons, contains by far the greatest industrial concentration. Here, more than 45 percent of the nation's industrial laborers work in 30 percent of the total number of industrial establishments to produce nearly half the value of Mexico's manufactures. And the concentration is still increasing. Almost the whole range of Mexican manufacturing is represented—from petroleum refining, iron and steel, and cement, through automobiles, textiles, chemicals, electrical products, and food processing, to jewelry, ceramics, and matches. The vast reservoir of cheap labor and the nearness to local markets in the densely populated Mesa Central are among the factors that may have caused this phenomenal concentration. The industrial concentration itself acts like a magnet, attracting into Mexico City more and more manufacturing plants and more and more job seekers. Decentralization of industry is one of Mexico's pressing needs.

Other growing manufacturing areas of central Mexico and adjacent sections include the textile towns and other industrial centers of the Puebla Basin and the eastern escarpment; the port of Veracruz, with its expanding metal industries; Cuernavaca and environs on the southern escarpment; Toluca, west of the Valley of Mexico; Guadalajara and nearby villages on the western side of the plateau; and the larger towns of the Bajío of Guanajuato. The Bajío is a likely area for the construction of new industrial plants in order to relieve the overconcentration in the Valley of Mexico. Moreover, the government is now engaged in the establishment of new towns for industry in various parts of the plateau. For example, the automobile and freight-car manufacturing center of Ciudad Sahagún, 60 miles northeast of Mexico City, was formed in 1952. More recently, in 1971, the new industrial city of Cuautitlán Izcalli was begun northwest of the capital. Many more such centers are in the planning stage.

Taken together, the manufacturing centers of the Mesa Central and adjacent escarpments, plus the main transport linkages, today form the *urban-industrial corridor* of Mexico. As shown in Figure 11.30, the corridor extends from Veracruz westward to Guadalajara for a distance of more than 500 miles. It includes three of Mexico's four largest cities and scores of smaller ones; it supports two-thirds of the nation's industrial workers and produces about two-thirds of the value of Mexican manufacturers; and it contains the country's busiest railroad lines and highways.

341

Although much smaller in area, population, and industrial productivity, the emerging Mexican urban-industrial corridor is comparable in a relative sense to the older North American manufacturing-urban belt that extends from New England to Chicago and beyond.

In northern Mexico, the Monterrey-Saltillo-Monclova zone is the only significant industrial concentration. However, around the cities of Torreón, Chihuahua, and some of the agricultural market centers of the northwest there are growing manufacturing districts. Moreover, in 1965, the Mexican government, as part of its National Frontier Program, agreed to permit United States companies to establish "in-bond" industries in the northern border cities. Under this arrangement parts manufactured in the United States, as well as raw materials, are carried duty-free across the border, where they are assembled or processed in United States–built plants within the border towns. The finished product is then returned to the United States for marketing. North American capital and technology are thus combined with cheap and abundant Mexican labor to create an expanding industrial program along the international border. By 1973, nearly 40,000 Mexican workers were employed in about 340 border factories, producing light industrial items that ranged from sophisticated electronic devices to toys and processed foods.

Despite its spectacular growth since the 1940s, Mexico's manufacturing industry, like so much of the economy, has its share of problems. Those of geographical over-concentration in the Valley of Mexico and the need for decentralization have been mentioned. Another problem involves overexpansion of many industries in relation to existing markets to the extent that some plants operate at half capacity, resulting in high operative costs and inflated prices. To this must be added the problem of poor quality production. Until Mexican manufacturers can improve technical skills, most of their modern products cannot compete abroad with those of established industrial countries. Perhaps Mexico's greatest problem in industry is its lack of a large domestic market for manufactured goods. The bulk of its population, especially in the rural areas, is still too poor to afford even those items considered necessities in the developed countries. Mexico thus looks abroad to export its industrial wares, only to find a highly competitive international market. Nonetheless, the Mexican government continues to encourage industrial growth by maintaining high protective tariffs on various imports, subsidizing some private companies, and partially nationalizing certain manufactures, such as petrochemicals and steel. The original national goals of industrial self-sufficiency (import substitution), creation of employment in cities, and increased export of manufactured goods remain unchanged.

The Cottage Industries. Traditional cottage industries of aboriginal or colonial origin still supplement the livelihood of many rural folk throughout Mexico. Most of these home occupations involve handicrafts, such as pottery making, woodworking, weaving, basketry, and others. They usually occupy the spare time of women and children in small agricultural villages.

As in times past, members of a given Indian or mestizo household may specialize in a particular handicraft, handing down the traditional techniques from one generation to the next. For example, the towns of Acatlán, Puebla, and Tlaquepaque, Jalisco, are renowned throughout central Mexico for their fine pottery; the towns of Olinalá, Guerrero, and Pátzcuaro, Michoacán, for their lacquered woodwork; and Teocaltiche, Jalisco, for its woolen blankets. Probably the villages most highly specialized in many handicrafts are those of the Tarascan Indians in the state of Michoacán. And practically every Mixtec Indian village in the highlands of western Oaxaca specializes in making hats from palm leaf.

Commerce in cottage industrial products is usually confined to regional markets and fairs, although many local handicrafts are now sent to the cities for the tourist trade. The cottage industries play an insignificant role in the national economy, but they represent an integral part of traditional Mexican culture held over from the past.

The Transport Network

The development of modern transportation in Mexico is, of course, closely bound up with the growth of commercial agriculture and industry that began during the mid-nineteenth century. Most of the trunk railway lines in use today were built during the period of Porfirio Díaz, and with North American and British capital; only a few key lines have been added since 1910. The country's impressive network of surface highways, however, is recent; more than two-thirds of the present system was constructed after 1940, by Mexicans and largely with Mexican capital.

The major pattern of both railroads and highways roughly follows the transport lines of colonial times. Most of the important routes converge on the Valley of Mexico, which has always been the economic and political nerve center of the country. Main routes also connect the central plateau with the Pacific and Gulf coasts, with the north and the United States, and with southern Mexico and Central America (Figures 11.31 and 11.32).

Railways. Mexico's first rail line, finished in 1872 after 30 years of construction, connected the capital with the main port of Veracruz. The two main trunk lines, to El Paso and Laredo on the United States border, were easily constructed

Figure 11.31   Railroad network of Mexico, 1970

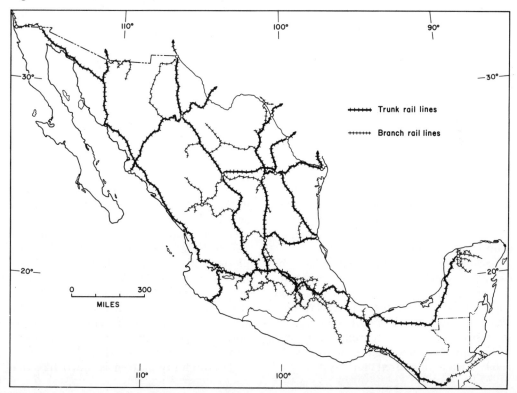

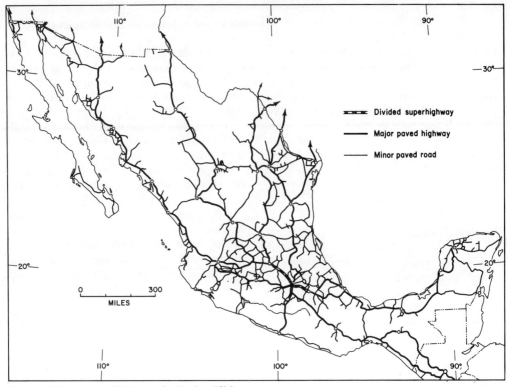

Figure 11.32 Paved highways in Mexico, 1970

through the flattish desert basins and rapidly completed by 1885. The Pacific coast line to Nogales, however, was not finished until the 1920s. These routes not only served the big mining centers and irrigated farming districts of northern Mexico, but also encouraged the growth of United States–Mexican trade. The two most recent additions to the railway network have been (1) the line that joined the Yucatan Peninsula with Veracruz and Mexico City for the first time, completed in 1950; and (2) the line between Chihuahua on the northern plateau and Topolobampo on the Pacific coast, the first railway to cross the Sierra Madre Occidental, completed in 1962.

Because of their importance to the country's economy, all Mexican railroads, except for a few minor lines, are now nationalized. The federal government strives to maintain the rail network, despite strong competition from the private truck and bus lines on the highways. By 1969, the nationalized rail system had been completely dieselized and through passenger service to the United States border had been improved.

The route between Mexico City and Nuevo Laredo, via Saltillo and Monterrey, is the most heavily used rail line in Mexico. This line carries twice the freight tonnage of any other trunk railroad to the United States. The second most important line, in terms of traffic volume, connects Mexico City with Guadalajara.

Roads. The most spectacular change in Mexico's transport system in the last 30 years has been the development of highways. Full-scale automobile traffic may be said to have begun in 1936 with the completion of the Inter-American Highway link from Laredo to Mexico City. Today, with over 40,000 miles of improved auto roads (one-half of which are paved) and with 1.5 million motor vehicles, Mexican auto transportation is exceeded, in Latin America, only by Brazil and Argentina.

The highway pattern is much like that

of the railroads. The densest net of paved roads is found in the Mesa Central, where modern farm roads have been constructed. Four paved highways radiate northward from the Valley of Mexico to the United States border; several run from the Mesa Central to the southern and southeastern parts of the country (for example, the Inter-American Highway to Guatemala and the Gulf Circuit Highway to Yucatan); and many short transverse roads lead from plateau cities down the steep escarpments to ports along the Pacific and Gulf coasts. Unfortunately, poor maintenance often detracts from the usefulness of the Mexican highways.

Two factors have significantly promoted the rapid growth of the highway system: the tourist trade from the United States; and the development of truck freighting, which now competes successfully with the railroads. In 1968, freight trucks in Mexico numbered nearly a half million; large, 12-wheeled, diesel-powered, truck-trailer combinations now carry farm and industrial products from one end of the country to the other.

Another aspect of modern transport in Mexico is the ubiquitous bus or passenger truck, heavily loaded with people and animals, bouncing along the most unlikely auto trails into remote areas of the mountainous countryside. Today there are relatively few towns and villages in Mexico that lack some kind of bus or truck service. On the paved highways, large Greyhound-type buses have become a major means of travel between the large cities of the country.

Ports and Foreign Commerce

Today, as in colonial times, Mexico's front door to overseas trade faces eastward on the Gulf coast. Since the early nineteenth century, the United States and northwestern Europe have replaced Spain as the main overseas market. At present, about 60 percent of all foreign overseas tonnage

Figure 11.33   Relative size of Mexican ports based on foreign tonnage, three-year average, 1965–1967

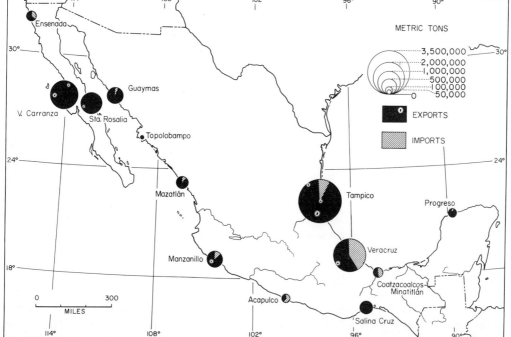

Figure 11.34 City and port of Tampico on the Río Pánuco. Oil refineries line both banks of the river; the main wharves for commercial shipping lie just off the photograph, lower left. The main business district of the city occupies the area between the river and the Laguna Carpintero. (*Compañía Mexicana Aerofoto*)

is cleared through the Gulf coast ports (Figure 11.33).

Veracruz remains Mexico's major port of entry, receiving half the country's imports, but Tampico now handles more foreign commerce, including the bulk of oil exports (Figure 11.34). Tampico is the port for northeastern Mexico, which contains the industrial zone of Monterrey-Saltillo-Monclova, the oasis of La Laguna, and the oil fields of Tamaulipas and northern Veracruz. Most of Mexico's sulphur and crude petroleum exports move from the fields of southern Veracruz and Tabasco through Coatzacoalcos on the Gulf and Salina Cruz on the Pacific.

The west coast ports are smaller and handle less traffic than those on the Gulf. However, since 1950, their share in the country's foreign maritime commerce has increased from 20 to 40 percent, due mainly to the growing trade with Japan and the Pacific coast of the United States. With the increase of cotton production in the river oases of Sonora and Sinaloa, Guaymas, on the Gulf of California, has become an important west coast port, shipping cotton chiefly to Japan. Cotton also leaves through the ports of Topolobampo and Mazatlán, but the exports of the Mexicali irrigation district pass either through San Diego, California, or are shipped directly out of the newly enlarged port of Ensenada. Other west coast ports engaged in foreign commerce include Santa Rosalía, in Baja California, from which copper concentrates are shipped; Venustiano Carranza, a new port on the west coast of Baja California, from which large quantities of industrial salt leave for the United States and Japan; and Manzanillo, the port for Guadalajara and the western part of the Mesa Central. Acapulco, one of the most renowned colonial ports on the Pacific coast of the Americas, no longer handles any significant cargo.

The bulk of Mexico's trade with the United States moves by rail and highway through 16 customs stations along the international boundary. In 1966, over half of Mexico's total imports (by both tonnage and value) and a third of its total exports passed through these border crossings, indicating the close commercial ties between the two countries. As shown in Figure 11.35, most of this trade crosses the border in northeastern Mexico and utilizes the major rail lines and highways that lead to and from the manufacturing and population centers in the eastern United States.

Prior to World War II, minerals, including crude petroleum, comprised three-quarters of the value of Mexico's exports, reflecting the continuation of the colonial overseas trade pattern. Since 1945, a dras-

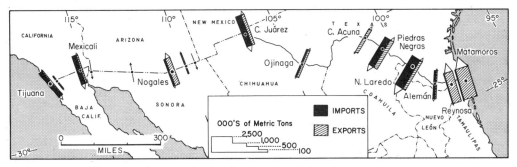

Figure 11.35 Movement of international trade across the United States–Mexican border, 1966–1967 average

tic change in Mexican exports has occurred, and agricultural commodities now account for 30 percent of the value of exports. Of these, cotton, sugar, and coffee account for a sixth of the total. The change in the export pattern clearly reflects the revolution in Mexican commercial agriculture during the last 30 years, as well as the decline of minerals in the national economy. Moreover, the fact that in 1974 manufactured products made up more than half of Mexican exports, by value, parallels the recent surge of industrialization and the government policy to encourage the sale of manufactures abroad. More significant is the overall diversification of export commodities, which has helped stabilize the Mexican economy.

Despite its goal toward industrial self-sufficiency, Mexico continues to import large quantities of manufactured wares. More than half the imports, by value, consist of machinery of all kinds, chemical products, precision tools, and motor vehicle parts.

Since the *Pax Porfiriana* of the late nineteenth century, the United States has been Mexico's best customer, followed by the north European nations. Recently, Japan, which imports a third of the Mexican cotton crop, has become second in Mexico's export list. Recent Mexican policy aims to increase trade with Asiatic countries, including Communist China,

and to establish closer commercial ties with other Latin American nations, especially the neighboring Central American states. As Mexico expands its foreign commerce to various parts of the world, the United States' share of its neighbor's international trade stands to decline. Between 1958 and 1970, for example, that share decreased from 78 to 66 percent.

The Tourist Trade

The significance of tourism to the economy and landscape of the Caribbean in the past 30 years was described in previous chapters. Mexico shares with the rest of Middle America many of the physical factors that have attracted tourists, particularly North Americans: geographical proximity, a benign winter climate, tropical seascapes, varied mountain scenery, and the like. Mexico may be even more attractive because of its exotic folk culture of Indian origin, its abundance of prehistoric Indian monuments, and its many colonial vestiges, such as religious structures and quaint, medieval-looking towns. The national capital, one of the world's great cities, is itself a special tourist attraction, and it is becoming a favorite locale for international conventions (Figure 11.36).

Tourism in Mexico began on a modest scale about 1938, after the completion of

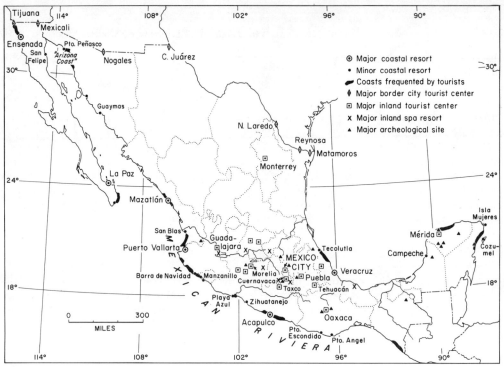

Figure 11.36 Tourist centers in Mexico

the highway from Laredo to Mexico City. Thereafter, except for the war years (1941–1945), the number of foreign visitors has steadily increased. In 1970, aproximately 2.1 million tourists who visited the interior spent nearly 600 million dollars within the country. Adding the amount spent in the border towns in 1970, tourists left a total of about 1.5 billion dollars in Mexico. As this sum accounted for more than half of Mexico's foreign exchange income, tourism has indeed become a significant factor in the national economy. Mexico, however, receives only 30 percent of the total number of tourists who visit Middle America, versus the 60 percent who vacation in the West Indies.

Nearly 90 percent of the tourists who visit Mexico are United States citizens, mainly residents of California, Arizona, and Texas. Most of those who travel inland from the border points head either for the beaches along the Pacific coast or for the cities and resorts of the central highlands. Somewhat more travel by air (50 percent) than by highway (41 percent),

Table 11.2 PASSENGER AIR TRAFFIC TO MEXICAN CITIES FROM NORTH AMERICA, 1973

City	Number of Weekly Flights	Percentage of Total Weekly Flights to Middle America from North America
Mexico City	493	16.5
Acapulco	187	6.2
Guadalajara	109	3.6
Mazatlán	74	2.5
Puerto Vallarta	39	1.3
Monterrey	31	1.0
Mérida	15	0.5
TOTAL	984	31.6

Source: Official Airline Guide, North American and International editions, 1973.

and the proportion that uses passenger planes is increasing. Table 11.2 indicates that half the weekly air flights from North

America to Mexico terminate in the capital, whereas about one-third go to the big resort centers on the Pacific coast.

To attract and accommodate the large influx of foreign visitors, the Mexican government has expanded its transport system. It has also encouraged the establishment of modern hotels in the larger towns, of United States–type motels along the main highways, and of resort areas in certain sections of the country. One of the most popular areas of Mexico is the formerly isolated southwest coast. This "Mexican Riviera," extending from Acapulco northward to Mazatlán, is rapidly becoming one of the world's foremost winter resort areas. A pleasant tropical climate, a scenic coast composed of rocky headlands that alternate with long stretches of sandy beaches, excellent fishing, and luxury accommodations now attract thousands of national and foreign vacationers to the main resort centers of Acapulco, Zihuatanejo, Puerto Vallarta, Manzanillo, Navidad, San Blas, and Mazatlán. Other rapidly developing resort centers include various sections of the warm southern escarpment of the Mesa Central, such as the Cuernavaca area immediately south of Mexico City and the hot-spring health resorts of San José Purúa in Michoacán and Ixtapan de la Sal in the state of Mexico. Easily accessible by air and highway, the large Mayan archaeological sites of Yucatan now attract a growing number of North American and European tourists. Likewise, the beach resorts along the Caribbean side of the Yucatan Peninsula, such as Cozumel Island, Cancún Island, and Isla Mujeres, are becoming increasingly popular.

The United States tourists spend more dollars in the Mexican border towns than in any other part of the country. Most of these visitors cross the border to shop and to "see Mexico" only for a few hours, but they leave in the border towns over half of Mexico's income from tourism. Although all the 16 major border crossings attract foreign visitors, Tijuana, Nogales, Ciudad Juárez, and Nuevo Laredo lead in tourist income.

Despite the spectacular growth of tourism in Mexico, various problems plague the industry. More and better hostelries are needed in many parts of the country, especially along the major highways that lead southward from the United States border. Partly because of such infrastructural deficiencies, the growth of tourism in Mexico has not kept pace with that in the West Indies and western Europe. Moreover, increasing numbers of Mexican upper- and middle-class urbanites now visit the United States and Europe, partially offsetting the gains in foreign exchange income earned by tourism at home. For this reason, the Mexican tourist bureau has attempted to increase the number of local tourists by appealing to national pride through such slogans as "See Mexico First."

SELECTED REFERENCES

BENASSINI, O. "Bases Para el Aprovachamiento Racional de los Recursos Hidráulicos en México." *Ingeniería Hidráulica en México* 25, no. 4 (1971):359–98.

BERMÚDEZ, A. J. *The Mexican National Petroleum Industry: A Case Study in Nationalization.* Stanford, Calif.: Institute of Hispanic America and Luso-Brazilian Studies, Stanford University, 1963.

CARR, R. "Mexican Agrarian Reform, 1910–1960." In E. L. Jones, and S. J. Woolf, eds. *Agrarian Change and Economic Development: The Historical Problem.* London: Methuen, 1969, pp. 151–68.

CHARDON, R. *Geographic Aspects of Plantation Agriculture in Yucatan.* National Research Council Publication no. 876. Washington, D.C., 1961.

CLINE, H. F. *Mexico: Revolution to Evolution, 1940–1960.* London and New York: Oxford University Press, 1962.

DILLMAN, C. D. "Urban Growth along Mexico's Northern Border and the Mexican National Border Program." *Journal of Developing Areas* 4, no. 4 (1970):487–507.

FREEBAIRN, D. R. "The Dichotomy of Prosperity and Poverty in Mexican Agriculture." *Land Economics* 45, no. 1 (1969):31–42.

GIERLOFF-EMDEN, H. G. *Mexico: Eine Landeskunde.* Berlin: Walter de Gruyter, 1970.

HENDERSON, D. A. "Arid Lands under Agrarian Reform in Northwest Mexico." *Economic Geography* 41, no. 4 (1965):300–12.

KENNELLY, R. A. "The Location of the Mexican Steel Industry." *Revista Geográfica* 14, no. 40 (1954):51–80; 15, no. 41 (1954):105–29; 16, no. 42 (1955):199–213; 17, no. 43 (1955):60–82.

LEWIS, O. *Life in a Mexican Village: Tepoztlán Restudied.* Urbana: University of Illinois Press, 1963.

———. *The Children of Sánchez; Autobiography of a Mexican Family.* New York: Random House, 1961.

McBRIDE, G. M. *Land Systems of Mexico.* New York: American Geographical Society, 1923.

McDOWELL, H. G. "Cotton in Mexico." *Journal of Geography* 63, no. 2 (1964):67–72.

MOSK, S. A. *Industrial Revolution in Mexico.* Berkeley: University of California Press, 1950.

SIMPSON, L. B. *Many Mexicos.* 4th ed. Berkeley: University of California Press, 1966.

STEVENS, R. P. "Spatial Aspects of Internal Migration in Mexico, 1950–1960." *Revista Geográfica,* no. 69 (1968):78–97.

STOLTMAN, J. P., and BALL, J. M. "Migration and the Local Economic Factor in Rural Mexico." *Human Organization* 30, no. 1 (1971):47–56.

TANNENBAUM, F. *The Mexican Agrarian Revolution.* Washington, D.C.: Brookings Institution, 1929.

UNIKEL, L. "The Process of Urbanization in Mexico: Distribution and Growth of Urban Population." In Rabinovitz, F. F., and Trueblood, F. M., eds. *Latin American Urban Research.* Vol. 1. Beverly Hills, Calif.: Sage Publications, 1971, pp. 247–302.

WHETTEN, N. L. *Rural Mexico.* Chicago: University of Chicago Press, 1948.

———. "Population Trends in Mexico." *Population Bulletin* 19, no. 7 (1963):180–84.

12

Geographic Regions of Mexico

In Chapter 11, we discussed the major features of Mexican culture that give expression to the geographical landscape, emphasizing the various changes in population and economy since the close of the colonial period. In this chapter we shall suggest two possible methods for dividing Mexico into areas or regions. One division, called *culture areas*, is based principally on present-day ethnic and cultural characteristics, many of which derive from the pre-Conquest and colonial past. The other division, called *city regions*, is based on the measurement of present-day interrelated human activities, which, through various means of transport and communication, bind the surrounding towns and countryside to a large city. Because of the historical emphasis of this book, the culture areas are herein presented at some length. The city regions, however, mainly because of the lack of pertinent measurable data, are only briefly considered at the end of the chapter.

CULTURE AREAS

Culture areas are geographical entities, within which particular cultural elements combine to pattern a landscape that is dis-tinct from that of adjacent regions. These areas are often hard to define and still more difficult to delimit precisely. Theoretically, such areas should be uniform in cultural elements and patterns, but in reality they are rarely so. In Mexico, culture areas in some cases coincide roughly with physical regions, for man's cultural manifestations within a given area are often closely associated with the nature of the land.

The largest and most fundamental cultural divisions of Mexico are the Indian-mestizo south and the European-mestizo north. The present boundary between these two divisions may be considered to be a wide zone, approximating the pre-Spanish borderland that separated the high Mesoamerican Indian farming cultures of southern and central Mexico from the nomadic hunting and gathering bands and primitive cultivators in the arid north. Figure 12.1 shows that the large regions are further divided into smaller culture areas, each with its particular cultural characteristics. Even these areas could be further divided, for the cultural scene of modern Mexico is almost as varied as its physical character. For this reason, the term "many Mexicos" is often used to denote the multitude of regional differences within the country. Here, as in many other

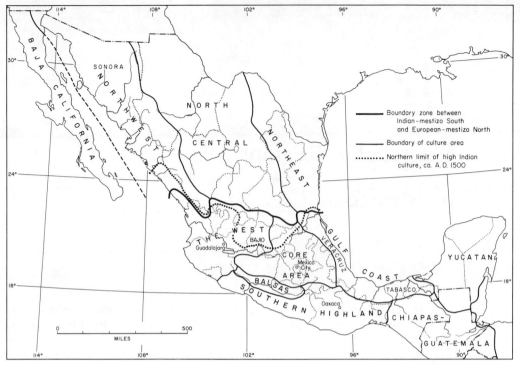

Figure 12.1   Culture areas of modern Mexico

Latin American nations, the local inhabitants often refer to their *patria chica* ("little homeland"), the small culture area to which they and their families feel that they belong, and most Mexican rural folk feel a stronger political allegiance to their *patria chica* than to the nation. In predominately Indian areas, the inhabitant usually views his individual village and surrounding lands as a cultural and geographical entity to which he professes a strong social attachment.

The Indian-Mestizo South

This area is by far the more important of the two large cultural divisions of Mexico. It had a large population before the Conquest, and even today it contains nearly three-quarters of the Mexican people. It was the locale of the ancient Mesoamerican civilizations and the main center of Spanish colonial activity. Today, its population is chiefly mestizo, but in many

sections the people are pureblood Indians; in others, unmixed Caucasians. The overall culture of the area is a mixture of Indian and Hispanic traits, but there are sizable sections, such as the Oaxaca highlands and the Yucatan Peninsula, in which most of the people are of Indian blood and culture.

The northern border of the Indian-mestizo south coincides only partially with the pre-Conquest limit of high Indian culture. The middle portion of the border has been pushed northward, to the vicinity of San Luis Potosí and Zacatecas, through migrations of people from the central part of the country. A closer correlation, perhaps, exists between the northern border and the transition between the volcanic Mesa Central and the arid Mesa del Norte. The southern boundary of the Indian-mestizo south is little affected by modern international limits; it extends beyond Guatemala and includes parts of Honduras and El Salvador. For convenience of presentation, however, these areas will be considered in the chapters on Central America.

The Core Area. The outstanding culture area within the Indian-mestizo south occupies the eastern and middle portions of the Mesa Central, including the eastern and southern plateau escarpments. For lack of a better term, we shall call this "the core area." Since before the Conquest, it has been the cultural center of all Mexico. It contained the hearths of the Aztec and Tarascan states and is still an area of much Indian tradition. During the colonial period, it was the political and economic center of New Spain. Today it contains the national capital and the densest population of the country. An important agricultural zone, it is also the industrial and transportation hub of modern Mexico and contains many large cities that have a veneer of modern European–North American culture.

The well-watered volcanic basins on the plateau form one of the significant physical features of the core area. Probably for more than 3,500 years, the fertile soils of the basins and lower mountain slopes have attracted a dense farming population, and the food available in the numerous lakes that occupy many of the basin floors has been equally attractive. The most important volcanic basin is the Valley of Mexico, flanked by those of Toluca and Puebla. Located more than 1.5 miles above the sea, most of the basins enjoy a bracing, tropical highland climate *(tierra fría)*.

The steep tropical escarpments bordering the plateau on the south and east form a part of the core area chiefly by reason of the close trade relations with the adjacent highland basins, which have existed since pre-Conquest times. In the course of this active trade, many elements of highland culture have penetrated the upper escarpment valleys. The tropical basins of Morelos, south of the Valley of Mexico, not only furnish the highlands with sugar, tropical fruits, and rice in return for wheat flour and manufactures, but they also have become sites for winter homes of the Mexico City elite and recreational areas for highland urban vacationers, much as they were for Aztec nobility nearly 500 years ago.

Racially, the bulk of the population within the core area is mestizo. A sizable portion, however, is of pure Indian blood, and about 10 percent, largely urban, is of Caucasian descent.

Enclaves of Indian speech and aboriginal mores dot the area. The total number of Indian-language speakers, however, is probably no more than one million, or about 7 percent of the core area population. The Otomí, who number around 185,000, occupy a large section north and northwest of the Valley of Mexico. One group, together with the closely related Mazahua (85,000), live in parts of Toluca Basin and adjacent mountain slopes, where semidispersed rancheria settlements and scattered hillside milpas have changed little since the Spanish Conquest. A still larger Otomí enclave covers the semiarid and highly eroded Mesquital Valley in Hidalgo state, one of the most forlorn of the *patrias chicas* in Mexico. Other important Indian groups within the core area include the Highland Totonac in northern Puebla state, the highland Huastec of easternmost San Luis Potosí, and the Tarascans of central Michoacán. Scattered throughout the area are small groups of Nahuatl speakers, highly fragmented remnants of a once-solid distribution, who now number perhaps 600,000. The sharp contrast between the remaining Indian strongholds and the modern urban centers is one of the important cultural characteristics of the core area, and one that makes it perhaps the most interesting of all Mexico for the student of human geography.

Prior to the agrarian reforms of this century, two rural settlement forms prevailed in the core area: (1) the colonial-type hacienda with its elaborate living center (*casco*); and (2) the agglomerated village, including the landholding Indian settlements and those of mestizos who had lost their land to the encroaching haciendas. The compact rural village still prevails, but the hacienda has been almost completely destroyed, for the ejido program of land redistribution has gone farther in the core area than in any other section of Mexico. Some large holdings still exist north of the Valley of Mexico for the cultivation of maguey (for pulque), and a few stock ranches (some for the breeding of fighting bulls) remain. Most of the villages and ejido farmers on the plateau raise maize, beans, and squash, as subsistence crops, and wheat and barley, as cash crops. Owners of small private holdings and some collective or individual *ejidatarios* in the escarpment areas cultivate commercial crops such as coffee and citrus.

Large urban centers form another component of the settlement pattern within the core area. Some of the cities, such as Puebla, Orizaba, and the federal capital, have a long history of industrialization, especially in textiles, and are now leading manufacturing centers. Modern Western culture has influenced the cities so greatly that they provide an exceptional contrast to the surrounding rural scene, still largely colonial or even pre-Conquest in character.

Mexico City. Greater Mexico City and its satellite towns in the Valley of Mexico form a special cultural region within the core area. With nearly 8.5 million inhabitants, the Mexican capital is one of the world's great cities and the largest in Latin America. This vast urban sprawl is unique in Middle America, the much smaller metropolitan area of Havana, Cuba (2.3 million) being its closest rival in size.

Mexico City occupies one of the least favorable sites in the nation for the development of a large urban center. It was a historical accident that Cortes and his men chose to build the administrative center of New Spain upon the ruins of Tenochtitlán, which occupied a low, marshy island near the western shore of Lake Texcoco. The Spaniards soon learned that the waters of the lake would flood the site yearly. Consequently, attempts to drain the lakes of the Valley of Mexico by artificial means were started during the seventeenth century, but this engineering feat was not completed until 1900, when the tunnel of Tequixquiac was opened in the northern part of the valley. Through this breach, the lake waters now flow northward to the upper tributaries of the Río Moctezuma and thence to the Gulf of Mexico. The draining of the lakes has decreased the danger of flood within the older part of the city, but the partially dried bed of Lake Texcoco has become the source of saline dust clouds that are swept into the urban area by easterly winds during the dry winter season.

An even more serious problem arises from the peculiar character of the subsurface alluvium on which the city is built. The top 200 feet of basin fill consists of fine silt and clay saturated with water. In the past 40 years, overpumping from deep wells has caused the surface to sink at a rate that, in places, has increased to about one foot annually. A large portion of the city's business section has been affected by this sinking, which has damaged buildings, water lines, and sewage disposal systems. Lacking a firm foundation, some of the tall, modern buildings in the city are constructed on gigantic steel drums that float in the spongy alluvium.

Mexico City's most pressing physical problem is the lack of sufficient local water to meet its growing requirements. Only short, intermittent streams drain the surrounding mountain slopes into the closed basin; the numerous springs that issue from the porous lava flows bordering the valley once supplied most of the city's water, but they now furnish only a small part. Since 1900, wells bored into the basin alluvium have supplied increasing amounts of water for the city; at present, one-third of the daily consumption is pumped from wells as deep as 1,000 feet below the surface. Even this supply has not kept pace with growing needs, and, as we have already noted, the rapidly lowering water table is causing the basin surface to sink. In the past few years, engineers have been forced to go outside the valley for water. In 1951, the Lerma aqueduct, which carries water to Mexico City from the copious springs of the upper Lerma River in Toluca Basin, was finally completed with the blasting of a tunnel through the Las Cruces range. This abundant source now supplies the city with nearly 30 percent of its needs, but the increasing demand will necessitate the further tapping of sources outside the valley, and at enormous cost.

For 350 years after its founding, Mexico City grew inordinately slowly. By midnineteenth century, the built-up section had reached beyond Alameda Park on the west; to the east, expansion was sharply limited by Lake Texcoco. By 1920, the more elite residential section had reached beyond Chapultepec Park to the lower foothills of the Las Cruces range. The city achieved its present phenomenal size in the past 40 years, during which it engulfed agricultural villages and market towns on the western side of the valley. The solidly built-up areas now cover approximately 180 square miles and, in places where industrial suburbs and slums are still expanding rapidly, extend far beyond the city limits (Figure 12.2).

The functional areas of Mexico City, as of many old European urban centers, form a highly complex pattern that has evolved with little planning. The traditional central business district lies between the Zócalo (the plaza that formed the center of the colonial city) and the Alameda to the west. Since 1940, the main hotel and office area has expanded southwestward along the famous Paseo de la Reforma, in lines of tall, ultramodern buildings. As in most cities of the world, retail and service activities line the main traffic arteries (Figure 12.3).

Most of the older residential areas are composed of closely spaced apartment buildings or European-type chalets enclosed by stone walls. Even in the elite residential suburbs along the foothills of Chapultepec Park, elaborate homes usually lack the spacious yards cherished by North American suburbanites.

Slums are found throughout the city (Figure 12.4). The recent arrivals from the countryside have spawned the largest squatter settlements, especially around the industrial districts and along the edge of the dry Texcoco lake bed on the eastern edge of town. There, the new "city" of Netzahualcoyotl, composed mainly of slum dwellings, in 1970 contained a half million people. In certain sections of the city, however, the municipal government has destroyed many of the worst slums to make way for community apartment units, such as that of Nonoalco, housing 90,000 people.

Although Mexico City's industrial areas are scattered in many parts of the metropolis, the greatest concentrations of plants cluster along the railroads and main highways in the vicinity of Tlalnepantla, Naucalpan, and Azcapotzalco, former agricultural towns northwest of the old city. Another important manufacturing district lies northeast of town, along the Laredo highway from Villa Madero to Ecatepec. The smoke and gaseous wastes from the industrial plants and from the exhausts of the thousands of automobiles that clog the city streets have created a serious air-pollution problem. The dull, grey haze and smog that envelop Mexico City most of the year obscure the beautiful views of surrounding mountains that one could enjoy 30 years ago.

Perhaps more than most large urban areas, Mexico City suffers from traffic con-

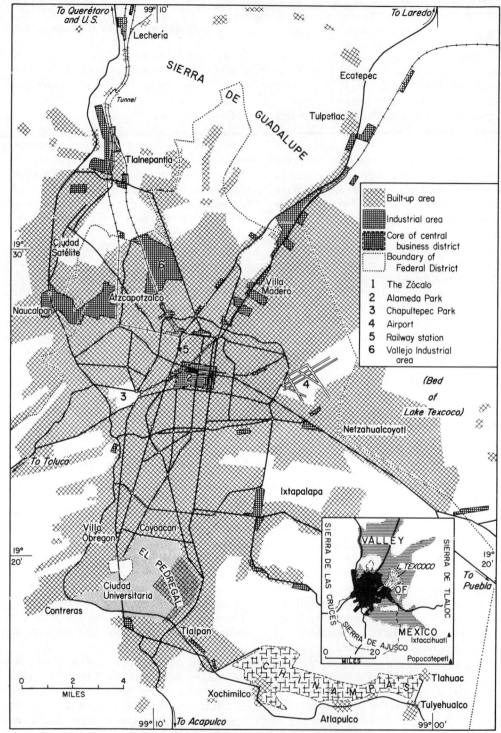

Figure 12.2 The metropolitan area of Mexico City. The heavy lines represent the main traffic arteries of the city. The floor of the Valley of Mexico is shown in the inset.

Figure 12.3   Aerial view of the central part of Mexico City. The scene looks eastward over the Valley of Mexico toward the dry bed of Lake Texcoco and the Sierra de Tlaloc. Snow-capped Ixtaccihuatl appears, upper right. In the foreground is the Alameda, a park formed in the seventeenth century. Beyond is the old section of the city, including the Zócalo, or main plaza, built upon the ruins of Tenochtitlán, the Aztec capital. *(Compañía Mexicana Aerofoto)*

Figure 12.4   Slum dwellings in the industrial district of Villa Madero, northern part of Mexico City. Squatters use old brick, adobe, and tin sheeting to erect semipermanent shelters, often on private property.

gestion. A network of freeways and a sub-way system have recently been completed to help relieve this problem and to speed the flow of people between the central business district and the suburbs. But, if the city's population and area continue to grow at the present rate, such measures must be constantly expanded to cope with the increased traffic flow.

The West. The western part of the Mesa Central and adjacent Pacific slope form another culture area within the In-dian-mestizo south. This culture area might be termed "the west" (*El Occi-dente*), as it includes the western part of Mexico's traditional heartland. Although in some respects similar to the core area, the west has sufficient cultural differences to set it apart as a separate region. Most of the area can be identified with the state of Jalisco, with Guadalajara as the regional capital. Peripheral sections include the states of Colima, Nayarit, Aguascalientes, and parts of Zacatecas and Guanajuato. Roughly, this area formed the core of the colonial province, New Galicia. Guadala-jara was the administrative capital and seat of a circuit court (*audiencia*) that had jurisdiction over most of western and northwestern New Spain. The present-day cultural distinctiveness of west-central Mexico derives mainly from its colonial history. Characterized by a dense popula-tion, large agricultural production, and growing industry, the significance of the west to Mexican economy and culture is second only to that of the core area.

The plateau surface of the west, like that of the core area, is composed of high-land basins filled with fertile lacustrine soils bordered by volcanic hills and moun-tains. In the west, however, the basin floors are 1,000 to 1,500 feet lower and consequently enjoy a milder tropical high-land climate (*tierra templada*). The pro-ductive Bajío of Guanajuato is the largest basin, followed in importance by those of Guadalajara, Ameca, and Sayula near the western edge of the plateau. Along the Pacific escarpment, at lower altitudes (2,000 to 3,000 feet), the attractive basins of Tepic, Autlán, and Colima form fertile spots of level agricultural land amidst a jumble of steep, rugged slopes. The Pacific coastal plain forms a narrow ribbon of *tierra caliente* in Colima and Jalisco states and widens considerably in Nayarit, where rich alluvial deltaic plains alternate with extensive tidal swamps.

The most distinctive cultural feature of the west is its lack of a strong Indian tradi-tion, in contrast to the rest of central and southern Mexico. Although it was part of the ancient realm of high aboriginal cul-ture, its pre-Conquest population was ap-parently never as dense as that to the east. Moreover, during the first years of Spanish Conquest, the mortality of the Indian pop-ulation of this area was very great so that Indians were few in number throughout the colonial period.

The mixing of Indian and Spanish cul-tures that was so characteristic of other parts of Central Mexico therefore occurred in the west only on a modest scale. Today, it is a land of predominantly Hispanic culture. The rural houses are of Andalu-sian and Extremaduran origin; the ox draws the wooden plow in the fields; and Indian slash-burn cultivation of wooded slopes is unimportant. Although the ab-original crop complex of maize-beans-squash predominates in subsistence agri-culture, the cultivation of wheat, barley, and the European horse bean (*haba*) is not insignificant.

Another distinctive feature of the west is its colonial land-tenure system. Until the Revolution of 1910, there were many large haciendas, chiefly for raising live-stock, and the small rancho, of 50 to 500 acres, is still a significant holding for both subsistence and commercial agriculture. The land is usually worked by a single family, either mestizo or of pure Spanish descent. The proud, Spanish-like peas-antry is best exemplified by the tall, blue-eyed men of the Los Altos district of northeastern Jalisco, around the towns of Arandas, Tepatitlán, and San Juan de los Lagos. The people of this *patria chica* are deeply religious Roman Catholics and are among the most conservative of all Mexicans.

Not all the *rancheros* of the west are farmers, however; many are small-scale stockmen of long tradition. From this group comes the famous *charro,* the distinctively costumed Mexican horseman who has been popularized in song and legend throughout the nation.

Although there are agricultural villages throughout the west, the dispersed ranchero dwellings are equally characteristic of the rural settlement pattern. Like the core area, the west contains a number of medium-sized cities overshadowed by a large urban area—in this case, Guadalajara (1.2 million population). Although its sphere of political and commercial influence is less than it was in colonial times, Guadalajara remains the metropolis of western Mexico, and is of growing industrial importance. Like Mexico City, it is connected to a seaport (Manzanillo, on the Pacific coast) by railroad and highway via a steep escarpment route. The smaller cities of the western area, as well as many medium-sized towns, have grown from pueblos or villas founded by Spanish settlers in the sixteenth and seventeenth centuries and still retain much of their colonial Hispanic flavor in architecture and custom. Most of the towns function as market centers for restricted areas. The largest and most rapidly growing cities are those of the Bajío, where León (350,000), Irapuato (135,000), Celaya (95,000), and Salamanca (57,000) form an urban cluster and a significant industrial belt.

The Bajío is a special geographical entity within the western culture area. Though its role as the breadbasket of Mexico has diminished in recent years, it remains one of the most productive agricultural sections of the country (Figure 12.5). Despite the abundance of ejido settlements created from expropriated haciendas within the basin, the Bajío is still a stronghold of the western *rancheros,* whose holdings, now reduced to small farms through divisions by inheritance, date from the colonial period.

The Gulf Coast Area. In terms of physical environment and economy, the coastal zones of Veracruz and Tabasco stand apart

Figure 12.5 Harvesting garlic near Apaseo in the eastern part of the Bajío of Guanajuato. Various parts of the fertile Bajío specialize in growing certain crops. For example, Apaseo is known for its garlic, Irapuato for strawberries, and Salvatierra for peanuts.

from the adjacent highlands. Yet these lowlands show many historicultural attachments to the core area. Before the Spanish Conquest, the central Gulf coast formed an integral part of the Aztec tribute state, supplying tropical and marine products to highland markets and the Valley of Mexico nobility—a function continued through the colonial period and retained still today. Many Indian language groups flourished before the Conquest, and Nahuatl was widely spoken in many lowland villages and was the trade language throughout the coastal zones. From the time of the Conquest, the port of Veracruz and the escarpment roads have closely bound the central Gulf coast to the core area.

The outstanding physical characteristics of the central Gulf lowlands include the tropical, practically frost-free climate (*tierra caliente*) and the fertile alluvial soils that border the numerous streams that flow from the highlands to the Gulf (see Chapter 2). Most of the area is hilly, and in some places low elevations are interrupted by mountains, such as the volcanic Sierra de Tuxtlas in southern Veracruz. Extensive plains occur only in Tabasco.

Like the core area, the Gulf coast is today mainly mestizo in race and culture. Only a few purely Indian groups remain. The lowland Huastec (about 25,000 native-language speakers) and the lowland Totonac (50,000) live in scattered pueblos and rancherias in northern Veracruz; small groups of Nahuatl-speaking folk are found on the lower escarpments; and the few remaining Popoluca occupy the eastern portion of the Sierra de Tuxtlas. Nevertheless, the mestizos (many of pure Indian blood) of Veracruz and Tabasco retain a large number of aboriginal traits in their largely Hispanic culture. One which is widely expressed on the landscape is slash-burn cultivation, especially on hillsides or, as in Tabasco, in level forested areas. Indian houses typical of the

tierra caliente (mainly of wattle construction) predominate throughout the lowlands.

The rural mestizos of lowland Veracruz are known as *Jarochos*. This folk name implies a number of culture traits peculiar to the Veracruzanos, including a distinct Spanish dialect and regional foods, dress, music, and attitudes. In northern Veracruz live the *Jarochos del Norte,* who are cattle herders and slash-burn cultivators, some with private holdings, others with individual ejidos. The *Jarochos del Interior* are farmers who cultivate the fertile stream alluvium and hillsides of the lower escarpment, west and southwest of Veracruz; and the people of the Sotavento, descendants of the colonial herders, are chiefly cattlemen who still run sizable herds on the savannas and coastal marshes between Veracruz City and the Tuxtla Sierra. Another subculture area corresponds to the Tuxtlas volcanic highlands, still largely an Indian enclave, which was opened to commercial agriculture (tobacco) in the last century and is now important for the cultivation of the famous small black beans of Veracruz. Steeped in the colonial tradition of cattle raising and commercial cacao production, the people of Tabasco have developed a kind of *patria chica* within the coastal lowlands; the local area called "the Chontalpa," the alluvial deltaic plain of the Mezcalapa River in the western part of the state, has a long history of cacao cultivation and subsistence farming on natural levees along the abandoned distributaries of the river.

Long neglected because of tropical diseases, the Gulf coast area has, within the last half-century, become one of Mexico's most rapidly developing economic regions. Various new developments in land use in Veracruz and Tabasco, mentioned earlier (Chapter 11) include: (1) the new growth of stock raising in northern Veracruz made possible by planting nutritious grasses for pasture and improving cattle breeds; (2) the increase in tropical commercial farming with cultivation of sugar cane, citrus fruit, and cacao on river flood plains and terraces; (3) the development of government-sponsored agricultural and industrial projects for colonizing and resettling the coastal areas, such as the Papaloapan Valley Authority in southern Veracruz and the Grijalva Commission in Tabasco; and (4) possibly the most significant, the growth of the petroleum industry, including the recent beginnings of petrochemical manufactures based on local oil, natural gas, salt, sulphur, and abundant supplies of water. Perhaps no other large region of Mexico has undergone such rapid and fundamental changes in the past three decades and holds greater promise for the future than the Gulf coast area.

The Balsas Lowland. Sandwiched between the Mesa Central and the southern highlands of Mexico, the Balsas lowland forms a distinct natural region characterized by a peculiar cultural pattern. This structural depression, 350 miles long, has the dubious distinction of being the hottest part of Mexico the year round. The highland Tarascan Indians still call it *jurío* ("the infernal region"). Deprived of moist air from both the Pacific and the Gulf, it is also quite dry, some rain falling only in the summer months. Consequently, low, tropical scrub covers most of the depression, including the lower slopes of the adjacent escarpments. Although it is low in elevation (500–1,500 feet), most of the surface is hilly, level land occurring as spots of alluvium along the Balsas River and its tributaries and as alluvial piedmont plains north of the Río Tepalcatepec.

In most of the lowland, a sparse mestizo population ekes out a precarious living on scattered ranchos and ejido plots by herding cattle, farming, and trading. Since the Spanish Conquest, cattle raising has been the most widespread activity of the Balsas. There the herder is completely clothed in tough leather, and even his horse wears an apron of rawhide as protection against the thorny bush.

Besides hides and dried meat, one of the most typical products of the smaller Balsas cattle ranchos is a soft, salty, white cheese (*queso blanco*), traded widely in the adjacent highlands. Subsistence farmers, using slash-burn techniques, plant maize, beans, and squash on hillside plots or till the fertile spots of alluvium along the rivers with the plow or the ancient *coa*.

Since the 1950s, commercial agriculture based on large-scale irrigation and mechanized equipment, has developed in the Balsas lowland. Irrigation in the Tepalcatepec piedmont plain, where cotton, rice, coconuts, and limes comprise the main crops has already been mentioned. With the completion of two large irrigation projects, the Mexican government hopes to increase the farming potential of the land along the Balsas River. In 1969, the Palo Alto reservoir in the middle Balsas was supplying water for cotton, sesame, and vegetable farms in the vicinity of Ciudad Altamirano, a rapidly growing market center. A much larger project is now underway in the lower Balsas, where water from the Villita reservoir will irrigate most of the fertile river delta. These government schemes, plus a planned steel mill near the river mouth may soon transform the impoverished Balsas Basin into a thriving tropical lowland.

The Southern Highlands. The rugged Sierra Madre del Sur of southern Michoacán and Guerrero state and the equally mountainous Mesa del Sur of Oaxaca comprise a culture area that is called "the southern highlands." As defined, it includes not only the cool uplands, but also the steep, scrub-covered Pacific escarpment, the hot coastal fringe, and the semi-arid plains and hills on the southern side of the Isthmus of Tehuantepec. Moreover, the northern edge laps over into the dry upper Balsas drainage, and the eastern border includes portions of the humid escarpment that overlooks the Gulf low-lands of southern Veracruz. The difficult terrain of this jumbled highland mass, as well as its relatively poor, overworked and eroded soils, help make it one of the most poverty-stricken parts of Mexico.

The Valley of Oaxaca, in the center of the Mesa del Sur, is the only extensive level section in the uplands. Intensively cultivated for over 2,000 years, the once fertile soils of the valley are now badly depleted. In terms of arable land, most of the southern highlands are overpopulated despite a low overall population density. The uneven distribution of people and lack of good communications are reflec-tions of the highly complex terrain. The recent irrigation developments in the Te-huantepec Isthmus and the spectacular growth of tourism along the Guerrero coast are the only bright spots in the picture.

The rugged surface of the southern high-lands has made it an ideal refuge for rem-nant Indian groups, and it is consequently one of the most aboriginal parts of the country. Its cultural core is the state of Oaxaca, where approximately 600,000 in-dividuals, 35 percent of the state's popula-tion, speak Indian languages and retain a good part of their aboriginal culture. Of a total of 14 different major Indian lan-guages spoken in Oaxaca before the Con-quest, 12 are still extant, and possibly 35

to 40 dialects and subdialects of these languages are still spoken. The two most important Indian language groups are the Zapotec (200,000 individuals) in the east-ern part of the state, and the Mixtec (185,000) in the western half. Other large aboriginal groups include the Mazatec (75,000) in northern Oaxaca; the Mije, (45,000) who inhabit the high, isolated mountains of east-central Oaxaca; and the Chinantec (30,000), who dwell on warm, humid eastern slopes of the Oaxaca pla-teau.

Culturally, the western part of the high-lands (the Sierra Madre del Sur of Guer-rero state and southern Michoacán) is peripheral to the Oaxacan core. Only in eastern Guerrero are Indian languages still spoken (Nahuatl, Tlapanec, and Amusgo), and only by a few thousand people. Never-theless, certain aspects of aboriginal life, such as primitive slash-burn cultivation, wattle-daub and thatch house construc-tion, Indian foods, and a fatalistic outlook characterize the mixbloods of the Sierra Madre del Sur.

Subsistence farming is the chief economy of the southern highlands. Except for the use of the plow on level-to-rolling terrain, cultivation techniques are essentially ab-original (Figure 12.6). However, some Old World farming practices, in particular, wheat cultivation and sheep rearing, have been adopted by the mountain Indians of

Figure 12.6 Cultivating maize with oxen-drawn wooden plows (ards) in a small valley in Oaxaca. Such scenes are typical in rural sections of Mexico.

Oaxaca. On mountain slopes above 8,000 feet, many Indians plant small patches of wheat as a cash crop. In all parts of the highlands, but especially around the Mixtec villages in western Oaxaca, the annual wool clip from small herds of sheep furnishes supplemental income. In addition, there are the usual cottage industries common in most Indian areas.

The few spots of modern commercial agriculture within the southern highlands occupy tropical or subtropical zones on the Pacific escarpment and coast. These include the Pochutla coffee zone along the southern escarpment, the irrigated plains of Tehuantepec, and the long stretch of coconut plantations along the beach ridges of the Guerrero coast.

In the Oaxaca and Guerrero highlands, the landholding village is the basic unit of settlement among the Indians and many mestizos. As in ancient times, the village lands are often worked communally, though many villagers now have legal title to individual plots. Usually a number of villages and their satellite rancherias (small groups of scattered dwellings on the mountainside) surround the larger market towns inhabited by mestizos and some whites; there the Indians hold the colorful weekly, or even daily, markets that are the delight of foreign visitors. There are few cities in the southern highlands. Oaxaca City (95,000 inhabitants) and Chilpancingo (28,000) are both state capitals and the largest urban centers in the mountainous interior. Modern Acapulco (175,-000), on the Guerrero coast, is an aberrant development and foreign to the native culture of southern Mexico.

Prior to the Agrarian Revolution of 1910, large haciendas controlled the best agricultural lands in the southern highlands, especially those in the Valley of Oaxaca. Similarly, the stock-raising districts in the Pacific lowlands of Oaxaca and Guerrero, as well as the pastures of Tehuantepec, were in large holdings. In the Mesa del Sur, however, the hacienda was never the important institution that it was in central Mexico. Today the federal government has expropriated most of the large estates within the Valley of Oaxaca, granting some lands to the surrounding Indian villages and creating ejidos with the remainder. Elsewhere in the uplands, the ejidos derived from expropriated haciendas are overshadowed in importance by communal Indian village lands.

A large number of *patrias chicas,* or small culture units, characterize the southern highlands. Most of these are based primarily on geographical area and aboriginal language; secondarily, on economy, dress, and social organization. All such culture units have particular names known to all the inhabitants of neighboring *patrias.* One of the best known is the Mixteca Alta, which covers the high mountains of west-central Oaxaca—the present stronghold of the Mixtec-speaking Indians and the center of ancient Mixtec culture. Immediately northward is the Mixteca Baja, which comprises the hot, dry hills of the upper Balsas depression. The highland Zapotec in eastern Oaxaca has formed several small cultural units, all distinct in landscape and culture from the lowland Zapotec of Tehuantepec, where the women are famed for their beauty and their colorful native dress.

Chiapas. Most of the state of Chiapas is culturally more closely associated with Guatemala than with Mexico. Except for the Soconusco Coast along the Pacific, pre-Conquest Chiapas formed part of the ancient highland Maya culture area. During the colonial period it was a province attached to the Captaincy of Guatemala, and it did not become a Mexican state until 1824.

Today, Chiapas is composed of two cultural units. One is the predominantly mestizo southern half, which includes the Valley of Chiapas (drained by the upper Río Grijalva), the Sierra Madre de Chiapas, and the narrow Pacific coastal plain. The other is the predominantly Indian plateau (the Meseta Central de Chiapas) and adjacent limestone ranges in the northern part of the state. The major cultural aspects of both areas stem from the colonial period. Except for some agricultural developments in the Sierra Madre and the Pacific coastal plain, the cultural landscape of Chiapas has changed little since the end of the eighteenth century.

Attracted by spots of savanna grasslands scattered through the tropical scrub, Spanish stockmen occupied the valley of Chiapas early in the sixteenth century. Spanish encomenderos also quickly assumed control of the native cacao groves along the Soconusco coast. In these lowland areas, the Indian population gradually dwindled. By the end of the colonial period, the people of southern Chiapas had become largely mestizo in blood and culture. The only remaining significant Indian area is at the eastern end of the Sierra Madre, where a Mam-speaking group extends across the Guatemalan border into Mexican territory.

Stock raising remains a major occupation in the valley of Chiapas, but with the redistribution of many hacienda lands to ejidos, the area devoted to subsistence agriculture has increased. This has been especially true on the gentle northern slope of the Sierra de Chiapas, where the *llanos,* the wide grassy valleys that were formerly pasture, are now fields of maize and beans. The present coffee zone along the steep Pacific escarpment of the sierra and the rapidly expanding commercial growing of bananas and sugar cane on the Pacific coastal plain around Tapachula are extensions of similar economic activities in neighboring Guatemala.

High and cold (6,500–9,000 feet elevation), and forested with pine and oak, the Meseta Central of Chiapas (sometimes called the Sierra de San Cristóbal) attracted few Spaniards during the colonial period. The administrative and religious centers of Ciudad Real (now San Cristóbal) and Comitán were the only important Spanish settlements on the plateau. Today, the northern Chiapas highlands are the refuge of numerous Indian groups, most of which speak languages related to Maya. Approximately 200,000 Indians, comprising about half the highland population, live in agglomerated villages and semidispersed rancherias scattered over the rough plateau surface. The Tzotzil and Tzeltal (about 125,000 people) are the most important aboriginal groups.

The international boundary between Mexico and Guatemala, which runs directly through Indian country, has little meaning for the related families on either side of the border. Long isolated from outside influences, the Chiapas Indians are perhaps the least Hispanicized in southern Mexico. The highly publicized Lacandon people who inhabit the rain forest of northeastern Chiapas now live more primitively than did their Mayan ancestors. Cultivation is of the slash-burn dibble variety; land is held by the village; houses are pre-Conquest types; and dress, particularly of the women, is typically Indian. Among the few elements of Old World culture that the Indians of Chiapas (like other highland aborigines) have integrated into their present way of life are sheep raising and the use of wool for making homespun cloth (Figure 12.7).

San Cristóbal de las Casas (25,000 population) is the only large town in the Chiapas highlands. It is the administrative and commercial center of the entire area, and its daily market draws Indian traders from most parts of the plateau. Located on the paved Inter-American highway, San Cristóbal is now sharing in Mexico's rich tourist industry.

Yucatan. Although physically a peninsula of the Mainland, Yucatan is culturally an island. It is probably the least Mexican portion of the country. Even today, many inhabitants of the peninsula

Figure 12.7 The Chiapas highlands near San Cristóbal de las Casas, showing pine-clad slopes and a mountain meadow, where Indian women and children tend flocks of sheep

numerous elaborate stone temples and palaces, this area was practically depopulated long before the Conquest. Since colonial times, the rain forest of this *despoblado* has served as a barrier to human movement, isolating densely populated northern Yucatan from direct contact with both Mexico and Guatemala.

An equally important isolating factor was the conservative and hostile attitude of the Maya Indians toward the Spaniards. Initially difficult to subdue, the Mayas of northern Yucatan rebelled many times against the Spanish encomenderos and *hacendados* who had usurped a large part of the best Indian lands during the colonial period. The last serious native rebellion occurred in 1847, when Mexican estate owners came close to losing the entire peninsula to the Indians.

Like most of the other culture areas of southeastern Mexico, Yucatan contains a large Indian population. About 300,000 Maya-speaking people, mainly poverty-stricken subsistence farmers, comprise nearly half the population of the northern part of the peninsula, including the state of Yucatan and parts of Campeche and Quintana Roo. These Indians retain a large number of aboriginal traits. Slash-burn dibble farming and the ancient maize-bean-squash crop complex form the basic subsistence economy. The Indians reject almost completely the Old World ox-drawn plow, both from conservatism and from the impracticability of the tool in the small, rocky milpa patches. Although the native apsidal, straw-thatched house is typical, the prevailing agglomerated village with a gridlike street plan stems from the Spanish resettlement program of the sixteenth and seventeenth centuries.

During the colonial era, Spaniards established large cattle haciendas in the northern part of the peninsula. By the end of the nineteenth century, most Indian villages had lost their anciently held lands to the encroaching haciendas, but

consider themselves Yucatecos, not Mexicans. This provincial attitude is the ultimate expression of the *patria chica* concept that has created so many Mexicos.

The limestone lowlands of Yucatan contrast with the mountainous character of most of Mexico. As mentioned earlier (Chapter 2), the porous character of the limestone in the northern third of the peninsula has led to the development of underground, rather than surface drainage. *Cenotes,* or steep-sided sinkholes, are the major landform and important sources of drinking water. Soils are red, thin, and not very fertile. The tropical scrub forest that covers most of northern Yucatan results from paucity of soil moisture and centuries of slash-burn farming.

The hilly southern part of the peninsula, including the Petén of northern Guatamala, receives more rainfall than the northern plains and is covered by heavy rain forest. Once the center of classical Mayan culture, and famed for its the villagers were permitted to till parts of the estate for subsistence crops. As explained earlier (Chapter 11), henequen cultivation and processing began on a large scale in northern Yucatan during the last quarter of the nineteenth century, the biggest plantations taking over the best agricultural lands in the vicinity of Mérida, the capital city of Yucatan state. This enterprise gave rise to a class of wealthy Yucatecos, mestizo and white, whose palatial houses in Mérida are now but a reminder of the days just prior to the outbreak of the Agrarian Revolution in 1910. Today, most of the large henequen plantations have been broken up into ejidos, and estate lands that rightfully belonged to Indian villages have been returned. Although henequen cultivation still forms an important part of the economy of northern Yucatan, the Maya Indians utilize most of the peninsula for subsistence farming, practicing ancient slash-burn cultivation on the thin soils, just as their ancestors did a thousand years ago.

In 1968, the federal government began a farming scheme, called the "Plan Chac," in southern Yucatan. The plan involves the commercial cultivation of tropical fruit and other crops by overhead irrigation on 10,000 acres of ejido and private lands. If successful, this pilot project may lead to a new agricultural development in the peninsula.

Except for the immediate coasts, where commercial coconut farming has developed in recent years, most of the southern part of the peninsula is a sparsely inhabited wilderness. Some lumbering of tropical timbers goes on, but the most widespread activity in the rain forest for the past half-century has been the collecting of *chicle,* the latex of the chicosapote tree (Achras sapota), which is used for chewing gum. Hundreds of Mayan *chicleros* wander through the unsettled forest, tapping trees for the latex which they bring to collecting stations for shipment

to processing plants in Campeche and Chetumal. Most of the chicle is sent to the United States, where chewing gum has been used since the 1890s.

The European-Mestizo North

More so than in the Indian-mestizo south, the landscape of northern Mexico reflects, in settlement forms, house types, and economic activities, the impact of Hispanic culture. Although the population is predominantly mestizo, the north contains a large number of whites, mainly members of proud families descendent of Spanish colonists. Only in northwestern Mexico are there some Indian groups, the remnants of a once sizable aboriginal farming population. Elsewhere in the north, the bands of primitive nomads that formerly scourged Spanish settlements have long since disappeared, leaving few traces of their culture.

Northern Mexico, which comprises 60 percent of the national territory, contains but a quarter of the country's people. In this arid to semiarid land, spots of dense rural population occur chiefly along river oases and in irrigated zones. Large desert areas in Baja California, northwestern Sonora, and on the Mesa del Norte are totally uninhabited, forming true *despoblados.*

Since the sixteenth century, northern Mexico has been an area of frontier expansion. The Spaniards, attracted by silver deposits and grasslands, spread northward from central Mexico, carrying with them their Hispanic culture (see Chapter 9). Today, as new irrigation districts are opened or expanded and as industry grows in the cities, Mexicans continue to migrate northward from the overpopulated central part of the country.

The European-mestizo north is here divided into four smaller culture areas: (1) the north-central area, corresponding generally to the Mesa del Norte; (2) the northeast, including the states of Tamaulipas, most of Nuevo León, and the northeastern part of Coahuila; (3) the northwest, principally the states of Sonora and Sinaloa; and (4) the peninsula of Baja California (Figure 12.1).

The North-Central Area. This highland desert-steppe area forms both a physical and cultural entity. Throughout the area, the Spanish economic complex of mining and stock raising, firmly established in colonial times, still prevails.

In this section, the large estates devoted to stock raising have been little affected by the agrarian revolution. The most favored area for the establishment of the ranch-mine complex was the wide belt of grassland that occupies the semiarid foothills and basins on the eastern side of the Sierra Madre Occidental. In this Silver Belt, the present cities of Zacatecas, Durango, Parral, and Chihuahua grew out of the administrative centers of colonial mining and stock-raising settlements. Eastward, Spanish miners and stockmen also colonized the less favorable areas of desert basins and ranges, founding centers such as Matehuala, Mazapil, and Saltillo.

Irrigated farming, begun on a modest scale in colonial times, has boomed in the Mesa del Norte during the present century. The productive Laguna area of central Coahuila and the Las Delicias district on the Conchos River in Chihuahua are now among the most productive mechanized farming areas of Mexico. In other desert oases that were settled during colonial days are found practices of Mediterranean origin, such as wheat and barley cultivation; vineyards and wine making; and the widespread use of the ox-drawn wooden plow and the two-wheeled cart. Such practices, plus the ubiquitous flat-roofed adobe rural house of Moorish origin, give the north-central area a definite Hispanic cast (Figure 12.8).

In contrast to the predominant Spanish cultural heritage in the Mesa del Norte,

Figure 12.8   A small hacienda near Saltillo, Coahuila state. Flat-roofed adobe structures and a small church contrast with the pretentious hacienda buildings of Central Mexico. In the background irrigated fields of maize, wheat, and grapevines occupy the central portion of the basin oasis.

an economy that may derive from the nomadic Indian still prevails in the desert. Here the wild desert plants are gathered for processing into useful products, an occupation that provides a livelihood for an estimated 40,000 families that live in small hamlets scattered throughout the desert basins and mountain slopes (Figure 12.9). One of the most important products

Figure 12.9   A typical desert house in a small community of *ixtleros,* or lechuguilla collectors, northern San Luis Potosí state, Mesa del Norte

is *ixtle,* a fiber obtained from the short, fleshy leaves of a small agave (lechuguilla) and from the spiny leaves of a yucca (palma). Both these plants are widespread in the eastern portion of the central desert south of Saltillo (Figure 12.10). Rope, twine, sacks, and huaraches, or native sandals, are made from *ixtle* fiber, and since the 1930s, foreign demand for twine and rope has greatly increased Mexican *ixtle*

production. Other desert plants gathered in north-central Mexico include *candelilla,* a small euphorb that produces a wax used in industry; *guayule,* which yields a rubber-producing latex; and *tuna,* the fruit of the pricklypear cactus, once an important Indian food, now processed to make nutritious confections such as *queso de tuna* ("tuna cheese"). The exploitation of these plants has been so intensive in the

Figure 12.10   Gathering of wild desert plants: Main areas of production.
(1) candelilla (wax); (2) lechuguilla (agave fiber); (3) tuna cactus fruit;
(4) guayule latex; (5) interior desert of northern Mexico.

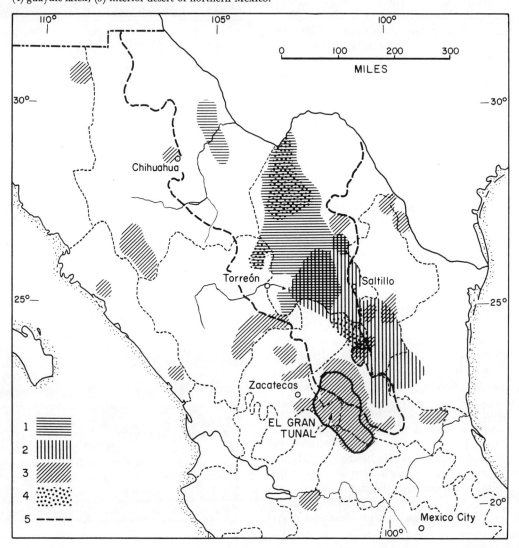

last few decades that some have disappeared from the scant vegetation of large sections of north-central Mexico. As a result, many desert gatherers have been forced to migrate to the cities to find other occupations.

Since the end of the last century, some religious groups have migrated to north-central Mexico. In 1885, Mormons from the United States formed several agricultural villages in the vicinity of Casas Grandes, northwestern Chihuahua. By 1912, the colonies contained 4,000 people, but the rigors of the revolutionary period forced most of the colonists to disband, and only a handful remain. In 1922, the Mexican government permitted the entry of several hundred Mennonites (of German-Russian descent) from Canada. They founded agricultural colonies near Cuauhtemoc, west of Chihuahua City; near Patos, north of Durango City; in Zacatecas State, northeast of Fresnillo; and in southeastern Tamaulipas, north of Tampico. Today more than 30,000 German-speaking Mennonites live in these colonies, but over half are concentrated in 67 villages near Cuauhtemoc, Chihuahua. So populous have these settlements become that many Mennonites are migrating to British Honduras to form new cells. The Mennonite settlements in Mexico are characterized by elongated, European-type street villages; by names such as Kleefeld, Blumengart, and Schanzenfeld; by north-German houses and barns; and by dairy farming, which emphasizes the production of cheese and butter. These villages contrast sharply with the surrounding Mexican cultural scene, and they represent one of the few examples of non-Hispanic European settlement in Mexico.

The Northeast. This region covers the subhumid coastal lowlands and the adjacent hill areas between the Pánuco River and the Rio Grande. An isolated, poverty-stricken land a century ago, it is today one of the most progressive sections of Mexico.

The state of Nuevo León and its capital and industrial city, Monterrey, form the regional hub, overshadowing the adjacent state of Tamaulipas and its administrative center, Ciudad Victoria.

Although Spanish stockmen settled the central part of Nuevo León in the late sixteenth century, the Crown did not effectively occupy most of the northeast until the mid-eighteenth century, when Spanish farmers entered after the defeat of the Indian nomads. Thus, the cultural landscape of the northeast (like the north-central desert area) is chiefly Hispanic in origin and character, and, except for the recently arrived mestizos from central Mexico, both the rural and urban families are predominately of Caucasian stock. One of the most interesting cultural features of the northeast is its distinctive rural house, with white stone or plastered walls, neatly thatched or tiled roofs, and quaint outside chimney—the latter possibly an introduction from Anglo-America (Figure 12.11).

Within the last 50 years, the northeast has become a leading industrial and agricultural section of Mexico. The exploitation of the Sabinas coal deposits, the lower Rio Grande gas fields, and the oil reserves north of the Río Pánuco have been significant factors in the rise of Monterrey and towns adjacent to it as the leading industrial center of the north. Iron and steel are two of the main products of this area. The recent development of mechanized farming on irrigated lands in the Rio Grande delta, and the opening of new agricultural areas on the rich calcareous soils in southern Tamaulipas, have also furthered the economic development of the northeast.

A particular feature of this area is its close economic and cultural ties with the United States. Three paved highways and two railways lead directly from Monterrey to the United States border. Another main highway leads from Brownsville to Ciudad Victoria and from Piedras Negras to Mon-

Figure 12.11   Typical rural house of northeastern Mexico

clova, Saltillo, and Monterrey. Four large border towns, each with its United States counterpart, are within the northeast. It is not surprising that Monterrey has many characteristics of a North American city, in contrast to the definite Hispanic cast of most other north Mexican urban centers.

The Northwest. Physically and culturally, the northwest is the most complex region of northern Mexico. As defined here, it includes all of Sonora, most of Sinaloa, the extreme western parts of Chihuahua and Durango, and the northeast corner of Baja California. The northwest comprises three major physical zones: (1) the dry coastal lowlands, which include fertile river flood plains and deltas; (2) the subhumid basins and ranges of eastern Sonora and Sinaloa; and (3) the moist, rugged, pine- and oak-covered Sierra Madre Occidental.

Despite its physical complexity, the area retains some cultural unity through its aboriginal heritage, now greatly modified by Hispanic peoples and traits. The northwest today is the most Indian area of northern Mexico. Before the Conquest, it

was the only significant part of the north that was inhabited by large groups of sedentary farmers. Today, the most numerous of these are the Mayo (28,000), who live in the flood plains and deltas of southern Sonora and northern Sinaloa, and the Tarahumar (45,000), primitive mountain farmers and hunters of the northern Sierra Madre Occidental in Chihuahua. Others, now reduced to small remnants, include the Yaqui (4,000) of southern Sonora and a few Pápago in northwestern Sonora, both flood-plain dwellers; a small number of Ópata and Lower Pima in the basins of eastern Sonora; and a handful of primitive Seri, who now fish off the desert coast of Tiburón Island in the Gulf of California. Except the Tarahumar and Seri, most Indian groups have been fairly well integrated into modern Mexican rural life. Indian culture, however, has left its mark on the landscape—the maize-beans-squash crop complex still dominates subsistence farming, and the aboriginal wattle-and-daub rural houses are the prevailing type.

More important in the northwest, however, is the mark of the colonial Spaniard. As in the Mesa del Norte, the mining of silver and the raising of livestock became the prevailing colonial economy, lasting in some places until the present time. Missions among the Indians, and garrisons placed at strategic points to protect settlement and trade from frequent Apache raids, were also features of Hispanic occupation in the northwest. Spanish control centered in the high grassy basins within the Ópata Indian area of northeastern Sonora (towns of Arizpe, Nacozari, and Bavispe) and in the flood plain of the Río Culiacán in northern Sinaloa.

The last half-century has brought great changes to the northwest—mechanized farming, new highway and rail transport, port facilities, and growing cities. Perhaps the most significant of these changes has been the rise of commercial agriculture in the coastal river flood plains and deltas (see Chapter 11).

Through government construction of dams and reservoirs for irrigation water, the arid coast from the Coloradao delta (Mexicali area) to central Sinaloa has become Mexico's foremost producer of cotton, wheat, and winter vegetables (Figure 12.12). This has resulted in drastic changes in the landscape of those coastal areas where water is available for irrigation. The scrub-covered range lands of the cattle haciendas were converted to large irrigated fields which now belong to ejido communities or to small private holders, who cultivate by modern, mechanized methods.

Large cities now service the expanding agricultural area. Among the more important market and administrative centers are Hermosillo (180,000 population) and Ciudad Obregón (100,000) in Sonora, and Culiacán (150,000) and Los Mochis (75,000) in Sinaloa.

The development of modern port facilities is another important change in the northwest. Guaymas (54,000) and Mazatlán (130,000), formerly small fishing villages, now export agricultural products and mineral concentrates and import machinery and Mexican petroleum for the mechanized farms. The growing fishing industry in the Gulf of California, encouraged by the new port facilities and processing plants, has enhanced the importance of the northwest in modern Mexican economy.

As we have already indicated, much of the impetus and the technical knowledge for the recent agricultural developments in the northwest derives from the United States. Similarly, the renascence of mining in Sonora came with the opening of the Cananea and Nacozari copper deposits by United States investors and engineers at

Figure 12.12 Irrigated lands of the deltaic plain of the Fuerte River, northwestern Mexico. These contrast with the dry, cactus-covered slopes of the surrounding hills. Tomato-packing plants are seen in the middle background.

the beginning of this century. Moreover, the proximity of the northwest to the stock-raising areas of southern Arizona, as well as the presence of American stockmen in Sonora, facilitated the introduction of the improved cattle breeds that are now replacing the rangy *criollo* stock in northern Mexico.

Baja California.   Far from central Mexico, effectively isolated from the Mainland by the Gulf of California, and poor in economic resources, the long, arid peninsula of Baja California has always stood apart from the rest of the country. Only since World War II, with the increase of rapid air travel, the establishment of regular ferry service, and the construction of a paved highway and railroad around the north side of the Gulf, has the peninsula become easily accessible to the Mexican heartland. Moreover, in 1973, a paved highway, running the entire length of the peninsula, was finally completed. Like Yucatan, Baja California, though physically a peninsula, was long a cultural island. But modern communications have now opened both to the world, for better or for worse.

Aridity is the basic characteristic of most of Baja California. Only the northwestern Pacific coastal plain and the adjacent interior mountains, which receive winter cyclonic rains, and the cape region at the peninsula's southern tip, which is moistened by late summer tropical storms, fall outside the area of desert climate. The central part of the peninsula, which receives less than four inches of rain annually, is the most arid section of Middle America. There are no sizable rivers like those of Sinaloa and Sonora to serve as a physical base for agriculture in Baja California. The scant settlement in the desert clusters around springs that issue from old lava flows.

During the colonial era, the Spaniards found little to attract them to the peninsula. The Catholic orders from the Mainland, founding mission settlements among the scant, nomadic, hunting and gathering Indians were the actual colonizers. The missions in the desert between the cape area and the moist northwestern sector were founded at spring oasis sites. After the near extermination of the Indian population in the early nineteenth century by European diseases, the mission settlements reverted to small stock-raising centers and producers of irrigated Old World fruits such as dates, figs, and citrus. Oasis towns such as Mulugé, Comondú, San Ignacio, and San José de Gracia, with their date and citrus orchards, resemble places in southeastern Spain or in the Sahara of North Africa. Most of the village farmers and stockmen are of Spanish or mestizo origin.

Mining has been relatively unimportant in Baja California. Only one mining center is of any significance—that of Santa Rosalía on the desolate Gulf coast, where copper ore has been extracted and smelted on a large scale since 1885. The demand for local agricultural products in the mining town is the sole economic basis for the continued existence of the old oasis farming settlements in the desert interior.

The cape region of Baja California, having climatic and cultural affinities with the adjacent Mainland coast, is geographically distinct from the rest of the peninsula. Although moistened by summer tropical rains (10–25 inches yearly), the area is semiarid. Cattle and goats browse over most of the scrub-covered hill lands; but tropical products such as sugar cane, plantains, and citrus, as well as truck crops, are cultivated by irrigation in the alluvial valleys and coastal lowlands. The largest urban center is La Paz (24,000), the capital of Baja California Sur territory and the center of a growing tourist industry based on deep-sea fishing off the coast.

Only one significant modern irrigation district has developed recently in the southern part of the peninsula—that of Santo Domingo, some 100 miles northwest of La Paz (Figure 11.18). Using water from deep wells dug by the federal government, recently arrived farmers from the Mainland grow cotton, wheat, and oil seeds with mechanized equipment. Most of the cotton is shipped to Japan from the new Pacific port of San Carlos.

Northwestern Baja California is more akin to southern California of the United States than to the rest of the peninsula. Winter rains and chaparral vegetation extend southward, beyond the United States border, as far as San Quintín on the coast. Moreover, California-type farming, of Spanish origin, including the cultivation of wheat, citrus fruits, olives, and the vine, are characteristic of northwestern Baja. Since the 1930s, wine production has become a major industry in this part of Mexico, and the vineyards around Ensenada and Tecate vie with those of Parras and Coahuila in north-central Mexico, both in output and in the quality of the wine and brandies. Northern Baja California, together with the Mexicali irrigated cotton area (here considered part of the northwest culture area), is the most populous and economically important section of the peninsula. The border city Tijuana (300,-000) and Ensenada (70,000) attract thousands of United States tourists yearly and also boast a growing industry.

CITY REGIONS

The concept of the city region is a relatively recent development in the social sciences. The city is a nodal point, into which flow products of the surrounding countryside for consumption or processing and out of which flow manufactured goods, information, and administrative authority. The city also attracts migrant labor from the surrounding area to work in industry or in various urban services; it draws customers to trade and to utilize such services as schools and medical facilities; and it allures, perhaps unfortunately, large numbers of impoverished rural people hopeful of a better life with urban amenities. The city is a center of eco-

nomic, social, and political action, as well as of innovations of all kinds. It thus influences a surrounding geographical area (the city region), the extent of which varies with the size, importance, and function of the urban center, the nature of transport facilities, and distance from the center. The city region can be measured and mapped by determining the quantity and areal distribution of such things as business transactions on the wholesale level, banking services, supply of raw materials to the city, newspaper circulation, transportation services, and the like. Such regions have been determined for advanced industrial countries, like the United States and those of western Europe, where the city has long been dominant economically and where statistical data are available.

With the recent growth of large urban centers in Mexico (see Chapter 11), the city region is becoming increasingly significant in the national economy and in the geography of human activity there. Unfortunately, the statistical data necessary for the study of such regions in Mexico are lacking or difficult to obtain. Nonetheless, several French geographers, headed by Claude Bataillon of the University of Paris, have recently made preliminary studies of Mexican city regions.

Although modern Mexican urban regions may now be evolving, the concept of the city region could be applied to the study of colonial or even pre-Conquest urban centers of Mexico. For example, archaeological evidence indicates that at its apogee (400–600 A.D.), the city of Teotihuacán held sway over a surrounding rural area tributary to it. Again, the tribute territory subject to Tenochtitlán during the Aztec period and the areas under economic and social control of the Spanish cities (villas) in sixteenth-century Mexico are cases in point. In fact, much of the structure of Spanish colonial conquest and settlement was based on the establishment of cities from which evolved urban regions.

Today, the largest and most easily delimited city regions of Mexico may be associated with the greatest cities: the federal capital, Guadalajara, and Monterrey. However, Mexico City, being a primate urban center, in a sense includes the entire republic as its region. For instance, because of the country's centralized system of government, political power flows outward from the capital to all parts of Mexico, and branches of governmental agencies in the provinces are subject to decisions made in the capital. Again, the major daily newspapers of the capital are sold in most of the provincial cities and towns; the large banks of Mexico City have branches in all parts of the republic; and wholesale transactions made in the capital cover most of the nation. On the other hand, other influences from Mexico City

extend to a much smaller area. Figure 12.13 shows bus service between the capital and its surrounding "satellite" cities, from one to two hours distant via the super highways. The hourly schedules permit commuting from the closer cities and regular shopping trips from all of them into the capital. The satellites in turn are connected by daily bus service to many smaller communities within their respective marketing territories. The entire transport network encompasses an area that closely corresponds to Bataillon's "east-central" region, or the immediate city region of the federal capital, which he determined by using other criteria (Bataillon 1971). This region includes the states of México, Morelos, Puebla, Tlaxcala, and Hidalgo. Because of the close transport ties between

Figure 12.13   Mexico City region, based on passenger bus service: (1) Mexico City metropolitan area; (2) city, over 50,000 inhabitants; (3) towns tributary to satellite cities within the Mexico City region; (4) hourly bus service from satellite cities to Mexico City (for at least 8 hours of a 24-hour period); (5) daily bus service from tributary towns to satellite cities; (6) boundary of the Mexico City region, based on bus service and modified from Bataillon's "Centre-Est" region (Bataillon 1971).

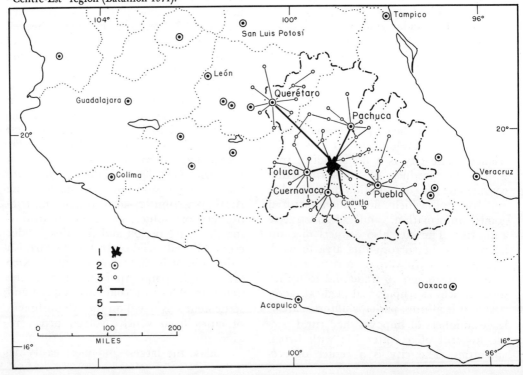

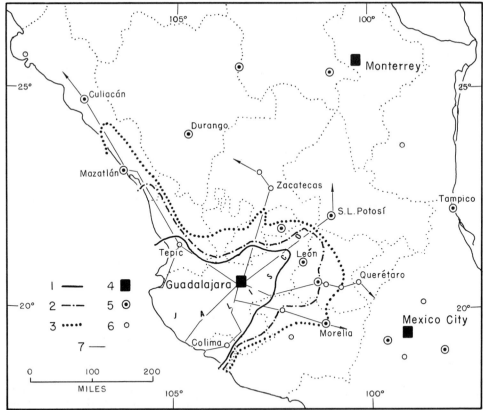

Figure 12.14 Guadalajara City region, based on three service criteria:
(1) area receiving its bulk of manufactured and processed goods from
Guadalajara; (2) area using Guadalajara as its major market for agricultural
products; (3) area receiving one of Guadalajara's major daily newspapers (*El
Informador*) on regular basis; (4) city, over 1 million inhabitants; (5) city,
100,000 to 1 million inhabitants; (6) city, 50,000 to 100,000 inhabitants; (7) main
transport routes out of Guadalajara. (*Sources:* symbols 1 and 2 modified from
Rivière d'Arc 1970: symbol 3 from México, D.F.: Asociación de Editores de los
Estados, 1965)

the capital and the city of Querétaro, we
have added the state of Querétaro to this
region.

In Figure 12.14, three criteria are used
to depict the city region of Guadalajara:
(1) the agricultural area tributary to the
city, (2) the area dependent on Guadalajara for most manufactured goods, and
(3) newspaper circulation from the state
capital. There is a lack of complete correspondence of these distributions, but a
vague city region does emerge. Moreover,
were the distributions of these same criteria plotted from other large cities, such
as San Luis Potosí or Mexico City, an
overlapping of influence would surely

occur in the eastern and northern parts of
the region. On comparing the Guadalajara city region shown in Figure 12.14
with the culture area called "The West,"
shown in Figure 12.1, a fair correlation
can be seen. Perhaps we may conclude that
the modern city region has superimposed
itself upon the older culture area.

As more statistical data on the functions
of Mexican urban centers become available, the city regions of the country can
be more precisely measured and useful
studies may be made for planning purposes. The city region concept offers abundant possibilities for future applied research.

SELECTED REFERENCES

BATAILLON, C. *Ville et Campagnes dans la Région de México.* Paris: Editions Anthropos, 1971.

BELTRÁN, E. *El Hombre y su Ambiente: Ensayo Sobre el Valle de México.* Mexico, D.F.: Fondo de Cultura Económica, 1958.

DICKEN, S. N. "The Basin Settlements of the Middle Sierra Madre Oriental, Mexico." *Annals of the Association of American Geographers* 26, no. 3 (1936):157–78.

FOX, D. J. "Man-Water Relationships in Metropolitan Mexico." *Geographical Review* 55, no. 4 (1965):523–45.

GIERLOFF-EMDEN, H. G. "Die Halbinsel Baja California: Ein Entwicklungsgebiet Mexikos." *Mitteilungen der Geographischen Gesellschaft in Hamburg* 55 (1964):1–160.

MEGEE, M. C. *Monterrey, Mexico: Internal Patterns and External Relations,* University of Chicago, Department of Geography. Research Paper no. 59. Chicago: University of Chicago Press, 1958.

PFEIFER, G. "Sinaloa und Sonora: Beiträge zur Landeskunde und Kulturgeographie des Nordwestlichen Mexico." *Mitteilungen der Geographischen Gesellschaft in Hamburg* 46 (1939):289–460.

REDFIELD, R. *The Folk Culture of Yucatan.* Chicago: University of Chicago Press, 1941.

REVEL-MOUROZ, J. "Monterrey et le Nord-Est Mexicain: Croissance Urbaine et Organisation Régionale." *Cahiers d'Outre-Mer* 20 (1969):161–90.

RIVIÈRE D'ARC, H. "Los Circuitos Comerciales en la Zona de Influencia de la Ciudad de Guadalajara." In *Memoria de los Trabajos de 1968 y 1969.* Vol. 1. Mexico, D.F.: Comisión Nacional de Salarios Mínimos, 1970.

SAWATZKY, H. L. *They Sought a Country: Mennonite Colonization in Mexico.* Berkeley: University of California Press, 1971.

SCHMIEDER, O. "The Settlements of the Tzapotec and Mije Indians, State of Oaxaca, Mexico." *University of California Publications in Geography* 4 (1930):1–184.

STANISLAWSKI, D. *The Anatomy of Eleven Towns in Michoacán.* Latin-American Studies, no. 10. Austin: University of Texas Press, 1950.

TAYLOR, P. S. *A Spanish-Mexican Peasant Community: Arandas in Jalisco, Mexico.* Ibero-Americana, no. 4. Berkeley: University of California Press, 1933.

WAGNER, P. "Parras: A Case History in the Depletion of Natural Resources." *Landscape* 5, no. 1 (1955):19–28.

WEST, R. C. *Cultural Geography of the Modern Tarascan Area.* Institute of Social Anthropology Publication no. 7. Washington, D.C.: Smithsonian Institution, 1948.

WEST, R. C., et al. *The Tabasco Lowlands of Southeastern Mexico.* Baton Rouge: Louisiana State University Press, 1969.

≡ 13 ≡

Main Characteristics
of Present-Day Central America

Smaller in area, less rich in natural resources, and less populous than Mexico, Central America has never attained the economic and political prestige of its northern neighbor. During the colonial period, except for the isthmian crossing point in Panama, Central America was an isolated segment of the Spanish Empire, virtually ignored by the Crown, mainly because of little mineral wealth and relatively few aboriginal peoples. The heritage of isolation, neglect, and poverty carried over into the nineteenth century, and only since the mid-twentieth century has Central America seen the beginnings of modernization in the form of highways, industry, large urban centers, and resource development.

The reasons for Central America's developmental lag are varied. One is its fragmentation into small nations, so small that the economic viability of some may be questionable. This viability is further lessened by the fact that each country, having similar physical characteristics, produces about the same agricultural products, and this has tended to stultify intraregional trade. Most commercial farm products, such as coffee, bananas, and cotton must be exported. Consequently, each country is dependent on foreign markets, and for that reason some have suffered from outside political influences, especially from the United States, Central America's major trade partner until recently. Perhaps the most fundamental reason for economic lag in Central America has been the lack of an integrated land transportation system. Because of mountainous terrain, transport has always been difficult in the isthmus. Throughout the colonial period and until recently the major transport lines were either trans-isthmian, such as the Panama route, or were oriented to the outside, connecting production and population centers with local seaports. Not until the 1960s were the Central American countries joined by a continuous auto road—the Inter-American Highway, constructed by United States engineers mainly with United States funds.

With the recent establishment of the Central American Common Market, most of the isthmian countries have made impressive advances in intraregional trade and industrialization. But none of them can boast of the large-scale growth of industry and transportation that has occurred in Mexico during the last 40 years.

POLITICAL FRAGMENTATION

The division of Central America into a number of tiny nations is indeed striking. What are the reasons for this political fragmentation of a contiguous land area whose major way of life is Hispanic?

After it became independent of Spain in 1821, most of the colonial Captaincy General of Guatemala devolved into five small independent states, while Chiapas became part of Mexico. Much later, in 1903, Panama, a former province of Colombia, was made a separate country. Belize, or British Honduras, long under English influence and a British colony since 1862, soon expects to be an independent nation.

It appears that the present political separation in Central America has its roots in the colonial provinces, for in each there developed around the provincial capital a single population cluster, usually separated from that of the neighboring province by sparsely peopled areas that were difficult to gain access to. Examples of such clusters include the small Meseta Central of highland Costa Rica, the lowland lake country of western Nicaragua, and the silver-mining area of the Honduran highlands. Largely neglected by a disinterested home government, the isolated Central American provinces were left much to their own devices. Moreover, the difficulties of travel between the provinces hindered cultural interchange. Thus, each population core tended to develop local loyalties and often distinctive culture patterns, to an even larger degree than in the *patrias chicas* of Mexico (see Chapter 12). More important, colonial authorities discouraged trade and contact between the provinces. It was Spain's economic policy that individual provinces could exchange most goods only with the mother country, and intraregional trade was effectively blocked by high internal custom duties and, in some cases, by outright prohibition. Among the few exceptions to this policy was the trade in livestock, which was permitted across provincial boundaries. Furthermore, the Central American region lacked a large urban center sufficiently strong to administrate the various isolated provinces effectively. Although Guatemala City was the seat of colonial administration for the Captaincy, it lacked the political prestige and power that enabled Mexico City, the traditional religious and administrative center of central Mexico since Aztec times, to hold together a large, diversified area.

Mainly for these reasons, the Spanish colonial provinces broke up into separate states despite attempts at political unification. Today, most of the isthmian countries are still dominated by a single population core which contains the national capital. In some, however (e.g., Honduras), secondary centers that have been developing since the late nineteenth century now threaten to eclipse the traditional centers in economic and political importance.

Even after independence, various forces tended to keep the Central American states apart. The paucity of intraregional trade, caused partly by similarity of production patterns and lack of adequate transport, has been mentioned. Moreover, it was in the interests of foreign powers (mainly the United States and England), concerned with the development of transisthmian canals and railroads, to keep the Central American countries divided and weak. It is also probable that the Central American people lacked a feeling of national unity because they were never forced to unite against a common enemy as were the Mexicans when invaded by the United States (1845 and 1917) and by France (1862). Even independence from Spain came easily to the Central American provinces, without undue military conflict or political strife.

Efforts to hold together the five Central American provinces after independence have included the abortive union with Mexico (1821–1822) and the longer-lasting but ineffective United Provinces of Central America, a federation that lasted from 1823 until 1839. By 1960 there had been no less than 25 separate attempts to revive political unity among the Central American republics, and all of them failed. The most recent attempt at intraregional cooperation was the establishment in 1960 of the Central American Common Market, a scheme for economic integration of all the isthmian countries except Panama.

Despite the obvious advantages that would accrue from political and economic unity, friction continues among the Central American nations. In the past such friction resulted from border disputes and alleged armed intervention by a neighboring country. The so-called Soccer War between El Salvador and Honduras in the summer of 1969 was the most serious recent armed conflict between Central American nations. Such conflicts highlight the continuing distrust that the people of these small countries have for one another, despite a common Hispanic heritage.

CENTRAL AMERICAN POPULATION

Today over 16 million people live in Central America. Most are concentrated on the Pacific side of the isthmus, where they occupy both tropical lowland and highland environments. In contrast, the rainy, forested Caribbean versant is, with some exceptions, sparsely populated. This general distribution pattern has persisted in Central America since aboriginal times.

Population densities vary greatly, even in the well-settled Pacific area, because of the traditional clustering of the population. Rural densities of over 1,000 persons per square mile occur in the Meseta Central of Costa Rica, and the overall density of little El Salvador is now 460 people per square mile. On the other hand, certain mountainous sections of the Pacific slope

may have population densities of 5 to 15 people per square mile, as low as those in most parts of the Caribbean sector.

The population of Central America, almost stagnant during much of the colonial period, is now increasing more rapidly than that of any other major region in the world. Yearly rates of increase vary from 3 percent in Guatemala to 3.5 percent in El Salvador and Nicaragua. At the present rates of increase Central America may have more than 23 million inhabitants by 1980 and over 40 million by the year 2000.

The rapid increase in numbers, added to the high rural densities that already exist in the overcrowded Pacific clusters has led to (1) the beginnings of colonization of the empty forests on the Caribbean slope, and (2) the sudden growth of urban centers.

Colonization of the Caribbean slope, which has progressed slowly in most of Central America, has gained momentum since World War II. Figure 13.1 shows the present frontiers. Pioneer colonization began first in Costa Rica (in the early nineteenth century) and has progressed furthest there. In Panama, peasants from the Pacific lowlands penetrated northward into the forest-covered mountainous interior, but the movement has stagnated at the continental divide. In Nicaragua, farmers from the densely settled lake lowlands and central highlands, encouraged by the government, are slowly moving into long unoccupied portions of the Caribbean versant. Similar movements have occurred in Honduras and are beginning in Guatemala, where the government has recently established agricultural colonies within the southern Petén in the northern part of the country. In overcrowded El Salvador, which has no Caribbean frontage, there has been movement toward the national frontier only to emigrate, but since the altercation with Honduras in 1969, that flow has ceased. Excepting El Salvador, Central America still has abun-

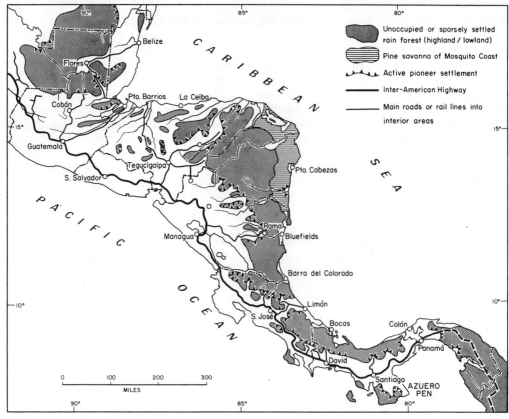

Figure 13.1 Status of settlement in Central America, mid-twentieth century (after G. Sandner 1964)

dant land (though much is of questionable farming quality) for its expanding population. However, a major problem is the reluctance of conservative rural folk, deeply attached to their crowded places of birth and to their local customs, to move to unfamiliar environments.

As in Mexico and most of the West Indies, since 1950 the Central American countries have experienced a rapid growth of urban population. This has occurred mainly in the capital cities, which, being centers of government and industry, offer more employment possibilities and other amenities for urban living than do the smaller provincial towns. The capitals thus attract the bulk of migrants from the countryside and maintain a high natural growth rate as well. They likewise attract the economic elite and the aspiring middle class, not only because of the op-

portunity for wealth, but also for the social prestige attached to living in the capital city. Such attitudes reflect the strong urban bias in Latin American life. Tables 13.1 and 13.2 indicate the growth and other significant characteristics of Central American capital cities. Guatemala City, for example, grew from 176,000 inhabitants in 1940 to an estimated 730,000 in 1970, retaining its long-held rank as Central America's largest urban center. Because of their rapid growth, most of the capital cities exhibit the characteristics of primacy, each containing a population several times greater than the next largest cities (index of primacy see Chapter 5 n. 3) as well as a large percentage (8 to 30) of the country's total population. In most of the Central American capitals rapid growth has intensified the usual problems associated with present-day Latin Ameri-

Table 13.1   POPULATION OF CENTRAL AMERICAN CAPITAL CITIES, 1940–1970

City	1940	1950	1960	1970 [1]
Guatemala City (Guatemala)	176,000	284,000	382,000	730,000
San Salvador (El Salvador)	102,300	162,000	231,000	337,200
Tegucigalpa (Honduras)	47,200	72,000	134,000	229,150
Managua (Nicaragua)	83,500	109,000	191,000	323,500
San José (Costa Rica)	65,000	87,000	102,000	205,600 [2]
Panama City (Panama)	111,900	128,000	253,000	425,000 [3]

[1] All 1970 figures are estimates, except for Panama City.

[2] San José's metropolitan area, which includes several nearby towns separated by rural zones, is estimated to contain 420,000 inhabitants.

[3] Includes the contiguous suburban town of San Miguelito, 70,000 inhabitants.

Sources: Official government censuses and statistical yearbooks.

Table 13.2   SOME CHARACTERISTICS OF CENTRAL AMERICAN CAPITAL CITIES

City	1970 Population Estimate	Percentage of Total Population of Country	Percentage of Total Industry by Value of Production	Index of Primacy
Guatemala City	730,000	13.1	60	7.1
San Salvador	337,200	9.6	60	1.9
Tegucigalpa	229,150	8.3	30	1.3
Managua	323,500	16.6	60	2.3
San José	205,600	11.5	45	2.5
Panama City	425,000	30.0	30	3.2
Mexico City	8,500,000	17.0	40	2.6
New York City	11,500,000	5.5		0.7

Sources: Official government censuses and statistical yearbooks.

can cities, such as slums, traffic congestion, inadequate municipal services, and, in some instances, air pollution.

Figure 13.2 shows the dominance of the capital city in each of the Central American countries. It also depicts the grouping of urban centers within the traditional population cluster of each country, except Honduras, where, since 1900, several cities have emerged in the banana and sugar-producing areas of the Caribbean lowland. These urban centers, especially San Pedro Sula, now compete with the inland capital, Tegucigalpa, for national economic and political hegemony.

As in many small developing countries today, the capital city in most of the Cen-

tral American countries is so dominant in the political, social, and economic fabric that the national territory is sometimes said to function as a city-state rather than as a nation-state. With its concentration of political power, the capital city tends to receive most of the government expenditures for economic and social improvements. Moreover, administrative control flows from the capital city to the limits of the national territory, while resources from the lesser towns and countryside flow into the capital for processing and redistribution.

Racially, the Central Americans are highly varied. About half of Guatemala's population is Indian, but only remnants

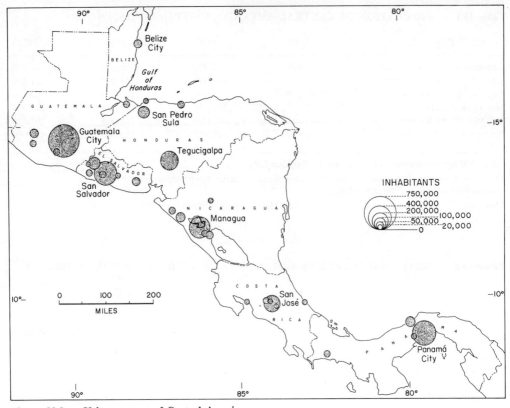

Figure 13.2 Urban centers of Central America

of aboriginal groups are found in the rest of the isthmus. The Costa Ricans, especially those who live in the highlands, are unique for their high percentage of Caucasian blood. Elsewhere in the well-settled Pacific versant, Central Americans are largely mixed Indian-white with occasional traces of black blood.

Much of the Caribbean coast is noted for its high percentage of Negroid population (Figure 13.3). Black slaves were brought to the Caribbean shores by English woodcutters and smugglers as early as the seventeenth century, but most of the present-day blacks descend from English-speaking West Indian islanders who came to work on the banana plantations and the Panama Canal at the beginning of this century. These blacks live in well-defined areas on the Caribbean side of Panama, Costa Rica, and Nicaragua. The Black Caribs, descendants of mixed black-

Indians from the Windward Islands whom the British forcibly marooned in the Bay Islands of Honduras at the end of the eighteenth century, form still another Negroid group. Nearly 35,000 of these curious people, who speak an Arawakan dialect, are subsistence farmers and fishers along the Caribbean shores of Honduras, Guatemala, and Belize.

THE ISTHMIAN FUNCTION
OF CENTRAL AMERICA

Because of its form and geographic position, the long, narrow land of Central America has played two important roles in the cultural history of the Americas. Central America served, first, as a land bridge connecting North and South America. In prehistoric times, it was a roadway over which plants and animals moved between the two continents. Later, American Indians used it for migrations and cultural interchange. After the Spanish Conquest, when the narrow land mass became a barrier to seafaring Europeans who wished to cross from one ocean to the next, the isthmus assumed a second role. The constrictions—the narrowest and lowest portions—of the mountainous isthmus became key points for the Spaniards; the same constrictions are still important crossing points today.

As mentioned in Chapter 10, the earliest and most significant crossing was Panama, the narrowest portion of the Central American isthmus. Other colonial crossings included the Nicaragua Rift, the Comayagua Depression in Honduras, and, occasionally, the Isthmus of Tehuantepec in southern Mexico. Owing to economic depression and political turmoil, however, transport over the isthmian crossings lagged in the eighteenth and early nineteenth centuries.

Traffic was suddenly revived after the discovery of gold in California in 1848. Rather than endure the long, dangerous trip overland across the United States, thousands of Europeans and eastern North American gold seekers took sea passage to California via the Central American crossings, particularly the route between Puerto Bello and Panama City. In 1855, to facilitate this growing traffic, North American interests completed the Panama Railway. The crossing via the Nicaragua Rift—up the San Juan River from Greytown and across Lake Nicaragua to San Juan del Sur on the Pacific—became another important route to the California gold fields. And, although less important, the Tehuantepec crossing was sufficiently used to instigate the construction of a transisthmian railway from the Pacific coast to Coatzacoalcos on the Gulf of Mexico, which was not completed until 1907. Because of the arduous trip by muleback, the long Comayagua route, from the Carib-

Figure 13.3   Distribution of Indian and negroid groups in Central America

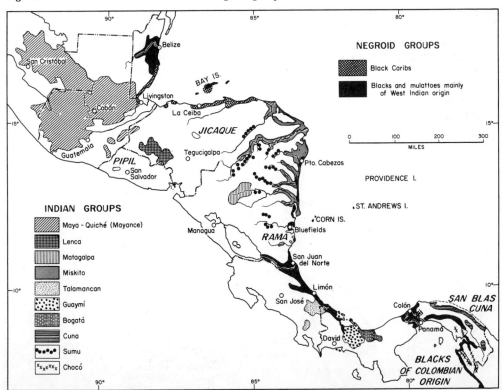

bean port of Puerto Cortés to the Gulf of Fonseca on the Pacific, was rarely used by California travelers.

Since colonial times, men had envisioned the construction of ship canals across the Central American isthmus, but it was only with the increase in oceanic traffic following the opening of the American West and the rise of the United States as a two-ocean sea power that serious consideration was given to such a gigantic undertaking. Between 1850 and 1900, United States and European engineers surveyed more than 30 transisthmian canal routes from the Isthmus of Tehuantepec to the Atrato River and its lower tributaries in northwestern Colombia. Of these, the old Panamanian route was favored, mainly because of its short 50-mile distance between the two oceans.

French interests first began excavations of a canal across this route in 1882, but yellow fever and inadequate machinery forced them to abandon the project. After political maneuvering and outright military intervention that resulted in the independence of Panama from Colombia, the United States, in 1903, obtained from the newly organized nation the right to build the canal. Completed in 1914, the Panama Canal, together with the Canal Zone, came under virtual United States sovereignty. In recent years the canal has become inadequate, and a new waterway, to be con-

continuous, well-traveled *camino real* that extended the length of the isthmus, constructed through one of the many possible transisthmian routes, is under consideration (Figure 13.4).

Central America's old isthmian role of land bridge between the two continents may soon be revived with the completion of the Inter-American Highway. However, a 400-mile stretch through sparsely populated rain forest in eastern Panama and northwestern Colombia (the Darien Gap) remains to be constructed before the highway can actually assume that function.

LAND TRANSPORT

Throughout most of its history, Central America has been plagued by inadequate land transportation. As mentioned previously, difficulty of communication appears to have been an underlying cause of political fragmentation within the isthmus. During the colonial period and into the nineteenth century, the better mule trails and a few cart roads connected the capital city of each province with the larger villages and haciendas located within the central population cluster. More difficult trails led to small ports, but only the transisthmian road across Panama boasted of traffic of any consequence. There was no

Figure 13.4   Transisthmian routes of Central America

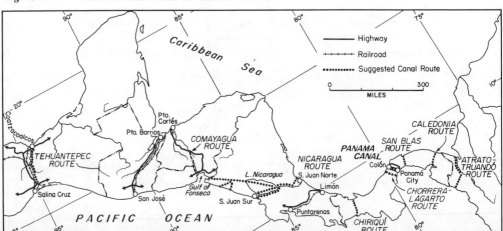

necting the provincial capitals, nor was there any real economic need for one.

hauling both freight and passengers is steadily declining.

Railroads

Introduced during the last half of the nineteenth century and financed mainly by British and United States capital, railroads were the first modern means of transport that appeared in Central America. Finished in 1855, the highly profitable Panama Railroad, which replaced the old transisthmian mule trail, was Central America's first rail line. In 1850, another transisthmian railroad was planned across Honduras and was to follow the old Comayagua route; but by 1868, only 50 miles of track had been laid inland from the Caribbean, and the project was never completed. Other early rail lines were begun in Costa Rica (1871), Nicaragua (1878), Guatemala (1883), and El Salvador (1892). All of these were built expressly to haul tropical products, especially coffee, to the ports and to bring in imported goods to the population centers. In the early 1900s, foreign banana companies laid hundreds of miles of rails and tramways to ship out fruit from plantations established on the Caribbean side of the isthmus. In 1912, a United States company, the International Railways of Central America (IRCA) purchased the lines of Guatemala and most of those in El Salvador. With the completion of a connecting line between the two countries in 1929, the IRCA system included the first and only international rail link to exist in Central America for public service.

Except in the banana areas, few railroads were built in Central America after the 1930s. Today they have been eclipsed by the more efficient highways begun after World War II. Many of the privately owned lines have become bankrupt; others have been nationalized. Most are so dilapidated and slow that they have ceased to be effective carriers, and their capacity for

Highways

As late as 1935, automobile roads in Central America were considered to be rudimentary. Generally, truck roads radiated outward for varying distances from the capital cities, encompassing the more populous areas in each country, as did the mule trails in colonial times. By 1940, Guatemala and El Salvador were the only isthmian countries linked by a graveled highway, and paved roads were nonexistent outside the main towns. Indeed, in most of Central America during the 1940s, travel from the capital city to distant parts of the country was more frequent and regular by air than by automobile; in Honduras, alone, 75 small air fields were in regular service.

The most ambitious road-building program in Central America has been the construction of the Inter-American Highway from the Mexican border to South America—a distance of 1,600 miles. Although short sections of the road were completed for local use in the late 1930s, it was not until after World War II that a unified construction program, financed mainly by the United States, was started. In 1964, it finally became possible to drive with comparative ease from the United States to Panama City over this highway; by 1973, the road had been completely paved. Optimists predict the construction of an auto road through the Darien Gap of eastern Panama and the final completion of the Inter-American Highway by 1978.

This highway has had a profound effect on the economy and perhaps on the politics of Central America. With its completion, the isthmian nations, for the first time, were linked by a continuous road. Intercountry travel by bus and private car increased greatly, but more important, the

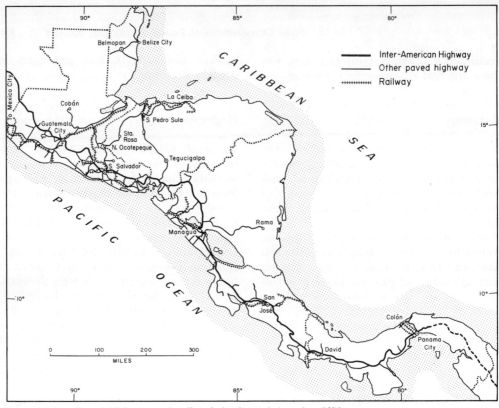

Figure 13.5 Paved highways and railroads in Central America, 1972

surge of intraregional trade since the start of the Central American Common Market in 1960 was facilitated by the highway. The Central American countries, aided by international financing, have constructed many all-weather regional and local feeder roads that link with the Inter-American Highway, thus revolutionizing road transport within the isthmian area (Figure 13.5). For example, ferry-trailer services now operate between two Caribbean ports (Santo Tomás in Guatemala and Puerto Cortés in Honduras) and Miami, Florida. Refrigerated trailers carrying shrimp, fresh beef, and other perishable produce are trucked over the Inter-American Highway and feeder roads to the ports from as far south as western Panama.

Despite the recent improvements in road transport, only the more populous Pacific side of Central America is adequately supplied with paved highways, as shown in Figure 13.5. Many parts of the mountainous interior and Caribbean lowlands still lack mechanized transport, and one of the aims of most Central American governments is the construction of penetration routes into the sparsely occupied areas to encourage settlement. In 1970, in all of Central America (an area the size of California), there were only some 200,-000 passenger cars and half as many commercial vehicles, such as trucks and buses, and most of those were in the cities.

THE CENTRAL AMERICAN ECONOMY

Agriculture

Since colonial times Central America's economy has revolved around agriculture. In recent years, however, as other sectors of the economy grow, such as industry and urban services, the relative importance of agriculture is decreasing in each of the Central American countries. Nonetheless, at present nearly two-thirds of the area's 16 million people still make their living by farming. Agriculture now contributes about 27 percent of the area's gross domestic product, and farm products account for 70 percent of the value of Central American exports—despite the fact that less than 15 percent of the land is under cultivation.

In Central America, food crops and techniques for subsistence cultivation have not changed appreciably since colonial, or even pre-Conquest times. Primitive slash-burn or dibble farming is even more widespread here than in Mexico. Maize, beans, and squash still form the major crop complex of subsistence farmers of Mesoamerican Indian heritage living in Guatemala, El Salvador, much of Honduras, and western Nicaragua; whereas in eastern Nicaragua, Costa Rica, and Panama, tubers of South American Indian origin are as important as maize in the rural diet, and Old World rice is now becoming more common than any of the aboriginal foods.

That part of Central American agriculture that has undergone the greatest change during the last 125 years is commercial farming. In Chapter 10 we saw that stock raising and the cultivation of indigo and cacao formed the economic cornerstone of most of the Central American provinces during the colonial period. This pattern continued until the midnineteenth century. Thereafter, the growing of coffee in the tropical highlands revolutionized commercial farming and changed the rural landscape of many Central American states. A second revolution in commercial farming came near the end of the nineteenth century, when North American fruit companies established large banana plantations in the Caribbean lowlands. A third change, the growth of mechanized cotton farming on large es-

tates in the hot Pacific lowlands, occurred after World War II. Finally, in several Central American countries the recent surge of improved cattle raising for the export of fresh beef to the United States may result in a fourth change in the agricultural economy of the isthmus.

Today, coffee, bananas, and cotton are Central America's most remunerative products. In 1960, the three crops constituted nearly 75 percent of the area's exports by value; in 1970, this percentage had dropped to about 53, indicating an increasing diversification of the Central American economy. However, these three crops occupy the best agricultural land, yet they supply no food for the area. Much of the foreign exchange that the Central American countries gain through the sale or taxing of these products must be used in many cases to import staple foods such as wheat and wheat flour, maize, and rice to feed their expanding urban populations.

Coffee. The central highlands of Costa Rica are the heartland of coffee cultivation in Central America. Although the plant was introduced there as a curiosity from Cuba in 1796, it was not until 1832 that the first coffee beans were exported. By 1850, the coffee farm (*finca*) was an established institution in the Meseta Central, and it still dominates Costa Rica's highland agriculture. From Costa Rica, coffee cultivation spread to El Salvador in 1840, to Nicaragua in the 1850s, and was introduced to the Pacific slope of Guatemala in the 1860s. In all four countries today this crop is a major export, and in all four the *fincas* occupy fertile lands along the volcanic axis of Central America (Figure 13.6). Honduras and Panama were the last of the Central American nations to enter the world coffee market. The crop was grown on a small scale in the Honduran highlands in the nineteenth century, but sizable amounts have been exported only since the 1940s. In Panama,

Figure 13.6 Coffee processing plant near Ahuachapán, El Salvador. The coffee fruits are depulped in the buildings at left, and the beans are spread to dry in the platforms, lower right.

coffee was first cultivated in the western highlands at the turn of the century, but exports are still relatively insignificant.

Today the economies of Guatemala, El Salvador, and Costa Rica are so closely tied to coffee that any considerable drop in the world price creates economic difficulties, just as a substantial rise brings prosperity. Traditionally, both the United States and western Europe (chiefly Germany) have been the main buyers of Central American coffee. The beans are of high quality and delicate flavor and are often blended with cheaper-grade Brazilian coffee. Since the mid-1950s, coffee production in Central America has more than doubled, reflecting improved cultivation techniques as well as the increase in consumption of quality beans in the United States and Europe.

Bananas. The story of the commercial banana industry in Central America is one of the most dramatic episodes in the cultural history of this area. The development of large-scale production of this delicate tropical fruit in Central America at the end of the last century was based chiefly on three factors: (1) the availability of large tracts of unoccupied fertile land in the hot, rainy Caribbean lowlands; (2) the establishment by North American interests of large tropical plantations, on

which efficient and standardized production was achieved by scientific agricultural methods and modern transportation techniques; and (3) the presence of a large nearby market in the heavily populated, industrialized eastern United States.

The many river flood plains of Caribbean Central America afforded almost ideal conditions for banana production. Highly fertile, friable, and well-drained, the alluvial clay-loam soils of the natural levees bordering the large rivers lacked only sufficient quantities of nitrogen for the exacting banana plant. Throughout most of the lowlands, continuously high temperatures and an average annual rainfall of 80 to 120 inches, with only a month-long dry season, insured year-round harvests.

Numerous individuals had experimented with commercial banana production as early as the 1860s near Puerto Bello, in Panama, and in the Ulúa-Chamelecón basin of northern Honduras. In the 1870s, small quantities were shipped out of the lowlands around Limón, in Costa Rica, in order to supply freight for a railroad under construction. Substantial exports, however, did not develop until the 1880s, after small North American and local companies had established plantations in the Matina valley of Costa Rica, the Bocas del Toro district of northwestern

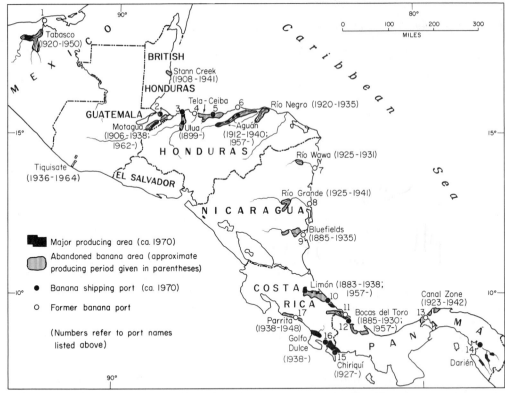

Figure 13.7 Major banana-producing areas in Central America. Banana ports are numbered as follows: (1) Frontera, (2) Puerto Barrios, (3) Puerto Cortés, (4) Tela, (5) La Ceiba, (6) Puerto Castilla, (7) Puerto Cabezas, (8) Rio Grande, (9) Bluefields, (10) Puerto Limón, (11) Sixaola, (12) Almirante, (13) Colón, (14) La Palma, (15) Puerto Armuelles, (16) Golfito, and (17) Quepos.

Panama, and along the Escondido River around Bluefields, Nicaragua. Figure 13.7 shows the major banana plantation areas of Central America and southern Mexico.

The vast tropical plantation usually associated with banana production in Central America did not fully develop until after the establishment of the United Fruit Company in 1899. Much later, in 1924, several small fruit companies merged to form the second big banana corporation, the Standard Fruit and Steamship Company.[1] Clearing of large forested tracts

and construction of drainage canals, railway networks, company labor and administrative towns, and shipping ports, as well as the maintenance of fleets of refrigerated fruit ships—were all undertaken by these United States companies and their predecessors. During this time, too, large numbers of West Indian blacks, chiefly Jamaicans, were imported to work on the Caribbean plantations. United Fruit established plantations in the Limón district of Costa Rica; Bocas del Toro, Panama; Ulúa-Chamelecón, Honduras; and the lower Motagua valley, Guatemala. Standard Fruit's holdings were mainly along the north coast of Honduras. Only El Salvador, whose coast is completely on the Pacific, failed to experience the big Central American banana boom of 1900–1930. Banana exports, mainly to the United States, grew steadily after 1900, reaching

1. In 1969, majority stock in the United Fruit Company was purchased by a large food concern, and the combined enterprise was renamed the United Brands. Later, the Standard Fruit and Steamship Company merged with a holding corporation. Despite these changes, hereinafter we shall use the old names United Fruit and Standard Fruit in reference to the corporate banana operations in Central America.

a peak in 1930. More than half of these exports came from the Caribbean coast of Honduras, which at that time produced one-third of the world's bananas.

By the 1930s, the Caribbean plantations were so ridden with Panama disease, a banana plague, that production suffered a serious decline. This disease, which affects the root systems of the commonly grown Gros Michel variety, was detected in Panama as early as 1880. By 1900, thousands of acres of banana lands had been abandoned throughout the Caribbean lowlands. In 1938, banana leaf blight, Sigatoka, entered the area, causing further damage. Sigatoka can be controlled with chemical spray, but no effective remedy has yet been found for Panama disease.

The most significant consequence of Panama disease was the partial shift of the Central American banana industry from the Caribbean to the Pacific lowlands, where the plague had not penetrated. This movement began in 1927, when United Fruit transferred its Panamanian operations from Bocas del Toro, on the Caribbean, to the Puerto Armuelles district on the Pacific coast. By the 1930s, the company had established plantations on the Pacific side of both Costa Rica and Guatemala, until recently the main banana-producing areas of those countries (Figure 13.7). However, both Panama disease and Sigatoka have since invaded the Pacific lowlands and caused abandonment of banana lands there. For example, in 1964, United Fruit closed out its banana properties at Tiquisate on the Pacific coast of Guatemala.

Considerable banana production, however, has been retained or reestablished on the Caribbean side. Plantations in the Ulúa district of Honduras were maintained through flood fallowing, which helped control Panama disease. But since 1960, practically all plantations in Central America have turned to the cultivation of banana varieties resistant to Panama disease, such as the Giant Cavendish, which

has now supplanted the traditional Gros Michel. In consequence, banana exports, from both the Pacific and Caribbean sides have reached all-time highs since World War II, with Honduras and Costa Rica leading all other isthmian countries. With the planting of the easily bruised Giant Cavendish variety, bananas are no longer shipped by stem; rather, the hands are cut and boxed for transport. Boxing adds to processing costs, but permits the salvage of fruit that was formerly rejected as unfit for marketing. Moreover, production systems are rapidly changing in the banana industry. The big plantation is still significant, but an increasing part of production comes from the small private fruit grower and workers' cooperatives that have acquired former company land. Both the private grower and the cooperatives sell their crop to the large companies that control overseas transport.

Like some other types of large-scale commercial farming in the tropics, banana culture in Central America is an unstable kind of land use. This can be seen in the high susceptibility of the banana plant to disease and in the frequent abandonment of cultivated areas; it can also be seen in the large financial risk involved in maintaining profitable production. However, some of the abandoned banana lands in both the Caribbean and Pacific lowlands have been converted to more stable plantation crops, such as African oil palm and cacao in Costa Rica, or to planted pasture for cattle production in other areas.

Cotton. The sudden rise of cotton production has been even more spectacular than that of bananas. After World War II, the great demand for cotton fiber and the consequent high prices prompted many large land owners on the dry Pacific side of Central America to invest in large-scale mechanized cotton cultivation. Since 1958, cotton has been Nicaragua's leading export, and in El Salvador and Guatemala it has become second only to coffee as the most remunerative commercial product; as yet, cotton is a minor crop in Honduras, Costa Rica, and Panama. Exports go mainly to Japan and western Europe.

Because cotton grown in the lowland tropics is highly susceptible to many insect predators, Central American planters must apply large amounts of pesticides to save their crops. Moreover, to maintain high yields, commercial fertilizers are liberally applied to the soil. These practices have so increased costs that most marginal cotton farmers in Central America have ceased operation, leaving production to the larger and more affluent land owners. The liberal use of pesticides has also adversely affected native wild life within the Pacific lowlands of Central America, where both bird and fish populations have been seriously reduced since the 1960s.

Fresh Meat Exports. In recent years a lucrative market for fresh meat in the United States has led to the rise of a new agricultural industry in Central America—the processing of chilled beef for export. It has also led to a start in the revitalization of stock raising, a traditionally backward occupation in the isthmian area.

Central America's share of United States imports of chilled beef rose from less than 2 percent in 1958 to nearly 15 percent in 1973. Chilled beef is now the third most valuable export of Nicaragua and Costa Rica, the largest Central American producers; the industry is growing rapidly in Guatemala and Honduras, but it has lagged in Panama and El Salvador. Barring unforeseen price declines or import restrictions by the United States, chilled beef exports may soon become one of Central America's main trade items.

Spurred by high prices for livestock, Central American cattlemen have recently taken steps to modernize. The more affluent ranchers have upgraded their herds with the use of imported pure-bred bulls, such as the Brahma; they have improved and expanded pastures by planting nutri-tious African grasses; and many now employ modern livestock management techniques. Nevertheless, low-grade criollo cattle still supply the bulk of the meat exports, nearly all of which is used for the making of hamburger, bologna, and other processed meats in the United States.

Modern processing and transport techniques characterize the chilled beef industry in Central America. Packing plants, approved by the United States, have been built in industrial centers or within the livestock areas. The chilled and boned meat, packed in cartons, is placed in refrigerated trailers that are hauled by truck principally to Caribbean ports and there loaded on freighters bound for Florida, although some is shipped by air to the United States. Lesser amounts of meat go directly to Puerto Rico or California.

Although many Central American ranchers are benefiting from the profitable chilled beef trade, increase in meat exports has been at the expense of domestic consumption of beef, which declined approximately by 30 percent per capita between 1958 and 1968. In view of their rapidly growing population, the Central American countries are now faced with a problem: whether to keep meat output for domestic supply, increasing the protein intake of the people; or to export meat for foreign exchange. Perhaps only by increasing cattle production through further modernization and expanding pastures within the forest-covered tropical lowlands might this dilemma be resolved.

Problems of Land Reform

Of the many problems that beset agriculture in Central America, none is more pervading than that of land tenure. As in much of Latin America, two contrasting forms of land ownership prevail in the isthmian area: (1) the large estates (latifundia) owned by a small number of rich families or by foreign corporations that occupy most of the good farmland and produce mainly crops for export; and (2) the great number of small individual plots (minifundia) cultivated chiefly for subsistence by poverty-stricken peasants who comprise the bulk of the rural population and who may own, rent, or simply occupy illegally their tiny parcels. In part, this agricultural dichotomy derives from colonial society, but the large estates have expanded in size and number during the last 100 years with the rise of large-scale commercial farming based on the cultivation of tropical products for the world market.

Inherent in the dual system are grave economic and social problems. In most cases a given subsistence holding is too small to feed a family, much less to supply a surplus for sale or to support the use of modern technology. And with the recent explosion of rural population, land available for subsistence farmers is becoming increasingly scarce. Moreover, owners of large estates often permit sections of good land to lie idle. Such conditions not only preclude the best use of the land; they also give rise to a restive, dissatisfied rural peasantry who have come to expect a better life. In recent years landless peasants have resorted in desperation to widespread squatting on unused national and private lands, creating serious confrontations with public authorities. All the Central American countries are affected by inequality of land distribution and its inherent problems. But the greatest inequality is seen in Guatemala and El Salvador; somewhat less in Nicaragua, Costa Rica, and Panama; and least in Honduras.

Unlike Mexico, none of the Central American countries has been successful in effecting true land reform. There have been serious attempts at reform, as in Guatemala in 1954, but the landed aristocracy has been sufficiently strong to prevent radical change. Thus, attempts to alleviate the lot of the subsistence farmers have proceeded along other routes, which include: (1) colonizing unused public lands,

(2) giving squatters legal titles to plots they have occupied, and (3) taxing idle portions of estates more heavily than land under use to force holders to liquidate such properties for government-directed settlement. Prodded by requirements set up under the Alliance for Progress, by 1962 all Central American countries had established government agencies (national agrarian institutes) to handle land problems. In most cases these agencies have found that colonization programs prove to be too costly and usually less than successful, that the legalization of squatting merely perpetuates the curse of minifundia, and that property tax laws have been difficult to enforce. Still, one of the chief aims of the land tenure programs is to give the subsistence farmer sufficient acreage to raise not only enough to feed his family, but to produce a crop surplus for sale—to create a "middle-class" peasantry. Without a real change in land tenure, including the power to expropriate large holdings, this goal may be illusory. In Chapters 14 and 15 the slight progress made in land reform is discussed for each country.

Sea Fisheries

Like the fresh beef industry, commercial fishing off the Central American shores has developed only recently and in response to a lucrative market in the United States. To date, the marine delicacies, shrimp and spiny lobster, which abound in the tropical waters off coast, have been the mainstay of this industry. Panama, El Salvador, and Belize are the leading producers in Central America, and in each, fish products now rank third in value of total exports.

As shown in Figure 13.8, the main shrimp beds lie off the Pacific coast and form a continuation of the Mexican shrimping grounds. Large white shrimp thrive in the shallow muddy bottoms of the narrow continental shelf, and the nu-

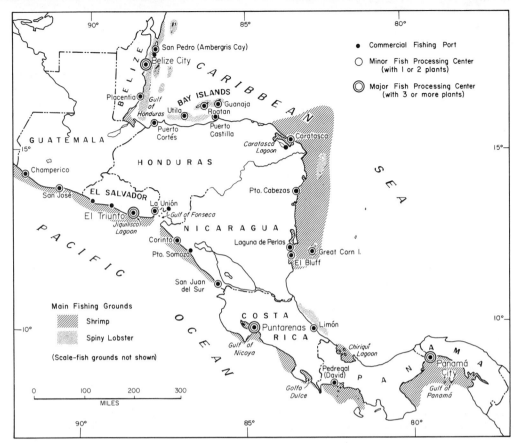

Figure 13.8 Central American fisheries

merous coastal lagoons and estuaries serve as nurseries for the juvenile form of the animal. Fewer shrimp beds are found on the Caribbean side; the largest extends along the Nicaraguan coast in the wide, shallow, coral-strewn banks, where pockets of mud and sand afford suitable habitats. In contrast, the spiny lobster lives chiefly within the coral reefs near the Caribbean coast. The main lobster beds are located along the barrier reef off Belize, around the Bay Islands off Honduras, and along the shore of Costa Rica.

Strongly influenced by modern fishing technology introduced from the United States in the late 1940s, Panama was the first Central American country to exploit commercially its shrimp beds along the Pacific coast. During the following decades the industry spread northward to other Central American countries because of the steady demand and high prices for

shrimp in the United States. Often aided by United States capital, locally owned companies assembled fishing fleets and built freezing plants in port towns and fishing villages, where shrimp are processed for export mainly via refrigerated trailer trucks to Caribbean ports. More recently, processing plants and trawler fleets have been established on the Caribbean coast in Nicaragua and Honduras to exploit the adjacent shrimp beds. Because signs of overexploitation on the Pacific side are already evidenced by decreasing yields, the Caribbean beds may one day become Central America's leading source of shrimp. In 1970, however, the Gulf of Panama on the Pacific side was still the most productive isthmian shrimping ground, with Panama accounting for more than half of the Central American shrimp exports.

Less developed than shrimping, commercial exploitation of the spiny lobster is confined largely to Belize, where the industry grew rapidly after World War II. Since 1960, Honduras, Nicaragua, and Costa Rica have begun to process lobster on a small scale. Only the lobster tail is considered edible, and these are frozen for shipment by air freight to Miami and New York.

Since the mid 1960s, Central American commercial fishermen have begun to exploit other forms of marine life. Panamanians, for instance, have established a sizable fish meal and oil industry based on exploitation of the vast schools of anchovies and thread herring that inhabit the Gulf of Panama. More significant, several Central American countries with technical help from Japan and Korea are forming cooperatives to fish for tuna and other deep-sea fin-fish in the tropical waters of the Pacific. Unfortunately, such projects are planned chiefly for exporting fish products abroad, not for the supply of cheap protein foods for local consumption. With the exception of Panama, the Central American countries, like Mexico, consume little fish, Guatemala having the lowest per capita intake of seafoods of any coastal country in the world.

The Central American Common Market

Within the last decade the Central American countries have been working toward economic unity. In 1960, five countries, all except Panama, agreed in principle to a Central American Common Market (CACM), which would endeavor to abolish tariffs on most goods traded among the member countries and to fix common tariffs on most items entering the five countries from abroad. It was further agreed to establish the Central American Bank for Economic Integration to promote, through loans, a "balanced economic development" among the CACM countries, especially in industry. By 1963 all five countries had signed the agreement.

The Central American Common Market is often cited as the most successful attempt at economic integration among the developing countries of the world. By 1969, intraregional trade had increased nearly tenfold among the CACM countries, and their dependence on foreign trade had been decreased. In addition, industrial development in most of the countries had greatly expanded under the common market arrangement.

Unfortunately, within the last few years various economic and political problems within the CACM have cast uncertainty over its future. Trade imbalances have arisen among the member countries. Honduras, Nicaragua, and Costa Rica have suffered serious trade deficits, while Guatemala and El Salvador have enjoyed corresponding surpluses. Even more discouraging for the future of the CACM was the regrettable military conflict between El Salvador and Honduras in 1969, which terminated all trade between the two and temporarily disrupted trade among the others. Finally, in 1970, Honduras virtually withdrew from the CACM by reimposing tariffs on imports from the other Central American countries. Although the organization still functions in part, without the full participation of all members, its effectiveness for regional economic integration is greatly reduced. Once considered a possible first step toward political union, the Central American Common Market may be no more than another attempt at international cooperation thwarted by the regional and political differences that have separated the isthmian countries since colonial times.

Industrial Development. Despite its uncertain future, the Central American Common Market has been responsible for impressive growth in the economies of the member countries. The increase in intraregional trade has especially furthered manufacturing and has thereby helped to diversify the Central American economy. The contribution of manufacturing to the combined gross national product of the CACM countries increased from 13 percent in 1962 to over 17 percent in 1970, while in the same period agriculture's share decreased from 37 to 27 percent.

Under the original CACM agreement, certain "integration industries," considered to be important for the whole of Central America, were to be established in each of the countries to maintain balanced growth. Guatemala, for example, obtained an automobile tire factory and Nicaragua, an insecticide plant, the products to be sold duty free to all CACM members. More important, various fiscal incentives, such as the reduction of tariffs on imported raw materials used in manufacturing has encouraged the establishment of subsidiaries of United States and

European companies that make a large range of consumer goods, from electronic devices to clothing and toys.

Industrial development in the Central American countries, however, has been uneven. Guatemala and El Salvador, already the most industrialized of the isthmian countries prior to the establishment of the CACM, have enjoyed the largest recent expansion. Honduras, traditionally the poorest of the countries, has grown the least. The uneven growth of industry was one of the underlying causes of the accumulation of trade deficits by the least favored countries, which in turn led to the partial breakdown of the common market system.

Figure 13.9 shows the distribution and relative size of industrial centers in Central America in relation to the power re-

Figure 13.9 Industry and power resources in Central America. Numbers refer to the names of hydroelectric plants: (1) Marinalá, (2) 5 de Noviembre, (3) Cañaveral, (4) Centroamérica, (5) Garita, (6) Cachí, and (7) Bayano.

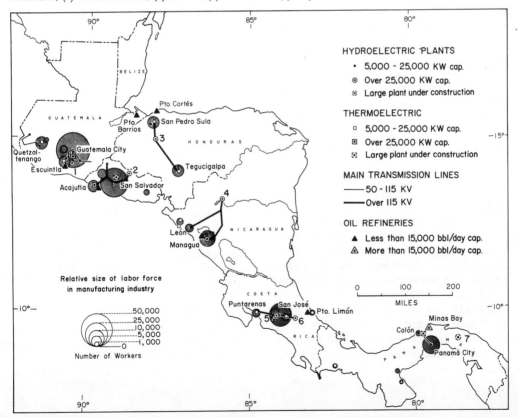

sources. Not surprisingly, manufacturing is concentrated in the capital cities and in smaller urban centers within the population cluster of each country.

The Central American nations are still on the threshold of industrial development. Unlike Mexico, the area lacks profitably exploitable deposits of hydrocarbon fuels. However, large reserves of industrial mineral ores, such as nickel in Guatemala, iron in Honduras, and copper in Panama have recently come to light. Moreover, there is a sizable hydroelectric potential for power to run light industry; many hydroelectric plants are now in operation, and several large ones are under construction or planned in every Central American country (Figure 13.9). Thermoelectric plants are generated with foreign fuel or with that refined locally from crude oil imported from Venezuela.

Tourism

Central America has never attained the degree of tourism equal to that of Mexico or the West Indies. Inadequate transport, hotels, and other tourist accommodations, as well as frequent political unrest, have been major reasons for this lag. More important, a general disinterest in the development of the tourist trade has long pervaded the Central American countries, and only recently have the governments and private agencies made serious efforts to attract foreign visitors, mainly United States citizens.

These belated efforts have been best developed in Guatemala and Panama, both favored by viable tourist attractions. Like Mexico, Guatemala has its Indian people and their colorful markets (such as Chichicastenango) in the southwestern highlands; famous archaeological ruins (such as the recently reconstructed Mayan site of Tikal) in the northern lowlands; quaint colonial towns (such as historical

Antigua) in the central part of the country; and striking volcanic landscapes (such as the areas around Guatemala City and Lake Atitlán). Panama's attractions center around the canal and the bazaars of the capital city and Colón, which draw thousands of tourists and seamen yearly. Its position as a "crossroads of the world" has made the transit zone across Panama a natural tourist haven. However, except for short visits to the San Blas Cuna Indian villages on the northeastern coast, there is little to attract the tourist in other parts of the country.

Only a rudimentary tourist trade has begun in a few other parts of Central America. The coral reefs, cays, and islands off Belize and Honduras, like other Caribbean areas, are ideal for the development of resorts featuring skin diving and deepsea fishing; but to date only small isolated

Table 13.3   PASSENGER AIR TRAFFIC TO CENTRAL AMERICAN CITIES FROM NORTH AMERICA, 1973

City	Number of Weekly Flights	Percentage of Total Weekly Flights to Middle America from North America
Panama City	104	3.5
Guatemala City	66	2.2
San José, Costa Rica	31	1.0
San Salvador, El Salvador	30	1.0
Managua, Nicaragua	29	1.0
San Pedro Sula, Honduras	20	0.7
Tegucigalpa, Honduras	11	0.3
TOTAL	291	9.7

Source: Official Airline Guide, North American and International editions, 1973.

guest houses provide accommodations of varying quality. Recently, a few resorts and housing projects have been started along the Pacific side of Costa Rica, where wide crescent beaches bounded by rocky headlands make this coast the most scenic in Central America. Poor roads, however, have prevented rapid development of this area. Fortunately, from an ecological point of view, little of the Central American coastline has as yet been ravaged by modern development, and in most of the countries, beaches are considered to be public lands.

Probably the best tourist accommodations in Central America are found in the capital cities, where luxury hotels, modern restaurants, and adequate transport facilities have recently been built. The capital city usually receives the most favorable tourist propaganda, is usually the first point reached by air travel from abroad (Table 13.3), and is therefore the single point that obtains the bulk of the tourist dollar spent in each country. Unfortunately, the capital city is the place least likely to give the foreign tourist the true flavor of the country he is visiting.

SELECTED REFERENCES

ADAMS, R. N. *Cultural Surveys of Panama, Nicaragua, Guatemala, El Salvador, Honduras.* Washington, D.C.: Pan American Sanitary Bureau, 1957.

CASTILLO, C. M. *Growth and Integration in Central America.* New York: Praeger, 1966.

CRAIG, A. K. *Geography of Fishing in British Honduras and Adjacent Waters.* Baton Rouge: Louisiana State University Press, 1966.

DOZIER, C. L. *Indigenous Tropical Agriculture in Central America: Land Use, Systems, and Problems,* Publication no. 594. Washington, D.C.: National Research Council, 1958.

HELBIG, K. M. *Die Wirtschaft Zentralamerikas.* Hamburg: Ubersee Verlag, 1966.

HILDEBRAND, J. R. "The Central American Common Market: Economic and Political Integration." *Journal of Inter-American Studies* 9, no. 3 (1967):383–95.

HOLBIK, K., and SWAN, P. L. *Trade and Industrialization in the Central American Common Market: The First Decade.* Austin: University of Texas, Graduate School of Business, Bureau of Business Research, 1972.

JONES, D. R. W. "The Carribbean Coast of Central America: A Case of Multiple Fragmentation." *The Professional Geographer* 22, no. 5 (1970):260–65.

KEARNS, K. C. "A Transisthmian Sea-Level Canal for Central America: Proposals and Prospects." *Journal of Geography* 60, no. 4 (1971):235–46.

MINKEL, C. W. "Programs of Agricultural Colonization and Settlement in Central America." *Revista Geográfica,* no. 66 (1967): 19–53.

PARSONS, J. J. "Cotton and Cattle in the Pacific Lowlands of Central America." *Journal of Inter-American Studies* 7, no. 2 (1965):149–59.

ROURK, J. P. *The Beef Cattle Industries of Central America and Panama.* Washington, D.C.: United States Department of Agriculture, Foreign Agricultural Service, 1969.

SANDNER, G. "Die Erschliessung der karibischen Waldregion im südlichen Zentralamerika." *Die Erde* 95, no. 2 (1964):111–30.

———. *Die Hauptstädte Zentralamerikas: Wachstumsprobeme, Gestaltwandel und So-*

zialgefüge. Heidelberg: Quelle and Meyer, 1969.

SMITH, R. S. "Population and Economic Growth in Central America." *Economic Development and Cultural Change* 10, no. 2, Part 1 (1962):134–49.

STOUSE, P. A. D. "Instability of Tropical Agri-culture: The Atlantic Lowlands of Costa Rica." *Economic Geography* 46, no. 1 (1970): 78–97.

TAYLOR, J. R. "Agricultural Development in the Humid Tropics of Central America." *Inter-American Economic Affairs* 24, no. 1 (1970):41–9.

14

Central America:
The Northern Sector

This chapter and the following one discuss the main characteristics of the land and people of each Central American country. For convenience of presentation the isthmus is divided into the northern and southern sectors. Guatemala, Belize (British Honduras), El Salvador, and Honduras are considered in this chapter; Nicaragua, Costa Rica, and Panama, in the next. Although a feeling of nationalism has developed in each of these political entities, most of them exhibit more than one culture area. Perhaps future study will reveal that each Central American country, Honduras excluded, forms a single urban nodal region, based on the dominance of the capital city.

GUATEMALA

Of the six small republics that comprise the isthmus of Central America, Guatemala is physically and culturally perhaps the most distinctive. Guatemala is smaller than the state of Louisiana, yet the physical landscape is almost as diverse as Mexico's. Culturally, Guatemala is the most Indian country of all Middle America. Of its 5.4 million people, about 43 percent are classed as aborigines who live

much as their eighteenth-century ancestors did. Like most Latin American nations, Guatemala has been much beset by political strife since independence from Spain early in the nineteenth century. The lack of political stability, the cultural conservatism of both the Indians and the landed aristocracy of Spanish descent, and a compartively poor endowment of natural resources have slowed the country's economic development. Much more than Mexico, Guatemala lives in its colonial past.

The Physical Landscape

The gross physical characteristics of the Central American countries have already been described (see Chapter 2). The following summary of the salient features of the land configuration, climate, and vegetation of Guatemala provides a review and reemphasis.

Mountainous highlands make up the southern half of Guatemala. These consist of two high ranges, geologically related to the Old Antillean tectonic belt that runs west–east through northern Central America. Between the ranges lies the deep, dry, scrub-covered Motagua River depression. The northern range, composed chiefly of limestone, extends eastward from southern Mexico into Guatemala as the Alto Cuchumatanes plateau (9,000–11,000 feet elevation) and the lower folded ranges of Alta Verapaz (Figure 14.1). South of the Motagua depression rises the high southern range, topped by a series of magnificent volcanoes interspersed with lava plateaus and ash-filled basins, forming the northwestern end of the Central American volcanic axis. The largest volcanoes (10,000–14,000 feet elevation) and the highest basins (6,000–8,000 feet) lie in the western portion of the southern range, aptly called "Los Altos." The uplands above 5,000 feet enjoy a cool, bracing tropical highland climate with well-marked dry (November–April) and wet (May–October) seasons. Remnants of a once-extensive pine and oak forest cover most of these highlands.

Facing southward toward the Pacific Ocean, the escarpment of the volcanic range descends abruptly to the coastal plain. Often called the "Boca Costa," or the "Piedmont," the lower half of the escarpment today forms Guatemala's most productive agricultural area. The upper portion of the Boca Costa (1,500–5,000 feet elevation) lies within the *tierra templada* altitudinal zone of the Middle American tropics. Rain-drenched and once covered with a dense tropical rain forest, the upper Boca Costa has, since the mid-nineteenth century, become Guatemala's major coffee belt. The lower Boca Costa (300–1,500 feet elevation), entirely within the *tierra caliente,* comprises the lower portions of the great alluvial fans that have been formed at the base of the escarpment by rivers flowing from the volcanic axis. Beyond the rolling landscape of the lower Boca Costa, the Pacific plain (locally called "La Costa") stretches seaward as a low, hot, flattish, grass-and-forest-covered surface to the coastal lagoons.

A much larger tropical lowland, the

Figure 14.1   Natural-cultural areas of Guatemala

Petén, forms the northern third of Guatemala. The flattish-to-rolling surface of this limestone area is a southern continuation of the Yucatan Platform. Covered by a dense rain forest and scattered savannas, it represents one of the great sparsely populated regions (*despoblados*) of Middle America.

People and Settlement

With 5.4 million inhabitants (1970 estimate), Guatemala is the most populous of the Central American countries. As in most of Middle America, the population increase has been extraordinarily rapid since 1940 (Figure 14.2), and between 1950 and 1964, it was 3.3 percent yearly. This rapid growth stems entirely from natural population increase, for immigration has been negligible since the colonial period.

Since pre-Columbian times, most of the people have lived in the southern highlands, the cultural core of the country. Although the overall population density of Guatemala averages 125 persons per square mile, some of the volcanic basins of the southwestern highlands, or Los Altos, have rural populations of over 300 persons per square mile. Indeed, nearly one-third of Guatemala's entire population is concentrated in the highland basins and on the lower slopes of Los Altos.

Since the introduction of coffee as a cash crop in the last century, population densities have greatly increased in the upper

Figure 14.2   Population growth in Guatemala, 1750–1970

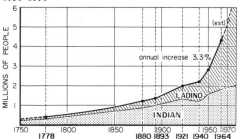

Boca Costa zone of the volcanic escarpment. In addition, portions of the Pacific coastal plain (La Costa), sparsely peopled during the colonial period, are today being cleared and settled. The lowest population densities occur in the northern third of the country. The vast, forest-covered lowlands of the Petén contain only two persons per square mile, a relative emptiness that dates from the abandonment of the area by the highly cultured Maya Indians more than a thousand years ago. The forested mountains and lowlands around Lake Izabal and within the lower Motagua Valley near the Caribbean coast are also sparsely populated, but the area has higher densities (10 to 20 persons per square mile) than the Petén.

Guatemalans, like Mexicans, are of two main racial groups: pure Indian stock and mixed Indian-Caucasian ancestry. In Guatemala, however, pure-blooded Indians probably make up more than half of the total population, while they are in a minority in the other Mainland countries of Middle America. Only an insignificant proportion of Guatemalans are Caucasian (chiefly in urban centers) or Negroid (mainly along the Caribbean coast).

The term "Indian" has a cultural rather than a racial meaning in Guatemala, as it does in most of Central America. Thus, Guatemalans comprise two main culture groups: (1) the Indian, who has usually retained his language and a large number of indigenous customs; and (2) the non-Indian, or *Ladino*,[1] who speaks only Spanish and whose customs are largely of Spanish origin. To be sure, most Ladinos are either mixbloods or Caucasians, but full-blooded Indians may become Ladinos on

1. The term "Ladino," used chiefly in Guatemala, El Salvador, and Honduras, has an even broader cultural connotation than "mestizo," which is employed in Mexico, Nicaragua, and Panama. Caucasians, as well as mixbloods and Indians, may be called "Ladinos," while pure whites are usually not referred to as "mestizos."

losing their Indian ways and adopting European modes of living. Figure 14.2 indicates that the Ladinos have increased from approximately 25 percent of the Guatemalan population, in 1893, to 57 percent in 1964. The Ladino element will probably continue to gain at the expense of Indian culture.

The Indians. The Guatemalan Indians are concentrated in the highlands, chiefly in Los Altos, west of Guatemala City, and in the isolated Alto Cuchumatanes Plateau and mountains of Alta Verapaz, where in many sections they comprise over 90 percent of the rural population. These areas, together with the northern highlands of adjacent Chiapas in southern Mexico, form the largest and most populous continuous aboriginal area of Middle America (Figure 14.3). The Indian languages spoken throughout the area belong to the large Mayance, or Maya-Quiché, family. Thus, the Guatemala-Chiapas Indian area in the south and the Maya-speaking section of Yucatan in Mexico form the two large aboriginal remnants of the pre-Conquest Maya culture area.

According to the 1950 Guatemalan census, 16 different Mayance languages are spoken in the country. The largest groups are the Quiché, Cakchiquel, and Mam, who inhabit the highland basins of Los Altos, the most densely populated area of

Figure 14.3   Present-day Indian language groups in Guatemala. Shaded areas represent those in which 40 percent or more of the total population speaks Indian languages.

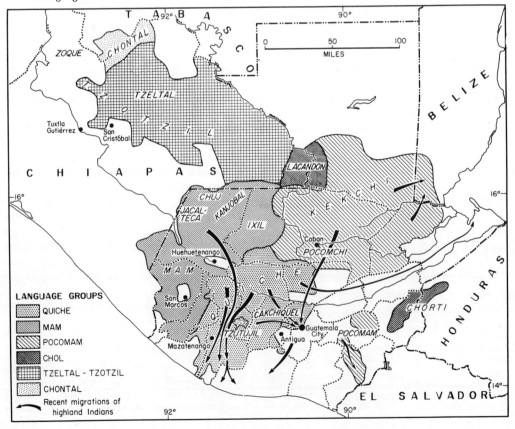

Figure 14.4 Terracettes (*surcos*) on a hillside near Totonicapán, Guatemala

Guatemala. The Kekchi, who occupy the isolated limestone ridges and valleys of Alta Verapaz and southern Petén, are among the least acculturated Indians of the country.[2]

Most of the Guatemalan Indians are subsistence farmers, cultivating maize, beans, and squash (the crop triad of Mesoamerica) much as their ancestors did in pre-Conquest times. Slash-burn farming is often practiced on steep slopes, but in the fertile volcanic basins and adjacent slopes of Los Altos, series of wide ridges and furrows, as well as elaborate terracettes, are laboriously constructed on permanent fields with a heavy metal hoe (Figure 14.4). Borrowed from the Spaniard, this instrument probably replaced the aboriginal wooden *coa*. Throughout most of the Indian area of Guatemala, as in Chiapas and Yucatan, the farmers have rejected the Spanish ox-drawn plow.

Hoe cultivation, however, often yields

2. Unfortunately, the 1964 Guatemalan census does not list aboriginal languages or the number of Indian-language speakers. According to the 1950 census, Quiché was spoken by 340,000 individuals over three years of age; Mam, by 178,000; Cakchiquel, 170,000; Kekchi, 134,000. In 1964, these figures probably would have been substantially greater.

surplus crops that can be sold for cash. At high elevations, wheat is now a cash crop, although Guatemala still imports wheat and flour for her bread-eating urban population. As in most highland Indian areas of Latin America, sheep raising is now an important subsidiary occupation, especially on the high alpine grasslands of the southwestern highlands. In the past 50 years, some Indian communities, such as those surrounding Lake Atitlán, have specialized in the cultivation of vegetables as cash crops, employing elaborate gardening techniques introduced by the Europeans.

Among most of the indigenous groups individual farms are small (one to ten acres) and are either privately owned or communal village lands, as in pre-Conquest times. In many instances, the plot of an Indian family is too small to produce enough food for one household. Indeed, some writers estimate that nearly 75 percent of the Indian farmers of Los Altos must rent additional land to cultivate sufficient food crops or must work for others to supplement the production from their own land. As indicated in Chapter 9, the colonial Spaniards established few large estates among the dense Indian population in the cold, pine-covered southwestern highlands of Guatemala. Today, in this

Figure 14.5 A portion of the pine- and oak-clad volcanic plateau of Los Altos, southwestern Guatemala. In the background at right are the twin volcanoes of Tolimán (10,400 feet elevation) and Atitlán (11,600 feet); to the left is the volcano of San Lucas (7,300 feet); all form part of the volcanic axis.

area, aboriginal land tenure systems prevail, along with newer, small private holdings (Figure 14.5).

As in most Latin American areas of high pre-Conquest culture, the Indians of the Guatemalan highlands supplement their farming activities with cottage industries. The pre-Conquest custom of community specialization persists throughout the Indian area, and pottery, baskets, reed mats, blankets, together with surplus farm prod-

Figure 14.6 Guatemalan Indian women weaving *rebozos* (shawls) on the traditional belt loom (*Delta Air Lines*)

uce, are carried on human backs to colorful weekly village markets. Often the artisans take their own handicrafts to market, but usually they are purchased by merchants who travel from village to village, buying the wares for resale. Surplus crops are usually carried to market and sold by women, who squat before their wares in long, colorful rows. Such market towns are centers of Indian economic, social, and religious activity, just as they were in the pre-Columbian period. Thus, the present Guatemalan Indian economy, though strongly aboriginal, is in many ways a market economy based on specialized production and on money as a medium of exchange (Figure 14.6).

Although the Indians of Guatemala retain a common culture, there is little social or political unity among the various language groups. In fact, the individual Indian community, which corresponds to the small political unit called the *municipio* ("municipality"), usually constitutes a distinct cultural grouping based on blood relation, local customs and, sometimes, dialect. The women of a given *municipio* all wear the same kind of native dress, distinct in color and design from that of neighboring communities. Such customs contribute to the kaleidoscopic cultural scene that so enchants the foreign visitor. The cultural distinctiveness of the Indian communities is also enhanced by physical isolation. This is especially true among the Kekchi in the rugged mountains of Alta Verapaz and in the southwestern highlands (Los Altos), where streams have eroded deep canyons in the soft volcanic ash, effectively discouraging communication between *municipios.*

A distinctive settlement pattern, partially derived from pre-Columbian times, characterizes most Indian *municipios* in Guatemala. There is one main settlement that functions as the administrative center and the market, and most of the rural population lives on farmsteads dispersed throughout the political unit. Some centers may be relatively large, nucleated towns containing 1,000 to 5,000 rural and urban inhabitants. Others may consist of only a market place and a few small public buildings, with the rural dwellers dispersed for miles around. Since they are usually vacant except on market days or religious holidays, they are sometimes called "concourse centers." These have been likened to the small pre-Conquest ceremonial centers, the ruins of which dot the Guatemalan highlands. In addition, small cities that serve as political capitals of departments (states) and as regional economic centers lie within the Indian areas. Administrative towns in colonial times, these cities, such as Quetzaltenango and Cobán, now contain large numbers of Ladinos, who compose the commercial and professional urban classes.

Since the Spanish Conquest in Guatemala, Indians have served as the main source of labor for commercial agriculture on large Ladino estates and for public works. As in Mexico, abuses of Indian labor continued after independence in the form of debt peonage, and even the colonial work levy (*repartimiento*) was not stopped until the end of the nineteenth century. Actually, all kinds of forced Indian labor, including debt peonage, continued to some extent in Guatemala until the enactment of the Constitution of 1945.

A gradual extension of Indian settlement, from the highlands into the western portion of the Pacific piedmont and coastal plain, has occurred within the past hundred years. Since the mid-nineteenth century, the most frequent use of Indian labor in Guatemala has been in coffee cultivation and harvest, chiefly in the upper Boca Costa of the Pacific piedmont. More recently, the developing sugar and cotton plantations on the Pacific coastal plain have also relied heavily on Indian labor for the adjacent highlands. Although the demand for workers during the coffee harvest is largely seasonal, many Indian families have settled in the coffee area. Moreover, the need for a permanent labor force on the cotton plantations in the coastal plain has steadily grown since World War II. In addition, many Indians now migrate seasonally to the coastal plain to clear small plots on public lands for raising maize; in this way they supplement their meager crops grown on the tiny, inadequate holdings in their highland homeland.

Figure 14.3 shows that the major language groups involved in the expansion of settlement from highland to lowland include chiefly the Quiché of the Los Altos district and the Mam of the Alto Cuchumatanes. Both groups have settled mainly in the coffee zone above Mazatenango and in the coastal plain below that city. Another migratory trend has been the movement of Indians from the rural areas to the national capital, Guatemala City, where they are attracted by the dubious amenities of city life and the expectation of well-paying jobs.

The problem of bringing the large Indian population into the stream of Guatemalan national life is much greater than it is in Mexico. The Indian's principal social and political allegiance is to his *municipio*—to his *patria chica*—not to the nation. On the other hand, although many are illiterate and speak little Spanish, most Guatemalan Indians are successful farmers, craftsmen, or tradesmen within their own communities. They may be considered as an aboriginal peasantry, proud of their Indian heritage, rather than as an abject and underdeveloped ethnic minority.

The Ladinos. In contrast to the Indians' occupance of the high, cool areas of the country, the Ladinos, or non-Indians, have generally settled in the lower, warmer and drier regions. The relatively low (3,000–5,000 feet) eastern highlands and, immediately northward, the hot, dry Motagua depression have formed the core of Ladino or Spanish settlement in Guatemala since the colonial period. Today only small islands of remnant Indian culture remain in these eastern areas, locally termed "El Oriente." Other predominately Ladino sections include the eastern part of the Pacific piedmont (Boca Costa) and the Pacific coastal plain. Moreover, the highland basins that contain the colonial and present political and administrative centers of Guatemala—Antigua and Guatemala City—are also predominately Ladino. These cities hold strategic positions between the Indian and Spanish sections of the country. In addition, a few enclaves of Ladino culture, such as those around Huehuetenango and San Marcos, surround some of the departmental capital towns in the predominately Indian western highlands.

The present concentration of Guatemala's Ladino population in the eastern part of the country stems mainly from early Spanish settlement in the low, dry areas which afforded abundant grass and scrub for raising livestock. Colonial cattle ranches centered in the hot, arid plains around Zacapa in the Motagua depression and in the higher grassy basins of Jutiapa and Chiquimula, in the eastern highlands,

where stock raising is still a major occupation. The non-Mayan Indians who inhabited most of the eastern area seem to have disappeared soon after the Conquest, leaving only small groups of Mayan-affiliated Chorti and Pocomam to resist Spanish settlement.

Today, the Ladinos of eastern Guatemala retain a Spanish colonial way of life that has been influenced by many Indian traits. Though most of the people are mixbloods, many families of pure Spanish ancestry live in small urban centers. Settlement follows the traditional southern European pattern of compact town and hamlet, in contrast to the dispersed dwellings of the highland Indians. Although some large cattle haciendas remain around Jutiapa, most of the land is in medium-sized holdings of 50 to 100 acres. Many landless farmers of the hamlets work as day laborers, sharecroppers, or cowherds on the larger farms, forming a socioeconomic system found in much of non-Indian Central America. Ladino farmers have adopted the aboriginal maize-beans-squash crop complex, and, as among the Indians, the maize tortilla is the staff of rural life. The main farming tools are the European, ox-drawn, wooden plow; the hoe; and a hook-shaped machete. Finally, the ox-drawn, two-wheeled cart for hauling farm produce and the small Spanish-style adobe, tiled-roof farmhouse complete the rural landscape of eastern Guatemala.

The national capital and its immediate surroundings form a special Ladino area. Guatemala City, founded in 1773 after a severe earthquake had destroyed the old colonial capital (Antigua), had a population of 730,000 in 1970, making it the largest urban center in Central America (Figure 14.7). The Indians who continue to flock into the city from rural areas soon lose their aboriginal ways, and many young ones intermarry with mixbloods. In this sense Guatemala City is a racial and cultural melting pot, but it is also the home of the conservative landed aristoc-

Figure 14.7   Aerial view of Guatemala City. The city has expanded to cover the flat surfaces between steep-sided barrancas that have been cut by streams into the soft volcanic ash of the valley floor. The barrancas form barriers to movement between the outlying areas of the city. The view looks southwest toward Agua Volcano (upper left). (*Instituto Geográfico Nacional de Guatemala*)

racy of Spanish descent, who still control the country.

Commercial Agriculture

More than two-thirds of the Guatemalans live by the soil. The Indian and Ladino farmers described above form two distinct groups of rural peasantry that have given rise to two contrasting cultural landscapes in Guatemala since the colonial period. Economically, both cultures are basically subsistent in character.

Large-scale commercial agriculture is far more significant to the Guatemalan economy. In terms of value, over half of the country's exports are coffee, cotton, and bananas. These crops are raised chiefly on large holdings owned and operated by a Ladino aristocracy of European descent. Commercial agriculture, much of it on tropical plantations, forms a third kind of cultural landscape in Guatemala.

Since colonial times, the main areas of commercial agriculture in Guatemala have been the Pacific piedmont, or Boca Costa, and the Pacific coastal plain (Figure 14.8). Favored by fertile, well-drained soils, derived from volcanic ash and alluvium, and by a humid tropical climate, these areas today form Guatemala's richest source of wealth. Another significant region of tropical commercial agriculture is the humid, lower Motagua Corridor, where the fertile alluvium of the wide river flood plain was first cleared of rain forests in 1906 for banana plantations.

Coffee. Guatemala's most important commercial crop is coffee, which alone accounts for one-third of the country's export revenue. Since the mid-nineteenth century, the upper Boca Costa of the Pacific escarpment has been the main coffee area; it now produces nearly 80 percent of the total crop. The isolated Cobán district within rugged Alta Verapaz is the second, but much less significant, coffee zone.

Local estate owners, following the lead of planters in other Central American countries, began coffee cultivation on the escarpment south of Guatemala City around 1860. It was a small group of foreign planters, however, aided by outside capital and agricultural acumen, who gave impetus to the Guatemalan coffee industry. Most successful were German planters who in 1869 established the first *fincas,* or coffee estates, in the Cobán area

of Alta Verapaz, using the local Kekchi Indians as laborers.

The upper Boca Costa coffee zone began to boom in the 1870s. German planters moved chiefly into the westernmost sector of San Marcos department, while local Guatemalans and a few Englishmen and North Americans opened fincas in the central and eastern parts of the escarpment. Rich volcanic soils, correct air temperatures at elevations between 1,600 and 5,000 feet, and plentiful moisture with a five-month dry season (December–April) for harvest and processing were almost ideal for coffee cultivation (Figure 14.9). And there was an abundance of long-unoccupied, forest-covered land, easily convertible to a tree crop. Moreover, transport along the lower piedmont to Pacific ports, and even to the Caribbean via the Motagua Corridor, was not difficult. Most important, however, was the abundant supply of cheap Indian labor close by in the adjacent highlands of Los Altos. By the end of the nineteenth century, the coffee industry of the upper Boca Costa was well established, and by World War I, the German planters had acquired approximately 30 percent of the producing estates.

The coffee farms, which range in size from approximately 25 to 4,500 acres, form the main landscape element in the upper Boca Costa. From a distance, the

Figure 14.8   Vertical cross-section of the Pacific slope of Guatemala

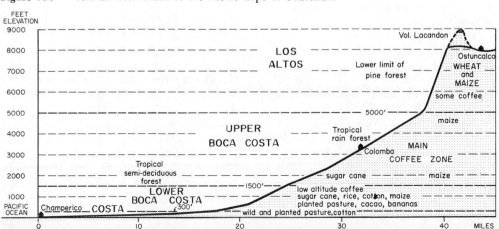

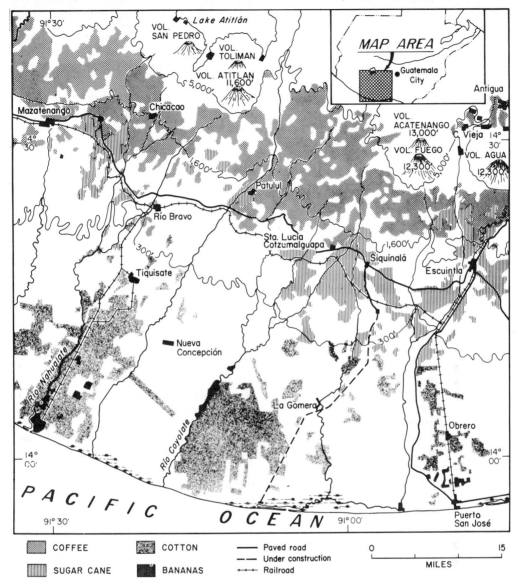

Figure 14.9 Commercial agriculture within a portion of the Guatemalan Pacific piedmont and coastal plain, 1965. Cotton farms have replaced the banana plantations of the Tiquisate area and much of the former native pastures of the coastal plain. The blank areas within the coastal plain are chiefly in pasture, forest, and small farms.

finca appears as a forested slope, for the coffee shrub is cultivated under the shade of large trees in Guatemala and other Middle American countries. This technique, as well as careful harvesting of the beans, is said to be responsible for the high quality coffee for which Guatemala is famous. Each finca has a household center of the owner or overseer, near which may be the huts of the Indian workers. A large estate may also operate a coffee processing plant. During World War II, the Guatemalan government expropriated all coffee and other holdings of German nationals, and the government still controls some of these "national farms," which produce around 25 percent of the country's coffee crop.

With the growth of coffee cultivation in the upper Boca Costa, a series of market towns developed along the major transport route that follows the great alluvial fans of the lower piedmont. The more important coffee market centers include Coatepeque, Retalhuleu, Mazatenango, and Escuintla, cities of 20,000 to 30,000. The pack trains of mules that once carried sacks of green coffee from the market centers to Guatemala City and Puerto Barrios have long since been replaced by rail or truck transport.

Other Commercial Crops. While coffee has been the mainstay of Guatemala's economy for the last century, the cultivation of other commercial tropical crops has had a chequered history. Since colonial times, sugar cane has been grown in the hot valleys of El Oriente and in the lower Boca Costa on the Pacific slope, but largely for local consumption. Today, the largest plantations, some over a thousand acres, are concentrated around Escuintla, just below the coffee zone (Figure 14.9). Since the cessation of trade between the United States and Cuba (1962), sugar production in Guatemala has doubled, owing to increased export quotas for the United States market.

BANANAS. The interesting history of the banana plantations in Central America is summarized earlier in this text. For nearly 55 years (1910–1964) Guatemala was one of the leading banana producers of the isthmian countries. Until the 1930s production was chiefly in the lower Motagua Valley in the Caribbean lowlands. At that time banana diseases forced the United Fruit Company to abandon most of its Motagua plantations and to shift production to the Tiquisate area in the Pacific lowlands. With the closing down of the latter area in 1964, banana production in Guatemala plummeted. Since 1962, however, the United Fruit Company has reestablished many plantations near Morales (Bananera) in the Motagua Valley by introducing disease-resistant varieties. Ba-

nana acreage and production in the Motagua area are now increasing rapidly and may soon reach pre-1930 proportions. The United States, however, is no longer the major consumer of Guatemala's bananas, for in 1970, more than 75 percent of exports from Puerto Barrios were destined for western European countries.

COTTON. Since 1950, cotton has become the most important crop produced in Guatemala's Pacific coastal plain, where it is grown mainly on large holdings and with modern farming techniques (Figure 14.9). For several years this crop has held second place in the country's agricultural exports, despite a temporary decline in production since 1966 because of low world prices and inadequate pest control. More than 80 percent of Guatemala's cotton crop is exported, chiefly to Japan and to western Europe, and the remainder is used in the country's growing textile industry.

RICE. Rice is another crop that is spreading into the Pacific coastal plain, as well as in the Caribbean lowlands near Lake Izabal and in the Petén. Unlike cotton, rice is cultivated on small holdings, as it is over most of the southeastern highlands, where it has been grown since colonial times. As rice is a prestige food of growing importance among the urban population in Guatemala, large amounts must still be imported from El Salvador, Mexico, and the United States.

Stock Raising. The greater part of La Costa, the hot Pacific coastal plain, is devoted to the raising of livestock on large haciendas, most of which are owned by wealthy Ladinos living in Guatemala City. In colonial times, La Costa's lush grasslands were fattening pastures for range cattle bred in the eastern highlands of Guatemala, in western and central Honduras, and even in Nicaragua. Still today, large herds from Honduras and El Salvador are driven or trucked annually into Guatemala and fattened on the coastal haciendas, within easy rail distance of the large meat processing plants in Escuintla and Guatemala City and the market in the national capital. Ranchers are rapidly replacing the natural savanna grasses by planting more nutritious African varieties; they are also upgrading herds by crossing the rangy criollo cattle with Brahman bulls. As in other Central American countries, such modernization has received impetus from the recently developed market for chilled fresh beef in the United States. Chilled beef now ranks fourth in value among Guatemalan exports, and the country's Pacific coastal plain is today a leading tropical livestock area of Central America.

Agrarian Reform and Colonization

Guatemala's agrarian problems are as acute as those in most of Latin America. The Indians' tiny, intensively cultivated plots in the western highlands contrast with the immense and often unused estates of the lower Boca Costa and the Pacific coastal plain; only in the eastern highlands, with its predominately Spanish peasant culture, do medium-sized farms prevail. According to the Guatemalan agricultural census of 1964, nearly two-thirds of the farmland is owned by only 2 percent of the farmers, and nearly half of the farmers work plots of less than 3.5 acres. The inequality of the land distribution underlies many of Guatemala's economic and social problems.

The first real attempt at agrarian reform in Guatemala did not occur until 1952–1954, when a scheme roughly similar to the Mexican ejido system was hurriedly started by the leftist-oriented Arbenz regime. Fearing Communist domination, the landed aristocracy, with outside help, succeeded in overthrowing Arbenz and ending the radical reforms. Today's approaches to the agrarian problem are more conservative, emphasizing colonization of unused lands and the resettlement of farmers from the densely peopled highlands. As part of the Rural Development

Program of 1956 (later reorganized under the Agrarian Transformation Law of 1962), several colonies, or "zones of farm development," have been established chiefly in the Pacific coastal plain on unused lands, national lands, and expropriated private estates. Within a given colony, each resettled family is given legal title to a farm of at least 50 acres, for which it must pay the government a nominal price on easy terms. Some colonies include as much as 87,500 acres of land and contain as many as 4,500 families. However, because of inadequate financial assistance, poor administration, and illegal land speculation, most of the colonies have been less than successful.

A second part of the present agrarian reform involves the disposition of the "national farms," mainly large coffee fincas that the Guatemalan government expropriated from German nationals during World War II. Since 1966, the government has been slowly transferring some of these estates to cooperatives formed by agricultural workers. By 1970, 10 out of 26 disposable estates had been transferred.

In addition to the colonization program, one of the fundamental aims of the Agrarian Transformation Law is to encourage owners to utilize the idle land that usually comprises a large part of the big estates. To implement this goal, the government threatens to expropriate unused lands and to impose high taxes on idle or inefficiently utilized estates. Whether or not such measures will improve agricultural production remains to be seen. In any case, such tactics do not directly tackle Guatemala's fundamental land problem—the need to alleviate the ills caused by overpopulation and minifundia among the highland Indians.

Development of the Petén

The vast rain forests of northern Guatemala—the Petén and much of the adjacent lowlands of Izabal and Alta Verapaz departments—to date have contributed little to the Guatemalan economy, except for the exploitation of forest products. The banana plantations of the lower Motagua valley and the small rice and coffee farms within the Polochic River and Lake Izabal areas are among the few commercial farming activities practiced in this sparsely peopled area. The only settlements of any significance in the Petén—the town of Flores (the departmental capital) and a few villages of Mayan and Ladino subsistence farmers which date from the seventeenth century—cluster around Lake Petén.

For many years the possibilities for agricultural colonization of the Petén appeared to be slim indeed. The heavy rainfall (80–150 inches), the short dry season, and the relatively poor limestone soils were not attractive, and the lack of roads and the long distances from markets were further deterrents. In 1970, however, the government completed an all-weather truck road that joins the town of Flores in the Lake Petén area with the lower Motagua. This road now serves as a penetration route for agricultural colonization

into the Petén. Another penetration route leads northward from the Cobán highlands into the lowlands of Sebol, in northern Alta Verapaz, where a government-sponsored colony has been established and where spontaneous agricultural settlement has taken place near the southern frontier of the Petén (Figure 14.10). Even so, the greater part of this forest-covered lowland still lies outside the national life of Guatemala. Its agricultural development lies far into the future.

The gathering of chicle latex from the wild chicosapote tree was once the most important economic activity in the Petén, just as it was in adjacent Mexican territory to the north (Campeche and Quintana Roo). This industry began on a large scale during the first decades of this century, but with the recent development of synthetics for chewing gum, chicle gathering has declined drastically.

Mahogany and many other tropical woods suitable for commercial lumber also abound in the Petén rain forest. Since the last century, these have been exploited chiefly by North American lumber companies, but few roads exist in the Petén

Figure 14.10   Gross transport pattern in Guatemala

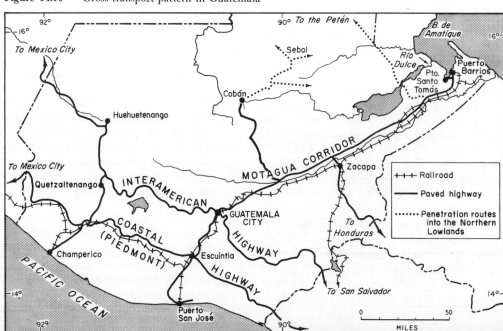

and the extraction of timber is costly. The few rivers sufficiently large for rafting flow either into Mexico or Belize. Thus, much timber was formerly floated down the Usumacinta River to the Mexican Gulf port of Frontera, and today mahogany rafts are often taken to the Mexican Caribbean port of Chetumal via the Hondo River. Present government plans call for the construction of truck roads, saw mills, and wood processing plants in various parts of the Petén to develop the lumber industry more fully.

Industry

Like other Central American countries Guatemala has developed a small but growing manufacturing industry. Except for the recent discovery and planned exploitation of vast nickel deposits in Izabal department, the country is relatively poor in mineral resources. Hydrocarbon fuels are either lacking or are insufficient for exploitation; almost all the needed petroleum must be imported. A hydroelectric power potential, however, exists on small streams as they drop down the Pacific escarpment from the volcanic highlands, and several plants now furnish electrical power to the urban centers (Figure 13.10).

Aside from the native cottage industries, most of Guatemala's industrial effort has been put into light manufacturing, such as food processing and textiles. Since the inauguration of the Central American Common Market, however, a spate of new industrial activity has begun: a large tire plant is now in production in Guatemala City; two small oil refineries have been completed, one in the new port of Santo Tomás de Castilla, near Puerto Barrios and another at Escuintla, south of Guatemala City; the textile industry has been greatly expanded; several electronic and pharmaceutical products plants have been established; and many more industrial enterprises are planned.

Thus, since 1960, a few small industrial centers have been emerging in Guatemala. The largest is Guatemala City and the nearby industrial suburbs of Mixco and Villa Nueva, with their large reservoir of cheap labor and growing urban market. Other centers include the towns of Escuintla and Amatitlán, both on the main line of communication between the Pacific coast and the national capital. These three centers now form a small industrial corridor which extends from the Pacific piedmont to Guatemala City. Industry is also growing in the town of Quetzaltenango in the western highlands.

Transportation and Trade

The pattern of Guatemala's main land routes for travel and commerce have varied little since colonial times. Three lines dominate the pattern: (1) a transisthmian route determined chiefly by the Motagua Corridor; (2) a highland route, mainly along the volcanic axis from Mexico to El Salvador; and (3) a Pacific piedmont route that follows the alluvial fans at the base of the volcanic axis from Mexico into El Salvador (Figure 14.10).

The transisthmian route, connecting the Pacific lowlands with the Caribbean ports via the national capital, contains Guatemala's most heavily traveled railroad and paved highways. It is the principal communication axis of the country. Leaving the Motagua depression in its middle sector, the road crosses the volcanic highlands through a gentle pass, the Valle de las Vacas, which is the site of Guatemala City (5,000 feet elevation). From there it continues down the Pacific piedmont via the long, gently sloping alluvial fan of Escuintla to the coastal plain. Both the old colonial capital, Antigua, and Guatemala City were strategically located in relation to the Motagua Corridor and the Escuintla fan.

Railroad construction began in the late

nineteenth century to transport coffee to the ports. Around 1890, North American contractors completed the Pacific coastal rail system connecting the ports of San José and Champerico with the coffee areas and with Guatemala City. Within the next two decades, the line was extended down the Motagua Corridor to the banana-shipping port of Puerto Barrios. The railways of Guatemala are now nationalized as the *Ferrocarriles de Guatemala*. Coffee and bananas destined for the Caribbean ports of Puerto Barrios and Santo Tomás comprise the main cargo on the transisthmian portion of the railroad.

All-weather auto roads date from the 1940s, when most of the highland portion of the Inter-American Highway was completed from Guatemala City; by 1970, the entire route had been reconstructed and finally paved. Between 1955 and 1963, the Coastal Highway and the Inter-Oceanic Highway through the Motagua Corridor were completely paved. Other major highways recently completed and paved include the highland-coastal connection between Quetzaltenango and the Pacific port of Champerico, and those that lead from the Motagua Corridor southeastward to the Honduran frontier and northward to Cobán.

Guatemala, like most of the Central American countries, depends on the Caribbean for its main contact with foreign commerce, a trade orientation which has obtained since the colonial period, despite the location of population centers close to the Pacific side of the isthmus. Guatemala's principal markets (the eastern United States and northwestern Europe) are on the Atlantic shore; equally important, her best harbors are on the Caribbean. Since the sixteenth century, the sheltered Bay of Amatique and the Río Dulce on the Caribbean have been the chief outlets for overseas trade, while the hazardous roadstead harbors on the straight, open Pacific coast have been less important.

After 1912, a United States company constructed modern port facilities at Puerto Barrios to export bananas and coffee and to handle much of Guatemala's import trade. In terms of tonnage, Puerto Barrios was, until recently, one of the leading ports of Central America, for its hinterland included not only Guatemala, but also El Salvador, which shipped much of its coffee over the former American-owned railway to the Caribbean terminus. Having incomplete control over the foreign-managed facilities, the Guatemalan government in 1952 began construction of a new port, called Puerto Matías Gálvez, a few miles south of Puerto Barrios. Recently renamed Puerto Santo Tomás de Castilla, the new port is now the country's main overseas outlet, leaving only the banana trade to Puerto Barrios. In addition, Puerto Santo Tomás has taken over the shipment of El Salvadorean coffee and most of the exports of Nicaraguan and Costa Rican chilled beef, which is trucked over the Inter-American and Inter-Oceanic highways. On the Pacific coast, San José serves as a major import port, through which move bulk goods such as wheat and petroleum products. This small roadstead consists of a single long pier for unloading lighters that transfer freight from ships anchored off coast.

BELIZE
(BRITISH HONDURAS)

The small English colony of Belize, formerly called British Honduras, represents the only successful north European foothold on the Middle American mainland. Once a part of the pre-Columbian Maya culture area, the colony adjoins Guatemala on its northeastern border, and Guatemala has continued to claim this Caribbean territory for more than a century. However, as indicated in Chapter 9, the early cultural history of Belize was quite distinct from that of Guatemala. The coastal sector of the colony is today chiefly English-speaking, black or mulatto in racial composition, and Caribbean in general cultural attitudes. Like much of the eastern coast of Central America, Belize is a mainland extension of the Caribbean island, or Rimland, cultural realm of Middle America.

Major Physical Characteristics

Physically, much of Belize is a continuation of the Guatemalan Petén—rolling limestone hills covered by a heavy tropical rain forest. The Maya Mountains, an igneous mass with maximum elevations of 3,000 to 4,000 feet, extend from the Petén into the west-central portion of the colony. Several rivers, flowing northeastward from the Petén across Belize, form narrow flood plains through the limestone hills. Near the coast, ancient beach ridges of sand and shell support stands of pine (Pinus caribea) and are consequently called "pine ridges." Thousands of coral and limestone reefs and islands fringe the swampy, mangrove-ridden coast. These coastal conditions make navigation hazardous, but favor an abundant tropical sea life. The heavy rainfall, dense forests, and leached, infertile soils of Belize have not been conducive to settlement and economic development; moreover, the colony lies within the Caribbean hurricane belt, and its coastal towns and forests are ravaged by frequent storms. Hurricane Hattie, in November 1961, almost completely destroyed Belize City, the main urban center, and seriously damaged northern settlements.

The People

About 120,000 people inhabit Belize, giving it an average density of only 12 persons per square mile. The population is unevenly distributed, however, one-third being concentrated in Belize City alone. The rest live in towns and villages along the coast and on farms inland along the river banks, with the greatest densities in the northern districts.

This small population has a highly varied racial and cultural makeup. English-speaking blacks and mulattoes, descendants of slaves brought in by British woodcutters in the eighteenth and nineteenth centuries, comprise approximately half of the population. They live mainly in the central coastal area, particularly in Belize District, which forms the cultural core of the colony (Figure 14.11). A quite distinct Negroid group, the Black Caribs, inhabits the coast south of Stann Creek

Figure 14.11   Selected economies and settlement in Belize

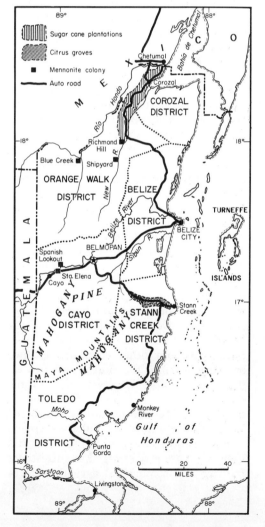

and continues into Guatemala to the town of Livingston. These people, who stem from mixed black-Indian exiles from the Lesser Antilles, have spread their settlements along the Caribbean coast from Nicaragua to Belize since the close of the eighteenth century. Among themselves, the Black Caribs use a curious language that is basically Arawak, but many are trilingual, speaking broken English and Spanish as well. In their almost total subsistence economy, the women do most of the farming, still cultivating the Antillean bitter manioc as the staple foodstuff, while the men engage in fishing off the coast.

A third culture group consists of Spanish-speaking whites and mixbloods, who make up 25 percent of the Belizean population and occupy the northern district of Corozal and the sparsely populated interior near the Guatemalan and Mexican frontiers. Those in the north are mainly descendants of Mexican refugees who fled Yucatan during the Indian wars of the last century. Those on the western frontier are Guatemalan immigrants from the Petén, now engaged in cattle ranching. Within the Spanish area of Belize, a fourth ethnic group consists of Indians—Maya-speakers in the northwest, and Kekchi, recent migrants from Guatemala, in the extreme southwest.

The most recently settled rural group consists of German-speaking Mennonite farmers from northern Mexico. The first of their closed communities was founded in 1958, on the upper Hondo River, where the elders had purchased a large tract of cutover forest across from the Mexican border. Later, the Mennonites established four other communities, two on New River in the north, and two on the upper Belize. Unaccustomed to the climate, soils, and diseases of the humid tropics, the Mennonites nearly foundered in the initial settlement, but they appear to have made a successful adjustment, and some 3,500 are now engaged in subsistence farming and commercial agriculture. For example, Mennonite farmers supply Belize City with vegetables, poultry, and dairy products.

The racial and cultural complexity of the colony reaches its maximum in Belize City. Representatives of all the groups mentioned above, plus North American businessmen, British military personnel, and East Indian, Lebanese, and Chinese merchants all reside within the city.

The Economy

Forest Exploitation. For three centuries, since the entry of the Baymen, or English pirates and logwood cutters in the seventeenth century, the commercial economy of Belize revolved around the exploitation of its forests. As late as 1955, over 60 percent of the colony's export revenue came from lumber and chicle. The once extensive commercial stands of mahogany, tropical cedar, and pine, however, are today so depleted that in 1968 the value of forest products had fallen to 5 percent of the total exports. The isolated Maya Mountains contain one of the last remaining stands of precious woods in the colony, and that is being rapidly cut. Despite plans for the forest conservation and regulation through large-scale planting of mahogany and pine in cutover areas, few positive results have been attained.

Commercial Agriculture. Within the past two decades, the mainstay of Belizean economy has changed from lumbering to agriculture. In 1968, farm products, mainly sugar and citrus, made up nearly 60 percent of the colony's export revenue, and the production of subsistence crops, such as rice, beans, and maize, had substantially increased. Despite this rapid economic shift, forests and cutover land still cover most of the colony, and much food must still be imported.

The sugar cane area in the northern

Figure 14.12   A grove of grapefruit, Stann Creek Valley, Belize

districts of Corozal and Orange Walk is the fastest developing farming zone of Belize. By 1940, Spanish-speaking growers had established several small plantations within this area, south of the Rio Hondo. Today many of these holdings have been consolidated into large plantations, and hundreds of small sugar growers have expanded southward along the alluvial soils bordering New River. A British concern now operates two large mills within the area, producing unrefined sugar for export to the United States and Canada.

Forty miles south of Belize City lies the famous Stann Creek Valley, a long, narrow trench cut into the northeastern flank of the Maya Mountains. This valley has enjoyed a number of agricultural booms. Between 1900 and 1910, it was the center of a profitable banana enterprise, but Panama disease caused its abandonment. Citrus orchards gradually replaced the banana groves in Stann Creek, and since World War II, the valley and adjacent slopes have been completely covered with groves of oranges and grapefruit (Figure 14.12). High-quality canned juice and frozen concentrate, the chief exports of the valley, bring premium prices on the British and Canadian markets.

Other instances of specialized commercial agriculture occur in various parts of the colony. One is a new and growing citrus area along the Belize River flood plain in Cayo District. Another lies along the Sibun River, immediately southwest of Belize City, where cacao groves have been established since 1950. (These were badly damaged by recent hurricanes, and production has declined.) Finally, in the far south of the colony, inland from the town of Punta Gorda (Toledo District), is a fertile section that has become significant for its rice production under government supervision. Sizable rice farms also occur in various sections of Belize District, near the main port city.

One of the goals for agricultural development sponsored by the present government of Belize is to make the colony self-sufficient in staple foodstuffs. In 1970, food still comprised 25 percent of the value of imports into the colony. The recent surge of farm development, however, has lessened the traditional dependence of Belize on imported food and has even made it self-sufficient in staples such as rice, maize, and beans.

Fishing.   The rich fish resource in the offshore tropical waters is gradually being developed commercially. Most of the catch is exported to the United States; as in so many areas of Middle America, little fish is consumed at home. Local fishermen make profitable hauls of red snapper, and

417

the take of the spiny lobster for many years has been the main source of income for the Belizean fisheries. More recently, conch meat, from a large tropical shell fish, has been added to the growing exports of marine products to the United States. And since 1966, Belizean fishermen have been exploiting the rich shrimp beds at the mouth of the Sarstoon River in the extreme southern part of the colony. Several freezing and packing plants for fin-fish, spiny lobster, conch, and shrimp operate in Belize City (Figure 14.13).

Future Development

In 1964, Belize attained internal self-government and may soon become an independent nation, despite its small size and meager population. In anticipation of independence, a new capital city, called Belmopan, 50 miles inland from Belize City, was planned and finally opened in 1970. The inland site, at the junction of two key highways, may serve for furthering the development of the new country's interior. The site also avoids the frequent tidal hurricane floods that so often have devastated the old coastal capital of Belize City. Although still not completed and now inhabited by less than 2,000 people,

Belmopan is to expand to 30,000 inhabitants, according to government plans.

Although its agriculture has expanded impressively in the last decade, the colony still has no industry of importance, and aside from small-scale food and wood processing, there is little likelihood that much will develop in the near future. The colony's recent attainment of membership in CARIFTA, a trade association of former British possessions in the West Indies, was intended to spur external trade with the islands, but Belize has little that its neighbors want. It remains to be seen if this colony can become a viable independent nation.

EL SALVADOR

El Salvador is the smallest mainland country of Latin America. It is also the most heavily populated, having in 1971 a density of 460 persons per square mile. Within all of Middle America, only some of the Caribbean islands have similar overall population densities.

El Salvador is the only Central American country without a Caribbean coast; it therefore lacks a port facing eastward toward its United States and European markets. It also lacks unsettled land for

Figure 14.13   Part of the Belizean fishing fleet tied up in Haulover Creek in Belize City

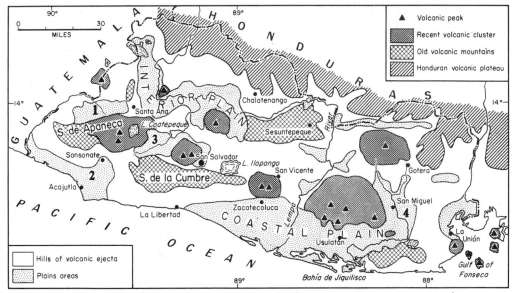

Figure 14.14 Surface configuration of El Salvador. Numbers refer to the names of plains: (1) Chalchuapa; (2) Sonsonate; (3) Zapotitlán basin; and (4) San Miguel basin.

its expanding population, unlike the other isthmian countries. Confined, overcrowded, and plagued by the evils of both latifundia and minifundia, El Salvador suffers some of the most acute social and economic problems in Middle America. Nearly 40 percent of its total territory is under cultivation (including fallow land) —the highest ratio in Latin America. Its natural vegetation cover has been almost completely destroyed or highly altered, and its originally fertile soils are greatly eroded in many sectors. As in most Latin American countries, the best lands are owned by a few rich families who raise commercial crops for export, not food for the nation. Despite overpopulation and widespread rural poverty, El Salvador's economy appears to prosper in many respects. Especially significant during the last two decades are the growth of industry, the diversification of commercial agriculture, and a start toward increased production of food crops for home use.

In contrast to neighboring Guatemala, El Salvador lacks great variety in its landscapes and cultures. Yet it possesses an individuality that has been derived largely from its colonial past. During the colonial period, most of the present national territory formed the province of San Salvador within the Captaincy General of Guatemala (see Figure 9.3). Like the eastern section of the Guatemalan Pacific piedmont, this province was settled by Spanish stockmen and growers of cacao and indigo, and lands were concentrated in the hands of a few Spanish families. Indians, whites, and some black slaves gradually intermixed to form, by 1800, a predominately mestizo proletariat, landless and poverty-stricken, with a mixed Indian and southern European culture. This colonial socioeconomic pattern still prevails in rural El Salvador.

The Physical Landscape

El Salvador is a land of volcanoes. Its entire territory lies within the Central American volcanic axis. Southeastward from Guatemala, the volcanic range decreases in elevation, so that in El Salvador individual peaks do not rise above 7,800 feet. Figure 14.14 depicts two rows of recent volcanoes that extend east–west through the country. The southern one contains the largest cones, which have spewed out vast quantities of ash and lava for miles around.

Several eruptions have occurred in El Salvador within historic times. Izalco, first formed in 1770, still smolders; in 1917, Volcán Boquerón, near the capital city of San Salvador, ejected a large flow of lava that destroyed many coffee plantations on its northern flank.

Between the large composite cones are low, flattish, alluvial basins and rolling hills eroded from ash deposits, which have formed sites favored for human settlement since pre-Columbian times. As in Guatemala, highly fertile soils derive from the recent volcanic ejecta. Other volcanic phenomena include fumerole and geyser fields, which are so abundant that plans for converting hot underground steam into electrical energy have often been suggested, and feasibility studies have now been completed. The northern frontier of El Salvador lies along the edge of the high, rugged volcanic plateau of southern Honduras, an area that is physiographically distinct from the lower Salvadorean territory.

Recent vulcanism has so disrupted normal drainage that El Salvador can boast of only one large river, the Río Lempa, which today is the source of hydroelectric power for local industry. The upper course of the river flows through a dry interior basin, but its lower course and other short streams have built up an alluvial coastal plain, 15 to 20 miles wide, in the southeastern part of the country. This plain, formerly the exclusive domain of cattle ranchers, is now one of the prime areas of commercial agriculture (chiefly cotton and sugar cane), which lie along the Pacific coast of Central America.

With most of its surface below 3,000 feet elevation, El Salvador lies almost entirely in *tierra caliente*. The higher slopes of the large volcanoes reach into the *tierra templada,* where coffee is the main crop. Like most of the Pacific side of Central America, El Salvador experiences a long dry season (December–April) to which most agricultural activity is closely adjusted.

The People

The official government census of 1971 gives El Salvador a population of over 3.5 million, which is increasing at the rate of 3.5 percent annually. If this rapid growth is maintained, by 1980 the country's population density will have grown from the present 460 to nearly 580 persons per square mile. Although the people are fairly evenly distributed throughout the country, there are heavy concentrations of both urban and rural dwellers in the central basins and adjacent volcanic slopes where the soil is most fertile.

The bulk of the Salvadoreans are a racial mixture of Indian and white, with some traces of black blood. It is estimated that perhaps 10 percent of the population may be of pure Indian blood, but fewer than 3 percent retain even a modified aboriginal way of life. These aborigines— the sole remnant of the Pipil-speaking Indians of Mexican origin who once covered western El Salvador to the Lempa River— occupy a few villages north of Sonsonate in the southwestern part of the country. Culturally, most other Salvadoreans are Ladinos who speak only Spanish but who practice many Indian as well as European customs. At the apex of the social system stand the few affluent, land-rich families, most of which trace their lineage from the colonial era.

The rapid increase of people, especially since 1940, has caused a number of significant migrations. One has been from the overcrowded rural areas into the cities, especially into San Salvador, the national capital, whose population grew from 105,-000 in 1940 to 337,200 in 1971. Even more significant was the large-scale migration of Salvadoreans into Honduras. Many emigrated temporarily to the north coast of

Honduras to work on the large banana plantations. Thousands of others rented small farms or illegally squatted on hillside plots in the southern and central highlands of Honduras, often causing international ill feeling. Indeed, one of the underlying causes of the recent military conflict between El Salvador and Honduras was the presence of some 300,000 Salvadoreans in the neighboring country's territory. After cessation of the 1969 hostilities, the Honduran government forced most of these immigrants to return to their homeland, further adding to El Salvador's population pressure. Salvadoreans have also migrated into Guatemala, where perhaps as many as 75,000 now live.

The Agricultural Economy

The economy of El Salvador varies little from that of its Central American neighbors. Agriculture and stock raising are basic; well over half (63 percent) of the Salvadorean people are farmers. Since 1960, however, the manufacturing industry, a possible solution to the nagging problem of overpopulation, has been growing rapidly. But the hydrocarbon fuels are lacking, and the mining of metals has never been outstanding.

The agricultural system is dualistic. On the one hand, commercial farming, which is done on the best lands, held in large tracts by the elite, produces chiefly for export (coffee and cotton) and gives the country much of its monetary wealth. On the other hand, subsistence cultivation of small hillside plots occupies the great majority of Salvadorean farmers, who produce the bulk of the food crops. Under such a system, the country has not been able to feed itself, and since the nineteenth century, El Salvador has imported basic foods —maize, beans, and wheat—from Honduras, Nicaragua, and overseas. Only in recent years has the country been able to

produce sufficient rice for home use and even some for export. One of the major economic goals of the Salvadorean government is to encourage small farmers to increase the production of basic food crops by extending them credit so that they might purchase fertilizer, improved seeds, and better tools.

Subsistence Farming. The poverty of the small subsistence farmer in El Salvador is indicated by the size of his holdings. Half of the farms are smaller than 2.5 acres, but they comprise only 2 percent of the total farmland. Many of the small farmers hold legal title to such plots, but most are tenants, paying rent in kind or cash to the landowner. The smallest plots are concentrated in the central and northern sections on generally poor soils. The steep slopes have been badly eroded by the complete stripping of the original vegetation and overcropping; and the fertility of much of the land used for subsistence farms was greatly depleted by large-scale cultivation of indigo during the eighteenth and nineteenth centuries.

In El Salvador, as in most of mainland Middle America, subsistence farming revolves around the cultivation of maize; the aboriginal maize tortilla and tamale are the staff of life. Other basic food crops include beans, rice, sugar cane, and sorghum. Within the last century grain sorghum (*maicillo,* of African origin) has become as important as maize in El Salvador; its cultivation now extends from eastern Guatemala to northern Nicaragua (Figure 14.15). It grows well in dry areas and on poor soils and is often interplanted with maize as insurance against drought. Probably because of its use by black slaves on the indigo plantations and in the mines during the colonial era, sorghum is regarded by most Central Americans as a poor man's food that carries a certain social stigma. Even a Salvadorean sharecropper will rarely admit that tortillas of

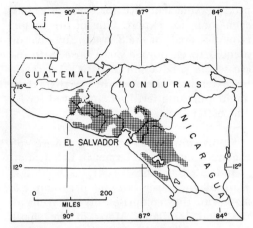

Figure 14.15   Area of grain sorghum cultivation in Central America

sorghum are served in his house. Nevertheless, in overcrowded El Salvador, as much sorghum as maize is harvested.

Depending on the terrain, the Salvadorean subsistence farmer practices either Indian-derived dibble tillage or southern European plow cultivation. The former is used on steep slopes, the latter on level-to-rolling land. The dibble, or planting stick, is normally associated with slash-burn, shifting cultivation.

In El Salvador, however, land is at such a premium that steep slopes are often tilled with the hoe and planting stick year after year, with the result that the soil becomes eroded and its fertility suffers. In plow cultivation, the ox-drawn wooden ard is still used in the traditional fashion, but fields are rarely fallowed or fertilizers applied. Although two or more consecutive maize crops per year are climatically possible in the *tierra caliente,* most Salvadoreans raise but one, during the wet season from May to September. At the onset of the dry period in December, large numbers of farmers leave their tiny plots and flock to the coffee or cotton estates to bring in the harvest, in this way supplementing their family income.

AGRARIAN REFORM.   The miserable lot of the small subsistence farmer in El Salvador cries for reform. Over 60 percent of the rural families are landless, and nearly half of the private holdings are too small for making a living. Yet, to date, little has been accomplished in land reapportionment. This situation exists despite the fact that since independence in 1824, the rural masses have more than once physically rebelled against the hold of the rich families. The last uprising occurred in 1932 and ended in the death of hundreds of peasants.

In 1962 the Salvadorean government established the Rural Colonization Institute to improve land distribution by subdividing large, little-used estates and by parceling out the few remaining public lands to landless farmers. Through this program, by 1967, some 4,000 rural families had been given small plots and some 30 agricultural colonies were formed. To date, however, all the productive private estates remain untouched. The government is now developing the country's first large-scale irrigation project in the Zapotitan Valley (formerly poor pasture land) between San Salvador and Santa Ana. Small irrigated plots are to be distributed to landless farmers, with the hope of increasing national food production.

SETTLEMENT PATTERNS.   The majority of Salvadorean subsistence farmers live in small hamlets or in farmsteads dispersed throughout the countryside. A century ago, however, most farmers in El Salvador lived in compact villages or towns in the old Spanish tradition, and the fields were located in the surrounding area. Apparently, the present semidispersed rural settlement pattern is a result of the pressure of population and a forced change from communal to private properties instituted by the government in the 1880s. The rural houses, essentially Indian in form and building materials, contrast sharply with the whitewashed adobe-walled and red tile-roofed town houses. Square or rectangular huts with wattle-daub walls, thatched roofs, and dirt floors predominate (Figure

Figure 14.16 Typical rural house assemblage in El Salvador. The kitchen is the separate structure to the right of the main house.

14.16). The two-wheeled cart is a far more common means of transportation in El Salvador than in Guatemala. The rural scene in the subsistence areas of El Salvador exemplifies the amalgam of aboriginal and south European traits that is so common in Latin America.

Commercial Farming. Agricultural exports have been the mainstay of Salvadorean economy since the colonial period. Then, it was cacao and indigo that gave the country its economic wealth. Today it is coffee and cotton.

Independence from Spain (1821) opened Central America to world trade and foreign investments, and the Salvadorean indigo industry reached its peak in the midnineteenth century, most of the dyestuff being exported to Germany. The plantations were concentrated in the low, hot lands around San Salvador in the central part of the country, and in the plain of San Miguel and the lower Río Lempa in

the east, where the ruins of the processing plants can still be seen. The perfection of synthetic aniline dyes in the 1860s, however, caused the indigo industry to decline. COFFEE. Fortunately for El Salvador, coffee was introduced in 1840. By 1870, it had become a significant export, eventually replacing indigo as the main commercial crop. Thereafter, for nearly a century (1880–1970), El Salvador's national economy depended on this one crop. Between 1880 and 1950, coffee furnished from 80 to 90 percent of the country's export revenue. With the recent rise of cotton farming and industry, however, that figure has fallen to approximately 45 percent. Nonetheless, El Salvador still produces more coffee than any other Central American country. Most of the crop is exported to West Germany.

The best coffee lands in El Salvador are areas above 2,000 feet elevation within the southern row of volcanoes (Figure 14.17). One-third of the entire crop comes from

Figure 14.17 Areas of commercial agriculture in El Salvador

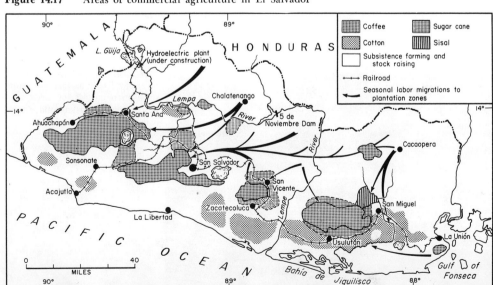

the highland west and south of Santa Ana; other areas include the highlands westward from San Salvador and, in the eastern part of the country, the slopes of the volcanoes San Vicente and San Miguel. As in Guatemala, the coffee farms vary greatly in size, but the larger and more productive ones are immense estates of 3,000 to more than 6,000 acres. Eighty percent of the land in coffee is said to belong to 14 leading Salvadorean families, who, until the 1932 peasant rebellion, controlled the country's politics as well (Figure 14.18).

The coffee landscape is quite similar to that of Guatemala. The permanent workers live in hamlets on the estates and grow their own food on small plots. With the beginning of the coffee harvest in December, an estimated 300,000 seasonal workers, chiefly men, women, and children from the subsistence farming areas, migrate to the estates as pickers. The provenience of the seasonal workers is shown in Figure 14.17).

COTTON. Cotton, presently the second most important commercial crop in El Salvador, was a minor plantation crop in the last century. But, as in other Central American countries, the present cotton boom did not get under way until after World War II. The plantations are largely in the east, for example, in the San Miguel basin and the southeastern coastal plain, where the towns of Zacatecoluca and Usulután are the main market and supply centers. Unlike coffee cultivation, cotton farming is mechanized on the large estates, but the smaller farms still employ ox-drawn plows. Cooperatives have been formed for dusting the cotton fields from airplanes and for ginning and marketing the crop, most of which is exported to Japan. Thousands of peasants are seasonal workers at harvest time, and since 1950, the lowland of southeastern El Salvador has developed from a sparsely settled cattle range to an intensely cultivated farming area containing many new hamlets and towns for the permanent laborers.

OTHER CROPS. Sugar cane, rice, and sisal are also grown commercially in El Salvador. Large sugar plantations and modern mills (*centrales*) were not organized in the country until the turn of the century, and until recently sugar was refined wholly for home consumption. Today a third of the sugar produced is exported to the United States. Encouraged by increased export quotas, the Salvadorean growers have doubled the acreage planted to cane since 1960. Most of the plantations and

Figure 14.18   The lower slopes of Volcano San Vicente in El Salvador are covered with fields of sugar cane and pasture, above which are coffee fincas that appear as wooded areas. Near the left peak farmers using slash-burn cultivation are destroying the last remnants of original forest.

mills are concentrated in the western Pacific lowlands near Sonsonate and in fertile basins near the national capital. Smaller, oxen-powered mills (*trapiches*), found throughout the country, make brown *panela,* the poor man's sugar, from locally grown cane, as in colonial times.

Long a subsistence food grown in many parts of the country, rice, likewise, has become a commercial export crop only recently. The increased production comes mainly from small farms in the Pacific coastal plain. The cultivation of sisal is closely connected with the local coffee industry, for, since 1900, several large plantations north of San Miguel have supplied fiber for coffee sacks.

Stock Raising. Despite its dense human population, El Salvador still maintains a large livestock industry, a heritage of the colonial period. About 30 percent of the total area is in permanent pasture. Cattle, which comprise 75 percent of the livestock, are raised in all parts of the country, for even the subsistence tenant farmer may own a few head. Commercial stock raising, however, is concentrated on the large haciendas in the coastal lowlands and in some of the dry interior basins, for example, the upper Lempa River plain. Although most of the beef produced is consumed locally, many cattle are exported to Guatemala for fattening, and Salvadorean ranchers are hopeful that chilled meat export to the United States will soon develop on a large scale, as it has in other Central American countries.

Nearly half of the pastures in the coastal areas grow nutritious grasses imported from Brazil and Africa. Some are even irrigated to provide green forage through the long dry season. Most of the interior grasslands, however, are so-called natural pastures. These include original savannas and grasslands culturally induced by cutting and burning the original forest. Near the coast are natural marshes, inundated during the rains, but dry and lush in the dry season. To further increase the cattle population (in 1970, 1.5 million head), Salvadorean ranchers must improve the carrying capacity of the pastures by planting better grasses and by using modern methods of range management. Even now, El Salvador's cattle population density (per unit area of pasture), like its human population density, is the highest in Central America.

Fishing

Fishing, based mainly on shrimp, has been a major part of the Salvadorean economy since the 1950s (Figure 13.8). The large lagoon called Bahía de Jiquilisco was El Salvador's initial shrimping ground, but local fishermen now trawl most of the catch from the clayey sea bottom off coast. Quick-frozen at small mainland plants, as at El Triunfo, the shrimp are exported to the United States. The steady and uncontrolled growth of shrimping in Central American waters, however, may deplete the beds, as it did in parts of the Gulf of California.

The further development of offshore fin-fisheries, such as tuna, for home consumption would be highly desirable, in view of El Salvador's dense population. However, high prices, as well as local prejudice, have kept this protein-rich food out of reach of the masses. In 1970, government plans to develop a tuna fishing fleet and processing plant, with South Korean aid, were under way. If successful, this venture may be a breakthrough in the solution of El Salvador's food problem.

Industry

El Salvador is usually considered the most industrialized country in Central America. About 14 percent of its working population engage in manufacturing—the highest ratio among the isthmian countries (Mexico, 16 percent; United States, 26 percent).

El Salvador's industrial growth, perhaps aided by population pressure, has been longer and faster than elsewhere in Central America. Between 1963 and 1968, the contribution of manufacturing to the country's gross national product increased from 16 to nearly 20 percent, while that of agriculture fell from 31 to 26 percent. Within that period both government aid and the trade increase engendered by the Central American Common Market were key factors in industrial growth.

The country's most important industry is cotton textiles. Most of the cloth is for national consumption, but much is exported to neighboring countries under the common market arrangement, and some even goes to the United States and Europe. Textile production, as well as other light industry including food processing, pharmaceuticals, plastics, and garment manufacture, are carried on around the national capital and in the large towns of Santa Ana and San Miguel, where abundant labor and local markets are close at hand. Since 1960, manufacturing has grown most rapidly in the new Ilopango Industrial Area, east of San Salvador, and around the port of Acajutla, where the country's oil refining complex (using crude imported from Venezuela) has attracted related industry. Lacking coal and petroleum deposits, El Salvador could not have developed its industry without hydroelectric energy. In 1954, the large dam and hydroelectric plant, *5 de Noviembre,* was inaugurated on the middle course of the Lempa River, and a second plant has been completed on Lake Güija in the northwestern corner of the country.

Transportation and Trade

Its small area, comparatively easy terrain, and intensive land utilization help explain El Salvador's highly developed transportation system. The rail network, which consists mainly of the North American-owned International Railways of Central America, was completed in the 1920s to transport coffee. As stated previously, the Salvadorean section of this railway connects with the Gualemalan portion, now nationalized as the *Ferrocarriles de Guatemala.* In addition, a short rail line, formerly British-owned and now nationalized, joins San Salvador with the port of Acajutla.

Two trunk highways traverse the country: one, part of the Inter-American Highway system, keeps to the southern line of volcanoes and passes through the coffee belt and the main population centers; the other, completed in 1962, forms the eastern extension of the Littoral Highway that runs from Mexico to the Gulf of Fonseca along the Pacific coastal plain. From these two arteries, paved feeder roads interconnect the important areas of commercial agriculture, giving El Salvador the best highway system in Central America. Most of the impoverished northern sections toward the Honduran border, however, still lack good roads. Except for a single paved highway that leads into extreme southwestern Honduras, trade across the northern border is today almost as difficult as in the last century.

Although much of El Salvador's coffee goes by rail and truck to Guatemala's Caribbean ports, three Pacific ports handle the bulk of Salvadorean overseas trade. Two of these are roadsteads: La Libertad and Acajutla. Acajutla is connected with the hinterland by both rail and highway. The new deep-water harbor, protected by large sea walls, opened there in 1961 and later enlarged, has made Acajutla the country's leading port as well as an industrial center. The third port is Cutuco, near the town of La Unión on the well-protected Gulf of Fonseca. Here a deep-water dock permits the direct loading of cargo, mainly coffee and cotton, onto large freighters.

HONDURAS

Honduras occupies a distinctive geographical and economic segment of Central America. Most of its surface is covered with the oldest and most highly mineralized rocks of the isthmus. Its land is mountainous and difficult to traverse. Its soils, except on the Caribbean coast, are generally infertile. Thus, from colonial times to the early twentieth century, Honduras was a land of mines and livestock, of little agriculture, of a scant and isolated population, and of indifferent colonial and unstable republican governments.

Among its sister republics, this unfortunate country has been regarded as the most backward economically and culturally of the Central American states. Much of the country still lives under almost colonial conditions. Honduras is also considered the prototype of the "banana republics," with commercial economies based on a single export crop under the control of large North American companies. This is, however, not correct, for the Honduran economy includes much more than the banana industry, although only since World War II has the country seen substantial economic diversification and growth of transportation and settlement.

The Physical Base

As indicated in Chapter 2, Honduras lies completely within the land mass of geologic Old Antillia, characterized by its east–west-trending mountain ranges of ancient crystalline rock often capped by limestone or sandstone. In southwestern Honduras, the ancient rock is covered by thick layers of old lava and other volcanics that have been highly eroded to form a rugged surface, parts of which rise above 9,000 feet. The volcanic axis of Central America skirts the southern edge of Honduras, leaving but a few volcanoes as islets within the Gulf of Fonseca. Honduras thus lacks the covering of recent volcanic ash that has created the fertile soils of Central America's Pacific versant. In the central and northern parts of the country, northeast–southwest-trending crystalline ranges rise to maximum elevations of 9,000 feet, with deep valleys between.

In terms of human settlement, the most significant physiographic features of the interior highlands are numerous flat-floored basins of 1,000 to 3,000 feet elevation, called *valles,* the more important of which are shown in Figure 14.19. One of the largest is that of Comayagua, some 5 by 25 miles in extent. This *valle* occupies part of a north–south structural depression which was a transisthmian land route from colonial days through the nineteenth century. Dry and hot, grass and shrub-covered, the *valles* have been centers for stock raising since the sixteenth century, and some have recently become important for commercial agriculture.

Much of the mountainous interior of Honduras supports an oak and pine forest, one of the most extensive in Middle America. Elevations above 7,000 feet, however, carry remnants of dense cloud forest, called "montañas." The southern and central highlands receive 30 to 60 inches of rain between May and December, the rest of the year being quite dry. The Pacific slope, somewhat wetter, carries a semideciduous tropical forest and patches of savanna. On the Caribbean side, heavy rains (70 to 100 inches a year) and a short dry season give rise to a tropical rain forest, now greatly altered by man, that once covered mountain slopes and valley floors.

The Caribbean lowlands, which the Hondurans call "La Costa," form a distinct physiographic unit. Narrow river flood plains extend like fingers far inland, following depressions between mountain ranges. The fertile alluvium of the valleys

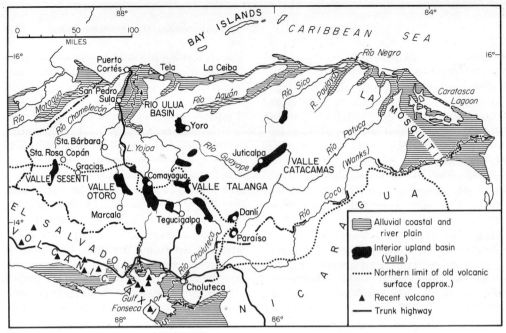

Figure 14.19   Selected landscape features of Honduras and adjacent areas

and adjacent coastal plains, cultivated since pre-Columbian times, now contain large banana plantations. Of these productive lowlands, the Ulúa River basin is the most intensively developed.

In the far northeast lies the most extensive Caribbean lowland, the Mosquitia, which continues southward into eastern Nicaragua. This sparsely peopled Honduran lowland and the adjacent mountain ranges comprise one of the least known sections of all Middle America.

Honduras reaches the Pacific only along the northern side of the Gulf of Fonseca. Back of the mangrove-fringed shore lie narrow coastal and river plains, the most extensive of which is Choluteca, famed for its savanna pastures and its livestock industry since the sixteenth century.

The People

One of the sharpest demographic contrasts in Central America is that between relatively underpopulated Honduras (58 persons per square mile) and overcrowded El Salvador (460 per square mile). About 2.6 million Hondureños—just under three-fifths the number of Salvadoreans—live in an area five times larger than its tiny neighbor to the south. This contrast in population has existed since aboriginal times, and before 1969 was reflected in the overflow of Salvadorean migrants into Honduras and in Honduras's traditional role of exporter of surplus food to El Salvador.

The Honduran people, like their neighbors, however, are increasing rapidly in numbers (3.4 percent annually). Partly because of the poor soil and the mountainous terrain, many rural sections of the interior are already overpopulated, although densities rarely exceed 150 per square mile. Thus, within the last 60 years there has been considerable migration of peasant farmers to the empty northern highlands and to the developing Caribbean lowlands.

Hondurans are distributed unevenly over their mountainous land, and more than half live in the western and southern highlands. Since the development of the banana plantations along the Caribbean during this century, the population of the lowland flood plains and the coast has grown remarkably; this area now contains a fourth of the total number of Hondurans. Thus, in terms of both population distribution and cultural pattern, there are now two Hondurases: (1) the mountainous interior of colonial tradition centered on the national capital, Tegucigalpa (229,000 population); and (2) the newly developed Caribbean lowlands, or La Costa, centered on the banana plantations and the commercial-industrial city of San Pedro Sula (112,000 population) in the Ulúa River basin.[3]

Racially, about 85 percent of the Hondurans are mixed Indian and white, with some black blood as well. Only 10 percent are considered full-blooded Indians, perhaps 2 percent black, and 2 percent white. Culturally the great bulk of the population is Ladino, having a mixed Spanish and aboriginal tradition.

Excepting its western portion, Honduran territory lay outside the area of aboriginal Mesoamerican culture. The pre-Conquest Indian population was never dense, and during the colonial period most of it was destroyed or greatly modified. At present, the so-called traditional Indians, who have been little influenced by Western culture, consist of a handful of Sumu and Paya riverine forest people in the far northeast. In the same area, several hundred Miskito Indians, now mixed with blacks, live along the Río Cocos. In southwestern Honduras, some 65,000 Indians, whose culture is now greatly modified, form a remnant of the once-extensive Lenca language group. Although they have lost their native language, the Lencas maintain many aboriginal customs and are considered to be Indians by their Ladino neighbors. In addition, several thousand Chorti-speaking Indians of Mayan affinity live on the Honduras-Guatemala border, and a few Jicaque are

found within the cloud forests on isolated mountain peaks in the north-central highlands.

The small black element in Honduras lives mainly along the Caribbean coast. One group consists of English-speaking descendants of Jamaican contract laborers who were imported from the West Indies early in the century to work on banana plantations. These people now make up a sizable element in the port towns and add to the West Indian cultural flavor that characterizes much of the Caribbean coast of Central America. The second Negroid group consists of several thousand Black Caribs, locally called *morenos,* who live in small villages and carry on a subsistence livelihood much as they do in Belize and Guatemala.

Off the northern coast of Honduras, the English-speaking white, mulatto, and black population of the Bay Islands adds to the cultural complexity of the Caribbean coastal scene. The Bay Islanders (some 10,000 in 1970) are descendants of English whites and blacks who migrated from Belize and the Cayman Islands in the 1830s. Although they have been under Honduran rule since 1859, these interesting people have maintained their Caribbean culture almost intact. Many are seamen who ship out on freighters that ply the world sea routes; others work for the fish processing plants recently established on the islands.

The Economy

In the preceding paragraphs we have noted that one of the fundamental features of present-day Honduras is its twofold physical and cultural division into the mountainous interior and the Caribbean lowlands. This dichotomy exists not only in population and settlement characteristics but also in types of economy. In the mountainous interior are found the traditional colonial occupations of stock

3. Population figures are 1970 estimates.

raising, mining, and subsistence farming; in the recently developed Caribbean lowlands, the tropical plantation system based on large-scale production of bananas and other commercial crops is dominant. The Caribbean lowlands have now surpassed the interior in economic wealth, rate of population growth, and rapidity of landscape change.

The Mountainous Interior

MINING. To understand better the present economic pattern of the interior, the Honduran mining industry should first be considered briefly. Although of little consequence today, the production of gold and silver was the mainstay of Honduran economy throughout the colonial period and the nineteenth century. As late as 1915, silver bullion led all other exports in terms of value.

After Honduras won its independence from Spain, mining companies owned by North American, British, and French interests began to take over the abandoned colonial silver mines in the interior and, by 1860, those around Tegucigalpa and Yuscarán were in full operation. Because

of its increasing economic importance, Tegucigalpa was made the national capital in 1880, gaining political ascendancy over its rival, Comayagua, the old colonial administrative center (Figure 14.20). Exploitation of the gold placers along the Guayape River, of colonial fame, was also revived at midcentury. After reaching a peak of production in the 1890s, the mining industry gradually declined, owing to depletion and to political instability. Today the mines of El Rosario, a few miles northeast of Tegucigalpa, and Morochito, west of Lake Yojoa, are the only large producers in the country. In the 1890s, silver and gold accounted for 75 percent of Honduran exports by value; by 1970, this figure had declined to 4 percent. In recent years, however, the mining and export of lead and zinc ores have maintained the total share of metals in Honduran foreign trade at 6 or 7 percent.

Many small mines still operate, and in the old silver centers, folk miners (*güirises*) grub for rich ores in abandoned shafts. Some also pan gold along the Río Guayape. But the picturesque mining towns such as Yuscarán, San Antonio, and Cedros in the central highlands, are, like

Figure 14.20   The central business district of Tegucigalpa in 1973. Since the late 1950s, tall modern buildings have replaced the low, tile-covered colonial-type structures that once characterized the architecture of the entire city.

Figure 14.21 The old mining town of San Antonio Oriente, in the central highlands of Honduras. The town retains much of its colonial architectural charm.

those in Mexico, mere reminders of a more prosperous past (Figure 14.21).

STOCK RAISING. As in northern Mexico, the mining industry in Honduras encouraged stock raising, for mining centers consumed quantities of animal products. From colonial times, therefore, the raising of cattle and mules has been a leading activity in the mountainous interior as well as in the Pacific lowlands. Since the sixteenth century, cattle haciendas have occupied the best lands—the grassy floors of the upland basins, such as those of Comayagua, Catacamas, and Yoro. In the Pacific lowlands, the lower Choluteca plain is still renowned for the production of mules and cattle. Within the last century, stock raising was developed on

a large scale in the wet Caribbean lowlands, especially in the Ulúa and Aguán river valleys, where the introduction of African grasses greatly increased the carrying capacity of the pastures. By mid-nineteenth century, cattle from the savannas of the Aguán Valley, destined for export to the West Indies, were being driven to Caribbean ports. Until recently, Honduran stockmen drove thousands of steers annually to the fattening pastures in Guatemala and El Salvador (Figure 14.22). Today most livestock is exported by truck.

Like other Central American countries, Honduras shares in the recently developed chilled beef export trade. Since 1960, several meat-packing and freezing plants have been established in various parts of

Figure 14.22 The cattle industry of northern Central America

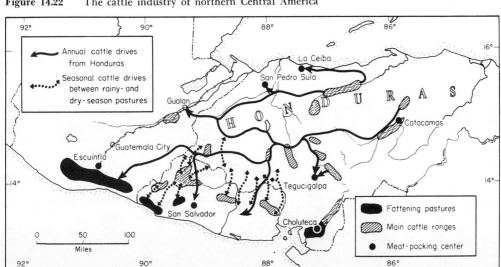

the country. The larger ones are in Choluteca, from where chilled beef is shipped to the United States via the Pacific port of Amapala, and in San Pedro Sula, where meat products are prepared for export through Puerto Cortés, the main Caribbean port. Despite the rapidly growing foreign trade in chilled beef, livestock and animal products now account for less than 8 percent of the total Honduran export revenue.

SUBSISTENCE FARMING. The most widespread human activity in the mountainous interior of Honduras is the cultivation of foodstuffs by peasant farmers. It, too, reflects the long influence of the colonial mining era. Because the cattle haciendas occupy most of the grass-covered basin floors, subsistence farming is ordinarily relegated to small plots on the mountain slopes where the soil is least fertile. Probably this agricultural pattern goes back even to aboriginal times, for, possessing only the stone axe, the dibble, and fire, the Indians could hardly have worked the tough grassy sod of the more fertile basins. The introduction of the plow did not have the effect of making farmland of the *valles,* however, for the colonial cattle barons forbade the cultivation of their hacienda lands. Hillside farming is still prevalent in many parts of Latin America, and it is one of the factors militating against increased food production.

Today two-thirds of the working population of Honduras are farmers, and most cultivate hillside plots of 15 to 25 acres. Many holdings are privately owned and worked by the owner and his family; others are sharecropped or leased. However, in the Indian-dominant southwestern highlands, most properties are ejido, or community, lands that belong to the municipality or village; plots are assigned or sold only to community members for use. The ejido concept has been legally recognized by the Honduran government since 1836, and its implementation predates the

Mexican ejido system by at least 50 years.[4] Finally, national lands, found on high mountain ridges and in the sparsely peopled northeastern lowlands are available for colonization, usually in 50-acre tracts per family. Since the writing of the Agrarian Reform Law of 1962, the Honduran government has established a few successful colonies, such as that of the upper Aguán Valley. Many landless farmers, however, simply squat on national lands without proper title, and some squatters have invaded the large private haciendas of the highlands, causing social strife.

Following the aboriginal crop pattern of most Central American countries, the Honduran mountain *campesino* cultivates chiefly maize and beans. At altitudes below 5,000 feet, sweet manioc (*yuca*) is an important staple, as are the African grain sorghum and cooking banana (plantain), rice, and sugar cane (for homemade *panela*). Wheat was formerly cultivated as a cash crop at elevations above 6,000 feet, but production has greatly declined in recent years.

In colonial times, the hillside Indian and Ladino farmers supplied food for nearby mining communities, and since the nineteenth century, Honduras has exported large amounts of maize and beans to overpopulated El Salvador. A surplus crop is normal in many parts of the Honduran highlands.

The dibble, hoe, and machete are the highlander's main agricultural tools, although southern Honduran subsistence farmers use wooden plows and oxen on

4. Ejido lands account for 34 percent of all farms and 17 percent of the total land area in Honduras. According to law, each municipality seat (large town) has the right to 8,750 acres of national land for ejidos, and each hamlet (*aldea*) of at least 100 inhabitants has the right to 4,000 acres. Each resident family within a settlement may have use rights to as much as 60 acres of such land, but today the average size of the ejido parcel is less than half that.

gentle slopes and valley flats. Modified primitive slash-burn cultivation, with only two to three years of fallow after an equal period of continuous cropping, is typical practice on the mountain slopes. As in El Salvador, this has caused serious soil erosion; in some places, the complete removal of the topsoil has turned sizable areas into reddish-colored wasteland, fit only for scrub pine. The best lands that remain to the highland farmer are the montañas, cloud forests on high mountain ridges of deep, rich soils. Unfortunately, the cloud-forest remnants are rapidly being destroyed by slash-burn cultivation. Erosion soon removes the topsoil, and the abandoned fields are colonized by pine rather than by the original broad-leaved evergreen forest.

The rural settlement pattern of highland Honduras resembles that of eastern Guatemala. Most of the subsistence farmers live in small hamlets with individual dwellings scattered about the mountainous terrain—a pattern well-suited to hillside cultivation. Larger compact villages and towns, often located within or on the edge of valleys and basins, serve as market and municipal administrative centers. The Lenca Indian settlements of southwestern Honduras parallel those of the aboriginal parts of Guatemala: dispersed farm houses, concourse centers for markets and religious functions, and Ladino towns as commercial and administrative centers. Craft specialization also characterizes the Lenca community, as it does many Ladino towns in the southern uplands near the Salvadorean border.

The poverty of Honduras is reflected in these upland rural people who comprise well over half the nation's population. Their primitive farming technology, small land holdings, low crop yields on poor soils, and physical isolation from ready markets create serious economic problems. COMMERCIAL AGRICULTURE. Since colonial times, parts of the Honduran highlands have specialized in the production of certain crops. One of the oldest is the tobacco area of Santa Rosa de Copán near the Guatemalan border, already famed in the eighteenth century for its high-quality cigar leaf. Since 1950 cultivation has expanded, most of the product being shipped to San Pedro Sula for the manufacture of cigarettes and cigars.

Parts of the large cattle haciendas in a few of the upland basins have recently been converted to farms producing cotton, maize, and beans. For example, sizable cotton plantations are now cultivated with mechanized equipment in the Comayagua Valley, and in the well-watered valleys of Danlí and Paraíso near the Nicaraguan border, small farms specialize in the commercial production of potatoes and beans.

The most significant cash crop of the highlands, however, is coffee. It has been important only since World War II, because Honduras was one of the last Central American countries to enter the world coffee market. Nearly half of the crop comes from the western and southern highlands. The coffee farms are concentrated in the high mountain slopes near the lower edge of the cloud forests where soil and moisture are favorable. Unlike those of Guatemala and El Salvador, the farms are small—25 to 50 acres—and many were started by Salvadorean immigrants, who introduced the industry into Honduras. Since 1950, the export value of coffee (10 to 18 percent of the total exports) has been second only to bananas. Three-quarters of Honduran coffee exports go to the United States, the rest go to western Europe.

The Caribbean Coastal Lowlands. The rapid rise of the western part of the Honduran Caribbean coast during this century is a remarkable example of modern economic and social development in the humid lowland tropics. Whereas in the mid-nineteenth century the Caribbean area was sparsely inhabited, forested, and disease-ridden, its western sector now contains nearly a quarter of the country's total population, accounts for half its export revenue, possesses its entire railway network, and has become its most industrialized region. Partly because of these developments, a sharp political and economic rivalry has evolved between the rich, progressive north coast and the poor, backward, mountainous interior.

The modern development of the north coast began with the rise of the banana industry in long, fertile valleys that extend inland from the sea. Of these, the largest and most intensively utilized is the Ulúa-Chamelecón river basin, in the northwestern corner of the country. Filled by rich, deep alluvium deposited by the rivers, this basin, 20 by 60 miles in extent, forms the northern end of the Comayagua transisthmian depression mentioned previously. San Pedro Sula, the second largest city of Honduras and rapidly growing, functions as an administrative and market center for the whole western lowland region. Farther east, the narrow river valleys of León, Aguán, and Negro, formerly all the largest banana producers, are now secondary to the Ulúa-Chamelecón basin.

The big banana plantation system was introduced into Honduras after the turn of this century by North American fruit companies, aided by government concessions of extensive lands in the coastal lowland. The United Fruit Company concentrated its efforts in the Ulúa-Chamelecón basin, the León River valley and adjacent coastal plain near Tela, and in the Río Negro valley and coastal area east of Trujillo. The Standard Fruit and Steamship Company developed plantations mainly in the long Aguán River valley and on the coastal plain near La Ceiba. Peak banana production was reached in Honduras from 1929 to 1931, when nearly 30 million bunches, about one-third of the world's exports, were shipped annually to the United States. To handle this enormous export, the fruit companies constructed port facilities at Puerto Cortés, Tela, La Ceiba, and Puerto Castilla (immediately north of Trujillo) and laid nearly 1,000 miles of standard and narrow-gauge railways throughout the lowland areas.

By 1945, however, disease had wiped out most of the eastern plantings in the Negro and Aguán valleys, and production had declined drastically in the Ulúa basin. By 1960, Honduran banana exports had fallen to 10 million bunches. But, despite adverse natural conditions (floods, hurricanes, and plant disease), the Ulúa-Chamelecón basin continues to be one of the major banana regions of the Central American Caribbean coast (Figure 14.23). Varieties of the disease-resistant Giant Cavendish bananas have completely replaced the Gros Michel, and industries subsidiary to modern banana culture, such as cardboard box factories, fruit canneries, and banana-chip processing plants, have become part of the industrial scene of the Caribbean coast. In the early 1930s, bananas constituted from 70 to 80 percent of Honduran exports by value and, through export taxes, virtually financed the Honduran government. Today this ratio has dropped to about 50 percent, not only because of the decrease in production but also because of the growth of highland exports, such as coffee and lumber.

People flowed from the interior of Honduras into the Caribbean lowlands to work on the banana plantations, and this influx continues, especially into the Ulúa-Chamelecón basin. There, the banana boom gave impetus to the commercial production of foodstuffs, sugar cane, and livestock; to the growth of market towns, such as San Pedro Sula, El Progreso, Puerto Cortés; and to the development of light industry, especially food processing. The United Fruit Company transferred large tracts of abandoned banana lands to subsistence and commercial farmers; it also introduced new plantation crops,

Figure 14.23 Banana plantation, Ulúa River floodplain, northern Honduras. The living quarters in the foreground are part of a "farm," one of the large blocks of land into which a plantation is divided. (*United Fruit Company*)

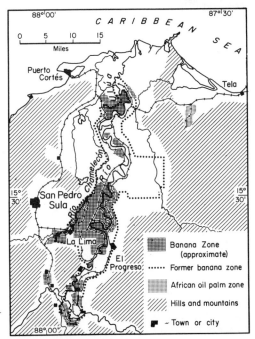

Figure 14.24 The Ulúa-Chamelecón River basin, northern Honduras

such as African oil palm and citrus. Between 1930 and 1970, the population of the Ulúa area increased more than sevenfold (approximately from 35,000 to 260,500), and San Pedro Sula increased as much (from 15,000 to 112,000 people). The population density of the area, around 260 per square mile, is one of the highest in Honduras. The cultural scene of this formerly forested tropical area is today one of intensive land use, a dense highway and rail network, and large numbers of agricultural hamlets and towns (Figure 14.24).

Forest Exploitation. Had they been wisely exploited, the extensive forest that once covered much of Honduras might have been that country's greatest resource today. Unfortunately, perhaps more senseless destruction of the forest cover has occurred here than in any other Central American area.

For nearly two centuries (1750–1930) Honduras was renowned for the fine mahogany of its Caribbean rain forest. Today, with practically no virgin trees left, the mahogany trade is insignificant. On the other hand, the pine forests of the mountainous interior and the northeastern lowlands, although somewhat depleted, are still an important part of Honduran natural wealth (Figure 14.25).

Much of the interior pine forest was altered or destroyed by slash-burn farming and by the firing of undergrowth and grass to improve pasturage for livestock. More serious are the epidemics of pine beetles, which between 1963 and 1965

435

Figure 14.25   Typical cutover pine forest in the central highlands of Honduras near Tegucigalpa

destroyed about 20 percent of the best trees. Today, however, scores of sawmills, large and small, are seen everywhere in the remaining pine stands, cutting timber for local use or for export. The most extensive stands left are in isolated mountains of Olancho department in the north-central part of the country. Since the 1950s, pine from Olancho and other interior forests has become the third-ranking export of Honduras. About half of the sawed lumber goes to the timber-poor West Indian islands, especially to Jamaica, the Dominican Republic, and Puerto Rico; the rest is shipped to western Europe. For many years foreign interests have planned a large wood pulp and paper plant on the Honduran northern coast, but, like so many costly developmental schemes in Central America, this project has been slow to materialize.

Manufacturing and Transport

The relative poverty of Honduras is reflected in its position as one of the least industrialized Central American coun-

tries. Only since 1950 has manufacturing employed more than 6 percent of the working population. Although it helped industrial growth in Honduras, the Central American Common Market has had a far greater impact on industrialization in other Central American countries. Food processing plants, textile mills, clothing factories, chemical manufacturers, and other consumer-oriented industries are concentrated in either Tegucigalpa or San Pedro Sula. San Pedro Sula has now surpassed the capital city in number of industrial workers, size of factories, and value of manufactures. Situated near the main port (Puerto Cortés) and within the most rapidly growing section of the country, San Pedro Sula appears to have the greater potential for further industrial expansion. The Lake Yojoa hydroelectric plant supplies power to both cities.

Formerly, an index of Honduras's economic backwardness was its rudimentary transport system, but this is no longer true. Since the 1950s, the Honduran government, with outside help, has constructed numerous all-weather highways in many parts of the country. In addition to the short portion of the Inter-American Highway that traverses southern Honduras, a transisthmian road from the Gulf of Fonseca, via Tegucigalpa, to San Pedro Sula and Puerto Cortés on the Caribbean, is now completely paved. Another recently paved highway leads from San Pedro Sula up the Chamelecón River valley to Santa Rosa de Copán in the western highlands and continues to Nueva Ocotepeque to connect with paved highways leading into Guatemala and El Salvador. Still another joins San Pedro Sula with the Caribbean ports of Tela and La Ceiba. In addition, hundreds of miles of all-weather feeder roads now connect once-isolated towns with market centers. Only the sparsely settled northeast now lacks transportation. As late as 1960, it was estimated that half the Honduran rural population traveled to market on foot or on horseback; probably less than 10 percent must do so today.

The main ports lie on the Caribbean. Puerto Cortés (formerly Puerto Caballos), the chief port since colonial times, still handles about half the country's foreign trade. One meager Pacific port, Amapala, which occupies a volcanic island in the Gulf of Fonseca, handles only a small part of Honduran imports and exports. However, the building of a new fully equipped deep-water port at Henecán on the Gulf of Fonseca is under way.

SELECTED REFERENCES

BROWNING, D. *El Salvador: Landscape and Society*. Oxford: Clarendon Press, 1971.

CHECCHI, V., *et al.*, eds. *Honduras: A Problem in Economic Development*. New York: Twentieth Century Fund, 1959.

CROSBIE, A. J., and FURLEY, P. A. "The New Belize: Prospects for British Honduras." *Scottish Geographical Magazine* 83, no. 1 (1967):53–63.

DAVIDSON, W. V. *Historical Geography of the Bay Islands, Honduras*. Birmingham, Ala.: Southern University Press, 1974.

GREGG, A. R. *British Honduras*. London: H.M. Stationery Office, 1968.

GUERRA BORGES, A. *Geografía Económica de Guatemala*. Guatemala, C.A.: Editorial Universitaria, 1969.

HIGBEE, E. "The Agricultural Regions of Guatemala." *Geographical Review* 37, no. 2 (1947):177–201.

HORST, O. H. "The Specter of Death in a Guatemalan Highland Community." *Geographical Review* 57, no. 2 (1967):151–67.

KEARNS, K. C. "Prospects of Sovereignty and Economic Viability for British Honduras." *The Professional Geographer* 21, no. 2 (1969):97–103.

McBRIDE, G. M., and McBRIDE, M. A. "Highland Guatemala and Its Maya Communities." *Geographical Review* 32, no. 2 (1942): 252–68.

McBRYDE, F. W. *Cultural and Historical Geography of Southwest Guatemala*. Institute of Social Anthropology Publication no. 4. Washington, D.C.: Smithsonian Institution, 1947.

MINKEL, C. W. "Colonization of the Sebol Region of North Central Guatemala." *Pacific Viewpoint* 9, no. 1 (1968):69–73.

RAYNOLDS, D. R. *Rapid Development in Small Economies: The Example of El Salvador*. New York: Praeger, 1967.

SEVERIN, T. "Pressure in El Salvador." *Geographical Magazine* 41, no. 4 (1969):278–86.

SQUIER, E. G. *Honduras: Descriptive, Historical and Statistical*. London: Trübner, 1870.

STOKES, W. S. "Land Laws of Honduras." *Agricultural History* 21, no. 3 (1947):148–54.

THOMAS, R. N. "The Migration Systems of Guatemala City: Spatial Inputs." *The Professional Geographer* 24, no. 2 (1972):105–12.

WHETTEN, N. L. *Guatemala: The Land and the People*. New Haven, Conn.: Yale University Press, 1961.

≡ 15 ≡

Central America:
The Southern Sector

NICARAGUA

Like Honduras, Nicaragua has had an unfortunate history. It was neglected by Spain in colonial times, was fraught with internal strife after independence, has been embroiled in wars and disputes with its sister republics, and its economy has developed slowly. On the other hand, two outstanding geographic features have given Nicaragua a much greater economic potential than Honduras: (1) the natural passway across the isthmus through the Nicaraguan Rift, and (2) the highly fertile volcanic soils on the Pacific side of the country. Nonetheless, the colonial past is still deeply entrenched in Nicaragua's social and economic patterns, which are reflected strongly in the present cultural landscape.

Perhaps more than any other Central American country, Panama excepted, Nicaragua has felt the direct influence of the United States in its politics and economy. American interests utilized the Nicaraguan Rift as a transisthmian route in the mid-nineteenth century. Between 1911 and 1932, actual military intervention in Nicaragua by United States forces was effected to protect American lives and investments, to manage the customs houses, and to supervise elections within the country. During this period Nicaragua was a virtual protectorate of the United States. Although needed health measures were introduced and North American investments and trade in Nicaragua sharply increased during the occupation, Latin Americans often point to this period of intervention as an example of United States "imperialism." The Nicaraguan Rift as a strategic canal route has been one of the significant geographical factors that has maintained the interest of the United States in this Central American country for the last 100 years.

Physical Patterns

Nicaragua is the largest country of Central America and as varied physically as any. The most salient physiographic feature is the great graben, the structural rift or depression that passes through the southern and western sections of the country, athwart the Central American isthmus. This lowland contains lakes Managua and Nicaragua, the two largest natural bodies of fresh water in Middle America. Both drain to the Caribbean via the San Juan River (Figure 15.1). Narrow plains surround the lakes, but the largest area of

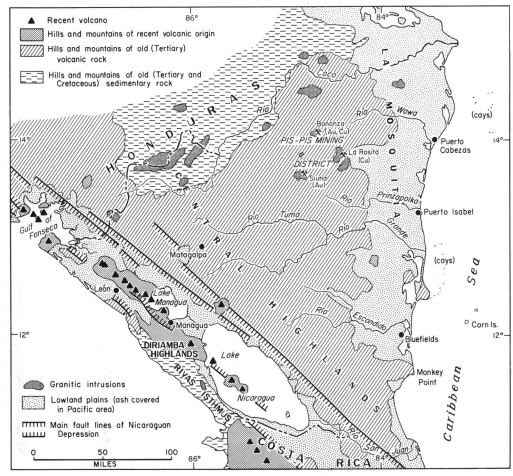

Figure 15.1   Nicaragua: Surface configuration and related geology

flattish lowland within the depression lies northwest of Lake Managua. From the Gulf of Fonseca to the southern shore of Lake Nicaragua, the depression is intruded by a single range of volcanoes—a part of the Central American volcanic axis. This range contains some of the most active volcanoes in Middle America. Among them are a line of low cones within the plain northwest of Lake Managua, including the beautifully symmetrical Momotombo; Nicaragua's most active volcano, Cerro Negro, which in 1968 and 1971 emitted great quantities of ash that was temporarily destructive to agriculture for miles around; and various volcanic peaks

that form islands within the lakes, such as Isla de Ometepe with its twin cones of Madera and Concepción. Concepción erupted in 1958, and the ashes caused widespread agricultural damage. The volcanic mountains of western Nicaragua are in part associated with the faults, or earth fractures, that underlie the lake lowland. Slippage along these fractures periodically causes destructive earthquakes, such as those of 1931 and 1972, both of which partially destroyed the capital city of Managua.

On the western side of the Nicaraguan Depression, a narrow upfaulted block of earth forms a series of uplands (Sierra de

Managua, Carazo Plateau) often called the Diriamba highlands. These, together with the low Rivas Isthmus to the south, separate the lakes from the Pacific Ocean. The Diriamba highlands, 700 to 3,000 feet in elevation, are thickly mantled with ash spewed from the adjacent volcanoes and blown westward by the prevailing trade winds.

Although the frequent eruptions and accompanying earthquakes have often been destructive, the volcanic ash that falls on the surrounding lowland plains and flanking uplands of the Nicaraguan Depression weathers into highly fertile soil. This, and plentiful rain (40 to 60 inches) from May to October, have attracted people to the northwestern portion of the depression and its adjacent uplands. For perhaps 2,000 years, the area has supported a dense population. In pre-Columbian times it was the locale of high Chorotegan Indian culture, the southernmost extent of Mesoamerican civilization. Today, it forms the core of Nicaragua in terms of people, agricultural production, and natural wealth.

Eastward from the lake and volcano-studded depression lie the central highlands. The higher mountain ridges reach 3,000 to 6,500 feet, and between them are deep valleys that drain eastward to the Caribbean Sea. Drenched by heavy rains (70 to 100 inches yearly), most of the crests and eastern slopes of the central highlands are covered by a dense rain forest; but in the north, near the Honduran border, extensive pine forests form the southernmost limit of the North American upland conifers. A semideciduous tropical forest once covered the drier western versant of the highlands, located in the lee of the prevailing trades. Since colonial times, settlers have pushed slowly eastward into the central highlands from the densely occupied Nicaraguan Depression. The drier western and northern portions of the highlands are now well settled, but the wet, forest-covered, eastern flanks are still pioneer country.

The extensive, sparsely settled Caribbean lowlands, sometimes called "La Mosquitia," comprise the eastern third of Nicaragua. This hot, humid area includes coastal plains of leached, infertile, gravelly soils; the lower eastern spurs of the central highlands; and the San Juan River basin. Receiving between 100 and 250 inches of rain yearly, with a short dry period in February and March, the lowland is the wettest section of Middle America. The pine and palm savannas that begin in easternmost Honduras extend southward along the coast to Pearl Lagoon, while the rest of the lowland is clothed in rain forest. Numerous rivers that drain the central highlands cross the Mosquitia as they flow to the Caribbean Sea. The area's only fertile soils are in the narrow floodplains of these streams, along which are concentrated the few lowland farming settlements. This great empty area contrasts sharply with the crowded western part of the country.

The People

Nearly two-thirds of Nicaragua's 1.9 million people live on the Pacific side of the country, mainly within the fertile plains of the lake lowlands and the adjacent Diriamba highlands and Rivas Isthmus. In these areas, population averages more than 150 persons per square mile; in some sections (as around Masaya, near Lake Nicaragua) rural densities reach beyond 500 per square mile (Figure 15.2).

The Nicaraguan Depression likewise contains most of the cities. Before the disastrous earthquake of 1972, the capital, Managua, had 323,500 inhabitants, 16 percent of the country's population. One of Latin America's youngest capitals, Managua was chosen in 1858 as a compromise site midway between the two rival colonial cities of León (now 65,700 population) and Granada (38,800). Although plans to move the capital from its present site have

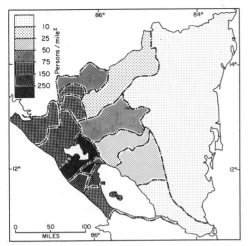

Figure 15.2   Population density in Nicaragua, by departments, 1970

been seriously considered, the city is already rebuilding from its ruins, as it did after the 1931 earthquake.

A secondary population center lies in the northern part of the central highlands. Only lightly settled by Spaniards in colonial times, this area began to receive an influx of settlers drawn by coffee cultivation during the mid-nineteenth century and has grown steadily since. The main settlements cluster around the towns of Estelí, Matagalpa, and Jinotega, where densities range from 50 to 100 persons per square mile. In sharp contrast, the Caribbean lowlands average less than 5 persons per square mile, and most of the interfluves are uninhabited.

The population distribution of Nicaragua has changed little since pre-Conquest times. At Spanish contact the lake lowlands and adjacent uplands supported a dense Indian population; a smaller number of less advanced aboriginal farmers lived in the central highlands; and the Caribbean lowlands contained a few small tropical forest tribes scattered along the river courses. Perhaps better than any other Central American country, Nicaragua illustrates the persistence of ancient patterns of population distribution.

Like the people of other Central American nations, Nicaraguans are increasing more than 3 percent annually. In order to relieve population pressure in the overcrowded Pacific area, the Nicaraguan government has encouraged colonization within the central highlands and the Caribbean lowlands. Since World War II, Nicaraguan farmers have been settling in the northern portion of the central highlands, but colonists from the Pacific area have made little headway into the Caribbean tropical forests.

Nicaragua is a land of mixbloods. Perhaps 75 percent of the people are mestizo, or mixed Indian-white, most of whom live in the populous Pacific area and the central highlands. At mid-nineteenth century, a third of the population of these areas was still Indian, but practically all of the purely aboriginal racial element has since disappeared from the lake lowlands, and only a small remnant of culturally modified Matagalpa Indians persists in the central highlands. In the Caribbean lowlands, however, a sizable number (about 25,000) of Miskito Indians (about half of whom are sambos, or mixed Indian-black) live as subsistence farmers and fishermen along the Cocos and other rivers (see Figure 13.3). In addition, small groups of Sumu Indians occupy isolated stretches of streams on the eastern flank of the central highlands. The Caribbean lowland is also the home of most of Nicaragua's black population (10 percent of the total), most of whom entered the country as laborers on banana plantations early in this century. About 10 percent of the Nicaraguan people are classed as Caucasian; these are mainly descendants of colonial families who live in urban centers and form the upper landholding and industrial class.

The Economy

Like its Central American neighbors, Nicaragua is a nation of farmers. About

60 percent of its economically active population is engaged in agriculture, and 80 percent of its exports by value are farm products, despite the fact that only 10 percent of the country is farmed. Most of the people are either landless laborers on large estates or subsistence farmers working hillside plots, and a smaller number own and cultivate medium-sized farms. The large hacienda owners possess most, and the best, of the arable lands and pastures. A heritage of the colonial past, this threefold rural class structure and land tenure system permeates Nicaraguan life.

Nicaragua's agricultural economy tends to coincide with the country's three distinct culture areas, which in turn reflect basic physical conditions. These areas are: (1) the Pacific area, including the lake lowlands and adjacent uplands; (2) the northern part of the central highlands; and (3) the Caribbean lowlands.

The Pacific Area. Since early colonial times, the densely peopled Pacific area has been Nicaragua's main center of subsistence and commercial agriculture. Most of the land is in large estates, or haciendas, on which the bulk of the rural people are employed as farmhands. Most of the farmhands and their families live in hamlets near hacienda lands in much the same way their Indian ancestors did in the colonial period. Most of their houses, Indian-like, have wattled walls and grass-thatched roofs. On rented subsistence plots near their settlements, many hacienda workers raise the native maize, beans, and squash, as well as rice and sorghum. The ox-drawn wooden plow and the two-wheeled cart are widespread. Thus, the rural cultural pattern of the Pacific area is a composite of Hispanic and Indian traits that have changed little from the colonial period, except for the growing of certain commercial crops.

STOCK RAISING. Since colonial times, most of Nicaragua's wealth has come from large haciendas. Livestock and indigo continued to be the country's main exports until the mid-nineteenth century. Today, indigo has disappeared, but cattle raising is still significant, and the main pastures are still centered in the hilly savannas of Chontales and Boaco on the eastern side of Lake Nicaragua. Nearly one-third of the beef cattle, however, is now found in the Pacific lowlands, where many former cotton haciendas have been recently converted to stock ranches by planting African grasses and irrigating them for pasture. The cattle barons have also begun to improve the traditional hide-and-tallow producing herds by crossing them with Brahma and other beef-yielding breeds. Today, chilled beef, shipped mainly to the United States, is the country's third most valuable export and in some years vies with coffee for second place. Begun in 1959 with the establishment of modern meat-processing plants, the chilled beef industry is the youngest and most rapidly growing part of Nicaraguan agriculture.

COMMERCIAL FARMING. The commercial crops produced on large estates in the Pacific area include coffee, cotton, bananas, sugar cane, rice, and sesame. Coffee and cotton are by far the most important.

In the 1850s Nicaragua's commercial agriculture was revolutionized by the introduction of coffee. First grown in the volcanic hills west of Managua, by 1860 coffee had spread into the fertile ash-covered Diriamba uplands between the lake plains and the Pacific. It is grown on estates of 100 to 4,000 acres, particularly in a small area of 1,000 to 3,000 feet elevation called "Los Pueblos," where the towns of Diriamba, San Marcos, and Jinotepe serve as market centers for the crop (Figure 15.3). In the 1920s, the Diriamba uplands produced 90 percent of Nicaragua's coffee. Today, it produces only a third of the total, owing to the expansion of cultivation in the more moist north-central highlands. For more than a century, coffee was Nicaragua's foremost

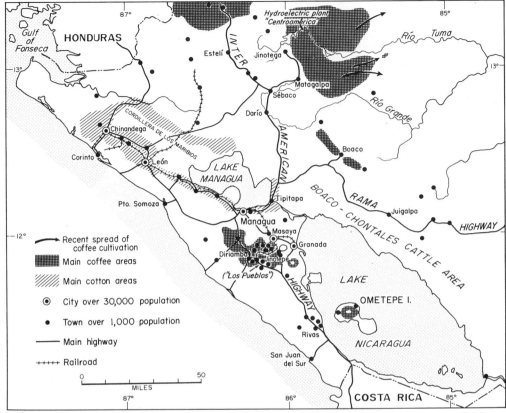

Figure 15.3   Commercial agriculture in western Nicaragua

export and one of the main sources of wealth for the estate owners.

Since 1962, however, cotton has been Nicaragua's most valuable export. As in other Central American countries, the cotton boom in Nicaragua began in 1950, reached maximum production and acreage in 1965, and after a short period of decline due to low world prices, expanded once again in the early 1970s. Production is centered in the northwestern lowland plains between Lake Managua and the Gulf of Fonseca. There, the deep, black soil, weathered from volcanic ash, is among the best in Central America. The most productive section lies around the booming market town of Chinandega, while a secondary cotton-growing area extends along the eastern side of Lake Managua around the town of Tipitapa. Although large holdings and a flattish terrain have facilitated extensive mechanization, a large labor force is still needed to harvest the crop, and new settlements for farm workers have mushroomed throughout the cotton zone. Practically all the crop is exported to Japan and western Europe through the new deepwater port of Corinto, constructed in 1958 near the old colonial harbor of Realejo.

The Central Highlands. During the colonial period, the central highlands underwent a cultural and economic development quite distinct from that of the Pacific area. Only the Nueva Segovia gold and silver deposits and the pastures for stock raising in the northern part of the highlands attracted Spaniards in any numbers, and the threat of pirate and Miskito Indian raids from the Caribbean caused frequent abandonment of these settlements. Moreover, the rugged terrain and the poor soils, as well as the scant and hostile Indian population, combined to

443

discourage agricultural developments similar to those of the Pacific lowlands. Thus, subsistence farming, small land-holdings, and dispersed settlement characterized the rural scene of the central highlands well into the nineteenth century.

COFFEE. The first significant change came in the 1890s, when German, North American, and English colonists introduced coffee cultivation into the hardwood forests of the Matagalpa and Jinotega areas. The success of these coffee growers attracted large numbers of peasant farmhands from the lake lowlands. Many of these, as well as the native Matagalpa Indians, established small coffee farms and slash-burn subsistence plots, pushing the settlement frontier eastward. Although interrupted by civil strife between 1911 and 1934, this eastward expansion has continued and has now reached well into the densely forested Caribbean versant of the central highlands.

Today, nearly two-thirds of Nicaragua's coffee crop comes from the northern part of the highlands, and nearly half is produced in Matagalpa and Jinotega departments alone. In contrast to the large, crowded estates in the Diriamba uplands, the coffee farms in the central highlands are small-to-medium holdings (25 to 75 acres), dispersed over wide areas between 2,000 and 5,000 feet elevation. Despite rugged terrain and poor transport, the high altitude and abundant rainfall afford better natural conditions for growing coffee than do the drier and lower Diriamba uplands.

STOCK RAISING. The middle and southern parts of the central highlands today constitute the main stock-raising area of Nicaragua. Over half the country's cattle graze on large estates within the savannas of Chontales and Boaco, northeast of Lake Nicaragua, and on extensive planted pastures recently formed in deforested sections along the Río Grande of Matagalpa. From these areas cattle are trucked to

Managua to be slaughtered for the chilled beef trade. Milk is also shipped from nearby dairies to a new established processing plant in Matagalpa, making this part of the highlands the leading supplier of milk and milk products for Nicaraguan cities. Since World War II, some cattle ranchers from the Boaco and Chontales savannas have penetrated the eastern slope of the highlands, felling the forest to plant grass for artificial pastures.

SUBSISTENCE FARMING. In addition to growing coffee, many small farmers of the central highlands plant subsistence crops of maize, sorghum, and rice in slash-burn hillside plots, with the dibble and hoe. Unfortunately, this activity has led to the destruction of the forest and to serious soil erosion on steep slopes. The scattered subsistence farms and the newly established cattle ranches in particular give the central highlands the ambience of a recently settled and expanding pioneer zone, a characteristic that sets them apart from the long and densely occupied Pacific belt of feudal Indian-Hispanic heritage. Like the vast, forested Caribbean lowlands, the eastern versant of the central highlands is an area for future colonization.

The Caribbean Lowlands. As noted in the first part of this chapter, the Caribbean lowlands of Nicaragua constitute a part of the eastern versant of Central America that falls outside the area of mainland Hispanic life. This is a territory whose littoral is a part of the Middle American Rimland (Caribbean Negroid culture) and whose interior still belongs largely to primitive forest Indian groups. As such, the eastern third of Nicaragua is, culturally and physically, a world apart from the rest of the country—a forested, sparsely peopled area that still lies outside the effective national territory.

The vast contrast between the Nicaraguan Pacific core and the Caribbean versant was equally pronounced in aboriginal times, for the civilized Chorotegans of the lake lowlands had little contact with the primitive fishermen and farmers of the Caribbean tropical forests. During the colonial period, the Spaniards normally shunned the Caribbean forests. In Chapter 10, we told how English pirates and smugglers used the unoccupied Caribbean coast for bases during the seventeenth and eighteenth centuries and how they organized the Miskito Indians into a kind of kingdom that lasted until the mid-nineteenth century. During this time, the English established the ports of Bluefields and Greytown (the site of San Juan del Norte) along the Caribbean coast to encourage trade and white colonization and to control their Indian protectorate. Although the Kingdom of Mosquitia was abolished by treaty in 1850, Nicaragua did not take formal military possession of the Caribbean coast until 1893.

Since the mid-nineteenth century, the economy of the Caribbean lowlands has revolved mainly around three activities, all of which have been largely in the hands of foreign interests: (1) exploitation of wild forest products, (2) gold mining, and (3) plantation agriculture. All three have been characterized by boom periods followed by decline and abandonment. Moreover, except for port towns, little permanent settlement has resulted from these activities.

FOREST EXPLOITATION. Between 1860 and World War I, the gathering of latex from wild rubber trees became a significant industry in the Caribbean rain forest. Thousands of mestizos from the Pacific belt, as well as local Matagalpa and Miskito Indians, ranged the forests in search of rubber, especially on the eastern slopes of the central highlands in the San Juan basin. By 1900, Nicaragua had become the leading producer of rubber north of the Amazon basin. With the rise of the rubber plantations in southeast Asia after 1915, the gathering industry collapsed in both Nicaragua and Brazil, reviving briefly during World War II.

Lumbering has been more permanent, particularly the cutting of mahogany and Spanish cedar, which are scattered through the tropical rain forest, and of slash pine, which grows in solid stands in the Mosquito Coast savannas. Early in the nineteenth century, English woodcutters were floating out mahogany logs along the many lowland rivers to the coast, and during World War I this tropical cabinet wood became Nicaragua's second most important export. In 1924, a company from New Orleans began lumbering slash pine in the Mosquito savanna and built a new port at Puerto Cabezas to handle exports to the Caribbean islands. Intensive logging still continues, but most of the better stands of pine are depleted.

MINING. Since the sixteenth century precious metals have been a significant Nicaraguan export. Until the latter half of the nineteenth century most of the mines of gold and silver were located in the central highlands. But, in the 1890s, the rich deposits of Pis-Pis were discovered in an isolated mountain spur 80 miles inland from Puerto Cabezas (Figure 15.1). Worked off and on by North American companies, it became Nicaragua's leading gold and silver district in the 1940s. Between 1938 and 1949, gold surpassed coffee as the country's leading export with more than half the production coming from Pis-Pis.

In the 1950s sizable quantities of copper ore were discovered in the gold mining centers of Siuna and Bonanza within the Pis-Pis district. Since 1965, the value of copper ore production has exceeded that of gold and silver, the ore concentrates being exported entirely to West Germany. However, production of all minerals in Nicaragua has declined in the past decade, despite the exploitation of newly discovered deposits of lead, zinc and copper in the central highlands.

PLANTATION AGRICULTURE. One of the most promising attempts to open the Caribbean lowlands to permanent settlement was the establishment of banana plantations along the lower flood plains of the Escondido, Grande, and Wawa rivers during the late nineteenth and early twentieth centuries. Commercial banana production in Nicaragua peaked in 1929, but disease adversely affected the industry after 1938, and the banana lands were completely abandoned by the end of World War II. During the height of production, English-speaking Jamaican blacks were brought in as plantation laborers. Many of their descendants now live in the major port towns of Puerto Cabezas, Río Grande, and Bluefields, where they have entered various trades; few have become farmers.

Despite varied economic activity in the Caribbean lowlands during the last hundred years, the land is relatively unpopulated. Since the close of World War II, the Nicaraguan government has encouraged mestizos from the Pacific to colonize the lowlands, but only one significant penetration has been made—along the new highway constructed from Managua through the central highlands to the town of Rama, a port for small ocean-going ships on the Escondido River (Figure 15.4). Along the alluvial floodplain,

colonists have established small subsistence and commercial farms. Although the paved highway to the population centers on the Pacific facilitates movement of produce to markets, the success of the colony is still uncertain.

FISHING. As indicated in Chapter 13, shrimping has become big business on both the Pacific and Caribbean coasts. Over half the shrimp and all the lobster exported to the United States are trawled and trapped off the Caribbean shores and are processed in Puerto Cabezas, Bluefields (El Bluff), and Laguna de Perlas. Shrimping is the newest, one of the most lucrative, and the fastest growing economic development in the Caribbean lowlands; it will probably remain so until overexploitation and decline of the marine resource occur. On the Pacific side, the main shrimping centers are Corinto and San Juan del Sur, but decreasing catches in recent years may already signal a permanent decline in shrimp population.

Land Reform. The familiar dichotomy of large and small land holdings, as well as the more serious social problem of the landless, poverty-stricken farm laborer, permeates Nicaragua's rural economy and

Figure 15.4   The town of Rama at the confluence of the Escondido and Rama rivers, in the Caribbean lowlands of Nicaragua. Rama, 50 miles from the coast, is the terminus of a paved road to Managua and a river port for Caribbean shipping. (*Instituto Geográfico Nacional de Nicaragua*)

national politics. It is estimated that nearly a third of all farm workers are landless tenants, sharecroppers, or squatters, and illegal possession of private and public lands by the latter group has been increasing at an alarming rate. Nicaragua's land problem is compounded by the clustering of well over half its population in the narrow Pacific zone, but it has possibilities for solution in the vast, empty lands of the Caribbean versant.

In accordance with similar measures taken by other Central American countries, Nicaragua, in 1963, established its National Agrarian Institute, whose main goal is to bring about a more favorable pattern of land distribution and tenure through the enforcement of land reform laws. To date, land redistribution has proceeded slowly, for only certain types of national or municipal lands and "underutilized" private estates of over 1,235 acres can be used for resettlement. Within the Pacific lowlands a few large private holdings that were deemed to be inefficiently utilized have been expropriated and the land distributed in 10- to 30-acre plots to landless peasants. It is in the Caribbean versant, however, that the agrarian institute has laid most of its plans for resettlement. There, immense tracts of national lands have been set aside for redistribution to individual families and for the formation of agricultural colonies.[1] Begun in 1967, the largest colonization scheme involves the settlement of more than a million acres of forested land on the eastern slope of the central highlands drained by the upper tributaries of the Escondido River and served by the Rama Highway. By 1970 some settlement had been made along the highway, the only major penetration route completed into the Caribbean lowlands; at that time, however, most of the project was still in the planning stage.

Industry

Before World War II, Nicaragua, like Honduras, was one of the least industrialized of the Central American countries. But, stimulated by the common market arrangement, industrial production has grown spectacularly since 1962. Industry now employs 15 percent of the country's work force and contributes about 25 percent of its gross domestic product.

Possessing the bulk of surplus urban labor and most of the country's electrical power, the capital city, Managua, produces more than 60 percent of the nation's manufactured goods, by value. Most of the remainder is scattered among the other cities within the Pacific zone: the port of Corinto, León, Chinandega, and Masaya. Only 10 percent of the manufacturing industry is found in the central highlands and the Caribbean lowlands.

Light industry prevails: nearly two-thirds involves the manufacture and processing of food and drink, and of clothing and textiles. However, the establishment of a small refinery in Managua in 1963 resulted in the growth of a fledgling chemical industry, especially the manufacture of agricultural pesticides and various other petrochemicals. With the recent completion of hydroelectric plants on the upper Tuma and Viejo rivers in the central highlands, the power base for industrialization and rural electrification has been greatly increased. Even so, more than half the power used in manufacturing comes from diesel and steam-operated thermoelectric plants located in the cities. Industry continues to expand, especially in the Managua area, where several new chemical and textile plants are currently

---

1. A head of a family may apply for clear title to a plot of national land up to 125 acres in size, provided he has occupied the plot for one year. Similarly, a squatter family may receive up to 250 acres of unused or private or municipal land.

being built or are planned. Fortunately, the earthquake of December 1972 did little damage to the industrial sectors of the city.

Transportation and Trade

Nicaragua's rail and highway network is another index of the concentration of economic wealth in the Pacific zone. The 216-mile rail system, now a government utility, was constructed piecemeal between 1878 and 1903, mainly to haul coffee from the Diriamba highlands to the port of Corinto. Owing to the relatively short haul, this railroad has proved to be uneconomical today and is gradually being replaced by the more efficient truck transport.

Few auto roads existed in Nicaragua before World War II, but in the late 1950s, paved roads were completed between Managua and the Pacific ports of Corinto and San Juan del Sur. The postwar period also saw the completion of the Inter-American Highway and of many all-weather feeder truck roads through the north-central highlands, linking the Matagalpa coffee area with the Pacific lowlands. The Rama Road, connecting the Pacific with the Caribbean lowlands and financed mainly by the United States, was started in 1942 as a military measure, but was not completed and paved until 30 years later. Other penetration routes into the Caribbean lowlands, such as that from Jinotega to the Pis-Pis mining district, have been planned for years, but are not likely to materialize in the near future.

Corinto is Nicaragua's only modern deepwater port, and it handles three-fourths of the country's foreign trade. Aside from Puerto Somoza, where petroleum is unloaded and thence carried by pipeline to the Managua refinery, all other Pacific ports are minor roadsteads served by lighters. The same is true for the Caribbean ports, all of which are on shallow water and lack modern facilities.

COSTA RICA

This delightful country is unique among Latin American nations. About 80 percent of the Costa Ricans claim to be unmixed white descendants of Spanish colonists, and most of these are small farmers in a confined highland area—the Meseta Central. The people also claim the highest literacy rate, the most democratic government, and the most comfortable living standard in Latin America. In striking contrast to its Central American neighbors, Costa Rica has suffered only one serious political upheaval (1948) during a long, peaceful period lasting from 1886 to the present. Unusual, also, has been the spontaneous colonization of the virgin forest lands from the surrounding, densely populated Meseta Central during the last 125 years, a vigorous and continuing pioneer movement.

Except for its northwestern province (Guanacaste), Costa Rica, in pre-Spanish times, lay outside the cultural influence of aboriginal Mesoamerica. Thus, the strong Indian heritage that Mesoamerican culture has given to Guatemala, El Salvador, and western Nicaragua is absent in most of Costa Rica. The Indians of South American (Chibchan) cultural affinity who lived in the Costa Rican highlands disappeared rapidly after the Conquest, leaving that area open to the Spanish colonists. Without a large number of Indians to work for them, the Spaniards in the highlands failed to develop the large landed estate and accompanying serfdom that is usually associated with Hispanic occupation. Rather, there arose, as the prevailing cultural pattern, a Spanish peasantry occupied with subsistence farming, a pattern that still dominates the

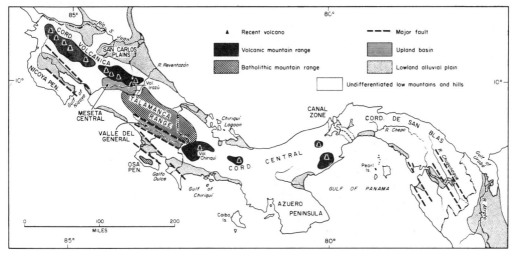

Figure 15.5   Costa Rica and Panama: Surface configuration and associated geology

rural scene of much of highland Costa Rica.

Physical Characteristics

Although of extreme local complexity, the physical structure of Costa Rica is roughly the threefold Central American division of (1) cool central highlands; (2) warm Pacific lowland and leeward mountain slopes with well-defined wet and dry seasons; and (3) Caribbean lowlands and eastward-facing escarpments, rain-drenched and forest-covered. Together with the Panamanian isthmus, the narrow Costa Rican land mass forms a bridge that connects Old Antillia with South America.

The Central Highlands. Figure 15.5 indicates that the Costa Rican highlands consist of a northern volcanic range (Cordillera Volcánica) and a southern mountain mass formed by the intrusion of a gigantic batholith of granitic rock (Talamanca Range). Between these two distinctly different mountain ranges lies a small upland known as the Meseta Central, the most significant physiographic unit of Costa Rica in terms of its cultural development.

The northern range, a part of the Central American volcanic axis, consists of a series of cones perched atop an elevated mass of lava and ash. The highest volcanoes are toward the southeast, where Irazú (11,500 feet elevation) suddenly erupted in 1963, causing temporary damage by ash throughout central Costa Rica. In 1968, Arenal volcano, in the middle portion of the range, emitted clouds of superheated gas (*nuées ardentes*), killing scores of people and spewing ash over a wide area toward the Pacific.

Immediately south of the highest volcanoes lies the Meseta Central, itself a product of vulcanism. Two small basins comprise this upland. The higher, eastern one is Cartago (4,500 to 5,000 feet elevation), drained by the headwaters of the Reventazón River, which flows to the Caribbean. To the west lies the lower and larger basin, San José (3,000 to 4,000 feet elevation), site of the present capital city and drained toward the Pacific by the headwaters of the Río Grande de Tárcoles. Between the two basins a low range of volcanic hills forms the continental divide. Ashfalls, avalanches of glowing cinders, and mudflows from the adjacent volcanoes have filled the basins to their present elevations. On this volcanic floor,

449

Figure 15.6 Basin of Cartago, which forms the eastern portion of the Meseta Central. Small fields of maize and pasture cover the surrounding slopes.

eroding streams have formed the rolling surface and numerous terraces that characterize the basins today. As elsewhere along the volcanic axis, the ash and cinder deposits have weathered into highly fertile soil. Situated in the *tierra templada* altitudinal zone, the Meseta Central enjoys one of the most equable climates in Middle America. Frost-free and sufficiently moist, the Meseta can produce a wide range of tropical and midlatitude crops and, since pre-Columbian times, it has supported a dense population (Figure 15.6).

Another upland basin, the Valle del General, lies between the Talamanca Range and the coastal mountains in southwestern Costa Rica. This isolated structural depression, composed of river floodplains, terraces, and rolling hills 1,000 to 3,500 feet above the sea, has been occupied only recently by farmers migrating out of the overcrowded Meseta Central.

The Pacific Lowlands. Unlike the straight Pacific shoreline of northern Central America, that of Costa Rica is indented by a series of peninsulas and gulfs, mostly as a consequence of faulting (Figure 15.5). The down-faulted blocks (grabens) produce the gulfs of Nicoya and Dulce as well as adjacent alluvial low-

lands; the up-faulted blocks (horsts) give rise to the mountainous peninsulas of Nicoya, Osa, and Burica with their steep, rocky shore lines. The alluvial plains afford fertile soils for tropical lowland farming and some, as the Golfo Dulce graben, contain large banana plantations. Despite a four-month dry season (January through April), the annual rainfall (80 to 120 inches) is sufficient to support a heavy rain forest. In the northwestern province of Guanacaste, where the interior plains receive less than 60 inches of rain, there are open deciduous forests, most of which man has transformed, by burning, into tropical grasslands.

The Caribbean Lowlands. The belt of heavy precipitation and tropical rain forest that characterizes the Caribbean lowlands of Nicaragua extends southward into Costa Rica, where the annual rainfall is 150 to 200 inches and there is a short or no dry season. Wetness and disease have discouraged modern settlement of these hot lands, despite the rich alluvial soils of many sections. Nevertheless, some parts, such as the Matina valley near Limón, have been occupied intermittently by Europeans since the colonial era and, between 1880 and 1940, other sections became centers of large-scale banana production.

Costa Rica's largest alluvial plain within the Caribbean lowland is the San Juan River basin, which borders on Nicaragua. This plain continues as the Llanos de Santa Clara southeastward along the coast, in a narrowing wedge to the vicinity of Limón. The vast accumulation of sediment that comprises both of these plains comes mainly from the numerous streams that drain the ash-covered northeastern slopes of the Cordillera Volcánica. Between the plain and the steep mountain escarpment, the same streams have created immense alluvial fans, and these have coalesced to form a continuous alluvial piedmont of fertile, well-drained soils, most of which are ideally suited for tropical agriculture. Farther south, along the Panamanian border, the Sixaola River forms a smaller alluvial plain, part of which extends into Costa Rican territory.

The People

Better than any other Middle American country, Costa Rica displays a single-cluster distribution of population. Well over half the country's 1.8 million people are concentrated in the Meseta Central, and the concentration used to be even greater. San José basin alone contains some of the most densely populated rural areas in Central America (300 to 1,500 per square mile); it also contains the country's largest towns and cities, including the national capital within whose metropolitan area live 420,000 people, 23 percent of Costa Rica's population. Within its city limits (Cantón Central), San José contains 211,000 inhabitants (1970 estimate). Moreover, between 1950 and 1960 Costa Ricans increased at the rate of 3.9 percent annually, one of the highest national growth rates in the world. By 1970, however, the rate had decreased to 2.7 percent, owing in part to the use of birth control measures popularized through family planning services. Rapid population growth, as well as the clustering within the Meseta Central, dates from the late colonial period. The small Meseta Central, only 15 by 40 miles, is truly the political, social, and economic core—and historically the cultural hearth—of Costa Rica.

The people who live outside the Meseta Central are scattered unevenly in various sections of the country that have been settled mainly since Independence (1821). The Pacific versant and the Reventazón River valley from Cartago basin to beyond Turrialba has received most of these settlers. In the Caribbean, only the former banana areas contain a sizable population;

the rest of the forested lowlands and eastern escarpments, with some exceptions, are still sparsely occupied. The greatest *despoblado* of Costa Rica, however, is the high, forested Talamanca Range.

Racial Composition. A characteristic in which the Costa Rican highlander takes special pride is his direct ancestry from colonial settlers who came chiefly from Extremadura and Andalusia in west-central and southern Spain. Within the Meseta Central and surrounding highlands, probably 90 percent of the people consider themselves pure Caucasians. An estimated 17 percent of the entire country's population is mestizo; most of these live in the northwestern province of Guanacaste and along the Pacific coast. Only 2 percent of all Costa Ricans are black; descendants of English-speaking Jamaicans, they are confined mainly to the former banana lands on the Caribbean coast. Isolated remnants of Indians who long ago fled into the remoteness of the Talamanca Range comprise today less than 1 percent of the population.

The Spread of Settlement. The spread of settlement that has occurred in Costa Rica is unique in Middle America. This outward movement has taken place without a decrease of population within the Meseta Central, the core area. Moreover, the settlers have come almost solely from the natural increase of the Costa Rican population. The national government has not controlled this expansion; it has been a spontaneous, unplanned movement of surplus peasants who were seeking new lands for subsistence and commercial farming. Generally, the more important movements have followed new lines of communication. Some colonists, however, have filtered into isolated, rugged hills and mountains far from established roads.

Today, about four-fifths of Costa Rica has been settled, while in 1860 less than one-fifth was occupied; and new settlement continues at an ever-growing pace. Large sections of the remaining frontier zones within the Caribbean lowlands and the high interior mountain areas may be occupied in the near future.

The exceedingly slow population growth and settlement of the Meseta Central during the colonial period was outlined briefly in Chapter 9. Figure 15.7 depicts the major lines of expansion during the nineteenth and twentieth centuries. With the spread of commercial coffee cultivation in the 1820s, the population of the Meseta Central began to

increase markedly, doubling between 1824 and 1844. At that time, settlement spread westward from the Meseta, following a cart road constructed to haul coffee to Puntarenas on the Pacific coast. During the next 20 years, farmers continued to settle northwestward into the Pacific escarpment and on the Guanacaste savannas along the foot of the Cordillera Volcánica. With the completion of a railroad between the Meseta and the Caribbean port of Limón in 1892, settlement expanded eastward along this route down the Reventazón valley, near which the

Figure 15.7   Rural colonization in Costa Rica, nineteenth and twentieth centuries

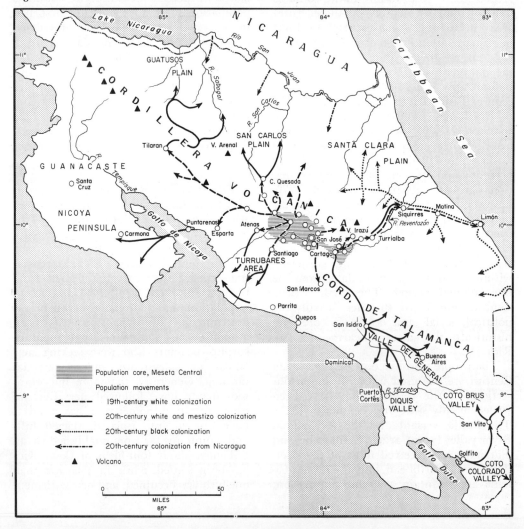

towns of Juan Viñas and Turrialba were founded.

By the close of the century, cattlemen and subsistence farmers had spilled northward across the volcanic range toward the San Carlos plain in the San Juan lowlands. Colonists had also pushed southward to settle the northern foothills of the Talamanca Range. Some penetrated as far south as the upper Valle del General, which later became a major route of expansion in southwestern Costa Rica. But few white peasant farmers from the Meseta Central ventured into the rainy, malarial Caribbean lowlands, and blacks imported to labor on the banana plantations there became the dominant racial group. For many years, the town of Turrialba (1,600 feet elevation) remained the lower limit of white colonization on the eastern escarpment. Since the 1930s, however, large numbers of white highlanders have settled on the abandoned banana lands northwest of Limón and have become successful tropical lowland subsistence and commercial farmers.

The greatest expansion of settlement in the entire history of Costa Rica took place between 1930 and 1960. During this time, the United Fruit Company shifted its banana industry from the Caribbean to the Pacific coastal lowlands. This change involved the inducement of large labor forces—mainly mestizos from Guanacaste and Puntarenas—into the previously sparsely peopled lowlands around Parrita and the valleys of Diquis and Coto Colorado in the southwestern part of the country. A more spectacular colonizing boom took place in the Valle del General, after the Inter-American Highway was completed through the northern end of the Talamanca Range. In 1927, the valley was almost a forested wilderness, containing only 4,800 people. In 1970, it contained more than 75,000 inhabitants, about 20,000 having immigrated from the Meseta Central, between 1950 and 1960, to farm and to pasture livestock on its fertile river floodplains and alluvial ter-

races. In the 1950s, the valley's market towns—San Isidro and Buenos Aires—reflected their recent establishment in their makeshift wooden stores, their muddy streets, and the noisy truck traffic. By 1970, San Isidro, the political and economic center of the valley, had grown to be a well-ordered city of 30,000. In 1962, the Inter-American Highway was completed to Panama, providing a connection to the Golfo Dulce banana area and opening new areas for settlement. A branch highway taps the Coto Brus Valley, where the once-thriving Italian agricultural colony of San Vito was established in 1952 near the Panamanian border.

Highland farmers continue to push northward into the forested lowlands of the San Juan basin. In 1957, a truck road was completed from the Meseta Central into the eastern portion of the northern lowlands along the Sarapiquí River to Puerto Viejo. However, the comparatively few highland farmers who have entered this extremely humid area have done poorly; only a small number of large-scale cattle ranches, sugar estates, and African palm plantations have been profitable. The less humid San Carlos Plain, to the west, has been more successfully colonized by both small farmers and big cattle ranchers. Connected with the Meseta Central by auto road in 1945, the town of Ciudad Quesada has become the area's administrative and market center. By 1972, a paved highway extended to El Muelle on the San Carlos River, and a truck road was being pushed northward into the Guatusos Plains near the Nicaraguan border. On the higher plains near the mountains, small farmers intensively cultivate coffee, sugar cane, and foodstuffs; at lower elevations, ranchers have converted big tracts of rain forest to lush planted pastures for large herds of cattle. The San Carlos Plain appears to be the most promising section of Costa Rica's northern humid lowlands for future settlement.

The Agricultural Economy

Costa Rica is basically an agricultural country. Nearly half the working population is directly engaged in farming; 90 percent of all exports, by value, are agricultural—chiefly coffee, bananas, chilled beef, and cacao; proceeds from crops and livestock make up about 40 percent of the gross domestic product. Patterns of agricultural land use in Costa Rica correspond closely with natural geographic regions and are usually synonymous with a given way of life.

Farming in the Meseta Central. The Meseta Central produces most of Costa Rica's coffee, sugar cane, commercial dairy products, and a substantial amount of the general food crops (Figure 15.8). Of these, coffee is outstanding; since the 1840s, it has been Costa Rica's main export, and its successful cultivation symbolizes wealth and prestige to the small, independent highland farmer.

The main coffee belt occupies the eastern portion of San José basin, including the valley floor and the surrounding mountain slopes up to about 4,200 feet elevation. Natural conditions are almost ideal for high-quality coffee: deep, friable, volcanic soils rich in organic matter; mild, frost-free temperatures; and an average rainfall of 70 inches, with a dry season between January and April for harvesting and processing the coffee beans. An important feature of the area is that the coffee farms are small or of medium size, averaging less than 25 acres. This system of *minifundia* also characterizes many of the newly colonized areas outside this particular area [2] (Figure 15.9).

2. According to the 1955 census, 44 percent of Costa Rica's farms are smaller than 17 acres, and another 36 percent are between 17 and 85 acres. Slightly less than 17 percent of the farms are between 85 and 425 acres. Only 3.5 percent exceed 425 acres, but this group includes the large haciendas and accounts for more than half the total farm acreage.

Figure 15.8   Land utilization: Meseta Central of Costa Rica. Figures indicate feet above sea level.

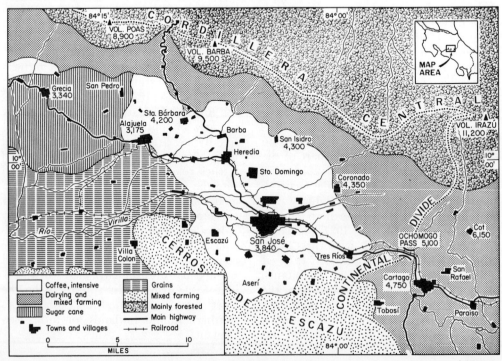

Small holdings within the coffee belt formerly were more numerous than they are today. As the cost of cultivation and processing has risen, many contiguous holdings have been purchased by individuals and companies to form larger and more efficient farms, and the former owners of the small farms often continue to work on the enlarged holdings as hired hands. Large coffee farms are even more common in the Reventazón valley, where some are larger than 500 acres. The consolidation of coffee lands has gone so far in Costa Rica that, today, less than 2 percent of the growers produce more than half the crop. Thus, the big agricultural estate in highland Costa Rica is of relatively recent development, unlike the haciendas in most other Central American countries, which originated in the feudal land tenure system introduced by the Spanish colonists.

In recent years, production on both small and large Costa Rican coffee farms has been substantially increased by more scientific methods—fertilizer, insecticides, and so forth. Between 1952 and 1962, for example, the coffee harvest was doubled, with no increase in acreage. Except for the war years, when trans-Atlantic shipping was curtailed, Costa Rica's best coffee market has been western Europe, especially Germany, where the high quality beans bring special prices. Since 1955, approximately one-third of the harvest has been shipped to the United States, two-thirds to western Europe.

The coffee belt of the Meseta Central contains an unusually large rural population. Most of the roads within the San José basin are bordered almost continuously by dwellings that form line settlements. These wooden, tiled- or tin-roofed houses, often brightly painted, are the homes of small coffee growers or of laborers who work on nearby farms. Each worker usually owns or rents a subsistence plot, of one acre or less, near his house, and grows food for his large family. For-

Figure 15.9　Portion of a small coffee *finca* near Alajuela, Meseta Central. Throughout Central America coffee is grown under shade. In this scene the low coffee bushes form the understory, and are shaded by the tall leguminous trees. (*Instituto Costarricense de Turismo*)

merly, each small coffee grower owned a *carreta,* a two-wheeled cart drawn by a yoke of oxen, to haul coffee and other products to the processing plant and market, but since World War II, the motor truck has come into use and the famed, brightly painted Costa Rican *carreta* is now common only in the more remote rural areas. Auto roads now form a dense network throughout the Meseta Central. Although they are dangerously narrow, most are paved or graveled and lead to the principal markets and administrative centers such as San José, and Alajuela.

In the dry, low, and hilly western part of the Meseta Central, the coffee farm gives way to small holdings on which maize, rice, and other cereal crops are produced. This cereal belt continues westward down the Pacific escarpment, following the Río Grande de Tárcoles valley. West from Alajeula to the town of Grecia, that portion of the Meseta below 2,500 feet is planted chiefly in sugar cane. This area, and the terraces that border the Reventazón River east of Cartago, produce the bulk of Costa Rica's sugar (Figure 15.10).

Figure 15.10 Sugar center of Juan Viñas, upper Reventazón Valley. Fields of sugar cane cover the rolling volcanic surface in the background.

On the high mountain slopes above the coffee belt is located one of the most distinctive economies of Costa Rica—a well-developed dairy industry based on introduced grasses planted at elevations between 4,500 and 9,000 feet. This belt now extends eastward to include the southern slopes of the Irazú and Turrialba volcanoes, as well as the basin of Cartago, which forms the eastern portion of the Meseta Central; it also extends northwestward along the slope of the volcanic chain as far as Tilarán. Settlers from the San José coffee zone began to form small dairy farms on the cool, wet mountain slopes in the 1880s. Since that time, the individual farms have been consolidated, and few small holdings remain. The herds include some of the finest dairy stock in Latin America, derived from Holstein, Jersey, and Guernsey breeds imported from Europe. Quite unlike his Central American neighbors, the Costa Rican highlander consumes large quantities of fresh pasteurized milk, butter, and cheese, mostly from the mountain dairy belt, which is connected with the larger towns in the Meseta by paved roads. A large cooperative does most of the processing in the area, including that of powdered milk and ice cream.

Southwestern Uplands. This large area has a pioneer character. It consists chiefly of low, rugged coastal mountains, the northern and western slopes of the Talamanca Range, and the Valle del General. Much of it was settled only in the past 40 years, and parts are still being colonized. The white subsistence farmers who first came to these mountains as squatters used primitive slash-burn cultivation, destroying large sections of the original forest to make clearings for their small plots of maize, beans, upland rice, and yuca (sweet manioc). On the higher slopes and crest of the Talamanca Range, the once magnificent oak forest has been partially destroyed by lumbermen and charcoal burners; the latter continue to eke out a precarious living and provide the towns of the Meseta Central with charcoal, still the main cooking fuel in the country. At lower elevations erosion has stripped the rather infertile red soil from many hillsides, but most of the cleared sections were converted to pasture after a few years of cropping. Produce is difficult to market, for few good roads exist in the mountainous zones, and farmers live in isolated homesteads or in small hamlets dispersed on the steep slopes.

Pioneer farming conditions are better in the Valle del General, where rolling land, fairly fertile soils, and good roads prevail. Here, in addition to subsistence agriculture, large-scale commercial production of maize, tobacco, coffee, and tropical fruits such as pineapple, has been developed (Figure 15.11). Cattle ranches, using both natural savanna and artificial pastures for grazing, are multiplying. Connected by paved highway to both the Meseta Central and the Golfo Dulce banana plantations, the once-isolated Valle del General now enjoys excellent truck transport for marketing farm products.

Guanacaste. The northwestern corner of Costa Rica—the province of Guanacaste—until recently was a world apart from the central highlands. Throughout the colonial period, this province belonged to Nicaragua, from which it received its major cultural patterns. Not until 1824 was it incorporated into Costa Rica, and only in the past half-century have portions of the area been settled by sizable groups of Costa Rican highlanders.

Guanacaste lies mainly within the *tierra caliente* and is composed of (1) the mountainous, forest-covered Nicoya peninsula; and (2) the savanna plains of the adjacent structural lowland and bordering volcanic mountain slopes to the east. Each of the two natural divisions presents a distinct cultural landscape.

Since the sixteenth century, the savanna lowland has been occupied by large cattle haciendas. Stock raising still dominates most of the savanna areas, and many herds have been upgraded with purebred stock imported from the United States. The ranchers of Guanacaste now supply much of the cattle slaughtered for the thriving chilled beef industry. In the Tempisque River valley, northeast of the Nicoya Gulf, many large landholders have turned to mechanized cultivation of rice and sorghum, having failed in cotton. Scattered throughout the plains are hamlets of subsistence farmers who cultivate maize, beans, and squash and prepare the traditional Mesoamerican tortillas and tamales as did their Chorotegan predecessors in pre-Columbian times.

Since 1890, large numbers of white highlanders, mainly landless peasants from the Cartago basin, have migrated to Guanacaste. Most of these people have settled in the Nicoya peninsula south and west of the traditional cattle country. Small, dispersed holdings on steep slopes, cultivation of beans and upland rice in slash-burn plots for subsistence, together with small fields of coffee and sugar cane for cash crops, raising of hogs and milk cows, use of the highland *carreta,* or two-wheeled cart—such are the Costa Rican traits and landscape features introduced

Figure 15.11   Landscape in the upper Valle del General along the Pacuar River, showing cultivation on stream terraces and hillslopes. Tobacco and maize are the main cash crops here.

by the Cartagos into the Nicoya peninsula. The development of such a cultural dichotomy in Guanacaste province within the last 70 years illustrates the changes that are taking place in Costa Rica, as well as the great diversity of the landscape.

The Caribbean Lowlands. By reason of their peculiar physical characteristics and settlement history, the Caribbean lowlands, including the San Juan River basin of northern Costa Rica, form a distinct economic region. About 10 percent of the country's people reside in this hot, rainy zone. Some lowland areas, such as parts of the San Juan basin, are almost unpopulated; others, in which tropical agriculture has been well developed, have population densities of over 100 people per square mile.

As mentioned earlier, effective settlement of the Caribbean coastal lowlands did not take place until the introduction of large-scale banana plantations in the 1880s. Banana planters considered the coastal section nearly ideal, for three reasons: it has an annual rainfall of 100 inches or more with no dry season; there is abundant, fertile, well-drained alluvial soil close to the coast; and windstorms are infrequent.

The Matina River valley, famed for its cacao groves in colonial days, was the first large area planted to bananas by foreign interests. Plantations next spread westward to the lower Reventazón River in the vicinity of Siquirres. After its incorporation in 1899, the United Fruit Company acquired almost complete control of banana production in Costa Rica and extended cultivation northwestward from the Reventazón along the lower alluvial piedmont within the Santa Clara Plain. Later, the company established plantations southward from Limón along the coastal plain to the Río Estrella and, in 1906, began the development of banana tracts on the Costa Rican side of the Six-

aola River valley across from Panama. Between 1880 and World War I, Costa Rica led all Central American countries in banana production. During this heyday, United Fruit extended rail lines throughout the producing areas to transport fruit to Limón, which was developed as a major Caribbean port. Along the railways, company towns were established to house the English-speaking Jamaican blacks imported as laborers. Thus, by 1910, the whole complex of Caribbean plantation economy had been implanted in the Costa Rican lowlands.

Chiefly because of plant disease, production declined steadily after 1913, and by 1926 United Fruit was forced to abandon large tracts of land in the Santa Clara Plain. In 1938, the company decided to shift its operations to the Pacific coast.

On their former banana lands in the Caribbean lowlands, United Fruit began large-scale cultivation of cacao between Limón and the Reventazón River. Management of the groves was turned over to former black plantation workers, who continued to live in the company towns and along the railroads. Today, cacao is an important product of the lowlands and ranks fourth in Costa Rican exports, after coffee, bananas, and chilled beef.

In 1957, the Standard Fruit Company revived commercial banana production near Limón on a 5,000-acre tract that had long before been abandoned by its rival, United Fruit. Growing the disease-resistant Giant Cavendish banana, the new Standard plantations and small independent holdings produced one-fourth of Costa Rica's total banana output in 1962, and nearly one-half of the total crop in 1970. The new variety has made possible a substantial revival of the banana plantations in the Caribbean lowlands and has helped double Costa Rica's banana exports since the late 1950s.

Since the 1930s, the subsistence farmer has become a significant part of the Caribbean coastal landscape. Many have settled on abandoned banana lands, especially in the upper Santa Clara alluvial piedmont, northwest of the Reventazón River. In 1933, the government purchased most of United Fruit's holdings in this area and parceled them out in small plots to former black plantation workers and to newly arrived white families from the highlands. Although some farmers cultivate cash crops such as cacao, most raise only maize, sweet manioc, and plantains. Blacks have also penetrated into the mountain slopes, where their primitive slash-burn fields, crops, and tools resemble those of their Jamaican homeland. Peasant settlement into the tropical lowlands is still continuing northeastward into the lower Santa Clara Plain, where virgin forest lands are being opened to subsistence cultivation and the grazing of livestock.

Plantation Zones of the Pacific Coast. The alluvial lowlands along Costa Rica's southwestern littoral have been the scene of one of the most recent developments of the tropical plantation in Central America. During 1938 and 1939, the United Fruit Company shifted its banana interests to two disease-free areas on the Pacific coast: (1) the Quepos-Parrita coastal plain and adjacent river valleys; and (2) the Golfo Dulce lowland, near the Panamanian border (Figure 13.7). Both areas are favored by fertile alluvial soils and over 100 inches of rainfall yearly, but a three-month dry season makes irrigation necessary in some sections. Moreover, the Pacific coast suffers from occasional violent storms.

Typical large-scale plantations, complete with a rail network, roads, and company labor towns, were laid out in both areas, and two new ports—Quepos in the northern section and Golfito in the Golfo Dulce—were completed by 1940 as banana shipping centers. The boom in the Parrita-Quepos area, however, was short-lived. After reaching peak production in

1948, most of the plantations became diseased and had to be abandoned. Subsequently, United Fruit planted much of the banana land near Parrita to African oil palm and cacao; other holdings, near Quepos, were reduced to small properties and sold to independent cacao and banana farmers.

Although it was eventually ridden by banana diseases, the Golfo Dulce area maintained production by clearing new land for planting as the plagues forced the abandonment of large tracts. Finally, in 1965, United Fruit converted completely to one of the Cavendish disease-resistant varieties (Valery), and instituted the new system of boxing bananas for shipment. Today, harvests come chiefly from two small alluvial plains: the lower Río Grande de Térraba north of the gulf (the Palmar section) and the Coto Colorado valley adjacent to the Panamanian border, where plantations of African oil palm have also been established. Banana exports leave the Golfo Dulce area through the port of Golfito on the eastern gulf shore. In 1970, one-third was shipped to Japan, the rest to the United States (Figure 15.12).

One of the most spectacular aspects of the banana boom in southwestern Costa Rica was the rapid influx of people into the coastal zone. Between 1938 and 1963, the population of the banana areas increased from a few hundred subsistence farmers to over 70,000 people (and to 90,000 in 1970). Migrants came mainly from Guanacaste and the Meseta Central, but thousands also entered from Nicaragua and adjacent Chiriquí province in Panama. They came as day laborers on the plantations and small merchants in the new port and administrative towns. Thus, a medley of mulattoes, sambos, mestizos, and whites now compose the population along the southwestern coast. Many have taken to subsistence farming in the hills, where the small, scattered slash-burn plots within the tropical rain forest pro-

Figure 15.12 Portion of the banana port of Golfito, on the Golfo Dulce, southwestern Costa Rica. The pier is equipped with modern cranes used to load boxes of bananas on refrigerated ships.

vide a contrast to the rectangular and well-regulated company plantations on the alluvial plains.

Agrarian Problems

For several decades Costa Rica has been plagued by problems of land tenure. Both the size of individual land holdings and the rural population have been steadily increasing. This situation has resulted in the creation of a large group of landless peasants, some of whom gain their livelihood as farmhands, but most have flocked to the cities or have become squatters, or *parásitos* (parasites), on both public and private lands, especially in the frontier areas. The prevalence of squatting by landless farmers has become Costa Rica's most pressing rural problem. The chief motive for the agrarian reform program of 1962 was to legalize the holdings of the present squatters and to attempt to halt further squatting and thereby preserve the remaining forests from destruction by the *parásito's* ax and fires.

One of the programs designed to halt squatting involves the creation of agricultural colonies on public lands or on private holdings purchased by the government in various parts of the country. Within a colony landless peasants are given small parcels of at least 20 acres,

to which they receive full title after making nominal payments. Unfortunately, few of these colonies have been successful; some have been abandoned and others have been invaded by squatters. No good solution of the squatter problem has been found, and the government is still obliged to purchase private land that has been invaded by the *parásitos* and to legalize their claims.

Industry

Like other Central American countries, Costa Rica aspires to industrialize in an attempt to diversify its economy, occupy the growing labor force of the urban areas, and raise the national living standard. Its industry has grown substantially since 1960 under the stimulus of the common market arrangement, and by 1970, about 16 percent of the work force was engaged in manufacturing. Nonetheless, the industrial effort remains on a small scale.

Predictably, industrial development is centered in the capital, San José, and in the neighboring towns of Alajuela, Heredia, and Cartago, where both the major labor supply and local markets are located. Here are concentrated food processing plants, textile mills, and many small shoe and clothing factories, which together produce more than 60 percent of

Geologically, most of the country that lies between the Canal Zone and the Colombian border is the northwestern-most extent of South America. Along the Caribbean coast runs the Serranía de San Blas (1,000 to 3,200 feet), an extension of a northern prong of the Andes. On the Pacific side, the Serranía de Baudó of northwestern Colombia extends into Panamanian territory and continues westward as low hills beyond the Gulf of San Miguel. Between these two low ranges lies a structural depression occupied by the Chepo and Chucunaque river systems. A yearly rainfall of 80 to 120 inches, with a dry period during February and March, is sufficient to support a heavy rain forest, similar to that of northwestern Colombia. Except for flurries of gold mining in Darien, Europeans and mixbloods alike have shunned the hot, humid, disease-ridden forests of eastern Panama since the Spanish Conquest, leaving the area to small groups of blacks and Indians.

The People

Most of Panama's 1.4 million people live in two well-defined regions. Over one-third are concentrated within the present transit area which includes the United States–administered Canal Zone and adjacent Panama City and Colón. Half the total population (and nearly three-quarters of the rural people) inhabit the Pacific lowland and adjacent mountain slopes west of the canal. These two areas of population concentration underscore the duality of Panama's geographical personality. The transit zone is chiefly urban and its people are cosmopolitan, of many races and nationalities; the western Pacific lowland is rural and its people are truly Panamanian, of mixed blood. This fundamental geographical pattern dates from the late sixteenth century, after the rise of Peruvian trade with Spain and the establishment of the transit route across the Panamanian isthmus near the present canal.

Whereas the overall population density of Panama is about 50 persons per square mile, that of the western Pacific lowland averages between 55 and 60; the savanna of Herrera province has rural densities exceeding 100 persons per square mile. Within the transit zone, in 1970, the capital, Panama City, alone contained 425,000 people, nearly 30 percent of the national total. The Caribbean slope of Panama and the province of Darien near Colombia are the least populated sections of the country. There, overall densities range from 3 to 20 persons per square mile, and many forested areas are completely uninhabited. The Caribbean coast has been settled to some degree, chiefly around the Chiriquí lagoon and the Changuinola and Sixaola river valleys, the locale of the Bocas del Toro banana plantations. Moreover, within the past 200 years, the San Blas Cuna Indians have effectively occupied the offshore coral islets along the Caribbean coast east of the Canal Zone. Elsewhere, both the Caribbean versant and the eastern forests remain places for future colonization.

The racial composition of the Panamanians is highly varied. Most of the rural people who live in the western Pacific lowlands are mixed Indian, white, and often black, a mixture which stems from colonial times when the few Spanish cattlemen and, often, their black slaves took Indian wives. More recently, the construction of the Panama Canal attracted English-speaking blacks from Jamaica and Barbados as laborers. Today, a large part of the 44,000 people in the Canal Zone are descendants of these blacks, and many of Jamaican descent now live in Panama City and Colón. A second English-speaking black concentration is found in the plantation zone of Bocas del Toro on the western side of Chiriquí lagoon. Since the 1940s, many of the blacks have migrated to the new banana plantations on the Pacific coast in the vicinity of Puerto Armuelles. Black communities also occur in Darien province, eastern Panama, mainly along the lower courses of rivers that flow into the Gulf of San Miguel. These, however, are Spanish-speaking migrants from the Colombian Chocó and differ from the aggressive Jamaicans in attitudes and customs. The 1940 census [3] classified almost 15 percent of the population of Panama as black.

Although Indians are now only 6 percent of the population, aboriginal groups occupy a large area of the country. Most have retained much of their individuality by retreating into the back country and refusing to blend their culture with the Hispanic (see Figure 13.3). The San Blas Cuna along the Caribbean coast of eastern Panama have already been mentioned; most of the 20,000 Cuna have isolated themselves on the offshore coral islands, where they cultivate maize and manioc for subsistence and coconuts for cash. Only a handful now occupy their original homeland along the rivers in the interior. The Guaymí, who have retreated into the forested slopes of the Cordillera Central in western Panama, are the largest Indian group in the country. Some 25,000 today form the remnant of a large pre-Conquest population that once occupied most of central Panama. A much smaller group, a few hundred Chocó, live on the upper river courses in Darien near the Colombian border; these forest people are the least acculturated Indians in Middle America.

Some 10 to 12 percent of the Panamanians are classified as Caucasians. Most of these are descendants of old Spanish families who form the upper class and live principally in Panama City.

The Economy

Panama's dual personality—the urban cosmopolitanism of the transit zone and the rural provincialism of the western Pacific lowlands—is reflected not only in popula-

tion distribution, but even more so in the nation's economy. Well over half of Panama's income derives directly from trade, transport, and related activities within the transit area. Only one-quarter of the country's wealth comes from agriculture and stock raising, mainly in the western Pacific lowlands and adjacent mountain slopes. Agriculturally, Panama is the least developed of the Central American countries. Less than 15 percent of the national territory is cultivated, although about 40 percent of the economically active population is engaged in farming or stock raising. Until recently, the country had to import large quantities of rice and maize, and the transit area, especially the Canal Zone, still imports much food from the United States. In 1970, however, farm products (chiefly bananas from foreign-owned plantations) accounted for two-thirds of Panama's total exports by value.

Agricultural Patterns. Since colonial times, the western Pacific lowland has been the country's most important farming and stock-raising area, supplying meat and some grains to the transit area. By the mid-sixteenth century, Spanish cattlemen occupied the rolling central savannas. By the end of the eighteenth century, a mestizo population of white, Indian, and black mixtures had developed in this area. Many were employed as cowhands on the large haciendas; others owned small tracts on which they raised food and cattle, shipping their surplus to Panama City. But most had become small subsistence farmers practicing the ancient Indian system of slash-burn cultivation on forested hill slopes inland from the savannas. Out of these elements has evolved the present-day peasant of the central savannas. This area is the hearth of Panamanian rural life. Here are still found most of the old food habits, house types, and social customs typical of the peasant during the last century; from here, migrants settled in other parts of the western Pacific lowlands in the early nineteenth century.

3. This was the last census taken in Panama that identified racial groups other than Indian.

Figure 15.13   The typical *bohío* of rural Panama. The wattle-daub walls and thatched roof derive from Indian culture; the attached kitchen with tiled roof may be of Spanish origin.

SUBSISTENCE FARMING. Most of the peasants of the western Pacific lowland, as elsewhere in Panama, are migratory slash-burn farmers who have inherited many Indian farming practices. Most of them hold no property titles, but squat on government land or rent plots from large owners. They live in scattered dwellings or small hamlets on forested hillslopes, raising rice, maize, beans, plantains, and a variety of root crops in small fields that are abandoned after two or three years of continuous cropping. Around their aboriginal-type dwellings *(bohíos)* of thatch and wattle, small patches of sugar cane and clumps of peach palms *(pejibaye)* or coconuts add to the typical rural scene (Figure 15.13). The machete and the dibble are the main tools, while ox-drawn wooden plows are rare.

Since the colonial period, rice, introduced by the Spaniards before 1600, has become the main food in both urban and rural Panama. Mixed beans and rice *(guacho)* is the national dish of the rural people. Of nearly equal importance are yuca (sweet manioc) and the Old World plantain, main ingredients of *sancocho,* a filling potage. Panamanian peasants eat much less maize than their Central American neighbors, chiefly in the form of the Mesoamerican tortilla and tamale and the South American maize cake *(arepa)* and mildly fermented corn beer *(chicha).*

The prevalence of primitive slash-burn farming in Panama is made evident by the fact that from the small hillside plots come 75 percent of the country's rice crop and almost all its maize, beans, plantains, and starchy tubers. With the improvement of roads, an increasingly larger part of this produce is reaching urban markets.

Today it is estimated that over 60 percent of all farms in Panama are small plots operated by slash-burn squatters mainly on national lands. Although the government's agrarian institute urges the peasants to take up permanent homesteads of 25 acres free of charge, few do so because their practice of migratory cultivation discourages permanent settlement, and few comprehend the concept of private ownership. With the increase of rural population, the habitual practice of slash-burn squatting may soon become a serious ecological and socioeconomic problem. For that reason a fundamental goal of Panama's Agrarian Code of 1962 was the legalization of tenure for squatters and changes in their farming practices to effect better use of the land. In addition to free cultivation of national lands, squatters may also gain legal rights to plots they have cultivated for 10 years on privately owned property. Moreover, in some instances, the government has expropriated large estates because of nonpayment of taxes, so that the land might be redistributed to squatters.

A variant of the slash-burn farming in the western Pacific lowlands occurs in the more level parts of the central savannas, where peasants combine crop cultivation with small-scale stock raising. Their holdings, of 50 to 100 acres, are chiefly planted pastures where as many as 100 head of cattle can graze. However, these farmers consider their small rice and maize fields to be their major source of food and cash. Such farms are characteristic of the dry eastern side of the Azuero peninsula near the market towns of Chitré and Las Tablas. This area is the center of Hispanic culture in the western Pacific lowlands, and here one finds a concentration of tile-roofed houses, ox-carts, and a large per-

Figure 15.14 Artificial pasture of pará grass near Chitré, central savannas of Panama (*R. H. Fuson*)

centage of Caucasians. It is likewise the most densely populated rural section of Panama, although many migrants are leaving the area for Panama City or slowly penetrating northward to colonize the forest lands along the crest of the Cordillera Central.

STOCK RAISING. The large stock ranch is the oldest agricultural enterprise of Spanish origin in Panama. Many cattle haciendas in the Pacific lowlands were settled in colonial times in the dry plains and hills within the central savanna. Since the mid-nineteenth century, many more prosperous stock ranches have been established in the cleared sections within the southern versant of the Cordillera Central and in the wet coastal plain of Chiriquí province near David. The principal

market for the cattle haciendas is the transit area—the slaughter houses and packing plants of Panama City, Colón, and the Canal Zone. Most of the animals destined for this market originate in the coastal pastures of Chiriquí, which also supplies cattle for the growing chilled beef export industry (Figure 15.14).

COMMERCIAL AGRICULTURE. Large-scale commercial farming began with the banana plantations of Panama's Caribbean coast during the 1880s. Plant disease caused this large enterprise to shift to the Pacific coastal plain in the late 1920s, and the western Pacific lowland has since become Panama's main producer of agricultural exports and the center of mechanized farming (Figure 15.15).

Mechanized farming is exemplified by

Figure 15.15 Commercial economy of Panama. Only selected items are shown.

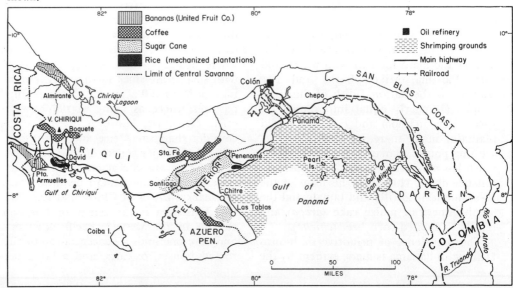

the large, irrigated rice plantations of the Chiriquí coastal plain, near David, and along the Coclé coast in the vicinity of Antón (Figure 15.16). Their high yields furnish a quarter of the country's rice, and they have made Panama a self-sufficient producer of its major staple food since 1953. Moreover, between 1960 and 1970, sugar cane production in Panama tripled, chiefly because of the increased quotas for the United States market. Over half the export crop is grown and milled on large holdings in the eastern part of the central savannas (Coclé province). Sugar for local rural consumption, however, is still harvested on small plots, and the energy-giving brown sugar *(panela)* is processed in crude animal-powered mills.

Coffee has never been a major commercial crop in Panama. It was first planted in the rich soils of the Boquete valley on the southern slopes of Chiriquí volcano about 1900 and became a significant crop only after World War II. As late as 1957, coffee was still being imported, but, with increased production in the Boquete area and the establishment of small coffee farms on the Pacific slope of the Cordillera Central in Veraguas province, Panama finally entered the world coffee market in 1958.

The United Fruit Company's banana plantations in extreme southwestern Panama, in the vicinity of Puerto Armuelles, are the most highly developed form of commercial agriculture in the country. This small area is an eastward continuation of the company's Costa Rican banana holdings in the Coto Colorado River plain and possesses the same natural advantages —heavy rainfall (120 inches annually) and fertile alluvial soils (within the Chiriquí River flood plain). By 1940, the Puerto Armuelles plantations were in full production, only to be curtailed by the lack of shipping facilities during World War II. Since 1948, banana exports from the area have increased steadily. In 1962, the old banana lands in the Bocas del Toro district on the Caribbean (mainly in the Changuinola River valley) were replanted with disease-resistant varieties. Today, this area accounts for one-third of Panama's banana production, which is shipped from the refurbished port of Almirante. Since 1964, bananas have accounted for more than half of Panama's exports by value.

Fishing. One of Panama's most spectacular economic developments since World War II is the rise of shrimping in

Figure 15.16   A field of irrigated rice near Divisa, central savannas of Panama (*R. H. Fuson*)

the shallow, muddy coastal waters around the Gulf of Panama (Figure 15.15). By 1960, shrimping contributed one-fourth of the country's total export receipts, but by 1971, this proportion had decreased to about 10 percent. The catch is frozen in six packing plants in Panama City, and most of it is shipped to the United States. A fleet of some 240 trawlers, chiefly of Panamanian registry, now operate in the gulf. Trash fish caught in shrimp nets, as well as commercial catches of anchovies and thread herring off the coast, are processed into fish meal and oil in plants near Panama City. As in Mexico and the neighboring Central American countries, the rapid rise of commercial fishing is a belated exploitation of a valuable Middle American coastal resource. It also illustrates the relation of resource development to the United States market, which fluctuates according to public taste and affluence.

Transportation and Trade

THE TRANSIT ZONE.   Even as a Colombian province, Panama lived mainly by the trade and transport conducted over its transisthmian road. This pattern continues today, for Panama has a special political and economic relationship with the United States and has become highly dependent on the canal. Moreover, because of its strategic position in world oceanic shipping and its military vulnerability, the Panamanian transit zone is now one of the world's most politically sensitive areas.

The present transit area, as here defined, includes the United States–administered Canal Zone, the terminal cities of Panama and Colón, and the area adjacent to the transisthmian highway, which passes through national territory a few miles east of the Canal Zone (Figure 15.17). Within this area live 600,000 people, 90 percent of whom are urban, and who comprise 40 percent of Panama's total population. Apart from the canal itself, the transit area is a complex of cities, towns, military installations, highways, and railroads. The bustling economic activity within the area generates over half the national income, partly in the form of wages paid to nationals working in the Canal Zone and partly through trade with United States citizens who are Canal Zone residents and through trade with tourists and foreign transients. Panama's growing manufacturing industries are also concentrated in or near the transit area.

THE CANAL ZONE.   According to the United States–Panama treaty of 1903, the Canal Zone comprises a strip of land extending five miles on either side of the canal, including Gatun and Madden lakes. This area, however, excludes Panama City and the coastal plain eastward thereof, as well as the city of Colón on the Caribbean. The treaty gave the United States what has amounted to "perpetual sovereignty" over the Canal Zone, but the interpretation of such rights has caused much friction between the two nations in recent years. In return, the United States now pays Panama an annuity of nearly two million dollars.

Today Panamanians resent American occupation of what they consider to be the most important segment of their national territory. This resentment, an outgrowth of intense nationalism, has increased to the extent that most Panamanians now favor the demand that the United States relinquish control of the canal and the Canal Zone to their country. The Canal Zone riots of 1964 led to an agreement with the United States to renegotiate the 1903 treaty. To date, little progress has been made toward a revision, but the United States has conceded in principle that the "in perpetuity" provision must be dropped.

The canal is a lock-and-lake type, with elaborate sets of locks that raise ships from ocean level to Gatun Lake level, normally 85 feet above the sea. Gatun Lake, a reser-

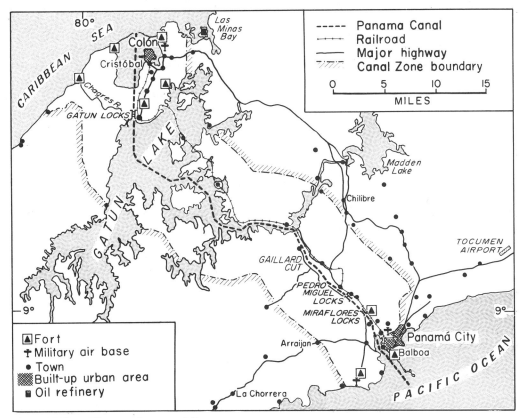

Figure 15.17   The transit zone of Panama

voir created by damming the Chagres River, supplies water for the locks and serves as a waterway for half the 51-mile distance across the isthmus (Figure 15.18). Hydroelectric plants at Gatun Dam and Madden Dam (completed in 1935) furnish power for the entire Canal Zone, including operation of the locks. The canal crosses the continental divide through the famous 8-mile Gaillard Cut, a 200-foot-deep trench constructed by United States engineers and British West Indian black laborers at the expense of many lives and after seven years of toil (1907–1914).

Figure 15.18   Miraflores Locks on the Pacific side of the Panama Canal. In the background is Miraflores Lake and the Pedro Miguel Locks, through which ships are lifted to the level of Gaillard Cut and Gatun Lake. (*Panama Canal Company*)

In recent years, the constantly increasing traffic (more than 14,000 ships in 1972) making the eight-hour trip through the canal has led to serious congestion. Moreover, the locks are too narrow (110 feet) to accommodate the largest ships. In addition, the locks are militarily vulnerable, and Panama is seriously challenging the United States' complete control of the Zone. All these factors have prompted serious planning for a new sea-level canal in some other part of the Central American isthmus. At present, the most likely choice for a new one is the La Chorrera–Lagarto route, only ten miles west of the existing canal.

As a United States–owned reservation, the Canal Zone's functions include the operation, maintenance, and protection of the canal and its installations. For this purpose about 44,000 people inhabit the Canal Zone; of these, 40 percent are blacks, chiefly descendants of West Indian laborers, and the rest are United States white residents, or "Zonians"—the administrators, engineers, and skilled laborers who operate and maintain the canal installations. They live in cities and towns scattered through the Zone, the largest being Balboa, adjacent to Panama City, and Cristóbal, which borders Colón on the Caribbean. Balboa and Cristóbal, the terminal stations of the canal, contain the main docks in the transit area for oceangoing ships. In addition, the Canal Zone bristles with military installations—army camps, forts, airfields, naval yards, and communication centers—all of which house a sizable personnel.

Both a railroad and a highway connect the terminal points of the isthmus. The Panama Railroad, which parallels the canal, was constructed as a convenience for transisthmian ship passengers and to facilitate maintenance of installations. As a military measure during World War II, the United States government built the Transisthmian Highway within Panama-nian territory a few miles east of the Canal Zone, cutting transit time from Panama City to Colón to less than two hours by auto.

PANAMA CITY AND COLÓN. That part of the transit area under direct Panamanian jurisdiction is dominated by two cities, the capital and Colón. Panama City, with 425,000 people, 30 percent of the nation's population, crammed into its confines, exemplifies the dominance of the primate city better than any other Middle American capital. The next largest urban centers are Colón, with 70,000 inhabitants, and then the small provincial cities of David (35,000) and La Chorrera (26,000), the latter located just west of the Canal Zone. Highly mixed racially and nationally, both Panama City and Colón live by trade. A free trade zone opened in Colón in 1951, creating an economic boom there that has enhanced the trade of the entire transit area and instigated the development of light industry in the Colón area.

Since World War II, Panama City and Colón have become industrialized. A substantial part of the nation's light industry is located in Panama City, which has food processing plants, wood products factories, and clothing manufacturing shops. Power for light industry comes from several local thermoelectric plants. With the completion of the large hydroelectric station under construction on the Bayano River east of Panama City, the country's industrial potential will be greatly increased.

Panama's first heavy industry (1958) was a small steel mill using local scrap; the latest, which is one of the most spectacular recent industrial developments in all Central America, is the petroleum refinery on Las Minas Bay, five miles east of Colón. This mainly United States–owned refinery began operations in 1962 with a 55,000 barrel-per-day capacity, which has been recently increased to 70,000. Using imported Venezuelan crude, the refinery supplies Panama's needs and furnishes many Central American countries with several kinds of petroleum products. The refinery has also attracted other industries, such as petrochemical plants, making Minas Bay a likely site for the development of an industrial center. Petroleum products now account for a quarter of Panama's export trade by value and are second to bananas as the country's chief earner of foreign exchange.

Future exploitation of mineral deposits recently discovered in Panama may increase the country's industrial potential. In 1969 and 1971, two huge copper deposits were revealed in the Cordillera Central, and negotiations are under way to develop both. Again, in 1972, a local firm began mining high-grade iron ore (magnetite) from the black sand beaches west of Panama City, but all the material is shipped to Japan for processing.

The development of Panama's manufacturing industry, however, is handicapped by a small domestic market. Closer trade ties with neighboring countries, including full membership in the faltering Central American Common Market, do not insure a wider market for manufactured goods. Panama's hope for industrialization perhaps lies with the increasing affluence of its large urban population, a doubtful prospect at best.

THE INTER-AMERICAN HIGHWAY. While the main axis of Panamanian transport is the transisthmian transit zone, a secondary axis trends east–west along the Pacific lowlands, where the Inter-American Highway has been completed through the settled part of the country from Costa Rica to Panama City. A number of feeder roads have been constructed from the highway northward into the lower slopes of the Cordillera Central and southward into the Azuero Peninsula. Eastward from Panama City the Inter-American Highway continues only 54 miles to the village of Chepo. Beyond lies the vast forest-covered wilderness of eastern Panama and the Chocó of northwestern Colombia, which forms today the only gap in the intercontinental road from Fairbanks, Alaska, to Buenos Aires, Argentina.

SELECTED REFERENCES

BIESANZ, J., and BIESANZ, M. *The People of Panama*. New York: Columbia University Press, 1955.

FUSON, R. H. "Land Tenure in Central Panama." *Journal of Geography* 63, no. 4 (1964): 161–68.

GUZMÁN, L. E. *Farming and Farmlands in Panama*. University of Chicago, Department of Geography Research Paper no. 44. Chicago: University of Chicago Press, 1956.

HILL, G. W. "The Agrarian Reform in Costa Rica." *Land Economics* 40, no. 1 (1964): 41–8.

INCER, J. *Geografía Ilustrada de Nicaragua*. Managua: Librería y Editorial Recalde, 1973.

LEÓN, J. "Land Utilization in Costa Rica." *Geographical Review* 38, no. 3 (1948):444–56.

NIETSCHMANN, B. *Between Land and Water: The Subsistence Ecology of the Miskito Indians, Eastern Nicaragua*. New York: Seminar Press, 1973.

NUNLEY, R. E. *The Distribution of Population in Costa Rica*. Publication no. 743. Washington, D.C.: National Research Council, 1960.

RUBIO, A., and GUZMÁN, L. "Regiones Geográficas Panameñas." *Revista Geográfica* 24, no. 50 (1959):53–66.

SANDNER, G. *Agrar-kolonisation in Costa Rica: Siedlung, Wirtschaft und Sozialgefüge an* der *Pioniergrenze.* Schriften des Geographischen Instituts der Universitat Kiel 19, no. 3. Kiel, 1961. Spanish trans.: *La Colonización Agrícola de Costa Rica.* San José: Instituto Geográfico de Costa Rica, 1962–1964.

SQUIER, E. G. *Nicaragua: Its People, Scenery, Monuments, and the Proposed Interoceanic Canal.* New York: D. Appleton, 1852.

TAYLOR, B. W. *Ecological Land Use Surveys in Nicaragua.* Managua: Instituto de Fomento Nacional, 1959–1961.

WAGNER, P. L. "Nicoya, a Cultural Geography." *University of California Publications in Geography* 12, no. 3 (1958):195–250.

= 16 =

Middle America:
Summary and Outlook

SALIENT PATTERNS
AND PROBLEMS

It is difficult to generalize about the lands and peoples of Middle America. The effect of a varied history on an equally varied physical environment has been to create a vast array of landscapes, cultures, and ways of life. No one economic model can portray the numerous ways in which the land is exploited; no single cultural description can embrace the ethnic, linguistic, and religious heterogeneity of the people; and no chart of organization can outline the many forms of government. The area's diversity is rooted in pre-Columbian times and in the Conquest (see Chapter 1); it has persisted and it has even been increased by poor communications, special economic interests, and political disunity.

Nor is it easy to classify or pattern the area's landscape and customs. Except in a few cases, such as Hispaniola, international boundaries are seldom a meaningful guide to cultural differentiation. Ways of life frequently vary more within the same country than between countries. Many of the ways of the southern Mexicans, for example, are more like the Guatemalans' than the northern Mexicans' (see Chapters 11, 12, and 13). Similarly, the patterns that create uniformity in the

Rimland as contrasted to the Mainland (see Chapter 1) have evolved with little regard to state boundaries.

Frequently, the most obvious common denominators in Middle America are its problems. Thus, the localism born of diversity has made it difficult to establish stable government almost everywhere. The same localism is also partially responsible for the fragmentation of the area into a multiplicity of states, most of which are too limited in size and resources to be economically viable. Note, for example, the failure of the West Indies Federation and the many obstacles that impede the progress of the Central American Common Market.

Cultural diversity and localism have also militated against the crystallization of a strong sense of nation in many territories. To what extent do the Indians of Guatemala or the Jamaican blacks of Costa Rica participate in national life? Is it realistic to consider the Creoles and East Indians of Trinidad as the same nation? The strong bond of nation that unites the people of the United States, or of Japan, or of most European states requires a degree of cultural uniformity, a sharing of common goals, a knowledge of history, and a communication of ideas that are largely lacking to the indigenous and peasant populations of most Middle American countries.

The most important problems that the peoples of Middle America share are economic. Chief among these are a history of exploitation by outsiders; a narrow commerce which is subject to the whims of foreign markets; a distribution of wealth so unequal as to create extreme poverty and great affluence; and, above all, an increase in population that is dangerously out of proportion to the countries' economic growth.

Population Problems

Many of Middle America's problems pertain directly to population. In most of the area, growth rates continue high, and the pressure of people on resources is increasing. Population pressure is compounded by the tendency, particularly on the Mainland, for settlement to concentrate in selected regions, separated by thinly populated areas. Within the settled regions, the gulf separating urban life styles from those of the countryside remains wide; and the flow of people from the rural areas to the towns and cities, especially to the primate city, is growing.

Growth Trends. One measure of the growing pressure of population in Middle America is the high rate of natural increase in recent decades. Virtually everywhere in the area the death rate is dropping while the birth rate is more than twice that of the United States. As a result, Middle America's total population, which was around 50 million in 1950, reached 60 million by 1960 and jumped to over 90 million by 1970.

People-to-land ratios are highest in the Antilles but, because of the irregular distribution of population, the pressure of population is almost as high in the settled sectors of the Mainland. In Mexico, the bulk of the inhabitants are still concentrated in the old Mesoamerican highland centers; the Mesa Central, only 16 percent of the country's area, contains over 55 percent of its population. Over 90 percent of the inhabitants of Central America live on the Pacific side of the isthmus, the highest densities being in the western highlands and in the foothills bordering the coastal lowlands.

Nucleation. Nucleation, initially begun by the selective occupance of the colonial Spanish, persists particularly on the Mainland, although it is also found on the larger islands of the West Indies. There are clear-cut concentrations of population, each forming the tributary area of a major city and separated by empty or lightly occupied areas across which transportation is often very difficult. Overlapping of tributary areas of the major urban centers, so common in Anglo-America and western Europe, where cities tend to develop specialized functions, is rare in Middle America.

In most political entities of Middle America, there is a single concentrated area of settlement, spreading out from the territory's chief city and capital. This is so everywhere in the West Indies, except in Hispaniola, and it is so in most of Central America, except in Panama where the canal has necessitated more than one nucleus, and in Honduras, which has a highland population clustered around Tegucigalpa and a Caribbean nucleus around San Pedro Sula, Tela, and La Ceiba. In Haiti and the Dominican Republic, there are two concentrated settlements—one in the north, around Cap-Haïtien and Santiago, and one in the south, around Port-au-Prince and Santo Domingo. In Mexico there are several concentrated settlements, each with its urban center, but most of these are on the Mesa Central and are less clear-cut. Where more than one concentrated settlement exists, the area which contains the territory's capital city is generally larger, has a greater population, and is more economically developed.

Urban-Rural Contrasts. An enormous socioeconomic gulf separates the urban centers from their rural tributaries. In the city, the streets are often crowded with automobiles; the stores are modern and well-stocked; beautiful buildings and monuments are much in evidence; and professional services compare favorably with those of Anglo-American centers. If one can overlook their beggars and the odoriferous shanties on their fringes, the cities of Middle America—like the cities everywhere in Latin America—create the impression of wealth and conspicuous consumption. But often, only a few miles outside the city, the conditions are those of another world and another era. Gone are the automobiles—not only because the country people cannot afford them but because the roads are inadequate. The well-stocked store is replaced by the little *kiosko* or *tienda,* which sells codfish or beans, work clothes, and cheap native liquor. The city's beautiful buildings give way to one-room *bohios* or adobe huts, and the only monuments are the scars of erosion on the misused land.

Consumption by the cities of Middle America of the wealth produced by their hinterlands is in keeping with the feudal tradition established by the early Spaniards and, to a lesser degree, by the northern European planters and merchants. From the first, their cities drew the landowners, the clerical and lay officials, and the other elements which were to become aristocracy, and they brought their colored and mestizo servants and their artisans. The early locus of wealth and activity, the city has had a magnetic attraction for the poverty-stricken people of the countryside ever since. As a result, the cities are too big, and the line of rural settlements too thin. The proportion of people who live in cities is surprisingly high. Not every city is equally magnetic, however. In each

country there is one city, usually the capital, which is several times larger than its runner-up.

The Middle American city is the collecting and distributing center, the administrative center, the educational center, and the religious center of the area around it. The city provides all the services available to its hinterland. Since urban areas rarely overlap and since the economy is based largely on agriculture, grazing, and mining, a city with specialized functions (such as Monterrey, in Mexico) is a great exception. In the Rimland, most of the chief cities are also ports. On the Mainland, where the chief urban center is almost invariably in the upland interior, twin cities, one a port, have evolved. Mexico City and Veracruz are such twin cities.

Although the urban population everywhere in Middle America is increasing more rapidly than the population as a whole, the great majority of Middle Americans, on the Mainland and the Rimland, still live in rural settlements. The economy would not permit otherwise. The percentage of rural population varies, however. On some of the West Indian islands, for example, the rural population may be as high as 85 percent of the total. In the crowded territories, such as Barbados and Haiti, it is often difficult to differentiate between urban and rural settlement—not only because of the high density of rural population but also because of the women, especially, who walk daily to the markets in the towns.

There are also wide differences in the type of rural settlement. The dominant rural settlement on the Mainland is an agglomerated one. Less than 1 percent of the Mexican people, for example, live in dispersed, isolated farmsteads; roughly 10 percent live in hamlets whose populations are under 100; more than half live in villages whose populations are 101 to 2,500; and the remainder live in even larger settlements. In the Rimland, the plantation manor houses were the core of agglomerated hamlets. Many of these remain, but dispersed settlement is more widespread than on the Mainland, for several reasons. In many of the West Indian islands, the terrain is mountainous. This confined the plantations to the coastal plains and valley bottoms, leaving the highlands to small holders and squatters. In Puerto Rico, for example, and in Cuba, to a lesser degree, a white peasantry invaded the less desirable mountain lands at an early date and developed a semisubsistence agriculture that included the growing of tobacco and, sometimes, coffee, for sale. Virtually everywhere in the West Indies, the emancipation of the slaves increased the dispersion of rural settlement. Wherever sufficient land was available, the emancipated blacks abandoned the estates in large numbers and established themselves as subsistence farmers. Generally, the land that was not already pre-empted was in the uplands, but, even in the lowlands, the subdivision and sale of some bankrupt estates provided the blacks with dispersed plots.

In most of Middle America, the trend seems to be toward agglomerated settlements. This may be partly due to the tempo of urbanization and partly to improved transportation and other factors. As roads penetrate into previously inaccessible areas, hamlets often string out along the artery. There are some exceptions to the general rule of increasing agglomeration, however, especially in El Salvador, Honduras, Costa Rica, and other Central American territories.

Economic Aspects

From the very beginnings of colonization, Middle America was regarded as a source of quick wealth either for the ruling metropolis or the small group of local aristocrats. Inevitably, the colonial economy developed in lopsided fashion. Only the exploitation of immediately profitable products and resources was undertaken long-range; systematic development of the territories and the welfare of the masses were disregarded by the privileged. More than four centuries after Columbus, a large part of the area's economy is still essentially colonial.

Agriculture. Nothing illustrates the imbalance and the colonialism of Middle America's economy more dramatically than agriculture, the area's chief occupation. In most territories, the economic structure is like an inverted pyramid resting on a few export crops, and it is so precariously balanced that any threat to the exports threatens the entire economic structure.

Equally serious problems stem from land use and tenure, from primitive agricultural techniques and practices, from plant disease, from erosion, from poor soils, and from other factors. The soil, for example, is not generally abundant or exceptionally fertile. Some soils, as in northern Mexico, receive too little rain and cannot be cultivated without costly irrigation; others, particularly the leached clays of the humid tropical lowland, cannot be permanently cultivated without heavy applications of fertilizer or frequent fallowing. Still others are on mountains too steep to cultivate.

As a result, agriculture in Middle America is spotty. Production is concentrated, for the most part, on narrow strips of coastal plains, on irrigated oases, on river valleys, or on suitable mountain basins. The volcanic soils of the upland areas and the riverine alluvial deposits are generally the most productive. Elsewhere the yield is low, because of natural infertility, long use and misuse, erosion, and inefficient farming. The percentage of land under cultivation varies widely, but it is generally much higher in the more densely populated West Indies than on the Mainland. In Mexico and Central America, the land in crops amounts to less than one-tenth of the total, though in a few crowded spots, such as El Salvador, it is as high as one-quarter.

Perhaps even more than the modest or poor soils, the traditional systems of land tenure account for the deficient state of agriculture in Middle America. These systems normally include (1) large landholdings *(latifundia)*, i.e., haciendas, plantations, or estates, which may be family- or corporate-owned and which are devoted to commercial production; and (2) small holdings *(minifundia)*, i.e., peasant-owned parcels, tenant worker plots on estates, communal lands, leased-lands, and share-cropped lands.

The best lands are owned by the large holders, a practice that has roots in both the Hispanic and northern European traditions in Middle America. On these large tracts are produced the commercial crops that may benefit a few and contribute little to the well-being of the area. True, some workers are employed and otherwise benefited, but the lion's share of the profits goes to the owners. The small farmer, the bulk of Middle America's population, is forced to cultivate the marginal lands. *Latifundia* also fosters the prestige of ownership. Land is bought for this reason or for possibly expanded operations, or simply in the hope that its value will rise. Much of this reserve land is put to little or no use.

On the *latifundia* sugar, coffee, cacao, cotton, sisal, animal products, and food crops such as wheat are produced. These products may be sold overseas, as is most of the Rimland produce and the coffee, cotton, and sisal produced on the Mainland, or they may be sold locally. In either case, they stimulate monoculture and retard, if not prevent, the emergence of a well-rounded agricultural economy. When the market is overseas, there is a slavish dependence on the vagaries of foreign demand and price. A drop of a few cents in the price of coffee on the New York Commodities Exchange creates widespread distress in the coffee regions of Central America.

The small holders grow food, primarily for their families but also for the local market. In Middle America as a whole, these small growers are the bulk of the agricultural labor force; yet food has to be imported into many areas, and most of the people are poorly nourished. The major food crops on most of the Mainland, particularly in the old Indian centers, are corn, beans, squash, and a variety of peppers. Crops may vary, especially in the different climatic zones of the highlands. In the Rimland, corn is less important. Starchy vegetable tubers, such as yams and manioc, and tree crops, such as breadfruit, plantains, and bananas, are grown. Rice is a staple in much of Middle America and is raised in many territories, but much is also imported from the Far East and the United States. Wheat is also widely grown and often imported.

Yields of the small holdings are low, partly because they are marginal lands and partly because they are not worked well. Most subsistence farmers are still using primitive techniques that originated with the Mainland Indians and on the Rimland with African slaves. Simple iron tools, such as the machete and the hoe are probably the most widespread technological innovations. The ox and the plow are not extensively used for food crops even on some of the haciendas.

Outside the grazing areas, farm animals are few, and here are often scavengers such as pigs, poultry, and goats. This scarcity of animals precludes the use of barnyard manure as fertilizer, and commercial fertilizer is beyond the means of the small holder. Crop rotation is known, but fertile land is so scarce that it is often under the same basic crops. The marginal land cultivated by small holders is often on hillslopes, and erosion is a major problem virtually everywhere.

Forests and Fisheries. The exploitation of the forests is locally important in a few areas, such as Hispaniola and parts of Central America and Mexico, but its contribution to the overall economy of Middle America is negligible. The more accessible forests have been virtually destroyed by the expansion of agriculture and the lack of conservation. This is particularly true of the once-extensive Caribbean lowland pine forests of Cuba. Even now, there is heavy and destructive cutting of Central American lowland pine, from British Honduras to Nicaragua. The mountain pine forests, which are less accessible, have been less exploited, but now highland pine forests, such as those of the Dominican Republic and Mexico, are being subjected to heavy cutting. Once-valuable areas of cabinet woods such as tropical cedar and mahogany, in the West Indies and Central America, have been logged dry.

Tropical forest industries, such as the gathering of drugs, resins, gums, and other items, have lost their markets to synthetic products. Despite the decreasing commercial importance of forestry in Middle America, however, the native subsistence economy relies heavily on the trees for buildings, fences, and charcoal fuel.

The history of the fisheries has been even more tragic. In pre-Columbian days, many of the circum-Caribbean tribes, such as the Caribs, relied heavily on the sea harvest to supplement the food produced by farming. Fish from the rivers, mollusks from the coast, and sea turtles and manatees were once important to the Europeans in the Rimland also. But overexploitation has erased this abundance, and, except possibly in Mexico, only a handful of part-time workers fish in each territory. In fact, much of the fish, such as the dried salt cod which is consumed in many areas, is imported from Canada, the United States, and Europe.

Minerals and Energy Fuels. The list of minerals in Middle America is a long one, but only a few are plentiful enough to warrant exploitation, and these are irregularly distributed. Mexico is easily the leading repository of mineral wealth. In Central America, except for the limited production of precious metals, especially in Honduras and Nicaragua, mining is negligible. Minerals are of only limited importance in Cuba and the Dominican Republic, but of notable importance to the economies of Trinidad and Jamaica. Petroleum, the fond hope of the Rimland, is produced in significant quantities only in Mexico and Trinidad. Other mineral resources of some importance are copper, lead, zinc, silver, and iron, in Mexico; bauxite, in Jamaica; and nickel and manganese, in Cuba. Water power is an important potential source of energy; but only about 1 percent has been actually developed. A deficiency of minerals and fuels is the rule in Middle America.

Manufacturing. The census data for most Middle American territories generally include a large number of factories. Most of these, however, are household enterprises or small establishments, which employ less than a dozen workers. They produce bricks, bread, and other items for their own localities. The larger establishments are often sugar *centrales* and other processing plants. In most of the large cities, where manufacturing is concentrated, the list of products includes beverages, matches, building materials, pharmaceutical products, and the like. Mexico's Monterrey and Monclova are the sole examples of industrial specialization.

No country in Middle America is industrialized in the modern sense, but industrialization is spreading. Virtually every territory is attempting to attract industry from abroad with offers of tax exemption, cheap labor, and other inducements. A few, such as Puerto Rico, are achieving surprising success, but industrial development is beset by too many obstacles to offer any immediate promise.

In addition, the resources, as we have observed, are inadequate for industry. Industrial development would have to overcome the same obstacles which have impeded agriculture: (1) the small populations, with limited purchasing power, spread over great distances, and with poor means of communication; (2) the lack of capital, of skills, and of facilities for generating power; (3) the prestige of landholding and the lack of prestige of manual labor; (4) the investor's preference for land, real estate, jewels, and precious metals; (5) an unwillingness to risk capital in untried enterprises and an expectation of large and rapid returns from investments; and (6) a strong and pervasive traditionalism, especially among the upper classes, who tend to view innovation as a threat to their status.

Transportation. Commercially and culturally, Middle America has faced the sea since the earliest colonial period. The sea orientation of the Rimland was inescapable, and the Rimland's destiny was repeatedly shaped by the particular power that controlled the sea lanes of the Gulf-Caribbean complex. Even in the interior Mainland settlements, an effort was made from the beginning to link the chief city and other centers with a coastal outlet. The sea, which was the major avenue for commerce and contact with the rest of the world, often became the principal means of contact with immediate neighbors as well. On the islands this was a matter of necessity, but on the Mainland it was chosen because of the difficulty of moving over land.

Land transportation is poorly developed even today. Dispersed settlements, the difficult terrain, the climate, and, above all, the lack of economic incentive are largely responsible for retarding transportation to the point where it is a major obstacle to economic development. Railroads, often financed by foreign capital, have made only the barest impression on most of Middle America. Mexico has about the best developed railroad system in Middle America, but the only zone with a dense rail network is the core area of the Mexican plateau. Mexico is connected with the United States system at several points along the border, and her railroads also join the Guatemalan line.

In Central America, short lines connect the upland populations with their coastal outlets. Some territories, such as Guatemala, El Salvador, and Costa Rica, have more miles of rails than, say, Honduras and Nicaragua, but nowhere do the railways serve the entire country. In the West Indies, Trinidad and all the Greater Antilles have railroads, many of which were built to transport sugar cane and other plantation crops to the *centrales* and to the ports. Cuba, which has the largest area and the strongest sugar economy, has the most extensive railways. The advent of highways and truck transportation, however, has rendered obsolete many of the West Indian railways on the smaller islands such as Puerto Rico and the Dominican Republic.

Middle America is now building more highways than railroads. On the Mainland, the interest in highways has been stimulated by the much-discussed Inter-American Highway; in the West Indies, highways have proved superior to rails. Again, however, development is spotty and, compared with the United States or western Europe, poor. Some of the islands, particularly Puerto Rico, Cuba, and the Dominican Republic, are developing excellent all-weather, paved systems. Considering its size and other difficulties, Mexico is also achieving a measure of success in road building. Americans may now motor into Mexico on at least three modern highways, one of which is the Inter-American Highway. In Central America, however, outside the major cities, the roads are nonexistent or rough, even if one includes the unpaved, fair-weather arteries and the extension of the Inter-American Highway.

With land transportation so poorly developed and costly, Middle America hailed the advent of air transport with great hope in the late 1930s. And the airplane was an immediate and outstanding success as a passenger vehicle. The movement of freight by airplane is costly, but land transport is so poor that many items, such as machinery and other valuable finished goods, are being flown in and out in increasing quantities. There are several international and national airlines, and many small operators offer common carrier services over short distances, linking even the most remote regions of the Mainland with its major centers. There are often more airports and landing strips than railroad stations, especially where land transport is poorest.

Commerce. The outstanding characteristics of Middle American commerce are: (1) its dependence on the exportation of a limited list of raw materials for the foreign exchange with which to buy finished products, fuel, and food; (2) the negligible importance of interregional trade as compared with extraregional trade; and (3) the dominance of the United States as the source of imports and the market for the exports of the entire area, except in a few territories which retain an association with European powers.

In varying degree, commerce spells economic life or death virtually everywhere, except in those local areas whose populations are almost totally subsistent. This dependence on commerce is more pronounced in the Rimland than in the Mainland, and in the Mainland, it is more pronounced in Central America than in Mexico. In Mexico the development of a more balanced economy during recent decades is making the country less vulnerable to the vagaries of international trade.

The cultural and physical diversity of the component units of Middle America has not created a basis for economic exchange within the area. Trade is still oriented outward, as it has been since the colonial period. Too often, the basic exports of the various territories are the same—sugar, coffee, bananas, or cotton. But even when they are not, they are raw materials from farm and mine, destined for use by more industrialized areas. The postwar industrial growth of Puerto Rico, however, has increased that island's trade with other territories of Middle America.

The dominant position of the United States in Middle America's trade is not surprising. Its geographic proximity, the differences in its climate which create corresponding differences in its agricultural products, its industrial production which requires raw materials, its heavy capital investment in many commercial enterprises of Middle America—all these conditions, and others, make the United States the logical area with which to exchange. It is perhaps less logical, although understandable, for Middle Americans to blame the United States for their economic ills.

The remaining European possessions in Middle America are integrated commercially with the mother countries because of political and economic expediency. Again, there are exceptions, chiefly the Dutch oil-refining islands, the Bahamas, and the British Virgin Islands.

THE OUTLOOK

Middle America is in ferment, and its transition is disquieting. Like much of the underdeveloped world, it is struggling against the inhibiting legacy of the past and toward modernization. This is not a new struggle. In Mexico, it has been continuously pressed since the Revolution of 1910. In the area as a whole, however, the fight to overcome the inertia of centuries has become intense only recently.

The tempo of modernization varies from place to place, but no major segment of Middle America is untouched by it. The threat, if not the impact, of change is being felt economically, technologically, politically and socially. Traditional patterns of settlement are being altered; there is a disturbing flow of population from country to town; new techniques of exploiting resources are being introduced; and new industries and other expressions of material culture are appearing on the landscape. An acute awareness of the need for change permeates every level of administration, from the national government to the village and community councils.

But the break with the past is neither complete nor painless. Modernization is hampered by the problems we have already mentioned, including the opposition of the upper classes. And the effort has become enmeshed in the conflict between the Communist countries and the West.

The ferment in Middle America requires reform or revolution. In the face of this dilemma, Cuba and, at an earlier date, Mexico chose revolution. Puerto Rico, with American aid, is taking the more peaceful path of reform. How will the others choose? The answer to this question may be as vital to the United States, and ultimately to the world, as it is to the peoples of Middle America.

Middle America's importance to the United States stems not only from economic and strategic considerations (see Chapter 1) but also from the challenge that it poses for American policy and leadership vis-à-vis the emerging nations. Because of its geographic proximity, its largely nonwhite population, and its lack of development, the area is a proving ground for America. Failure of American policy so close to home would not enhance its image elsewhere in Latin America, or in Asia, or in Africa. To date, however, our record in Middle America is less than brilliant. The United States' lack of sympathy for the goals of the Mexican Revolution during its early, critical stage added little to America's reputation as a champion of *Los de abajo*.[1] Cuba is a more recent illustration of U.S. failure and the dispatching of American troops to the Dominican Republic in 1965 was not a signal of success.

Too frequently we have addressed ourselves to the problems of Middle America in terms of their relevancy to our own contemporary political values and economic interests. Unfortunately, the problems of the area and the unrest to which they give rise are too deeply rooted in its geography and history to be approached within the context of current political and economic self-interests. To grasp the meaning of Middle America's struggle for modernization, it is essential to know the particulars—what was, what is, and where. Such a perspective reveals that the social unrest is primarily a mass revolt against the inequities of the past, particularly against the institutions that have perpetuated the exploitation of land and labor. To the privileged groups of Middle America and some Washington policy-makers, the revolt looks like a radical conspiracy, but this view may be both naïve and dangerous. "Revolution is a mettlesome horse. One must either ride it or be trampled to death by it" (Toynbee).

1. *Los de Abajo (The Underdogs)* is the title of Mariano Azuela's classic novel of the Mexican Revolution.

Index

References to figures and tables are indicated by italics.